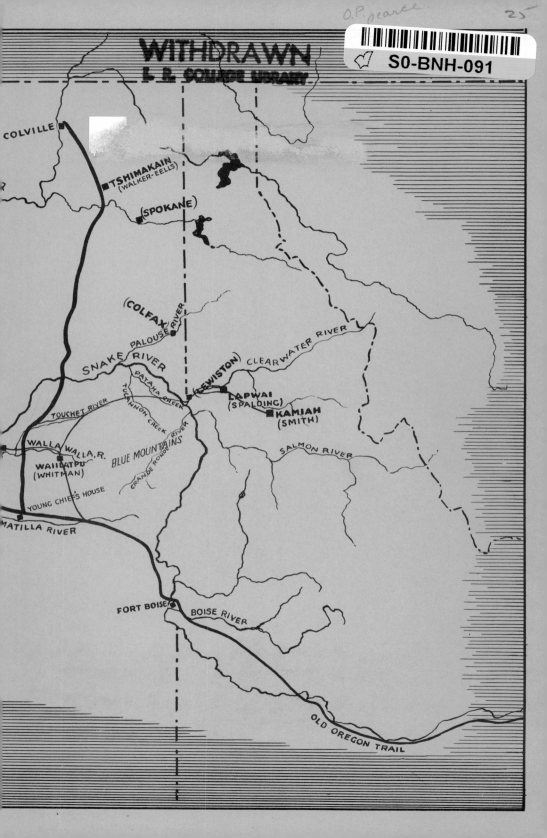

O.P. pearce.

25

MARCUS WHITMAN, M.D.
PIONEER AND MARTYR

CLIFFORD MERRILL DRURY, Ph.D.

AUTHOR OF
HENRY HARMON SPALDING
PIONEER OF OLD OREGON

STATUE OF WHITMAN ON WITHERSPOON BUILDING,
PHILADELPHIA, PENNSYLVANIA.

(An imaginary likeness.)

Marcus Whitman, M.D.

Pioneer
and
Martyr

By
Clifford Merrill Drury, Ph.D.

The Caxton Printers, Ltd.
Caldwell, Idaho
1937

COPYRIGHT 1937 BY
THE CAXTON PRINTERS, LTD.
CALDWELL, IDAHO

Printed, lithographed, and bound in the United States of America by
The CAXTON PRINTERS, Ltd.
Caldwell, Idaho
50316

TO MIRIAM

ACKNOWLEDGMENTS

SUCH a work as this is impossible without the interested co-operation of many people, and I hereby wish to acknowledge my indebtedness to the following institutions and individuals:

Whitman College—Dr. Stephen B. L. Penrose, Dr. H. S. Brode, and Prof. Melvin Jacobs.

American Board of Commissioners for Foreign Missions—Dr. Enoch Bell and Miss Dorothy Cole.

Washington State College—Dr. E. A. Holland and Mr. W. W. Foote.

Oregon Historical Society—Miss Nellie Pipes and Miss Irene Upson.

Dr. F. C. Waite, Cleveland, Ohio.

Dean J. G. Eldridge, Moscow, Idaho.

Mr. Robert Moody, Rushville, New York.

Miss Charlotte Howe, Prattsburg, New York.

Dr. T. C. Elliott, Walla Walla, Washington.

Dr. T. C. Pears, Philadelphia, Pennsylvania.

Mrs. Earl David, Moscow, Idaho.

Miss Eleona Underwood, Salt Lake City, Utah.

Mr. Charles Kelly, Salt Lake City, Utah.

Mrs. Ruth Karr McKee, Grand Coulee, Washington.

Dr. Hugh Moran, Ithaca, New York.

Dr. A. H. Limouze, New York City, New York.

Miss Martha Barrett, Evanston, Illinois.

I am also indebted to the following libraries and wish to express my appreciation for courtesies received from staff members:

University of Idaho, Moscow, Idaho.

University of Washington, Seattle, Washington.

University of California (Bancroft Library), Berkeley, California.

Congressional Library, Washington, D. C.

Hammond Library, Chicago Theological Seminary, Chicago, Illinois.

Cornell Library, Ithaca, New York.

Spokane Public Library, Spokane, Washington.

Some courtesies have been acknowledged in the footnotes. To all others whose names I have not mentioned but who have rendered valued assistance, I wish again to say: "Thank you."

C. M. DRURY.

FOREWORD

UNTIL Dr. Clifford M. Drury's critical mind and facile pen clothed Henry Harmon Spalding, Marcus Whitman, and Elkanah Walker with life and action, they were shadowy historical figures about whom tradition was already weaving a veil of unreliable romance.

The centennial of the Whitman-Spalding heroic journey to Oregon gave rise to Dr. Drury's valuable biography of Henry Harmon Spalding, which is based on an intelligent and discriminating study of the available sources and will bear the tests of the most rigid canon of historical criticism. As a result the real Spalding with all his faults and virtues stands revealed as an intriguing frontier personality.

But the volume on Spalding left many questions about the Oregon Country unsettled. It was highly necessary that Dr. Drury, having reintroduced Spalding to the American people, should proceed to interpret his superior co-laborer, Dr. Marcus Whitman, for their better understanding of the Oregon question.

This physician, missionary, pioneer, and national expansionist was a product of the first generation of pioneer settlers who rushed into western New York from New England after the Revolution. He was the son of Beza Whitman, six generations removed from his immigrant ancestor who arrived in Massachusetts in 1638. Born in Rushville, New York, in 1802, and educated in Massachusetts and New York, Marcus Whitman was awarded his M.D. at the age of thirty. After eight years of practice in Canada, Pennsylvania, and at Wheeler, New York, he offered his services to the American Board for Foreign Missions, and was sent West in 1835 with Samuel Parker to scout the Oregon region. Dr. Drury, after careful gleanings from printed sources, manuscripts, and aged persons still living, which necessitated extensive travels in the United States and Canada, has reconstructed for the first time this significant early period of Whitman's life, showing him to be an industrious, persistent, bright boy and young man with a pious strain and a pleasing personality. Some of the same New England influences—cultural, religious and social—that moulded the mind of William Cullen Bryant and John Brown, likewise moulded young Marcus Whitman.

Although inclined towards the ministry, upon attaining his majority he began "riding with Doctor Bryant," of Rushville, a distant cousin of William Cullen Bryant. Dr. Drury has discovered new sources bearing on Whitman's medical studies, thus correcting a number of errors in previous accounts. He shows that while studying with Dr. Bryant, Whitman also taught school, and worked in a shoeshop, a tannery, and a sawmill.

In 1830 Whitman gave up the practice of medicine for a time and began a preparatory course for the ministry; but only for a year, because in 1831 he re-entered the medical college at Fairfield, New York, and received his degree the next year as a full-fledged physician.

Not the least important portion of this book is the new interpretation of the life of Narcissa Prentiss, Whitman's plucky wife, a personality of charm, lively intelligence, and loyalty. The author has woven together out of many scraps of information her biographical sketch, making it one of unusual interest. The passion of Henry Harmon Spalding for Narcissa, which left embarrassments for both of them, is handled with strict truthfulness and a satisfying thoroughness. Her devotion to her husband and to the cause they both served, in the midst of extraordinary hardships, runs like a golden thread throughout the volume from her marriage in 1836 to her tragic death eleven years later.

This volume presents in detail the life of a man whose outstanding traits were physical vigor, persistence, courage, self-reliance, resourcefulness, and optimism. He gladly devoted his life to a great cause with zeal and faithfulness. If his judgment was not always reliable, his heart was. A typical pioneer with a dynamic body, he will be remembered not so much as a physician or a missionary as an American empire builder. Dr. Drury has written the fullest and the most accurate life of Whitman. The material is well organized, the presentation is judicial, the style is dignified and yet sympathetic. Controversial questions are handled impartially, and the conclusions are based on solid foundations. As a study in American pioneer heroism the book should be read by every citizen of the nation.

In 1936 Archer B. Hulbert and Dorothy P. Hulbert in their MARCUS WHITMAN, CRUSADER (Vol. 6 of the series, *Overland to the Pacific*) published a valuable collection of primary sources dealing with Dr. Marcus Whitman. Interested readers will find his letters printed in full in that work, when completed. Dr. Drury found and used 115 Dr. Whitman letters and 107 of Mrs. Whitman's letters. He includes in the Appendices a survey of the literature on "The Whitman Controversy," which lists all the earlier writers and also modern contributions like those of Professor Herbert D. Winters, of Keuka College, Keuka Park, New York; and a hitherto unprinted, illuminating letter on the Whitmans by the Rev. H. K. W. Perkins, who knew them well. The bibliography of printed books, pamphlets, and articles in periodicals is exhaustive. The numerous illustrations, all visual sources, add to the attractiveness and value of the book. All in all the volume is one to satisfy the scholarly historian and to inform the general reader.

It is gratifying to know that the trilogy of Oregon pioneers will be completed by the author with a biography of Elkanah Walker.

ALEXANDER C. FLICK,

May 25, 1937.   *State Historian of New York.*

TABLE OF CONTENTS

LIST OF ILLUSTRATIONS

MARCUS WHITMAN, M.D.
PIONEER AND MARTYR

CHAPTER ONE

THE FIRST EIGHTEEN YEARS
1802-1820

IN THE latter part of November, 1834, a cultured Congregational minister made his way in a light wagon over the muddy roads of Steuben and Allegany Counties in western New York. He was on a strange mission, for he was seeking missionaries to go to the Indians beyond the Rocky Mountains. Incidentally, he collected such money as he could to support the mission.

That man was the Rev. Samuel Parker[1] (1779-1855). While pastor of the Congregational church at Middlefield, Massachusetts, he had read in the March 1, 1833, issue of the New York *Christian Advocate* the thrilling story of the arrival in St. Louis of four Indians from beyond the Rockies who sought the white man's Bible and Christian teachers. Parker was then fifty-four years old and had a wife and three children, yet he dared to dream of going himself to the Pacific Coast in response to the Macedonian appeal. It was a bold plan, for no missionary had yet made the hazardous trip over the Continental Divide.

The American Board of Commissioners for Foreign Missions,[2] to whom Parker applied, felt that he was too old to go and treated his offer with some coldness. But Parker was not to be discouraged. He persisted even to the point of raising sufficient funds in the First Presbyterian Church of Ithaca, New York, to guarantee the mission. In the spring of 1834, with the permission of the Board, Parker and two associates left for the Rocky Mountains.

In those days professional men wore a fine type of top-hat made of beaver skins. The beaver hat was a sign of prosperity or elegance and remained in style until after the

---

[1] The Rev. Samuel Parker did not have a doctor's degree. He had a son, Samuel J. Parker, M.D., who was known as Dr. Parker.

[2] Sometimes referred to as the A.B.C.F.M. Organized in 1812 with the Congregational and the Presbyterian Churches co-operating from 1826 until 1837, at which time the Old School branch of the Presbyterian Church withdrew. The New School branch withdrew in 1870. The Dutch Reformed and the German Reformed Churches also co-operated in the Board for many years.

Civil War. One of the chief sources of supply of beaver skins was the Rocky Mountain area. Enterprising fur companies, with headquarters in St. Louis, Missouri, sent hundreds of men into the mountains to trap the fur-bearing animals. Each summer a caravan would carry supplies from civilization to these mountain men. The caravan would meet the trappers at an appointed place, not always the same from year to year, but usually west of the Continental Divide, called "the rendezvous." After exchanging the supplies for the beaver skins, the caravan would return to St. Louis.

Parker and his companions had planned to cross the plains and the mountains under the protection of the caravan, for it was not safe to go without escort. However, Parker reached St. Louis too late to go with the caravan. He left his two companions to begin missionary work among the Pawnee Indians, and he returned to look for more workers.

Thus it was that the late fall of 1834 found Samuel Parker holding missionary meetings in western New York, where, some twenty-five years earlier, he had begun his ministry. He noticed that the settlements had grown. Large areas had been cleared and were under cultivation. Some of the churches which he had founded had reached the stage of self-support, and were promising sources of gifts of both money and lives for the Oregon mission cause.

Parker paused one day in the little village of Wheeler, Steuben County, where he held missionary meetings. He issued his appeal for funds and for that which was more important than funds—missionaries.

Among his hearers was a country doctor, then thirty-two years old, who told Mr. Parker that he was willing to go if the Board should see fit to send him. The doctor mentioned the fact that he had offered his services to the Board the previous June, but had been rejected because of poor health. Learning that the doctor's physical condition was much improved, Parker advised him to try again.

Parker continued his journey and a few days later spoke at Angelica, in the neighboring county of Allegany. There he repeated his missionary appeal. Among his hearers was a charming young woman, twenty-six years of age, from the near-by village of Amity (now known as Belmont), who likewise offered to go.[3] Mr. Parker was not sure that the

---

[3] Bath *Plaindealer*, Dec. 31, 1892, article by Dr. Samuel J. Parker: "At Wheeler, Steuben County, a young physician came to him after one

Board would appoint "unmarried females," but he promised to make inquiry.

Writing to his family from Franklinville, Cattaraugus County, just west of Allegany, on December 5, 1834, Parker first described his fatiguing ride over the muddy roads and then referred to the success of his trip. "I have found some missionaries," he wrote. "Dr. Whitman, of Wheeler, Steuben County, New York, has agreed to offer himself to the Board to go beyond the mountains. He has no family. Two ladies offer themselves, one a daughter of Judge Prentiss of Amity, Alleghany County."[4] The name of the judge's daughter was Narcissa.

Although Parker did not realize the full significance of the drama then in its preliminary stages, we now know that one of his greatest services to the cause of both church and state was to find these two characters and to interest them in Old Oregon.[5]

THE ANCESTRY OF MARCUS WHITMAN

Following the Revolutionary War a restless urge sent many New Englanders over the Alleghenies into what was then known as the Connecticut Western Reserve, which included what is now northeastern Ohio. Among these was a young man who bore the unusual name of Beza Whitman. Beza was of the sixth generation of the descendants of John Whitman, who arrived in the Massachusetts Bay Colony some time prior to December, 1638,[6] and settled at Weymouth, some twelve miles south of Boston. It is believed that John Whitman came from Norfolk, England, where the family name was originally spelt Whiteman.

Samuel Lincoln, the ancestor of Abraham Lincoln, came to the same colony also from Norfolk, England, in 1637, or at about the same time as did John Whitman. Lincoln settled at Salem, Massachusetts. One of his sons, Mordecai, married Sarah Whitman Jones, the granddaughter of John Whitman. Their son Mordecai, was the great-great-grand-

---

of the meetings." "My father said that at a meeting held at Angelica or Amity, probably the former, a young lady. . . . "

[4] *W.C.Q.*, Vol. 2, No. 3, pp. 12-13.

[5] Oregon Territory included the present states of Washington, Oregon, Idaho, and those parts of Montana and Wyoming west of the Continental Divide.

[6] Farnham, *History of the Descendants of John Whitman.*

father of Abraham Lincoln. It is of interest to note that the martyred President and the martyred pioneer-missionary of Old Oregon were both descendants of John Whitman.

Beza Whitman was born May 13, 1773, at Bridgewater, Massachusetts, the son of Samuel. During the years 1765 to 1780, many of the residents of Bridgewater and of the adjoining towns[7] of Abington and Weymouth, stirred by the restless urge to migrate, moved to northwestern Massachusetts. As early as 1795, Beza Whitman and his younger half-brother Freedom had settled at Cummington in the heart of the Berkshires.

In the adjacent town of Windsor lived the family of Hezekiah and Alice Green.[8] Records show that Hezekiah saw military service in the battle of Saratoga in October, 1781, as a soldier from Windsor. Like the Whitmans, the Green family had long been in America. Hezekiah Green was of the sixth generation of the descendants of Thomas Green, who settled at Wenham, Massachusetts, about 1636.

Beza Whitman had not been long at Cummington before he won the heart and hand of Alice Green (1777-1857), of Windsor, the youngest child of Hezekiah and Alice. They were married on March 9, 1797. Their family Bible with the family record is still extant, and in it we read the following account of the birth of their first-born:[9]

Augustus Whitman was born in the town of Windsor AD 1798. January the 7th

About 1796, Henry Green (1763-1849),[10] an older brother of Alice, had moved from Windsor to Ontario County, New York, and had become one of the early settlers of Naples. He moved in 1799 to a settlement known as Federal Hollow, located partly in the present township of Gorham, Ontario

---

[7] The word "town" is still used as a synonym for township in certain parts of the East.

[8] Greene, *Genealogical Sketch of the Descendants of Thomas Green*, p. 43, states that the family originally lived at Killingly, Conn., where eight children were born. Farnham, *op. cit.*, p. 236, states that Alice, the youngest child, was born at Mumford, Conn. There is no such place now. The Whitman family Bible says that she was born at Thompson, Windham County, Conn.

[9] Now owned by Mrs. Minnie A. Dayton, of Rushville. The Bible was printed in 1808. Regarding the place where Alice was born, we read: "His wife Alice Whitman was born in the year of our Lord 1777, Dec. 5th in the town of Thompson County of Windham, Connecticut."

[10] A family tradition states that Henry Green served in the Revolutionary War and was one of the group to guard Major André the last night of his life.

County, and partly in Potter of Yates County. In 1818 the
name Rushville was bestowed upon the settlement by the
village doctor, Ira Bryant, who sought thereby to honor his
friend, the famous Revolutionary War patriot, Dr. Benjamin Rush, one of the signers of the Declaration of Independence.[11] In order to avoid confusion, the name Rushville
will be used even though it was not the official designation of
the village until nearly twenty years after Henry Green
moved there.

In Rushville, Henry, later known as Captain Green,
operated a sawmill and gristmill on a stream known as West
River, which empties into the southern end of Lake Canandaigua. As a child, Beza Whitman accompanied his
family in its migration to the Berkshires of western Massachusetts. Shortly after his marriage to Alice Green, he
moved westward again, this time going about two hundred
and fifty miles to Ontario County, in which Henry Green
was already established.

According to one report, Beza and Alice settled first in
Hopewell,[12] although the record of the birth of their second
son indicates that in 1799 they lived for a time in Canandaigua. According to another report, Beza and his family
paused in the town of Middlesex.[13] The Whitman genealogy
states that Beza arrived in Rushville with all of his earthly
possessions loaded on a wagon pulled by a pair of oxen. His
wife rode a horse and held Augustus in her arms. If this
account be true, it was after the death of their second child
on October 14, 1800.

A tradition which still lingers in Rushville states that
Henry Green had completed a frame dwelling about the
time Beza arrived, and consequently Beza and his family
were able to occupy the log cabin vacated by the Green
family. Another Rushville tradition tells the story of how
one day a bear raided the pigpen near the log barn which
stood behind the Whitman home. This tradition throws
some light upon the primitive life which surrounded the
struggling settlements.

Beza was an industrious and capable worker. He built a
tannery on West River. He also plied his trade as a shoe-

---

[11] *Centennial Celebration of Rushville Church*, p. 13.

[12] Letter of Mary Alice Wisewell, granddaughter of Beza, to Myron
Eells, March 10, 1882, Coll. W. (*See* Appendix 1 for list of abbreviations used to designate collections of source material.)

[13] *Yates County Chronicle*, June 8, 1871.

maker. An interesting item in the possession of Whitman College, Walla Walla, Washington, is the following receipt made out in Beza Whitman's handwriting:

March 14, 1807. This Day we the subscribers have made a full settlement by exchanging fifty Dollars and parted in friendship witness our hands

(Signed)   WILLIAM FANNING
            BEZA WHITMAN

Julia Fanning, a daughter of William Fanning, wrote on July 24, 1897: "He probably paid fifty dollars for his instruction in the trade of tanner & currier. . . . After Beza Whitman's death . . . my father & a son Augustus Whitman worked the tan yard in company for three years."[14]

BIRTH AND EARLY LIFE OF MARCUS WHITMAN

In that humble log cabin, the third son was born to Beza and Alice Whitman on Saturday, September 4, 1802.[15] They called him Marcus. The Whitman genealogy indicates that James Whitman, a first cousin of Beza, had a son born August 15, 1796, whom he named Marcus. About 1797 James Whitman and his family moved to Belchertown, Massachusetts, which is in the same county and thirty miles east of Cummington. It is probable that Beza was a frequent visitor in the home of his cousin James and was an admirer of the first Marcus Whitman, a babe but a few months old when Beza and Alice were married. Perhaps from this source came the name of Marcus for the third son of Beza.

We know virtually nothing about the very early life of our Marcus Whitman. One of the most authentic incidents is recorded by Mary Alice Wisewell, a niece of Marcus Whitman. She wrote:

His parents lived in a log house—the country was new and wild, and as his father was a tanner and currier his mother being lonely often used to go and sit with her husband in the little shop opposite the house binding shoes. Having left him a baby in his cradle one evening she was much startled to find on her return that a log had fallen from the fireplace and burned the lower end of the cradle, and that he was nearly suffocated by the smoke.[16]

Perhaps her timely return saved the infant Marcus from a premature death.

---

[14] Coll. W.

[15] Drury, *Spalding*, p. 95, states that Marcus was the second son. The Whitman family Bible was subsequently discovered.

[16] Letter of Mary Alice Wisewell, Coll. W.

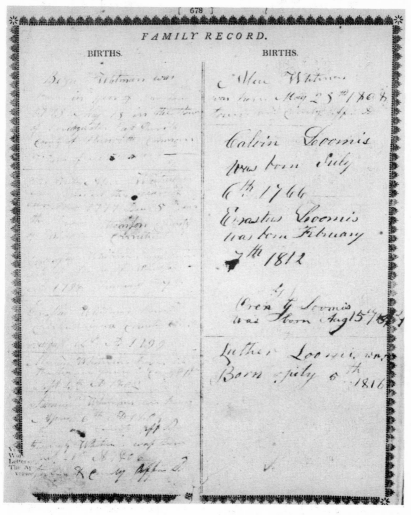

A PAGE FROM THE BIBLE OF BEZA AND ALICE WHITMAN.
The fifth entry on the left records the birth of Marcus.
By courtesy of Mrs. Minnie A. Dayton.

ALICE WHITMAN WISEWELL.

AUGUSTUS WHITMAN.

HENRY WHITMAN AND HIS SON

SAMUEL WHITMAN.

The likeness of Whitman's brother Henry was taken about 1847. The other photographs were much later. Samuel was blind in one eye.

The picture of Whitman's sister, Alice, is by courtesy of Whitman College. The other pictures are by courtesy of J. C. Fox, Rushville, N. Y.

MOSES HALLOCK'S HOME.

From *Magazine of American History*, Vol. 17, p. 219. "The house is a low, old-fashioned, one-story building, but of ample width, securing a large amount of room upon the lower floor and a spacious chamber above."— *History of the Connecticut Valley in Massachusetts*, p. 436.

THE PLAINFIELD CHURCH.
From Dyer, *History of Plainfield.*

MARCUS WHITMAN'S MOTHER.
Picture identified by the late Mrs. Marion B. Williams, of Middlesex, New York. Taken about 1847.

Two other sons and a daughter came to that home—namely, Samuel (1804-1875), Henry (1806-1854), and Alice (1808-1887). The home in which these children were reared must have been like the other pioneer homes of that period. Luxuries were unknown, and necessities were barely obtainable. Domestic industries, in which the children were obliged to assist as early as possible, made the home self-sufficient in most things.

Beza Whitman prospered in his trade sufficiently to warrant the building of a new frame house, which was used as a public inn as well as a home. According to one report this was the first "public house" in Rushville,[17] and was built upon or near the site of the log cabin in which Marcus was born. Another evidence of his success is the record of the purchase of about forty acres of land in December, 1809, for $450.[18] This land was located about one-half mile south of the village.

Marcus Whitman spent the first eight years of his life in Rushville. Among his playmates was a lad about his own age whose name was Jonathan Pratt, Jr. The two used to play under a big elm which stood at a crossroads about a mile northeast of Rushville in a place now called Baldwin Corners. Daniel Gates kept a tavern there. Below the crossroads on West River was Captain Joseph Blodgett's sawmill. Three miles to the west was Canandaigua Lake, where possibly the boys sometimes went fishing. The kind of life Marcus lived during those first eight years in that frontier settlement was an important preparation for life in a frontier far more primitive than western New York.

Mrs. Whitman, the mother of Marcus, is reported to have been a woman of great energy to whom laziness was a cardinal sin. The Rev. S. W. Pratt, D.D. (1839-1910), who served as Moderator of the Presbyterian Synod of New York in 1907, described her as follows:

Marcus was said to have derived much of his vigor and energy and resoluteness from his mother, who was physically very strong and

---

[17] *Yates County Chronicle*, June 8, 1871. The house remained standing for about one hundred years. Robert Moody, of Rushville, states that it was torn down before 1909. Some of the big wide boards from this house were used in the erection of a barn still standing at Rushville. A man who assisted in tearing down the house told the author at the centennial celebration held at Rushville, June 4, 1936: "If I had known that so much fuss would be made about Marcus Whitman, I would never have done it."

[18] *See* record of deeds, county courthouse, Canandaigua, N. Y.

untiring, weaving for her household, making cheese and performing other industrial duties. She had no patience with laziness, and to a girl who would work for her she said, "You must have pluck as big as a brass kettle if you live with me." Her cap border would shake with energy when she spoke. She never spent any time in sentiment, but abounded in deeds.[19]

While the author was collecting material for this book, an old daguerreotype was discovered which is owned by J. C. Fox, of Rushville, who is a grandson of Henry Whitman, the brother of Marcus. At the time of discovery, no one could identify the picture. Circumstantial evidence suggested that it was a likeness of Mrs. Beza Whitman. The picture was shown to Mrs. Marion B. Williams, of Middlesex, New York, who celebrated her one hundred and first birthday on May 24, 1936. She said: "I knew her. That is Mrs. Loomis. I used to go to church in Rushville with her."[20] Since Mrs. Beza Whitman married Calvin Loomis after the death of Beza, we have the satisfaction of knowing that we have a picture of Marcus Whitman's mother. The picture shows a face of much force and character. A lock of her blonde hair is in the archives of Whitman College.

TEN YEARS IN MASSACHUSETTS

Sorrow came to the Whitman home in Rushville on April 7, 1810, when Beza Whitman died in his thirty-seventh year. He was buried in the Baldwin Corners cemetery near the village, where one can still read on the brown sandstone marker the following epitaph, characteristic of that period:

> Stop here my friend and think on me
> I once was in the world like the
> This is a call aloud to the
> Prepare for death and follow me

The widow was left with five children, the eldest, Augustus, but twelve years old. The financial burden was too great for her slender resources, so she turned to relatives for assistance. In the fall of that year Marcus, then eight years old, was sent to live with his father's half-brother, Freedom Whitman, at Cummington, Massachusetts.[21] Thus Marcus

---

[19] *Sunset Magazine*, Aug., 1909, p. 186. Article reprinted in Corning (N. Y.) *Leader*, Oct. 9, 1909.

[20] *See* Rochester *Democrat & Chronicle*, May 19, 1936, for story about Mrs. Williams. *See* p. 131.

[21] Letter of Mary A. Wisewell, Coll. W.

suffered a double tragedy. He was not only bereft of his father, but was also separated from his mother, his brothers, and his infant sister. However, in the light of later events to be set forth in their proper place, it is safe to say that Marcus Whitman would never have gone to Old Oregon as a medical missionary, had it not been for the chain of events that started with the death of his father, Beza Whitman.

When Marcus wrote his letter of application to the American Board on June 3, 1834, he stated:

I was sent to reside with my Father's Brother in Massachusetts where I received my early education and Religious instruction, my Grand Father (for he resided in the same family) and Uncle were both pious and gave me constant religious instruction and care. I was under their care mostly for ten years.[22]

These two pious men, grandfather and uncle, left an indelible impression upon young Marcus. It was his good fortune to come under their influence during some of the most important years of character development.

Grandfather Samuel Whitman and his wife moved from Bridgewater to Cummington about 1799. Mrs. Whitman died at Cummington on September 19, 1816, after which Samuel probably went to live with his son Freedom. When Marcus reached Cummington he found other relatives also present in the village. His father's sister Mehitabel, who married Abner Bates, Jr., lived there with her family. The uncles and aunts and cousins were strangers to the eight-year-old lad who was often homesick for the familiar surroundings of Rushville.

Marcus Whitman met in Cummington a youth a few years his senior who was named William Cullen Bryant. A year or so after Marcus went to Cummington, Bryant wrote his famous *Thanatopsis* in which the poet used for the first time in American literature the name "Oregon."

> Take the wings
> Of morning, pierce the Barcan wilderness,
> Or lose thyself in the continuous woods
> Where rolls the Oregon, and hears no sound,
> Save his own dashings.... [23]

---

[22] Whitman letter 3. *See* Appendix 1 for list of Whitman letters. Hereafter all references to Whitman letters will be made in the text only. To distinguish these numbers from footnote references, the number of the Whitman letter referred to will be in brackets, *i.e.*, [Letter 3.].

[23] For a discussion of the meaning of the name "Oregon" see Bancroft, *Oregon*, Vol. 1, p. 19.

The Columbia River was once known as the Oregon, although Captain Robert Gray, who discovered it in 1792, named the river after his ship, Columbia. However, Bryant was not then acquainted with that fact.

After a residence of about five years amid the beautiful Berkshires of western Massachusetts, Marcus returned to Rushville to visit his mother and other relatives. He was then thirteen years old and had changed much during the years he had been away from Rushville. His niece, daughter of his sister Alice, describes the visit as follows:

When thirteen years old he unexpectedly returned home for a visit of three weeks. Coming in at evening he went up to his mother and reached out his hand, saying—"How do you do, Mother?"—and she drew back thinking herself no mother to him. This so grieved him that he burst into tears. My mother says that it was during this visit that she first saw him to know him—being six years younger.[24]

During the absence of Marcus, his mother, in 1811, had married Calvin Loomis (1766-1840). To this marriage, the second for both, three children were born—Erastus[25] (1813), Oren Green (1814—1881), and Luther (1816-1837). Calvin Loomis carried on the shoeshop and tannery business, and continued to conduct the tavern. It was to this house that the thirteen-year-old lad came on a visit to his mother, and to it he later returned to reside for several years.

Whitman's experience as a boy was somewhat similar to that of Henry Harmon Spalding, with whom he was associated for eleven years in the Oregon mission. Spalding was bound out as a babe to strangers when he was but fourteen months old. Whitman was in his eighth year before he had to undergo the shock of being wrenched from familiar surroundings and taken from the side of a mother to whom he must have clung with childish dependence. Though he was placed with relatives, they were strangers to him. There is pathos in the story of the boy, who, separated from his mother for five years, came back only to be unrecognized.

---

[24] Wisewell letter, Coll. W. This letter gives us the most authentic glimpses into the early life of Whitman, for it was written during the lifetime of Whitman's only sister, Alice, and was in part dictated by her to her daughter.

[25] Erastus was also the name of her second born. In that day it was quite customary to use a name the second time if the first child with the name died. Whitman genealogy, p. 236, erroneously states that Mrs. Whitman married Chester Loomis. Calvin Loomis lies buried in the French Cemetery at Rushville beside his first wife. Mrs. Loomis was buried by her first husband.

After his visit in Rushville, Marcus returned to Massachusetts. It appears that about this time he enrolled as a student in the excellent classical school conducted in Plainfield by the Rev. Moses Hallock, pastor of the church there. Plainfield is only about seven miles from Cummington, near enough for Marcus to have made frequent trips, while attending school, to see his uncle and grandfather. At Plainfield, Marcus lived in the home of Colonel John Packard, who was a man of considerable influence in the village and the church.[26]

The two villages, Cummington and Plainfield, are located in the northwest corner of Hampshire County, Massachusetts, on the crest of the Berkshires. These beautiful tree-clad hills form a southern extension of the Green Mountains of Vermont, but fifteen miles to the north. Near Plainfield is West Mountain, more than two thousand feet above sea level, the highest point in western Hampshire. Near by is Mill Creek, on which were located a number of mills and other establishments needing water power. There are two natural ponds in the vicinity of the village, the largest of which, North Pond, is about a mile long and a half mile wide in the widest part. When Marcus was a boy the hills contained much wild game, and the ponds and the stream were well stocked with fish. Marcus with the other lads of his age roamed those hills in search of game, and he tried his luck with the pole. Gradually he acquired those characteristics of industry, courage, and self-reliance which were to be of such value to him in later years.

The first settlers had come to Plainfield about 1770. Previous to the incorporation of Plainfield in 1785, the inhabitants attended the church at Cummington, which had been organized in 1771. The Plainfield church was organized August 31, 1786, and a few years later a building was erected which measured 55½ x 42½ feet. In the records of the church is found the following interesting item for April 23, 1792:

Voted that the owners of pews in the meeting-house provide rum to raise said building.[27]

---

[26] Dyer, *History of the Town of Plainfield*, p. 93.

[27] The comparative value of the church and the school in the eyes of the citizens of Plainfield is to be seen in the following item from the town records for March 13, 1786: "Voted to raise twenty pounds to here preaching for the present year. Voted not to raise money for to support a school."

The church was finally completed in 1797. It boasted of
forty-four box pews below and nineteen in the gallery. The
pew occupied by Colonel John Packard and his family, and
therefore by Marcus Whitman, was in the southwest corner
of the church.[28] The church had no stoves until 1822, when
two were placed near the pulpit, and then, so we learn, "not
... without considerable opposition." During the winter
weather the women carried with them the common charcoal
foot stoves, which are still used in Holland, while the men
frequently imbibed "a little good old rum internally to prevent the cold from piercing their vitals."

During the "long prayer," it was the custom for the congregation to stand. The seats in the box pews were hinged
and movable. When the congregation arose, these seats were
folded back in order to give more room. When the "Amen"
was pronounced, the seats all fell back into place with a bang
and a clatter that would astonish a present-day congregation.

In 1792 the church extended a call to the Rev. Moses
Hallock (1760-1837), who had served as a soldier in the
Revolutionary War and had been graduated from Yale in
1788. Hallock was a native of Goshen, Massachusetts, a
town adjacent to the east of Cummington. He was already
acquainted with the Whitman family for he had as his
pastor in Goshen the Rev. Samuel Whitman, a third cousin
of the Samuel Whitman of Cummington. Moses Hallock
had studied for the ministry under his direction; and when
he was installed pastor of the Plainfield church on July 11,
1792, the Rev. Samuel Whitman preached the installation
sermon. This sermon was published, and copies can still be
found in Eastern libraries. His text was from Ezekiel 44:23.

Hallock served as pastor of the Plainfield congregation
for forty-five years. He was a remarkable man in many
ways, and certainly left a lasting influence upon the life of
Marcus Whitman. Shortly after his installation Hallock
opened a school in his home, which he conducted with great
effectiveness until 1824. More than three hundred students
received the benefit of his training, of whom thirty were
girls. The nonresident students paid a dollar a week for
board and tuition. This school was established a year after
the founding of Williams College, thirty miles distant. One
hundred and thirty-two of Hallock's students went to col-

---

[28] Dyer, *op. cit.*, p. 7, gives detailed information about the church,
including a floor plan, etc.

lege, most of them to Williams College, but some went to Amherst, also about thirty miles distant, and to Harvard.

Among the students later to become well known were such men as William Cullen Bryant from near-by Cummington, and John Brown of Harpers Ferry fame. The former has left for us the following account of his experiences as a student under Moses Hallock:

> I was early at my task in the morning, and kept on until bed-time; at night I dreamed of Greek, and my first thought in the morning was of my lesson for the day, at the end of two calendar months I knew the Greek New Testament from end to end almost as if it had been English.[29]

Many of the same influences which flowed into the life of William Cullen Bryant likewise moulded his younger contemporary, Marcus Whitman, who shared with him the life of the same communities. They lived in the same environment; they knew many of the same people; they worshiped in the same church and studied under the same renowned schoolmaster.

John Brown's contact with the Hallock school was of short duration. About 1818, Brown, who then lived at Hudson, Ohio,[30] decided to enter the ministry. His attention was naturally directed to the Hallock school, because Hallock was a relative of his mother. John Brown was two years the senior of Marcus Whitman, and it is probable that the two were schoolmates for a short time in the Plainfield school.

Marcus Whitman summed up the story of his early education in a letter written to the American Board on June 3, 1834, when he stated: "My preliminary education consists of the english Branches together with some knowledge of Lattin and some little of Greek." In the Hallock school Whitman received the education then given to all students preparing for the Gospel ministry. Since he, also, planned to enter the ministry, it is well for us to review in some detail the religious influences which enveloped him during the impressionable years of adolescence.

In both Cummington and Plainfield the church played a central rôle in the life of their respective communities. There was a time in Cummington when membership in the church

---

[29] Bradley, *Wm. Cullen Bryant*, pp. 22-23.

[30] John Brown's father, Owen Brown, is buried in the Hudson cemetery. H. H. Spalding attended Western Reserve College at Hudson during the years 1831-1833, and undoubtedly knew both Owen and John Brown, since both were active in the religious life of the village.

was a necessary condition for full privileges as a citizen of
the community. While Marcus lived at Plainfield all of the
prominent people of the town were likewise prominent in
the church.

The Sabbath began at sundown on Saturday and continued until sundown on Sunday. The day was strictly observed according to the custom of the time. In 1800 the
Plainfield church acquired a bell which weighed 650 pounds,
whose tone was the key of D. The ringing of this bell called
the people of the village to public worship, and woe unto any
who absented himself without good cause! Going out in a
boat or standing idly on the river bank on Sunday was
strictly forbidden!

Among the devout members of the church was a miller
by the name of Joseph Beals, who died July 20, 1813. Though
Marcus Whitman may never have known him, yet the reputation of his piety was certainly a fact of which Marcus was
aware. His fame was greatly increased through a tract
written by the Rev. William Hallock, a son of Moses Hallock,
which was published by the American Tract Society in 1831
under the title, *The Mountain Miller's Home.*[31] During the
first year of its publication, some 140,000 copies were dis-
tributed. In 1833, another edition of 168,000 was issued.
People throughout the United States and across the seas
read the story of the piety of the Mountain Miller of
Plainfield.

The strong religious influence which Moses Hallock ex-
erted over the young men who studied in his school is especially evident from the number of his students who entered
the ministry or the mission field. Fifty out of 304 students,
including two of his own sons, entered the ministry, and
seven became foreign missionaries.[32] Is it any wonder that
Whitman dreamed of entering the ministry when he too was
under such an influence?

The Plainfield church started a Sunday school in May,
1819. Since the Sunday school movement did not become
a national force until 1825, it is to the credit of the Plainfield congregation that this form of religious activity was
adopted so early. Marcus was in his seventeenth year when

---

[31] Tract No. 254. Copies of this tract are to be found in several
Eastern libraries. One is in the Widener Library of Harvard
University.

[32] The list given in Dyer does not include Whitman's name as a
foreign missionary.

the school was organized. He entered a class taught by Deacon James Richards. In regard to the Sunday school, Whitman wrote: "I have attended as a schollar, teacher or Superintendent ever since." [Letter 3.]

All three of Deacon Richards' sons entered the ministry, which again reflects credit upon the strength of the Deacon's faith. One of these sons, James Richards, Jr., also a student of Moses Hallock, was graduated from Williams College in 1809. In 1806, while at the college, James Richards, Jr. and four others, Samuel J. Mills, Francis L. Robbins, Harvey Loomis, and Byram Green, assembled one day in a near-by grove to pray. A rainstorm caused them to seek shelter in a haystack. It was there that this small group under the leadership of Mills solemnly dedicated themselves to the cause of foreign missions. A monument has been erected on the site, on the present campus of Williams College. The names of the five young men are inscribed on the monument with the words: "The Field is the World Birthplace of American Foreign Missions 1806."

We can believe that the enthusiasm for foreign missions was carried back to his native village of Plainfield by James Richards, Jr., later sent by the American Board to Ceylon. If Marcus did not meet him, surely the story of his work in Ceylon would have been told to Whitman by James Richards, Sr., his Sunday school teacher.

In 1819, a religious awakening touched many of the communities of New England, and also many communities outside of New England which had been settled by New England people. Revivals were the order of the day. This awakening was felt in Plainfield, and among those affected was Marcus Whitman. Of that experience he wrote: "I attended the ministrations of Rev. Moses Hallock at which time I was awakened to a sense of my sin and danger and brought by Divine grace to rely on the Lord Jesus for pardon and salvation." [Letter 3.] Marcus was then in his seventeenth year.

There is no record of Whitman's joining the Plainfield church. It may be that he expected soon to return to Rushville and felt it wise to delay joining a church until he had reached his native town. More probably Whitman found himself caught between conflicting loyalties. On the one hand was the Congregational influence of Plainfield; on the other were the Baptist convictions of his grandfather and uncle in Cummington.

Marcus Whitman's failure to join the Congregational

church of Plainfield may have been due to his consideration of the Baptist ideas held by his grandfather and uncle. Records of the period frequently show that members of a Congregational church were dismissed for holding the "Baptist error." Marcus waited until he returned to Rushville before he joined the church.

Just what event or combination of circumstances caused Marcus to return to Rushville in 1820, after ten years' residence in Massachusetts, is not known. [Letter 4.] At this time he should have completed as much of the schooling as was offered by Moses Hallock. He was then ready for college. With his heart set upon the Christian ministry, it may well be that Marcus returned to see if the necessary financial assistance could be secured to permit him to continue his studies. A more probable explanation is that his stepfather and mother felt that since he was eighteen he was old enough to bear an active part in the work of the shoeshop and tannery. Augustus was then married and had his own home. Marcus, as the second eldest son in the family, was needed. Greatly disappointed but obedient, Whitman turned from his schoolbooks to assist his stepfather.

When Marcus returned to Rushville, he found that a new brick meetinghouse had been erected in 1818. This building is still in use, although it has been remodeled and repaired several times during the past years. The pastor of the church was the Rev. Joseph Merrill. Unfortunately the minutes of the church for its early years have been lost, but in a recently discovered record book of Samuel Whitman, the brother of Marcus, we find the following item: "Nov. 1870. Fifty years this month since I profest to love God and to love his people. Brother Marcus Whitman profest to love God the same time. S. Whitman."[33] This means that Marcus Whitman joined the Rushville church in November, 1820, and harmonizes with his statement: "I did not united with the Church until I returned to Rushville (my native place.)" [Letter 3.]

A new chapter in Whitman's life opened when he returned to Rushville to assume a man's labor in the work of the world.

---

[33] Original owned by Mrs. Maude Walker, of Wayland, N. Y.

CHAPTER TWO

WHITMAN'S MEDICAL TRAINING
1820-1832

MARCUS WHITMAN returned to Rushville with the hope of studying for the ministry. However, in this ambition he was disappointed. In the letter of Mary Alice Wisewell, to which reference has already been made, we find the statement:

> His heart was set on studying for the ministry, but he was opposed by his brothers who thought his limited means would compel him to be a charity scholar, and persuaded him against his will to take up the study of medicine. My mother says many a time she has seen the big tears on his face as he thought of his disappointment in his course of life.[1]

To this statement Joel Wakeman (1809-1898), whose personal reminiscences of Marcus Whitman appeared in a Prattsburg, New York, newspaper in 1893 and again in 1898, took exception. Wakeman wrote:

> If Marcus Whitman felt it was his duty to enter the ministry ten thousand brothers could not have changed his mind. A clear conviction of duty was with him the voice of God, and no power on earth could restrain him from prompt obedience.[2]

Whatever the truth may be, the financial difficulty suggested by Mary Alice Wisewell was a real obstacle. In Whitman's day the minister was the best educated man in the community. The Congregational and the Presbyterian denominations, with which Whitman had contacts, frowned upon an uneducated ministry. It was expected that a minister should have a full college course and three years of seminary work. There were exceptions to this general rule, but on the whole these two denominations insisted upon a thorough scholastic training. Seven years of college and seminary work were costly. It seems probable that the family could offer little or no financial assistance to Marcus in the fulfillment of his cherished plans.

---

[1] In the Naples *Record*, Sept. 24, 1913, there is an article by Frank Wisewell which contains a similar statement.

[2] Prattsburg *News*, Feb. 3, 1898. Wakeman's original MSS. are in Coll. Wn.

From available evidence it is also possible that Whitman's mother was unsympathetic to the idea of her son's becoming a minister. In Whitman's first letter to the American Board he wrote: "My Mother is living and professes a hope but is not attracted to any church." The Congregational church of Rushville was organized in 1802 with fifteen charter members,[3] and although Beza and Alice Whitman were then living in Rushville, they were not numbered among the fifteen. There is no record that either of them ever joined. However, Captain Henry Green, Mrs. Whitman's brother, was one of the organizers and later became a deacon. Oren Green, the son of Noah, another of her brothers, was also an active worker in the church.

An extract from a letter which Marcus wrote to his mother on May 27, 1843, closed with the following appeal:

Let me say in conclusion that I feel most desirious to know that my Dear Mother has determined to live the rest of her days witnessing a good profession of godliness. What keeps you from this. Is it that you are not a sinner, or if not that is it that there is no Saviour of sinners, or is it that you have not too long refused & neglected to love & obey him. Has not his forbearance & his mercy been very long expended towards you. [Letter 134.]

If the mother did not desire her eighteen-year-old son to enter the ministry, it would have been easy to find a satisfactory excuse for opposing his plans in the financial burden involved. In spite of his deep disappointment, Marcus was obedient. We surmise that for the next three years he lived in his mother's home and rendered such assistance as was possible to his stepfather in his business.

From the evidence at our disposal we have every reason to believe that Marcus took an active part in the work of the Rushville church. He was received into its membership on confession of faith by the Rev. Joseph Merrill (1777-1846), who had been installed as the first settled pastor of the church on July 5, 1809.[4] Mr. Merrill was, therefore, Whitman's first pastor. Perhaps he had officiated at the funeral service of Beza Whitman. Because of the inability of the people of Rushville to pay a sufficient salary, Mr. Merrill also served a Presbyterian congregation at Hopewell in an adjacent township, and in 1821 severed his rela-

---

[3] *Centennial Celebration*, p. 5.

[4] A. B., Dartmouth, 1906. No record is given of his theological seminary, if any. Chapman, *Sketches of the Alumni of Dartmouth College.*

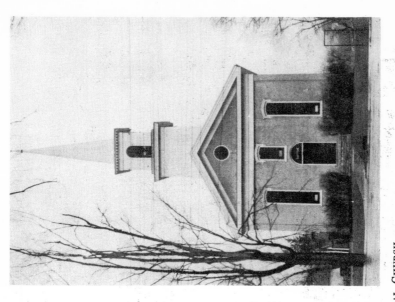

RUSHVILLE CONGREGATIONAL CHURCH.

This brick building, erected in 1818, is still standing. Changes were made in 1845, 1860, and 1899. Here Marcus Whitman joined the Church in 1820, and here he worshipped when in Rushville. From the *Centennial Celebration, Rushville Church.*

MARCUS WHITMAN'S HOME IN RUSHVILLE.

The drawing was made from an old faded photograph. This house, so it is believed, was erected by Beza Whitman shortly before his death. Here Marcus lived 1820-1825.

tionship with the Rushville church in order to give full time
to the Hopewell group.

On May 2, 1821, the day after Mr. Merrill left, the Rev.
David Page (1790-1855) was installed.[5] Mr. Page was a
Presbyterian. In 1814 the Rushville church united with the
Presbytery of Geneva under the "Plan of Union," which had
been devised in 1801 by the Congregational Association of
Connecticut and the Presbyterian General Assembly. This
agreement made it possible for members of both denominations in small communities to work together in one organization. The Rushville church withdrew from the presbytery
in 1855 and thus again became fully Congregational.

Both Merrill and Page were graduates of Dartmouth
College. They were educated and capable pastors, who, no
doubt, supplemented the fine Christian training Marcus had
received in Massachusetts. According to one report, Marcus
studied Latin under Mr. Page.[6]

The only contemporaneous record which throws definite
light upon Whitman's activities from 1820-1823, inclusive,
is the original record book of the Sunday school of the Rushville church,[7] in which the name of Marcus Whitman occurs
twice. He is listed as a teacher in June, 1822, and again in
1823, when his name appears first on a list of seventeen
teachers. His brother Augustus was then serving as the
secretary. Marcus taught a class of boys whose ages ranged
from eight to sixteen. Nearly twenty-five years later one of
the boys from his Sunday school class, Newton Gilbert,
visited the Whitman home in Oregon. [Letter 178.] The
history of the Rushville church written for its centennial in
1902 states that upon his return to Rushville, Marcus "immediately interested himself in the welfare of the church
by conducting sunrise prayer meetings in company with
two other young men."[8]

The church was not without its missionary enthusiasm,
although at that time the foreign missionary movement had
touched but few of the American churches. On October 23,
1819, the American Board sent seven missionaries and their
wives on the brig *Thaddeus* to begin missionary work in the
Hawaiian Islands, then known as the Sandwich Islands. The

---

[5] A. B., Dartmouth, 1817. Attended Andover Theo. Sem. for one year,
1818-1819. Chapman, *op. cit.*, p. 188.

[6] *Sunset*, Aug., 1909, p. 186.

[7] In care of Mrs. Ellen Bates, of Rushville.

[8] *Centennial Celebration*, p. 28.

group reached Honolulu on April 19, 1820. Among these
pioneers of the cross was Elisha Loomis (1799-1836), then
only twenty years old, of Rushville. He was a distant relative of Calvin Loomis, the stepfather of Marcus Whitman.
Loomis was a printer and took with him a printing press
valued at $450. The historical sketch of the Rushville
church contains the following interesting item about the
press:

> It is interesting to add, in view of the fact that Mr. Loomis and
> Dr. Whitman were both members of this church, that in 1839, the
> mission at Honolulu having been presented with a finer outfit, pre-
> sented the printing press, ink and paper to the Whitman mission at
> Waiilatpu.[9]

Loomis was influential in helping reduce the native
language to writing, and in the translation and printing of
the Gospel of Matthew into Hawaiian. After rendering
faithful service until 1827, he was obliged to return to his
home with his wife, because of his ill-health.

Loomis had gone before Whitman returned to Rushville
in 1820, yet it is possible that they knew each other as boys.
Certainly they were friendly after Loomis returned from
the Islands, for when Marcus sent in a list of references to
the American Board in the summer of 1834, he mentioned
"Elisha Loomis, former Missionary Printer to the Sandwich
Islands." [Letter 4.] In tracing out the roots of Marcus
Whitman's missionary interest, we should remember Elisha
Loomis. Without question Marcus spent hours listening to
the wonderful tales that his friend Elisha could tell, and at
times there came over him the old longing to be a minister
and go as a missionary to the benighted heathen in distant
lands.

"RIDING" WITH DR. BRYANT

Marcus Whitman celebrated his twenty-first birthday
on September 4, 1823. Legally he was free to follow his own
inclinations, and it appears that he then began "to ride" with
Dr. Bryant. In those days, when a young man aspired to be
a doctor, he usually began his studies under some local
physician, who would take the student with him when he
visited his patients. In the colloquialism of the time this
was referred to as "riding with the Doctor." From the

---

[9] *Centennial Celebration*, p. 28. Elisha Loomis is buried in the
French Cemetery near Rushville. The cemetery gets its name from a
family of that name who once lived in the vicinity.

meager evidence available, it appears that Marcus Whitman began riding with Dr. Ira Bryant, of Rushville, soon after Whitman reached his majority.

Frustrated in his plan to enter the Gospel ministry, Marcus turned to the medical profession as a promising field for altruistic service. One hundred and more years ago the medical profession did not demand the extensive educational background that it exacts now. A medical course was comparatively inexpensive. All that was needed in preparation was a good English education. Whitman had more than was required, in that he had studied both Greek and Latin. He was better prepared to pursue his medical studies than were the majority of the students of his day. Although the financial burden of a theological course might have been too heavy for him at the time, such was not the case with a medical course.

Dr. Ira Bryant (1786-1840), supposed to have been a distant cousin of William Cullen Bryant, settled in Rushville sometime prior to 1818.[10] He became a member of the county medical society and remained at Rushville, practicing medicine until he died in 1840. Whitman began his medical studies in Rushville under Dr. Bryant, as is indicated in his first letter to the American Board, wherein he wrote: "In my profession I studied and practiced regularly with a good physician."

Whitman does not state just how long he "rode" with Dr. Bryant. In view of the fact that he entered a medical school in the fall of 1825 and received a license to practice medicine the next spring, the assumption is that he must have had at least two years' experience with the local physician. This period would have included the years from the time he was twenty-one until he was twenty-three.[11]

One of Whitman's childhood playmates, and later a schoolmate, was Jonathan Pratt, Jr. (1801-1880). In the summer of 1936 some new material bearing directly and indirectly upon the life of Marcus Whitman was discovered

---

[10] *Centennial Celebration*, p. 41. The first doctor in Rushville, and for many years the only doctor, was Dr. Buffum Harkness (1773-1817). The fact that he died in 1817 may suggest the time when Dr. Bryant settled in the village.

[11] Wisewell letter, Coll. W.: "He took up a three years course of study with Dr. Ira Bryant of Rushville and received his diploma at Fairfield in 1824." Miss Wisewell was in error as to the date when her uncle received his license, and this error was repeated in Eells, *Marcus Whitman*, p. 23.

in the home of Carlton Pratt, the son of Jonathan. This material included two letters written by Marcus to Jonathan in 1827 and 1828, which are the oldest Whitman letters known to be extant. It also included Jonathan's diary, which began with an entry for January 1, 1824, and closed with one for May 2, 1838. The diary is not complete, for frequently weeks and even months passed without an entry. However, the eight double foolscap sheets of closely written material throw much new light upon some obscure years in the life of Marcus Whitman. The fact that Jonathan Pratt and Marcus Whitman were both students of Dr. Ira Bryant during a part of the period covered by the diary gives us added interest in what happened to Jonathan.

In his old age Carlton Pratt was sick and infirm. Shortly before the new Whitman material was discovered, he sold an antique desk to a collector. The contents of the drawers were dumped on the floor when the desk was removed, and amid the resulting debris the Whitman letters were later found. On November 19, 1936, the old house burned with all of its contents. Carlton Pratt lost his life in the fire.[12] The Whitman source material was discovered none too soon.

From the documents secured from the Pratt home we learn that on November 10, 1823, Chester Loomis and Augustus Whitman gave Jonathan Pratt a letter of recommendation to teach a common school. They testified to his good moral character and to the fact that he possessed sufficient literary requirements for the position. It appears that Jonathan alternated between teaching school and "riding with Dr. Bryant." In all probability Marcus Whitman did the same. A resident of Portland, Oregon, recently wrote: "When I was a young girl my grandmother, Lavina Lindsley born in Middlesex, New York, 1810, told me several times that she had been to school to Marcus Whitman."[13] In 1845 Whitman referred to the visit of Newton Gilbert and said that he was "formerly my day & Sabbath School Schollar." [Letter 178.] So for a time Marcus Whitman must have taught school.

There is also the tradition that Marcus assisted his brother Henry in the operation of a sawmill near Potter

---

[12] Rochester *Democrat & Chronicle*, Nov. 20, 1936. Source material which the author secured from this home is now in Coll. Wn.

[13] Mrs. Isaac Lee Patterson to the author, July 17, 1936. This Lavina Lindsley is not to be confused with the Levina Linsley to whom H. H. Spalding was once engaged.

Center.[14] Such experiences as teaching school, assisting in the shoeshop and tannery, and working in a sawmill gave Whitman some skills which proved to be of the utmost value to him in later years when circumstances made it necessary for him to provide for himself or do without.

Jonathan Pratt's diary opens with a statement that he had been to Canandaigua, the county seat of Ontario County, where he heard an oration by Mr. J. C. Spencer, who was a lawyer of that city. Mr. Spencer later became Secretary of War and then Secretary of Treasury in President Tyler's cabinet and was of great assistance to Marcus Whitman in 1843 when he was in Washington. In all probability Whitman also knew Spencer at the time mentioned by his friend Jonathan.

After completing a term of school teaching on February 23, 1824, Jonathan began his medical studies under Dr. Bryant. On March 5 he went to Bethel, now called Gorham, where he got a "cranium or scull." On March 15 he wrote: "Friday amnesty declared between J. P. & M. W." Nowhere in the diary is the name Marcus Whitman mentioned, but twice he gives the initial letters "M. W." which seem to refer to Marcus. Perhaps in this entry of March 15 we can assume that the amnesty was declared between Jonathan Pratt and Marcus Whitman.

On April 4, Pratt described what was expected of the medical student:

Saturday finished Anatomy & was pleased to get through for I found a great part of it verry dry study, but think of the different parts of which it is composed, viz. Muscles, bloodvessels, Lymphatics and Nerves, that the Muscles is the most perplexing. When shall I get through with my studies; two long years (if I live) before I can attend a course of medical lectures one course of which being three months will complete my studies.

Here Jonathan states quite clearly that a medical student was expected to study two years under a local physician and then have three months in a medical school before receiving his license. This was the procedure followed by Marcus Whitman.

On July 1 Pratt wrote: " ... heard a controversy between Dr. C. and M. W. respecting some observations made by the latter." From other references we learn that Dr. C. is Dr. Chatterton, and we can believe that M. W. is Marcus Whit-

---

14 Eells, *Marcus Whitman*, p. 23.

man. No further information has been discovered about Dr. Chatterton, and we are left in doubt regarding the nature of the controversy. A few days later Jonathan himself had a controversy with the same doctor and wrote: " . . . think he is not a verry likely fellow considering the stories."

After spending the summer and fall of 1824 "riding with Dr. Bryant," Jonathan returned to school teaching at Middlesex in December, 1824. In May of the next year he resumed his medical studies. On the 29th of that month he rode to Penn Yan "to hear a student examined for the purpose of getting a diploma and entering into the practice of physic." By an act of the New York Legislature in 1806, county medical societies were given the authority to examine all who desired to practice "physic and surgery" and if judged competent to license the same. Jonathan Pratt referred to the license as a "diploma."

No mention is made of Whitman, nor even of his initials, in Pratt's diary for 1825. Since Jonathan did not begin his studies with Dr. Bryant until May 22, and since Whitman enrolled in the medical college at Fairfield, Herkimer County, on October 3 of that year, it is possible that Whitman had received from Dr. Bryant all the training the local physician could give. In November, 1825, Jonathan returned to school teaching, and in April of the following year he "concluded to recommence the study of physic." On September 2, 1826, Dr. Ira Bryant addressed the following communication to Doctor Cleveland, of Benton:

Dear Sir Doct Pratt the bearer of this has been a student of mine his term of study being Towards a completion he wishes to come under the wing of some practioner that he may gain a livelyhood. Doct Pratt is a man well informed in Physic and I can recommend him to you a(s) a man of good morals and strict veracity. If you could help him to a place you would confer a great favor on him and oblige your friend and humble servant.

From this it appears that Jonathan had secured sufficient training under Dr. Bryant to enable him to secure a license from the county medical society. The title "Doct." was used even by those who did not have an M.D. degree. The title then signified an occupation and not an education.

WHITMAN AT FAIRFIELD

Not one of the several biographers of Marcus Whitman has given correctly the facts regarding his medical training. It is commonly reported that he was graduated with an M.D.

ON SURGERY.

Samuel Cooper's First Lines of the Practice of Surgery, 4th ed. ; Dorsey's Elements of Surgery; Boyer's Surgery.

ON OBSTETRICS.

Burns' Principles of Midwifery, by Dr. James; Denman's Midwifery, by Dr. Francis ; Dewees' Abridgement of Baudelocque's Midwifery, or Dewees' Midwifery.

ON CHEMISTRY.

Brande's Manual of Chemistry, or Gorham's Elements of Chemical Science ; Thomson's System of Chemistry, by Dr. Cooper ; Parkes' Chemical Catechism, and Hare's edition of Henry's Chemistry.

ON MATERIA MEDICA.

Beck's Murray's Materia Medica, and the Pharmacopœia of the United States.

ON PRACTICE.

Cullen's Practice of Physic, with Notes by Dr. Caldwell ; Armstrong's Works ; Bedingfield's Compendium.

ON ANATOMY AND PHYSIOLOGY.

Bell's, Fyfe's or Wistar's Anatomy : Baillie's Morbid Anatomy ; London Dissector : Magendie's Elements of Physiology.

EXPENSES.

Tickets for attending the Lectures are as follows:
For Anatomy and Physiology, $12
Chemistry and Materia Medica, 12

PAGE FROM THE CATALOG OF THE FAIRFIELD MEDICAL COLLEGE.
Medical textbooks recommended by the Fairfield Medical College catalog of 1825-26.

Surgery,   10
Midwifery,   10
Practice and Medical Jurisprudence,   10

To be paid on taking out the Tickets.

This regulation will hereafter be strictly and invariably inforced.

The whole expense for Tickets, Board, Wood, &c. during a course, need not exceed 100 dollars.

Any further information that may be desired respecting the regulations of the institution, either as to the Lectures or the requisitions for graduation, may be readily obtained by applying to the following individuals :

Joseph White, M. D. President of the College, &c. Cherry-Valley, Otsego county.

Westel Willoughby, M. D. Vice-President, &c. Newport, Herkimer county.

James Hadley, M. D. Fairfield, Herkimer county.

T. Romeyn Beck, M. D. Albany.

James M'Naughton, M. D. Albany.

JAMES HADLEY, *Register.*

N.B. A summer course on Chemistry, will be delivered by **Dr.** Hadley, to commence on the first Monday in June next, and to continue six weeks.— Ticket fee $6.

Dr. Lewis C. Beck, of Albany, will on the 3d Monday in June, commence a course of Lectures on Botany, to continue four weeks.—Ticket fee $4.

ANOTHER PAGE FROM THE FAIRFIELD MEDICAL COLLEGE CATALOG OF 1825-26.

degree from Fairfield in 1824, whereas he did not actually
receive this degree until 1832. Some writers state that he
attended the Berkshire Medical Institution at Pittsfield,
Massachusetts.[15] Recent research has uncovered source material which removes all doubt of when and where Whitman
received his professional training.[16]

Marcus Whitman enrolled in the College of Physicians
and Surgeons of the Western District of New York, located
at Fairfield, Herkimer County, New York, on October 3,
1825. Among the source documents that tell the story of
Whitman's medical training is the original ticket given by
Dr. Westel Willoughby to Marcus Whitman on October 3
upon the payment of ten dollars as tuition for "Lectures on
Midwifery." On the back the ticket bears the endorsement
of Dr. Willoughby in his handwriting.[17]

Fairfield College was chartered in 1812 and was called
the College of Physicians and Surgeons of the Western District of New York to distinguish it from the College of
Physicians and Surgeons of the Southern District of New
York, located in New York City. When Whitman enrolled
at Fairfield early in October, 1825, he found on the faculty
—Doctors Westel Willoughby, Joseph White, T. Romeyn
Beck, James Hadley, and James McNaughton. Dr. Willoughby was one of the founders of the school and its head
for nearly thirty years. Under his leadership the Fairfield
school grew until it reached its peak enrollment of 217
students in the year 1833-34.[18]

In the sixteen-week session of 1825-26, when Whitman
first enrolled, there were 130 students. When he returned
for the 1831-32 session, Fairfield College ranked third among
the medical schools of the nation in point of size, for it then
had an enrollment of 205. In 1839 the trustees voted to close
the school after the graduation in 1840, for they realized
that the school's greatest usefulness was over. Fairfield was
out of the way and could not provide the clinical facilities
found elsewhere. Competing schools, more favorably lo-

---

[15] Mowry, *Marcus Whitman*, p. 62. Dyer, *History of Plainfield*,
p. 93. Dr. F. C. Waite, of Cleveland, examined the complete list of students of this institution without finding Whitman's name.

[16] *O.H.Q.*, Sept. 1936, carried an article by Dr. F. C. Waite on
"The Medical Education of Marcus Whitman."

[17] Coll. U.

[18] *Transactions of the Med. Soc. of the State of N. Y.*, Vol. 4, Par.
3, p. 160.

cated, were attracting the students. The school closed while its reputation was still high.[19]

Among the graduates and faculty members of the Fairfield College were many who won enduring fame. Asa Gray (1810-1888) received his M.D. from Fairfield in 1831 and afterwards lectured there to the medical students on botany. Possibly Whitman was one of his students. Gray afterwards served at both the University of Michigan and Harvard University. Daniel Brainard, once a student at Fairfield, founded Rush Medical College with a faculty almost all of whom were Fairfield men. One of these men was Dr. N. S. Davis, who organized the American Medical Association in 1847. Altogether about twelve hundred men attended the Fairfield Medical College for one or two years. Among them, in 1835-36, was Martin, the son of President Van Buren. His father was at that time Vice-President under Jackson. Many of these men went West and became doctors in frontier communities.

Dr. F. C. Waite, of the Western Reserve Medical School, Cleveland, Ohio, who is an outstanding authority on the history of the early medical schools of our country, states:

I say advisedly and with much familiarity with all the medical schools of that period that *no other school in the United States* could have trained Whitman for the work he was to do as a frontier physician as could Fairfield, for that was the purpose of the school, namely, to train men for frontier work.[20]

It was natural for Whitman to decide on Fairfield. The school was nearer to his home than any other medical college. The cost was reasonable. The catalog for 1825-26 advertised: "The whole expense for Tickets, Board, Wood, &c. during a course, not to exceed 100 dollars." The cost of the tickets alone for the courses offered that term amounted to fifty-four dollars.[21]

Regarding the books to be used in the different courses, the catalog declared:

It is recommended to Students, that they furnish themselves with some of the most approved works on each branch of instruction, as a sufficient number of copies may not be at hand to supply a large class.[22]

---

[19] *O.H.Q.*, June, 1936, contains an article on the history of Fairfield College by Dr. O. Larsell, of Portland.

[20] Letter to author, July, 1935.

[21] A copy of the catalog is in the New York State Library, Albany, N. Y. Photostat copy in Coll. Wn. This shows that Whitman registered from Gorham, the township in which his native place was located.

[22] Medical colleges then rented textbooks to the students.

ONE OF WHITMAN'S MEDICAL "TICKETS."

These "tickets" were issued to medical students to show that they had paid the tuition for the lectures indicated. This is made out in Dr. Willoughby's handwriting. Original owned by Miss Underwood.

THE FAIRFIELD MEDICAL COLLEGE.
From Benton, *History of Herkimer County*, p. 229.

Only the central building is now standing, being used as a grange hall. The two buildings to the right belonged to the medical school. A monument erected in 1923 on the site bears the following inscription:

"On this campus Fairfield Academy was founded in 1802, the funds being raised by a committee headed by Captain Moses Mather. In 1803 was incorporated by the Regents of the University of the State of New York and in 1812 the College of Physicians and Surgeons was established continuing until 1839 and graduated 555 physicians. The academy was continued and reorganized as Fairfield Seminary in 1839 for the higher education of both men and women conducted as a military academy from 1891 to 1902."

Dr. Westel Willoughby, Jr.
(1769-1844).

Photographed from oil portrait in possession of a descendant of Dr. Willoughby. Artist and date of portrait is not known.

Dr. Joseph White (1763-1832).

From *Williams, Descendants of Thomas White of Weymouth, Mass.* Only twenty-five copies of this book were printed.

Dr. T. Romeyn Beck (1781-1855).

From *American Journal of Insanity*, Vol. 12, 1855.

Dr. James Hadley (1785-1869).

From picture in the possession of the widow of his grandson, former President Hadley of Yale.

Dr. James McNaughton
(1769-1874).

Taken about 1862. From *Tribute to Memory of Dr. James McNaughton*, Albany 1875.

Dr. John Delamater (1787-1867).

From Cleve's *Medical Biography*.

WHITMAN'S PROFESSORS AT THE FAIRFIELD MEDICAL COLLEGE.
By courtesy of Dr. F. C. Waite, Cleveland, Ohio.

The popular prejudice against the use of human bodies for dissection by medical students was still strong in the days of Whitman's medical preparation. Sometimes the students would resort to "resurrection," as they called it, of recently buried bodies. Others with less imagination referred to the practice as "grave robbing." The public naturally resented such practices, and oftentimes the medical schools as well as the individual students became involved in trouble. In the light of this knowledge, we can appreciate the following action taken by the Board of Trustees of Fairfield College on January 19, 1819:

A resolution was passed by the board of trustees dismissing any student who should be concerned directly or indirectly in digging up any dead human body, for the purpose of dissection in the college.[23]

The State of New York by legislative act of March 30, 1820, gave to the college the bodies of convicts dying in the Auburn prison which were not claimed by relatives or friends. Dissection of a human body was, therefore, incidental and depended upon the success of the faculty in securing an occasional cadaver. Even so, Fairfield College was the only medical school in New York State where cadavers could legally be used for dissection.

Anatomy was taught largely by lectures, accompanied by charts or demonstrations on a skeleton. The college had three buildings when Whitman first attended. One built of stone was called the Laboratory. In spite of such a name, the students had virtually no laboratory facilities as we now know them. Since the school was located in a village, which never had over two thousand inhabitants, there was no hospital or clinic near by in which the students might learn the art of healing from practical experience. In fact it was not until 1840 that medical students began to use a clinic even in the larger centers of study.

Usually not more than one of the faculty members lived in Fairfield. The others came from a distance, sometimes as far away as New York City, to give an intensive series of lectures, sometimes two a day, and then depart. From time to time the State of New York gave financial assistance to the school. In 1812, an endowment of fifteen thousand dollars was given, and in 1820 an appropriation of one thousand dollars annually for five years was made.[24]

---

[23] Benton, *History of Herkimer County*, p. 226.
[24] *Ibid.*, p. 225.

In all probability William H. Gray, who later was associated with Marcus Whitman in the Oregon mission, was a fifteen-year-old boy living in the village of Fairfield when Whitman was a student at the medical school. Gray was born September 8, 1810, at Fairfield.[25] His father died in the winter of 1825-26, and in the following summer Gray moved to Springfield, Otsego County, New York.[26] If Gray spent his youth in the place where he was born, then the dates of his residence in the village overlap with those of Whitman. It is possible that the two at least knew each other's names, although no reference has been found in later records of any meeting during this time.

THE NEXT FIVE YEARS

Whitman finished his first sixteen-week session at Fairfield Medical College on January 23, 1826. He enrolled again about the 4th of October, 1831. We can trace out only partially his movements during that interval of more than five years.

According to the custom of those days, a medical student could begin independent practice after attending but one session at a medical school. It has been estimated that about one half of the medical students of that period never returned to attend a second session and thereby earn an M.D. degree. Yet these freely spoke of having been "graduated" from a medical college, for then graduation was not always a synonym for having completed the full requirements. There were no graded courses in American medical schools until after the Civil War. A student who returned for the second session would hear the same lectures over again, unless there had been a change of professors in his absence. This caused many students to migrate from one school to another for the second session.

Frequently a student would stay out of school for a year or more and engage in practice, and then return to the medical college. If successful in his examination, he would then receive the M.D. degree. If not successful, the student still practiced under the title of "doctor."

On May 9, 1826, the Herkimer County Medical Society, of which Dr. Westel Willoughby was then president, granted a license to Marcus Whitman to practice medicine within

---

[25] Eells, *Marcus Whitman*, p. 320.
[26] Gray to the American Board, Feb. 17, 1836, Coll. A.

the State of New York.[27] By courtesy such a license was usually good anywhere in the United States or Canada. There were no state licensing medical boards before 1841, so the only legal license a doctor could have was that issued by the county society which received him. Since it was contrary to the usual custom for a county society to license a student who had spent but one session in a medical school, it seems that special recognition was given to Whitman because of his training under Dr. Bryant. These circumstances support the belief that Whitman studied at least two years with the Rushville physician. The date of Whitman's license is probably the date of the annual or semiannual meeting of the society. Perhaps the examination itself came at an earlier time.

The next authenticated date in the life of Marcus Whitman is September 11, 1827, when Whitman wrote from Rushville to his friend Dr. Jonathan Pratt, then located at Sugargrove, Warren County, Pennsylvania, that he was then "Making preparation for going into the practice." Just what Whitman was doing during the eighteen months after leaving Fairfield, we do not know.

Judging by some entries in Pratt's diary, it seems that Jonathan wrote to Marcus and begged him to take over the practice at Sugargrove for a short time. Jonathan was not in good health and wanted a vacation. In a history of Warren County we find the following interesting item:

His successor [i.e. Dr. Hiram Alden's] was Dr. Jonathan Pratt, a single man, who boarded with Henry Catlin three years, and then returned to Ontario County, N. Y. Then arrived another bachelor physician, Dr. Marcus Whitman, who boarded at Willson's Hotel. Several years afterward he was followed by Dr. Noah Weld.... [28]

This is the only direct statement that has yet been discovered to indicate that Marcus Whitman ever practiced medicine in Sugargrove. An examination of the tax rolls for Sugargrove shows that Dr. Jonathan Pratt was assessed as a physician one hundred dollars in 1828, and also for a horse worth forty dollars. In Pratt's diary we find the following notation for March 8, 1828: "Sold out my ride to Dr. N. Weld for one hundred dollars." The next year Dr.

---

[27] Original owned by Mrs. Dudley Voorhees, Middlesex, N. Y.

[28] Schenck and Rann, *History of Warren County*, p. 435. The author visited Sugargrove in June, 1936. A sign on the edge of the village stated: "Sugargrove named for vast original Maple Forest. Founded 1797."

Weld's name appears on the tax list, and for many years following.[29]

From a due consideration of the above facts and in the light of other well-established dates in Whitman's life, it appears safe to say that Whitman's medical practice in Sugargrove was of short duration. It did not cover a period of several years as intimated in the *History of Warren County*. Indeed were it not for the discovery of the two letters from Whitman to Pratt and some items in Pratt's diary for 1827, we should have reason to doubt that Whitman ever lived in Sugargrove.

In August, 1827, Jonathan complained in his diary about his ill health, and sometime during the latter part of the month or the first part of September, wrote to Dr. Whitman, asking him to go to Sugargrove. Dr. Whitman replied on September 11, saying in part:

> Friend Jonathan: I received your letter yesterday; it probably lay in the office several days I being absent to the east.
>
> I have been Making preparation for going into the practice: had calculated to go westward but not as soon as you require but as your health is so ill & you wish me to come and assist you I will endeavor to get ready the latter part of this or by monday of next week. I wish you to stay till I come. I have a hors and probably shall ride him....

Without any mention of the arrival of Dr. Whitman, Pratt wrote in his diary for September 27: "My health still very poor—Set out for Ontario. Arrived Oct. 7th." Pratt wrote of his departure from Rushville on November 26 and of his arrival at Sugargrove on December 13 "after a long and tedious journey owing to bad roads." On the 20th of the month he resumed his practice. Hence it is safe to say that Dr. Whitman practiced medicine in Sugargrove for a period of about two months, merely supplying for his friend Jonathan.[30]

WHITMAN IN CANADA

Following Dr. Pratt's return, Whitman went to Upper Canada[31] to look for a good place to settle. One of Whitman's

---

[29] Courtesy of Frank Miller, Sugargrove, Penna.

[30] The original records of the Presbyterian church of Sugargrove, organized January 25, 1821, make no mention of Whitman.

[31] Canada was divided into two parts by the Ottawa River, Lower Canada and Upper Canada, the terms having reference to the course of the St. Lawrence River. The present province of Ontario is in Upper Canada.

schoolmates at Fairfield, Dr. James Hunter,[32] was practicing medicine in the Niagara Peninsula, and it may be that Whitman went to see him. The following extracts are from Whitman's second letter to Pratt written from Rushville on February 5, 1828:

I write you, yet not as soon as I expected, or had ought; yet owing to staying so long in Canada it was not convenient to write as soon [as] we talked.

I had a good journey with some exceptions but found it necessary to stay longer than I expected in Canada, I found my friend well and reddy to assist me as far as I could wish. I intend going to Canada but as to what particular place I shall occupy I do not know, or whether I shall take license this spring or go into copartnership with Hunter. I intend to return to Canada in a few days, as to the prospects in Canada I cannot say precisely but I think they are better than at Sugargrove.

A record in the minutes of the Rushville church to the effect that Marcus Whitman reunited with that church on November 6, 1830, by letter from "the Presbyterian church in Gainsboro Upper Canada" supplies the information regarding where he settled.[33] This harmonizes with the last entry in Pratt's diary, dated May 2, 1828. Pratt wrote: "Went to Canada crossing the river at Lewiston and continued on in a Southwestern course to near forty mile Creek." It is quite possible that Pratt went to visit his friend Whitman, who might then have been settled in the little village of Snyders Mill, in Gainsboro township, which was located in a southwestern direction from Lewiston.

Upper Canada at that time had no medical schools, and consequently looked either to Great Britain or to the United States for its doctors. Many of the students from Fairfield Medical College settled in Upper Canada, and likewise many of the Fairfield students came from that region. An examination of the minutes of the Upper Canada Medical Board revealed the following:

July, 1829—Present: Widmer, Powell and Deihl. Peter Schofield of Johnston District; J. E. Rankin of Ottawa District; William McMahon of Hallowell; *Marcus Whitman, Niagara District*, and John Hutcheson of Port Hope received certificates.[34]

This action gave Whitman official permission to practice

---

[32] Hunter was registered in the 1825-26 term at Fairfield as being from Niagara, Upper Canada.

[33] No mention has been found of Whitman's dismissal from the Rushville church because those minutes were lost.

[34] Canniff, *The Medical Profession in Upper Canada*, p. 56. Italics, the author's.

medicine in Upper Canada, although it appears that he was following his profession there before he received his certificate. The phrase, "received certificates," means that Whitman and his companions were licensed without the necessity of being examined. Their training and previous experience elsewhere were found to be an acceptable substitute. It is quite possible that this license by a British medical board was of value to Whitman in his later contacts with Hudson's Bay officials in Old Oregon.

The little village of Snyders Mill in Gainsboro is now called St. Anns and is about twenty-five miles west of Niagara Falls. A visit to St. Anns in the summer of 1935 helped to reconstruct the story of Whitman's experiences in Canada. The road from Niagara Falls to the village, now almost nonexistent, crosses the Welland Canal. The canal was opened in 1833; and, therefore, Whitman must have seen men at work upon the project. A reference to the 1829 census of Upper Canada shows that the County of Lincoln, in which Gainsboro was located, and which then included the present County of Welland, had less than twenty thousand inhabitants. The settlements were largely along the two lake shores and along the Niagara River. The digging of the canal undoubtedly stimulated the whole region and may have been a factor which led Whitman to settle there. Pratt states that he found the country "altogether more pleasant than I had anticipated. Inhabitants are generaly wealthy."

All memory of Whitman's residence there has been forgotten. Not a single tradition lingers of the young doctor from the States who once ministered to the bodily needs of the inhabitants.

After a residence of about two years and a half in Canada, Whitman returned to Rushville.[35] He wanted to go back to his first love, the ministry. We are somewhat surprised at such a decision, for Whitman was then twenty-eight years old. His later success as a doctor can be taken as an indication of his skill in his earlier years. It was unusual for a man of his age to think of taking the required seven years of college and seminary work for ordination. Just why did he go back?

Again we must surmise. It may be that a new doctor had moved into his community, bringing undesirable competi-

---

[35] This is in correction of the statement made by Mary Alice Wisewell to the effect that Whitman spent four years in Canada.

tion. Our only definite information comes from Whitman's letter of June 27, 1834, wherein he wrote: "In the fall of 1830 I gave up the practise of my profession and entered upon a course of study preparatory to the ministry."

HE RETURNS TO RUSHVILLE

According to a tradition held by some of the descendants of Thomas Saunders (1764-1846), a pioneer resident of Rushville, Marcus Whitman was married to Persia[36] Saunders, a daughter of Thomas. This is extremely unlikely, for Persia's tombstone in the French Cemetery at Rushville gives her maiden name and states that she was born July 12, 1807 and died March 28, 1830. Surely if this marriage had taken place, it would have been remembered by Rushville residents who lived on into the period when Whitman had become a national figure. It is possible that Marcus Whitman was engaged to Persia Saunders and that with the passing of the years the tradition became confused in regard to some of the facts. The fact that Christopher Saunders, a brother of Persia, and Augustus Whitman each married into the Putney family, thus becoming brothers-in-law, may have added confusion to the theory.

Whitman's pastor in Rushville, under whom he may have resumed his theological studies, was the Rev. Joseph Brackett (1781-1832). Mr. Brackett had been installed pastor on February 23, 1826, succeeding Mr. Page. Records show that Mr. Brackett died September 24, 1832, after a period of ill-health. The minute book of the Rushville church carries the record: "He was a man of piety, of amiable deportment and faithful in the discharge of ministerial duty." His successor was the Rev. H. P. Strong, who was not installed until January, 1833.[37]

We know little of Whitman's activities from the time he returned from Canada in the fall of 1830 to the time he re-entered Fairfield Medical College in October, 1831. As has been mentioned, he reunited with the Rushville church on November 6, 1830. In his letter of June 27, 1834, Whitman wrote as follows regarding his theological studies: "I had not continued long, when for want of active exercise I found my health become impaired by a pain in the left side

---

[36] Tombstone located by Robert Moody, of Rushville. This tradition was called to the author's attention by A. L. Saunders, of Canton, Ill. Persia's name was pronounced Per-sī'a.

[37] *Centennial Celebration*, p. 7.

which I attributed to an inflamation of the spleen." For a
time he gave up his studies and then went back only to find
the old trouble recurring. "Then I used exercise," he wrote,
"and continued it for a number of months when I found I
was not able to study and returned to the practice of my
profession." [Letter 4.] A question naturally arises—if his
health prevented his continuing his theological studies, how
was he able to return to his medical studies? For want of
fuller information we must leave this unanswered.

HE RETURNS TO FAIRFIELD

In October, 1831, Whitman again enrolled in Fairfield
Medical College for another course of sixteen weeks. Perhaps he had realized the folly of trying to prepare for the
ministry at his age. He was convinced that his best policy
was to continue in the work in which he had been trained.
He coveted the M.D. degree for the added prestige it would
give.

Whitman found that the medical school had grown during the five years and more in which he had been away.
Only one change had been made in the faculty. Dr. White
had retired in 1827 and was succeeded by Dr. John Delamater. Dr. Delamater was an eminent physician and a successful teacher. Whitman was highly favored in having the
opportunity to study under such men as Willoughby and
Delamater, the latter of whom taught in eight different
medical schools between the years 1823 and 1843. Delamater founded the present School of Medicine of Western
Reserve University at Cleveland, Ohio, in 1843.[38]

Whitman returned to the medical school with that new
zest for learning that comes after one has been out in the
world for several years. He was older. He had had experience. His perspective was changed. No longer was he
dealing with mere theories; he was dealing with facts that
might mean life or death to his patients in later years.

The session ended in January, 1832, when thirty-nine re-
ceived their medical degrees. The recent discovery of the
minutes of the Board of Trustees completes the picture of
Whitman's medical training.[39] His thesis was entitled
"Caloric." The word caloric was then applied, according to
Dr. F. C. Waite, "to some subtle influence that caused the

---

[38] Waite, "John Delamater," *Bulletin of the Cleveland Academy of
Medicine*, May, 1930.

[39] Discovered by Dr. Waite in the New York State Library, Albany.

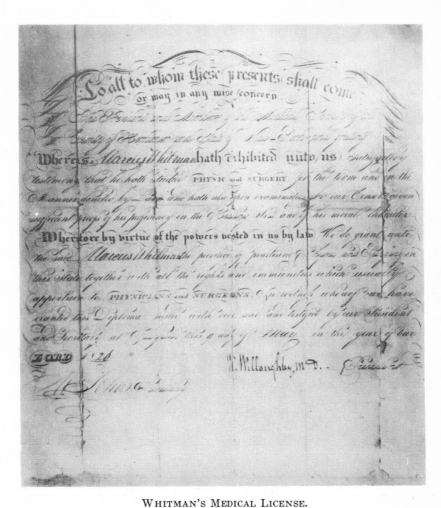

WHITMAN'S MEDICAL LICENSE.
The original was discovered in a farm home near Rushville, N. Y., in the summer of 1935.
Picture by courtesy of Mrs. Dudley Vorhees.

THE RECORD OF WHITMAN'S GRADUATION THESIS.

The above picture was taken from the original records of the trustees of Fairfield Medical College showing Whitman's name (third from the bottom) as being one to receive a degree in 1832. His thesis title was "Caloric." The name at the top, Robert Treat Paine, was probably the most famous of Whitman's classmates.

heat of the body." Whitman was studying normal temperatures and fevers. He was pioneering in medical thought
for, strange as it may seem to us now, the doctors then
failed to appreciate the value of bodily temperatures as a
factor in the diagnosis of disease. Would that we had a
copy of his thesis.

In the minutes of the trustees for January 24, 1832, we
can read:

After the reading of the Thesis by the candidates for graduation,
and it being certified by the Register that they had individually complied
with the requirements of the Laws of this state and the ordinances of
the college, It was resolved that they be recommended to the Regents
of the University for the Degree of Doctor of Medicine.

Thereafter Marcus Whitman could rightfully, and not
merely by courtesy, be called Doctor Marcus Whitman. He
was a well-trained physician, much better qualified than
the average doctor of his day. He had studied under capable
men. His academic work had been supplemented with years
of actual experience, and finally, his degree came from the
University of the State of New York, which added to his
medical reputation. Thus, at the age of twenty-nine, Marcus
Whitman found himself equipped for his life's work, but
the stage on which he was to play a major rôle was not then
quite ready for his appearance.

CHAPTER THREE

THREE YEARS AT WHEELER
1832-1835

THE village of Wheeler, New York, is to be found in Steuben County, nine miles north of Bath and six miles south of Prattsburg. It is located in the valley of Five-Mile Creek, a tributary of the Cohocton River. Low glaciated drumlin hills line the two sides of the valley, which is about a mile wide at that point.[1]

At a crossroads in the village today is a big boulder on which is fastened a memorial plaque to inform all who will pause to read that once on that spot stood the medical office of Dr. Marcus Whitman. The original building has been moved across the street and converted into a garage and woodshed.

On the highway about two miles south of the village is a marker which points out the place where Henry Harmon Spalding was born on November 26, 1803. At that time Marcus Whitman was a babe a little more than a year old with his parents at Rushville, twenty-five or thirty miles to the north. How strange that these two, who were to be associated for eleven years in the Oregon mission of the American Board, should each have had contacts with the little village of Wheeler.

Even in 1832 Wheeler was still a pioneer community. The population was small, probably not over one hundred. Round about were scattered families who were farming the clearings. The people had little ready money. Like other professional people of his time, Whitman must have been obliged to accept produce in payment for his services, or go unpaid. According to one tradition, Whitman lived in the home of Thomas Aulls, located on the north edge of the village.[2]

Whitman's practice was largely in the country. Roads

---

[1] The first settlers arrived there about 1800, among them Captain Silas Wheeler, who gave his name to the village. Drury, *Spalding*, p. 20.

[2] Aulls died in 1846. His son Ephraim (1809-1880) had the saddle-bags of Dr. Whitman. These passed into the possession of the Presbyterian Historical Society in June, 1936.

were poor, and buggies few and expensive. Hence we can
believe that Whitman rode horseback most of the time. He
might have had to ride ten or fifteen miles in one direction to
see a patient and find upon his return home a call to go
a similar distance in the opposite direction. If a doctor could
keep up his practice by keeping but one horse, it was evident
that his ride was not extensive and that he could not be a
popular or competent doctor. Such a man was designated a
"one-horse doctor," and the expression "one horse" came to
be applied generally as a derogatory term to indicate mediocrity.

Whitman's methods, medicines, and instruments, like
those of the other doctors of his day, were as primitive as
the community in which he lived. He carried no thermometer, for medical schools did not teach the value of temperature in diagnosis. Very few stethoscopes were used by the
doctors, so it is doubtful if Whitman had one. A set of amputating knives cost about fifty dollars. Whitman probably
secured such a set early in his professional career, together
with such other instruments as lances and scalpels. The
doctor was the dentist as well, and with the aid of a turnkey
would extract a tooth, frequently leaving a splinter of the
tooth in the jaw. The cost for such a service was usually
ten cents.

It is safe to say that Dr. Whitman did not have any
obstetrical forceps, because his professor of obstetrics, Dr.
Westel Willoughby, was much opposed to their use. The
germ theory of disease was unknown. Sometimes the doctors would boil their instruments, but usually they were
merely wiped clean and put away. Some of the instruments
had wooden handles. It was the common belief that suppura-
tion was essential to healing, and much was said about
"laudable pus" until as late as 1870. The properties of iodine
as a disinfectant were somewhat appreciated, although the
real reason for its effectiveness was unknown. Sometimes
a weak solution of lye was used.

Because of the belief that disease was caused by an excess
of blood, the doctors of that day practiced bleeding. It was
a remedy which had been used for centuries. No anesthetic
with its merciful power of producing unconsciousness was
then known. In amputation cases, the patient might be made
drunk with liquor, or in case of women or children stupefied
with heavy doses of opium. Frequently they were held by
strong men while the doctor worked as fast as he could.

Skillful surgeons boasted that they could amputate an arm in three minutes, and a leg in five. Only a favored few doctors had a surgical saw. They usually used the ordinary carpenter's fine-toothed saw.

The physician of a hundred years ago had to be his own apothecary. Only the largest towns boasted drug stores, so the doctor had to know how to prepare his own pills. Very few medicines were given in liquid form. The doctor would buy his drugs in bulk in crude form, and then would pulverize them in a hand mortar. Inventories of the drugs used a century ago indicate that a good doctor would have about fifty different kinds. Great reliance was placed on calomel. When Dr. Whitman rode his district, he would take with him quantities of various kinds of drugs. These would be carried in his saddlebags. Thus he was able to supply the medicines needed at the time.

False teeth were reserved only for the wealthy, and even so, they were ill-fitting and uncomfortable. Spectacles were available for those who had weak eyes, but these were fitted by the trial-and-error method, usually with no consideration of the fact that one eye might be out of adjustment with the other. Thus a pair of spectacles often did more harm than good. Sometimes the same pair would be used by several members of the family, as by turn they read the weekly newspaper.

Such were the medical conditions of one hundred years ago.

The business side is of interest. A doctor usually received twenty-five cents for a call at his home, and the fee included the medicine. The fee was doubled if the doctor called on the patient, provided the patient lived within five miles. Beyond that distance he charged six and one-fourth cents for each mile. An obstetrical case would pay from two to five dollars. Ten dollars was the usual fee for amputating a leg.[3]

Yet in spite of the limitations and handicaps under which Whitman worked, as compared with modern-day conditions, we know that Whitman was equipped as successful physicians and surgeons must ever be equipped, in that he had a personality which inspired faith and confidence. The people

---

[3] Dr. F. C. Waite furnished most of the material regarding this section on medical conditions of a century ago. *See* his article, "The Equipment of a Country Doctor of Northern Ohio in 1822," *Ohio State Medical Journal*, July, 1936.

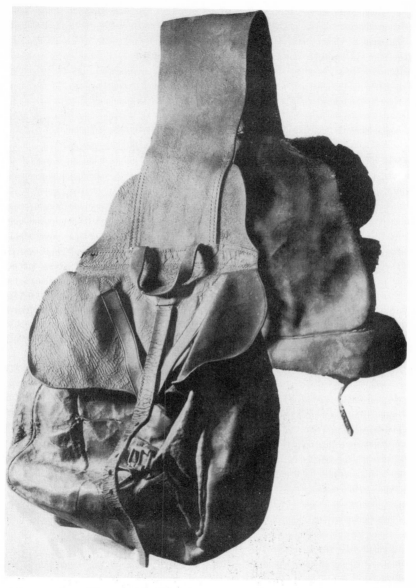

WHITMAN'S SADDLEBAGS USED AT WHEELER.
By courtesy of the Presbyterian Historical Society, Philadelphia.

WHITMAN'S MEDICAL OFFICE AT WHEELER.

The central building is said to be the building Dr. Whitman used, perhaps, as his home as well as his office, while in Wheeler. The building clearly shows that windows were once in the upper story. It is now used as a barn and garage.

By courtesy of Er. Brode.

of Wheeler and vicinity grew to trust and to love him. After
Whitman had practiced medicine at Wheeler for about three
years, the rumor started that he was going to Oregon with
the Rev. Samuel Parker. The following quotation from a
letter written by Parker, January 1, 1835, to the American
Board reveals the attitude of the Wheeler citizens to the
proposition:

I am afraid that the people in Wheeler and the vicinity on account
of their [being] unwilling to spare one whom they so highly esteem as
a physician and Christian, will dissuade him from offering himself.
I shall write him without delay.

Little did Marcus Whitman suspect as he rode the byways
of Steuben County during 1832, 1833, and 1834, that he was
preparing himself for the first great emergency in the
settlement of Old Oregon. If any year in the history of our
country tried the souls of its physicians, it was 1832. In that
year Asiatic cholera came to the United States.

During the World War of 1914-18, Spanish influenza
spread from city to city, from country to country, across the
oceans and around the world with terrifying rapidity, leaving behind millions of newly made graves. A century
earlier, or, to be exact, in 1817, Asiatic cholera sprang up in
Bengal, and began its death march around the world. Transportation was slower then, but the march once begun never
stopped even though at times it was delayed. It swept across
Russia and Poland and by the summer of 1831 reached Berlin. There the epidemic claimed seven thousand lives. By
November of that year it had reached Scotland. In February, 1832, the dread disease had spread to London, and by
March it was in Liverpool. In June it crossed the Atlantic in
a boat from Belfast bound for Quebec, and within a week
after its arrival in America, it was in Montreal, whence it
spread southward through the waterways down to New York,
and across New York State along the Erie Canal to the
Great Lakes. Cases were reported in Detroit on July 5, and
soldiers going to the Black Hawk War carried the epidemic
to Chicago. Others were convenient carriers, spreading the
disease along the Mississippi River, and by mid-September
it was epidemic in New Orleans.

The terror of the people was nearly as dreadful as the
disease itself. And they had reason to be afraid, for the
disease struck with fearful rapidity. Oftentimes people left
their homes in the morning apparently in the best of health,
only to be dead before sundown. From the records of reliable

contemporary physicians, we learn that not more than one in three cases ever recovered in 1832. In following years, as the doctors learned more about it, they were able to save a higher percentage of their patients.

Among the manuscripts of Joel Wakeman is one entitled "The Fearful Scourge of 1832," which began with this statement: "No summer in the history of the American people has ever equaled 1832 for excitement and general prostration of all enterprise." Joel Wakeman lived to be an old man and wrote his account of the plague sometime after 1890. He knew the dark days of the Civil War from personal experience, and yet even such memories could not blot out the terror of the summer of 1832. Wakeman wrote further:

> Every newspaper was freighted with the number of the dead and dying in the city—every breeze that swept by our doors, brought rumors (and often greatly exaggerated rumors) of the rapid increase of the scourge in the villages and inland towns. . . . The plague was bad; so exceedingly bad that the present generation can form no adequate conception of its fearful ravages, and prostrating effects upon the country. . . . [4]

Business was paralyzed for a time. Merchants were afraid to travel to the cities to buy goods. Because of the lack of knowledge about disease germs, all kinds of foolish superstitions swept the country. Some believed that articles of food were responsible for the disease, and for a time melons, cucumbers, green corn, and other vegetables were rejected, and in some places their sale was forbidden by law.

People did about all they could do—they fled. It was noticed that many of the towns in the interior escaped the contagion, and to these the refugees went. Some towns of five thousand people located in the midst of the epidemic lost half their population in a single day because of the evacuations.

The helplessness of the physicians was as great as the terror of the people. Marcus Whitman, who had received his M.D. degree in January of that year, had received no information whatsoever upon the subject of cholera. Ordinary remedies had no effect. The physicians bled their patients, but this only left them less able to combat the disease. The doctors then began to make observations. Deaths were notably prevalent among the lower strata of society, especially among those who lived along the waterways. These people had no sanitary toilet facilities. The

---

[4] Coll. Wn. contains the original manuscript.

rivers and canals, from which they got their drinking water, were soon polluted, but they did not know it. It was also observed that those addicted to intoxicating liquors were most subject to the disease. This we now know to be due to the fact that the saloons were usually along the water fronts, and the customers were provided with drinking water dipped up from some convenient river or canal. We can marvel that the virulence of the disease was not greater than it was.

The doctors slowly learned some things. They advised cleanliness, isolation, and the use of copperas and chloride of lime in drains, cesspools, and outbuildings. In Scotland the members of the famed medical faculty of the University of Edinburgh made some important discoveries which were published in pamphlet form. This pamphlet reached the United States soon after the disease, and was reprinted in many of the newspapers. It was not unusual to see a doctor using a country newspaper as the latest authority in treating the epidemic.

In all probability Wheeler was sufficiently distant from the Erie Canal to avoid the contagion, and yet it was near enough to be troubled with the reports which spread from the afflicted areas. We can be assured that Marcus Whitman read everything he could find pertaining to the treatment of this disease, and it is possible that he was called upon to minister to some isolated cases. The epidemic continued in this country with lessening fury during the next three years. The fact that Dr. Whitman was able to recognize the symptoms of the disease and that he knew something of the best-known methods of treatment proved to be of far-reaching importance in 1835.

"ESTEEM[ED] AS A ... CHRISTIAN"

When Parker wrote to the American Board about Dr. Whitman he said that the people of Wheeler highly esteemed him both as a physician and as a Christian. As was to be expected, Whitman took an active part in the church during his residence in Wheeler. The Rev. James H. Hotchkin, pastor of the Prattsburg church, began religious services in Wheeler in 1815. A church was organized in 1824, which reported twenty-three members to the Presbytery of Bath the following year, but internal dissension developed, which gradually stifled the life of the organization. On October 19, 1831, five men and four women banded themselves together into a new church group.[5] It was called the Wheeler Presbyterian Church.

Detailed information regarding the church is to be found in a collection of documents[6] gathered about forty years ago by the Rev. S. W. Pratt, D.D., who wrote an informing article on Marcus Whitman which was published in the August, 1909, issue of *Sunset*. These documents tell the story of a small struggling congregation, which by considerable sacrifice was able to erect a new building in the spring and summer of 1832. This church was in the process of being built when Marcus Whitman arrived in Wheeler. The dedication services were held on January 10, 1833. The building was used for religious purposes until 1867 and has since been torn down. Among the original records of General O. F. Marshal, long the main supporter of the church, was found the following entry under date of March 11, 1834:

Recd fifteen dollars from Doctor Whitman to pay M H Brown for ballance due on stove & pipe for Meeting house[7]

Whitman was elected a trustee of the church on December 29, 1832, and re-elected to the same office at the business meeting held a year later. A minute in the records of the Auxiliary Bible Society of the County of Steuben for December 11, 1833, states that: "Resolved that Doct. Whitman be and hereby is appointed agent for the town of Wheeler to collect funds for the Society."[8]

In the month of February, 1833, the Rev. James H. Hotchkin began his duties as pastor of the Wheeler church.[9] He was formally installed September 17. It thus fell to Mr. Hotchkin's lot to have been the pastor of Narcissa Prentiss, who became Mrs. Marcus Whitman, and of Henry H. Spalding in earlier years at Prattsburg, and then of Marcus Whitman at Wheeler. There can be no doubt that Whitman was highly favored in the type of men he had for his pastors. Merrill, Hallock, Page, Eastman, Brackett, and Hotchkin were all well-trained, consecrated, and devoted men. To this list we should add the name of the Rev. Henry P. Strong

---

[5] Hotchkin, *History Western New York*, pp. 474-476.

[6] Now in Coll. Wn.

[7] In the possession of General Marshal's grandson, O. F. Marshal.

[8] Original records owned by James McCall, of Bath, N. Y., by whose courtesy this information has been received.

[9] Drury, *Spalding*, p. 26, gives a picture of Hotchkin and more information regarding his life and ministry.

(1785-1835), who succeeded Brackett as pastor of the Rush-ville church in 1832.[10] It was Mr. Strong who first drew the attention of the American Board to Dr. Whitman in a letter written April 25, 1834.

After living at Wheeler for about a year, Whitman trans-ferred his church membership from the Rushville church to the Wheeler church. He was dismissed from the former on February 8, 1833, and joined the latter on Sunday, February 10.[11] About a year later he was elected to the office of elder, and was ordained on Sunday, June 1, 1834.[12] Whitman's loyalty and devotion proved of great value to the small struggling congregation. He worked in the Sunday school, and perhaps it was at this time that he served as Sunday school superintendent. [Letter 3.] The fact that the church made him both a trustee and an elder is testimony to the esteem in which he was held by the members. Minutes of the Bath Presbytery show that he attended a meeting of the presbytery held at Bath, August 26, 1834, as a delegate from Wheeler.[13]

In spite of having such a pastor as James H. Hotchkin, and in spite of the loyal and valued services of such laymen as Marshal and Whitman, the Wheeler church was never large. It reached its peak of membership in 1838, when thirty-eight members were reported. It was a mission church, for the pastor received aid from the American Home Missionary Society. Hotchkin's quarterly reports to the Society are now on file in the Hammond Library, Chicago Theological Seminary. One by one the old faithful band either died or moved away, until General O. F. Marshal alone remained. His refusal to permit the church to be disbanded kept it on the roll of Bath, later known as Steuben, Presby-tery until 1894. It was in the Wheeler church, perhaps in the new building reported to have been erected in 1870, that the Rev. Henry Harmon Spalding preached when he re-turned to the scenes of his childhood in the winter of 1870-71.[14]

The quarterly reports of Hotchkin indicate that the

[10] Received his A.B. from Yale in 1808, and attended Andover Theo. Sem., 1808-1810.

[11] The Pratt MS. in Coll. Wn. gives a copy of the church letter from Rushville.

[12] Eells, *Marcus Whitman*, p. 22, states that Whitman was made an elder in 1833. Pratt says that this office came to him in 1834.

[13] Miller, *Presbyterianism in Steuben and Allegany*, p. 7.

[14] *See* Drury, *Spalding*, pp. 24 and 394.

temperance movement was strong in Wheeler. On April 1,
1835, Hotchkin stated that there were five different societies
in the township, with 227 members. In Joel Wakeman's
reminiscences of Whitman, he gives the following incident
which shows Whitman's intense interest in this cause:

> He was in the habit of appointing temperance meetings in the school
> districts and of calling on the students of Franklin Academy to assist
> him. One evening he had an appointment in a new settlement where
> they were lumbering. It was a terrific night, the snow was deep and
> still falling and the winds were piling it up in huge drifts. I felt like
> abandoning the enterprise. Not so with Whitman; his motto was, "If
> we have an appointment it is our duty to fill it." We had out six or
> seven and we delivered our speeches, circulated the pledge, secured
> three or four names and returned home.[15]

Whitman never lost interest in the temperance cause, and
in later years did what he could to promote temperance in
Oregon.

Whitman's medical and religious interests carried him
beyond the vicinity of Wheeler. He made friends in near-by
Prattsburg, where he met members of the Prentiss family.
Judge Stephen Prentiss and his wife Clarissa were active
workers in the Prattsburg church and also strong advocates
of temperance. They had a family of nine children—four
boys and five girls. Their third child and eldest daughter
was Narcissa, and their second daughter was Jane. Since
the Prentiss family moved to Amity in Allegany County in
June, 1834, the event below described must, therefore, have
taken place before that date.

It seems that Whitman was invited to attend a prayer
meeting held in the Prentiss home in Prattsburg, which was
conducted by a Mr. Hamilton. Whitman attended and met
for the first time some members of the Prentiss family. Jane
was there, and Whitman was attracted to her. Narcissa was
then at Butler,[16] Wayne County, nearly one hundred miles to
the north of Prattsburg where she may have been teaching
school. In a letter written to Jane on May 17, 1842, Marcus
refreshed her memory of their first meeting in the following
words:

> I was just telling Narcissa when an interest I had taken in yourself
> ever since I was introduced to you at your father's house by Mr.
> Hamilton at the close of a prayer meeting. That was the first intro-

---

15 Original in Coll. Wn.
16 The town of Butler was founded in 1826 and was named for
General William Butler, a Revolutionary officer. The township has no
railroad through it, and in 1860 had but five hundred people.

duction to the family. From that moment my heart has been towards the family. But you smile, I suppose, and say it was Narcissa; no, it was Jane; Narcissa was in Butler. I presume you will have no recollection of the introduction; if so, let it rest on my recollection, which is vivid.

While we have no record that Marcus and Narcissa ever met while the Prentiss family lived at Prattsburg, yet in the light of later events it appears that they must have then become acquainted. Even though Narcissa taught school in other places during some of the time that Whitman lived at Wheeler, she would have spent her vacations with her parents. Whitman had many contacts in Prattsburg and was sufficiently well acquainted with her pastor, the Rev. George Rudd, to request his endorsement upon the application which Whitman sent to the American Board in December, 1834.

"WELL QUALIFIED . . . AS A MISSIONARY PHYSICIAN"

In the spring of 1834, the secretaries of the American Board learned for the first time of the young doctor at Wheeler, who was described to them by the Rev. Henry P. Strong, of Rushville, as one "well qualified to act as a Missionary Physician." The files of the Board contain the originals of Whitman's letters and of others interested in his appointment. They also contain copies of the replies sent by the Board. From such sources we can reconstruct the story of what took place.

On April 25, 1834, Mr. Strong wrote:

> I write at this time to make known to you the request of Doct. Marcus Whitman. He is a young man of about 30 or 35 years of age, of solid, judicious mind, of, as I hope and believe, more than ordinary piety and perseverance, a regular bred Physician, has practiced several years with good success and credit. He is, in my opinion well qualified to act as a Missionary Physician. Although I know not that he thinks of it, yet I think he might, if thought expedient after a time, be ordained to advantage. He has formerly been in poor health, but is now better, and thinks a station with some of our western Indians would be useful to him. He has thought of being a Missionary for some time past, and I think him better qualified to do good in that capacity than most young men with whom I am acquainted. He would be glad to hear from you soon, as, should he go, he would have some worldly concerns to arrange.
>
> Yours Respectfully
> HENRY P. STRONG.

This letter very clearly indicates that Whitman had talked to Mr. Strong of his going as a missionary physician and had evidently received encouragement. The two had dis-

cussed the advantages of an arid climate for his health. The
Board was glad to learn of such a person, for the secretaries
were having a difficult time finding men qualified to go to
the American Indians. One of the secretaries, the Rev. David
Greene, wrote September 10, 1834: "Very few candidates for
missionary service are willing to go among the Indians." The
reason was that most candidates preferred to go where a
language was spoken by tens of millions rather than to a
small tribe "of sparsely settled migrators."[17]

The Board replied to Mr. Strong through Dr. B. B.
Wisner on May 1, 1834:

> Your account of him is so far satisfactory as to induce me to request
> you to suggest to him to address me a letter in which he shall give some
> account of himself; his parentage, education, religious history, views
> and feelings on the missionary subject &c &c. We wish also to be
> informed whether he is married; and if he is, whether he has children,
> and if so, how many; if not married, whether he expects to be. We
> shall be glad to receive such a communication soon.

Strong then wrote to Whitman, perhaps enclosing the
Board's letter. Whitman replied from Wheeler on June 3,
1834. In this letter he reviewed briefly his early life and
education. He mentioned having studied under the Rev.
Moses Hallock. It is this part of his letter which is so helpful
in reconstructing the story of his early life. The latter part
of the letter is as follows:

> I regard the Missionary cause as based upon the Atonement, and
> the commands and promises of the Lord Jesus Christ to his Ambassa-
> dors and Church; and that it involve the holiness and happiness of all
> that may be reclaimed from Sin. I regard the Heathen as not having
> retained the knowledge of the true God and as perishing as described
> by St. Paul. I esteem it the duty of every Christian to seek the ad-
> vancement of the cause of Christ more truly than they are wont to their
> own favorit objects. I pray that I may have only such feelings in
> desiring to be received as a helper in the Missionary Cause. I am ready
> to go to any field of usefulness at the direction of the A. Board. I will
> cooperate as Physician, Teacher or Agriculturalist so far as I may be
> able, if required.
>
> I am not married and I have no present arrangement upon that
> Subject. Yet I think I should wish to take a wife, if the service of
> the Board would admit.
>
> I am in my thirty second year. My mind has long been turned to the
> missionary subject. For the last Six months I have been more intent
> upon it than before. I wish soon to have definite course.
>
> Yours in Christian fellowship,
> MARCUS WHITMAN.

---

[17] Quoted by Hulbert and Hulbert, *The Oregon Crusade*, p. 207.
This volume prints in full the early correspondence of Whitman with
the Board.

The letter was satisfactory in every respect save one. Whitman said nothing about the state of his health. Wisner wrote to Strong on June 14, making inquiries about this. He also said in part:

It seems from his letter that his preparatory education is quite deficient. What do you think, and what is generally thought by those who know him well and are qualified to judge of his talents, and mental improvement, and ability to appear respectable among sensible and respectable people, and to make a general good impression, to require the respect of others, and to get and keep any influence over others. . . .

I have asked him what he should think of going to the Washington Islands, for which we are now in want of a missionary physician. If he goes on a mission, he had better be married & in that case I hope may get a good missionary wife.[18]

On the same day Wisner also wrote to Whitman and asked for fuller information regarding his health. Wisner asked Whitman what he thought about going to the Marquesas Islands and referred him to the March, 1834, issue of the *Missionary Herald.* Wisner also recommended that if Whitman thought of being a missionary he ought to get "a good missionary wife."

Whitman replied on June 27, saying: "I have one of the best constitutions and have enjoyed almost uninterrupted health untill within three or four years." He then told of the pain he had had in his left side in 1830 which had caused him to give up his plan to study for the ministry. After using remedies and following a plan of exercises, he had resumed his study of medicine. Whitman wrote:

I have not used remidies but in some few instances since and except for the last two or three weeks I have had but trifling inconvenience and nothing of organic or functional deranges. I have not been for any length of time without a slight pain and for the last two or three weeks there has been an agravation of pain and soreness so that I have used remidies and shall have to use more skill. I have thought for the last year or more that my health was nearly restored and I am in hopes that I shall still find my expectation realized in this respect. [Letter 4.]

He stated further that he felt his health would not be a handicap for work in a temperate climate. He objected to the Marquesan mission because of the climate. The mission

---

[18] Strong, *The Story of the American Board,* p. 68: "A new mission to the Washington or Marquesas Islands was therefore undertaken in 1833." These islands are in the South Pacific and were taken over by France in 1842.

in those islands proved to be of short duration because of the bloodthirsty cannibals.

Whitman gave the names of several people at the close of this, his second letter to the Board, to whom the Board could write for further information. This list included the following: Erastus Bates, Whitman's first cousin, the son of Abner and Mehitabel Bates, who had served in the Massachusetts Legislature during the years 1822-34; the Rev. Moses Hallock; the Rev. J. H. Hotchkin; Elisha Loomis; and the Rev. Chauncey Eddy, agent of the Board for western New York State. The mention of Elisha Loomis is rather significant, for it shows that Whitman had talked with Loomis, a returned missionary, on this subject.

In this letter we also read: "I have some lands in possession which I should wish to sell & considerable business to settle if the Board should approve of me.[19] All efforts to locate any land in Whitman's name have so far proved fruitless. An examination of land records in the county seats of Steuben, Allegany, Ontario, and Yates Counties has been made, together with a search of records in Canada. Of course Whitman may have owned land in some other county, or possibly have had a share in some property recorded in the name of another.

Pratt wrote:

About this time Whitman bought a farm of 150 acres of the Pulteney Estate, lying about midway between Wheeler and Prattsburg, and now owned by Julius Stickney, on this he built a log house where he dwelt for a time, which is yet standing, and planned also to build a saw mill. This he sold later to Grattan H. Wheeler.[20]

A call was made on Mrs. W. C. Lewis, a daughter of Julius Stickney mentioned by Pratt, who also stated that her father had purchased the farm from Grattan H. Wheeler. She remembered the log house and claimed that it stood back from the highway and on the bank of Five-Mile Creek. It fell into ruin about twenty-five years ago. Mrs. Lewis had no memory of Marcus Whitman's ever living there.[21] If Pratt's account is correct, then it seems evident that Whitman had an equity in this property and that Grattan H. Wheeler took over those interests. Frequently no legal record was made until certain financial conditions had been

---

[19] Gray, *Oregon*, p. 317, states that Whitman disposed of some property in 1843.

[20] Pratt MS., p. 5, Coll. Wn.

[21] Information by courtesy of James McCall, of Bath.

fulfilled. The failure to find a record may be due to the fact that Whitman had but partially fulfilled those requirements.

Strong delayed in answering Wisner's letter until August 12. Wisner, on the basis of Whitman's letter of June 27, wrote, advising Whitman to give up the idea. In this letter, dated July 17, we read: "On the whole, I feel constrained to conclude that duty to the cause requires me to advise you to give up, or at least to defer, till it shall be certain that your health is restored and established, the plan of going on a foreign mission."

Strong's letter of August 12 did not change matters. Strong explained that he had delayed writing because he wanted to see some people who were better acquaintd with Whitman than he was. Having secured the necessary information, he wrote:

I find that his talents are above mediocrity, his mental improvement respectable [*i. e.* commendable], in his profession above ordinary Physicians; in appearance, among respectable people, rather forbidding at first, but makes a good impression soon and is respected. Is pretty well calculated to acquire & retain influence, will be a pleasant mission companion, cooperate well with others. Upon the whole, his acquaintance with the world is respectable & his friends think he will do well as a missionary.

This is a good letter and gives a splendid analysis of Whitman. However, nothing more was done in Whitman's case for the time being. As far as the Board was concerned, Whitman's ill-health made it inadvisable for him to be appointed. So the matter rested.

SAMUEL PARKER

During 1834 important events were taking place elsewhere which, toward the end of that year, injected their influence into the life of Marcus Whitman and suddenly wrenched him out of the peaceful and quiet surroundings of Wheeler and sent him on an adventuresome tour of exploration to the Rocky Mountains.

In the winter of 1831-32 four Indians from beyond the Rockies had made the long trip to St. Louis in search of the white man's religion. The story of that trip was made known in the March 1, 1833, issue of the New York *Christian Advocate*. Among the first to volunteer to go as a missionary was the Rev. Samuel Parker, of Middlefield, Massachusetts. Various circumstances prevented Parker's going in 1833, but in 1834 he made the trip to St. Louis with two associates, expecting to cross the plains with the caravan. However, for lack of information, they reached St. Louis six weeks too late. Leaving his associates to work among the Pawnees, Parker turned back to look for more workers. He planned to make another effort in 1835.

With the knowledge and consent of the American Board, Parker spent the fall and early winter of 1834-35 in western New York, holding missionary meetings. He wanted more men and money. Thus it happened that Parker visited Wheeler in the latter part of November, 1834, where he found Marcus Whitman. Parker learned that Whitman had volunteered to go to the American Indians as a medical missionary, but had been rejected because of ill-health. Being assured that Whitman was then in fine physical condition, Parker advised him to try again, and promised to write in his behalf.

Parker wrote to his family on December 5 and mentioned his good fortune in finding Dr. Whitman. On December 17, he wrote to the Board from Dansville, New York, stating: "Doct Marcus Whitman of Wheeler, Steuben County, N. Y. whom I saw a few weeks since made up his mind to offer himself. . . . He has the name of being a good physician and a devoted Christian. I think there can be no doubt in his case."

On the 25th, Parker was back at his home in Ithaca and on that day wrote again to the Board concerning Dr. Whitman. He said in part:

I wrote you in regard to Doct. Marcus Whitman whatever may be the fulness, or want of fulness, in the testimonials which may accompany his offer of himself to your Board, his general reputation in regard to all the particulars required and into which I have made particular inquiry, I think place his case beyond any particular doubt. He wishes to accompany me in my expected tour.

WHITMAN IS APPOINTED

On November 27, 1834, the Rev. James H. Hotchkin sent to the Board his letter of recommendation for Dr. Whitman. It is possible that this date indicates Parker's visit to Wheeler. Parker had encouraged Whitman to try again. Whitman, no doubt, went to his pastor, and Hotchkin in turn wrote the following letter to the Board:

Whereas Doct. Whitman has declared his intention to offer himself to the American Board of Commissioners for Foreign Missions, to be employed as an Assistant Missionary to the Indian tribes beyond the Mississippi river, and has requested of me a testimonial of his character and standing in the church, I hereby certify that I have been intimately acquainted with him, for about two years past, during the time that I have sustained the office of Pastor of the Presbyterian church of Wheeler (N. Y.) and that he is a member in good standing, and a Ruling Elder in said church, highly esteemed as a Christian of hopeful piety and possessing in a good degree the spirit of active benevolence.

In his medical profession he has deservedly been held in estimation and has had a good share of practice. I consider him as possessing in a good degree missionary qualifications and have no doubt that he will be esteemed by those who may be associated with him in missionary employment.

Whitman's offer to go as "an Assistant Missionary to the tribes beyond the Mississippi river" seems to be a clear indication that he had talked with Parker. This letter of Hotchkin's was endorsed by Marshal, Stryker, and Aulls, elders in the Wheeler church.[22] The letter was then sent to Prattsburg, where on Saturday, November 29, the Rev. George R. Rudd, pastor of the Prattsburg church, signed a short statement in which he said he concurred in the above testimonial.

In all probability Whitman himself carried the letter to Prattsburg, and then continued his journey to Rushville. He wanted to talk matters over with his mother and other relatives. He also wished counsel with Mr. Strong. On Monday, December 1, Strong wrote to the American Board, saying:

Doct. M. Whitman informs me that he still entertains the expectation of going on a mission. I have simply to say, as before, that the most judicious friends of Missions think him well qualified for the undertaking. His professional skill is good, his piety consistent and persevering, and his talents and acquirements quite respectable. Should he be sent, I may say that it will be thought, where he is known, a judicious appointment.

On the back of Strong's letter Whitman wrote on December 2:

I have had an interview with the Rev. Samuel Parker upon the subject of Missions, and have determined to offer myself to the A. M. Board to accompany him on his mission or beyond the Rocky Mountains. My health is so much restored that I think it will offer no impediment. I find no sensible inconvenience from my former difficultys, and think I shall not from the climate and labours of such a Mission.

In accordance with Mr. Parker's direction I send some testimonies. I think I have deliberately and prayerfully considered the subject and shall acquiesce in the decision of the Board.

This letter, with the testimonials, was mailed from Rush-

---

[22] In this letter Strong requested that the *Missionary Herald* be sent to Augustus Whitman, Oren Green, and others "who pay more than $10 a year." This indicates that Whitman's brother and cousin had a real interest in missions.

ville on December 2. It was received in Boston on December
9. The various recommendations, together with the assurance that Whitman's physical condition was no longer a
difficulty, cleared the way for his appointment. The Board
met on January 6, 1835, at which time Dr. Whitman was
appointed a missionary physician, with the view that he
should accompany Mr. Parker on his trip to the Rockies that
summer. Mr. Greene wrote to Whitman the next day, informing him of the action taken and giving him some good
advice:

> On such a tour as this, as well as in missionary labors among any of
> the wandering tribes of our continent, great patience, fortitude &
> perseverance are necessary. You must be willing to encounter hardship,
> dangers, self-denials in almost every shape & discouragements without
> being moved by them from your purpose. Nothing but an unquenchable
> desire to do good to the souls of the Indians, originating in and
> cherished by a supreme love to Christ and firm faith in the promises,
> can sustain you and carry you through.

Whitman was advised to get in touch with Mr. Parker,
who would give him detailed information regarding the trip.
He made immediate preparations to visit Ithaca. By the
2nd of February, he was back in Wheeler. On that date he
wrote the following letter to Greene:

> I received yours containing a notice of my appointment with which
> I shall cheerfully comply. I visited Mr. Parker and made such arrange-
> ments as we thought necessary. He had left the instruction of last year
> with Mr. Dunbar. I was somewhat disappointed that we were not
> likely to have a sufficient number of associates to make an establish-
> ment. I shall acquiese however in whatever the committee thinks most
> advisable. I wish to be informed as fully as possible of the intention
> of the committee as to the extent and design of our commission. I design
> to start by the 16th instant, if I obtain your answer in time so that I
> shall have an opportunity of visiting some friends in Ohio and Illinois.
> My health is generally good. I design to travel to St. Louis on horse-
> back and leave my baggage with Mr. Parker.
>   Yours affectionately
> P.S. Direct to Rushville, N. Y.   MARCUS WHITMAN

Whitman made haste to settle his affairs at Wheeler. In
the archives of Whitman College, Walla Walla, Washington,
are two documents of peculiar interest, each of them dated
February 5, 1835. One is a receipt given by Dr. Whitman
to E. S. Taylor. It reads:

> Received of E. S. Taylor eleven dollars in full of all account
>   MARCUS WHITMAN
> Wheeler, February 5th, 1835[23]

---

[23] This receipt was sent to Whitman College, October 21, 1929, by

The second document is Whitman's church letter signed by the Rev. James H. Hotchkin. It reads as follows:

This certifies that the bearer, Marcus Whitman, M.D. is a member in good standing and a Ruling Elder in the Presbyterian Church of Wheeler, N. Y. and as he has lately received an appointment from the American Board of Commissioners for foreign missions to go on a mission to the aborigines of this country, he is hereby on his request [dismissed] from his particular relation to the church of Wheeler, and affectionately recommended to the christian regard of any of God's people wherever he may travel and to the fellowship and communion of any particular church wherever God in his providence may cast his lot.

Greene wrote to Whitman on February 9, 1835, and reported the death that day of Dr. Wisner. Because of the pressure of business, he wrote briefly, and again referred Whitman to the instructions sent to Parker the previous year. "The objects of the Com." he wrote, "is to learn as fully as possible the condition & character of the remote & secluded tribes, that they may more effectually call upon the Christian church to furnish them the men & the means in other respects for giving them the gospel." Greene promised to send Whitman's commission to him at St. Louis.

Upon the receipt of this letter on February 19, Whitman mounted his horse and started westward. He spent several days at Amity, New York, including Sunday, February 22, and when he left he had the consent of Narcissa Prentiss to become his wife. His cup of happiness was running over. He was an appointed missionary of the American Board. Adventure, travel, service, the lure of the unknown, lay before him and beckoned him on! All this was in the service of the Church and for the Christ whom he served. And at the same time he craved the companionship of the one he loved, who in turn loved him. Fortunate man—to have won the heart and hand of Narcissa Prentiss! Conflicting emotions struggled for supremacy in his heart. Duty commanded him to go; love bade him to stay.

Marcus was not one to allow sentiment to rule over duty. With a glad, but heavy heart, he mounted his horse again and began his nine-hundred-mile ride to St. Louis.

George W. Howe, of Elmira, N. Y. It was given to him by J. Emmet Taylor, of Dundee, N. Y., who at that time was eighty years old. Mr. Taylor said: "When ten years old I distinctly recollect Dr. Marcus Whitman doctoring me for scarlet fever." J. Emmet Taylor was a son of E. S. Taylor.

CHAPTER FOUR

NARCISSA PRENTISS
1808-1835

NARCISSA PRENTISS, who became Mrs. Marcus Whitman, is one of the best-known and best-loved characters in the history of the Pacific Northwest. This popularity is based in part upon the fact that nearly one hundred of her letters and her diary have been published in whole or in part.[1] Most of these appeared in the 1891 and 1893 issues of the *Transactions of the Oregon Pioneer Association*. These letters, which were never written for publication, are like windows which give us intimate glimpses not only into the home life of Narcissa, but also into her heart and mind. From them we know what she did, how she felt, and even what she thought.

We have also frequent references to her in the letters and diaries of others who knew her. The combined evidence presents for us a beautiful character. She was refreshingly wholesome and human. Like most human beings, she had her faults, but even these faults throw into bold relief her admirable characteristics.

ANCESTRY AND BIRTH

Narcissa was the eldest daughter and third child of Stephen and Clarissa Prentiss, who settled in Prattsburg, Steuben County, New York, about 1805. Her descent can be traced to Henry Prentice,[2] who came from England and settled at Cambridge, Massachusetts, prior to 1640. The line of descent from Henry, through two Solomons and three Stephens, is as follows:

        Solomon (1646-1719)
            Solomon (1673-1758)
                Stephen (1720-   )
                    Stephen (1744-   )

---

[1] Appendix 1 gives a list of her letters, together with those of her husband.

[2] *W.C.Q.*, Vol. 1, p. 24, has an article on the Prentiss family by the Rev. Levi Fay Waldo, once a resident of Prattsburg. He states that old English records show that the family name was once spelt Prentiz. This might be a derivative of "apprentice."

THE PRESBYTERIAN MANSE AT PRATTSBURG.
Built in 1832 by Stephen Prentiss.
By courtesy of Dr. Limouze.

THE BIRTHPLACE OF NARCISSA PRENTISS, PRATTSBURG, NEW YORK, AS IT APPEARS TODAY.

By courtesy of H. S. Brode, Walla Walla, Wash.

This house was purchased in the summer of 1936 by Dr. Arthur Limouze of the Presbyterian Board of National Missions, who intends to restore it for a shrine, and for a home for missionaries.

Stephen, the third son of the last-named Stephen, was born at Walpole, Massachusetts, October 26, 1777.[3] When he came of age he migrated to Onondaga County in western New York, where he married Clarissa Ward on January 3, 1803. It was this Stephen Prentiss who changed the spelling of the family name from Prentice to Prentiss, although it appears that the change was also made in other branches of the family. Their first-born was a boy whom they called Stephen Turner.

About 1805 the Prentiss family settled in Prattsburg, a village named after the Pratt family, who were the first owners of the land and among the first settlers. Captain Joel Pratt[4] secured title to the whole township in which the village of Prattsburg is located, and in order to obtain settlers granted favorable terms to desirable people. The fact that Stephen and Clarissa named their second born Harvey Pratt is indicative of the respect they had for the Captain.

Stephen Prentiss and his family were among the earliest settlers in the whole county. The most primitive conditions surrounded them. Roads were almost nonexistent. There were no schools or churches. People were scattered on small clearings, from which they endeavored to make a living. For a time Stephen farmed on West Hill near Prattsburg, but it appears that very soon after his arrival he was operating a sawmill and flour mill on the banks of the little stream which flows through Prattsburg.[5] He was a carpenter and joiner and, no doubt, used the products of his sawmill to provide homes for the rapidly growing community.

About the time Stephen took over the mills, he moved his family into a frame house which measured about twenty-two by thirty-two feet. The house, which is still standing, is a story and a half high, thus providing rooms upstairs with windows at the gable ends. Stephen Prentiss located his home about half a mile southeast of the public square and near the stream which furnished the power for the mills.

If local tradition is correct, it was there in that unpretentious pioneer home that Narcissa was born on Monday,

---

[3] Binney, *Genealogy of the Prentice or Prentiss Family*, p. 75, states that Stephen was born at Walpole, N. H. While members of the Prentiss family did live there, from other evidence, it is apparent that Binney was mistaken. Stephen was born at Walpole, Mass., which is about twenty miles southwest of Cambridge.

[4] Jared, a brother of Joel Pratt, was an ancestor of the Mormon Apostles, Orson Pratt and Parley P. Pratt.

[5] *W.C.Q.*, Vol. 1, No. 3, p. 25.

March 14, 1808. Narcissa is such an uncommon name that we wonder why it was selected.

Six more children were born to Stephen and Clarissa Prentiss while they lived in Prattsburg. They were Jonas Galusha, Jane Abigail, Mary Ann, Clarissa, Harriet Rebecca, and Edward Ward.[6] Thus we find nine children in the Prentiss family, four boys and five girls. Narcissa, being the eldest of the girls, was undoubtedly a valued helper in the home as soon as she was able to assume responsibility.

NARCISSA'S PARENTS

Joel Wakeman has left for us the following description of Stephen Prentiss:

In the early spring of 1832 I became a resident of Prattsburg. I very soon made the acquaintance of Judge Stephen Prentiss, the father of Narcissa, who was then engaged in erecting the Presbyterian parsonage. . . . He was an architect, a master builder, and followed that occupation as he had calls. . . . He was quite tall, finely proportioned, a little inclined to corpulency, a well formed head, ruddy countenance and a sharp, penetrating eye. . . . He was remarkably reticent for a man of his intelligence and standing. It was not common for him to commence conversation, but free to communicate when others led off, and it was a rare thing for him to indulge in laughter.[7]

The interest aroused in Prattsburg and community when the centennial celebrations were held on June 4, 1936, brought to light many interesting documents, including the original contract for the building of the Presbyterian parsonage by Stephen Prentiss. The contract is dated May 15, 1832. The cost of the building was to be $835, which included both materials and labor.[8] The fact that the house is still in use and is in good repair is evidence of the fine workmanship with which it was constructed. There are other buildings in Prattsburg still standing which were also built by Stephen Prentiss.

An examination of the courthouse records at Bath shows that Stephen Prentiss bought eleven acres of land in 1810 for which he paid two hundred dollars, and a year later he bought ten acres for which he paid one hundred dollars. The land was located in or near the village. He served at least one term as County Supervisor, being elected in 1824. He

---

[6] Binney, *History and Genealogy of the Prentice or Prentiss Family.*

[7] Prattsburg *News*, Jan. 20, 1898. Original MS., Coll. Wn.

[8] The Rev. Marshal Scott, of Prattsburg, has charge of the document.

was made an Associate Judge for the County, thus winning for himself the title of Judge by which he was thereafter known. Narcissa was proud of this title, and when she addressed letters to her father, she usually included the title: "Hon. Stephen Prentiss."

Several years ago a local historian found some old court records from which he secured his information for the following story:

A disgraceful and cowardly act had been perpetrated by one of our citizens for which he had been arraigned before Esq. Prentiss and confronted by Judge Porter. The nature of the crime charged was such that in legal strictness, a justice's jurisdiction of it could only consist of an investigation, and commitment upon sufficient proof of guilt; but Esq. Prentiss doubtless from mistaken views concerning the extent of his authority, proceeded to try the issue and deeming the proof sufficient to pronounce judgment, was as follows: "To bind the culprit to Bidwell's signpost and there score his bare back with forty lashes!" Thus was justice satisfied, so were the population.[9]

The Judge's interests appeared to have been many and varied. According to one report he operated a distillery along with his mills. The Rev. Levi Fay Waldo, a descendant of an old Prattsburg family and a relative of Narcissa, wrote:

From my earliest recollection he was always known as Judge Prentiss, having served one term as County or Probate Judge. He carried on his business about one-half mile southeast of the public square, where he had a saw-mill, a gristmill and a distillery (!) My mother was for years a domestic in her uncle's family, and my uncle, Prentiss Fay, a most excellent Christian man, worked for his uncle in the distillery, where I am told they kept the Bible depository and held mid-week prayer meetings.[10]

In 1825 or 1826 a temperance lecturer arrived in Prattsburg. Prentiss attended the lecture, as probably did most of the citizens of the village, and according to Wakeman, left the building "very angry feeling he had been personally abused and insulted." Wakeman further states that Stephen Prentiss finally gave up the business because he was fearful of the effects of the trade upon his sons. "If I remember correctly," wrote Wakeman, "the good old parson embraced the reform at that time, and also the merchant that presented him occasionally with five gallons of rum."[11]

---

[9] Prattsburg *News*, Oct. 1, 1924. By courtesy of Miss Charlotte Howe, of Prattsburg.

[10] *W.C.Q.*, Vol. 1, No. 3, p. 26.

[11] Wakeman MS., No. 25, Coll. Wn.

Joel Wakeman gives the following description[12] of Narcissa's mother:

Mrs. Clarissa Prentiss, the wife and mother, was quite tall and fleshy, and queenly in her deportment. She was intelligent, gifted in conversation, and possessed great weight of Christian character. Her influence was potent in her family and the community. She was remarkably sedate, never excited, always master of the occasion whatever occurred. She also, like unto her husband, seldom laughed. As familiar as I was in the family I do not remember of ever seeing her laugh.[13]

Absence of laughter was then a sign of piety. Laughter was considered ungodly, especially on Sunday. This attitude was a part of the Puritan inheritance, and Wakeman felt that the lack of humor was a serious defect characteristic of many of the older citizens of Prattsburg. In many respects Narcissa resembled her mother more than she did her father. She too was "queenly in her deportment" and "gifted in conversation," but in one respect at least she differed—Narcissa had a sense of humor.

Mrs. Prentiss took the lead in religious matters, for she joined the Prattsburg church in 1807, while her husband did not join until 1817.[14] Waldo wrote of their interest in music:

Judge Prentiss and all his family were all singers. My earliest recollections of him are as choir leader, setting the tone with an old-fashioned pitch pipe, and now and then giving it a toot between the stanzas to make sure that they were keeping up to the pitch.

Yet the minutes of the Prattsburg church show that Judge Prentiss was not always directing the choir for the Sunday services. According to an item in the minutes of the church dated April 14, 1829, Judge Prentiss was asked to explain why he had absented himself from the Presbyterian church to worship with the Methodists. The record declares: "His reasons were. He was best edified in attending with the Methodists, and was not wholly pleased with the administrations in this church, particularly with respect of discipline."[15]

On May 5 of that year Judge Prentiss joined the Methodist Church, but two years later, or on January 19, 1831, he returned to the Presbyterians after acknowledging his "fault." If one may be allowed to read between the lines,

---

[12] See also Wakeman MS., No. 34, Coll. Wn.
[13] Prattsburg News, Jan. 20, 1898.
[14] Original records still extant at Prattsburg.
[15] Minutes of the Prattsburg church, Vol. 2, p. 144.

he may see in the reference to the "discipline" of the Prattsburg church an allusion to the action taken by the Bath Presbytery, of which the Prattsburg church was a member, on
August 28, 1828, in regard to Freemasonry. The presbytery,
affected by the anti-Masonic agitation of the time, viewed
Freemasonry as "hostile to the interests of the Church of
Christ" and called upon all members of Presbyterian
churches within its jurisdiction to "abandon the institution."[16]

While we lack confirming evidence, it may be that Judge
Prentiss was a Mason and left the Presbyterian Church because he objected to the action taken by the presbytery. The
Methodists were more lenient in this respect and permitted
their members to be Masons. Thus for a time the Prentiss
family was divided in its church allegiance. It appears that
the original Masonic lodge in Prattsburg was not able to
weather the storm. It disbanded and years passed before
another lodge was organized.[17]

We have every reason to believe that Narcissa was highly
favored in her parents and in her home life. Years later from
distant Oregon she wrote in affectionate terms of the beautiful fellowship of the home she had left behind. In one letter
she speaks of reading to her mother, and asked her sister
Harriet:

What books do you read? Do you comfort ma by reading to her such
books as Dwight's Theology, Dodridge's Rise and Progress, Milner's
Church History, etc., as Narcissa used to do in her younger days?
[Letter 81.]

Rather heavy reading for leisure hours! But those were
serious-minded days. Regardless of the type of books read,
we have a pleasing picture here of Narcissa reading to her
mother.

NARCISSA'S SPIRITUAL EXPERIENCES

The very first entry in the record of baptisms of the
Prattsburg church is the following:

Lords Day July 17th 1808 Baptised by Rev. Solomon Allen Willis
Gilbert Hayes, son of Simeon Hayes Grove More Bacon son of Samuel
Bacon Narcissa Prentiss, daughter of Stephen Prentiss

The Rev. Solomon Allen had been sent by the Ontario

---

16 Miller, *Presbyterianism in Steuben*, p. 9.

17 The Grand Secretary of the Grand Lodge of New York wrote to
the author August 24, 1935, stating that the Grand Lodge had no
records of Stephen Prentiss' being a Mason. However, the records for
the early years are incomplete.

Association to act at the installation of the Rev. John Niles
in the Bath church. Eight days after Mr. Niles had been
installed, Mr. Allen performed the above-recorded baptisms
in Prattsburg.[18] Narcissa was then a little over four months
old and she had the distinction of being the first girl baby
to be baptized in Prattsburg. Here is additional evidence
regarding the early date of the settlement of the Prentiss
family in that community.

The pastor of the Prattsburg church during most of the
time that Narcissa lived there was the Rev. James H. Hotchkin, who remained in Prattsburg from 1809 to 1830. The
church building in which Narcissa was probably baptized
was a wooden building about the same size as her home,
twenty-two by thirty-two feet. In 1809, this building was
enlarged by an eighteen-foot addition at one end. This long
rectangular structure, with the pulpit "stuck to the northern
wall like a bird's nest," was the first church building that
Narcissa remembered.[19]

In Mr. Hotchkin's old age, he wrote a book entitled: *A
History of the Purchase and Settlement of Western New
York and of the Rise, Progress, and present state of the
Presbyterian Church in that section.* The book was published
in 1848. In this work he tells of the religious revival which
visited his church in Prattsburg during the winter of 1818-
19 and which reached a climax in February, 1819. Mr.
Hotchkin wrote:

February. The first Sabbath in that month was a day of unusual
solemnity. At an appointed weekly meeting the house of worship was
filled to overflowing, and from the necessity of the case, and the
powerful state of feeling existing, it became necessary to continue the
meeting from day to day for several days in succession. Individuals
were seen trembling on their seats, and the silent tear trickling down
their cheeks, but entire stillness reigned. Nothing was heard but the
voice of the speaker imparting instructions, addressing exhortation to
the assembly, or lifting up the prayer unto God. More than thirty, it is
believed, were born again during that eventful week.[20]

Hotchkin then continues his account by telling us how all
of the new members won in this revival were received into
the church on "the first Sunday of June following," which
fell that year on June 6. On that day "fifty-nine individuals
stood before a great congregation" and made their public

---

[18] Information secured from Miss Sarah Parker, of Bath, N. Y.

[19] Drury, *Spalding*, pp. 277 ff., gives a more detailed description of
the church.

[20] P. 465.

confession of faith. People from the neighboring towns came for the big occasion. Knowing that the church was too small to hold the anticipated crowd, preparations were made in advance to hold the services in a neighboring grove. The day was a perfect June day with a clear sky and no wind. Mr. Hotchkin took for his text the words found in Isaiah 53:11: "He shall see of the travail of his soul, and shall be satisfied." The text reveals the joy that Mr. Hotchkin felt upon that auspicious occasion.

Among the new members welcomed that day was golden-haired Narcissa Prentiss, who was then but eleven years old. Her two older brothers, Stephen and Harvey, were with her. By an interesting coincidence, a revival was held about the same time in Plainfield, Massachusetts, where Marcus Whitman experienced a spiritual awakening.

About five years later, when Narcissa was in her sixteenth year, she had another religious experience, which caused her to consecrate herself to the missionary cause. Of this she wrote in her first letter to the Board as follows:

I frequently desired to go to the heathen but only half-heartedly and it was not till the first Monday of Jan. 1824 that I felt to consecrate myself without reserve to the Missionary work awaiting the leadings of Providence concerning me. [Letter 7.]

Narcissa must have had a very impressive experience, since it caused her eleven years later to remember that it occurred "on the first Monday of Jan. 1824." According to one report, Narcissa read the life of Harriette Boardman, a missionary to India, and was much influenced by it.[21]

Waldo in his reminiscences published in the *Whitman College Quarterly* wrote as follows concerning Narcissa:

She seems to have been peculiarly gifted in speech, and especially in prayer and song. I well remember her clear sweet voice, as a leading soprano, in the old church at home. And one who afterwards used to hear her pray, testifieds: "She could offer up the finest petition to the Throne of Grace of any person I have ever heard in my life."[22]

Several have written about Narcissa's beautiful voice. The Rev. Joel Wakeman wrote:

Her voice was an important factor in the social prayer meetings and missionary concerts that were held monthly in those days.[23]

---

[21] Douthit, *Souvenir of Western Women*, article by Catherine Sager Pringle.

[22] *W.C.Q.*, Vol. 2, No. 1, p. 38. Waldo was then a Congregational minister at Canon City, Colo.

[23] Prattsburg *News*, Aug. 10, 1893. Church people then frequently called a prayer meeting a "concert."

Years later in distant Oregon, the natives traveled many miles just to hear her sing. In a letter to her mother dated March 30, 1837, Narcissa wrote: "While I was at Vancouver, one Indian woman came a great distance with her daughter, as she said, to hear me sing with the children." The Cayuses at Waiilatpu felt the charm of that same voice, so much so that Narcissa also wrote: "I was not aware that singing was a qualification of so much importance to a missionary." [Letter 40.]

Joel Wakeman in one of his articles tells of a revival which visited Prattsburg in the summer and fall of 1832 under the ministry of Mr. Rudd. Sunrise prayer meetings were held during the summer months, in which the Prentiss family took an active part. Of Narcissa's efforts at this time, Wakeman wrote: "No one devoted more time in personal efforts to win souls to Christ than Narcissa. There are some still living who can trace their first serious impressions to her charming singing and tender appeals to yield to the overtures of mercy."

At that time the Prentiss family had moved from the house in which Narcissa was born, and was living in "a large two story framed house, with a hall in the centre" which was located on the west side of the village green. During the month of October, 1832, an intensive four-day evangelistic effort was made, with two visiting ministerial brethren assisting Mr. Rudd. These men were entertained in the Prentiss home. During these "protracted meetings," the following incident took place:

One evening, Mr. Higby preached on final judgment, and by a previous arrangement Miss Narcissa, with two or three leading singers, took their seats near the pulpit and the moment the speaker closed his sermon they struck in and sang the old judgment hymn. The reader can more easily imagine the effect than I can describe it. Christians were melted to tears, and hardened sinners bowed their heads and wept bitterly; many of whom yielded to the claims of the gospel.

She had a clear, strong voice, and by cultivation it was under perfect control and as sweet and musical as a chime of bells.[24]

A good index to the vitality of the spiritual life of the Prattsburg church is to be found in the long list of the sons and daughters of that church who gave their lives to full-time Christian service. Up to 1876 the church had sent twenty-six men into the ministry, and it was then reported that: "Not far from a score of ministers' wives have also gone

---

[24] Prattsburg *News*, Jan. 27, 1898.

Mrs. Narcissa Prentiss Whitman.

From 3rd edition of Nixon's *How Marcus Whitman Saved Oregon.* While
not a drawing from life, yet it is the best likeness
that we have of Mrs. Whitman.

MRS. HARRIET PRENTISS JACKSON.
Sister of Mrs. Marcus Whitman.
By courtesy of Mrs. Edmund Bowden of Seattle, who got the picture from one of the Sager girls.

HARVEY PRATT PRENTISS.
Older brother of Narcissa.
This picture was taken by Platt and Hawley, Oberlin, Ohio.
By courtesy of Miss Charlotte Howe.

out from this church."[25] Most of these young people belonged
to the generation of Narcissa Prentiss and Henry Spalding.
The presence of Franklin Academy in the village added to
the notable list of ministers and missionaries who at one
time were members of the Prattsburg church. In this environment of piety Narcissa grew to womanhood.

Narcissa was vivacious and popular. The Prentiss home
was the center of many a happy gathering of young people,
in which Narcissa was a leading spirit. Sometimes Mrs.
Prentiss would say: "I wish Narcissa would not always have
so much company." Years later when Narcissa found her
own home in Oregon crowded with guests, she felt moved to
write: "It is well for me now that I have had so much experience in waiting upon company, and I can do it when
necessary without considering it a great task." [Letter 78.]

NARCISSA'S EDUCATION

Narcissa Prentiss received what can be considered a very
good education for a young woman of her generation. She
began her training in the common school of Prattsburg.
Waldo is the authority for the statement that Narcissa
studied for a time in Mrs. Emma Willard's (1787-1870)
famous "Female Seminary" at Troy, New York.[26] Mrs.
Willard founded her school in 1821 and soon attracted pa-
tronage from all parts of the country. Within fifty years
more than thirteen thousand young women studied there.[27]
The school seemed to have majored on the training of
teachers and was what we would now call a normal school.
It became a pattern for later women's schools as, for instance, Mt. Holyoke.

Mrs. Willard was born in New Berlin, Connecticut, where
Eliza Hart, who later became Mrs. Henry Harmon Spalding,
was also born. Mrs. Willard's maiden name was Hart, and
she was a third cousin to Mrs. Spalding. Emma Hart was
married to Dr. John Willard in 1809. Left a widow, she
turned her talents and energies to the field of higher education for women and pioneered along new lines. In a day

---

[25] Pratt, *Historical Sketch*, p. 18.

[26] *W.C.Q.*, Vol. 2, No. 1, p. 39.

[27] Sylvester, *History of Rensselaer Co.*, pp. 233-4. In 1898 Fairbanks
published his *Emma Willard and Her Pupils, or Fifty Years of Troy
Female Seminary, 1822-1872*, which makes no mention of Narcissa
Prentiss. However, no record of any graduates prior to 1843 is given.
Only fragmentary records were available for the earlier years.

when young women did not have the same educational advantages as young men, her school became famous for its advanced stand.

Mrs. Willard was a woman of commanding personality, who left an indelible impression upon the thousands who came under her influence. She wrote on many subjects and was the author of "Rocked in the Cradle of the Deep," which song, incidentally, bespeaks her religious faith. She was a member of the Episcopal Church, and was active in such reform movements as the temperance cause.

Just how long Narcissa was a student of Mrs. Willard's is not known, but in 1827 an extension was added to Franklin Academy in Prattsburg to accommodate the boarding department for "female" pupils. The records of the academy show that Narcissa was enrolled there for the term ending April 6, 1828.[28]

Among the treasured documents in the possession of the academy today is the original list of subscribers. The list contains the names of fifty-three who signed under the following statement:

We the subscribers do hereby promise to pay to Stephen Prentiss, Noah Niles and Robert Porter, or their order the sums set opposite our names, for the purpose of establishing a permanent fund for an Academy to be erected in the town of Prattsburg in the county of Steuben, and payable in ten equal annual installments, with the interest payable annually on each installment, to be paid in wheat at one dollar per bushel, on the first day of February in each and every year. This obligation becomes binding, when the amount of two thousand dollars is subscribed as above or in lands—witness our hands this 20th day of March A. D. 1823.

Stephen Prentiss, who was active in the establishment of the academy and later one of its builders, pledged fifty dollars. The original minutes of the trustees show that Judge Prentiss assisted for many years in the management of that institution. He was kept on the list of trustees even after he moved to the adjoining county.[29]

The academy, which was named after Benjamin Franklin, opened its doors in the spring of 1824, with William Beardsley as its first principal. Beardsley (1797-1866) was a graduate of Hamilton College in 1823. It appears that he

---

[28] Drury, *Spalding*, pp. 30-31, gives a brief history of the academy with pictures.

[29] Catalog of the academy, 1837, contains the name of Judge Prentiss as one of the trustees. In possession of Miss Charlotte Howe, Prattsburg, N. Y.

attended Auburn Theological Seminary following his teaching experience in Prattsburg and was ordained in 1829. He later went to Illinois, where he taught in a church school at Quincy. Beardsley was undoubtedly the reason for the presence of Edward and Jane Prentiss at Quincy in 1843, of which mention will be made later. He was a professor in Wheaton College from 1859 to the time of his death in 1866.

An old tuition bill in the archives of Prattsburg High School and Franklin Academy for the term ending April 5, 1826, shows that twenty girls were then enrolled in the female department. When Narcissa was a student for the term ending April 6, 1828, there were twenty-eight girls and thirty-four boys in the academy. Miss Clarissa Thurston was then in charge of the girls. The tuition fee for the term of twenty-one weeks was six dollars.

Another tuition account for the term ending September 28, 1831, gives the names of fifty-four boys, including that of Henry Harmon Spalding, and of forty-six girls, including Narcissa Prentiss. Thus for one term, at least, these two were students together in the same school at Prattsburg.[30] The principal was Seymour Gookins, A.M., and Mrs. Sarah Cooke was in charge of the girls. In November of that year the trustees of the academy inserted an advertisement in the Steuben *Messenger* of Bath in which it was stated that the academy library had over one thousand volumes, "and also several expensive articles of aparatus, among which is a Telescope, of sufficient magnifying power to display the Sattellites and Belts of Jupiter and the Ring of Saturn."[31]

Some writers have developed the theory that Henry Spalding was a suitor for the hand of Narcissa Prentiss. The theory gave a plausible explanation for some dissension which later grew up in the Oregon mission. It was based upon an ambiguous phrase in one of Narcissa's letters. [Letter 79.] On the other hand, the theory was vigorously denied by Prattsburg residents, and, moreover, evidence was found which showed that Spalding was once engaged to another Prattsburg girl. After this engagement was broken, he entered into a correspondence with Eliza Hart, of Holland Patent, New York, whom he later married. In view of the fact that documentary evidence was lacking to prove that

---

[30] Correcting the statement made in Drury, *Spalding*, p. 38. Since the publication of the Spalding book, the tuition bill for Sept. 28, 1831, was discovered. Owned by James McCall, of Bath.

[31] Original paper owned by Miss Howe, of Prattsburg.

Henry was a suitor of Narcissa, the author of this work in his biography of Henry Harmon Spalding rejected the theory. However, new evidence has been discovered which seems to show conclusively that Henry was indeed a rejected suitor. On January 11, 1893, Narcissa's youngest sister Harriet (Mrs. J. W. Jackson) wrote from Oberlin, Ohio, and said regarding Henry Spalding:

He was a student when a young man in Franklin Academy, Prattsburg the place of our nativity, and he wished to make Narcissa his wife, and her refusal of him caused the wicked feeling he cherished toward them both.[32]

The consequences of this love affair were far-reaching, as shall be explained later.

The academy had many students who later became well known in the affairs of the world. One of them, David Malin, became pastor of a prominent church in Philadelphia. In October, 1837, he was married to Mary Porter, a close friend of Narcissa. Out in Old Oregon, Narcissa named a forlorn half-breed Indian boy whom she took into her home, David Malin.

Narcissa's experience as a schoolteacher should be included as a part of her education, for therein she received a training which was of the greatest value to her in Old Oregon. We have the record of two people who speak of their experiences as pupils under Narcissa. O. P. Fay, of Vermontville, Michigan, writing on January 16, 1898, to the Prattsburg *News* said:

I well remember Marcus Whitman's wife Narcissa Prentice; she taught our district school when I was quite a lad, and she seemed to me then as a woman of rare abilities, with qualifications sufficient to teach in any academy instead of in a common school which showed that she was willing to labor wherein she could find work to do. She had a class in natural philosophy and wanted to start one in chemistry also, but that was more than we could venture to try until we had graduated in philosophy. She taught the best school of any teacher in our district.

Natural philosophy was the term then used to designate what we now call physics. It was then unusual for a woman to be interested in science.

The second report of Narcissa's work as a schoolteacher comes from Miss Alice C. Pratt, of Prattsburg, whose mother attended an "infant school," that is, kindergarten, which Narcissa conducted in Bath. Miss Pratt's mother was four

---

[32] To Mrs. Eva Emery Dye, Coll. O.

years old at the time and although she lived to be nearly ninety she never forgot the song taught by her teacher.[33]

·Chil - dren go to and fro In a mer - ry pret - ty row,

Foot - steps light, fa - ces bright, 'Tis a hap - py, hap - py sight.

Swift - ly turn - ing round and round, Do not look u - pon the ground,

Fol - low me full of glee, Sing - ing mer - ri - ly.

Sing - ing mer - ri - ly, mer - ri - ly, mer - ri - ly, Sing - ing mer - ri - ly, mer - ri - ly, mer - ri - ly,

Fol - low me full of glee, Sing - ing mer - ri - ly.

Perhaps we can see a reference to another school that Narcissa may have taught at Butler in the letter Marcus wrote to Jane Prentiss, of which mention has already been made. Marcus is not explicit; he merely states that Narcissa was then in Butler.

Available records do not permit us to reconstruct with accuracy the events of those years from April, 1828, when she finished a term in Franklin Academy, to the summer of 1833. Wakeman states that "she taught district schools

---

[33] In a letter from Miss Pratt dated Feb. 2, 1936, to the author. *See* also Waldo in *W.C.Q.*, Vol. 2, No. 1, p. 39.

several years with marked success," and that soon after he became acquainted with the family, Narcissa was giving her time to home duties.[34]

"ARE FEMALES WANTED?"

Wakeman tells us that the people of Prattsburg were troubled with rumors in the spring of 1833 to the effect that the Prentiss family was considering moving from the village. The long residence of some twenty-seven or twenty-eight years was to be terminated. Just why this move was considered advisable is not known, but in all likelihood it was due to business reasons. Judge Prentiss was a carpenter. Other and newer settlements then developing may have offered more opportunities for his craftsmanship than did Prattsburg, which by that time was assuming the character of a settled community, with little new building.

So it was, according to Wakeman, that the Prentiss family moved to Amity in Allegany County, which adjoins Steuben County on the west. Amity was about fifty miles from Prattsburg. It is assumed that the move was made sometime during the latter part of 1833. At Amity, Judge Prentiss erected some dwelling houses and built a bridge over the Genesee River which flows near the village. Life in Amity was more primitive than it was in Prattsburg, for it was a newer community with fewer people.

At Amity, Narcissa gave herself to the little church that had been organized one year previous, or on January 30, 1832, by the Rev. Moses Hunter, of Angelica. The church had but few members and held its meetings for nine years in a log schoolhouse. During the years 1833 to 1835, the Rev. Samuel May served as pastor of the struggling congregation, supplying also at the same time other congregations in the vicinity.

A minute from the record book of the Prattsburg church shows that on Sunday, April 27, 1834, letters of dismission were issued to Stephen and Clarissa Prentiss, and to Jonas G., Narcissa, Clarissa, Harriet, and Edward "to join the Presbyterian Church in Amity, N. Y."[35] In January, or the early part of February, 1835, the Rev. Oliver S. Powell, a

---

[34] Prattsburg *News*, Jan. 27, 1898.

[35] The original minutes of the Amity church were also examined. A record was found of Mr. and Mrs. Stephen Prentiss, Jonas G., and Edward being members but no indication of when they joined. No mention was made of Clarissa, Harriet, or Narcissa.

brother-in-law of Samuel May, became minister of the
Amity church. Mr. May had become pastor of the Angelica
church in December, 1834. Narcissa was a welcomed guest
in the homes of both of these pastors and became friendly
with them and their wives.

In the latter part of November, 1834, the Rev. Samuel
Parker made his way over the muddy roads into Allegany
County. He had been holding missionary meetings in western New York and was looking for workers who would be
willing to go to the Indians beyond the Rocky Mountains. He
also sought to raise as much money as he could to support
the mission. Parker had just come from Wheeler, where he
had interested Dr. Marcus Whitman in the project. According to Parker's son, a meeting was held at Angelica, at which
Narcissa Prentiss was present.[36]

We do not have the record of their meeting, but we may
imagine Narcissa's going to Mr. Parker and telling him of
her desire to be a missionary and then asking: "Is there a
place for an unmarried female in my Lord's vineyard?"
Parker was not sure about that. He had been looking for
men, or possibly a married couple, but had not expected to
find a young unmarried woman who was ready to go. In a
letter to the American Board written on December 17, he
asked.

> Are females wanted? A Miss Narcissa Prentiss of Amity is very
> anxious to go to the heathen. Her education is good—piety conspicuous
> —her influence good. She will offer herself if is needed.

A few weeks later, on January 1, 1835, Parker again
wrote to the Board and referred to Miss Prentiss and to a
Miss McCoy. He explained his caution in giving advice. "I
think," he wrote, "I said nothing about their going among the
Indians, or to any particular part of the world, but only they
would offer themselves if their services are needed. I recollect that I told them if they offered themselves it must be to go
anywhere the Board should choose."

Greene, replying to the first letter of Parker's above
mentioned, wrote on December 24: "I don't think that we
have missions among the Indians where unmarried females
are valuable just now." Parker must have been rather dis-

---

[36] Parker MS., p. 180: "The finding of Miss Prentice, if my memory
is correct was at Angelica, N. Y. where my father held meetings and
she was present." *See* Powell to Green (Coll. A.) Dec. 6, 1834: "The
Rev. Mr. Parker visited this place a few weeks since & urged upon our
attention the need of a missionary to go among the Omaha Indians."

couraging to both Miss Prentiss and Miss McCoy, for Greene
wrote again on January 7, 1835, saying that no word had
been received from them. The idea of using single women
in the mission work of the Board was somewhat new. Greene
took the idea under consideration. On January 2, 1835, he
wrote to Henry Harmon Spalding, who was then planning
to go to the Osage Indians, and said:

> Female teachers our missionaries have all along supposed could
> not be employed usefully, except at boarding schools. I am not certain
> that their opinion is correct, even at the present time; and I am quite
> confident that the way may be opened for them in a year or two, if
> the Osages should become settled.[37]

Narcissa herself felt such doubt on the subject that she
did not send in her letter of application until February 23,
1835, and then it was with the prospect of going as a married
woman.

At the time Parker met Narcissa, he met Mr. and Mrs.
O. S. Powell, who also volunteered. Parker was much pleased
with their qualifications and recommended their appointment. The Board accepted the application of the Powells,
and they were appointed missionaries on January 6, 1835.
Circumstances prevented their going to a field that spring,
and after that other causes prevented their departure.

According to the testimony of one of Parker's sons, it was
Parker who first told Marcus Whitman about Narcissa's
offer. If this be true, we know the suggestion came at an
opportune time. Whitman had informed the Board that if
he were appointed, he would consider getting married. Narcissa had learned that the Board was not much interested
in "unmarried females." We do not know when Whitman
first met his future wife. Certainly they were not strangers
to each other when Parker suggested to Whitman that he
call upon her. It is reported that Narcissa later said: "We
had to make love somewhat abruptly, and must do our courtship now we are married."[38]

Narcissa was getting along in years. She was then approaching her twenty-seventh birthday and not married. In
those days she was already considered an old maid. But she
was not one to marry just to be married. Unless she found

---

[37] Quoted in full in Hulbert & Hulbert, *The Oregon Crusade*, pp.
289 ff.

[38] *W.C.Q.*, Vol. 2, No. 3, p. 13: "It is the impression of Dr. S. J.
Parker, son of Rev. S. Parker, ... that his father wrote Dr. Whitman
that he had better go and see her at her father's house."

NARCISSA'S LETTER OF APPLICATION.
By courtesy of the American Board.

WHITMAN'S COMMISSION FROM THE AMERICAN BOARD.
By courtesy of Whitman College.

a companion who would share with her the religious convictions of her heart, she would probably have preferred to
remain single. A common purpose was instrumental in
drawing the two together.

THEY PLIGHT THEIR TROTH

Marcus Whitman learned of his appointment by the Board
about the 14th of January. He then made the trip to Ithaca
to see Parker, where, incidentally, he learned more about
Narcissa, and was back in Wheeler by the 2nd of February.
Whitman planned to leave Wheeler by February 16. [Letter
6.] He went to Rushville to say farewell to his mother, other
relatives, and friends. He did not receive Greene's final instructions until February 19 and left the same day for the
West. [Letter 9.] He spent the week end over Sunday, February 22, at Amity, where he was the guest, for part of the
time, in the home of the Rev. and Mrs. O. S. Powell. Amity
was about a day's ride from Rushville.

Powell wrote to Greene on March 18, 1835, making mention of Whitman's visit in these words: "About 3 weeks since
Dr. Whitman spent a Sabbath with me while on his way
west." Sometime during this visit to Amity, Marcus proposed marriage to Narcissa and was accepted. The next
Monday, February 23, Marcus started for St. Louis. It was
on that day that Narcissa reached into her desk for a sheet
of her pale-green letter-paper, on which she wrote in a beautiful script her letter of application to the American Board.
The opening part of the letter is as follows:

To the Secretaries of the A.B.C.F.M.
Dear Brethren
Permit an unworthy sister to address you. Having obtained
favour of the Lord and desiring to live for the conversion of the
world I now offer myself to the American Board to be employed in their
service among the heathen, if counted worthy. As it is requested of me
to make some statements concerning myself I shall endeavour to be
as brief as possible knowing the value of your time especially under
the late *afflictive bereavement*.

The reference to a bereavement was to the death of one
of the secretaries of the Board, Dr. B. B. Wisner, who died on
February 9. Greene had made mention of the death of Dr.
Wisner in his letter of that date to Whitman. The fact that
Narcissa knew about it on the 23rd of the month is clear
proof that Whitman had either told her, or had let her read
Greene's letter.

Narcissa briefly reviewed her early life. She closed her letter with these words:

> Feeling it more my privilege than my duty to labour for the conversion of the heathen, I respectfully submit myself to your direction and subscribe   Your unworthy sister in the Lord
>   NARCISSA PRENTISS

On the back of the letter are three short testimonials. The Rev. Samuel W. May, who signed himself "Minister of Angelica," wrote:

> Dear Brethren: Having been acquainted for some time past with Miss Narcissa Prentiss—I therefore most cheerfully recommend her to your Board as well qualified for usefulness in instructing the heathen in the way to Heaven.

The Rev. William Bridgman, pastor of the Presbyterian church at Cuba, wrote:

> Having been requested to express my opinion of the qualifications of Miss Narcissa Prentiss as an assistant missionary I would cheerfully say that from a personal acquaintance with Miss Prentiss I do consider her well qualified for usefulness in that station.

The Rev. Oliver S. Powell wrote:

> I fully concur in the above recommendations. I would add that Miss Prentiss is a member in good standing of this 1st. Pres. Church of Amity of which I now have the charge. I am happy in the prospect of having so efficient a fellow labourer in the missionary service.

And then Powell added this illuminating footnote:

> P.S. As it is probable that Miss Prentiss will hereafter become the companion of Doct. Marcus Whitman (should he be established missionary beyond the Rocky Mts.) it may be proper to add that he expressed a desire that she might accompany us on our mission as it will be a field of usefulness & an opportunity presented for becoming acquainted with the labors of a missionary.

Ellis May, Elder in the Amity church, also wrote:

> I concur in the above recommendations.

Thus the story unfolds. The Powells were half expecting to be sent to some tribe west of the Mississippi that year, and Marcus and Narcissa had discussed the possibility of Narcissa's accompanying them. Out of the 222 letters written by either Marcus or Narcissa which were consulted in the preparation of this work, there is only one which was written by Marcus to Narcissa, and the original of this was not located. Marcus wrote to his fiancée from Liberty, Missouri, on April 30, saying:

I had not given up the hope that you would have come on with Mr. Powell until I received your letter. I regret very much that he did not come.

From this letter we assume that Narcissa had suggested that they be married when Marcus was with her in Amity so that she might go with him, for Marcus wrote:

In reading your letter I was surprised exceedingly that you should have conceived it practicable for you to have crossed the mountains this spring. Had I known one half as much of the trip as I now do, when I left you, I should have been entirely willing, if not anxious, that you should have accompanied us.

This letter is printed in Mowry's *Marcus Whitman*, and at this point Mowry indicates that Narcissa had written on the margin of the letter:

Mr. Parker said I could go just as well as not. N. Prentiss.

Whatever the advice of Parker may have been regarding the feasibility of taking "females" over the mountains, Marcus with his sound common sense was taking no chances until he had investigated. White women had never crossed the Rockies. Was it possible? Was it wise? Marcus decided to make certain before taking Narcissa with him.

Narcissa's letter of application was sent to Mr. Parker, who forwarded it to the Board on March 5, with a letter of his own, in which he wrote as follows regarding the future Mrs. Marcus Whitman:

I enclose you Miss Narcissa Prentiss' offer of herself to become a missionary. I have for some time been acquainted with Judge Prentiss' family. Their standing as intelligent Christians in public estimation is *good*. Narcissa's education, talents, person, disposition, conciliatory manners, and sound judgment promise well for usefulness in a mission field.

As a result of such testimonials and her own letter of application, Narcissa was appointed on March 18, 1835. In the letter of notification, nothing definite was said about her destination. It was to be to some tribe west of the Missouri. It seemed to have been understood that she was to wait until Dr. Whitman returned, or until some report had been made about the explorations that he and Parker were making.

CHAPTER FIVE

TO THE ROCKIES

1835

A FTER Whitman had settled up his affairs at Wheeler, he went to Rushville to await final instructions from Greene. The letter arrived on Thursday, February 19, and Whitman left that same day for Amity. Whitman had planned to be in St. Louis on April 1, so he was eager to be on his way. We can assume that he was in Amity not later than Friday, and that he was on his way again the next Monday. Writing to Greene from Liberty, Missouri, on May 13, Whitman declared that he had furnished his own horse, equipage, and such outfit as he felt it necessary to take. His other baggage he left with Mr. Parker, who made the trip from Pittsburgh to St. Louis by boat. Whitman drew upon the Board for one hundred dollars to cover expenses.

Since Whitman mentioned to Greene his desire to visit relatives and friends in Ohio and Illinois [Letter 6], we can trace out the approximate route he took. After leaving Amity, he probably proceeded westward until he came to the Buffalo-Cleveland highway, which passed through Kirtland, Ohio. There he must have seen the Mormon temple then in the process of construction. In 1835 the Mormons were still a main topic of conversation for the non-Mormons of the vicinity.

At Kirtland, Whitman turned south to Chester where he found many old friends and relatives from western Massachusetts. Among these were John Packard,[1] with whom Whitman had lived at Plainfield when he attended Moses Hallock's school, and his foster parents, Freedom and Sally Whitman. Two of his father's sisters, Mehitabel Bates[2] and Sally Richmond, and their families had also moved to the same vicinity.

The records of the Baptist church of Chester bear testi-

---

[1] His tombstone is in the Chester Center cemetery. He died April 11, 1843, aged 59 years.

[2] Farnham, *Descendants of John Whitman*, p. 245. A fifteen-foot monument in the Chester County cemetery bears her inscription and also that of her son Erastus.

mony to the character of Freedom Whitman. Page after page tells the story of his influence and ability. For more than ten years he continued to occupy positions of trust and responsibility. From these entries we learn much of him who was a father to Marcus Whitman longer than Beza Whitman or Calvin Loomis. We know that Marcus, during the impressionable years from eight to eighteen, was under the influence of a godly man of talent and ability.

A striking evidence of the esteem in which Marcus Whitman was held by those of his own generation is to be found in the fact that four boys were named after him during his lifetime. His sister Alice married Henry F. Wisewell, and to this union was born a son on May 23, 1838, who was called Marcus Whitman Wisewell. At Chester, Ohio, Marcus visited his cousin Abner C. Bates, the son of Mehitabel. Abner's son, born April 26, 1840, was called Marcus Whitman Bates. Even those who were not related to him, honored him by giving their sons his name. A son of Whitman's co-workers in Old Oregon, the Rev. and Mrs. Elkanah Walker, born at the Walker mission station, March 16, 1842, was named Marcus Whitman Walker. A fourth namesake was Marcus Whitman Saunders, born May 8, 1846, at Rushville, New York. In later years many have been named after Dr. Whitman.

While en route from Chester, Ohio, to St. Louis, Whitman undoubtedly paused at Danville, Vermilion County, Illinois, to call on his brother Samuel, who had married Mary Jenkins Peabody, of Rushville, on April 3, 1929. There on March 4, 1830, a son was born to them whom they called Perrin Beza after his two grandfathers. Two other children besides Perrin had arrived at Samuel's home before Marcus visited there sometime in March, 1835, but our interest centers in Perrin, who, in 1843, accompanied his uncle out to Old Oregon.

PARKER AND WHITMAN

Whitman reached St. Louis on Wednesday, April 1, where he received a letter from Greene which contained his commission. Parker did not reach St. Louis until Saturday, April 4. Together they called upon the officials of the American Fur Company and secured permission to go with the caravan across the plains that summer. The two left St. Louis on the steamboat *Siam* for Liberty, Missouri, on April 8. The boats usually made the trip between these points in seven or eight days, but this time, because of an accident, it took them a full two weeks.

On account of unfavorable weather conditions the caravan was unable to leave Liberty before May 14. Whitman and Parker, therefore, found they had plenty of time to complete their arrangements. At first Whitman deferred to the years and the previous experience of Parker, but he soon came to distrust Parker's judgment in matters pertaining to their travel. Parker, who knew from personal experience the difficulty of raising money for missions, was too cautious in his expenditures. None of the contemporaneous letters of Whitman's reveals his uneasiness on this point, but several years later when word reached Whitman of some criticisms that Parker had made of the expenses of the Oregon mission, he was stimulated to write a long and revealing letter to the American Board. [Letter 62.]

Parker wanted to limit their personal baggage to fifty pounds each and to take but one pack animal. "One mule," wrote Whitman, "was to pack all the provisions necessary to take us that long route, including the different items of clothing, etc., besides cooking furniture, bedding, tent, etc." Whitman urged the purchase of a fourth animal, but Parker then refused. Some extra baggage was placed in one of the wagons belonging to Lucien Fontanelle, who was the captain of the caravan. So the matters stood on the eve of their departure from Liberty.

On the morning of the 14th, the caravan started for Bellevue, which was located about twenty miles south of the present city of Council Bluffs, Iowa. The trail led up the east bank of the Missouri, crossed the river at Bellevue, and then continued westward along the north bank of the Platte. Whitman gives a vivid description of their departure:

> And now for the task of packing, a thing I have never seen done and had no example before me, as the Company was to go up to Bellevue before arranging their bags transporting all their goods in a ... boat. This task Parker performed alone in the streets of Liberty, and after putting all of our possessions on the poor old mule, Parker started alone, but did not get far before all [was] in disorder and needed repacking, a scene often occurring and for which I was often blamed by Mr. Parker for my unskillful management. [Letter 62.]

At Liberty Whitman and Parker met the Rev. Moses Merrill, who had a wagon heavily loaded with supplies for his mission station at the Otoe Agency. Merrill had opened his work in 1833 at the Agency, which was located about twelve miles south of the present city of Omaha, Nebraska, and about a mile and a half north of the Platte River. Continuing with Whitman's description of the trip from Liberty to Bellevue, we read:

It was not long before we found Mr. Fontennelle did not wish to take the trouble of our provisions and we were forced to put them into Mr. Merrill's waggon, although he was obliged with a loaded ox team to keep up with Mr. Fontennelle with ... mules and empty waggons. In order to do this I assisted him in taking out his bags at every bad place and carrying them on our backs, or else lifting up the wheels in the mud, etc.

In addition to these difficulties, the rough and ungodly men of the caravan did not appreciate the presence of the two missionaries, and forcibly expressed their disapproval. Whitman wrote:

Very evident tokens gave us to understand that our company was not agreeable, such as the throwing of rotten eggs at me.

Whitman did his best to offset this disapproval by helping the men get their wagons over the difficult places.

I used to labor with extreme exertion with Mr. Fontennelle's men in crossing rivers, making rafts and bridges, etc.

By the time they reached Bellevue, Whitman found himself "very much exhausted in health."

Parker, in the third edition of his *Journal of an Exploring Tour from Beyond the Rocky Mountains,* likewise speaks of the hostility of the men of the caravan, who "so disliked the restraints which our presence imposed upon them that as they afterwards confessed they had plotted our death & intended on the first convenient occasion to put this purpose into execution."[3] Surely a word needs to be spoken in behalf of Mr. Parker. He was not by nature or disposition qualified to be a frontiersman. He was then fifty-six years old, a man more suited to the study than for roughing it on the plains. It was, indeed, a strong sense of duty which caused him to give up the comforts of his Eastern home for the life of an explorer.

WHITMAN'S JOURNAL

Whitman began his journal on May 14, the day they left Liberty. The journal was kept with more or less regularity until October 26, when Whitman was back at Cantonment Leavenworth after his trip to the Rockies. He took the journal with him to his home in Rushville, where, it appears, he copied it and sent the copy, with a letter, to the American

---

3 P. 46.

Board on December 17. This copy, now in the files of the
American Board, appeared in the September, 1927, issue of
the *Oregon Historical Quarterly*, edited by F. G. Young. A
comparison between the original journal[4] and the copy sent
to the Board reveals the fact that Whitman made many
changes, mostly of a minor character. The following is a
good example:

ORIGINAL JOURNAL

(May) 24 The Sabbath. Rested
in company with Rev. Moses Merrill. How refreshing is the rest of
the Sabbath and how delightful
is social worship in this uncultivated Prairie. Mr. Fontanell's
men went on.

26th Started and crossed the
big Tarkoo with raft. Came up
with Mr. Fontanell at evening.

27 Spent the day in crossing
the River on the raft

28th Made a raft and crossed
the west branch of the Nishnibat-
lon (?) Mr. Fronsa (?) has Waggons which he crosses on the raft.
We swim our animals over. The
water was rising so fast we had
great difficulty to get off the bottom after crossing

29th Made a bridge over the
five barrel creek.

30th Bridged the maraguim
creek and crossed. the mission
and came to Bellvue. We stopped
at the government agency under
the hospitality of Mr. Merrill.
The Brethren Dunbar and Allis
of the Pawnee mission are here
awaiting the arrival of Maj
Dockerty agent for the Pawnees.
They speak encourageingly of
their reception among the Pawnees.

10 June I was called to visit
one of Mr. Fontanell's men sick
with cholera Spent much of the
night with him

11th Patient much relieved

AMERICAN BOARD COPY

24. The Sabbath. We rested in
company with Mr. Merrill. Mr.
Fontanelle's men went on. How
refreshing is the Sabbath and
how delightful social worship in
this uncultivated prairie. I bled
myself for the pain in my side
which is quite severe.

30. We arrived at Bellevue
after a very fatigueing journey.
The rains were excessive and the
streams high. Most of them had
to be bridged or crossed by rafts.
We put up with Mr. Merrill at the
agency. Messrs. Dunbar and
Allis are here waiting for Maj.
Dockerty, agent for the Pawnees.
They speak encouragingly of
their reception among the Pawnees.

31st. Sabbath. Mr. Parker
preached in Mr. Merrill's house
in the morning & in the evening
prayer meeting.

1st June. Attend concert with
Mr. Merrill's family and the
Brethren of the Pawnee mission.
How blessed is the consideration
of union and concert in such a
cause.

10. I was called to visit one of
Mr. Fontanelle's men sick with
cholera. Spent much of the night
with him.

11th. Patient much relieved.

---

[4] Coll. U. The author had the privilege of studying this in the
original in November, 1935. The part the author saw was incomplete,
for it took the entries only to July 13. The Dunbar and Allis mentioned in the entry for May 30 were the Rev. John Dunbar and Samuel
Allis who went out with Mr. Parker in 1834.

THE MERRILL MISSION HOUSE.
Built in 1834 on the north bank of the Platte River three miles west of North Platte, Nebraska, by the Rev. Moses Merrill, a Baptist missionary from Maine.
By courtesy of Louis R. Bostwick, of Omaha.

CHOLERA

The dread cholera first visited St. Louis in the summer of 1832. It reappeared in the following summer with lessened force, but in 1834 it was worse than it had been in 1832. On June 10, 1835, Dr. Whitman was called to minister to a sick man of Fontanelle's caravan and diagnosed the case as cholera.

Whitman himself was not in good health. The trip from Liberty proved to be the hardest part of the whole journey. Whitman had been more willing to share the burdens of that trip than his physical strength permitted. Although afflicted with his chronic ailment, he was called upon to relieve the pains of others. On the 14th Whitman wrote in his journal: "I am much afflicted with pain in my head and side. Used remedys." On the 16th he felt strong enough to see some patients. Of this he wrote:

16th My (health) improved. Went to see the man for whom I was called last night. I found him past hope of recovery in collaps of Cholera, he died soon after I saw him. Another case without Shelter, upon the ground and much neglected for nursing. Exposed to a severe shower in the evening soon after which he died.[5]

During the following days others were taken ill, including Mr. Fontanelle himself. At least three cases were fatal. On Sunday, June 21, Whitman wrote the following:

For the last twelve days have been attending upon Mr. Fontanille's men; the cholera has raged severely among them; three only have died. Mr. Fontanille is sick with it himself, but now convalescent.

It is not strange that they should have the cholera, because of their intemperance, their sunken and filthy situation. They have been removed for some days out upon the Bluffs where they have a clean, healthy situation. [Letter 12.]

The hostility of the men toward Parker and Whitman now completely disappeared. Parker reported to the Board that had it not been for the successful practice of Dr. Whitman, the caravan would probably have been unable to cross the plains that summer.[6] Whitman, in his letter to Greene of December 17, 1835, made mention of the gratitude of Mr. Fontanelle. He wrote: "We received the kindest treatment from Mr. Fontanell especially after we left Bellvue."

Thus by a strange set of circumstances we find that the knowledge and experience which Whitman acquired as a

---

[5] Original diary, Coll. U.
[6] Parker to Greene, June 21, 1837, Coll. A.

village doctor in Wheeler became an important factor in opening up Oregon for the missionaries of the American Board. If there had been no cholera epidemic at Bellevue, would Parker and Whitman have been able to get to the rendezvous? Certainly we know that the good-will and co-operation of the men of the caravan, and especially of the leader, were essential to the missionaries, and these Whitman won by his efficient ministrations at Bellevue.

After the unexpected delay occasioned by the sickness, which extended to three weeks, the caravan proceeded again on June 21. That being a Sunday, Parker and Whitman refrained from traveling and so spent the day with Merrill. They easily overtook the caravan on Monday.

BELLEVUE TO THE RENDEZVOUS

Whitman demanded of Parker the purchase of another pack animal at Bellevue, and after some debate on the subject, succeeded in persuading him to buy it. Thereafter, most of the labor connected with packing and unpacking these animals fell upon Whitman.

According to Whitman's journal, Fontanelle had "between fifty and sixty men, six waggons, three yoke of oxen, and nearly two hundred horses and mules." Whitman was especially interested in the wagons. Wherever they could go, women could go, for if the women wearied of riding on the sidesaddles, they could ride in the wagons. Later, when Whitman wrote to Greene about the feasibility of taking women across the Plains, he stated: "We can go as far as the Black Hills with a waggon for the convenience of females." [Letter 14.]

On June 22 Whitman referred to his health as then being "still feeble." On the 24th a heavy shower of rain drenched the caravan as the men were preparing to camp. "The water ran like a brook through our tent," wrote Whitman in his journal, "so that we were unable to lay down untill late and then with wet blankets." The Elkhorn River was crossed on the 26th. To accomplish this they converted a wagon box into a boat by covering it with skins. The Fourth of July, then the major festival day for the whole nation, was spent with the Pawnee Indians. "We were invited to three feasts two made of corn and one of dry buffalo meat," wrote Whitman of this experience.

It was the custom of the fur men to carry with them only enough food to enable them to reach the buffalo range, which usually took from two to three weeks. After that they lived almost entirely upon buffalo meat and other wild game. Because of the delay at Bellevue, they ran short of food before they found buffalo. The first of the shaggy beasts of the prairies was killed on July 13.

Whitman was sick for the week beginning July 7. The exposure to wet, the cold nights, and a bad case of dysentery so sapped his strength that he could ride only with the greatest difficulty. He did not go into detail in his journal regarding this experience, but in his letter of May 10, 1839, he wrote:

Soon after passing the Pawnees, I was taken sick with a painful bowel complaint. Being often obliged to stop, I fell in the rear of camp and was unable to overtake them again until they had been encamped, for I was too weak to ride faster than a walk. I must have failed by the way had it not been for one of the Companies Clerks who kindly kept me company and assisted me in mounting and dismounting my horse. [Letter 62.]

By this time Fontanelle had realized that the presence of a physician in the caravan was a distinct asset and perhaps delegated one of his men to assist Whitman. Whitman bemoaned the fact that he and Parker did not have a man in their employ to help them, especially since Parker was so ill fitted for camp life. "I do not recollect," he wrote, "that Mr. Parker ever got a meal during my sickness either for himself or me, but went to eat with Mr. F., and it was only by the favour of his cook that I obtained a little food occasionally."

On the 16th of July the caravan passed the forks of the Platte and continued up the north bank of the North Fork to Fort Laramie, which they reached on the 26th. There the missionaries met a delegation of the Ogalalla Sioux Indians. On the 30th Mr. Parker held a conference with one of the chiefs, who expressed a desire for Christian teachers. In an interesting letter to his family, written August 19, 1835, Mr. Parker tells of his singing the song, "Watchman, tell us of the night," to the Indians, who no doubt were attracted by the novelty of a white man singing for them. Parker, however, gives the following interpretation to the incident:

They wished me to sing the hymn again, and when I had done so, they took me by the hand to express their satisfaction. Some others came around, and those who came first wished me to sing the hymn for them to hear, and when I had done so, they again took me by the hand. It moved my heart, and it would have moved the hearts of the Christians of the east, had they witnessed the scene. Can they not now be moved, and send missionaries to teach these very interesting people the way of salvation. Are there no young men who are willing to take up the cross and come.[7]

The caravan continued the journey on August 1. The wagons were left at the Fort and the baggage transferred to pack animals. Thomas Fitzpatrick took over the command at Fort Laramie, relieving Fontanelle. With him Whitman formed a friendship which was to prove of value the following year. The Continental Divide was crossed on August 10. The trail led through South Pass, which came to be known later as the gateway to Oregon. The ascent of the pass is very gradual, though the elevation is about 7,500 feet at the summit. The pass is several miles wide and is flanked on both sides by snow-capped mountains. Whitman noted that there was no reason why wagons should not go through it, and indeed learned that wagons had been taken to the rendezvous on a previous occasion. In his journal he wrote: " . . . we could cross the mountains with a waggon. There were 20 waggons at one time from St. Louis at the place where the company rendezvoused last summer." Whitman's interest in the wagons is one indication of his desire to marry and to take Narcissa over the Rockies.

It was cold in the mountains at night. The day after they crossed the divide the thermometer read 23°F. in the morning. On the 12th the caravan reached the rendezvous, which was located that year on the Green River, a branch of the Colorado. There they found most of the trappers and traders of the mountains and several thousand Indians impatiently awaiting their arrival. Whitman said that there were "about two thousand Shoshoni or Snake Indians, and forty lodges of Flathead & Napiersas [Nez Perces], and a few Utaws." [Letter 11.]

AT THE RENDEZVOUS

The annual gathering at the rendezvous was the one big social event in the life of the mountain men. It was a time for business, when the trappers traded their furs for the supplies which had been brought out from civilization, and it was a time for social pleasure when old friendships were renewed. Always there was much carousing, for one item of trade was liquor, which was carried in kegs built to fit the backs and sides of the horses or mules. Prices were high for the goods brought from St. Louis, while comparatively low

---

[7] Owned by Mr. L. Alexander Mack, a great-grandson of Parker.

prices were paid for the furs. G. W. Ebberts in his "A Trapper's Life in the Rocky Mountains" states that tobacco was sold for two dollars a pound; whisky at two dollars a pint; three awls cost fifty cents; and a red and green blanket sold for twenty-five dollars. In return the Company allowed five dollars a pound for furs, five dollars for a small beaver skin, and seven dollars for a large one.[8]

Both Parker and Whitman were dismayed to see the demoralizing effects of the liquor traffic, not only upon the white men but upon the Indians as well. Upon Whitman's return he wrote on December 28 to Greene at some length in regard to this problem. "All the present regulations upon this point are disregarded or evaded," he declared, "and I fear all further regulations will be equally ineffectual." Whitman felt that the Government should take some steps to curb the evil, but realized that it was a delicate problem for missionaries to handle because of their dependence upon the traders for various favors. He wrote: "You are aware of the delicacy of this subject to one who is liable to be exposed to opposition of traders." [Letter 15.]

On the 13th of August, the day after their arrival at the rendezvous, Dr. Whitman removed from the back of Bridger a three-inch iron arrow point which had been embedded there three years previous in a battle with some Blackfeet Indians. Parker, describing the operation, wrote as follows:

> It was a difficult operation, because the arrow was hooked at the point by striking a large bone and a cartilaginous substance had grown around it. The Doctor pursued the operation with great self-possession and perseverance; and his patient manifested equal firmness.[9]

The operation was performed in the presence of many witnesses, including some Indians, who admired both the skill of the surgeon and the endurance of the patient. Medical science then knew nothing of anesthesia, so Jim Bridger had to grin and bear it. Thus began a friendship between Whitman and Bridger which continued until death separated them. Years later, Bridger sent his half-breed daughter, Mary Ann, to the Whitman home at Waiilatpu to be educated.

Whitman's reputation as a competent physician and surgeon was firmly established by the success of the Bridger

---

8 Ebberts MS., Bancroft Library, Berkeley, Calif., pp. 8-9.

9 Parker, *Journal*, p. 76. Hafen and Ghent, *Broken Hand*, p. 103, gives the story of how Bridger was wounded in 1832.

operation. Others who had arrowheads embedded in their
flesh came and begged for their removal. Even some of the
Indians came forward. Here was a medicine man greater
than any they had ever seen, whose skill was as magic in
their eyes. Whitman sent one of these extracted arrow
heads as a souvenir to a friend in the East.[10] Parker stated
that "calls for medical and surgical aid were constant every
hour in the day.[11]

Due attention has never been given to the important connection which existed between Whitman's medical and surgical ability and the founding of the Oregon mission of the
American Board. It has often been stated that some foreign
mission field has been opened at the point of a lancet, referring to the pioneer labors of a missionary doctor who had
won the confidence of the natives through his medical and
surgical skill. So may it be said of Oregon. Dr. Whitman
was the first American-trained physician ever to cross the
Rocky Mountains. Jason Lee and his companions, who were
the first Protestant missionaries to cross the Rockies, had
the good fortune to go out with the Wyeth Expedition in
1834. But such expeditions did not go out every year. The
American Board was dependent upon the good-will and
co-operation of the American Fur Company and of the
Hudson's Bay Company for the establishment of its Oregon
mission.

If the Board had sent out some tactless individuals in
1835, the way would have been closed for any further effort.
But, instead, the Board sent Parker and Whitman. While
Parker was not a frontiersman, he did have an attractive
personality that won friends for him all along the way.
Sometimes he imposed upon these friendships, not from any
selfish motive, but for the sake of saving money for the
Board.

In Whitman, however, the Board had unknowingly chosen
a man superbly qualified for the very task that had to be
done. More important than spying out the country was the
winning of friendships among those whose co-operation was
the key to the success of the enterprise. And this is what
Whitman did. At Bellevue, when cholera struck the men
of the caravan, it was Whitman who saved many of their
lives and made the trip that summer a possibility. And at

---

[10] Owned by Miss Alice Wheatley, Clifton Springs, N. Y. Reported
to have been taken from the back of an Indian.

[11] Parker, *op. cit.*, p. 77.

the rendezvous, it was Whitman's medical skill which made him the most popular man at that mountain gathering.

On Sunday, August 16, Parker and Whitman met with the principal men of the Flathead and Nez Perce Indians and explained the object of their visit. A mountain man by the name of Charles Compo, who had married into the Nez Perce tribe, was secured as an interpreter. Without a doubt, the missionaries made reference to the Nez Perce delegation which visited St. Louis in the fall of 1831 in search of the white man's Book. They told of the possibility of having missions established, provided the Indians were willing to extend the necessary protection and co-operation. Whitman's account of the conference, as found in his journal, is as follows:

16. We had a talk with the chiefs of the Flathead and Napiersas tribes, in which they expressed great pleasure in seeing us and strong desire to be taught. Little Chief of the Flatheads said he was greatly rejoiced when he heard there was a teacher from the Almighty and physician coming among them; that he immediately set out to meet us; that on their way they were robbed by the Crow Indians and that he lost a horse he loved very much, but that since he had seen us he did not lament the loss of his horse. He had been told some things he said about the worship of God but he did not practice them. But now, if a teacher would come among them, he and his children (meaning all over whom he had authority) would obey all that he should say.

Parker and Whitman were deeply stirred by the earnestness and sincerity of the Indians. They made inquiries and found that the Methodist missionaries had settled in the Willamette Valley. After serious discussion and prayer, Whitman dropped the remark that " . . . if we had another associate with us I should like to return, and if the Board should approve, come out next year with others to establish a mission among them." Whitman added in his journal: "I did not at this time think it practicable for him [Parker] to go without me." Somewhat to Whitman's surprise, Parker insisted that it would be perfectly satisfactory to him to go on alone. Whitman raised objections by asking what the people in the States would think if some accident befell Parker. "I told him to give himself no uneasiness upon this subject," wrote Parker, "for we could not go safely together without divine protection, and with it, I could go alone."[12] It was a courageous attitude to take. All honor to him!

Gray, in his *Oregon,* states that the two men separated

12 Parker, *op. cit.,* p. 78.

because Parker was "rather fastidious" and could not "put up with the off-hand, careless, and, as he thought, slovenly manner in which Dr. Whitman was inclined to travel."[13] Gray felt that this subdued friction which existed between the two men was the primary reason for Whitman's return. While it may have been a contributing factor, it was hardly the main cause. Both Parker and Whitman had a deep and sincere desire to benefit the Indians and, whatever their personal feelings might have been, these were subordinated to their high sense of duty. It might have been that Whitman, convinced that women could cross the plains, wanted to return to marry Narcissa and take her with him to the Northwest.

On the 17th Parker and Whitman met with the Indians again to discuss the idea of Parker's going with them. Parker asked if they would give him safe escort to Walla Walla if Whitman returned "and made known their wishes to the Fathers (the Board)." The Indians were quick to give this assurance. They promised to assist in packing and caring for Parker's animals. The decision was final. Parker was to go on alone and continue the exploring trip, while Whitman was to return for more workers.

Since the Indians were eager to be on their way the missionaries found that they had but four days in which to complete their arrangements. Letters had to be written for Whitman to carry back. Whitman turned over both pack animals to Parker with nearly all of their equipment, and Whitman bought "a horse for five dollars which was a disgrace to any man to pack on account of his extreme sore back." [Letter 62.] The price of an ordinary horse at the rendezvous was one hundred dollars, which was more than Whitman felt he could pay. However, his pack was light.

The services of Charles Compo were secured as interpreter and servant for Parker, which relieved Whitman's mind considerably. Whitman found a Nez Perce boy named Tackitonitis, who had some knowledge of the English language, and he conceived the idea of taking the boy with him back to the States. "My reason for taking him is," wrote Whitman in his journal, "that he . . . by being with white people . . . will soon speak so as to interpret or assist in learning his language." It was a good idea. Two years previously Captain Wyeth had taken two Indian boys East with him.

---

[13] P. 108.

A few days after Whitman secured permission to take Tackitonitis, whom he renamed Richard, one of the Nez Perce chiefs came with his son, Ais, and begged Whitman to take him also. Ais had a horse and the necessary equipment. Of this experience Whitman wrote:

> The father said he had but one more son, but he was willing to part with this one that he might be taught the religion of the whites or the Christian religion. I did not like to take him as I had one already, but at the request of Mr. Parker I consented that he might come along with me and go to his family and the people of Ithaca. [Letter 11.]

Parker wrote to his family on the 19th, and on the 20th added a postscript to his letter in which he too wrote about Ais, whom he renamed John. Parker wrote: "There was an affecting parting between him and his father. His father pointed upward and then separated."[14] Thus Whitman found himself responsible for two Nez Perce boys.

On Friday, August 21, the Indians moved their camp three miles. Whitman went along and spent the night with Parker. The next morning the two men parted, never to meet again. It has been supposed by some that Whitman visited Parker in Ithaca in the spring of 1843. Recently discovered evidence, which will be introduced in its proper place, shows that this was not so. With a heavy heart Whitman mounted his horse and returned to the rendezvous to be ready to return with the caravan. On that day Whitman wrote in his journal:

> 22. Mr. Parker went on this morning, after we had unitedly sought the blessing and guidance of God. He went on with firmness. I regretted exceedingly to see him go alone, but so we have decided, hoping more fully to advance the cause of our divine master.

The caravan laden with furs did not get started until August 27. During the interval Whitman was busy not only with his medical service, but also with the task of gathering such information as he could regarding the various Indian tribes, their languages, customs, and the nature of the country in which they lived. This information he embodied in the report that he submitted with his journal to the Board after he had returned.[15]

Whitman was not a man of many words. For the most part his letters are short, frequently confined to one letter

---

[14] Parker to his family, Aug. 19, 1835. Owned by Mr. Mack.

[15] *See* critique of the journal by F. G. Young, in *O.H.Q.*, Sept., 1927.

page. Parker with considerable literary skill wrote a book
of his experiences on this trip which went through five
American editions and one English edition. Whitman never
dreamed of writing a book. In a scrawl rather difficult to
read, with some misspelled words, he penned his concise
statements to the Board. His keenness in picking out the
essential facts and his accuracy of statement more than com-
pensated for his lack of literary ability.

He classified the Indians into tribes that spoke the same
language. He advised against the establishment of a fixed
mission station among some of the tribes who still depended
upon buffalo for their food. Regarding the possibility of
a party of missionaries crossing the plains and the mountains in 1836, he wrote that Fontanelle had assured him the
Company would furnish them with meat after they reached
the buffalo range. He investigated the possibility of securing
supplies in the Oregon Country and wrote:

> We could drive cows and other cattle without much if any expense
> and I would advise to take enough so that in case of necessity we might
> kill some for beef after we arrived at our destination. For a time,
> untill we could cultivate, we should have to depend upon the Northwest
> Fur Company for flour and corn meal. . . . Besides the country abounds
> in salmon. . . . Cattle and horses may be wintered in the plains beyond
> the mountains with moderate attention.

It was just the kind of report the Board wanted. They
acted upon his recommendations, and the plans outlined
in 1835 were followed to a remarkable extent in 1836.

Whitman included in this report an account of the Indian
delegation that visited St. Louis in the fall of 1831. Whitman
claimed that he received his information direct from Fontanelle, "under whose protection they came and returned."[16]
No doubt the Indians went to St. Louis with the returning
caravan of 1831, but they returned a different way, for the
two survivors went up the Missouri on the first steamboat
that ascended that stream as far as the mouth of the Yellow-
stone. George Catlin, the Indian painter, was also a passenger on that boat, and painted their pictures. According to
Whitman, three of the four Indians who reached St. Louis
were Nez Perces, and one was a Flathead. This harmonizes
with other contemporary information and adds to Whitman's
reputation for being a keen observer and a careful writer.

Whitman forwarded his journal and report to the Board

---

[16] Drury, *Spalding,* Chapter 3, gives a detailed study of the
delegation.

from Rushville, New York, on December 17, 1835. Greene received it on December 23.

THE RETURN TRIP

The caravan made good time on its return trip. Fort Laramie was reached on the 8th of September. On the 23rd of the month the caravan was in the buffalo country, and three days were spent in killing buffalo and in drying enough meat to take them to civilization. On the 10th of October, Whitman met Dunbar and Allis again near Council Bluffs. He wrote of the joy he had in "social worship and intercourse." Whitman told of his plan to take out missionaries for an Oregon mission in 1836 and undoubtedly mentioned his desire to be married. Both Dunbar and Allis were engaged, and they asked Whitman to escort their fiancées the next spring to Liberty.

Whitman continued his journey on the 12th. He visited Fort Leavenworth on the 26th, where he had a conference with Colonel Henry Dodge, who had just returned from a military expedition that had taken him as far west as the Rockies. The fact that Colonel Dodge had taken wheeled cannons with him confirmed Whitman in his belief that wagons could be taken to Oregon.

On the 4th of November, Whitman was in St. Louis. From there he wrote a letter to Greene dated the 7th. In this letter he told of Parker's going alone to the Columbia and of his own return for missionaries. Although Whitman said nothing definite in this letter of his desire to be married and take his wife with him, yet Greene was able to read between the lines. On December 8, Greene replied to the letter, addressing it to Rushville, and asked:

Have you carefully ascertained & weighed the difficulties in the way of conducting females to those remote & desolate regions and comfortable sustaining families there? How are the common & what are usually deemed the indispensable articles of furniture used in housekeeping to be obtained or transported? How are annual supplies to be obtained, with such certainty that a family may safely depend upon them?

In this letter Greene wrote further: "We have a number of candidates who have expressed a desire to go to the remote western tribes. Rev. Oliver S. Powell & wife, now at Fowlersville, Rev. Daniel Clark & wife, agent of the Am. Bible Society...." When Greene received Whitman's journal and report he found answers to many of his questions and doubts.

In the closing paragraph of Whitman's report, mailed from Rushville on December 17, he stated: "I received fifty-five dollars from Mr. Trueman, Cincinnati, for which I gave a receipt, and twenty dollars from the Presbyterian church at Erie, Pa., which I desire you to acknowledge in the Herald as a donation to the Board." This gives us the necessary information by which we can outline a part of Whitman's return trip. He proceeded by boat up the Ohio River to Cincinnati, then by stage to Cleveland, and then by boat or stage to Erie. Since he received a donation at Erie from a church, it is probable that he spent a Sunday there and attended the Presbyterian church, of which the Rev. George A. Lyon was then pastor.

Whitman's next stop was at Angelica, where the Prentiss family then lived. With high hopes Marcus and Narcissa discussed the possibility of their marriage. They agreed that it was essential for them to have another married couple in the party. Perhaps Marcus learned from Narcissa the fact that Henry and Eliza Spalding were under appointment and were to go to the Osage Indians in western Missouri the next spring. Whitman wrote to Spalding to find out if he were willing to go to Oregon and received a reply at Rushville on December 16. In Whitman's letter to Greene, written the next day, he said:

> I received a letter yesterday from H. H. Spalding saying he would be ready to accompany me across the mountains if the Board should approve of it.
> I hope you will appoint Mr. Spalding or Mr. Clark, if he has been approved by the Board and is not appointed to a particular station. Mr. Spalding said he knew of farmers and mechanics that would go

We do not know with certainty just when Whitman reached Rushville. According to a statement made by Mrs. Mary Alice Wisewell Caulkins,[17] a daughter of Whitman's only sister, Marcus reached his mother's home with the two Indian boys late on a Saturday night, perhaps December 11.[18] The family had gone to bed when Marcus arrived. Mrs. Caulkins described the meeting as follows:

> His Mother, then Mrs. Loomis, hearing a noise, recognized his step and went out in her nightclothes to meet him, and Marcus said, "How do you do, Mother?"

---

17 Caulkins MS., Coll. Wn.

18 Whitman's letter of Nov. 7, mailed from St. Louis, reached Boston by the 8th of Dec. Since Whitman evidently wrote soon after his return, it appears that he was home by the 11th.

They sat around the fireplace and talked late into the night. It takes but little imagination to recreate that circle of eager listeners, absorbing every word of a fascinating tale. Mrs. Caulkins also gives the following incident which took place the next day:

A brother, Augustus, lived only across the street, but the Sabbath was so strictly observed that there was no communication between the two families on that day, so Augustus and his family were already in church without knowing that Marcus was in town, and when he walked in followed by the two Indian boys, the niece, Deborah Whitman, jumped up and cried, "Why there's Uncle Marcus."[19]

Deborah was sixteen years old when she broke the decorum of the assembled congregation by crying out, "Why, there's Uncle Marcus."

After a short visit with relatives in Rushville, Whitman took the two Indian boys to Ithaca. When Whitman wrote to Greene on December 17, he added this postscript: "I have the two Napiersa boys with me, one of which design to take to Ithaca in a few days." In the library of Cornell University, Ithaca, New York, is a manuscript of about seventy thousand words written by Samuel Parker, M.D. (1818-1898), the son of the Rev. Samuel Parker, who writes of the arrival of Dr. Whitman with the Indian boys at Ithaca.

My recollections are that one day late in the fall of 1835, he came to my father's house (now mine in which I write this) and there was at the door the two Indian boys, that he said he had been a few days with his brothers family at Rushville; and that the Indian boys could not bear to be separated, that he talked over the missionary matter with my mother; and called together the Ithaca Presby. Church and town mission committee; and after a few days consultation, left the Indian boys both in this house.[20]

Dr. Parker then relates several interesting anecdotes about Richard and John. The Rev. Samuel Parker's two sons, Samuel and Henry, were then lads of about the same ages as the Indian boys and they endeavored to show the Indians a pleasant time. When the creeks were frozen and

---

[19] Caulkins MS., Coll. Wn. This was in an envelope addressed to the Rev. S. W. Pratt, D.D., postmarked Naples, Oct. 8, 1902. Mowry, *Marcus Whitman*, p. 63, gives a different version, stating that it was his mother who exclaimed: "Well, well, there is Marcus Whitman." Ells, *Marcus Whitman*, p. 30, gives the same story.

[20] Pp. 446 ff. The Parker home was partially burned in 1934; but was soon rebuilt. Another Parker house, at 404 Seneca St., is still standing. The June 21, 1929, issue of the Ithaca *Journal-News* contains an article, with picture of the house, by L. Alexander Mack, describing the dwelling.

snow was on the ground, the Nez Perces were taken out for some winter sports. "Nothing would persuade the Indian boys," wrote Dr. Parker, "to put on a pair of skates; or ride down hill on a 'coaster sled.' " He also related this interesting incident:

... and what was amusing these Indian boys were ever on the look out for being murdered. As one day they came home on the most rapid run, having seen a 'codger' with a gun just above Spring St. And another [time] while four or five boys of us were sporting on skates ... a man with a gun hunting partridges, sent them off like the wind; into the cliffs of the creek, while we skated undisturbed.

The Indian lads, who had been taught to be suspicious of all strangers, and especially strangers with guns, found it difficult to adjust themselves to the security of civilized life. We do not know how long both boys remained at Ithaca. Dr. Parker states that they attended a school taught by Miss Emeline Palmer, "who lived near the head of Seneca St. on Eddy St." Miss Palmer was engaged to Samuel Allis, and took a special interest in the boys because of her expected employment in the mission field. It appears that Whitman took Richard back to Rushville and placed him in a school there sometime during the winter. The boys acquired a considerable knowledge of the English language and were useful as interpreters and teachers in 1836.

Greene looked upon the experiment with doubtful eyes. Writing to Whitman on December 30, he said:

I think you will have cause to regret that you brought the two Indian boys with you. Our whole experience is against such a measure. The boys will probably be ruined by the attention which they will receive, and the high notions which they will get by being among white people and seeing their ways. It will probably do the church rather hurt than good, although it may increase their donations somewhat for the time being. . . . They can hardly fail to occasion considerable expense.

The two boys rendered valuable services to the mission party which crossed the Plains in 1836, for they helped in caring for the cattle. However, after their arrival in Oregon, Richard gave Whitman considerable trouble, of which mention will be made later.

The year 1835 closed with Whitman engaged in doing what Parker had been doing just a year before—looking for missionaries who would be willing to go to the Indians beyond the Rocky Mountains. The Board's reply to Whitman's letter of November 7, written from St. Louis, was received after Whitman had sent in his journal on the 19th. Whitman wrote again from Cohocton on December 28. Greene had asked about the advisability of taking "females to those remote & desolate regions." Whitman replied:

In answer to yours of 4th Dec. I would say that I think the questions are substantially answered by my communication already forwarded to you. We should expect to take pack animals sufficient to carry every absolutely necessary article of cook utencil, furniture and clothing.

He pointed out the fact that heavier articles could be sent by boat around the Horn, and that many items could be purchased at Fort Vancouver from the Hudson's Bay Company. The arguments presented by Whitman were convincing, for the Board thereafter co-operated with Whitman in finding a married couple to go with him. Greene wrote on December 30, even before he had received Whitman's letter of the 28th, but after the receipt of the journal, suggested that Whitman communicate with the Rev. Chauncey Eddy, agent of the Board for New York State, "relative to suitable persons to accompany you on yr return."

Thus the year 1835 came to an end without the appointment of any missionaries to return with Whitman. Since he wanted to be on his way by the middle of February, he had then but six weeks in which to find his associates.

CHAPTER SIX

WHITMAN IS MARRIED
1836

SOMETIME during the spring or summer of 1835, the Prentiss family had moved from Amity to Angelica, about seven miles distant but within the same county. The minute book of the Angelica church shows that on Sunday, September 27, 1835, "Stephen Prentiss and Clarissa his wife, Narcissa, Clarissa, Harriet R. and Edward W., their children presented a letter with the request to be received into the church and their request was granted." The Rev. Leverett Hull was then pastor of the church. Another entry for Sunday, November 1, of the same year states that the Prentiss family was that day formally received into the membership of the church at a communion service.[1] Narcissa's younger brother, Jonas Galusha, who had his membership transferred with the others to the Amity church, did not join the Angelica church. He entered the mercantile business at West Almond, Allegany County, where later Judge and Mrs. Prentiss spent the declining years of their lives.

Narcissa with characteristic enthusiasm gave herself to the activities of the Angelica Presbyterian church. She sang in the choir and taught a class of girls in the Sunday school. In the spring of 1835 the church experienced a revival under the leadership of the pastor and the Rev. Samuel W. May, which added about 90 members,[2] including the family of William Geiger, of particular interest because several years later, a William Geiger, of Angelica, perhaps William, Jr., entered the employ of Dr. Whitman at the mission station in Old Oregon. According to the 1836 *Minutes of the Pres-*

---

[1] P. 55 of minutes. In the summer of 1935 the author examined the the original records of this church at Angelica. Miller, *Presbyterianism in Steuben and Allegany*, p. 64, gives a brief history of this church. The organization is no longer in existence.

[2] Mr. Hull's quarterly reports to the American Home Missionary Society are in the Hammond Library, Chicago Theo. Sem. His salary was $500 a year. His reports indicate much activity.

byterian General Assembly, the Angelica church had 185 members.[3]

Stephen Prentiss was quickly recognized as a leader by the members of the Angelica church. He was elected to the office of elder on January 21, 1836, and was ordained on Thursday evening, February 18. Both he and his pastor were sent as commissioners to the Presbyterian General Assembly which met at Philadelphia that year. He and his wife remained members of the Angelica church until May 9, 1842, when they were dismissed to the Presbyterian church in Cuba, Allegany County, New York.[4]

A letter written by Narcissa to Mrs. Sarah Hull, wife of the Angelica pastor, gives evidence that Narcissa was early aware of the necessity of finding associates for the Oregon mission. The letter was printed in Mowry's *Marcus Whitman* but without date or place of writing. From internal evidence, it is apparent that it was written from Amity in the summer of 1835. She wrote:

> I received a letter last week from Rev. D. Clark, New York, which has greatly relieved my mind from that state of suspense in which it has long been laboring. . . . You will see that his heart, as our hearts, is on the Astoria mission.

It seems that the Board had written to Clark about some "obstacles." Clark had in turn written to Narcissa, perhaps sending her a copy of his reply to the Board.

> What can be the obstacles which the Board of Missions speak of? Is it want of funds or missionaries? Or is it want of faith and prayer in the churches? Surely the obstacles cannot be with the Indians, when they have sent over to us and invited us to carry them the Word of Life.
>
> At times my mind labors excessively on this point, and I have been well-nigh crushed with an unsupportable load for want of strength to roll it upon the Lord. But I can say, notwithstanding the clouds of darkness that overshadow the future, and the obstacles that roll up before the mind like waves of the sea, that I am permitted to believe that a mission will be established there soon, at least before many years shall have passed away. . . . Will not the dear Christians in Angelica remember this Oregon mission at their monthly concert of prayer? [Letter 10.]

---

[3] The Rev. Gilbert Reid, A.M., for many years a missionary in Peking and Shanghai, China, went out from this church. Mr. Reid founded the International Institute in Shanghai.

[4] Narcissa's first known letter addressed to her parents at Cuba was dated Feb. 7, 1843. Thereafter all letters to her parents were sent there. Spalding sent his letter of April 6, 1848, telling of the massacre to West Almond, N. Y., which shows that Spalding had learned that the Prentisses had moved.

When Marcus visited Narcissa at Angelica in November, 1835, it is reasonable to believe that she told him of the appointment of the Rev. and Mrs. H. H. Spalding to Boudinot in western Missouri. The Spaldings had expected to leave for their field in the fall of 1835 but were delayed. An entry in the Spalding family Bible, now in the library of Pacific University, Forest Grove, Oregon, states that Mrs. Spalding gave birth to a stillborn baby girl at Prattsburg on October 24, 1835. Mrs. Spalding's serious illness made it necessary for them to postpone their departure until spring. Undoubtedly all of this was known to Narcissa.

Whitman mailed his rewritten journal to the Board from Rushville on December 17. In a footnote he wrote: "I received a letter yesterday from H. H. Spalding saying he would be ready to accompany me across the mountains if the Board should approve of it." It was Whitman's hope to be on his way to Oregon by the latter part of February or the first part of March, 1836. He knew there was no time to lose. It then took from a week to ten days for a letter to go from Rushville to Boston.

Greene answered Whitman's letter of November 7, written from St. Louis, on December 8. He, too, knew the necessity of haste in finding proper associates and suggested several names, including those of the Rev. and Mrs. Oliver S. Powell and the Rev. and Mrs. Daniel Clark. Both of these couples had previously signified an interest in the Oregon mission. He also suggested that Whitman get in touch with the Rev. Chauncey Eddy, agent of the American Board for New York State.

Greene wrote again on December 30, acknowledging receipt of Whitman's journal. In this letter he gave some good advice regarding the qualifications of suitable workers, but failed to give any more names. The whole burden of finding the desired associates was shifted to Whitman's shoulders. Greene closed his letter with these words:

Let us hear from you soon relative to yr progress in obtaining associates. It seems to me that one or two ordained missionaries, a teacher, and perhaps a farmer and mechanic are as many as ought to go the coming spring. No families of children should go, and probably, the more of the men who go without wives, at first, the better.

The Board's committee responsible for Indian missions met in Boston on Tuesday, January 5, and authorized Whitman's return to Oregon, taking with him "an ordained missionary, a teacher or catechiest, & a man able to labor as a farmer, & mechanic to accompany." The committee felt that one married couple in addition to the Whitmans would be enough. "Families of children," wrote Greene to Whitman the next day, "cannot be taken." That was a wise provision. Miss Palmer and Miss Smith, the fiancées of Dunbar and Allis, were given permission to go out to their destination with the Whitman party. Dr. Benedict Satterlee, who attended Fairfield Medical College, 1835-36, and his wife were appointed missionaries to the Pawnee Indians. They, too, were to go out with the Whitmans as far as their field. Greene had little to offer in the way of helping Whitman find the Oregon workers. He even confessed his ignorance of Clark's address, and Clark was then considered to be the one best qualified to go with Whitman. Greene gave this word of caution: "Better go alone than with unsuitable associates, therefore use great caution in finding & recommending men."

It is easy to imagine that by this time Whitman was getting anxious. He felt the necessity of returning to the mountains. He had promised to meet Parker there. He had given the most solemn assurances to the fathers of the two Indian boys that he would return them in the summer of 1836. Moreover, he had told the Nez Perces that he would return with workers the next summer. He knew it was unwise to marry Narcissa and go out with her alone.

On the same day that Greene wrote to Whitman, that is, January 6, 1836, Whitman wrote to Greene. He informed Greene that the Powells were disqualified because a child had been born to them. He had written to both Eddy and Clark without receiving a response from either. Twice in the letter he mentions Spalding:

I have as I mentioned before received encouragement from the Rev. H. H. Spalding who is (as I said) designed by the Board for Boudinot among the Osages that he would go with me if the Board would alter his designation.

P.S. I hope the Board may think best to alter the designation of the Rev. H. H. Spalding as he expresses a willingness that they should.

Greene answered this letter of Whitman's on January 15. He wrote that he was still hopeful of getting Clark's consent to go. Regarding the Spaldings, he said: "The same objection we suppose to lie against Mr. & Mrs. Spalding, which you mention in the case of Mr. Powell. Besides these, we have no missionary candidates as preachers, who can be ready to proceed as early as will be necessary." As far as

Greene was concerned, the outlook was dark for Whitman. Only six weeks remained before Whitman should be going— and still no one else was appointed!

It so happened that the very day Greene was writing to Whitman, telling of his hope to get Clark, Clark was writing to Greene. Clark had his heart set upon a station which he felt should be established at Astoria. He did not want to go into the interior of Oregon. Thus Clark eliminated himself. Greene received Clark's letter on the 22nd and at once wrote to Whitman:

> I have today received a letter from Rev. D. Clark Jr. declining to go to the Flatheads and Nez Perce Indians. He states that his mind is fixed on Astoria. . . .
>
> I do not know where to look for a missionary to accompany you, unless Mr. Spaulding should go. His child (as I understand he has one) will be a hindrance; and it seems to me that no person with an infant child should go to such a work.
>
> Besides I have some doubt whether his temperment well fits him for intercourse with the traders and travellers in that region. As to laboriousness, self-denial, energy and perseverance, I presume that few men are better qualified than he.[5]

Matters were swiftly approaching a crisis. Whitman wrote to Greene from Rushville on January 29. He had received Greene's letter of the 15th but not his letter of the 22nd. Whitman stated that he felt it necessary to leave for St. Louis "by 25th. Feb. or at furtherest the 1st of March." He said that he had written to Eddy and "have been in constant expectation of an answer." Whitman was worried. Precious time was slipping by. He had found a man at Cohocton, David Weld, who expressed a willingness to go, only the time then was too short for him to make ready. Regarding Spalding, Whitman wrote:

> Your allusion to Mr. Spalding is not correct; they lost their child by death some time since. They expect to be at Prattsburgh where I can see him if desired.

Greene received this letter on February 5 and replied at once. In his letter of December 30, Greene had listed the desirable qualifications for an Oregon missionary and added: "these are the persons wanted for such a service; and such I hope you may find the finger of Providence pointing to."

---

[5] Hulbert & Hulbert, *Marcus Whitman, Crusader*, prints most of the correspondence between Whitman and Greene in full, but Greene's letter of January 22, 1835, is unfortunately omitted. The letter is to be found in Coll. A., Vol. 17, Domestic Correspondence, pp. 523-524. *See* Drury, *Spalding*, p. 112.

The "finger of Providence" was pointing to Henry Harmon Spalding. One by one all possible candidates had been eliminated except Spalding, who had expressed his willingness to go when Whitman first approached him upon the matter. Greene, now that he was informed of the death of Spalding's child, found no other objection to a change of destination, and yet he was a bit vague in his reply. He wrote: "I know not who will accompany you, unless Mr. Spalding should; and respecting the change of his destination, we are held in suspense by the uncertainty which still hangs over the fate of the Osages." There was nothing definite about that! Yet Whitman was quick to read into the words permission for him to intercede with Spalding.

Whitman received the letter on the 12th, possibly the 13th, of February. He left at once for Prattsburg, twenty-five miles to the south. There he found to his dismay that the Spaldings had already left for their field in western Missouri. Spalding had converted his light wagon into a sleigh by the use of temporary runners, for it was winter and the snow was deep in places. But Whitman learned that the Spaldings intended to spend Sunday, February 14, at the village of Howard, about twenty miles to the southwest. He immediately set out in pursuit.

THE SPALDINGS

Henry Harmon Spalding was graduated from Western Reserve College, then at Hudson, Ohio, on August 28, 1833. He received the A.B. degree. He was married on Sunday evening, October 13 of that year, at Hudson, to Miss Eliza Hart, of Holland Patent, New York. Eliza was born at Berlin, then Kensington, Connecticut, August 11, 1807, the daughter of Captain Levi and Martha Hart. She was less than a year older than Narcissa Prentiss.

The Hart family had moved to Holland Patent, Oneida County, New York, in 1820. Eliza became a member of the church there and was active in its work. For a time she attended a "female seminary" in Clinton, New York. Very little is known of her early life and education. She was in Hudson, Ohio, during Spalding's last year at Western Reserve, and may have attended one of the seminaries for young women then being conducted in that town.

After their marriage, Henry and Eliza had gone to Cincinnati, where both of them took work in Lane Theological Seminary, a Presbyterian institution, of which the famed

Dr. Lyman Beecher was then president. There they remained for two years. Eliza took in boarders at three dollars
a week for both board and room. Henry worked in a printing
shop and elsewhere. They were thus enabled to earn enough
to pay their expenses. From a Spalding letter still extant,
we learn that Eliza studied both Greek and Hebrew at Lane,
and even took some courses in theology under Dr. Beecher.[6]
She was unusually well educated for a young woman of her
generation.

Spalding was a man of strong physique, of unquestioned
devotion to the Christian cause, and of great versatility and
energy. He was a man of many talents. In one of the letters
of recommendation sent to the Board concerning him, we
read: "Few men are willing to labor more abundantly or
endure more fatigue, or make greater sacrifices than he."[7]
On the other hand, Spalding was inclined to be censorious
and critical of those who did not agree with him. The fact
of his having been born out of wedlock was a greater stigma
in his generation than in ours. Because of this he was sen-
sitive, and it probably was an important factor in the in-
feriority complex which he often unquestionably displayed.
Spalding was an individualist who did his best work alone.
Both Henry and Eliza were admirably qualified by tempera-
ment and training to be missionaries to the Indians.

Hoping to secure a position under the Government as
a teacher among the Choctaw Indians, Henry had decided
to leave the seminary in May, 1835. He thus had completed
two years of seminary work, and lacked a year for graduation. He and his wife returned to New York State to bid
their relatives and friends goodbye. After a visit at Holland
Patent, they went to Prattsburg. There Spalding learned of
the failure of his appointment by the Government, so on
August 7, 1835, he sent in his application to the American
Board. He and his wife were accepted and appointed to a
station among the Osage Indians, but because of the birth
of their child in October, they had been unable to leave that
fall.

We are not certain whether or not Whitman had the
opportunity for a personal conference with Spalding in
regard to the Oregon mission prior to February 14. In a
footnote to his journal, mailed December 17, 1835, Whitman
speaks about having received a letter from Spalding the day

---

[6] Spalding letter, Mar. 31, 1834, Presbyterian Historical Society.
[7] Bullard to American Board, Aug. 14, 1835.

before. Spalding wrote to the Board on December 28 from Holland Patent, New York, where his wife's parents lived. Yet there are records which indicate that Spalding served as temporary supply minister for the near-by churches of Cohocton and Tyrone during the fall and winter of 1835-36, so it is possible that Whitman saw Spalding in regard to the matter.[8]

In view of an impetuous remark that Spalding made about Narcissa, evidently before February 14, it seems that Spalding had discussed with some of his friends the possibility of going to Oregon. The fact that he was once a suitor for Narcissa's hand created some embarrassment in his own mind. His first reaction to the proposal of going with the Whitmans to the same mission seems to have been negative. Yet, in Spalding's letter of December 28, 1835, to Greene, he asked: "If the Board and Dr. Whitman wish me to go to the Rocky Mountains with him, I am willing. Act your pleasure." Greene replied on January 2, and, not knowing that the Spalding child had died, wrote: "It does not seem to me desirable that yr designation should be changed to the Rocky Mountain Indians at this time unless you strongly desire it." From this it appears that Spalding had discussed the possibility of changing his destination sometime during December.

The following quotations tell the story of the far-reaching consequences of a few words lightly spoken.

Spalding's diary, July 9, 1840: That the root of all the difficulties in the Mission lay between us, viz: in an expression I made while in the states respecting his wife before she was married to Dr. Whitman, Viz.: that I would not go into the same Mission with her, questioning her judgment.

(Rev. A. B. Smith to Greene, Sept. 3, 1840) Mr. Spalding had published from town to town before he left the States that he would not go on a mission with Mrs. Whitman.

(W. H. Gray to Greene, Oct. 14, 1840) Dr. Whitman stated that he thought, or believed, that the whole difficulty originated between him and Mr. Spalding before they left the United States. . . . He said that the difficulty was between Mr. Spalding and his wife. Mr. Spalding had said more publicly that it would be for him to repeat it hear That he (Mr. Spalding) would not come on a mission with Mrs. Whitman. He felt he had been injured by Mr. Spalding by the reports he had circulated from town to town in the United States.

---

[8] *Minutes of the Presbyterian General Assembly* for 1836 and 1837, pp. 325 and 537. Just why Spalding's name should appear in the 1837 record as supply pastor for Tyrone is not clear, for Spalding left for the West on February 12, 1836. When Spalding wrote to Greene on Dec. 28, 1835, he referred to some visits he had made to churches in the vicinity of Bath.

We know that when the Spaldings left Holland Patent on February 1, 1835, they never dreamed that their destination would be changed at that late date. They drove in their light wagon, a gift from Captain Levi Hart, to Prattsburg, where they remained about a week. On the 12th of February they started for Howard, New York. According to Spalding, Whitman overtook them on the road shortly before they reached Howard with the hail: "We want you for Oregon."[9]

We do not know with certainty that Whitman was aware of Spalding's foolish remark about Narcissa's judgment when he besought Spalding to go with him to Oregon. If he was, the urgency of the occasion made him overlook the statement. Whitman wanted missionaries, and the Spaldings were the last and only possible companions. He either had to persuade them to go with him to Oregon or give up the mission.

Whitman continued with the Spauldings into Howard, where the Spaldings engaged a room in the inn. Whitman was importunate. He quickly reviewed the course of events and showed how "the finger of Providence" had pointed to them. He spoke of the superior qualifications of the Oregon Indians, who had asked for the Gospel, in comparison with the Osages, who were then considered to be among the most decadent of all American tribes. He showed them Greene's letter—the way was clear if they were willing. If Whitman knew that there had been a love affair between Henry and Narcissa, it seems that he was quite willing to let bygones be bygones.

The argument of duty, which Whitman stressed, struck a responsive chord in the hearts of both Henry and Eliza. They were not afraid of the journey, having been satisfied by Whitman that it was feasible for women. Henry was a little hesitant, because he felt his wife would not be physically strong enough to endure the trip, but Eliza pluckily declared: "I like the command just as it stands, 'Go ye into all the world,' and no exceptions for poor health."[10] The three sought God's guidance by taking turns praying alone in a room at the inn. It was then decided, contingent upon the final approval of the Board, that the Spaldings would go with the Whitmans.

Both Whitman and Spalding agreed to write to Greene about the new developments and ask for his decision, which

---

[9] *U. S. Senate Document No. 37,* p. 9.
[10] *Ibid.*

THE INN AT HOWARD, NEW YORK.

Where the Spaldings made the decision to accompany Dr. Whitman to Oregon. According to local residents, the building was torn down about 1920.

By courtesy of Mrs. Josephine Bennett, Howard, N. Y.

Whitman's Letter to the Board Announcing His Marriage to Miss Narcissa Prentiss on February 18, 1836. Whitman also wrote: "I have not received an answer to mine in which I speak of Spaldings willingness to go and of Hotchkin wishes...."

could reach them at Cincinnati. The Spaldings were to continue their journey and wait at Cincinnati for the Whitmans.
Their route took them through Jamestown, and from that
place Spalding addressed his letter to Greene on Wednesday,
February 17.

From a statement in Mrs. Whitman's letter to her
father, written October 10, 1840, it appears that Judge
Prentiss had an interview with Spalding regarding the advisability of both couples going to the same station. This
conference may have taken place after the Howard meeting, for the natural route for the Spaldings to have taken
from Howard to Jamestown would have gone through
Angelica. Narcissa wrote: "This pretended settlement with
father, before we started, was only an excuse, and from all
we have seen and heard, both during the journey and since
we have been here, the same bitter feeling exists." This we
know—the antagonism which existed between Henry Spalding and Narcissa Prentiss had important consequences in
Old Oregon.

NARCISSA AND MARCUS ARE MARRIED

Marcus Whitman must have breathed a sigh of relief
as he mounted his horse at Howard and started for Angelica,
about twenty-five miles to the westward, to tell Narcissa.
With a little haste plans could still be made for their marriage. What a bridal tour lay before them! A trip to Oregon!

It so happened that Judge Stephen Prentiss and two
other elders-elect were to be ordained to the office of elder
at a congregational meeting to be held in the Angelica Presbyterian church on Thursday evening, February 18. Proper
notice of such a meeting had been given by the pastor, the
Rev. Leverett Hull, at the Sunday services on February 14.
Thus when Marcus arrived at the Prentiss home and tri-
umphantly announced that he had secured the consent of the
Spaldings to go with them, someone suggested that the marriage take place at the church when Judge Prentiss would be
ordained as an elder. It was an opportune time, for all of
their Angelica friends would be there. Marcus would have
time to go to Rushville and return, bringing with him those
of his family who could attend.

Marcus Whitman rarely traveled on Sunday, and then
only when stern necessity overruled his religious convictions. Since Whitman was writing a letter at five o'clock in
the afternoon of Monday, February 15, from Canandaigua

to Greene, and since Canandaigua is about seventy miles from Angelica, we are forced to the conclusion that Whitman left Angelica on Sunday, or very early Monday morning. In this letter we read:

> I saw Mr. Spalding on his way to the Ossages. He consented to accompany me if the Board saw fit to alter his designation.... I am willing to accompany Mr. Spalding as an associate yet I know little of his peculiar addaptedness to that station.

Still on the search for more workers, Whitman had visited Canandaigua to see Samuel Hotchkin, a son of the Rev. James H. Hotchkin, with the hope of securing his services as a lay assistant. Hotchkin expressed a willingness to go under certain conditions, but time proved too short to make the necessary arrangements. Whitman with Richard, the Nez Perce boy who had been attending school in Rushville, was back in Angelica on or before Thursday the 18th.[11] We are not told whether his mother or any other relative or friend returned with him.

In the meantime, Narcissa, with the help of many of the women of the Angelica church, was busy with her trousseau. Her wedding dress was made of black bombazine.[12] She had made several brightly colored print dresses, believing that the bright colors would please the Indians.[13] In those days locks of hair were greatly treasured. On her wedding day, Narcissa clipped a lock of hair and gave it to one of her dear friends, Harriet Whitcomb Russell.[14]

The minute book of the Angelica church gives us the story of what happened before the wedding took place in the following record:

> The church met agreeably to previous notice for the ordination of Elders elect, when the following individuals were set apart to this office in due form and order to wit Stephen Prentiss, Jacob Schoonver, and Charles Patrick, and session ordered a letter to our sister Narcissa Prentiss who is destined to the Mission beyond the Rocky Mountains. Adjourned closed with prayer. L. Hull Moderator.

There is the picture, first of the ordination of the three

---

[11] In Mrs. Whitman's letter (No. 23), mention is made of Richard as "the one you saw at our wedding: he calls me Mother."

[12] Letter of Matilda Sager Delaney to Mrs. Bowden, March 26, 1928, copy, Coll. Wn.: "I never saw her in a gray silk nor any other colored silk—had no use for silk—her best dress was a black bombazine—it was her wedding dress and her whole family wore black at her wedding."

[13] The author heard of two persons in the vicinity of Rushville who still had bits of these print goods.

[14] Given to her daughter, Mrs. Harriet Nobles, who in turn gave it to Mrs. Dudley Voorhees. A part is now in Coll. Wn.

men as elders, and then of the session meeting which followed in the presence of the congregation, when Stephen Prentiss sat as an elder and voted with the others to give "Narcissa Prentiss" a letter of dismissal. In one of Narcissa's letters she refers to the communion service which was held that evening. [Letter 44.] Judge Prentiss for the first time in his experience would then have assisted in the serving of the elements to the members of the congregation. Perhaps he was given the privilege of passing the bread to Marcus and Narcissa. According to the custom of the time, they drank from the common cup served by the pastor, Leverett Hull.

Then followed the wedding, when through the exchange of vows Marcus and Narcissa were made one. A short courtship had reached its joyful fruition. Sometime during the evening Mr. Hull preached a sermon. According to the custom of that day, it is possible that the sermon came after the wedding with the bridal couple still standing before the altar. Of that sermon Narcissa later wrote:

Brother Hull, you know not how much good that sermon I heard you preach for the last, the which you gave me, does me now in this desert land. O that I had more than one! I read it, meditate upon it in my solitary hours until the truth of it burns upon my heart and cheers my soul with its blessed promise. [Letter 37.]

As the closing number of the evening's program, Mr. Hull announced the hymn, "Yes, My Native Land! I Love Thee," which was written by the Rev. Samuel F. Smith,[15] the author of "America." The hymn was sentimental, but appropriate for the occasion. The first three stanzas are as follows:

Yes, my native land! I love thee;
All thy scenes I love them well;
Friends, connections, happy country,
Can I bid you all farewell?
Can I leave you,
Far in heathen lands to dwell?

Home!—thy joys are passing lovely—
Joys no stranger-heart can tell;
Happy home!—'tis sure I love thee!
Can I—can I say—Farewell?
Can I leave thee,
Far in heathen lands to dwell?

---

[15] Samuel F. Smith, A.B. Harvard, 1829, graduated from the Andover Theo. Sem. in 1832. Several tunes have been associated with this hymn, including Newton, Wellwood, Smyrna, Latter Day, and Greenville.

Scenes of sacred peace and pleasure,
Holy days and Sabbath-bell,
Richest, brightest, sweetest treasure!
Can I say a last farewell?
Can I leave you,
Far in heathen lands to dwell?

One by one the members of the choir and congregation found their throats constricted with emotion and their cheeks dampened with tears. Only a few, including Narcissa, sang the fourth stanza:

Yes! I hasten gladly,
From the scenes I love so well;
Far away, ye billows! bear me;
Lovely native land!—farewell!
Pleased I leave thee,
Far in heathen lands to dwell.

By the time the last stanza was reached, muffled sobs could be heard. Narcissa in her clear soprano voice, which Wakeman described as being "as sweet and musical as a chime of bells," sang the last stanza alone:

In the deserts let me labor,
On the mountains let me tell,
How he died—the blessed Saviour—
To redeem a world from hell!
Let me hasten,
Far in heathen lands to dwell.[16] [Letter 37.]

The next day Marcus and Narcissa left for Ithaca. Imagination alone must supply the details of the last farewell. Many of their Angelica friends were filled with fears as they saw the Whitmans leave. Narcissa asked for their prayers. Later she wrote to the Hulls: "I told you and Brother Bridgman that if we ever got over the mountains it would be in answer to your prayers." [Letter 37.] Narcissa, like Mrs. Spalding, never returned. Both Dr. Whitman and Mr. Spalding subsequently visited their homes in the East,

---

[16] Winchell's *Additional Hymns*, 1832, concluded the hymn with a sixth verse: "Bear me on thou restless ocean, Let the winds my canvas swell. Heave my heart with warm emotion, While I far hence do dwell. Glad I bid thee, Native land, Farewell, Farewell." Whitman letters 19 and 44 both refer to the marriage date as Feb. 18. Bashford, *Oregon*, p. 234, erroneously gives it as Feb. 7. Eells, *Marcus Whitman*, p. 30, gives a picture of the Prattsburg church and Franklin Academy and states that the Whitmans were married there—another error. The Angelica building burned in 1868. No public records of marriages were kept in New York State prior to January 1, 1886. The incident of the hymn is mentioned in *Golden Rule*, Jan. 12, 1893. There are people living in Angelica who heard the story from their grandparents.

Whitman in the spring of 1843 and Spalding in the winter of 1870-71.

From a reference in one of Mrs. Whitman's letters, [Letter 35] we know that the Whitmans spent a Sunday in Ithaca, perhaps February 21. Narcissa appeared before the Sunday school of the Presbyterian church there and promised to send back from Oregon an account of her experiences, which promise she kept. Dr. Samuel Parker wrote of this visit to Ithaca as follows:

Dr. Whitman made addresses in the churches; and Mrs. Whitman in the Sunday Schools, especially the Presby. and the Dutch Reformed Churches.[17]

After spending a few days in Ithaca, the Whitmans went to Rushville, taking the Nez Perce boys with them. There is a record of their stopping en route at Geneva, New York, where Dr. Whitman spoke in the Presbyterian church on the subject of Oregon missions.[18] Sunday, the 28th, was spent at Rushville. But few references to the events of those last days in New York State are to be found in the Whitman correspondence. In one letter Narcissa speaks of having had a pair of "gentlemen's boots" made for her in "Brother Augustus' shoe store in Rushville." [Letter 21.] Marcus also provided himself with footwear at the same time. The women of the Rushville church presented Marcus with some shirts, which Marcus was later tempted to leave, behind as surplus baggage. Narcissa, however, persuaded him to keep them. [Letter 26.]

In Whitman's letter of March 3, written the day they left Rushville, he reported the receipt of $26 from the Angelica church and $200.07 from the Rushville church. He wished due credit to be given for these gifts. In addition he drew upon the Treasurer of the Board for $126 and wrote that he would need more when he got to Cincinnati. [Letter 19.] According to the financial report submitted to the Board on September 5, 1836,[19] Whitman had $166.96 when he reached Cincinnati, which means that the cost to the Board for traveling expenses for himself, his wife, and the two Indian boys from Rushville to that point was but $185.11. This covered a period from March 3 to March 18, and probably included the cost of some supplies.

17 Parker MS., Cornell University.

18 *Centennial Celebration*, p. 42. *See* also Whitman letter 19 for another reference to the Geneva visit.

19 Coll. A.

The Whitmans said their farewells on March 3 and started for Cincinnati. At Elmira, Whitman engaged a man by the name of J. S. Seeley to drive them in his sleigh to Hollidaysburg, Pennsylvania. Fifty-nine years later, in 1895, Seeley, then living at Aurora, Illinois, wrote to Dr. Oliver W. Nixon, who was then writing his book *How Marcus Whitman Saved Oregon,* saying:

> I drove Dr. and Mrs. Whitman from Elmira, N. Y., to Hollidaysburg, Pa., in my sleigh. This place was at the foot of the Allegheny Mountains (east side) on the Pennsylvania canal. The canal boats were built in two sections and were taken over the mountains on a railroad.
>
> They expected to find the canal open on the west side and thus reach the Ohio River on the way to Oregon. I was with them some seven days.[20]

Near Williamsport, Pennsylvania, the Whitmans overtook Dr. and Mrs. Benedict Satterlee, who were under appointment by the Board to go to the Pawnee Indians. Mrs. Satterlee, also a bride, was formerly Miss Martha Ann Mather, of Fairfield, where Dr. Satterlee had attended medical college. With them was Miss Emeline Palmer who was on her way to Liberty, Missouri, where she was to meet her fiancé, Samuel Allis. This party of three had left Ithaca on Tuesday, March 1. However, because of the ill-health of Mrs. Satterlee, they were delayed in their journey, so that the Whitmans overtook them. The party of seven rested at Williamsport over Sunday, March 6. Dr. Whitman and Dr. Satterlee held a consultation over Mrs. Satterlee. They debated whether or not she could proceed, and finally agreed that she could. They had fine sleighing to Hollidaysburg. [Letter 22.]

They reached Pittsburgh on Saturday, March 12. The next day Marcus and the two Indian boys went to a church, where the Nez Perces created somewhat of a sensation when their identity was made known. Narcissa suffered from a severe headache, so remained in her room. [Letter 20.] The party secured passage on the steamboat *Siam,* which left Pittsburgh 10:00 A. M., Tuesday morning, March 15.

---

[20] P. 67. *See* also Nixon's *Whitman's Ride Through Savage Lands* (1905), p. 44: "The late Eli G. Coe of Illinois then a young man drove them in his sleigh to the mountains en route for Pittsburgh where they were to take the boat for St. Louis." It is hard to reconcile these two accounts. Perhaps Nixon relied on memory and got the name of the man confused with another. Perhaps there were two men, or two sections of the journey. The earlier account is to be preferred because there Nixon quotes from a letter.

THEIR PERSONAL APPEARANCE

No authentic picture remains of either Narcissa or Marcus. However, we do have several good descriptions of their personal appearance which date back to the time of their marriage and even before. Joel Wakeman described Narcissa as follows:

She was of medium height, symmetrically formed, very graceful in her deportment and general carriage, slightly sandy complexion, a brilliant, sparkling eye, peculiarly so when engaged in animated conversation. She was not a beauty, and yet, when engaged in singing or conversation there was something in her appearance very attractive.[21]

The Rev. Levi Fay Waldo, who also knew Narcissa, wrote of her:

She was a beautiful blonde, of fair form and face and well rounded features, dignified and stately, yet modest in her bearing, kindly and Christian in social life, honoring and gracing every station that she was called to fill.[22]

The people of Rushville remembered the bride of Marcus Whitman as being "of slight build, a little above medium height, blue eyes, pretty, with beautiful blond hair."[23] Narcissa weighed herself a few weeks after her marriage and informed her sister Jane that the scales tipped at 136 pounds. [Letter 21.] On October 9, 1844, in a letter to her parents she declared that she then weighed about 150 pounds, "much higher than ever before in my life."[24]

Several attempts have been made to produce a portrait of Narcissa. Probably the best known of these idealized pictures is the oil painting by Mrs. Orville R. Allen which hangs in Prentiss Hall at Whitman College. This is a life-sized study which shows her clad in a gray silk dress with flowing sleeves and a low neck. The artist was guided by some hazy tradition that she wore such a dress and "fluffed her hair" once when about to greet her husband upon his return from a trip to the mountains.[25] According to Matilda

---

[21] Wakeman, Prattsburg *News*, Jan. 27, 1898. On Sept. 29, 1838, Narcissa wrote: "Please tell me what has become of Joel Wakeman. Has he given up to be a missionary?"

[22] Waldo, *W.C.Q.*, Vol. 2, No. 1, p. 39.

[23] Told to the author by Mrs. Abram, of Rushville, who remembered the description given by her mother. Another said her eyes were gray. *O.H.Q.*, Vol. 2, p. 266.

[24] *W.C.Q.*, Vol. 1, No. 3, p. 20.

[25] From clipping of *Times Sun*, May 8, 1927, loaned by Mrs. Ross, of Portland. This idealized picture was dedicated May 16, 1927.

Sager Delaney, who spent several years in the Whitman mission home, Mrs. Whitman never had a silk dress. The sleeves used for a model for the picture are authentic, for they once belonged to Narcissa.[26] Mrs. Delaney wrote:

> ... Mrs. Whitman was so severe both in dress and in the way she dressed her hair. She had a reddish colored hair parted in the middle and combed back and twisted in a knot and wore a high backed comb. Most of her dresses had either gathered or pleated pointed waist and had collar like in picture or a fancy neckerchief—never had her bare neck exposed—the flowing sleeves with undersleeves and a coat heavier for winter and the old mutton leg sleeves.[27]

When Nixon issued his *How Marcus Whitman Saved Oregon* he included an idealized picture of both Narcissa and Marcus. This book first appeared in 1895 and it was so popular that a fifth edition appeared the following year. Nixon wrote to the Rev. S. W. Pratt on March 8, 1898, stating that a sixth edition was then being prepared and that the largest of previous editions had numbered 3,800 copies.[28] The book was written in the month of April, 1895, and Nixon frankly confessed that it was not intended to be an authentic Whitman biography.

The first and second editions give the idealized pictures without any word of explanation of how they were made or by whom. It is quite evident that many wrote to Nixon criticizing the pictures, for the third edition included different conceptions with some of the most apparent anachronisms, especially in regard to Dr. Whitman, removed. In this third edition, Nixon inserted the following statement under the new picture of Mrs. Whitman:

> No authentic picture of Mrs. Whitman is in existence. This portrait of her has been drawn under the supervision of a gentleman familiar with her appearance and with suggestions from members of her family. It is considered a good likeness of her.

In the March, 1898, issue of the *Whitman College Quarterly* is an article by Waldo, who remembered Mrs. Whitman. He makes the following statement regarding Nixon's picture of Mrs. Whitman, although he does not state which edition he used: "It is much to be regretted that no likeness of her can be found, for the one in Dr. Nixon's book, though bearing

---

26 Mrs. Edmund Bowden, of Seattle, had the pair, one of which she presented to Whitman College.

27 Delaney to Bowden, March 26, 1928.

28 Original in Coll. Wn.

some resemblance, is far from doing her justice."[29] The Whitman College collection contains a letter from Nixon to the Rev. Myron Eells which was evidently written shortly after the first edition of his book appeared. In this letter Nixon wrote:

I find also the janitor of his home church is living at Baraboo, Wis—& sends me word that he is delighted with the book—& that after our laborious work that "the picture of Whitman upon his marriage day is good." As you know all these pictures were composite & under the manipulation of the best artists have been going the rounds of all that knew the Dr & his wife for criticism & change. The picture of Mrs. Whitman her sister has mainly directed & says "it is entirely satisfactory to herself & family."[30]

From this it appears that the picture of Narcissa which appeared in the third edition of Nixon's book represents the final criticism of those who knew her, including Mrs. Harriet Jackson, Narcissa's youngest sister, who was then living at Oberlin, Ohio. This conception bears a striking family resemblance to the pictures of Harriet and to her older brother, Harvey Pratt Prentiss. It represents the best endeavor to present Narcissa's personal appearance.[31]

Nixon's first idealized portrait of Dr. Whitman had him clothed in the ministerial garb of 1870. The retouched picture which appeared in his third edition corrected this apparent anachronism, yet left the type of beard, known as burnsides, which were unknown in 1836. Under this second picture, Nixon gave the following information:

No picture of Dr. Whitman is in existence. The above portrait is made from the basis of a photograph of Rev. Marcus Whitman Montgomery, who resembled Dr. Whitman very closely. Changes have been made under the supervision of the family, who now pronounce this a very correct likeness.

A redrawing of this picture appeared in Miller's *Presbyterianism in Steuben and Allegany*[32] which came to the

---

[29] P. 39. The fifth edition of Nixon's book does not have the picture of Mrs. Whitman. The author was unable to locate the 4th or 6th editions.

[30] Dated Mar. 4, 189..... Exact year not given, but undoubtedly 1896.

[31] Other descriptions of Mrs. Whitman can be found in Gray, *Oregon*, p. 109, and elsewhere. Locks of her hair are to be found in Collections, O., W., Wn., and in the Ferry Museum, Tacoma, Wash. Several locks are still in private possession. These show that her hair had an auburn tinge.

[32] P. 48. The author called on Dr. Miller, pastor of the Presbyterian church, Huntsville, Ohio, in the summer of 1935.

attention of the Rev. Joel Wakeman who wrote an article which was published in the February 3, 1898, issue of the Prattsburg *News*. Wakeman wrote:

> The picture in the "History of Presbyterianism" is a misnomer; there are only a few points of resemblance. The eyebrows, the manner of parting his hair, and the outline of the upper part of his face; otherwise there is nothing that really belonged to Whitman.

Wakeman gave the following description of Dr. Whitman:

> His stature was medium, compactly built, well proportioned, muscular, but not fleshly, a finely formed head, and according to phrenological science, large veneration, benevolence and combativeness, which manifested itself in his firmness and strict adherence to principle; a bright, penetrating eye that seldom failed to read human character correctly, an aquiline nose, a benignant expressive countenance, moderately social, not a rapid talker, and what he said, sensible and to the point. . . . [33]

Phrenology was much in vogue in Wakeman's day, especially when he was younger than when he wrote this description. An undated clipping from the Corning, N. Y., *Leader*[34] comments on a picture of Samuel Whitman, the brother of Marcus, as follows:

> There was a marked family resemblance, and the picture shows how Dr. Whitman would have looked had he lived to an old age. He had a larger head and overhanging eye brows, and a strong chin, and high cheek bones as described by those who knew him.

A lock of hair given by Dr. Whitman to his sister when he was East in the spring of 1843, now in the museum of Whitman College, Walla Walla, Washington, shows that he had brown hair.[35] It is supposed, therefore, that he had dark eyes.

Another good description is that of B. F. Nichols, who as a lad eighteen years old spent a winter at the Whitman station. He wrote:

> I think he was a man that would weigh one hundred and seventy-five pounds, being what we would call a raw-boned man. He was muscular and sinewy, with broad shoulders, neck slightly bent forward and firm set limbs. His eyes were blue, rather dark, I think; his hair was brown, his forehead massive and broad, and his nose, though not large, was straight and prominent. His cheekbones were high and

---

[33] Original MS. in Coll. Wn.

[34] Coll. Wn. Believed to be from the Corning, N. Y., paper, 1905.

[35] Locks of hair were frequently carried in jewelry made especially to keep them; thus the name locket.

prominent, and his mouth was nearer like General Grant's than any one else I know of, denoting firmness and determination.

As an illustration of the Doctor's strength I might mention that on one occasion I was sitting on the rails of a corral where they had a lot of wild young cattle that they wanted to brand. The Doctor walked into the corral amidst the young steers, many of them three-year-olds, and moved around till he got a favorable opportunity, when he caught one by the under jaw and the near horn. He made it jump around and when its feet were off the ground he gave it a sudden wrench, throwing it upon its back on the ground, where he held it until it was branded. He did this time and again, and we were amazed at the strength which he displayed on this and similar occasions. He was one of the most unassuming men I ever met.[36]

"Bulldogging" steers is still practiced in Western rodeos and indicates skill as well as strength.

Pictures of all three of Whitman's brothers, Augustus, Samuel, and Henry, together with one of his sister, Alice, have been found. While the pictures of Augustus and of Samuel were taken in their old age, the picture of Henry was taken about 1847 and perhaps represents the nearest likeness to Marcus that we will ever find. On May 23, 1936, a daguerreotype of Whitman's mother was identified by Mrs. Marion B. Foote Williams, who was born at Rushville on May 24, 1835. Mrs. Williams, who possessed a keen active mind even though she was 101 years old, looked at the daguerreotype and said: "That's Mrs. Loomis. I used to go to church with her." Since Mrs. Williams was twenty-two years old when Mrs. Loomis died, it is reasonable to believe that her identification is correct.[37]

Mary Alice Wisewell, the daughter of Whitman's only sister, wrote to Myron Eells on March 10, 1882, saying:

Mother says that Uncle Marcus never had a picture taken except a profile for his wife—that he told by sending to R. K. Cummings Boston she [i.e. Whitman's mother] could get one like it. This she never did, as the picture was only a black outline, and very unsatisfactory.[38]

All efforts to locate one of these silhouettes have failed.

An idealized portrait of Dr. Whitman was recently

---

[36] W.C.Q., Vol. 1, No. 3, p. 19.

[37] The daguerreotype is owned by Charles Fox, of Rushville, a grandson of Henry, the brother of Marcus Whitman. The picture was taken about 1847 at the same time as that of Henry and his son. The identity of the picture was unknown until Mrs. Williams said it was of Mrs. Loomis. This identification was made in the presence of her son, Lewis C. Williams, Robert Moody, of Rushville, and the author. She died on July 11, 1936.

[38] Coll. Wn.

painted by Ernest Ralph Norling and presented by a group of physicians and surgeons of the Pacific Northwest to Whitman College, on Thursday, August 13, 1936, at the time of the Whitman Centennial celebration. This is a life-size study and shows Whitman clad in frontier garb, with a beard. It avoids the errors of both of Nixon's pictures as far as the anachronisms of dress are concerned. It is probably as good an idealized picture of Whitman as ever can be secured.[39]

The twelve-foot statue of Marcus Whitman by Alexander S. Calder which is on the Witherspoon Building in Philadelphia is said to have been modeled after Perrin, the nephew of Dr. Whitman, who bore some resemblance to his famous uncle.

W. H. Gray, who came West with the Whitmans in 1836, remembered him as being "above medium height; of spare habit; peculiar hair, a portion of each being white and a dark brown, so that it might be called iron-grey; deep blue eyes, and a large mouth.[40] Much as we desire an accurate picture of both Narcissa and Marcus, we find ourselves obliged to be contented with such descriptions as have come down to us from the past.

---

[39] *The Journal of the Department of History,* Presbyterian Church U. S. A., Dec., 1932, printed a supposed picture of Marcus Whitman, claimed to be from an "original ambrotype." An ambrotype was a transparency on glass. The process was not invented until 1846 and was patented in 1855. There is no evidence that it was retaken from an earlier picture.

[40] Gray, *Oregon,* p. 107.

CHAPTER SEVEN

THE TRIP TO OREGON

1836

THE WHITMANS, the Satterlees, Miss Palmer, and the two Indian boys secured passage on the steamboat *Siam*, which left Pittsburgh Tuesday morning, March 15. They reached Cincinnati on Thursday noon of that week, where they found the Spaldings eagerly awaiting their arrival. The day the Whitmans left Pittsburgh, Narcissa began one of her journal letters to her loved ones. These letters were written with more or less regularity as she journeyed westward. Sometimes Narcissa made daily entries, and again she would summarize the events of a week or more.

Narcissa's first entry in the first of these journal letters is as follows:

Dear, Dear, Mother:—Your proposal concerning keeping a diary as I journey comes before my mind often. I have not found it practicable while traveling by land, although many events have passed which, if noted as they occurred, might have been interesting. We left Pittsburg this morning at ten o'clock, and are sailing at the rate of thirteen miles an hour. It is delightful passing so rapidly down the waters of the beautiful river. The motion of the boat is very agreeable to me, except when writing. Our accommodations are good; we occupy a stateroom where we can be as retired as we wish.

To avoid traveling on Sunday, the missionaries decided to remain in Cincinnati until Tuesday, March 22, when the *Junius* was due to leave for St. Louis. Whitman and Spalding spent several days purchasing supplies, drawing for this purpose upon the treasurer of the American Board for two hundred dollars. On Sunday the Whitmans heard Dr. Lyman Beecher, then president of the Lane Theological Seminary, preach. Narcissa wrote that after their short sojourn in the city, they felt strengthened and comforted "as we left them, to pursue our journey into the wilderness." [Letter 20.]

The party expected to reach St. Louis before Sunday, but Saturday night found them still eighty-nine miles from their destination. The boat, as was the custom, was tied up at night. The next day the missionaries disembarked at their first opportunity, which was at Chester, Illinois. After spending the day with a small group of Christians, they were fortunate enough to secure passage on the *Majestic* on Monday morning for St. Louis. Fog delayed them so that they did not actually reach their destination until Tuesday evening, March 29.

As soon as possible after their arrival, Dr. Whitman hurried to the post office for their mail.[1] Whitman received a letter from Greene, and Spalding received a communication from the United States Secretary of War which gave official permission for him and Whitman to establish missions in the Indian country.[2]

Narcissa was disappointed in not receiving letters from her home. "Why have they not written?" she wrote in her journal, "seeing it is the very last, last time they will have to cheer my heart with intelligence from home, home, sweet home, and the friends I love." A week later she was delighted to receive a letter at Liberty, Missouri, written by her brother-in-law, the Rev. Lyman Judson. That was the only letter she received from any member of her family for over two years, or until July 11, 1838. [Letter 51.]

FINAL INSTRUCTIONS

In response to the letters of both Spalding and Whitman, written after their Howard meeting, Greene wrote to the former on February 25 and to the latter on the 27th, in which full approval was given to the change of destination for the Spaldings.[3] Writing to Whitman at St. Louis on March 4, 1836, Greene gave some sound advice on a number of points. He cautioned them in their relationships with the mountain men, and advised them to keep the Sabbath with great strictness. "Live near to God," urged Greene in his concluding remarks. On the whole, it was a good letter, filled with wise and kindly counsel.

THOMSONIANISM

While at St. Louis, under date of March 30, 1836, Narcissa wrote:

---

[1] The St. Louis *Missouri Argus* for April 8, 1836, printed a list of unclaimed letters at the St. Louis post office on April 1. The list included a letter for "Doct Marcus Whitman" and one for "Rev. Henry H. Spalding." It is evident that this list was prepared shortly before Whitman called. The next published list does not include their names.

[2] Drury, *Spalding*, p. 124.

[3] Greene's letter to Spalding is in Coll. W. Many of Greene's letters to Whitman have been published in Hulbert and Hulbert, *Marcus Whitman, Crusader.*

I think I should like to whisper in mother's ear many things which I cannot write. If I could only see her in her room for one-half hour. This much I can, mother. I have one of the kindest husbands, and the very best every way. Tell father by the side of his calomel he has taken a quarter of a pound of lobelia and a large quantity of cayenne, which will answer my purpose better than some of the apothecary medicines.

The average reader entirely misses the significance of the reference here made by Narcissa to lobelia and cayenne pepper. But to the student of America's medical history, these words stand out like words on a telegram. They are the code words for Thomsonianism, a medical cult founded by Samuel Thomson[4] in 1808. Thomson, an illiterate New Hampshire farmer, built up a system of medicine which called for two things. First, the patient was to take lobelia, which acted as a powerful emetic. Because of this the regular school of doctors called the Thomsonian practitioners "puke-doctors." Then the patient was made to perspire. This was induced by prescribing "hot-drops" and steam baths. The "hot-drops" were prepared by a formula which Thomson patented, the principal ingredient of which was cayenne pepper.

Thomson wrote a book entitled *Guide to Health or Botanic Family Physician* in which he prescribed for the symptoms for which each of six secret formulas of his were to be used. The following quotation regarding cayenne is taken from this volume:

This is a medicine of great value in the practice, and may be safely used in all cases of disease, to raise and retain the internal heat of the system, cause a free perspiration, and keep the determining powers to the surface....

For a dose, take from half to a teaspoonful, in hot water, or a tea of No. 3 sweetened.... The dose should be repeated every ten or fifteen minutes till the desired object is effected, and continued occasionally till health is restored.[5]

Thomson sold his book, together with a diploma, which entitled the purchaser to be a "Botanic Physician," for thirty dollars, and it is reported that a hundred thousand of these books and diplomas were sold between 1813 and 1836. The book went through nineteen editions. The fad was especially popular in central New York. Thomson called the

---

[4] *See* article by Dr. Harold M. F. Behneman in *California and Western Medicine*, Vol. 44, No. 2, on Thomsonianism.

[5] P. 80. Many of the facts herein given concerning Thomsonianism were supplied by Dr. F. C. Waite.

regular doctors "mineral murderers," and especially condemned calomel, then much used. He claimed that all medicines other than those of vegetable origin were poisonous.
In view of such claims it is easy to see how a bitter rivalry
grew up between the "puke-doctors" and the "mineral
murderers." Lobelia and cayenne pepper were anathema to
the regular profession.

This one paragraph in Narcissa's letter in which she
refers to her lobelia and cayenne, along with her husband's
calomel, throws a spotlight upon a hitherto unknown fact of
Narcissa's home life. Her father was a Thomsonian. Narcissa was a Thomsonian. Yet she had married one of the
"mineral murderers." Think of Marcus—great was his love
for Narcissa and tolerant was his spirit if he would permit
her to pack along her lobelia and cayenne pepper. We wonder
what would have happened to their love affair if they had
not gone to Oregon, but instead had settled down in some
New York community.

ST. LOUIS TO LIBERTY

The missionaries were in St. Louis from Tuesday evening until Thursday noon, when they left on the steamboat
Chariton for Liberty. During this short visit, the Whitmans
saw some of the sights of the city and met several old friends,
including the Rev. Milton Kimball, who took Narcissa to see
the Roman Catholic cathedral. The building was dedicated
in 1834 and was one of the attractions of the rapidly growing city. It was Narcissa's first contact with Catholicism,
and she looked upon the people assembled in worship with
considerable curiosity.

Writing to her sister Jane, Narcissa described the service
as "idolatry," and referred to the "nuns" (perhaps a vested
choir) who sang "in an unknown tongue." The following
quotations from her letter, here published for the first time,
reveal the anti-Catholic attitude which was entertained by
the Whitmans as well as the Spaldings:

> While sitting there and behold their Idolitry, I thot of the "Whited
> Sepulcher which indeed appears beautiful to men but within are full
> of dead mens bones and all uncleanness." ... What cause of gratitude
> have I that I am not of the number who willfully shut my eyes to the
> truth, deceiving and being deceived.[6]

It should be remembered that the Whitmans and the

------

[6] Whitman letter 21. This was published in the *T.O.P.A.*, 1891,
pp. 83 ff. but about three hundred words were omitted, which includes

Spaldings were reared in a Protestant community where the
anti-Catholic spirit was especially strong.

Whitman had vivid memories of the trip between Liberty
and Bellevue, made the previous year. The heavy rains had
turned the prairies into a sea of mud. He recalled how he had
toiled with Merrill's wagon, and how at times he had felt
obliged to assist the men of the caravan with their wagons.
Therefore, while at St. Louis, Whitman made every effort to
arrange for boat transportation as far as Bellevue. He
called at the offices of the American Fur Company, where
doubtless the good services he had rendered their men the
preceding year were recalled. Arrangements were made
for the members of the mission party to take passage on the
Chariton, which was to leave on the 31st for Liberty. It was
agreed that the *Diana,* then at St. Louis for repairs, would
follow within several weeks and take the mission party
from Liberty to Bellevue.

The *Chariton* left St. Louis "immediately after dinner"
on the 31st. At twilight the steamer left the wide sweep of
the Mississippi and entered the narrower channel of the
Missouri River. Narcissa wrote of the beautiful evening,
with the moon shining in all of its brightness. The two new-
lyweds remained on the upper deck until Spalding, with
more religion than romance in his soul, called them to evening prayers.

Their boat reached Jefferson City on April 2. Whitman
pointed out the fact that they were a week earlier at that
point than he and Parker had been the previous year. On
Monday, April 4, they saw a steam sawmill on shore which
Narcissa called "a great curiosity," as it indeed was to her,
for the mills she had seen in New York State were all run
by water power. The three-hundred-mile journey from St.
Louis to Liberty was ended on Thursday, April 7. The missionaries disembarked on a raw spring morning with the
thermometer registering 24° at nine o'clock.

In her letter to her sister, begun on March 31, Narcissa
referred to the continued illness of Mrs. Satterlee. Her
letter is filled with interesting items. She reported that she
then weighed "136 pounds" and was standing the journey
very well. "Mrs. Spaulding," she wrote, "does not look nor
feel quite healthy enough for our enterprise.... Sister S

Narcissa's description of her visit to the cathedral. Mrs. Spalding, who
visited the cathedral the same day, wrote in a similar strain in her
diary.

is very resolute no shrinking with her. She possesses good fortitude. I like her very much, she wears well upon acquaintance."[7]

Liberty, Missouri, represented the farthest point west of American civilization. It was about halfway between the Eastern home of the missionaries and their final destination in Old Oregon. Spalding estimated that the distance from Prattsburg to Liberty was nineteen hundred miles. Most of that distance had been made by water. The most difficult part of their journey was before them. Narcissa wrote: "The way looks pleasant notwithstanding we are so near encountering the difficulties of an unheard of journey for females." [Letter 21.]

On the 19th of the month, while they waited for the boat to take them to Bellevue, William Henry Gray unexpectedly arrived on the *St. Charles* and announced that he had been appointed by the American Board to the Oregon mission as a mechanic. Gray was born in Fairfield, New York, September 8, 1810, where Whitman had attended the Medical College in 1825-26 and in 1831-32. It is possible that the two were known to each other, at least by name, for Gray is supposed to have resided in Fairfield until the death of his father in 1826. Gray was sluggish of mind and therefore was called "an extremely dull scholar."[8] It so happened that when Whitman was searching frantically for missionaries he wrote to the Rev. Chauncey Eddy, of Utica, who was acquainted with Gray. Through Eddy's influence the Board hastily approved Gray's application and sent him on his way to overtake the Whitman-Spalding party if possible.

The Whitmans and the Spaldings were greatly encouraged with his arrival. Providence, so they thought, had smiled on them again. The three men turned their attention to the task of assembling their equipment and buying the necessary livestock. On September 5, 1836, Whitman, Spalding, and Gray signed their financial report from which we are able to obtain a good idea of the outfit they had deemed essential for the overland journey. The report, made out in Whitman's handwriting, lists total receipts at $3,273.96, and a total expense of $3,063.96. The balance on hand September 5, 1836, was $210.00.

Among the cattle were four milch cows and two calves.

---

[7] Whitman letter 21. This was printed with many discrepancies in the *T.O.P.A.*, 1891, pp. 83 ff.

[8] Drury, *Spalding*, p. 128, gives more information about Gray.

Marcus gave his wife the choice of a horse or a mule to ride. Narcissa chose the horse. Richard, who was inclined to judge the value of a riding animal in terms of speed, took one look at the mule and exclaimed: "That very bad mule, can't catch buffalo." [Letter 21.] Sidesaddles were provided for the women.

Spalding's light wagon was reserved for the lighter baggage and for the women. This is the wagon which was taken, in a reduced form, as far west as Fort Boise, and Dr. Whitman usually gets the credit both for owning the wagon and for taking it that far west. New information about the wagon is to be found in a letter written March 20, 1888, by J. S. Griffin to the Rev. Myron Eells, from which the following is taken:

Touching the question of wagons from the East to this coast.... I will say, that on the 5th day of July, 1835 in the town of Holland Patent (I think that was the place) in the state of N. Y. I worked with H. H. Spalding on the barn floor of his father-in-law a Mr. Hart, in putting the top on a small wagon, in which he was soon to leave for the west to engage in Indian Mission. He started with his wife in that wagon, first plan was for the Choctaws ... sufficient to say the wagon came west as far as the H. Bay Co's station at Boisie; & in the summer of '40 (the wagon having come through in '36) I saw the man at that Fort hauling adobies on that wagon. That was the first wagon that came that far Westward.[9]

Narcissa wrote, saying that the light wagon had no spring seats, but that they found it quite comfortable to sit on the baggage. [Letter 26.] The missionaries secured a heavy farm wagon for some of this baggage. They did not plan to take along food supplies for the entire trip but followed the plan of the men of the caravan and took only enough to enable them to reach the buffalo range.

Whitman found that the cost of the trip was mounting to more than he had expected. Writing to Greene on May 5, he declared: "Our expenses have been much worse than I expected; horses and cattle are much higher than last year." Their livestock alone cost over $1000. This was a large item, and yet in the light of later events, it was a wise expenditure. After deducting this item, the total cost of taking the five

---

[9] Original, Coll. W. *See* also Perrin Whitman's statement about the wagon in *W.C.Q.*, Vol. 2, p. 36. Perrin wrote: "It had been one of the old fashioned Deerborn wagons, with wooden springs from one axle to the other made out of hard wood.... The bed was of a dark brown color, and the wheels were yellow with blue strips. It was a light two horse wagon." By an interesting coincidence the college colors of Whitman College are yellow and blue.

missionaries from their homes in the east to Fort Walla Walla was about $1800, or about $360 a person. That sum included all moneys spent for transportation, clothing, medicines, Indian goods, and incidentals. The time involved was about six and a half months, for the financial report was rendered on September 5, 1836. The missionaries received no salaries, but were content with the assurance that the Board would pay their necessary expenses. Nothing was said about special allowances for children, or for furloughs, or for retirement pensions.

Whitman and Spalding hired a young man by the name of Dulin to assist them, and also secured the services of another Nez Perce boy whom they called Samuel Temoni. After they had started, a red-headed, nineteen-year-old lad from New Haven, Connecticut, attached himself to the party. His name was Miles Goodyear.[10] Thus the party grew to ten— five missionaries, three Nez Perces, and two hired men. Dulin left the party at the rendezvous, but Goodyear continued until they reached Fort Hall.

On Thursday, April 21, Samuel Allis arrived at Liberty, coming down the river by boat from Bellevue. On the Saturday following he was married to Miss Emeline Palmer, the Rev. H. H. Spalding officiating.

LIBERTY TO THE OTOE AGENCY

On Thursday, April 28, Spalding, Gray, the Indians and the hired men started with the wagons and the livestock overland to the Otoe Agency, which was about 250 miles distant. They planned to cross the Missouri River near Fort Leavenworth, where there was a ferry, and go up the west side of the Missouri to the Platte. Whitman was to remain at Liberty for several days and then follow. Allis was to go with the women on the boat, according to the arrangements made with the American Fur Company.

Mrs. Satterlee, who had been sick the entire journey, passed away late Saturday night, April 30, at the age of twenty-three. Dr. Whitman and her husband were at the bedside. Writing to Greene on May 5, Whitman reported:

---

[10] A biography of Miles Goodyear by Kelly and Howe was published in 1937 by Western Printing Company, Salt Lake City, Utah. It contains a wealth of new material about this young man who became the first white settler in what is now the State of Utah. Gray in his *Oregon*, p. 113, states that he was sixteen years old. Goodyear was born Feb. 24, 1817.

JAMES BRIDGER, about 1866, from the only known portrait.

JOSEPH L. MEEK (by Joseph Buchtel). Trapper and Indian fighting companion of James Bridger.

Used by permission of the Shepard Book Company, Salt Lake City, from Alter's *James Bridger*.

Whitman's expense account showing cost to the Board of sending the Whitman-Spalding party to Oregon in the summer of 1836. Original in Coll. A.

By courtesy of the American Board.

"From the post mortem appearances we were satisfied that the foundation of her disease was of long standing."

The funeral service was fixed for Sunday afternoon at three o'clock. Just as they were to begin the service, the *Diana* appeared in sight. To the dismay and consternation of the small mission band, the captain of the boat refused to stop. With frantic gestures the missionaries hailed the boat, but the captain shouted back that he could take no one else on board and steamed by.[11] As the missionaries returned to complete the sad duty of burying the earthly remains of Mrs. Satterlee they felt they were burying at the same time all hope of establishing an Oregon mission that year. They knew it was inadvisable to attempt to cross the Plains without escort. Their only hope lay in overtaking the caravan.

Whitman hired a man with a team and wagon. It appears that the women had their riding horses. As soon as possible the party set out in pursuit of Spalding, whom they hoped to find at Leavenworth. Since the tent and other camping equipment had been sent on ahead, the women were obliged to spend their first nights on the prairie sleeping in the open with nothing more than their blankets for protection. When they arrived at Fort Leavenworth, they were disappointed to learn that Spalding had not tarried there but had proceeded on his way. Allis was sent ahead to overtake Spalding, which he succeeded in doing when Spalding was about halfway to the Platte. The light wagon was then sent back for the women and Dr. Whitman.

Within a few days the party was reunited, and continued the journey over the prairies. Good weather favored them, for on June 4 Whitman wrote: "We have not been once wet even to this time, and we are now beyond where the rains fall much in the summer." Whitman was so anxious about getting across the Platte in time to go West with the caravan, that he and his associates pushed on ahead of Mr. and Mrs. Allis, with their heavily loaded wagon drawn by three yoke of oxen.

By Saturday, May 14, the Whitman-Spalding party was within eighteen miles of the Otoe Agency, then located on the north bank of the Platte, about twelve miles south of the present city of Omaha. The trading post of Bellevue

---

[11] Some writers have felt that the fur company was loath to give any assistance to the mission party because of the presence of women. Allis to Greene, July 14, 1836, stated that there was a new captain on board, the inference being that the captain knew nothing of any arrangement with the missionaries.

was about eight miles northeast of the Otoe mission. Even though pressed for time, the missionaries rested over Sunday.

The caravan of the American Fur Company that year was under the direction of Thomas Fitzpatrick, who was known to Whitman, for Fitzpatrick had had charge of the caravan from Fort Laramie to the rendezvous and return the previous year. On Sunday, May 15, Fitzpatrick and his men left Bellevue for the rendezvous. On that day a messenger arrived at the missionary's camp from Major Dougherty, of the Indian Agency, asking for Dr. Whitman. Major Dougherty's brother was sick and needed a physician. Whitman responded to the call and while across the Platte called on Fitzpatrick on Monday. The caravan was then twenty-five miles from Bellevue, and Fitzpatrick was ready to continue his journey the next morning. Whitman urged him to tarry a few days to permit the mission party to join him before they reached the villages of the Pawnee Indians. Fitzpatrick, while professing willingness to have the mission party along, insisted on continuing the journey. He felt that the members of the mission party could overtake the caravan before hostile territory was reached.

Whitman hurried back to the crossing on Tuesday expecting to find his associates there, but to his dismay they had not arrived. The guide whom Whitman had sent to lead them in had himself got lost in the uninhabited prairie, and consequently the party did not reach the south bank of the Platte until Wednesday morning, May 18. [Letter 28.]

Realizing that every hour was important, Whitman set to work with frantic zeal to get the party across the river. A boat which would carry about six hundred pounds to a load was used. Spalding was sick and unable to do much. The brunt of the work fell on Whitman's shoulders, and Narcissa wrote, saying: "Husband became so completely exhausted with swimming the river on Thursday, May 19th that it was with difficulty he made the shore the last time swimming it." [Letter 26.] It was not until Friday night that everything was safely across.

Since it was realized that they had too much baggage, a number of articles were abandoned at the crossing or given to Dunbar and Allis. Spalding reluctantly parted with many of his theological books. After repairing one of the wagons, the party got started again on Saturday noon, with the caravan then more than four days in advance. The outlook was dark indeed, but they pressed on in hope.

ON THE MARCH

They traveled all day Sunday, May 22, necessity making excuses for their troubled conscience. The Elkhorn River was crossed on Monday. The next day the party made a hard drive of about sixty miles. Those with the wagons were able to reach the Loup Fork about eleven o'clock that night, but as Narcissa wrote: "it was too much for the cattle." [Letter 26.] Seeing that the cattle could not keep up, Dr. and Mrs. Whitman elected to spend the night with Richard and John, who were in charge of the livestock. The next morning they drove the cattle to camp before breakfast. To their joy they saw the caravan on the opposite side of the river. They had won their race! Later they learned that the caravan had met with some unexpected delays; otherwise they would have been too late.

It took the mission party half a day to cross the Loup Fork, and on Wednesday afternoon they made another forced march late into the night in order to join the caravan. They drove until one o'clock Thursday morning. With thankful hearts they camped with the sleeping caravan. Marcus wrote: "We then felt we had been signally blessed, thanked God and took courage." [Letter 24.]

The next day the caravan, with the mission party in the rear, passed the Indian villages. Mrs. Whitman and Mrs. Spalding experienced for the first time the sensation of being the object for curious eyes. They were the first white women the Indians had ever seen. Mrs. Whitman wrote: "We ladies were such a curiosity to them they would come and stand around our tent—peep in and grin in their astonishment to see such looking objects." [Letter 26.] This was an experience which was repeated many times thereafter as they met with the different tribes of Indians.

The caravan was like a great moving village with its four hundred animals and some seventy men. After joining the caravan, life settled into a routine. When on the march, they covered from fifteen to twenty miles a day. On June 3 the caravan passed the forks of the Platte. On the 6th they met someone returning to St. Louis who was willing to carry back letters to be mailed. Three of the Whitman letters written at this time are extant.

The first buffalo was killed on June 2, which means that the ten members of the mission party had been obliged to live for twelve days after they left the Otoe Agency on the food they brought with them. Narcissa once wrote of the difficulty of baking for ten people out-of-doors, and she boasted of her husband's skill in cooking buffalo meat. [Letter 26.]

When on the march the Whitmans and the Spaldings frequently rode together in the light wagon, resting on top of the baggage. Mrs. Spalding was not very strong and preferred that method of travel as long as it was available. Gray drove a four-horse team, hitched to the heavy wagon; the Indian boys took care of the cattle; Dulin and Goodyear assisted with the horses. [Letter 26.] Narcissa's letters are some of the most human and revealing documents ever produced by any of the many thousands who went over the Oregon Trail and are filled with interesting details concerning their experiences.

The caravan reached Fort Laramie on Monday, June 13, which meant that it was about five weeks earlier than was the caravan of the preceding year. Here they remained for eight days, leaving on Tuesday, June 21, for the rendezvous. During this interval the women had an opportunity to wash their clothes. Narcissa noted in her journal that only three such opportunities came to them en route; once at Fort Laramie, again at the rendezvous, and the third time at Fort Boise. [Letter 29.]

Whitman and Spalding decided that it was best to leave the heavy farm wagon at Fort Laramie and repack the baggage on the animals. The mules were given an average load of 250 pounds, while the horses sometimes carried heavier burdens. No buffalo were to be found west of the Continental Divide, so dried buffalo meat was taken along. Narcissa wrote: "We have meat and tea in the morn and tea and meat at noon—all our variety consists in the different ways of cooking." [Letter 26.]

The caravan followed the usual route which took them by famous Independence Rock, a landmark along the Oregon Trail. Gray later wrote that nearly all the prominent persons of the caravan carved their names on the rock, a common practice of the day.[12] The caravan crossed the Continental Divide on July 4. A monument erected by the Wyoming Trail Commission now marks the place where the first white women crossed the crest of the Rockies. They reached the rendezvous on Wednesday, July 6. It was held that year on

---

[12] Gray, *Oregon*, p. 118.

the Green River in the vicinity of what is now Daniel, Wyoming.[13]

Under the leadership of Joseph L. Meek, one of the most famous of the mountain men, the trappers gave the mission party, and especially the two women, a rousing welcome. Meek never lost an opportunity to be in the presence of Mrs. Whitman, and regaled her with his stories of battles with Blackfeet Indians and grizzly bears. The welcome given by the Indians was none the less cordial. The Indian women gathered around the two white women and saluted them not only by shaking hands, but also "with a most hearty kiss." Both Mrs. Whitman and Mrs. Spalding were much affected by this unexpected demonstration on the part of the Indian women.

The first part of a long and difficult journey was over. On July 16 Whitman wrote to Greene, saying: "I see no reason to regret our choice of a journey by land." However, the most hazardous part of the journey was yet before them.

AT THE RENDEZVOUS

The presence of the white women at the rendezvous in the summer of 1836 created a real sensation. Some of the mountain men had not seen a white woman for years and were quick to accept the invitation of the missionaries to join them in their daily devotions. Frequently from fifteen to twenty of the trappers were present on such occasions. There was an amazing interest in Bibles. Narcissa wrote that if they had packed one or two animals with nothing but Bibles she believed all would have been sold or given away. [Letter 27.] Wonder of wonders—a revival of religion had broken out among the mountain men at the rendezvous!

Another Bible story of a different type is found in a newspaper clipping in the archives of the American Board, from which the following extract is taken:

St. Louis Oct. 3, 1838
For the Bulletin. "Astonishing Disclosure" Messrs. Editors: As a citizen of St. Louis I have been grieved and mortified by reading an article in the Missouri Saturday News with the above heading.

The writer then referred to the fact that the article had called "the Rev. Mr. Spalding all manner of hard names, because he had said that packs of cards had been bought of unprincipled white men, by the Indians, for a Bible." It

[13] *Ibid.*, p. 121.

appears that at the rendezvous Spalding had learned of
instances where the mountain men had indeed sold packs of
cards to the unsuspecting Indians for the "white man's
book." Such cases were considered as a good joke by the
mountain men, but Spalding thought it was sacrilegious and
lost no time in sending back to his friends in the States a
sharp criticism of the practice.

More Indians were present at the 1836 rendezvous than
at the one held the previous year. Whitman wrote that the
Indians were especially interested in "our Females, cattle
and wagon," [Letter 28] these being the first that most of
the Indians had seen. Considerable rivalry developed among
the Nez Perces and Cayuses, for each tribe wanted the missionaries to settle with them. Narcissa wrote:

> This reminds me of a quarrel among the women while we were at
> Rendesvous. The Nes Perces women said we were going to live with
> them, and the Cayouses said, No, we were going to live with them.
> The contradiction was so sharp they nearly came to blows. [Letter 34.]

The Rev. Samuel Parker did not return to the rendezvous
in the summer of 1836, as was expected. Parker returned to
Fort Walla Walla in the spring of that year, but, as he
thought of the long and perilous trip with the Indians back
to the rendezvous, his heart failed him. He decided to go
to Vancouver and return to the States by boat. He wrote to
Whitman from Fort Walla Walla on May 16, explaining his
decision. The missionaries were deeply disappointed, not
only in the failure of Parker to meet them, but also in his
failure to send them the information they so much desired
regarding the country and mission prospects.[14]

The question of a suitable escort to Fort Walla Walla
from the rendezvous gave Whitman and Spalding considerable concern. The Indians wanted the mission party to go
with them by the northern route, as Parker had done the
preceding year. This way was very mountainous in places
and therefore more difficult. It would have taken two
months longer than the shorter route across what is now
southern Idaho. This factor alone was sufficient to induce

---

[14] *Ibid.*, p. 119, states that Parker was afraid of giving details
for fear his letter would be intercepted by the Hudson's Bay officials and thus "did not deem it prudent to write or to give any
advice." Contemporaneous documents do not support such a theory,
for the Hudson's Bay men were uniformly courteous and helpful to the
missionaries. Gray's unfair criticism grew out of some later unhappy
experiences with the Company.

the missionaries to favor the southern way. They wanted to reach their mission field in time to make some preparation for the winter, and every week counted.

As early as July 8, two days after their arrival at the rendezvous, Spalding wrote to Greene that they had decided to take the southern route, which he estimated to be six hundred miles from the rendezvous to Fort Walla Walla. Fortunately for the mission party, John L. McLeod and Thomas McKay, of the Hudson's Bay Company, arrived at the rendezvous on July 12. This Company had purchased from Captain Nathaniel J. Wyeth the fort which Wyeth had built in 1834, known as Fort Hall, near the present city of Pocatello, Idaho. Wyeth was on his way back to the States and was escorted to the rendezvous by McLeod and McKay. Parker, learning of the intention of the Company to purchase Fort Hall, had sent a second letter to Whitman by these men, in which he advised the mission party to travel under their protection. The missionaries looked upon this arrangement as another token of Divine favor and hastened to make their plans accordingly.

On Thursday, July 14, the mission party moved to the encampment of McLeod and McKay. The Nez Perces and Flatheads, as though fearful of losing their missionaries, also moved to the same vicinity. Before leaving the camp of Fitzpatrick, Whitman asked for his bill to cover the favors received from the Company. In turn Fitzpatrick asked Whitman for his bill to cover medical services rendered, and when Whitman stated that he had no bill, Fitzpatrick declared that the Company also had none. Whitman wrote to Greene: "We have received nothing but favours & kindness from this company while with them." [Letter 28.]

Among Whitman's patients at the rendezvous was a negro by the name of Hinds, who attached himself to the mission party and remained with them until they reached Fort Walla Walla. He rendered some assistance in the construction of buildings on the mission site. Narcissa referred to him in one of her letters as: "A black man who came on account of his health and for the purpose of taking medicine." [Letter 34.]

TRAVEL EXPERIENCES

On July 18 the McLeod and McKay caravan began its journey to Fort Walla Walla. On that day Narcissa started another diary which she kept with more or less regularity until October 22 of that year. This diary, intended at first for her parents, was copied and the duplicate sent to her husband's mother. For the sake of designation, the first diary will hereafter be referred to as diary A and the second as diary B. Diary A passed into the possession of Mrs. Harriet Jackson, the youngest sister of Narcissa, and was given by her descendants in 1932 to Whitman College. This diary was published in some local paper in the vicinity of Narcissa's home shortly after it was received by her parents. On September 18, 1838, in a letter to her sister Jane, Narcissa wrote: "I regret you should have it printed, or any of it, for it never was designed for public eye." The paper containing the first published copy of the diary has not been located. This diary also appeared in the June, September, and December, 1936, numbers of the *Oregon Historical Quarterly*, being edited by Dr. T. C. Elliott, of Walla Walla.

Diary B is still owned by a descendant of the Whitman family.[15] It appeared in the 1891 issue of the *Transactions of the Oregon Pioneer Association*, although a poor transcription was made. The same diary was better printed in the *Chronicle Express* of Penn Yan, New York, beginning January 8, 1931. As would be expected, diary A contains some family references which Narcissa did not copy for her mother-in-law. For the most part the differences between the two versions are of a minor character.[16] All of the following quotations from Narcissa's diary will be from the first mentioned version.

The matter of securing sufficient food after leaving the rendezvous was a real problem. A few elk and antelope were killed en route; occasionally, along the Snake River below the American Falls, fresh salmon was secured, and sometimes edible berries were found. McLeod shared with the mission party a supply of rice brought from Fort Walla Walla. However, the main item on their menu was dried buffalo meat purchased from the Indians. Spalding wrote that this dried meat was "the poorest kind of buffalo bull meat, sour, mouldy, & full of all manner of filth, such as I once would not have fed to a dog."[17]

---

15 Coll. U.

16 Another copy, claimed to be an original, is owned by Mrs. Ginera Whitman Lutz, of Bellingham, Wash. *See* Bellingham *Herald*, Dec. 20, 1936. Judging from the printed photograph of one page of the diary, this was written by another.

17 Spalding to Greene, Sept. 20, 1836.

In the first entry of the journal, which was begun on July 18, Narcissa had the following comment to make about her food:

I thought of Mothers bread & butter many times as any hungry child would, but did not find it on the way. I fancy pork & potatoes would relish extremely well. Have been living on fresh meat exclusively am cloyed with it. I do not know how I shall endure this part of the journey.

On July 27 she wrote again:

We have plenty of dry buffalo meat which we purchased of the Indians, & *dry* it is for *me*. I can scarcely eat it, it appears so filthy, but it will keep us alive, & we ought to be thankful for it.... (Girls do not waste the bread, if you knew how well I should relish even the dryest morsel, you would save every piece carefully.)

From the rendezvous to Fort Hall the missionaries accommodated themselves to the Indian's method of travel, which was to make but one camp a day. While crossing the plains, the caravan had stopped for a two-hour period at midday for rest and refreshment. The Indians, however, did not stop after they started in the morning until they were ready to camp for the night. The women found this rather trying and were glad to be able to resume their former way of traveling after the Indians left them at Fort Hall.

On Saturday, July 30, they passed by the small geysers and soda springs in the vicinity of what is now Soda Springs, Idaho. Spalding looked into the future and saw the time when a railroad would cross the Rockies and bring visitors from "the far east ... to visit the West & see the great Soda fountain of the Rocky Mountains."[18]

Several references are to be found in Narcissa's diary to the light wagon which the men were determined to take with them. As has been stated, this wagon was not the first wagon to cross the Rockies, but it was the first to go west of the rendezvous. Little did they think of the significance to be attached to that event. Whitman and Spalding then thought only of the utilitarian value of a wagon at the mission station. The following is a typical reference to the wagon to be found in Narcissa's diary. She wrote on the 25th of July:

---

[18] Spalding to Greene, Sept. 20, 1836. The Rev. Samuel Parker also prophesied the building of a railroad across the Rockies. When the Union Pacific first conceived the idea of doing this, some of the officials wrote to Mr. Parker for information. The originals of this correspondence are in the possession of L. Alexander Mack.

Husband has had a tedious time with the *wagon* today. Got set in the creek, this morning while crossing, was obliged to wade considerable in getting it out. After that in going between two *mts.* with side of one so steep that it was difficult for horses to pass, the wagon was upset twice. Did not wonder at this at all. It was a *greater* wonder that it was not turning somersault continually.

On the 28th one of the axletrees broke when the party was still several days east of Fort Hall. Narcissa was a little rejoiced for she felt that then it would be left behind, but the men converted the back wheels into a cart, lashed the fore wheels to it, and proceeded. "They are so resolute & untiring in their efforts," wrote Narcissa, "they will probably succeed." This two-wheeled cart was taken to Fort Boise where it was left because of the fatigue of their animals. [Letter 31.] Whitman and Spalding expected to send back for it, but they never did.[19]

The party reached Fort Hall on the morning of August 3. There they met Captain Thing, one of Wyeth's men who was left in charge of the Fort. The missionaries were given a cordial welcome. Narcissa wrote that they were much cheered by the view of buildings again. They inspected the small vegetable garden and Narcissa mentions the pleasure of eating fresh turnips for dinner.

The main body of the Indians turned north at the Fort while the McLeod and McKay caravan followed the south bank of the Snake westward. Chief Rotten Belly, of the Nez Perces, and a few other Indians decided to go with the missionaries to render such assistance as was possible. The caravan got started again on August 4. Near Fort Hall the missionaries saw the Snake River, one of the largest rivers of the West, a tributary of the mighty Columbia.

Great areas in what is now southern Idaho are nothing more than a sun-parched desert, where only the sage can grow. During the months of July and August the sun beats down with merciless intensity, making travel a trying experience even in motorcars over hard-surfaced roads. It took the missionaries a full two weeks to make the journey from Fort Hall to Fort Boise, a trip that can be accomplished now with ease in one day in a motorcar.

The letters and diaries of the members of the mission party speak about the "sandy desert," and the "scarcity of

---

[19] Other references to the wagon are to be found in Farnham's *Travels*, p. 142, and Cannon's *Waiilatpu*, p. 25. The wagon was still in use in the early sixties at the Fort.

grass and water." Such expressions as "heat very great," "came fifteen miles without seeing water," and Whitman's statement: "Imagination can hardly equal the barrenness of the main route along the Snake River," [Letter 29] give some idea of the hardships they endured. The day before they reached Fort Hall, Narcissa wrote in her diary: "Heat excessive. Truly I tho't, 'The Heavens over us were brass & the earth iron under our feet.' "20

The hard sharp rocks made traveling difficult for the animals. Some of the cattle had to be shod even before the party reached Fort Boise. Five of the cattle had to be left there because they were too weak to be taken over the Blue Mountains. Some satisfactory exchange must have been made with the Hudson's Bay Company for these cattle left behind.

The Snake River was forded on August 13 at Island Ford, which is about three miles below the present site of Glenns Ferry, Idaho. At that point two islands break the main channel of the Snake into three parts, thus making it possible to ford the river on horseback. Dr. Whitman had a hard time to get the cart across, because the swiftness of the current turned the cart over and entangled the mules in the harness.

Several times Whitman and Spalding found it necessary to reduce their baggage load. At the rendezvous Whitman wrote: "The one thing I regret is that we brought any supplies except such as we wanted for our immediate use on the journey." [Letter 28.] When the light wagon broke down, other things had to be given away or left behind. The night before the party crossed the Snake, Marcus informed Narcissa that the little trunk, given by her sister Harriet, would have to be left. Narcissa wrote a little farewell to the trunk in her diary and added: "Thus we scatter as we go along."

After reaching the north bank of the Snake, McLeod and McKay pushed on ahead of the missionaries, who found their progress delayed by the cattle. The trail led in a northwesterly direction across the desert to the Boise River, which was followed to its mouth, where Fort Boise was located. This fort was established in the summer of 1834 by Thomas McKay, who remained there after his return from the rendezvous in the summer of 1836.

The mission party reached the Fort on Friday noon,

20 Irving, *Astoria*, gives a thrilling story of the hardships endured by the Hunt party, which crossed this desert in 1811 and 1812.

August 19, and remained there until the following Monday. The women welcomed the opportunity to rest. A further reduction in their baggage was made there, including the wagon. Narcissa wrote: "The custom of the country is to possess nothing, then you will lose nothing while traveling."

The Snake River was crossed again after leaving Fort Boise. Here a rude canoe was found, made of rushes and willows. This was large enough to carry the two women across the river. Two Indians on horseback, with a rope attached to the canoe, towed it to the other bank. The missionaries with their reduced herd of cattle remained with McLeod until the 26th, when it was decided to divide the party. McLeod, the Whitmans, and Gray pushed on ahead, while the Spaldings remained with the Indians and the animals. Their trail led them from the Powder River Valley into the Grand Ronde Valley, which they followed to the summit of the Blue Mountains.[21] After spending so long a time upon the treeless prairies and the desert wastes, the forests which cover the beautiful Blue Mountains came as a welcome change.

The Whitmans reached the summit of the Blue Mountains in the afternoon of Monday, August 29. Before they camped for the night, the party came to a vantage point, where they were able to see down into the valley of the Columbia. Here is Narcissa's account:

While upon this elevation, we had a view of the valley of the Columbia R. It was beautiful. Just as we gained the highest elevation & began to descend, the sun was dipping his disk behind the western horizon. Beyond the valley we could see two distant mts. Mt. Hood & Mt. St. Helens. These lofty peaks were of a conical form, & separate from each other by a considerable distance. Behind the former the sun was hiding a part of his rays, which gave us a more distinct view of this gigantic cone.

McLeod left the party on the 31st and rode on ahead to notify those at the Fort of the approach of the missionaries. The Whitmans camped that night on the Walla Walla River, a tributary of the Columbia, about eight miles from the Fort. Under the heading of September 1, 1836, we read in Narcissa's diary:

You can better imagine our feelings this morning than I can describe them. I could not realize that the end of our journey was

---

[21] *O.H.Q.*, June, 1936, carried an article by T. C. Elliott, entitled "The Coming of the White Women," which gives in some detail the route followed.

so near. We arose as soon as it was light, took a cup of coffee ate of the duck, we had given us last night, then dressed for W. W. Started when it was yet early for all were in haste, to reach the desired haven. If you could have seen us now you would have been surprised, for both man and beast appeared alike propelled by the same force. The whole company galloped almost all the way to the Fort.

The fatigue of the long journey was forgotten as they saw signs of civilization again. First they passed the vegetable gardens, two miles from the Fort, and then the Fort itself appeared in sight. It was located on the east bank of the Columbia River near the mouth of the Walla Walla River. When the party was sighted from the Fort, McLeod, Pierre Pambrun, the trader in charge, and J. K. Townsend, a traveling naturalist, rode forth to greet them. After the usual salutations, the weary travelers were invited to partake of breakfast. Again the Whitmans sat in cushioned armchairs! For breakfast they had fresh salmon, potatoes, tea, bread and butter. "What a variety!" wrote the grateful Narcissa.

The Whitmans were ushered to the southwest bastion, which was to be their bedroom. Narcissa was thankful for the privacy of a room again. They inspected the Fort and the surrounding grounds. Narcissa noticed that the dooryard was filled with "hens, turkeys, and pigeons." Elsewhere she saw "cows, hogs & goats in abundance, & I think the largest & fattest cattle & swine I ever saw." Later in the morning they enjoyed a feast of melons. Narcissa wrote that they were the finest she had ever seen.[22]

They dined that afternoon at four o'clock on "pork, potatoes, beets, cabbage, turnips, tea, bread and butter." The Pambruns were as cordial in their hospitality as could be expected. Mrs. Pambrun was a native woman, who spoke some French in addition to her mother tongue, and very little English.

On the morning of Saturday, September 3, Townsend and McLeod left for Fort Vancouver, about three hundred miles down the river. Whitman had decided that a trip to Vancouver was necessary, and so it was decided that he would follow with Pambrun.

The Spaldings arrived on Saturday noon and were given the same cordial reception as that extended to the Whitmans and Gray. Out of the seventeen head of cattle with which

---

[22] Diary B., in *T.O.P.A.*, 1891, p. 58, states: " . . . the first, I think I ever saw or tasted." Correct reading is "the finest."

they had started, only eight got as far as Fort Walla Walla. Two calves were eaten; two cattle were lost; and five were left at Fort Boise. Whitman in his letter of September 5 to Greene, written from Fort Walla Walla, lists thirteen head of cattle. If the Hudson's Bay Company replaced the five left at Fort Boise, the small herd belonging to the missionaries would have numbered thirteen. Writing to Parker, Whitman stated that they had "five cows, seven heiffers, and one bull." [Letter 31.] These cattle were highly prized, for the Hudson's Bay Company had a policy of not selling any cattle. The only way to get cattle into Old Oregon was to drive them overland from the States, or to get some inferior Spanish breed from California.

FORT VANCOUVER

After the arrival of the Spaldings at Fort Walla Walla, it was decided that all should go to Fort Vancouver. Whitman wanted to meet Dr. John McLoughlin, Chief Factor of the Hudson's Bay Company in Old Oregon. New provisions had to be secured, and arrangements made for getting such necessities in the future. The party left with Pambrun on Tuesday at 2:00 P.M. in a boat which Gray described as being "30 feet long and 8 wide in the center, coming to a point at each end propelled by 5 oares and a stearsman, of sufficient depth to carry 2500 pounds."[23] They reached Fort Vancouver on Monday, September 12.

The first person they met upon landing was Mr. Townsend, the naturalist, who led them to the Fort. Dr. McLoughlin and others noticed the arrival of the party and hastened forth to greet them. In addition to the white-haired Dr. McLoughlin, whose reputation for kindly courtesy has grown with the years, there came Sir James Douglas and Dr. William Fraser Tolmie. The missionaries were invited into Dr. McLoughlin's home and presented to Mrs. McLoughlin[24] and Mrs. Douglas, both of whom were half-breeds.

John McLoughlin (1789-1857) is one of the most picturesque figures in the history of the Pacific Northwest. He arrived in Oregon in 1824 and built Fort Vancouver. He stood six feet four inches high. His white hair was worn

---

[23] Gray to Ambler, Sept. 9, 1836. Original, Coll. O.

[24] Mrs. McLoughlin was first the wife of Alexander McKay, who lost his life on the ill-fated *Tonquin* in 1811. She was left with three girls and one boy, Thomas. It was this Thomas McKay who met the missionaries at the rendezvous.

long, so that it touched his shoulders. His commanding personality and his reputation for fair dealing won the respect of native and white, English and American.

Sir James was Dr. McLoughlin's chief associate, and later his successor. William Fraser Tolmie, M.D. (1812-1886), was a young Scottish physician who had received his medical education in Glasgow.[25] He first reached Fort Vancouver in May, 1833, having been sent out by the Hudson's Bay Company to relieve Dr. McLoughlin of his medical cares.

Dr. McLoughlin was quick to appreciate the significance of the overland trip made by the two women, and complimented them upon their achievement. Spalding wrote that he called upon "his powers of invention to confer upon them some title of honor as due to their heroism."[26] He did all within his power to make his guests welcome and personally guided them through his extensive gardens and his establishment.

Among those who were present when the mission party arrived was William McKay, then a lad thirteen years old, the son of Thomas McKay. Later he was sent East, and on the advice of Dr. Whitman, went to Fairfield, New York, to study medicine. He became a doctor and was for many years a resident of Pendleton, Oregon.[27]

Two other residents of the Fort should be introduced— the Rev. and Mrs. Herbert Beaver, who had but recently arrived from England on the *Neriade,* then in port. Mr. Beaver was an Episcopal clergyman sent out by the Hudson's Bay Company to be chaplain at Vancouver. In spite of the appropriateness of his name for a fur-trading post, he was not a success and returned with his wife to England in 1838. Another English woman at the Fort was a Mrs. Capendel, the wife of one of the employees of the company. "This is more than we expected," noted Narcissa in her diary, "that we should be privileged with the acquaintance & society of two English ladies."

After considerable discussion, it was decided to have the women remain at Fort Vancouver while the men would return to the upper Columbia country, pick out the mission

---

[25] His son, Simon Fraser Tolmie, became premier of British Columbia.

[26] Spalding to Greene, Sept. 20, 1836.

[27] His reminiscences appeared in *History of the Synod of Washington,* p. 234.

sites, and begin building. Dr. McLoughlin was most willing to sell the needed supplies. Whitman and Spalding sought his advice as to the best place to locate the two stations which they had then decided to establish. A bill of goods, amounting to £371.8.1, was purchased. This included household furniture, clothing, farming utensils, building supplies, Indian goods, books, stationery and other provisions. Out of this total Whitman assumed £188.7.2; Spalding accepted £172.13.1; and Gray took £10.7.10. Gray's bill was smaller because he was unmarried and had no house to erect for himself.

On March 18, 1837, Whitman again drew upon the Board to the extent of £102.13.1, of which his share was £26.12.10; Spalding's was £32.13.1, and Gray's was £45.7.2. These two bills, including the expenses of all of the missionaries, totaled £474.1.2. According to the rate of exchange then prevailing, the two drafts cost the American Board about $2,560.00. When this is added to the $3,273.76 incurred before the missionaries left the States, we find that the American Board paid out nearly $6,000.00 to establish the Oregon mission. A considerable sum could have been saved by a wiser selection of supplies before they left the States. "We see now," wrote Narcissa, "that it was not necessary to bring anything because we find all here." [Letter 38.] Even so, Dr. McLoughlin assured the missionaries that the cost of their trip across the country, covering a period of about seven months, was less than their expenses would have been had they gone by boat around South America. [Letter 38.]

Writing to Greene from the rendezvous, Whitman had said that he did not regret the decision to go overland, and that: "For safety I would as soon risque a land as a sea voyage." After the trying experience in crossing what is now southern Idaho, Spalding came to the opposition opinion. In his letter of September 20 to Greene, he wrote: "I can never advise females, notwithstanding, to venture a rout over the mountains so long as a passage to this country is so easy by sea."

Narcissa expressed her opinion of the overland journey in a letter to Mrs. Parker written from Vancouver, in which she said:

Do you ask whether I regret coming by land? I answer, "By no means." If I were at home now, and expected to make this journey again I would choose *this way* in preference to a seven months' voyage

PIONEER HUDSON BAY CO'S OFFICIALS AND STEAMER BEAVER.

DR. JOHN McLOUGHLIN,
(THE OREGON PIONEER- 1822.)

SIR JAMES DOUGLAS.

DR. Wᵐ F. TOLMIE.

STEAMER BEAVER.
FIRST STEAM SHIP TO ROUND CAPE HORN

The *Beaver*, of 110 tons register, arrived in the Columbia River in the spring of 1836. She was used in coastwise trade until 1888. See *Pacific Northwest Quarterly*, Oct., 1936, pp. 347 ff. From Evans, *History of the Pacific Northwest*, Vol. I, p. 16.

Picture by courtesy of Whitman College.

Perhaps the one best qualified to judge the relative comforts and discomforts of the two routes was Samuel Parker who went out to Oregon by the overland trail and returned by sea. Writing to Greene from Honolulu on November 14, 1836, Parker discussed the merits of the two routes and said:

On this question, I want to say, do not on any consideration send them this way. It is a *very long tedious way* at best. And there is no knowing how long they would be detained here, unless a vessel should be chartered, at great expense, to take them into the Columbia river. There may not be a ship going into that river for years, which would take missionary passengers. . . . I think going with the caravan is not forbidding.

Here I am shut up, like a prisoner, more than four months waiting for a passage to the United States, although several vessels have sailed for the States, since I have been here. Probably you will ask, why I cannot obtain passage? I am engaged in missionary service. . . . I thought I did right in adopting the course which I did; but if I had known what I now do, I would rather have thrown myself upon the mercy of the Blackfoot Indians, than to have come here.

Parker did not succeed in obtaining a passage until the first of January, 1837. After a five-month trip around the Horn, he reached New London, Connecticut, on May 18. Two years after the members of the Whitman-Spalding party crossed the plains and the mountains, the Board sent out another party with women to make the same long and difficult trip overland. The Methodist Board never sent any women workers that way, and but one party of men. The Lees went overland in 1834, but all others went by sea.

We of this generation do well to remember the fortitude and courage of the first two white women to make the hazardous journey across the continent. It was, as Narcissa described it in her diary, an "unheard of journey." Narcissa and Eliza have won for themselves an important place in the history of the Pacific Northwest if for no other reason than that they were the first of a long line of pioneer women to venture over the Oregon Trail. But their fame rests on other reasons as well, which will be told in the chronicle of their labors as missionaries for eleven years in Old Oregon.

CHAPTER EIGHT

WAIILATPU

1836-1837

THE BOAT which took Whitman, Spalding, and Gray back to Fort Walla Walla left Fort Vancouver on Wednesday, September 21, 1836. It was heavily laden with supplies and was manned by eleven men. Pambrun and a Cayuse chief, who had gone to Vancouver with the mission party to see how the white men lived, were also on board.

Mrs. Whitman and Mrs. Spalding were reluctant to see their husbands depart. "One thing comforts us," wrote Narcissa in her diary, "they are as unwilling to leave us as we are to stay & would not, if it was possible for us to go now." Narcissa also mentions the fact that Dr. McLoughlin gave her husband "a pair of leather pantaloons" for riding.

The returning party reached the Cascades on the 22nd, where a portage was necessary. Another portage of about half a mile was necessary at The Dalles. Sometimes the boats could be pulled through the rapids by ropes, but at other times they had to be carried. The Indians native to the region were always willing to help if paid by a little tobacco. It took from thirty to forty Indians to carry the empty boat.

On the 28th, Pambrun and Spalding left the boat and, having secured horses, completed the journey to Fort Walla Walla by land. They reached the Fort the next day, and the boat arrived on Sunday, October 2.[1] By the following Tuesday the men were ready to search for suitable locations for the mission stations.

THE WHITMAN STATION LOCATED

Even before Whitman left the East he had considered the possibility of locating his station in the Grande Ronde Valley, on the east side of the Blue Mountains, but the scarcity of game and the difficulty of getting supplies made such a location impractical. Since it was agreed that Spald-

---

[1] Drury, *Spalding*, p. 157, states that the party reached the Fort on the 30th. This was due to an ambiguous statement in the *Missionary Herald*, 1837, p. 426.

ing was to settle among the Nez Perces on the Clearwater, the next best place for Whitman was in the vicinity of Walla Walla.

There were two good reasons for such a choice. To begin with, the Cayuse tribe lived in that region. Though this tribe numbered only about three hundred altogether, yet it was composed of an aggressive and influential people.[2] Near by were two other tribes, the Walla Wallas and the Umatillas. The members of these three tribes were able to speak the Nez Perce language. Today the remnants of all three tribes are to be found on the Indian reservation near Pendleton, Oregon.

A second consideration was the strategic location of Fort Walla Walla. Before it rolled the majestic Columbia, the main artery of trade and travel in Old Oregon. Even though the great Northwest was then crisscrossed with Indian trails, the white man preferred the canoe and the bateau whenever possible. Each spring an express was sent from Fort Vancouver to Montreal. Most of the route was by water. The express ascended the Columbia, stopping at the Hudson's Bay Company's forts along the way—Fort Walla Walla, Fort Okanogan, and Fort Colville. After reaching the waters of the upper Columbia, the men crossed the divide to the Athabasca River, and then, later, over other portages into the Saskatchewan River, through Lake Winnipeg and the Great Lakes into the St. Lawrence River, and thence to Montreal. It took six months or more to make the trip one way. A second express was sent eastward later in the season, and two were sent westward each year from Montreal.

Fort Walla Walla was, therefore, at the crossroads, on the main line of communication which linked Vancouver with Montreal. It also marked the end of the trail that led over the Blue Mountains to Fort Boise, Fort Hall, and the rendezvous. Whitman must have been impressed with the strategic value of such a site. Future years disclosed its importance, for the old Indian trail broadened into a highway over which came the covered wagons by the hundreds and thousands. At first the immigrants passed Whitman's station, but after 1845 most of them followed the Umatilla to the Columbia, which was a shorter way to The Dalles.

---

[2] Eells, *Marcus Whitman*, p. 96, notes that early writers differed widely in their estimates of the number of Cayuses.

On Tuesday, October 4, Whitman, Spalding, Gray, and Pambrun set out to explore the Walla Walla River for a suitable site for the Whitman home. The Walla Walla River (literally Little River), which emptied into the Columbia at Fort Walla Walla, is not a long stream. It rises in the Blue Mountains about forty miles away. The men rode about twenty-five miles upstream and then camped. Spalding noted in his journal:

> Found plenty of timber, cottonwood, birch, balm of Gilead, & thorn; pine on the mountains in sight, perhaps 15 miles distant. Soil on the river & its branches appears to be good. This will probably be Doct Whitman's location.

Spalding called it "a beautiful country, not mountaneous but rolling." A heavy growth of bunch grass covered the ground. The timber grew only along the banks of the streams, thus leaving the soil back from the streams free for cultivation. On October 5, Whitman selected a spot in the bend of the river on the north bank, where, by building about eighty rods of fence, he could enclose some three hundred acres. The Indians called the place, Waiilatpu, "the place of the rye grass."[3] Whitman selected for his home a place near the mouth of a small creek that flowed into the Walla Walla River. This creek was called Pasha by the Indians, and later Mill Creek by the missionaries, because Whitman used its waters to turn his mill.[4]

The next day the men returned to the Fort. On the 8th Whitman wrote to Parker and emphasized the importance of his location. "You are well aware," he stated, "of the importance of the field as to its future influence on the civilized world. It is undoubtedly before the Willamette or any point on the Columbia." [Letter 32.] Later, Whitman was to see the immigrants pass by the Walla Walla region in favor of the Willamette, yet it is rather significant to find him at the very beginning of his residence in Old Oregon looking forward into the future and speculating on the importance of that fair country to the civilized world. Was he not even then dreaming of the day when the United States of America would extend its authority beyond the mountains to the shores of the Pacific?

---

[3] According to Dr. Stephen B. L. Penrose, formerly president of Whitman College, Myron and Edwin Eells, sons of the Rev. Cushing Eells, differed as to the correct pronunciation of Waiilatpu. One placed the accent on the second syllable, and the other on the third. The pronunciation usually heard is "Wy-ee-lat'-poo."

[4] Warren, *Memoirs*, p. 110.

THE SPALDING STATION LOCATED

True to his promise, Chief Rotten Belly with a company of from twenty to thirty Nez Perces arrived at Fort Walla Walla on October 7 to conduct the missionaries to the Nez Perce country. The Nez Perces were deeply disappointed to learn that the Whitmans were not also to settle among them. They told Dr. Whitman that the Cayuses were always in difficulty with the white people and warned him of trouble. In contrast, they referred to their good record and again entreated him to live with them. Marcus wrote of these statements in a letter to Narcissa which Spalding carried to Fort Vancouver a few days later. Upon that information, Narcissa wrote in her diary on October 18:

> The Nez Perces are exceedingly anxious for the location. Make many promises to work, & listen to instructions. They do not like to have us stop with the Cayuses. Say *they* do not have difficulty with the white men as the Cayuses do, & that we shall find it so.[5]

Prophetic words! Would that the Whitmans had heeded the warning! Several years later, when Spalding was asked why two stations were established instead of one, he is reported to have said: "Do you suppose I would have come off here all alone a hundred & twenty miles if I could have lived with him or Mrs. Whitman."[6] Of course, Dr. Whitman could not go into detail and explain to the Nez Perces the real reason of the missionaries' deciding upon two stations. They had to be content with having the Spaldings live with them. Nevertheless the Nez Perces shook their heads doubtfully and repeated their warning: "The Cayuses are bad people."

Whitman and Spalding with their escort left Fort Walla Walla on Saturday, October 8. They remained in camp over the Sabbath. The two men were highly gratified to see how faithfully the Indians observed the day. They also noted the fact that daily devotions were practiced, a custom perhaps learned from Mr. Parker. On the 11th the party camped at the confluence of the Snake and the Clearwater Rivers, where Lewiston, Idaho, is now located. The next day they reached the Lapwai Valley, about ten miles up the Clearwater from its mouth. Parker had favored the location

---

[5] *See* also Whitman letter 34, where Narcissa wrote in a similar manner of the Cayuses.

[6] Gray to Greene, Oct. 14, 1840.

of a mission station at the mouth of the river, but the Nez Perces preferred the Lapwai Valley.[7]

Along the Lapwai Creek, which flows into the Clearwater, the missionaries found some good farming land. Spalding chose a site on the south side of Thunder Hill about two miles up the creek from its mouth. The Nez Perces, who numbered about three thousand, showed great enthusiasm, quite in contrast to the lack of interest on the part of the three hundred or so Cayuses. Having made the necessary selection, the men again turned their horses toward Fort Walla Walla, which they reached on Friday, October 14.

The next day the Hudson's Bay express from Montreal arrived, and arrangements were made for Spalding to return with it to Vancouver. Whitman wrote at least two letters which Spalding carried. One was to his wife, a copy of which we do not have; the other was to Samuel Parker. Whitman had written this under the date of October 8, and then after his return from Lapwai had added a postscript on the 15th, in which he told of the selection of Lapwai as the home for the Spaldings. He repeated to Parker the warning of the Cayuses: "The Nez Pierces do not like my stopping with the Cayous; and say that the Nez Pierces do not have difficulties with white man, as the Cayous do; and that we will see the difference." He also wrote: "We expect to build both our houses this fall and winter, and be prepared for crops next summer." [Letter 32.] This letter reached Vancouver in such a damaged condition, that Narcissa felt it best to copy it before sending it on. [Letter 36.]

The express left the Fort for Vancouver on Sunday, October 16, at 4:00 A.M., and made the trip down the river in the record time of less than three days. Assisted by favorable winds, the express arrived at Fort Vancouver on Tuesday, October 18, at 2:00 P.M. Spalding wrote in his journal about the extent of his travels as follows:

I have now since the 3rd of Sept traveled 1200 miles which added to our journey over the Mountains makes 5300 since the first of Feb last. There is yet 425 miles to travel before myself & wife reach our location.

McLoughlin was surprised to see Spalding back so soon. Spalding had made the round trip in less than a month. Dr. McLoughlin was disappointed to learn that the women

---

[7] Lapwai is a corruption of the Nez Perce words meaning "Butterfly Valley." The Indians have a tradition that long ago myriads of small white butterflies were found in the valley at certain times of the year.

intended to go up the river with Spalding as soon as the
necessary arrangements could be made. "The Dr.," wrote
Narcissa, in her diary, "urges me to stay all winter. He is a
very sympathetic man." Dr. McLoughlin was probably
aware that Mrs. Whitman was then in the fifth month of
pregnancy and felt that the care and comforts she could
receive at Fort Vancouver would be much better for her
than the privations and hardships attendant upon the establishment of a pioneer home in the wintertime. But in
spite of his repeated invitations to spend the winter at Vancouver, the women decided to go back with Spalding.

In the meantime Whitman and Gray were busy at
Waiilatpu erecting a house. Gray had started a building
while Whitman and Spalding were making the trip to
Lapwai. He secured the assistance of several men from the
Fort, including Charles Compo, who had served Samuel
Parker the previous year as an interpreter. Compo, who
was married to a Nez Perce woman and knew the Nez Perce
tongue, was of great value to the mission group. He lived in
the vicinity of Whitman's station for several years and was
frequently in Whitman's employ. The negro, Hinds, also
went out to Waiilatpu, but his physical condition was probably such as to make him of little use.

THE WOMEN AT VANCOUVER

Narcissa and Eliza had spent four happy weeks at Vancouver, waiting for Spalding to return. During this time
they had received much attention from Dr. McLoughlin and
the other residents at the Fort. Narcissa wrote:

Since we have been here, they set a table for us in Dr. McLoughlin's
sitting room, and we have the company of Mrs. Douglas, Miss Maria
(McLaughlin) and two of the Gentlemen. Mr. and Mrs. Beaver occupy
a part of Mr. Finlinson's house; and a Mrs. Carpendel eats by herself
in her own room. . . . [Letter 36.][8]

Mrs. Whitman wrote of the great variety of items on
their menu. She mentioned the various kinds of vegetables,
including tomatoes. There were also wild game, fish, rice,
cheese, and fruit. The fact that she and Mrs. Spalding belonged to the "tee total Society" did not prevent Dr. Mc-
Loughlin and the other gentlemen from raising their glasses

---

[8] Samuel Parker, M.D., the son of the Rev. Samuel Parker, copied
these letters in a manuscript history of the Oregon mission he wrote.
A copy of this is in the library of Cornell University, Ithaca, New
York.

frequently to drink toasts to their lady guests. There must have been some good-natured banter about the table, for Narcissa wrote that the men never gave them the opportunity of refusing the toasts. "We have many talks about drinking wine," she wrote, "but no one joins our society."

The presence of the two cultured white women, especially of Mrs. Whitman, who was more socially inclined than Mrs. Spalding, was an oasis in a desert land to Dr. McLoughlin. He did all within his power to make their sojourn a happy one. He begged Mrs. Whitman to tutor his daughter, which she was glad to do. At his suggestion Narcissa sang to the children of the school for an hour each evening.[9] It is easy to believe that Dr. McLoughlin was present whenever possible for those informal concerts, for he, too, had succumbed to the charms of her sweet voice. Three times in her diary, Narcissa speaks of singing to the children of the school.

I could employ all my time in writing, & work for myself if it were not for his wishes, I sing with the children every evening also, which is considered a favor.

I sing about an hour every evening with the children, teaching them new tunes, at the request of Dr. McLoughlin.

They have improved much in their singing, & learned very many tunes, for the short time I have been here. Dr. thinks it is a great assistance to them, in learning to speak the English language.

Writing to Mr. Parker on October 25, Narcissa referred to the trouble that had already developed between Dr. McLoughlin and his chaplain:

Mr. Beaver arrived only a few days ago, before us. He preached twice every Sabbath, and I wish I might say to the acceptance of the people of Vancouver; but it is otherwise. There is a difficulty between Dr. McLoughlin and this Rev. Mr. Beaver; such that they neither speak to each other. Neither the Dr. nor the Gentlemen of the Fort have attended his services for several Sabbaths past.

Beaver did not remain long at Fort Vancouver. He and his wife returned to England in 1838. In spite of his trouble with his chaplain, Dr. McLoughlin was a deeply religious man. Narcissa wrote in her diary:

The most of the gentlemen of the Fort are Scotch Presbyterian & but very few that are Episcopalians. The great mass of labourers are

---

9 Johnson, *John McLoughlin,* p. 118: "The first school west of the Rocky Mountains was opened by McLoughlin, November 17, 1832." Johnson should have said in the Pacific Northwest, for the Catholics had long been in California, where they no doubt had a few schools for the natives.

Roman Catholics, who have three services during the Sabbath, one of which is attended at this house, in which Dr. McL. officiates in French, translates a sermon or a tract, & reads a chapter in the Bible, & a prayer.

When the missionaries were ready to return to Fort Walla Walla on September 21, it was Dr. McLoughlin who suggested that they seek God's guidance in prayer, and he joined his petitions with theirs.[10]

As time permitted the women wrote or sewed or made other preparations for their return to the upper Columbia country. Occasionally they rode horseback. One day Mrs. McLoughlin sought to persuade the white women to give up the sidesaddles and ride astride like the native women. Of this suggestion Narcissa wrote in her diary: "We have never seen the necessity of changing our fashion."

In one of Narcissa's letters we obtain a good idea of the conditions and difficulties of shopping at Vancouver. She wrote:

The Company let us have goods as cheap as can be afforded & cheaper probably than we can get them from the States. They only charged us a hundred per cent more than the prime cost, or England prices. All their goods are of the best quality & will be durable. Husband has obtained a good stove of Mr. Pambrun of W. W. & we take up sheet iron enough for the pipe. My tinware has all been made within a week past of the first rate block tin. I have only six large milk pans, coffe & tea pots, Candlesticks & moles, covered pails & a baker, very good, the first of the fashon seen here, etc. etc.

And besides this the blacksmiths have all been employed in making our farming utensils, etc. and are mostly or quite finished, so that we shall be able to have our accounts closed & goods boxed ready to leave tomorrow.

There are a few deficiencies in the cloth line. No provisions is made for beding, except blankets & these are dear. No sheets, nothing for shirting except striped calico. I have found a piece of bleach linen which I take for sheets, the only one in the store price 75 cents per yard. I miss the cotton batting for quilts & comfortables very much, but can make the blankets do me very well, only it will be heavy washing for they are all white. [Letter 38.]

Narcissa was also disappointed in not finding geese either at Fort Walla Walla or Fort Vancouver, but managed to secure enough feathers from wild fowl for a feather bed, which was ready when Spalding returned to Vancouver on October 18 to escort the women up the river. The feather bed was highly valued a hundred years ago. It was one of the insignia of culture. Frequently a feather bed was

---

[10] Spalding to Greene, Sept. 20, 1836.

given by the mother of the bride at her wedding. Women boasted of the number of feather beds they owned, and sometimes an obituary notice would contain such a record. The fact that Narcissa managed to acquire a feather bed in Oregon indicates a high cultural status.[11]

Before leaving Vancouver Narcissa copied her diary for her husband's mother. Both were left at the Fort ready to be sent on the first boat that would sail for the States. In her closing words she referred to her health: "I think every time I look into the glass, if Mother could see me now, she would not think my cheek bones were very prominent." She made a plea for letters. Her last paragraph was as follows:

> Husband is so filled with business that he writes but little. He often speaks of writing you, but says I must write *for* him, until he is less hurried in his business. He is far away now, poor darling! Three hundred miles, (if I had wings I would fly). I intended to have written this so plainly that Father & Mother could read it. Adieu!
>
> NARCISSA WHITMAN

Two boats loaded with supplies and passengers left Fort Vancouver, Thursday noon, November 3. Mr. McLeod and Mrs. Whitman were in one boat, and the Spaldings were in the other. Eight of the boatmen were Iroquois Indians. The rainy season had begun. On October 22, Narcissa noted in her diary that the rain which fell that day was the first she had seen since the 22nd of July. It rained again on the 4th and 5th of November. On the 6th it rained all day. The women succeeded in keeping dry by staying under oilcloth. Of that return trip Narcissa wrote:

> At night, when a great fire was made, our tents pitched and the cloth spread for tea, all was pleasant and comfortable. I rolled my bed and blankets in my India-rubber cloak, which preserved them quite well from the rain, so that nights I slept warm and comfortable as ever. My featherbed was of essential service to me in keeping my health this rainy voyage. [Letter 39.]

They arrived at Fort Walla Walla on Sunday, November 13, after a disagreeable trip of ten days. Whitman and Gray were working at the mission site, where they remained until the 18th. Whitman had secured the services of two Hawai-

---

[11] There were grades of feather beds. The most desirable was the goose-feather bed, next the hen-feather bed, and last of all the turkey-feather bed. There was also a language of feather beds. It was considered inhospitable to put a guest, especially a woman, in a room without a feather bed. If a guest wore out his or her welcome, the fact could be made known by substituting a straw tick for the feather bed. The guest would be sure to go the next day.

ians by courtesy of the Hudson's Bay Company, who brought the Islanders to Oregon as laborers.[12] Hinds, the colored man, died some time after the 18th. "Already," wrote Narcissa to her mother on December 8, "death has entered our home, and laid one low." [Letter 39.]

The women spent the week beginning November 13 as the guests of Mr. Pambrun at Fort Walla Walla. Mrs. Whitman busied herself in teaching Mrs. Pambrun and her daughter Maria to read. Of this she wrote: "We consider it a very kind providence to be situated near one family so interesting, and a native female that promises to be so much society for me. She is learning to speak the English language quite fast." [Letter 39.]

Whitman returned to the Fort on the 18th, and on Sunday all five of the missionaries were together again for a religious service. On Tuesday of that week the Spaldings and Gray left for Lapwai. About 125 Nez Perces formed the escort. It was a long and colorful cavalcade that left the Fort that day, for, in addition to the Indians, Spalding took with him eight head of cattle, his share of the small herd driven from the States. His baggage, totaling about two and a half tons, was loaded on some twenty horses. The Spaldings expected to live in a buffalo-skin lodge until a suitable dwelling could be erected.

Mrs. Whitman remained with the Pambruns until her husband had time to finish the house he was building. Being a physician, he realized the necessity of giving her the best possible care, so he labored from early in the morning till late at night on the rude dwelling which was to be their home.

THE WAIILATPU HOME

On Friday, December 9, Whitman returned to the Fort for his wife. The next day he escorted her to Waiilatpu and for the first time she gazed upon the spot which was to be her home for eleven years. Let her describe for us her first impressions:

Dec. 26th,—Where are we now, and who are we that we should be thus blessed of the Lord? I can scarcely believe that we are thus comfortably fixed, and keeping house, so soon after our marriage, when considering what was then before us. We arrived here on the tenth—distance, twenty-five miles from Walla Walla.

---

[12] The Hawaiians were called Owyhees. One of the counties in Idaho received its name from this source.

Found a house reared and the lean-to enclosed, a good chimney and fireplace, and the floor laid. No windows or door except blankets. My heart truly leaped for joy as I alighted from my horse, entered and seated myself before a pleasant fire (for it was now night.)

The next day she was able to view her surroundings in the daylight. About four hundred yards to the northeast was a hill some two hundred feet high, which is cone-shaped when viewed from that angle. From the top of that hill Narcissa could have found a good view of the surrounding country. From that vantage point she could have traced out the course of the Walla Walla River as it curled in a half loop around the south and west sides of the acreage which her husband had selected. Fifteen miles or more to the south and east were the tree-covered slopes of the Blue Mountains, the upper parts of which were then covered with snow.[13]

Today the Whitman monument crowns the top of that hill.

In another journal letter for her mother, started December 5, Narcissa described her location and summed it up with these words: "It is indeed a lovely situation." From the unpublished portion of this letter we can glean many interesting facts regarding that first American home to be established west of the Rocky Mountains.

On Friday, December 16, Narcissa wrote:

Mr. Pambrun sent us a table & window sashes which he kindly offered to get made for us. The sashes were made with a crooked knife by a frenchman. I have taken the liberty to prime them & set some of the lights, & while engaged in it thought a great deal about *Father* how handily he used to do such work, & could have wish him here to assist in many things difficult & perplexing to hands unacquainted.

There was so much to do and so few to do it! The Whitmans soon learned that they could not depend upon the Cayuses for manual labor. Spalding was more fortunate in that respect, for the Nez Perces were eager to assist.

The winter of 1836-37 was unusually severe. Snow began to fall on the 16th of December, and before the storm had passed eighteen inches had fallen. This snow remained

---

[13] Whitman letter No. 39. This letter was started on Dec. 5, 1836, and included entries for many days until March 30, 1837. The letter was supposed to have been published in full in the *T.O.P.A.* for 1891, but a comparison with the original shows that about twelve thousand words of the most interesting part were omitted. Hulbert and Hulbert, *Marcus Whitman*, likewise omits this section, for they followed the *T.O.P.A.* version. The full letter is to be found printed in the March, 1937, issue of *O.H.Q.*

on the ground for several weeks. Lapwai likewise reported an eighteen-inch fall at the same time. The Spaldings were then living in the Indian lodge, and did not move into their home until December 23. As late as February 16, 1837, Spalding reported to Greene that his house lacked "two doors, two windows, and a part of the under floor." Gray assisted Spalding until the 28th and then returned to Fort Walla Walla.

Gray met Mr. and Mrs. Francis Payette at the Fort and with Mr. Payette rode out to Waiilatpu to see the Whitmans on Wednesday, January 4. In his journal, Gray wrote:

> We remained with him fixing his doors, etc. the 5th, 6th, 7th and over Sabbath, the 8th; during Sabbath evening the Doctor and I had a long conversation about the past.[14]

Gray and Payette returned to the Fort the next day.

It is difficult to deduce from the available source material an accurate picture of the Whitman home. It appears that Whitman and Gray had started to build a house thirty by thirty-six feet, but soon discovered that they would be unable to complete a building of that size before winter. Perhaps one wall was finished and the frame erected before Whitman decided to confine his efforts to the building of a lean-to, which seems to have measured twelve by thirty feet. In Whitman's first letter to Greene, written from Waiilatpu, May 5, 1837, he had this to say about his house:

> Brother Gray & myself commenced to build at Wiiletpoo 14th Oct. The frame of my house is thirty by 36 built in a substantial manner with good chambers. The leanto only is finished making two bed rooms kitchen and pantry. We commenced house keeping the 10th Dec. The remainder of my house I intend to finish in the fall.

A good description of their home is to be found in Narcissa's journal letter to her mother under the date of February 18. This entry throws so much light upon their manner of living that it is here quoted in full:

> Feb 18th Anniversary of our Marriage. I find it perfectly natural to suffer my thoughts to dwell upon scenes that transpired one year ago from the present time. One year, since I have heard a lisp even of my beloved friends in Angelica, & who can tell how many are sleeping in their graves by this time. Ah! it would be like cold water to a thirsty soul indeed, to know how you all do. It is delightful weather now; The birds sing sweetly, & the frogs croak; familiar sounds these; the same I used to hear in my native land. The Husbandmen are making arrangements for plowing immediately. The snow remained only

---

[14] *W.C.Q.*, June, 1913, contains Gray's *Journal*.

about six weeks upon the ground, Feb. so far, has been as warm, and pleasant as April at home, even more so.

In addition to my other conveniences we have now 3 chairs & a bedstead. & all our doors are made & hanging. These are exceeding comfortable although not of the finest order. My chairs two of them are of my Husband making; with deer skin bottoms woven as the Fancy chairs of the States are & very durable. Our bedstead is made of rough boards & nailed to the wall, according to the fashion of the country.

Perhaps a more minute description of our house is demanded. The upright part is a story & half, faces the east. As I said before the leantoo only is enclosed. The siding is made of split logs fitted into grooved posts. & the spaces filled with mud. The roof is made of poles, first covered with straw then with 5 or 6 inches of mud. The fire place & chimney is of the same. The size of the whole building is 30 by 36 feet, the leantoo 12 feet between joints. My room is in the south end of it, a small bedroom & pantry on the north end, and a very pleasant kitchen in the Middle. On the west side of the kitchen, is the fire place with a twelve lighted window on each side, & the outer door. At present the Indians have full liberty to visit the kitchen, but as soon as we are able to prepare a separate room for them, they will not be allowed to come in any other part of the house at all.

You will scarcely think it possible that I should have such a convenience as a barrel to pound my clothes in for washing so soon; in this part of the world, & probably mine with Mrs. Pambrun are the only two this side of the Rocky Mountains. I am indebted to her for mine, & she never knew the use of one, untill I suggested it. I am not without a dog and good cat even. My dog was a present from Mr. McLeoud. These may appear small subjects to fill a letter with, but my object is to show you that people can live here, & as comfortably too as in many places east of the mountains. A few lodges of Indians have come to this place & the whole tribe will be here before many weeks.

Whitman received a small heating stove from Pambrun on January 2, by which they were able to keep their rude dwelling quite comfortable. Indeed Narcissa wrote that she suffered less from the cold that winter than in many winters spent in New York State.

FOOD SUPPLIES

Until the first harvest was gathered in, both the Whitmans and the Spaldings were dependent upon the Indians and the Hudson's Bay Company for food. The Indians furnished wild game and fish, for which the missionaries sometimes paid. Spalding had eight head of cattle, including the bull and two calves, while Whitman had five cows. Two of the cows calved about the first of February, so after that they had plenty of milk. [Letter 41.] In the letters of 1837, written to the Board by members of the mission, mention is made of chickens and pigs. These must have been purchased from the Hudson's Bay Company.

Writing to her mother on May 2, 1837, Narcissa said that they had brought with them "a good supply of pork, flour, butter, etc., from Vancouver," and had secured corn and potatoes at Walla Walla. She also reported that up to that date ten wild horses had been butchered to supply meat for their family, including their hired men, and for their visitors. She wrote:

This will make you pity us, but you had better save your pity for more worthy subjects. I do not prefer it to other meat, but can eat it very well when we have nothing else.

On May 10, 1839, Whitman wrote in a letter to Greene: "We have killed and eaten twenty-three or four horses since we have been here."

While in Cincinnati, the men purchased seven dollars' worth of seeds, which they intended to take with them over the mountains. These seeds may have been part of that which was scattered along the way. When Whitman wrote to Parker on October 8, he suggested that Mr. Parker might send "all kinds of grains and seeds for experiment and variety, and particularly a large quantity of seeds of the locust, chestnut, and walnut trees." [Letter 32.] About the same time Narcissa also wrote:

Husband has sent for the seeds of the Large Locust, Chestnut and Walnut trees. I should like to have the butternut included, for experiment.

When Brother Weld comes, please remember and fill his pockets with peaches, plums and pear seeds, some of the best kinds, and some good apple seeds. What they have here is not of the best kind, nor a great variety. Another very important article for us housewives, some broom corn seed. We brought a little, but we are afraid it will not do well. They have nothing of the kind here, but use hemlock boughs for broom. Hemlock, I say, there is no such tree known here. It is balsam. [Letter 34.]

While at Vancouver, Narcissa carefully saved all of the seeds of the grapes and apples which she ate. "This is a rule at Vancouver," she wrote in her diary, and added: "I have got collected before me an assortment of garden seeds, I take up with me, also, I intend taking some young sprouts of Apple, peach & grapes, & some strawberry vines, etc. from the nursery here."

Whitman in his letter to Greene of May 5, 1837, reported on his agricultural activities. He began plowing the first week of March. He wrote:

I have two acres of peas sowed 9 acres of corn planted & intend to plant 3 more & have planted & intend to plant 2 acres of potatoes, in all 16 acres. If associates come I think they will have little to fear for want of provisions. I hope to obtain wheat for fall sowing.

Whitman lent fifteen hoes to the Indians and encouraged them to make a beginning of agriculture. In this letter he reported that he had been obliged to expel Richard, one of the boys he took East with him in 1835, from his house for bad conduct. John went with the Spaldings. The two boys were able to help some in interpreting. John died a year or so later, and Richard thereafter remained unmentioned in the Whitman correspondence.[15] Thus we find that Whitman's experiment of giving the two boys special training by taking them East did not prove to be very successful.

Unfortunately, we have but three Whitman letters written in 1837, and none of these were written in the fall of that year. From a letter of Mrs. Whitman's, written April 11, 1838, we learn that her husband harvested about 250 bushels of potatoes and 200 bushels of corn, besides an abundance of garden vegetables. However, because Spalding's crop that year was not very successful and because of the demand of the Indians for seed, the Whitmans were very sparing in the use of what they had raised. Mrs. Whitman wrote that they had refrained from eating peas, had taken but few potatoes, but had used freely of the corn. Whitman had received but little assistance from the Indians, so most of the labor of cultivating his fields rested on his own shoulders.

By the fall of 1838 the gardens, both at Lapwai and at Waiilatpu, were producing in such abundance that the missionaries felt free to use the products of their fields without restraint. The food problem was then solved. A few years later they were able to butcher hogs and cattle. Sheep were introduced from the Hawaiian Islands in 1838. The small band of eight head quickly multiplied, for the ewes were able to drop their lambs twice a year.

Gray was a disappointment to both Whitman and Spalding. After returning from Lapwai, he spent several weeks at Fort Walla Walla. On February 1 Whitman visited the Fort, and Gray returned with him to Waiilatpu and remained

---

[15] Spalding to Parker, Feb. 21, 1837: "The Dr's boy ran away last fall, taking considerable property; which with the clothing and books given him, in the States, he has gambled away. He is a profane, gambling youth." Parker MS., Cornell Univ., Ithaca, N. Y. Eells, *Marcus Whitman*, p. 30: "After the death of Dr. Whitman Richard was appointed Chief by Indian Agent H. A. G. Lee, but later was killed by another Indian."

there until the 9th. He then went back to Fort Walla Walla, where he met Francis Ermatinger, of the Hudson's Bay Company, and the two went to Fort Vancouver in the latter part of February. Gray was restless and wanted his own station. He had written to Greene from Vancouver the previous September, suggesting the possibility of making an exploring trip for the Board.[16] Without waiting for the approval of those plans, Gray went ahead and made arrangements to go with Ermatinger through the Flathead country in the spring of 1837.

Gray returned to Walla Walla on March 14, and after a short visit to the Whitman station, was on his way to Spokane Falls. The heavy snow delayed him, but he arrived there on the 29th. Spalding also visited Spokane, arriving there on March 31.[17] He was en route to Fort Colville, where he hoped to get some swine and some seeds. Gray proposed to Spalding his plan of taking some horses back to the States and bringing out more cattle. Gray also spoke of his intention to return to Boston and see if the Board would not send out more workers. Four Nez Perces with some Indian horses were to go with Gray as far as the frontier. This trip of Gray's, about which Whitman appears not to have been consulted, resulted in much grief for him and the mission. Of this, mention will be made later.

RELIGIOUS ACTIVITIES

The Whitmans found that their mission site was on the ground claimed by Chief Umtippe of the Cayuses, whom Narcissa described as being "a savage creature in his day." She also wrote:

His heart is still the same; full of all manner of hypocracy deceit and guile. He is a mortal beggar as all Indians are. If you ask a favour of him, sometimes it is granted or not just as he feels, if granted it must be well paid for. A few days ago he took it into his head to require pay for teaching us the language & forbid his people from coming & talking with us for fear we should learn a few words of them.[18]

Even before the missionaries arrived, the Indians were accustomed to assemble twice a day for daily devotions.

---

[16] Gray to Greene, Sept. 19, 1836.

[17] Hulbert and Hulbert, *Marcus Whitman*, p. 282, footnote, states that the site of Gray's and Spalding's meeting was unidentified. They met at Spokane.

[18] Whitman letter No. 39, from the portion not published in the *T.O.P.A.*, 1891.

Samuel Parker may have been responsible for this, yet Narcissa wrote:

The Cayuses as well as the Nez Perces are very strict in attending to their worship which they have regularly every morning at daybreak & eve at twilight, and once on the Sab. They sing & repeat a form of prayer very devoutly after which the Chief gives them a talk. The tunes & prayers were taught them by a Roman Catholic trader. Indeed their worship was commenced by him. [Letter 39.]

Narcissa may have here referred to Pambrun, the Hudson's Bay trader in charge of the post at Walla Walla, who was a devout Catholic.

On Sunday, March 6, Narcissa noted that their Indian congregation had grown considerably, because of the return of many of the natives. "Last eve," she wrote, "our room was full of men & boys, who come every eve to learn to sing." The whole tribe would have come to the room if it had been large enough. She wrote: "Indeed I should not attempt to sing with them, were it not for the assistance my Husband renders. You will recollect when he was in Angelica he could not sing a single tune." That must have been a disappointment to Narcissa. Gray wrote that Mrs. Whitman found considerable enjoyment on the trip across the country in teaching her husband to sing.[19] Her perseverance was sufficiently rewarded in that Dr. Whitman was able to lead in the singing of several tunes. "This," wrote Narcissa, "saves me a great deal of hard singing." [Letter 39.]

In Whitman's report to Greene of May 5, 1837, he stated that the Cayuses showed a strong desire to be taught, but that little had been accomplished outside of teaching them to sing. Marcus and Narcissa were still laboring under an imperfect understanding of the language. A mountain of difficulties had piled up before them. The Indians seemed to be constantly on the move. They had no building large enough to accommodate them in a comfortable worship service. They had no school building, no books, and no other helpers to assist them. Marcus had a farm to cultivate with very little help there, while Narcissa had her household duties, and was likewise handicapped by the lack of competent assistants.

ALICE CLARISSA

On the evening of Narcissa's twenty-ninth birthday, or on March 14, 1837, a daughter was born to the Whitmans. They named her Alice after the mother and sister of Marcus,

---

[19] Gray, *Oregon*, p. 109.

and Clarissa after the mother and a sister of Narcissa. She was the first white child born of American parents west of the Rockies.

Mrs. Pambrun was present at the time of the birth but was not able to render much assistance, on account of her ignorance of the ways of white people. Narcissa described the dressing of the babe by her husband and Mrs. Pambrun as follows:

> It would have made you smile to see them work over the little creature. Mrs. P. never saw one dressed before as we dress them, having been accustomed to dress her own in the native style. I was able to lend a helping hand and arrange the clothes for them, etc. Between us all, it was done very well.

> Thus, you see, beloved sisters, how the missionary does in heathen lands. No mother, no sister, to relieve me of a single care—only an affectionate husband, who, as a physician and nurse, exceeds all I ever knew. [Letter 40.]

Narcissa called her babe "a treasure invaluable."

Dr. Whitman was exceedingly busy during the days of his wife's confinement. Mrs. Pambrun was not very well, and in addition had her two children with her, so she was of little assistance. He found it necessary even to attend to the washing of the clothes himself. During the week the Indians returned from a hunting expedition, so that the mission house was "thronged with company," to use Narcissa's expression. Moreover, it was seedtime, and Dr. Whitman was trying to teach the Indians the first principles of agriculture. He had started plowing the first week of March and was eager to get his seed into the ground.

With the responsibility of caring for Narcissa and the child, the supervision of the house and the fields, and the entertainment of guests all resting upon the broad shoulders of Marcus, it is no wonder that Narcissa wrote: "He was excessively pressed with care and labor during the whole time of my confinement."

Narcissa in her letter to her parents, dated March 30, gave the following description of the child:

> Her hair is light brown, and we think she will be like her aunts Jane and Harriet. She is plump and large, holds her head up finely, and looks about considerably. She weighs ten pounds.

The Indians were intensely interested. In the above-mentioned letter, Narcissa wrote:

> The little stranger is visited daily by the chiefs and principal men in camp, and the women throng the house continually waiting an op-

portunity to see her. Her whole appearance is new to them. Her complexion, her size and dress, etc., all excite a great deal of wonder; for they never raise a child here except they are lashed tight to a board, and the girls' heads undergo the flattening process.

Among the chiefs who called was Tiloukaikt, who told Mrs. Whitman that the child should be called a "Cayuse te-mi (Cayuse girl)," because she was born on "Cayuse wai-tis (Cayuse land)." [Letter 40.] He told her that the Indians of all the surrounding country had expected the baby's coming and that the whole tribe was very much pleased. Nearly eleven years later it was that same chief, Tiloukaikt, who took a leading part in the final tragedy.[20]

Mrs. Whitman made a rapid recovery. Within a week she was up again and dressed, and by the 26th she was able to walk out of doors. [Letter 41.] Mrs. Pambrun returned to the Fort on the 24th but left her twelve-year-old daughter, Maria, with Mrs. Whitman to be taught the English language. Dr. Whitman requested Dr. McLoughlin to send up one of the orphan girls from the school at Vancouver. In due time a sixteen-year-old girl arrived, who appeared no larger than one of twelve years. "You have no idea," wrote Narcissa to her family, "how difficult it is to realize any benefit from those who do not understand you." The two Hawaiians who worked for Whitman sometimes assisted in housework as well as in outside tasks.

---

[20] Whitman letter 46 gives the identification: "He is the Indian Teloukike, that gave our baby the name of Cayuse tenni, spoken of in a former letter."

CHAPTER NINE

THE VERSATILE DOCTOR

1837-1838

THE WHITMANS at Waiilatpu, like the Spaldings at Lapwai, lived and labored alone for nearly two years after their arrival. The restless Gray left Spokane on April 5 for the States; consequently many of the tasks which he was supposed to do were of necessity passed to the doctor and the minister. Both Whitman and Spalding found that they had to spend much of their time in manual work. Fortunately, both men were versatile and could turn their hands with success to many different tasks. Whitman was not only the mission doctor; he was also farmer, carpenter, miller, teacher, and preacher, as occasion demanded.

With infinite patience and unending love the Whitmans and the Spaldings gave themselves to a people far below them in culture—literally to wild, ignorant savages.

Our chief source of information regarding the kind of life the Whitmans lived at Waiilatpu is to be found in the correspondence of the members of the mission. It is rather amazing to realize that about three hundred of the letters the Whitmans wrote are still extant.[1] Nearly sixty of this number were sent to the American Board, and, fortunately for us, the American Board has the habit of keeping the correspondence of its missionaries. However, most of the letters which we have were sent to individuals. Many of these letters went around South America, while others were carried overland by trappers or by the Hudson's Bay express. These letters have survived the vicissitudes of a century and after being passed from one generation to another are now, for the most part, safely cared for in the archives of such institutions as the Oregon Historical Society and Whitman College.

We turn to such letters to find information regarding the three major activities of Dr. Whitman during those first two years; namely, the medical, the agricultural, and the educational.

---

[1] *See* Appendix 1 for the catalog of the Whitman letters.

WHITMAN THE DOCTOR

Although Whitman was sent out primarily as a missionary physician, we find that he rarely referred to the details of his work in his letters. In his letters to the Board he would sometimes refer to the health of his associates, but seldom would he refer to the ailments of the natives. Here even Narcissa fails us. If the theory of her father's being a Thomsonian is correct, then we can understand why she would hesitate to say much about her husband's medical work to the members of her family. Under such circumstances the tactful thing was to say nothing about a subject over which there was such pronounced disagreement. However, we do find a few statements of a general nature which throw some light upon the conditions which Whitman faced as a missionary doctor.

Both the Nez Perces and the Cayuses had their medicine men, whom they called *tud-ah-tee-wats* or *te-wats*. Like all medicine men of primitive peoples, they relied upon sorcery, superstition, and deception for their cures. In one of Narcissa's first letters to her Eastern home she described in detail an experience with old Chief Umtippe, which, incidentally, throws much light upon the superstitions of the Indians.

Early in the spring of 1837 a number of Indians "were taken sick with an inflamation of the lungs." Among the afflicted was the wife of Chief Umtippe, who nearly died. Narcissa wrote:

For a season they were satisfied with my husband's attention, and were doing well; but when they would over-eat themselves, or go into a relapse from unnecessary exposure, then they must have their te-wat doctors; say that the medicine was bad, and all was bad. Their te-wat is the same species of juggling as practiced by the Pawnees, which Mr. Dunbar describes—playing the fool over them, and giving no medicine. They employed them over and over again, but they remained the same. Soon they became weary of these, and must have a more noted one. [Letter 41.]

Chief Umtippe was greatly concerned over the condition of his wife and bluntly told Dr. Whitman that if she died while under his care "he should kill him." That threat rested back upon an Indian custom. Frequently the *te-wat* was killed when the patient died. The threat came at the beginning of the Whitman residence at Waiilatpu, and pointed like a dark shadowy finger across the eleven years to the final tragedy, when the life of "the white *te-wat*" was indeed taken. "The contest," wrote Narcissa, "has been sharp between him and the Indians, and husband was nearly sick with the excitement and care of them."

Chief Umtippe, losing faith in Dr. Whitman, called in a famous *te-wat* from the Walla Walla Indians, who came and after chanting his incantations pronounced the woman well. But, alas, the next day she was worse. The presence of the *te-wat* relieved Dr. Whitman of responsibility. Chief Umtippe went into a rage over the Walla Walla *te-wat's* failure and declared that he ought to be killed. Fortunately for the *te-wat*, the woman recovered.

However, a little later this grim superstition of the Indians wrought its vengeance upon him. Narcissa described the incident as follows:

Last Saturday the war chief died at Walla Walla. He was a Cayuse, and a relative of Umtippe; was sick but six days; employed the same Walla Walla te-wat Umtippe sent for, but he died in his hands. The same day Ye-he-kis-kis, a younger brother of Umtippe, went to Walla Walla; arrived about twilight, and shot the te-wat dead. Thus they are avenged. [Letter 41.]

About that time Chief Umtippe himself was taken ill and went to Dr. Whitman for medicine. "Notwithstanding all his villany," wrote Narcissa, "he came to my husband to be doctored. He was very sick, and we thought he would die; but the medicine given him soon relieved him."

In one of Spalding's letters we find mention of the many cases of lung complaint among the Indians occasioned by "bare feet in the wet and snow." Another common trouble was due to overeating. When food was plentiful, the Indians would gorge themselves, and then perhaps half starve before more food would be found. They alternated between feasts and famines. For gluttony Spalding prescribed cathartics, a simple and effective remedy.[2]

On Monday, May 1, 1837, another influential chief visited Dr. Whitman and asked for medical attention. He was Stickus, who proved to be a valuable and faithful friend. Stickus was to Whitman what Timothy was to Spalding. Narcissa called him "an excellent Indian," and stated that he was half convinced that the methods of the *te-wats* were all wrong. The Whitmans took Stickus into their home, where they could supervise the treatment. At times Stickus was doubtful of the efficacy of the new method. The Whitmans were as sympathetic as possible for they realized the

---

[2] Warren, *Memoirs*, pp. 72 ff.

struggle involved, and the risk they ran if Stickus died.

Throughout Tuesday and Wednesday, Stickus remained in the Whitman home. Narcissa sat up late Wednesday night to minister to the sick Indian's needs. It was then that she finished her long newsy letter of May 2 to her parents. In that letter she made the plea for additional workers, a plea which is to be found in nearly every letter the Whitmans sent home.

> Who will come over and help us? Weak, frail nature cannot endure excessive care and anxiety any great length of time, without fall under it. I refer more particularly to my husband. His labor this spring has affected his health considerably. His old complaint in his side affects him occasionally.

The letter closes with this postscript:

> You are indebted to little Alice Clarissa's quiet disposition for this sheet. I have no cradle yet, and she has lain in my lap all day; for she does not like to be where she cannot see her mother, long at a time. She receives many kisses for her grandparents, uncles and aunts, every day. She is now in bed with her father, sleeping sweetly. She is pleasant company for me here alone.
>
> One o'clock, and I retire, leave the sick Indian to himself the remainder of the night. [Letter 41.]

Stickus recovered, and it may be that his abiding friendship to the Whitmans can be traced back to the tender care he received in their home at this time. Years later it was Stickus who guided the first great emigration over the Blue Mountains, and a few years after that it was Stickus who warned Dr. Whitman that certain Indians had "a bad heart."

WHITMAN THE FARMER

Both Whitman and Spalding saw the necessity of teaching the Indians the arts of civilization. There were two outstanding reasons. In the first place, the type of life the Indians followed gave them a precarious livelihood. The buffalo east of the mountains were being slaughtered by the thousands. The missionaries saw that the day was coming when the wild life would not furnish sufficient meat for the Indians. Narcissa wrote: "We are anxious to give them the means of procuring their provisions in a more easy way, so that there may be less starving ones during the winter." [Letter 46.] It was therefore necessary to teach them to cultivate the soil.

In the second place, any consistent educational or religious work was made extremely difficult when the tribe was constantly on the move. The sensible plan was to settle the

Indians. Hence Whitman's interest in agriculture was two-
fold. By it he expected to raise much of his own food, and
by it he hoped to change the habits of the Indians, to whom
he had dedicated his life.

Whitman found the soil and the climate admirably fitted
for agricultural purposes. He had a plow for his own use
the first spring, but had only hoes to give to the Indians.
Whitman wrote to Greene in May, 1837, asking for more
hoes. A year later, he wrote again, saying in part:

I have written to several gentlemen of my acquaintance to send us
fifty ploughs & three hundred hoes, & in case of failure I have ordered
my Brother to appropriate two hundred dollars on my account to that
object. But this is not enough, what are three hundred hoes & fifty
ploughs. We ought to have at least seventy five or one hundred ploughs
& six hundred hoes immediately to save this starving multitude from
an untimely grave.

He also added:

Had I one doubt of the disposition of the Indians to cultivate I
would not thus write: But having seen them for two seasons breaking
ground with hoes & stickes & having given them trial of the plough,
I feel an entire confidence in their disposition & ability. [Letter 48.]

The fact that Whitman stood ready to contribute two
hundred dollars from his meager resources proves his faith
in his endeavors to settle the Indians. The first year Whitman boasted of having sixteen acres under cultivation. Reporting on his activities for the second spring, Whitman
wrote: "I have six acres of potatoes two & half of wheat &
peas oats & corn enough to make forty acres probably." It
is assumed that this acreage did not include the lands cultivated by the Indians.

At first no question was raised about the proprietary
rights of the land. The Indians had never cultivated, and
hence the idea of private ownership was never raised. Later
this was an issue which caused Whitman considerable
trouble. The Indians who cultivated the first year found that
some of their own number helped themselves to the crops
raised. The next spring all who planted were anxious to
cultivate in the vicinity of Waiilatpu, where Whitman could
watch their crops, "for," wrote Whitman, "they say the
Indians fear me but do not fear them." [Letter 43.] This
fear of others' stealing from them was a real hindrance in
the development of Whitman's agricultural program.

WHITMAN THE TEACHER

Whitman's educational and religious activities can be considered together. Before much could be done along these lines, it was first necessary for the Whitmans to master the language. This was a difficult task, for the language had never been reduced to writing, and they had no trained teachers to assist them. Richard, from whom they expected much, proved to be unworthy and was expelled from the Whitman home. Chief Umtippe tried to force Whitman to pay for instruction. In the winter of 1838-39, Chief Lawyer of the Nez Perces tutored the members of the re-enforcement of 1838. It is altogether possible that Whitman had discovered this man's ability as a teacher, and had already used him in that capacity.

By the fall of 1837 the Whitmans had sufficient mastery of the language to begin a school and to give some consistent religious instruction. Writing on April 11, 1838, Narcissa declared: "We have had a school for them for about four months past, & much of the time our kitchen has been crowded & all seem very much attached." Spalding had made a beginning in the reduction of the language to writing and had submitted a primer of some seventy-two pages to the Whitmans for their approval. Mrs. Whitman copied this primer before the original was sent to the American Board mission in the Sandwich Islands to be printed. Whitman knew that a printing press was there, because his friend, Elisha Loomis, had taken one out to the Islands in 1820. Later it was discovered that the alphabet which Spalding devised was not adaptable. The primer sent to the Islands was never published there in full; only a few proof sheets were run off.

Whitman sent the following description of their religious services to Greene on March 12, 1838:

We have two meetings for the Indians on the Sabbath & in the evening what we call a sabbath school for the children & youth. The attention on religious instruction is good & solemn. Worship is strictly maintained in the principal lodges morning & evening. Lately I have been explaining the ten Commandments & our saviours first & great commandment to which they listen with great attention & from their inquiries I think they understand them. They say they do not worship Idols but still I think many of their traditions are evidences of idolatrous worship of some Animals & Birds. [Letter 43.]

Narcissa pointed out one interesting reaction to an educated conscience. "Some feel almost to blame us," she wrote, "for telling them about eternal realities. One said it was good when they knew nothing but to hunt, eat, drink & sleep, now it was bad." [Letter 46.]

Names, for the most part from the Bible, were given to the children who attended school. Among these children were two sons and a daughter of Tiloukaikt. Narcissa named them Edward, David, and Jane. She induced Mrs. Pambrun to name her baby, born in August, 1837, Harriet. And then Narcissa was able to write: "Pa and Ma will see that I have my Jane, my Mary, and my Harriet, too." [Letter 46.] Sometimes names of old friends in the East were bestowed upon the Indians. Narcissa had a girl helping her with the housework whom she called Sarah Hull, after the wife of her pastor, the Rev. Leverett Hull.

The Indians were like children in many ways. They were capricious, now dutiful and obedient, again petulant and threatening. They had the idea that manual labor was beneath their dignity and were fearful that the missionaries would make the children work if sent to school. "Gratitude," wrote Narcissa, "has no place in their hearts." [Letter 46.] On the other hand, Narcissa spoke of their respect for property. "I have let my clothes remain out over night, feeling just as safe in doing it as I used to in Prattsburgh." [Letter 11.] Even the extent of the family wash later became a focal point of trouble, for the Indians looked with envious eyes upon what they considered the excessive amount of clothing owned by the Whitmans.

In Whitman's letter of March 12, 1838, he made reference to Cayuse Halket, who had been sent to the Red River mission school where Winnipeg, Canada, is now located. In 1825, Sir George Simpson of the Hudson's Bay Company sent two boys, one from the Spokane tribe and the other from the Kootenai tribe, to this school. Each was given the name of his tribe and the name of a Hudson's Bay official. The former was called Spokane Garry[3] and the latter Kootenai Pelly. According to one report, these two boys returned to their people in 1828 and took back with them to the Red River school five more boys from as many different tribes. One of these was from the Cayuse Indian tribe and was called Cayuse Halket.[4]

In 1834 Cayuse Halket returned to his people, but, being unhappy with the lot of his people and their manner of life,

---

[3] Drury, *Spalding*, pp. 76 ff.
[4] Tucker, *The Rainbow in the North*, pp. 70-71.

he went back to the mission school, where he died some two years later.[5] Dr. McLoughlin wrote to Mr. Spalding on November 28, 1837, saying in part:

In my opinion, Indians ought never to be taken from their Lands to a Civilised Country, as they will see so many things new to them, that they may form very mistaken opinions, and if any thing happens to displease them, they may give those who take them there an Immensity of trouble; you see the return we get for sending the young Cayuse Chief [Cayuse Halket] to be educated at Red River, now that he is dead, his Relations, at least some of them give it out that we killed him.[6]

According to William McKay, Halket aroused considerable interest in the Bible among his people when he returned from the mission school. In his letter to Greene of March 12, 1838, Whitman wrote:

The young Cayuse who had been about seven years at the Mission School at Red River died about a year since just as he was about to return to his People We had looked for his return with much interest as he had been home on a visit & behaved very well.

ELIZA SPALDING BORN

Dr. Whitman's letter to Greene of March 12, 1838, and Mrs. Whitman's letter to her parents, written two days later, give us an account of their first visit to the Spalding home at Lapwai, at the time a baby girl was born to the Spaldings. Realizing that the Whitmans would have to bring with them their eight-month-old daughter, Spalding sent three of his Indians to Waiilatpu with a "leather lodge" for the Whitman's use.

The Whitmans left home on Tuesday afternoon, November 7, 1837. Before leaving, Whitman nailed up all of the windows and locked the door of his house. He took with him one of the Hawaiians besides the Indians Spalding had sent. The first day they made ten miles in a rainstorm, then camped for the night. They found the Indian lodge very comfortable, although they suffered somewhat from the smoke of the fire which was built Indian-fashion within the lodge.

On Wednesday they made a good day's journey and camped on the Touchet, a tributary of the Walla Walla

---

[5] Dr. Wm. McKay, *Hist. Synod of Wash.*, p. 231, stated that he thought Halket returned in 1831. Miss Tucker states that he returned in 1834.

[6] Published with the permission of the Governor and Committee of the Hudson's Bay Company. *See* also *T.O.P.A.*, 1891, p. 141, for attitude of Indians when a Nez Perce died at the school in 1841.

River, perhaps to the northeast of what is now Dayton,
Washington. Whitman followed the old trail which connected the Clearwater Valley with Fort Walla Walla. Lewis
and Clark had gone over the same route, long before there
was any fort at Walla Walla, in the spring of 1806.

It rained so much Wednesday night and on Thursday
that they were able to travel but six miles that day. They
camped Thursday night upon the same stream. On the 10th
of November they awoke to see two inches of snow on the
ground. The snow melted during the day, but the traveling
remained rather cold and miserable. It was hard to take a
baby with them on such a trip. That night they camped on
the banks of either the Tucannon or the Pataha Creek; if
on the latter, it would be about where Pomeroy, Washington,
is now.

The next day they passed over a divide, where they encountered both snow and rain until about two o'clock in the
afternoon. The trail led them down to a stream which is now
known as Alpowa Creek, on the banks of which, near its
mouth, Chief Timothy of the Nez Perces had his village.
Timothy called his village Alpowa from the Indian word
meaning "sabbath." His was the sabbath-keeping village.

There at Alpowa the Whitmans found a letter from
Spalding awaiting them, in which he urged them to press on
with all possible haste. Mrs. Whitman described the crossing of the Snake River at Alpowa as follows:

We rode all day in the wind and rain and came to the Snake river
about the middle of the afternoon and thought to stop, but it cleared
away, and after making a fire and warming a little, we started again
and came to the crossing place, and when the sun went down it found
me sitting by the root of a large tree on stones with my babe in my
arms, watching by moonlight the movements in crossing our baggage
and horses. This was the only piece of wood in sight and with a few
bunches of wild sage a fire was made against it to warm me while
waiting to cross. Soon I was seated in a canoe with my babe and
landed across safely. [Letter 44.]

They were then more than twenty miles from Lapwai
but dared to try to finish the journey in the night. The next
day was the Sabbath, and they wanted to reach their destination before that day. After traveling twelve miles in the
night Mrs. Whitman confessed that she was too fatigued to
ride the remaining distance, so they camped on the north
side of the Snake River near the present site of Lewiston,
Idaho. It was agreed that the next day the Whitmans should
continue their journey while the men with the baggage
should follow on Monday.

The Whitmans and the Spaldings had been separated for nearly a year. "It was with no common emotion," wrote Dr. Whitman, "that we met after a years absence & so far as Mrs. Spalding was concerned the year was spent without seeing any civilized friend after Brother Gray left the December previous." The Whitmans were pleased to see how well Spalding had developed his station, working as he had singlehanded except for the aid rendered by the Indians. Mrs. Whitman wrote: "We found Sister Spalding very comfortable and were not a little rejoiced to meet them after a separation of a year."

The baby, a girl, arrived on the morning of Wednesday, November 15. She was the first white child to be born within what is now Idaho, and was the first white child born west of the Rockies of American parentage, who lived to maturity.[7] On Sunday, November 29, Mr. Spalding baptized his daughter and the Whitman child, and administered the Sacrament of the Lord's Supper, "a blessing," wrote Narcissa, "which we have not enjoyed since we sat at the table with our beloved friends in Angelica on the eve of our marriage." [Letter 44.] The Whitmans spent about three weeks at Lapwai, remaining until Mrs. Spalding was strong enough to carry on her domestic duties.

The weather remained cold and disagreeable during the time the Whitmans were with the Spaldings. Narcissa felt appalled as she thought of the long trip back to her home with her baby. It was therefore decided to return by canoe down the Clearwater to the Snake, and thence down the Snake to Fort Walla Walla. That was perhaps a more comfortable way, and yet Narcissa described the return trip as "a tedious journey."

They left the Spaldings on Saturday, December 2, and reached the mouth of the Clearwater that night. There they camped in the snow over Sunday. One wonders why they left the Spaldings on Saturday. The presence of a large encampment of Nez Perces at the mouth of the Clearwater might have been the reason. Whitman in his letter to Greene stated that the Indians were very attentive to religious instruction.

The Whitmans embarked in their canoe on Monday morning with a minimum of baggage and only one Indian for a guide. The river was low, and navigation was dangerous

---

[7] Mrs. Eliza Spalding Warren died in Coeur d'Alene, Idaho, June 21, 1919.

in places. At night they were obliged to camp in the snow. They reached Fort Walla Walla on Thursday, December 7, and, after spending a day there, completed the remaining twenty-five miles of their journey on horseback. Dr. Whitman took his little daughter on his horse with him on the trip to Waiilatpu. Narcissa wrote that they stopped but once to nurse and change her, "which she did not relish quite so well." [Letter 44.] It snowed the whole day. They reached their home after dark, and were, as Narcissa wrote, "not a little rejoiced to see it again."

THE ADOBE HOUSE

During the summer and fall of 1837, Dr. Whitman managed to build his adobe[8] house, which promised to be more comfortable than the lean-to. We regret that none of the Whitman letters written during the fall of 1837 have been saved for posterity. Since not even the American Board has a letter of Whitman's written during this time, it is supposed that all he wrote were lost in transit.

Narcissa's letter of April 11, 1838, was published only in part in the 1891 issue of the *Transactions of the Oregon Pioneer Association*. The following extract is taken from the hitherto unpublished portion and describes the troubles the Whitmans had with their adobe dwelling.

But I must talk a little to Father about our house. Our letters of last fall showed that we had a fair prospect for a comfortable house soon. In this we are disappointed. We mentioned that it was built of dobies made of mud, both the walls of the cellar & of the house. The last week in Dec it was so warm & melted the snow in the mountains in such quantities as to cause the waters of the rivers to rise to a great height and in many places to overflow their banks, both above and below us the waters were running in every direction.

On the eve of the 28th the waters entered our cellar, the walls settled, the props gave away one after another, & for the whole night we were in the utmost anxiety, fearing the consequences to our whole house. Soon after dark our men & Indians went to work diping out the water & throwing earth against the walls & continued it all night long. In great mercy to us our house was preserved to us standing, although the wall is materially injured. Towards morning the water began to fall a little. We were obliged for several days & nights in succession to keep the water bailed out.

---

[8] Adobe comes from the Spanish verb *"adobar,"* meaning "to pickle." It has the derived meanings—"to tan hides" and "to plaster." Eells, *Marcus Whitman*, p. 112, quoting T. J. Farnham: "The old mission house stands on the northeast bank of the river, about four rods from the water side, at the southeast corner of an enclosure containing about two hundred and fifty acres."

In March the river rose again and, as Narcissa declared, "gave it another stroke." During the winter, Whitman sent some men to the Blue Mountains to saw some pine boards. He had been able to lay a rough pine board floor in the fall of 1837 which was uneven enough to give Alice Clarissa, when she began to walk, many an occasion for stumbling. While at Lapwai, Whitman induced Spalding to make the window sash.

After the crops were planted in the spring of 1838, Whitman visited Spalding at Lapwai, and helped him build his new home on the banks of the Clearwater. Narcissa was somewhat perturbed over the turn of events which gave the Spaldings a new house before they could build one at Waiilatpu. Writing to her sister on September 25, 1838, she said: "Mr. Spalding . . . persuaded my husband to believe that he needed a house more than we did, and prevailed on him to go over and assist in building."

In the fall of 1838 the first and only re-enforcement for the Oregon mission of the American Board reached Waiilatpu. In that group was Mrs. Cushing Eells, who has left for us the following description of the Whitman home as she first saw it:

Dr. W's house . . . is built of adobe (mud dried in the sun in the form of brick only larger) I can not describe its appearance as I can not compare it with anything I ever saw. There are doors and windows, but they are of the roughest kind; the boards being sawed by hand and put together but by one who knew nothing about such work, as is evident from its appearance.

The furniture is very primitive. The bedsteads are boards nailed to the side of the house, sink fashion, then some blankets and husks make the bed; but it is good compared with traveling accommodations.[9]

Perhaps Mrs. Eells did not realize that the best carpenter in the world could not have kept the green and unseasoned wood used in the woodwork, window sashes, and floors, from shrinking and warping in the hot summer days.

McLOUGHLIN VISITS WALLA WALLA

Dr. John McLoughlin visited Fort Walla Walla in the latter part of March, 1838, en route to London. In the hope that he might be able to visit Boston, Spalding prepared a letter of introduction, which Whitman signed. However,

---

[9] *T.O.P.A.*, 1889, pp. 88-89.

circumstances prevented Dr. McLoughlin from visiting Boston.[10]

The Whitmans were expecting Dr. McLoughlin to call on them at Waiilatpu, but on March 27 he sent word saying that he was behind in his schedule and could not come. He requested them to call instead at Fort Walla Walla. The Whitmans with their baby left early Wednesday morning, the 28th, but a heavy rain caused them to return. It was then decided that Marcus should go alone.

Dr. Whitman carried his wife's letter, dated March 14, to which a postscript was added on the 28th. This was given to Dr. McLoughlin, who took it with him and mailed it in the East. The opening sentence of that letter, written on her thirtieth birthday and on the first birthday of her little girl, paints a pathetic picture:

More than two years have passed since I left my father's home and not a single word has been wafted hence, or, perhaps I should say, has greeted my ears to afford consolation in a desponding hour. This *long* long silence makes me feel the truth of our situation, that we are far, very far removed from the land of our birth and Christian privileges. I am weary of writing so much about ourselves without receiving a response, and yet I am anxious that father and mother should know all about us.

The only letter of which we have record that the Whitmans had then received from loved ones in the East after their departure was the letter from the Rev. Lyman Judson, which reached them at Liberty, Missouri. The first mail from their relatives did not reach Waiilatpu until July, 1838—two years and five months after they had left for Oregon. Who can measure the heartaches and the disappointments of those years as the months rolled by without a word from loved ones? They were as completely cut off as though they lived on another planet.

All evidence points to a very cordial relationship between the Whitmans and Dr. McLoughlin. It must have been with real regret that Dr. McLoughlin gave up his visit to Waiilatpu, and also when he learned that Mrs. Whitman was unable to make the trip to the Fort. In Whitman's letter to Greene, which Dr. McLoughlin also carried East, was this statement: "We cannot speak to[o] highly of his kindness to us since we have been in this country." [Letter 43.]

---

[10] Spalding wrote to Greene, Mar. 17, 1838, saying in part: "We have only to mention his name, to call to your recollection the numerous favors your unworthy missionaries have received, since their arrival in this country, from this gentleman. . . . "

WILLIAM CAMERON McKAY

Thomas McKay and his three sons, William, John, and Alexander, reached Fort Walla Walla before the Montreal express which brought Dr. McLoughlin. As shall be mentioned later, it is evident that Thomas had his daughter Margaret with him also. Thomas McKay was then in charge of Fort Hall and was en route to his station. He planned to send his eldest son, William Cameron McKay (1824-1892), to Scotland with Dr. McLoughlin to study medicine.

McKay and his sons[11] rode out to Waiilatpu to visit the Whitmans, and while there Dr. Whitman strongly urged McKay to send William to the Fairfield Medical College. "Make an American of him," he told McKay, and prophesied that the day was coming when Oregon would certainly belong to the United States. Oregon was then held under a joint-occupation treaty which the United States and Great Britain had signed in 1818. Dr. Whitman felt that the boy would have a much better chance for a successful career as a doctor in Oregon if he were educated in the States and "became an American in thought and feeling."[12]

Whitman's arguments prevailed. McKay knew that Jason Lee was due to arrive soon and that the Lee party would go with the Hudson's Bay party as far as Fort Hall. It was decided to have the boys go on with Lee.

JASON LEE

On Friday, April 13, 1838, Jason Lee reached Fort Walla Walla on his way to the States. The next day he rode out to Waiilatpu, where he met the Whitmans for the first time. Jason Lee had missed seeing them at Fort Vancouver, for he left the Fort the Saturday before the Whitman-Spalding party arrived. Lee in his diary speaks of how Dr. Whitman met him and conducted him to the house, where Mrs. Whitman met them at the door.[13]

Lee remained at Waiilatpu until the following Thursday, April 19, when he left for Lapwai to see Spalding. In the unpublished portion of Mrs. Whitman's letter of April 11, she wrote: "Our visit with him has been a very refreshing

---

[11] Since McKay was married to a native, his children had but one-quarter white blood.

[12] *T.O.P.A.*, 1889, pp. 91 ff.

[13] Lee's *Diary*, *O.H.Q.*, Vol. 17, pp. 417 ff.

one. He is the first christian brother that has visited us since Mr. Gray left last March, 1837."[14]

Lee spent Sunday, April 22, with Spalding, and the two started back for Waiilatpu on Monday. By riding seventy-five miles in one day they were able to get to Whitman's station by the 24th. Lee, in a letter written to his nephew on April 25, confessed that he felt a bit sore from his long ride the previous day. He frankly stated that he considered it very rash for Whitman and Spalding to settle so far apart, thus putting themselves "so entirely into the hands of the Indians when there was not absolute necessity for it."[15] It is evident that Lee had not learned the real reason for the separation.

From this letter of Lee to his nephew and from his diary we find that he was favorably impressed with what Whitman and Spalding had accomplished. On the 16th, while at Waiilatpu, he wrote: "Visited the In's [Indians] Farms and was surprised that they had done so much in the absence of almost every tool necessary to do with. Some had two or three acres, wheat, peas, corn & Potatoes."

To his nephew he wrote:

Both the Kioose and the Nez Perce are doing a great deal in cultivation, the former with wooden ploughs with a little bit of iron nailed upon them, and hoes, and the latter with hoes alone. Some of the Nez Perces came to the Doctor's for potatoes to plant, a distance of 300 mi. I was astonished to see the industry of these Indians. The fact is they are starving, and they will be forced to work their land. . . .

Both Mr. W. & Mr. S. use highhanded measure with their people, and when they deserve it let them feel the *lash*. Now my Dear Brethren . . . be strong in the Lord, be firm, and let not the Indians trifle with you. . . .

Lee was convinced that the Indians of the Upper Columbia were much superior to those of the Willamette Valley.

Some explanation should be given about what he said in regard to the lash. In Whitman's letter of May 5, 1837, to Greene we read: "A system of punishment for crime established also by the traders has done much good." In a country where there were no jails or law-enforcing agencies, the white men adopted the lash as an effective way to punish

---

[14] About thirteen hundred words of this letter were omitted when the rest of the letter was published in the *T.O.P.A.*, 1891. Although the letter was dated April 11, it contains several entries for later dates.

[15] Brosnan, *Jason Lee*, pp. 94 ff. It is possible that Spalding did not return with Lee but followed a few days later. Evidence is not clear on this point.

wrongdoers and at the same time to inculcate a little respect. Spalding in his diary makes reference to the use of the lash by the Indians themselves upon wrongdoers.[16] It is doubtful that the missionaries ever used the lash, but may have requested its use from the chiefs.

In McLoughlin's letter to Spalding of November 28, 1837, we find this interesting passage in regard to the lash:

You also see the return Ellice is making us for the expenses we have ... upon him, and you know how Garry has acted; When he came he found that the chiefs were in the habit of Flogging, at our suggesting, those who stole &c and by which in a great measure they had put a stop to their evil practices, and made their followers live more correctly than before. . . .

Because of the objections to the use of the lash raised by the young men who had been at the Red River school, it was gradually given up, although Dr. McLoughlin in this same letter stated: "last year the Cayouse Chief told me, that he now saw they were wrong in giving up flogging, as the Young Men would not attend to anything."[17]

Lee gave Whitman and Spalding such a glowing account of the work of the Methodist mission and the liberality of his Board in sending workers to the field that he aroused their envy. The Methodists had sent out a re-enforcement of twenty in 1837, and yet Lee was then on his way to the States for more. The next year he succeeded in bringing out fifty-one additional workers by sea.

When Lee was with Spalding at Lapwai, he so fired the imagination of Spalding that on Saturday, April 21, Spalding wrote to Greene and made the following amazing request:

To occupy these fields immediately, we ask as the least possible number which God & our consciences will admit us to name, for 30 ordained missionaries 30 farmers, 30 school teachers, 10 physicians & 10 mechanics, with their wives.

A total of 220 additional workers! These Spalding wanted the American Board to send out as soon as possible. Spalding carried that letter with him to Waiilatpu, and there the three men discussed the future of the Oregon mission of the American Board. Undoubtedly Lee encouraged them to make big requests from the Board, and for a time Whitman shared in their enthusiasm. He signed Spalding's letter, thus making it a joint letter to the Board. Whitman then filled out a blank requesting supplies.

---

16 Drury, *Spalding*, p. 216.

17 Published with the permission of the Governor and Committee of the Hudson's Bay Company.

One is amazed at the extravagance of Spalding's letter, and one is equally amazed by Whitman's requests. He asked for: "Several tons of iron and steel . . . 2,000 gun flints, fifty gross Indian awls, 100 dozen scalping knives . . . two best cook stoves, six box stoves." What must Greene have said when he received that letter?

The most sensible request in Whitman's long list was for two cookstoves, for both Mrs. Whitman and Mrs. Spalding were cooking over an open fire. Another reasonable request was for mill machinery, for both Spalding and Whitman appreciated the importance of being independent of the Hudson's Bay Company. They argued that a mill would save them much money, for flour was costing them ten dollars a hundred. [Letter 62.] The awls and scalping knives were used in trading with the Indians or as payment for labor received. Whitman also asked for crockery, and for "1 Websters octavo Dictionary 1 doz Watts Hymns 2 doz Village hymns . . . 2 doz Parleys Geography."

Ordinarily Whitman was not so unreasonable. Usually he was deliberate in his judgment. The combination of Spalding's impetuosity and Lee's success swept him off his feet. Both Whitman and Spalding felt that the American Board ought to be as generous with them as the Methodists were with Lee. Whitman wrote: "I hope we may not be left unsupported while our Methodist Brethren devise so liberal things. . . . I would urge that blacksmiths farmers mechanicks & teachers be sent as soon as possible." [Letter 48.] Later Whitman regretted that he had joined in the request for 220 additional workers and goods in proportion. He was inclined to blame the extravagant nature of their requests on the impulsiveness of Spalding. Yet the fact remains that he signed the letter, wrote out the bill for goods, and also wrote on May 8: "I have had the pleasure of signing a joint letter to yourself prepared by Brother Spalding."

On May 15, Whitman added a postscript to the letter of April 21, in which he requested the following items:

Add to your bill Shoes No 7 female, 8, 9, & 10, male six pair each Boots No 9 & 10. two pair Shoes for children of the age two and four years six pair each Hats 25 & 26 one of each 12 palm leaf hats for summer candle sticks & snuffers 12 each six large cow bells four pair coarse wool cards—2 hetchels [hatchels]

Because it sometimes took two years to receive a reply to a letter, Whitman felt the necessity of ordering in quantity and for the future.

Another matter which the three missionaries certainly discussed was the future development of the country. They saw that the day was swiftly coming when white settlers would enter the country. Whitman in his letter of May 8, 1838, expressed a fear that the wrong kind of colonists would come. Lee was carrying with him a memorial signed by twenty-seven Americans and French Canadians living in the Willamette Valley, asking for the extension of the jurisdiction of the United States over that territory.[18] The memorial declared: "The agriculture and other resources of the country cannot fail to induce immigration and commerce." Both Whitman and Spalding were undoubtedly in sympathy with the memorial, and we wonder why their names do not appear with the others. Perhaps it was felt that they were too far removed from the Willamette Valley. Lee became a missionary colonizer, and his services in that respect far overshadowed what he was able to do for the Indians of the Willamette Valley.

Lee bade his friends at Waiilatpu mission farewell on May 12. In his diary he described their parting: "We kneeled upon the bank of a small stream, and Mr. S. commended us to the throne of grace, we then took the parting hand, and they returned to their arduous labors; and I pensively pursued camp, thankful for the pleasing acquaintance then formed." Lee carried with him several of the Whitman letters, including Mrs. Whitman's interesting letter dated April 11.

MADAME DORION

Among the visitors to Waiilatpu in the spring of 1838 was Madame Dorion, the heroine of Washington Irving's *Astoria*. In the above-mentioned letter of Narcissa's, she wrote on April 19:

Saturday Mrs. Pambrun came with her three daughters, Maria, Ada, & Harriet, also two daughters & a son of an Iowa, the Old woman spoken of in Washington Irving's Astoria, (Perhaps Father has not seen the book, it contains a more just representation of this country than any other written previous.) She is now the wife of a Frenchman now residing at the Fort. She was here with the rest & spent the Sabbath & left today. Mr Lee arriving at Walla Walla on Friday came with them.

Madame Dorion married John Toupin, a French Canadian, who was once used by Parker as an interpreter. They

---

[18] Bancroft, *Oregon*, Vol. 1, p. 169. The memorial was printed in 25th Cong., 3rd Sess., H. Rept. 101.

lived at Fort Walla Walla, where the Iowa woman became friendly with Mrs. Pambrun. In July, 1841, Father Blanchet performed a marriage service for Madame Dorion and John Toupin, thus putting the seal of the church upon a relationship which had existed for some time. Toupin also served as Pambrun's interpreter.[19]

Life at the Whitman mission station was not dull when such interesting guests were coming and going. It is most interesting to see how the influences of the lives of such well-known characters as Dr. McLoughlin, Tom McKay and his son William, Jason Lee, and Madame Dorion mingled with those of the Whitmans and the Spaldings. Like the bright strands of a richly ornamented tapestry, the shuttle of time wove them together in an historical picture of Old Oregon.

THE SUMMER OF 1838

The summer of 1838 passed swiftly for the Whitmans. So many tasks in the field, in the home, among the Indians, and elsewhere called for their strength and their attention. Whitman went to Lapwai in June to assist Spalding in building his new house on the banks of the Clearwater. Some sheep arrived from the Hawaiian Islands that summer. Evidence is rather conflicting regarding the number. On October 30, 1836, Whitman wrote to the Rev. Levi Chamberlain of the American Board mission in Honolulu and reported that: "Five of the six sheep reached here in safety for which we feel very thankful as we value them highly." Writing to Judge Prentiss on April 8, 1845, Whitman said: "We have above eighty sheep. . . . All these came from one ewe brought from the Sandwich Islands in '38 and two more brought in '39." It may be that most of the sheep received in 1838 were sent to Lapwai, for Spalding once referred to receiving eight sheep in 1838.[20]

During the last week of June, Mr. and Mrs. McDonald and their family, of Fort Colville, spent a week with the Whitmans. Mrs. McDonald favored Mrs. Whitman in January, 1838, with a gift of twelve fine pickled buffalo tongues. Narcissa found Mrs. McDonald, who was a native, to be an intelligent woman with a fair command of the English language.

---

[19] Defenbach, *Red Heroines of the Northwest*, has a chapter on Madame Dorion. Dates given for her life are 1786-1853. She married Toupin in 1824. Toupin was among the witnesses at the hearing of the murderers of Whitman.

[20] Drury, *Spalding*, p. 186.

Mrs. Whitman made two visits to Fort Walla Walla during the summer, called there by the illness of Mrs. Pambrun. Dr. Whitman was called to The Dalles early in August to see Mrs. Perkins, of the Methodist mission, who was critically ill. During his absence Sarah Hull, the Indian girl who had been living with the Whitmans for more than a year, died. "If ever I felt the presence of my husband necessary," wrote Narcissa, "it was while passing through such a scene." [Letter 52.]

Mrs. Whitman also had in her home Margaret McKay, the daughter of Thomas McKay. Margaret is mentioned in Mrs. Whitman's letter of March 12, 1838, and probably was left at the mission station by her father when he was there with his sons. She remained at Waiilatpu assisting Mrs. Whitman in the household duties for more than a year. Later she is reported to have married Charles Roe, an American.[21]

Wednesday, July 11, 1838, was a red-letter day at Waiilatpu, for on that day arrived the first home mail. Writing to her sister Jane on September 18, Narcissa said: "You know not with what feelings of inexpressible joy I received your letter dated January and August, 1837, and sent from Leroy." Narcissa received letters from her father, her sisters Jane and Mary Ann, her brother-in-law, Lyman Judson, and from Mrs. Mather, the mother of Mrs. Satterlee. Dr. Whitman received several from his friends and relatives and at least two from Greene, of the American Board. Narcissa wrote: "Letters from Mr. Greene in July caused our hearts to sink, and we gave up all hopes of a reinforcement very soon joining us. [Letter 51.] In her letter to Judson, Narcissa gave the interesting news that Spalding had received a letter from "L Lynsley Prattsburg and his sister." Spalding had once been engaged to a Miss Levina Linsley, of Prattsburg.[22]

The Hawaiians who had been assisting Whitman from the very beginning of his work returned to Fort Vancouver, and two other men from the Islands arrived on June 28. [Letter 54.] One went to assist Spalding, while the other, Joseph Maki, remained at Waiilatpu. Maki was married and had his wife with him.

---

[21] Hines, *History of Oregon*, p. 139. Bancroft, *Oregon*, Vol. 1, p. 159, states that Roe married a Nancy McKay.

[22] Drury, *Spalding*, p. 39. The engagement was broken because of Miss Linsley's continued ill-health. She died Dec. 21, 1838. It is possible that the word "his" in the quotation should be "her." Spalding's writing is difficult to decipher at times.

At the request of Whitman, the Spaldings came to Waiilatpu, arriving there on Monday, August 13. Mrs. Spalding and their daughter accompanied him. Fearful of leaving his precious sheep behind at Lapwai, Spalding drove them all the way to Waiilatpu and back again.[23] He also drove along some milch cows. It is possible that Spalding reached Waiilatpu in time to take charge of the burial of Sarah Hull, who died on the 11th.

On Tuesday, August 14, Spalding began a series of religious meetings, which climaxed on Saturday, August 18, in the organization of the First Church of Oregon. It appears that the members of the Methodist and the American Board mission were observing Tuesday evenings for prayer in their separate stations. At the meeting held in the Whitman home July 24, Compo and the Hawaiian showed signs of a spiritual quickening. Narcissa called it a "melting season," referring to the tears of repentance. [Letter 54.] This induced Whitman to write to Spalding and urge him to visit Waiilatpu. Narcissa states that her husband then suggested the organization of a church.

The charter members of the church were the four missionaries and Mr. and Mrs. Joseph Maki, who presented letters from the mission church in Honolulu which had been organized by the American Board missionaries there. Spalding was chosen pastor, and Dr. Whitman was the ruling elder. On Sunday, August 19, Charles Compo was married to the Nez Perce woman with whom he had been living, the mother of his eighteen-month-old son. Spalding officiated. Having thus fulfilled a necessary requirement as far as his private life was concerned, Compo was baptized and received into the church. According to Spalding's record in the minute book, Compo was "the first fruit of our missionary labor in this country."[24] The little boy was baptized and given the name John.[25]

The seven members of the newly organized church then observed the Lord's Supper. "It was a solemn and interesting season for us," wrote Narcissa. [Letter 54.] Pam-

[23] Spalding to Greene, Sept. 11, 1838.

[24] Drury, *Spalding*, pp. 186 ff., gives details about the church, including a picture of the first record. The original minutes were published in the 1903 *Minutes of the Synod of Wash.*, and republished by the Synod in their 1936 records.

[25] Seymour, *Story of the Red Man*, states that Billy Compo was still alive when that book was written (published in 1934). Billy Compo was evidently a younger son, for the eldest was named John.

brun was present and strongly advised Compo not to join the Protestant church, for Compo, like Pambrun, had been reared in the Roman Catholic faith.

On the evening before the special meetings closed, word was received from Gray that he was arriving soon with re-enforcements. Spalding, who was eager to be on his way back to Lapwai, decided to stay a few days longer and help welcome the new missionaries. On Tuesday, August 21, W. H. Gray, and his wife, formerly Mary Dix, of Ithaca, New York, reached Waiilatpu, having ridden ahead of the others in their party. It was just like Gray to push on in advance. With joy and eagerness, the Whitmans and the Spaldings received the two and heard their account of the trip. Gray told of the coming of the Rev. and Mrs. Elkanah Walker, the Rev. and Mrs. Cushing Eells, the Rev. and Mrs. A. B. Smith, and Mr. Cornelius Rogers. By that re-enforcement the personnel of the Oregon mission of the American Board grew to thirteen. It was never any larger.

This sudden re-enforcement was more than the Whitmans and the Spaldings had dared to expect in the light of Greene's letters. The new workers were warmly received. Fortunately the gardens about Waiilatpu were bearing well, and the newcomers reveled in fresh vegetables, melons, and so forth, as had the Whitmans and Spaldings two years earlier.

CHAPTER TEN

THE THIRD year of the Oregon mission of the American
Board was a year of peculiar trial and difficulty for the
Whitmans. It was a time of necessary and painful adjustments. During the year they tasted of the overflowing cup
of joy, and they drank the dregs of the most poignant sorrow that can come to any mother and father.

Gradually they learned from Gray the story of his
eventful trip East. Gray had ventured to cross the prairies
ahead of the fur company's caravan, with the result that his
party was attacked by Sioux Indians at Ash Hollow, Nebraska, on August 7. His four Indian companions were
killed, and Gray himself narrowly escaped being shot. The
Sioux stole his horses. Through the intercession of a white
man who happened to be with the Sioux, Gray was permitted to continue his journey.

Greene was displeased when he learned of Gray's return.
However, Gray assured the Board that it would be under no
expense as far as his sojourn in the East was concerned. He
returned to his native town of Fairfield, New York, where
he enrolled in the Medical School, giving his home address
as "Columbia, Oregon." It so happened that the Board had
appointed two clergymen, the Rev. Elkanah Walker (1805-
1877) and the Rev. Cushing Eells (1810-1878), as missionaries to the Zulus in Africa, but because of native disturbances these men had been unable to go to their fields.
Learning that they were willing to have their destination
changed to Oregon, the Board, therefore, commissioned them
to return with Gray.

Gray wrote to Walker from Fairfield on December 18,
1837, and gave information about the proposed journey
across the mountains. From this letter we learn that the
Board had promised to send out five couples in the summer
of 1838, and had allowed three thousand dollars for expenses.
Gray also stated that the Rev. Lyman P. Judson and his
wife, Mary Ann Prentiss, a sister of Narcissa, were hoping
to be in the party. Gray also wrote: "You will remember me

in love to Mrs. Walker in the present or in prospect. Mrs. G. is yet to be found."[1]

Gray's perplexity as to "Mrs. G." was suddenly solved when he visited Mr. Parker at Ithaca, New York. According to one report, "he met Miss Mary Augusta Dix, a handsome stately brunette, on the evening of the 19th of February, 1838, and became engaged to her the same evening. Six days later they were married, and on the morning of the 26th started westward to join the caravan of the American Fur Company."[2]

On March 5, Elkanah Walker married Miss Mary Richardson (1811-1897), at Baldwin, Maine. On the same day at Holden, Massachusetts, Cushing Eells wedded Miss Myra Fairbanks (1805-1878). The two couples met for the first time on Saturday, March 17, 1838, in New York. The next day a special service was held in their honor in the Brick Church, of which Dr. Gardiner Spring was then pastor. The Rev. David Greene was present and gave them their instructions.

The next day they met the Rev. Asa Bowen Smith (1809-1886) and his wife, Sarah Gilbert White Smith (1813-1855), who were also appointed to the Oregon mission. The Smiths were married March 15, so with the Grays, the re-enforcement consisted of four newly married couples. At Cincinnati, a young man twenty-three years old, Cornelius Rogers (1815-1843),[3] joined the party, although he did not receive his appointment as a missionary of the American Board until after his arrival in Oregon. The Judsons were unable to go, much to the Whitmans' disappointment when they heard of it.

Parker wrote to Walker from Ithaca on February 19, 1838, and gave the following advice in regard to travel:

Brother Gray has put into my hands yours of the 8th ult. for the purpose of making a few statements from the experience I have had in traveling both routs, across the continent and around Cape Horn. I shall not go into detail, but only say, by all means go across the continent by land. I had rather go across the continent three times than around the Cape once, and probably it would not take more time, nor be attended with half the dangers and hardships, as to go by water.

---

[1] Original, Coll. Wn.

[2] Obituary notice of W. H. Gray, Portland *Oregonian*, Nov. 15, 1889. Also Gray to Walker, Feb. 21, 1838: "I have not known till yesterday that I was to have a companion to go out with me." Original letter in Coll. Wn.

[3] Eells, *Marcus Whitman*, gives a brief biographical sketch of the members of the re-enforcement, pp. 320 ff.

You might be detained six months in the hot climate of the torrid zone, before an opportunity would present to go from the Sand. Isles. There need be no hesitation which way to go. A lady can go with far more comfort by land than by water.[4]

So the American Board sent its second party of Oregon missionaries, women included, overland. The trip of the four women with their husbands across the plains and over the mountains in 1838 would be far better known had it not been that Mrs. Whitman and Mrs. Spalding anticipated them by two years. The travel conditions and attendant dangers were so similar that all of the praise spoken in behalf of the fortitude and courage of Mrs. Whitman and Mrs. Spalding can be applied to the women of the 1838 re-enforcement as well."[5]

Judging from the letters and diaries of the members of this party, the trip was a most trying experience. Mrs. Walker made frequent mention in her diary of Mr. Smith's faultfinding. Gray was so domineering that no member of the re-enforcement would consent to live with him in the same station after their arrival on the field.

On August 15, Gray and his wife left the party, pushed on ahead, and reached Waiilatpu a few days before the others. All were there by Wednesday, August 29. Since the Spaldings were eager to be on their way back to Lapwai, a mission meeting was called for Saturday, September 1. Thus, after only a two days' rest from a long and arduous trip and before they could grasp the real problems which confronted them, the three new clergymen were called upon to help determine some vital policies for the mission.

Spalding was chosen Moderator and Walker was made Secretary. The original record, kept with a lead pencil on a piece of letter paper, was recently discovered.[6] In view of the issues decided, this meeting proved to be one of the most important ever held in the Oregon mission of the American Board.

It was voted to give instruction to the natives in their own language. Whitman and Spalding had tried teaching the natives English but soon realized that this was impractical. This vote was qualified by the statement: " . . . but for

---

[4] Coll. Wn.

[5] A detailed account of this trip will be given in the author's forthcoming book, the third of this series, on Elkanah Walker.

[6] Owned by Sam T. Walker, youngest son of Elkanah Walker, who still lives at Forest Grove, Oregon (April 4, 1937). These original minutes, with other important Walker records, are now in Coll. Wn.

their permanent benefit of the peoples we will introduce the English language as fast as expedient." Whitman and Spalding told of their experience in trying to get a book published by the missionaries of the Sandwich Islands, and of the offer of these missionaries to send to the Oregon mission the old press, undoubtedly the one that Elisha Loomis took out in 1820. Hence the following action: "Voted that the press printer type paper & binding apparatus offered by the S. I. Mission be accepted." The fact that the mission on the Islands had a larger press made it possible for them to part with the old and smaller one.

Considerable discussion centered about the distribution of the new workers. Because of the interest the Spokane Indians had manifested in having Christian workers live among them, it was decided to have Walker and Eells establish a station there. The Smiths and Rogers were to live at Waiilatpu, and since nobody else wanted the Grays, Spalding consented to their living with him at Lapwai. It was also voted to establish a corn and flour mill, and a blacksmith shop at Lapwai because it was most centrally located. Since new supplies were urgently needed, Dr. Whitman was appointed to visit Fort Vancouver to make the necessary purchases. A salary of twenty-five pounds per annum was voted for Rogers.

Both Whitman and Spalding saw the necessity of settling the Indians, although Spalding was more enthusiastic on this point than Whitman. In Walker's first letter, sent back to Greene after his arrival at Waiilatpu, he stated: "It is too about made certain by actual experience that we must use the plough as well as the Bible if we do anything to benefit the Indians. They must be settled before they can be enlightened much." Later, serious differences of opinion developed in regard to this point and caused considerable friction within the mission. At first, however, the new arrivals accepted the judgment and experience of Whitman and Spalding.

Monday, September 3, the men resumed their activities. Spalding made haste to leave for Lapwai; Walker and Eells prepared to go to the Spokanes; and Whitman turned his attention to the many tasks that had to be completed before he could leave for Vancouver. On that day the women organized a Maternal Association, modeled after similar associations which were common at that time in the East. The following officers were chosen: President, Mrs. Spalding; Corresponding Secretary, Mrs. Whitman; Recording Secretary, Mrs. Gray; and Vice President, Mrs. Walker. This association was kept alive all during the history of the Oregon mission. The membership was enlarged to include the native wives of some of the Hudson's Bay men. Mrs. Whitman was diligent in securing subscriptions for the *Mother's Magazine* and on one occasion sent in eighteen dollars for this purpose. [Letter 193.]

On Tuesday the Spaldings, the Grays, Charles Compo, James Conner, a number of Nez Perces, together with Spalding's milch cows, sheep, horses, and pack animals started for Lapwai. Rogers remained at Waiilatpu until the 20th of the month, and then he, too, went to Lapwai. Walker and Eells left on September 10 to explore for a mission site among the Spokane Indians. The women remained with Narcissa. The men did not return to Waiilatpu until October 13, coming back by way of Lapwai, where they found Spalding digging his potatoes. Walker wrote in his diary on October 8, 1838: "Mr. S. has a fine lot of potatoes; and I think he will have at least 1500 bushels, 500 to the acre. I never saw any that turned out so well."

Walker and Eells picked out a site on the trail which connected Fort Walla Walla with Fort Colville, about seventy miles south of the latter, and about twenty-five miles northwest of the present city of Spokane, Washington. The Indians called the place Tshimakain, or "place of springs." The men started to build their cabins, and before they left were able to erect the walls for the two houses, each measuring about fourteen feet square.

Whitman left for Fort Vancouver on Monday, September 17, and was away for about a month, returning October 13. After his return to Waiilatpu, Whitman superintended and assisted in the erection of another adobe house. Profiting by his experience in being too near the stream, Whitman chose a site farther removed. The plans for his new house called for the erection of a story-and-a-half unit, which measured nineteen by forty feet, with the main axis running north and south. To the east was a one-story unit, which measured twenty-two by thirty feet. The two units joined to make a "T." That fall Whitman harvested "three hundred bushels of corn, seventy-five of wheat, and a thousand bushels of potatoes, besides a large supply of turnips and garden vegetables." [Letter 62.]

FINANCIAL PROBLEMS

On March 27, 1838, Whitman made out his financial report, covering the period from his previous report, which was dated March 18, 1837. He acknowledged receipt of two boxes of goods, shipped from Boston on January 18, 1837, which contained clothing, bedding, books, paper, and other supplies. The books formed the nucleus of the mission library, of which Spalding was librarian.[7]

Whitman then reported on his expenditures of £63.14.2½ and itemized his account as follows:

Supplies Clothing & Indian Goods to pay for Provision &c& Transportation	29- 1- 1
Farming utensils & Building Materials	11- 5- 9
Clothing &c for a Boy living with me	3-14- 1
Flour & Seeds & Hogs	10- 3- 6
Bill at Walla Walla for last year Seeds & provisions &c	5- 8- 9
One half of Mr. Grays expenses in the Flat Head Country & at Rendezvous	4- 1-½

Whitman subtracted from this total the sum of £9.19.4½ which was his share of a cash contribution to the Oregon mission made by the "Society of Honolulu." Spalding received a like amount. Whitman also reported: "The avails of the sale of salt contributed by the King and his sisters at Oahu (one half) the other being reported by Mr. Spalding £17-5-10." It is most interesting to find King Kamehameha III and his royal sisters listed among the contributors for the evangelization of the Oregon Indians. After subtracting these two cash gifts from the total required, Whitman found it necessary to draw upon the board for £130.15.11, to meet the balance of his and Spalding's expenses.[8]

To this bill Whitman added another charge of £58.3.10 to pay wages due two men who worked for him from September 21, 1836, to June 1, 1838, for £17.0.0 each per annum, and £0.12.0 due some Indians for such services as carrying letters.

When we add Whitman's various expense accounts together, we find that up to March 28, 1838, he drew upon the Board for £336.18.½. According to Hill, treasurer of the American Board, every £100 cost the Board about

---

[7] Coll. W. contains a volume of *Pilgrim's Progress*, on the flyleaf of which in Spalding's handwriting is written: "Colm. Mission Library No. 44).

[8] Treasury Books of the American Board. Photostat copy, Coll. Wn.

$540.[9] This means that the cost of the Waiilatpu branch of the mission was somewhat more than $1,800 during the first two years. However, it must be remembered that this included everything—building materials, wages, machinery, food supplies, Indian goods for trading, transportation, and salary (if indeed it is possible to speak of salary for either Whitman or Spalding). Considering the high rate of exchange and the excessive cost of transportation up the river, we must admit that this figure is very low.

Conservative as these figures were, still they brought dismay to the secretaries of the American Board. While Whitman and Spalding were making their extravagant demands upon the Board for 220 missionaries and goods in proportion, together with their legitimate claims for expenses, a letter was on its way to the Oregon mission from the Board, limiting each family to $500 a year. This letter was received in July, 1838, and bore the date of June 23, 1837. The original was found in the archives of Whitman College and was addressed to: "Rev. H. H. Spalding & Associates." Perhaps it was this letter which caused Narcissa to write: "Letters received from Mr. Greene in July caused our hearts to sink. [Letter 51.]

We should remember that the financial depression of 1837 seriously affected the receipts of the American Board. Faced with a heavy debt and lowered income, they simply had to retrench. The circular of June 23, 1837, which the Board sent out to Oregon, was likewise sent to all of its stations throughout the world. The draft which Spalding drew at Fort Vancouver on November 20, 1836, for £371 reached the Board on July 5, 1837, a few days after the circular of June 23 had been prepared. Greene and Hill were dismayed to see the amount demanded. On July 6, each of them added a postscript to the circular. Greene wrote: "We were greatly surprised at your draft of £371 received by Mr. Hill yesterday. It is quite impossible for us to go on meeting such drafts in present circumstances."

Greene exhorted them as follows: "More of the Brainard & Eliot mode of labor and extent of expenditure must be introduced and followed out." Brainard and Eliott were well-known missionaries to the Indians of the East of an earlier day. They made no efforts to settle the Indians and to introduce the arts of civilization but shared the nomadic

---

[9] American Board to Spalding, June 23, 1837.

life of the Indians and taught and preached as occasion permitted. Such advice was contrary to the convictions of
both Whitman and Spalding, who saw the necessity of settling the Indians. The fact that Whitman and Spalding
each had a family made their situation far different from
that of Brainard and Eliott.

Samuel Parker had, perhaps unconsciously, placed both
Whitman and Spalding in a bad light before the Board. It
seems evident that soon after reaching the States in May,
1837, he visited the Board rooms in Boston. He arrived at a
time when the Board was struggling with finances. Perhaps
he was there when Spalding's draft for £371 arrived. This
we know, Greene quoted Parker in his note of July 6, 1837,
to Spalding and Whitman. Greene wrote: "I write also of
a remark of Mr. Parker, which he made on being informed
of the expenses of your outfit and journey, without expressing any opinion respecting its correctness: He remarked
that he would pledge himself to outfit a mission of equal
numbers, take them across the country, and sustain them
in their work three years for the same amount, i. e., about
$7,000.00."

Parker appears to have been rather outspoken on the
subject. A letter which he wrote to Greene from Ithaca,
New York, dated October 16, 1837, tells of a visit he made
to the Geneva Synod the first week of October. Parker was
called upon to speak. Of this he wrote to Greene as follows:

I told them that I was confident with judicious and economical
management, the out-fit and expense of traveling through the States
need not exceed 1500 dollars—nor did I doubt from what I know of
the Country with reference to what the mission might do for themselves,—kindness of the H.B. Co.—that the mission might be sustained without additional expense for three years to come.

Parker felt that Whitman and Spalding were far too
free with their expenses. Greene and Hill, faced with stern
realities in the Board rooms, were very susceptible to such
suggestions. What would they have said if they had then
known that additional drafts already drawn for a total of
nearly sixteen hundred dollars were then on their way?

And what did Whitman and Spalding say to each other
when they read the circular of June 27, 1837, with the postscripts by Greene and Hill, and remembered that in addition
to the extra drafts sent in was the demand for 220 additional missionaries and goods in proportion? It would probably be even more interesting if we knew Greene's reaction
to that joint letter of April 21, 1838.

Spalding sent in a lengthy letter to Greene on September 10, 1838, in which he argued in favor of their policy to settle the Indians. He pointed out the necessity of the missionaries' becoming self-supporting, thus being independent of the Hudson's Bay Company. Therefore, the necessity of heavy initial expenses for livestock, mill machinery, and so forth. He ventured to assert that he and Whitman could make their stations self-supporting within ten years.

Parker's remark roiled him, and Spalding made some uncomplimentary statements about Parker's methods. Nor did he approve of the suggestion that they practice the methods of Brainard and Eliot. We can sense his indignation as he pushed his quill pen across the paper: "Did they take their wives hundreds of miles into the wilderness & then go off for supplies of provisions 100 or 200 miles & leave them perhaps with young babes for weeks alone among the savages, I have done this. . . . Did they eat horse beef, so do we."

Whitman wrote to Greene on October 30 and said: "I think Brother Spalding & myself will find no difficulty in getting on with $1000. between us & taking that as a guide the other Brethren intend to govern themselves by it & not exceed $500 a piece." The heavier initial expenses having already been met, both men felt they could live on the stipulated sum. Figures show that some years they did not draw the full amount allowed.

In May, 1839, Francis Ermatinger, of the Hudson's Bay Company, visited the Whitmans, and repeated some gossip common among the men of his company regarding Mr. Parker. This seems to have been the reason why Whitman wrote his letter of May 10 to Greene, which is the most caustic letter that we have, penned by him. Whitman rarely wrote long letters, yet here he wrote twenty-six hundred words. Whitman rarely engaged in criticism of others, yet this letter was biting in its judgment of Parker. He wrote:

As there has been many incorrect representations concerning the facilities for obtaining supplies, etc., in this country, I hope you will pardon me while I represent in some measure our situation and the policy by which we have been governed. And in the first place, as you introduce Rev. Samuel Parker as authority for stating we might have saved expense, I will venture to make a few statements respecting his policy in this country and in his general tour of exploration.

Whitman refuted Parker's criticism by telling of Parker's methods. "If Mr. Parker," he declared, "was to contract to take a party across the mountains and sustain them in this field, I think no one would be found satisfied with the arrangements he would make." In brief, both Whitman and Spalding were in full agreement as to their policy. Both felt the necessity of making their stations self-supporting, and both saw the importance of settling the Indians. Therefore, they felt fully justified in making the large initial expenditures.

According to Whitman's financial report, dated May 10, 1839, the mission kept its total expenses for that year down to £595.1.0, which was a little less than an average of £100.0.0 for each of the six families. Of this amount Whitman took £118.19.10 as his share, which was itemized as follows:

> Family supplies building materials Farming Da.,
> Provisions Medicines Indian Goods Trans-
> portation £67- 8-4
> One sixth of the General Expense for Black Smith
> Shop Mill Irons, Steel for ploughs, Hoes, Chains,
> etc. Bolt Cloth Hire of a Smith, Transportation........17-17-2
> Labour 21- 3-4
> Passage of an Hawaiian & wife from the Sandwich
> Isl. 12-10-0

Whitman's expenses included the cost of boarding the three clergymen of the re-enforcement and their wives during the winter of 1838-39.[10]

MEN IN THE KITCHEN

More difficult than even the financial problem was that of making the necessary personal adjustments with the members of the re-enforcement with whom the Whitmans were obliged to share their home. The primitive conditions under which they were living made it easy for personalities to rub against each other. The fact that these people were missionaries did not mean that they were perfect. They all had their faults, and these sometimes became most annoying to others. No better test of Christian forbearance has ever been devised than that of making two or more families live under the same roof and share the same kitchen. It is especially difficult when surrounded by peoples of another culture, race, or tongue, thus forcing them upon each other's society all the more. Modern-day missionaries on the foreign field will testify to this point.

During the beautiful days of the early fall, Narcissa did

---

10 *See* Appendix 2 for a summary of Whitman's expenses for each year of the mission.

not mind the crowded conditions so much. She was happy to have the new workers present. The men were outside most of the time. After Whitman's return from Vancouver, the men worked hard on the new adobe house and were able to finish a part of it before the winter started. Mr. and Mrs. Smith moved into it on December 4. The Walkers and the Eells stayed with the Whitmans. There was no other place for them to go.

When the winter rains came and the days grew cold and disagreeable, all naturally sought the warmth and comfort of Narcissa's kitchen. Mr. Walker smoked, much to Narcissa's disgust. Narcissa wrote to her sister Jane and mentioned her difficulties. She asked: " . . . now how do you think I have lived with such folks right in my kitchen for the whole winter?" [Letter 63.]

The other side of the picture is to be found in some of the Walker correspondence and in Mrs. Walker's diary. After Walker and Eells left for their exploring trip, Mr. Walker wrote back to his wife and gave the following good advice: "Remember that you are not Mistress of the house & you have nothing you can call your own that you are entirely dependent upon others."[11] Mrs. Walker in her diary mentions several little points of friction. She complained about the necessity of doing her washing in the afternoon. Another time she mentioned Mrs. Whitman's being "quite out with Mr. Smith" over the services of a hired man. Writing to her husband on October 8, Mrs. Walker declared that she felt more reconciled to her lot than did Mrs. Eells. "She does not seem to like Mrs. Whitman very well." She also stated:

Mr. Roger writes us that Dr. Gray is the same as ever & so far as we can discover is trying to prejudice Mr. Spalding against him as much as he can. I am glad we are going to the new station. Hope we shall be able to enjoy more peace than these the other stations have.

It is rather interesting to see Mrs. Walker refer to Gray as Dr. Gray. In looking through her diary, covering the trip out from the States, we find the title occurring several times. Gray induced the Board to list him as a "Physician and Mechanic" in the *Missionary Herald* for 1838. Whitman was irritated when he learned of it and wrote to Greene on October 22, 1839, saying in part: "I cannot conceive how you have been imposed upon to report him a physician. What can a man learn in sixteen weeks of public lectures (which

---

[11] Originals in Coll. Wn.

is barely all he can boast), to entitle him to that distinction."
Evidently Dr. Whitman corrected Mrs. Walker, for she
dropped the title "Dr." soon after their arrival and thereafter referred to Gray as "Mr. Gray."

One cannot help being impressed with the consistency
with which the various members of the mission referred to
each other in their letters and diaries. They never used one
another's first name. They always used the proper title with
the last name, although sometimes Dr. Whitman would be
called "Doct."

These letters and diaries throw considerable light upon
the Whitman home. Mrs. Eells, writing on October 4, 1838,
stated: "Mrs. W. & S. have obtained some earthern dishes
but think it is doubtful whether we can have any untill we
order them from England or the States."[12] Mrs. Walker
wrote in her diary of Mrs. Whitman's making soap, dipping
candles, washing, and ironing. Mrs. Walker's diary is most
revealing of the difficulties which developed in the crowded
household at Waiilatpu. On Friday, December 7, Mrs.
Walker gave birth to a son who was called Cyrus Hamlin.
He was the second boy born west of the Rockies of American
parentage, who lived to maturity.[13] Of course Mrs. Walker's
confinement meant extra work for Mrs. Whitman.

In view of all of these circumstances, we can read the
following extract from one of Narcissa's letters with a
sympathetic spirit:

> We need help very much, and those who will pray, too. In this we
> have been disappointed in our helpers last come, particularly the two
> Revs. who have gone to the Flatheads. They think it not good to have
> too many meetings, too many prayers, and that it is wrong and
> unseemly for a woman to pray where there are men, and plead the
> necessity for wine, tobacco, etc.; and now how do you think I have
> lived with such folks right in my kitchen for the whole winter? If you
> can imagine my feelings you will do more than I can to describe.
> [Letter 63.]

On the whole this is an unpleasant side of the Whitman
story, but in the light of later events it is too important to
be omitted. The friction which developed within the mission
had important consequences.

---

[12] Eells, *Father Eells*, p. 76. The Oregon Historical Society has a
piece of broken plate found at Waiilatpu after the massacre. It is white
with a blue border, presented by Nineveh Ford, a pioneer of 1843.

[13] The first boy born of American parents west of the Rockies who
lived to maturity was Joseph Beers, born Sept. 15, 1837. Cyrus Walker
died at Albany, Oregon, May 5, 1921.

TUCANNON

Spalding began some special meetings in December, 1838, which continued into the following January. His first two converts were influential chiefs whom he called Joseph and Timothy. In later years Joseph "returned back to Egypt," but Timothy was true to the end.[14] The response in these meetings was so encouraging that Spalding sent Lawyer, whom he and Whitman met at the rendezvous in the summer of 1836, to Waiilatpu for Whitman.

Whitman left for Lapwai on January 1, and arrived there on the 4th. He found some two thousand of the Nez Perces present, and taking the greatest interest in the religious services. Many of them showed genuine signs of repentance and conversion. Whitman admired Spalding's ability to use the language and became convinced of the necessity for him to spend more time in its study. He felt that this was almost impossible as long as he was burdened with so many duties at Waiilatpu.

Whitman and Spalding talked about the matter. The details of the conversation are lacking, but from subsequent events it appears that an arrangement was made with Timothy, whose people lived on the creek now called Alpowa,[15] about twelve miles west of the present city of Lewiston, Idaho. Timothy was a faithful soul and on many occasions showed his friendship for the white man. It was agreed that Whitman would return for his wife and child and that the three would then meet Timothy and his people on the Tucannon Creek, a tributary of the Snake on the south. Whitman would then have uninterrupted time for language study.

Whitman left Lapwai on January 10 and reached his home on the 15th. He found his wife most agreeable to the plan. Writing to her sister Jane, she declared: "He had no difficulty to persuade me to accompany him, for I was nearly exhausted, both in body and mind, in the labour and care of our numerous family."

Preparations were made at once to leave, and on Tuesday, January 22, 1839, the Whitman family started on its journey of fifty miles or more to the Tucannon. Alice Clarissa was

---

[14] McBeth, *The Nez Perces Since Lewis and Clark*, p. 63.

[15] Alpowa is a derivative of the Nez Perce word for "sabbath." Timothy named his village Alpowa because his people kept the Sabbath. Today the bridge spanning the creek is dedicated to Timothy.

then nearly two years old. Mr. and Mrs. Eells, Margaret McKay, and Mrs. Walker accompanied them for about three miles on their journey. The Whitmans were glad for the vacation, and the following extract from Mrs. Walker's diary describes her feeling: "Mrs. W. has dealt so largely in powder and balls of late that perhaps her absence will not detract much from our happiness."

The weather was mild, even quite warm for that time of the year. After a pleasant journey of three days, the Whitmans encamped among the Nez Perces on the Tucannon. Soon afterwards the weather turned cold, and snow fell. The Whitmans lived in a tent which Marcus tried to make comfortable by building a fire at its entrance. For a time the smoke affected Alice's eyes. Marcus then built a small lodge over the fire to draw off the smoke.

Sunday, January 27, was an interesting day. Narcissa gave the following description of one of the services:

At midday I was present. Husband talked to them of the parable of the rich man and Lazarus; all listened with eager attention. After prayer and singing, an opportunity was given for those who had heavy hearts under a sense of sin, and only those, to speak if they wished it. For a few moments all sat in silence; soon a prominent and intelligent man named Timothy broke the silence with sobs weeping. He arose, spoke of his great wickedness, and how very black his heart was; how weak and insufficient he was of himself to effect his own salvation; that his only dependence was in the blood of Christ to make him clean and save his soul from sin and hell. He was followed by a brother, who spoke much to the same effect. Next came the wives of the first and of the second, who seemed to manifest deep feelings.

Several others followed; one in particular, while confessing her sins, her tears fell to the ground so copiously that I was reminded of the weeping "Mary who washed her Saviour's feet with her tears." All manifested much deep feeling; some in loud sobs and tears; others in anxious and solemn countenance. You can better imagine my feelings than I can describe them on witnessing such a scene in heathen lands. They had but recently come from the meeting at Brother Spalding's. [Letter 63.]

Narcissa liked the Nez Perces. She wrote that they were "not so hardened in sin; or, rather, they were not so proud a people as our people, the Wieletpoos." It was with great thankfulness of heart that Marcus and Narcissa witnessed the first fruits of their mission labors among the natives. That evening Narcissa sat in the door of her tent and wrote the following to her sister Jane:

O, my dear Jane, could you see us here this beautiful eve, the full moon shining in all her splendor, clear, yet freezing cold, my little one sleeping by my side, husband at worship with the people within hearing, and I sitting in the "door of the tent" writing, with my usual clothing except a shawl, and handkerchief on my head, and before me a large comfortable fire in the open air. Do you think we suffer? No, dear Jane; I have not realized so much enjoyment for a long time as I have since I have been here. [Letter 63.]

The Whitmans stayed at Tucannon into the third week and returned to Waiilatpu on Saturday, February 9. Mrs. Walker noted their return in her diary and added: "Adieu to peace and order."

MISSION BUSINESS

On Monday, February 11, Walker and Smith left for Lapwai. Mrs. Walker's letters and diary speak of the unhappy situation in the Whitman home. On February 12, she wrote to her husband, saying in part:

Mrs. W. presented herself at table this morning which if I am not silly to mention it is spread without a cloth. I was so provoked at this fresh mark of disrespect as I deem it that I was half tempted not to eat. It was true she had no brown cloth ironed but she has plenty white ones. If she does not begin to put away her bad heart now I am resolved to call her to account & if I have wronged her know what my offense is. Tomorrow is our maternal meeting & if she wears as much of Cain's countenance as usual I do not think I will unite with her in prayer.

That evening Mrs. Whitman in great agitation went to Mrs. Walker and sought a reconciliation. It appears that Mrs. Whitman felt that Mrs. Walker had been unappreciative of things done for her. The frank heart-to-heart talk eased much of the tension, yet Mrs. Whitman remained in her room most of the remainder of the week. Mrs. Walker wrote a full account of what took place in her letter of February 17 to her husband.[16]

In the meantime the men of the mission who had gathered at Lapwai found that since there were so many differences of opinion on important points, it was best to call a special meeting of the mission to settle them. Consequently a messenger was sent to Waiilatpu, requesting the presence at Lapwai of Whitman and Eells. When this messenger reached Waiilatpu, Mrs. Whitman decided to accompany her husband. They left for Lapwai on February 22. Alice Clarissa was taken along. It was her second visit to Lapwai.

Spalding's diary throws considerable light upon the difficulties which then existed. He speaks of the ill feeling existing between Mrs. Whitman and Mrs. Gray. Soon after the arrival of the re-enforcements, Mr. Gray, without his

---

[16] Coll. Wn.

wife's knowledge or consent, let it be known that they were expecting an addition to the family. According to Spalding, Mrs. Gray blamed Mrs. Whitman for communicating the fact to others. Mrs. Gray seemed to think that it was another case of a doctor's wife telling secrets. "A very little matter," wrote Spalding, "to cause such a difficulty."[17]

It is rather interesting to note how Mrs. Whitman became a focal point of difficulty during those months following the arrival of the re-enforcements. We happen to have source material to show how Mrs. Walker and Mrs. Gray felt toward her. If similar material were available, perhaps we would learn that Mrs. Eells and Mrs. Smith felt the same. On several occasions it appears that Mrs. Whitman inspired her husband to speak up in defense of what she thought were their rights.

The men gathered in their mission meeting on February 22. Spalding was again the Moderator, and Walker was the Scribe. Spalding was reproved for marrying a white man to a Nez Perce woman. Spalding's defense was that since the two were already living together, he thought a marriage service would help. A difficulty which had arisen between Whitman and Smith had to be settled. Spalding wrote to Greene on October 15, 1842, of this incident as follows:

Mr. Smith declared that he would leave the Mission rather than be connected with Dr. Whitman, and when it was found impossible to associate the two together Dr. Whitman consented to leave the station to Mr. Smith and commence a new one on the Tukana, where he would be central as physician.

There was a long debate on this point. Spalding was in favor of Dr. Whitman's being more centrally located. Smith wanted to move to Kamiah, about sixty miles up the Clearwater from Lapwai, but this proposal was rejected. Finally it was decided to have the Smiths take over the Waiilatpu station, while the Whitmans would move to the Tucannon, or to the Palouse, a stream which puts into the Snake from the north. Later Mrs. Whitman was of the opinion that Spalding was largely responsible for this vote. She wrote to her father on October 10, 1840, and said: "Every mind in the mission that he has had access to, he has tried to prejudice against us, and did succeed for a while, which was the cause of our being voted to remove and form a new station."

The mission also voted to locate the printing press at

---

[17] Spalding's diary, unpublished, is in Coll. W.

Lapwai when it should come. Perhaps the fact that Spalding was acquainted with the printing trade influenced this decision. The mission closed its meeting on Tuesday, February 26. Outwardly it appeared that all problems had been solved, but later events proved that this was not the case.

Walker and Eells returned to Waiilatpu as soon as they could and began making arrangements to leave for Tshimakain. Dr. Whitman was detained at Lapwai. Since he desired Spalding to accompany him in searching for a new location, it was agreed that Mrs. Whitman should remain with the Spaldings while he would return to Waiilatpu. They fixed upon a meeting place for Thursday, March 7, and then Whitman hurried back to Waiilatpu.

He reached his home about sunrise on March 5. Mr. and Mrs. Walker and their son Cyrus and Mr. and Mrs. Eells left at noon that day for their new station. Mrs. Walker wrote for that day in her diary. "Dr. W. accompanied us to our first encampment, about five miles. We talked with him all that time would allow and he left us feeling much better than when he came home." Dr. Whitman was troubled over the lack of harmony which existed.

Dr. Whitman met his wife and the Spaldings as they had agreed. On the 8th, the Walker-Eells party arrived. The four men discussed the advisability of having the Whitmans move.[18] It seems evident that there was a lack of enthusiasm on the subject. The next day Whitman and Spalding explored the region about the mouth of the Palouse but found it unfavorable. They spent Sunday with the Indians, and on Monday the Spaldings started back to Lapwai, leaving Dr. Whitman undecided.

On the 23rd of the month we find Spalding writing in his diary that Whitman and Smith had arrived at his station. He speaks of the "long consultation" which was held. They left again on the 25th. On April 1, Spalding noted that the Whitmans had written of their decision to remain at Waiilatpu. "Everything seems to be settled," wrote Spalding. "Hope it will remain so and that they may work together."

April was seedtime, and the men in all of the stations were busy with farmwork. On the 24th, the Spaldings

---

[18] Mrs. Walker's diary for Sat., March 9: "Dr. W. and wife and Mr. Spaulding with the babes came to meet us at our crossing place. Had not a remarkably pleasant interview with them. Parted without a social prayer."

started for Waiilatpu to meet Mr. and Mrs. E. O. Hall, who were bringing the printing press and equipment from the Sandwich Islands. To Spalding's joy he found that Whitman and Smith had settled their difficulties and were on good terms. Spalding wrote in his diary: "Doubtless they have all prayed more & talked less. May the Lord continue this peace." The Smiths were then planning to spend the summer in Lawyer's country at Kamiah. Lawyer was very serviceable as a teacher, and Smith soon came to have the best mastery of the language of any in the mission. He was an able scholar.

The Halls arrived at Walla Walla on April 29. Mrs. Hall was an invalid, being afflicted with a spinal irritation which left her almost helpless. She could sit up only a little. It was thought that the trip would be beneficial to her health, although we are somewhat amazed to think that Mr. Hall would take an invalid wife on such a long and difficult journey. Narcissa mentioned in her letter of May 17 to Jane, that Mrs. Hall "appears just like L. Linsley."[19]

The members of the Oregon mission were happy over the arrival of the press. The Spalding party with the press reached Lapwai on May 13. There it remained until 1846, when it was taken to The Dalles. After the Whitman Massacre it was taken to the home of the Rev. J. S. Griffin near Hillsboro, Oregon, and used to print the eight numbers of an early Oregon newspaper called the *Oregon American and Evangelical Unionist*.[20] The press is now on display in the rooms of the Oregon Historical Society.

ALICE CLARISSA WHITMAN

On March 14, 1838, Narcissa wrote to her parents, in which letter we find this sentence: "Mother will see from the date of this letter and remember with interest the events of it, thirty years previous, as I do but one year ago to-day." Alice was then one year old. What a joy she was to her mother! Narcissa reported that the little girl was able to say a number of words, including "Papa," "Mamma,"

---

[19] Levina Linsley to whom Spalding was once engaged.

[20] According to Edward Eberstadt, of New York, there were nine numbers printed on this press. For a time the press was stored in Griffin's barn and moved to Portland about 1888. Dr. E. E. Hubert, of Portland, examined the wood base of the press for me. The two large blocks to which the metal parts are fastened are white oak. The legs and supporting framework are Douglas fir. No pieces of wood in it originated either in Hawaii or Idaho.

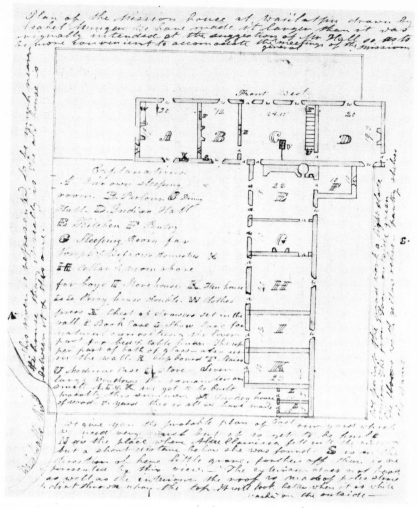

GROUND FLOOR PLAN OF THE WHITMAN HOME AT WAIILATPU.
Sent by Mrs. Whitman to her mother in her letter of May 2, 1840. Original in Coll. O. An imperfect copy appeared in *T.O.P.A.*, 1891, p. 137. The plan was drawn by Asahel Munger. Mrs. Whitman wrote the explanation. One of the Sager girls called it a "large white house." Clark, *Pioneer Days*, Vol. 2, p. 508.

HENRY HARMON SPALDING.
With the Bible and the Hoe.

It is believed that this is the earliest of a number of Spalding photographs and that this is the first time this picture has been published. On April 21, 1838, Spalding wrote to the American Board: "... while we point them with one hand to the Lamb of God which taketh away the sins of the world, we believe it to be equally our duty to point with the other to the hoe, as the means of saving their famishing bodies from an untimely grave & furnishing the means of subsistence to future generations." This photograph demonstrates Spalding's philosophy of his missionary work.

By courtesy of Pacific University, Forest Grove, Oregon.

"Sarah," and "pussy." She was also learning to walk. Narcissa wrote:

She is as large and larger than some of the native children of two years old. Her strength, size and activity surprises the Indians very much. They think it is owing to theirs being laced on their te-cashes (as they call the board they use for them), motionless night and day, that makes their children so weak and small when compared with her.

On April 11, Narcissa wrote again to her parents and again spoke of her child. "My Clarissa is my own little companion from day to day, and dear daughter." Again, "She is her mothers constant companion, & appears to be very lonely if she is out of her sight but for few moments. . . . Dear child, she is a great solace & comfort to her mother in her lonely hours & God grant she may live still to continue so."[21] In this letter Narcissa ordered flannel dresses, shoes, and some ready-made clothing for her daughter. She also requested that "the name of Alice Clarissa Whitman, born Wieletpoo, O. Territory, March 14, 1837, be placed in father's family Bible."

The letters which Narcissa sent to her loved ones in the fall of 1838 bear frequent reference to little Alice. The following is typical:

Yes, Jane, you cannot know how much of a comfort our little daughter, Alice Clarissa, is to her father and mother. O, how many melancholy hours she has saved me, while living here alone so long, especially when her father is gone for many days together. I wish most sincerely that her aunts could see her, for surely they would love her as well as her parents. She is now eighteen months old, very large, and remarkably healthy. She is a great talker. Causes her mother many steps and much anxiety. She is just beginning to sing with us in our family worship. The moment singing commences, if she is not in her mother's arms, she comes to me immediately and wishes me to take her, especially if it is a Nez Perces hymn that we are singing. We have but three or four of them, and sing them every day, and Alice has become so familiar with them that she is repeating some part of them most of the time. Situated as I am, I know not how I shall succeed in training her as I ought. So many Indians and children are constantly in and about our house, and recently I discover her much inclined to imitate and talk with them, or they with her. It makes them very much pleased to think she is going to speak their language so readily. They appear to love her much. [Letter 51.]

As Narcissa was writing about an eleven-year-old boy by the name of Mungo Mevway,[22] who was living with them,

---

[21] From Whitman Letter 46. This was printed in *T.O.P.A.*, 1891, but at least a thousand words were omitted. The quotation above is from the part not published.

[22] Mungo Mevway is mentioned in Whitman Letter 54. His mother was a native and his father a Hawaiian. He had been living with the Whitmans for about a year.

Alice interrupted and laid a soiled childish hand upon the letter paper. "You see, Jane," wrote Narcissa, "Alice has come and laid her dirty hands on this paper, and given it a fine mark. I send it as it is, so that you may have some of her doings to look at, and realize, perhaps, there is such a child in existence." The originals of most of the Whitman letters published in the *Transactions of the Oregon Pioneer Association* are in the archives of the Oregon Historical Society. But when search was made for the original of this letter to see the handprint of Alice Clarissa Whitman, it was discovered that the original was missing.

Judging from a proud mother's letters, Alice was unusually bright. She knew some Bible verses when she was but two years old and was able to repeat them at family worship. Frequently she called for the hymns which were to be sung. Narcissa spent many an hour with the little girl, talking about all of her grandparents, aunts, uncles, and cousins far away in the States. The bond which binds parent to child is always strong in normal, healthy individuals, but it is especially so when circumstances deny either or both the inspiration of suitable companions. In lonely hours a mother will hungrily monopolize the child's attention; so was it with Narcissa and little Alice. An appreciation of this situation will aid us in understanding the poignancy of sorrow which came to Narcissa on Sunday, June 23, 1839.

As has been mentioned, the Walla Walla River flowed a few rods from the Whitman home. Marcus and Narcissa were aware of the danger of the stream as they saw their little girl learning to walk and watched her active feet carry her about the house and dooryard. On the Friday before the tragedy, the Doctor and his wife were working in their vegetable garden with Alice trying in her baby ways to be of assistance. Dr. Whitman happened to pull up a radish which Alice picked up and ran away with. Her parents supposed that she had gone to the house and when they returned they were startled to find that she was not there. They hurried to the stream, where they found the little girl washing the radish in the water.

Narcissa once wrote that in order to frighten the child, her father had once put her into the water. "We had lost," wrote Narcissa, "that feeling of anxiety for her in a measure on its account." [Letter 64.] Marcus and Narcissa were "horror-stricken," to use Narcissa's term, to find the child by the stream. They both talked to her of the danger of the stream. Some weeks before, Dr. Whitman had felt obliged to drown a sick dog, called Boxer, with which Alice had often played. Alice had witnessed the event, so that evening after her mother had repeated the warning, the child said: "Alice fall in water, Alice she die like Boxer—mamma have no Alice." Narcissa clasped the child to her breast as she thought of the dreaded possibility, and repeated the warning. [Letter 67.]

On Sunday morning, June 23, Narcissa awakened her daughter with a kiss. The child slowly opened her eyes, and then, seeing her mother, stretched up her pudgy arms. Narcissa bent over and permitted the arms to encircle her neck. Alice gave her mother a long kiss. Narcissa then hurried to prepare a bath, while Alice objected. Later a sorrowing mother felt that the objection was due to a change of routine, for the bath usually came on Saturday.

That morning Alice selected "Rock of Ages" to be sung at family worship. They sang the first verse and then Alice said: "Mamma, should my tears forever flow?" It was her way of calling for the second verse. That noon the Whitmans held worship for the Indians. Because the main Indian village had moved, only four or five were present. The Whitmans invited them into the house, and "Rock of Ages" was sung again. That was the last time they heard Alice sing.

After the worship Dr. Whitman took her out into the garden and cut for her a stalk of rhubarb, of which she was very fond. He then returned to the house and began reading. Narcissa was likewise reading. For a time Alice amused herself with the stalk of rhubarb. About two-thirty Margaret McKay set the table preparatory for their main Sunday meal. Later Narcissa had a dim recollection that Alice said: "Mama, supper is almost ready; let Alice get some water." [Letter 68.] She went to the table and got two cups, hers and Margaret's, and left the house. "This was like a shadow that passed across my mind," wrote Narcissa, "[it] passed away and made no impression."

In a few minutes Narcissa realized that the child was gone and asked Margaret to look for her. Margaret went out, and not being able to find the child, went to the garden for some vegetables instead of returning to report her failure. Mungo also went out to look. Soon he returned and said that he saw two cups in the river. "How did they come there?" asked Narcissa. "Let them be," said Marcus, "and get them out to-morrow because of the Sabbath." But Narcissa again asked as to how they got there. Marcus then said: "I suppose Alice put them there." He laid aside his book and went out to get a pole to retrieve the cups. Mrs. Whitman, in the meantime, walked around the house looking for the child. She saw Margaret with some radishes going to the river to wash them, but the child was not with her. Then a flash of fear passed through Narcissa's mind, and she ran for the river. Marcus was then alarmed. Some of the Indians who had been with them but a little before in the worship service joined in the search.

Marcus and Narcissa ran down the bank, passed the point where some roots of a tree held the body under water, but they knew nothing of that. Frantically they retraced their steps. The Indians plunged into the stream, but at first all entered below the spot where the body was found. As the fruitless search continued, all realized that if she were in the water, it was too late to hope to resuscitate her. Finally, with leaden hearts Marcus and Narcissa started to return to the house, hoping that the child might be found elsewhere. On the way, Narcissa paused to look back. She saw an old Indian preparing to enter the river at the point where the cups were found. She waited and saw him go down with the current. He passed the point opposite them, and just a little below, he found the body in the roots of a tree. "She is found," he shouted.

Narcissa ran, eager to clasp the dripping body to her breast, but Marcus got there first. Hurriedly and with all the skill known, the doctor worked over the limp body. Finally they admitted the dreaded reality—the child was dead. Her short life on earth of two years, three months, and nine days was over. With a fine Christian spirit, Narcissa said: "Lord, it is right; it is right; she is not mine, but thine; she has only been lent to me for a little season, and now, dearest Saviour, thou hast the best right to her; 'Thy will be done,' not mine." [Letter 68.]

A messenger was sent at once to notify the Spaldings and those with them at Lapwai. The messenger made the 120-mile trip in 25 hours. E. O. Hall, the printer, started at once for Waiilatpu on horseback. He rode all night and made the trip in one hour less time than had the messenger. Spalding was then recovering from some injury to his ribs which made it impossible for him to go so far on horseback. Consequently he, his wife, and their little daughter left Lapwai on Monday evening by canoe. They reached Fort Walla Walla, Wednesday evening at eight o'clock and the next morning rode out to Waiilatpu, arriving there about nine or ten o'clock in the morning.

Narcissa prepared a shroud for the body, while her husband prepared the rude coffin.[23] A grave was dug in the plain, a little to the north of the new T-shaped mission house, and around it a picket fence was later built.[24] The funeral service was held on Thursday afternoon, June 26. Mr. Spalding took the words found in II Kings 4:26 for his text: "Is it well with thee? is it well with thy husband? is it well with the child?" Only a few were present. There were the parents and the members of their household, the Spaldings, Mr. Hall, Mr. Pambrun, and a few Indians.

The great sorrow which came to the Whitmans, in which the Spaldings sincerely sympathized, was the cause of bringing about a better feeling between the two couples. It appears that Mrs. Whitman had blamed Spalding for the vote of the mission which asked them to move from Waiilatpu. The old antipathy which existed between the two colored not only her attitude toward Spalding, but also her husband's. According to a letter written by Whitman to Greene on October 15, 1840, they were actually planning to leave the mission. Whitman wrote: " . . . so strong was this feeling that I should have left previous to the convening of the Mission in 1839 had not the Providence of God arrested me in my deliberate determination to do so, by taking away our dear child in so sudden a manner by drowning."

Mrs. Whitman in her letter of October 10, 1840, made reference to the same determination. She wrote:

He [i.e., Whitman] felt as if he must leave the mission, and no doubt would have done it, had not the Lord removed from us our beloved child. This affliction softened his feelings and made him willing to suffer the will of the Lord, although we felt that we were suffering wrongfully. The death of our babe had a great affect upon all in the mission; it softened their hearts toward us, even Mr. S's for a season. I never had any difficulty with his wife. . . .

Gray also mentioned the reconciliation which took place between Spalding and Whitman in his letter to Greene of

---

[23] There is a tradition that Mrs. Whitman used her "gray silk wedding dress" to line the coffin or to make the shroud. Comment has already been made upon the unlikeliness of Mrs. Whitman's owning a gray silk dress. It is most probable that she used some other dress for this purpose.

[24] Hines, *History Oregon Mission*, p. 176.

October 14, 1840. In the fragment of Whitman's letter of June 30, 1839, he said: "I had concluded to take the consequences of leaving the mission." In that letter he speaks of "reading Henry on Meekness."[25]

The Spaldings remained at Waiilatpu until July 4, when they started for Lapwai. They persuaded the Whitmans to return with them. Several matters, including that of deciding upon a proper alphabet, needed the combined wisdom of the men working in the Nez Perce language. So the Whitmans decided to go. The party reached Lapwai on Saturday, July 6.

On the Monday following, the Whitmans, Spalding, and Hall made the sixty-mile trip to Kamiah to see the Smiths. They stayed there two days while the men settled the alphabet question. The alphabet which Spalding had devised had proved too cumbersome, and the men agreed that the Pickering alphabet was better adapted to their needs.[26] This matter was formally decided to the satisfaction of all by vote of the mission in September of that year.

The Whitmans spent Sunday, July 14, at Lapwai and on the following Tuesday started back to their lonesome home. They reached their destination on Friday morning. That day word came from Tshimakain that Mrs. Eells was seriously ill. Her husband even despaired of her life and begged Dr. Whitman to go at once. Dr. Whitman was reluctant to leave his wife alone, yet duty called, and Mrs. Whitman had to pay the price of being a doctor's wife. "It was then," wrote Narcissa, "that I fully realized the full reality of my bereavement." [Letter 68.] On April 30, 1840, in a letter to her father, she said: "The lovely tender plant which our Heavenly Father gave us to rear for Him He has transplanted to His own Paradise above. It is almost a year since He took her, yet our hearts do not cease to bleed at the fond recollection of her innocent smiles and fond caresses."

The long distance which separated Waiilatpu from loved ones in the East, with the consequent length of time required for a letter to be sent and its answer received, was a cause of the frequent freshening of the Whitmans' sorrow. While the body still remained unburied, Narcissa wrote to Mrs. H. K. W. Perkins, the wife of one of the Methodist missionaries recently arrived at The Dalles. Mrs. Perkins had

---

25 *See* notes of Myron Eells in Coll. W.

26 Drury, *Spalding*, p. 225, gives a fuller account of the alphabet question.

written, making inquiries about the child, but before Narcissa could answer, the child was dead.

Then finally in the fall of 1839 letters came from their loved ones with congratulations; another year passed, and the dresses and shoes ordered by Narcissa in 1838 arrived; and still another year was to elapse before condolences arrived. The child was then in her grave for more than two years. No wonder it was hard for Narcissa to forget, when each of these letters served to open anew the great sorrow.

Dr. Whitman returned from Tshimakain on Saturday, July 27, and Mr. Walker came with him. During the third week in August, the Whitmans were agreeably surprised when William Geiger, of Angelica, suddenly appeared at their station. With him was a Mr. Johnson, who was on an exploring expedition of some kind. They were the first of a long line to stream by the Whitman station on their way to the Lower Columbia country. The Whitmans had received no letters from their home after those which arrived on July 11, 1838, more than a year previous. We can imagine the eagerness with which they questioned Geiger. After a short stay their visitors continued their journey to the Willamette.

On Sunday, August 25, little Eliza Spalding got an obstruction in her throat which greatly alarmed her parents. The next day an emergency call was sent to Whitman. By riding all night after receiving word, Dr. Whitman was able to reach Lapwai on the 28th. He found Eliza recovered. Since the annual mission meeting was scheduled for Lapwai during the early part of September, Dr. Whitman had arranged for his wife to follow with Mr. Walker before he left Waiilatpu.

While waiting for her coming, Dr. Whitman made himself useful at Lapwai. Spalding recorded in his diary that on August 30, the doctor performed an operation on an "old mare."

That evening Dr. Whitman expected Narcissa to arrive. With little Eliza Spalding mounted on his horse with him, the doctor set out to meet his wife. They rode down the trail on the south side of the Clearwater. His wife and her party happened to go up the north side, so the two missed each other. Mrs. Whitman reached Lapwai at sunset, while the doctor and Eliza did not return until after dark. Is it hard to guess some of Whitman's thoughts as he rode the trail with little Eliza Spalding?

CHAPTER ELEVEN

THAT MAN SPALDING

1839-1840

THE ANNUAL meeting of the Oregon mission of the American Board for 1839 was opened in Spalding's home at Lapwai on Monday, September 2. Whitman, Spalding, Gray, and Smith were present. Walker and Eells were absent. Hall, a member of the Sandwich Islands mission, was present and was invited to sit as a corresponding member. Rogers joined the group on the 4th when he returned from the buffalo country. Spalding was again elected Moderator, with Smith as Scribe.

The mission reversed two decisions made the preceding February. In the first place Whitman was to remain at Waiilatpu. Spalding expressed his feelings in his diary. "I do not approve of this." He felt that Whitman should be more centrally located.

Gray was eager to have a station of his own. After considerable discussion he was given permission to explore for a site. Again Spalding disapproved. This particular vote of the mission caused much trouble, for Gray interpreted it to mean that he was authorized to establish another station. As soon as possible after the meeting closed on the 5th, the Grays started on their tour of exploration. Mrs. Walker in her diary speaks of the Grays' being at Tshimakain on September 16-18. After being away from Lapwai for more than a month, they returned on October 18 and informed Spalding that they had selected a site "about a day above Walla Walla on a small stream putting in from the S.W."[1]

Gray began to make immediate preparations to move, and Spalding with characteristic bluntness told him that the mission had not authorized him to move but merely to explore for a site. The argument waxed warm. Gray was thoroughly discouraged and resented what he thought was his inferior status in the mission. Consequently he left for Fort Vancouver on October 21 with the hope of finding other employment in the Hudson's Bay Company. This he was unable to do because he could not produce satisfactory evidence

---

[1] Spalding diary.

that his withdrawal from the mission met the approval of his associates.[2] It seems quite clear that Gray's subsequent animosity to the company can be traced to this event.

Disappointed in his endeavors to find employment elsewhere, Gray returned to Fort Walla Walla and sent word to his wife at Lapwai to join him. Mrs. Gray with her seven-month-old baby left on November 11 with only an Indian escort. Gray was thoroughly provoked with Spalding and decided to remain at Fort Walla Walla until another meeting of the mission could be called to reconsider his case.

During Gray's absence from Lapwai, Spalding had time to write to Walker and Eells about the matter and learned from them that they, too, felt it was unwise for Gray to start a new station.

Mrs. Spalding was expected to give birth to a child about the middle of November. Dr. Whitman went up to attend her. He reached the north bank of the Clearwater opposite Spalding's home on Thursday night, November 14. Not being able to attract attention and not wishing to swim the river, Whitman rolled out his blankets on the sandy beach, which is still at that point, and spent the night.

On Sunday, November 17, Whitman was present when Spalding baptized and received into the membership of the First Church of Oregon three new members. They were James Conner, the mountain man assisting Spalding at Lapwai, and two influential chiefs, to whom Spalding gave the names of Joseph and Timothy. Before receiving the two Indians as members, Spalding first performed the Christian marriage service for each of them. After their reception into full membership, the sacrament of the Lord's Supper was observed, when for the first time the missionaries had fellowship in that sacred rite with Indians.

Spalding had time to discuss the Gray affair with Whitman. Gray had demanded that another mission meeting be called to settle his status. Both Whitman and Spalding felt that this was impractical at that time because of the cost and trouble involved. They wrote a joint letter on November 25 to Gray, pointing out these facts, and "respectfully requested" him to proceed immediately to Waiilatpu, where Dr. Whitman was to provide him with living quarters and where he was to assist in the erection of buildings and do such other mechanical work "as Doct Whitman shall direct."

---

[2] Marshall, *Acquisition of Oregon*, Vol. 2, p. 101.

On November 24, Mrs. Spalding gave birth to a son, who was called Henry Hart Spalding. Whitman started back to Waiilatpu on November 26, which happened to be Spalding's thirty-sixth birthday.

Gray was infuriated when he received the joint letter from Whitman and Spalding. He replied on December 2, saying:

In regard to your orders or request, I have only to say; Gentlemen, I have not yet nor shall I put myself under the control of any Committee of our Mission to answer individual demands any further than labor properly coming under the care and control of the Mission. The proposition to which you refer was gratuitous and does not relate to Doct Whitman in any way except that he is bound equally with myself to assist the Ordained Ministers (not Doct Whitman) in building and furnishing their permanent houses. . . . I protest against your right as a Committee of this Mission to order me to obey the private order or direction of any member of this Mission, or any body else in any way, shape, or manner.[3]

Whitman wrote to Walker from Waiilatpu on December 3 in regard to the Gray affair, saying in part:

What is to be the course of Mr. Gray, I know not. He is with his family at Walla Walla. I invited him here & offered to arrange a house for him. Mr. Spalding and myself as the only way to make known the views of the mission wrote to him as the Credential Committee of the mission requesting him to fulfill his resolution to build by coming to Waiilatpu to assist to build a school house and at the same time laid before him the views of the mission as to his locating but he objected to all we propose either as individual & denies all right on our part as Committee. [Letter 72.]

While Gray was embittered against Spalding, yet he was more aroused over the "request" to go to Waiilatpu. So he was obliged to return with his family to Lapwai, where he arrived on December 28, very much out of humor at the turn of events. He sulked through the rest of the winter of 1839-40, criticizing the constructive efforts Spalding was making and in other ways making trouble.

THE INDEPENDENT MISSIONARIES

Another source of perplexity and difficulty arose with the arrival in the fall of 1839 of the independent missionaries. On the day the mission meeting opened at Lapwai, a messenger arrived from Walla Walla with letters from David Greene which brought the news that missionaries independent of any board or church organization were to go to Oregon that year.

---

[3] Copy, Coll. O.

Following the mission meeting, the Halls returned with the Whitmans to Waiilatpu. It was time for the Halls to return to Hawaii, but Mrs. Hall, an invalid, was pregnant, and it was thought best for them to remain at Waiilatpu, where they could be near Dr. Whitman. Because of Mrs. Hall's condition, the Whitmans and the Halls went down the Clearwater and the Snake by canoe rather than attempt the overland trip. They reached Fort Walla Walla at noon on Monday, September 9, where they met Mr. and Mrs. Asahel Munger, who had arrived together with the Rev. and Mrs. J. S. Griffin as independent missionaries. The Griffins had already left for Lapwai, Mr. Griffin being an old friend of Mr. Spalding.

Griffin had started for Oregon with the Mungers as a single man, but while passing through St. Louis had met, courted, and married Desired C. Smith. According to an entry in the Griffin family Bible, they were married by "Rev. Mr. Braybrook in St. Louis, Mo. on the 10th of April, 1839, & at once left on our way across the continent."[4]

Munger was a carpenter and joiner from Lockport, New York. He was one of the first Oberlin colonists of 1833. Munger had sought the support of the Oberlin Congregational church for his proposed Oregon mission, but, according to the following record in the church minutes, this support was withheld:

Resolved, that under *present circumstances* the church can not feel justified in recommending to Br & Sister Munger to embark in their proposed missionary expedition.[5]

The Mungers were not discourged by this rebuff and secured the support of a Congregational Association of North Litchfield, Connecticut. As will be related later, Munger became insane in Oregon. Perhaps the Oberlin church was aware of some instability on Munger's part at the time it refused to assist him in his enterprise.

The two couples crossed the country in somewhat the same manner as had the missionaries of the American Board.[6] Upon their arrival at Fort Walla Walla, they soon realized

---

[4] Griffin family Bible is at Pacific University, Forest Grove, Ore. Mrs. Griffin died Sept. 22, 1884, in her eightieth year. J. S. Griffin was remarried on Oct. 4, 1887, to Mrs. Sina Kenyon. On May 15, 1853, H. H. Spalding was remarried to Rachel J. Smith, a sister of the first Mrs. J. S. Griffin.

[5] Information given by Prof. Robert S. Fletcher from the MS. of his book, *Oberlin, 1833-1866*.

[6] Munger's diary was published in *O.H.Q.*, 1907, pp. 387-405.

the difficulties of their situation. It was absolutely necessary for them to find employment, for they had virtually no financial resources of their own. The Hudson's Bay Company had no place for them, so they turned to the missionaries of the American Board, who suddenly found themselves faced with the problem as to what they should do with their uninvited guests.

Mr. and Mrs. Griffin reached Lapwai on September 9. Spalding found there was nothing to do but to hire Griffin, who proved to be a faithful and agreeable worker. The Griffins spent the winter of 1839-40 at Lapwai. They tried to start a mission at Fort Boise in the spring of 1840 but were unsuccessful. They then moved to the Willamette Valley.[7]

On the morning of September 10, Whitman entered into a bargain with Munger by which Whitman agreed to furnish board and room for the two and pay eight dollars a month until March 1, 1840. The Mungers then accompanied the Whitmans and the Halls to Waiilatpu. Mrs. Hall had to be carried from Fort Walla Walla to the mission station in a hammock. [Letter 68.]

Munger was a skilled workman, and his services were, therefore, greatly appreciated by the Whitmans. Within a month he had finished a room in the new mission house for the Halls. Writing on April 30, Narcissa said: "A part of the house is nearly finished and will be a very comfortable and clean house to what this has been." And a little later she wrote again: "It seems as if the Lord's hand was in it in sending Mr. and Mrs. Munger here just at this time, and I know not how to feel grateful enough." [Letter 76.] The Halls remained until March 1, 1840, and then they returned to the Sandwich Islands.

The pathetic and straitened circumstances in which the independent missionaries found themselves are revealed in a letter written by Mrs. A. B. Smith from Kamiah to Mrs. Walker and Mrs. Eells. The letter is dated December 18, 1839, and therein we read:

What is best for us to do about giving to Mrs. Griffin? What they can do I know not, or how they can get things to make them comfortable I know not, unless some one gives them. I would give her with all my heart if it is right. Mr. Smith, Mr. Hall & others say that they have come in opposition to the Amr. Board & ought not to be assisted. But the poor woman has come without a sheet or pillow case, & with

---

[7] Drury, *Spalding*, p. 239, gives more details.

little bedding & with no crockery. These things they must have & how they will get them I don't know.

Mrs. Spalding while I was there gave her three *broken plates* for her to use (?) & enough wide striped cotton to make a pair of sheets. If husband will consent I shall give her a pair of sheets. She has plenty of clothing probably more dresses than *I* shall have after mine get here. She has two pretty silk dresses several muslin & fine calico, & two or three pieces unmade. She has more neck dresses than she will ever need & all *very pretty*. Mr. G. has enough But *sheets pillow cases paper & crockery* they need. Would you give them Shall you do it?[8]

This letter indicates the differences of opinion which existed among the members of the mission regarding the treatment which should be extended to the independent missionaries. Smith was hard-hearted. Spalding was inclined to be more generous, and for this was severely criticized.

THE MISSION HOUSE

When Munger's term of service expired on March 1, 1840, Whitman rehired him for another six months, and raised his wages to £3 per month. "He is a good house carpenter," Whitman wrote to Greene on March 27, 1840. "In that time I hope he will finish our house & make us some comfortable furniture & some farming implements." The Whitmans were then still living in the first house they built, although they were fearful that the walls would collapse should the river rise as it did the first winter they were there.

On May 2, 1840, Mrs. Whitman wrote to her mother and enclosed a plan of their house, which was drawn to scale by Mr. Munger. The west front on the plan measured about seventy-two feet, while the east addition was supposed to be eighty feet long. The rooms A, I, and K were never built. Narcissa added a legend to the plan, indicating the use of each room.

On April 30, she wrote:

All our boards are sawed by hand with a pit saw, which dear father must know is very hard work, and besides this, the smoothing, daubing and whitewashing of an adobe house is very tedious work and requires much time and labor. Husband is now engaged in it, preparing it for painting. We feel ourselves highly favored that we could obtain oil and paint enough and at a reasonable price, to paint the wood work and floors, so as to save my strength and labor.

Since glass was so hard to get, Dr. Whitman planned to make Venetian blinds to protect his windows. Narcissa

---

[8] Coll. Wn. The words in italics are underlined in the original.

noted on the plan of the house drawn by Munger that the exterior of their home did not look as nice as the interior. The roof was made of poles, grass, and dirt. The outside woodwork was to be painted green. This with the white-washed adobe walls would perhaps give a slight resemblance to the neat colonial-type buildings back in New York State which were so frequently painted white and trimmed in green. Regarding lime, Narcissa wrote: "There is no lime stone to be obtained anywhere near us and our alternative is to burn clam shells, which we hope to make answer the purpose." [Letter 75.]

Writing to her mother on May 2, 1840, Narcissa again referred to her difficulties in her old house.

Could dear mother know how I have been situated the two winters past, especially winter before last, I know she would pity me. I often think how disagreeable it used to be to her feelings to do her cooking in the presence of men—sitting about the room. This I have had to bear ever since I have been here—at times it has seemed as if could not endure it any longer. It has been the more trying because our house has been so miserable and cold—small and inconvenient for us—many people as have lived in it.

But the greatest trial to a womans feelings is to have her cooking and eating room always filled with four or five or more Indians—men—especially at meal time.

A special room for the Indians was planned for the new house, with the understanding that certain rooms were to be reserved for the private use of the missionaries. Another trial as far as the Indians were concerned was the fact that they frequently brought in lice and fleas. No wonder Narcissa looked forward with eager anticipation to the privacy which she hoped the new house would afford.

In May, Dr. Whitman was called to Tshimakain, 140 miles to the north, to attend Mrs. Walker. Mrs. Whitman decided to go with her husband. Tiloukaikt, the principal Cayuse chief in the vicinity of Waiilatpu, could not understand the consideration that Dr. Whitman gave to his wife. "Why do you not go alone?" he asked. "What do you make so much of her for?" This gave Dr. Whitman the opportunity to explain the Christian conception of womanhood and of marriage.

The Whitmans reached Tshimakain on Thursday, May 14. Mrs. Walker gave birth to a daughter on Sunday, the 24th, who was named Abigail. While in that vicinity, the Whitmans visited Fort Colville. They began their return trip on May 26. The trip going and coming took about three weeks. Upon their return, they moved into their new home, much to Narcissa's joy.

Mrs. Munger was confined on June 25 and gave birth to a daughter. [Letter 78.] The Mungers continued to live at Waiilatpu until the spring of 1841. At that time we find Narcissa writing to Mrs. Perkins at Waskopum, or The Dalles, saying: "We are in deep trial and affliction. Our Brother Munger is perfectly insane and we are tried to know how to get along with him." [Letter 84.] Munger was obsessed with the idea that he was the divinely appointed agent for Christ's church and that all should obey him. He even claimed ownership of the Waiilatpu property.

FARNHAM'S VISIT

After his return from the fall mission meeting of 1839, Whitman wrote a letter to Greene in which he summarized the affairs within the mission. He acknowledged the arrival of twenty-eight boxes of goods for the mission, which were then still at Vancouver. Whitman like Spalding was not in favor of having the Smiths go to Kamiah, as Smith then desired. He felt that Smith should have remained at Waiilatpu to assist him.

In this letter we find indication that Whitman was realizing the strategic importance of the location of Waiilatpu. He wrote: "I do not think it proper for me to hold the most difficult & responsible station in the mission where all contact with Traders Catholics Travellers & adventurers of every description come in immediate contact & where I have to discharge all the duties of Minister & Physician to the Mission." The next spring we find Narcissa writing: "We are emphatically situated on the highway between the States and the Columbia river, and are a resting place for weary travelers, consequently a greater burden rests upon us than upon any of our associates." [Letter 76.]

Those visiting Whitman's station in the fall of 1839 were but the vanguard of a great host to stream by his door. Geiger and Johnson came first; then the Mungers and the Griffins; and then on September 23, J. T. Farnham and associates arrived. The Farnham party, also called the Peoria party, started fourteen strong with the avowed intention of beginning American settlements in Oregon.[9] The expedition was torn by dissension, with the result that only

[9] Bancroft, *op. cit.*, Vol. 1, p. 227.

four got into the Columbia River Valley that fall. They
were J. T. Farnham, A. M. Blair, Sidney Smith, and Robert
Shortess. Blair went to Lapwai, where he worked for Spalding. Smith went to the Willamette Valley. Shortess, who
reached Waiilatpu after Farnham, entered Whitman's employ for the winter of 1839-40 at six dollars a month. [Let-
ter 77.]

Farnham returned to the States, where he issued a volume describing his travels in which we find an interesting
account of his visit to Waiilatpu.[10] Here is his description
of the breakfast he enjoyed in the Whitman home:

> The morning of the 24th opened in the loveliest hues of the sky.
> When the smoking vegetables, the hissing steak, bread white as snow,
> and the newly churned butter, graced the table, and the happy coun-
> tenances of countrymen and countrywomen shone around, I could with
> difficulty believe myself in a country so far distant from, and so unlike
> my native land and all its features. But during breakfast this pleasant
> illusion was dispelled by one of the causes which induced it. Our steak
> was horseflesh! On such meat this poor family live on most of the
> time. It enables them to exist, to do the Indians good, and thus
> satisfied them.

Dr. Whitman escorted his guest about the mission premises. Farnham noted tomatoes in the garden. He saw
Munger at work on the new house. Whitman proudly
showed Farnham the new mill. Farnham called it: "a crazy
thing, but for it the Doctor was grateful. It would, with the
help of himself and an Indian, grind enough in a day to feed
his family for a week." On the whole Farnham was deeply
impressed with the progress that Whitman had made and
praised his industry and untiring energy. He marveled that
within three years the Whitmans should have been able to
learn the Indian language, establish a home, and begin a
farm in a wilderness, and reap the success that then crowned
their labors, when at the same time the Doctor was serving
as mission physician to widely separated stations.

Farnham visited the school which Dr. and Mrs. Whitman conducted. Some forty or fifty children between the
ages of seven and eighteen were present on the shady side of
the new mission house. After observing Mrs. Whitman at
her work for those several days, Farnham wrote in his
journal: "Mrs. Whitman is an indefatigable instructress."

---

[10] Farnham, *Travels*, pp. 147 ff. His description of Waiilatpu is
too long to be included here. Farnham gives a detailed account of the
gristmill.

WILLIAM H. GRAY.
From *Whitman College Quarterly*, June, 1913.
Used by permission.

1. Mill.   2. Mansion House.   3. Blacksmith Shop.   4. The Mission House.

THE WHITMAN MISSION.

From Mowry, *Marcus Whitman.* Several drawings have been made of the Whitman mission site after the mission was closed. This is one of the best although it does not show the various outbuildings which were on the grounds. The mission house erected in 1836 was near the mouth of Mill Creek, and near the Walla Walla River.

He stayed over Sunday, September 29, and saw Dr. Whitman conduct religious services for the Indians.

Regarding the use of horseflesh, we find Whitman writing to Greene on October 22, 1841, two years after Farnham's visit, saying: " . . . we had killed our first beef only grass fed a steer of four years old last summer which gave us one hundred and twenty eight pounds of tried tallow." Narcissa wrote that same month: "Seven hogs have been butchered today. . . . We do not need to kill any more horses for meat; for we killed a very fat beef a short time ago." [Letter 97.] Thus we find that the Whitmans ate horseflesh for five years after their arrival in Oregon.

MISSION WORK

On the whole Marcus and Narcissa were pleased with the attitude of the Indians during the winter of 1839-40. The school was kept going through the winter, although Dr. Whitman wrote that the average attendance fell to ten. Mrs. Whitman continued as teacher. In the spring the attendance again went up to about fifty when more of the Indians returned to Waiilatpu to prepare for their spring planting. [Letter 74.] Both Whitman and Spalding found it difficult to do consistent work with the Indians when they were constantly on the move. After three years of teaching and example, Whitman was encouraged to see an increasing number of the Indians prepare for planting in the spring of 1840.

In an unsigned report sent to Greene under date of July 6, 1840, Whitman reported on the number of livestock at the Waiilatpu station. The number included: " . . . five cows, two one year old heifers & three heifer calves. One pair Oxen, two pair of steers, two yearling bulls & two bull calves, twenty in all." He also reported having seventeen head of horses.

Regarding his medical work, he mentioned an unusual amount of sickness among the Indians and their reluctance to give up their native superstitions. Narcissa wrote that the sickness of the Indians caused them much "perplexity, care and anxiety." [Letter 75.] Sometimes the Whitmans had their moments of discouragement, yet Narcissa could write in May, 1840: "They are an exceedingly proud, haughty and insolent people, and keep us constantly upon the stretch after patience and forbearance. . . . Notwithstanding all these there are many redeeming qualities in them, else we should have been discouraged long ago. We are more and more encouraged the longer we stay among them." [Letter 76.]

Narcissa besought her loved ones to write, and we wonder why they should have been so negligent. On October 9, 1839, she wrote: "I have not received a single letter from home for more than a year except one from Cousin Jeremiah Butler, who is now at Oberlin." Again on April 30, 1840, she said to her father: "It is almost two years since we have received a single letter from home, and I have written several times since."

On the first of June, 1840, an Indian arrived at Waiilatpu from Fort Walla Walla with some letters. The Whitmans had retired, but they eagerly arose, lighted a candle, and read the latest news from their homes far away to the east—news that was then about a year old. One letter was from Narcissa's mother, the first she had received, and she was overjoyed. She wrote of that experience, saying: "It was enough to transport me in imagination to that dear circle I loved so well, and to prevent sleep from returning that night.... O, could my dear parents know how much comfort it would be to their solitary children here, they would each of them fill out a sheet as often as once a month and send it to the Board for us." [Letter 78.]

DISCORD

Would that it were possible to write the story of the Oregon mission without the necessity of describing the discord within it which came to a focus in 1840. The consequences of this trouble have been too far-reaching to be overlooked. As will be shown, this dissension started a chain of events which resulted in Whitman's mounting his horse on October 3, 1843, and starting for Boston.

For a variety of reasons Henry Spalding became the center of the turbulent eddy around which the personal jealousies, suspicions, fears, and criticisms swirled. To begin with, there was the old antagonism between Henry and Narcissa which dated back to her rejection of his suit. Because of it, Henry and Marcus had several differences of opinion on the way across the country in 1836. Because of it two stations were established, 120 miles apart. Under ordinary conditions the two families would have lived in one station.

We must also remember that some of the members of the 1838 re-enforcement were captious and hypersensitive.

No one wanted to live with Gray after enduring his overbearing attitude on the way out. Smith, afflicted by ill-health, was grouchy. Rogers likewise found it easy to criticize. In reviewing these unpleasant quarrels we should be charitable enough to remember the difficult conditions under which they lived. A sharp word or a ruffled disposition comes all too quickly when one is physically exhausted or mentally ill at ease. The missionaries could not give vent to their feelings upon the natives. Their only outlet was upon their associates.

With the exception of Walker and Eells, who lived peacefully together at Tshimakain, all of the other families wanted separate stations. Smith refused to live with the Whitmans at Waiilatpu, which would have been the sensible thing to do. Gray was ambitious for his own location and sulked like a spoiled child a whole winter because his wishes had been thwarted. Gray blamed Spalding for the attitude of the mission. Spalding was blamed by the Whitmans for the endeavor to have the Whitmans move to a more central location.

It was Spalding's unfortunate lot to have Gray live with him during the winter of 1839-40. Gray was in the mood for finding fault, and he found a ready listener in both Smith and Rogers. Spalding had objected to the Smiths' moving to Kamiah, and perhaps this lay at the root of Smith's critical attitude toward Spalding. Be it said to the credit of the members of the mission, they were deeply troubled about the situation and spent many an hour upon their knees in prayer about it. But at first their repentance was not deep enough to effect a full and frank discussion.

Whitman visited Lapwai during the latter part of January, 1840, and while there he had a talk with Gray, Hall, and Rogers about Spalding. Gray had much about which he complained. He criticized Spalding for spending so much time on secular activities. Spalding had a burning passion to settle the Indians. He wanted to teach them to farm, to raise cattle and sheep, and to become independent of the hunt. In general, this conviction was shared by Whitman but at first not to the same extent.

According to a letter of J. S. Griffin written on February 4, 1884, both Whitman and Gray opposed Spalding in his desire to get the Indians to raise sheep. Griffin claimed that Gray and Spalding accused him during the winter of 1839-40 of giving too much encouragement to Spalding in this respect. Griffin wrote:

Instead of yielding my influence in that direction, I did all in my
power to get him (Whitman) into the same. . . . In that last part of the
season of '40 in about the last discussion with him (Whitman) on the
subject, & he became almost abusive to me for my influence with
Spalding & in my justification of him (Spalding) in the nomadic work,
I declared that I would no more discuss the matter after I should add
one more sentence, *i.e.*, "*Dr. your Indians are all going to Hell on
horseback.*"[11]

Whitman felt that the Indians were too avaricious and
that it would only make more trouble if the missionaries
were to give them chickens, pigs, sheep, or cattle, even as
pay for services rendered. Griffin claimed that later Whitman changed his views on this question and became convinced that the Indians were doomed unless they became
settled. But at first these questions of mission policy were
bones of contention.

On February 6, 1840, Smith sent the first of a series of
complaining letters about Spalding to the American Board.
A few weeks later, Gray visited Smith, and when Gray returned to Lapwai, he, too, sat down and wrote to Greene
about "that man Spalding." On March 16, 1840, Hall joined
the chorus of disapproval. Gray sent in a second letter on
April 15. On March 27, Whitman wrote. On the whole,
Whitman was more charitable in his attitude and refrained
from being as outspoken in his criticism of Spalding as
were Smith, Gray, and Hall. Yet Whitman did write:

I feel to regret the joint letter sent by Mr. Spalding & myself in
1838 as containing a forced view of things calculated to excite hopes
not to be realized. This I have wished to avoid in all my correspondence.
The letter was written in Mr. S. peculiar stile for which I do not feel
responsible. But the signing I regret & also that such a bill of Indian
goods was asked for & fear you may have sent them.

Whitman was shifting to Spalding all of the blame for
the extravagant demands made upon the Board which were
inspired by the visit of Jason Lee. In the meantime, Spalding was ignorant that such criticisms were being sent to
Greene. His letters to Greene during this same time were
free of discussion regarding the difficulties within the mission. One must read his diary to see how he felt.[12]

The 1840 annual meeting of the mission was held at
Lapwai, beginning Saturday, July 4. All of the missionaries
were present and all sensed the tense situation. This time
Walker was elected Moderator, and the men condescended

---

[11] Griffin to Myron Eells, Coll. W.
[12] Spalding's side is given in more detail in Drury, *Spalding*.

to invite the women to attend the sessions although there is no record that they had the privileges of the floor. They were permitted merely to listen.

Gray's case came up again for discussion. Again the mission reversed itself. Permission was given to Gray to establish a station at the mouth of the Yakima River, about twenty miles up the Columbia River from Fort Walla Walla. The place was called Shimnap. Some of the mission objected to the way in which Spalding and Whitman had received Joseph and Timothy into the membership of the Church, and so it was voted that all who worked among the Nez Perces be a committee to pass on the fitness of the candidates.

Most of Tuesday and Wednesday, July 7 and 8, were given over to a discussion of the personal differences. According to Spalding's diary, Whitman arose on Tuesday "in great agitation" and stated that either he or Spalding would have to leave the mission. It seems that Spalding had discussed too freely the issues existing between himself and the Whitmans with the other brethren, and of course the Whitmans learned of it. Spalding's impetuous statement made in the States before leaving for Oregon about Mrs. Whitman's "judgment" was also discussed. It was the echo of an unfortunate love affair!

After two days' frank talk, a better feeling existed. Spalding was penitent, and Whitman was forgiving. Spalding wrote in his diary on the 9th: "About all present said they felt they had been more or less guilty in respect to the lamentable state of things that had existed sometime and wished now to forget everything and labor as one heart."

Smith, the secretary of the mission, sent in a report to Greene on September 2. He wrote a long letter of fifty-two pages, forty of which were taken up with adverse criticism of Spalding. He went into detail regarding the quarrel between Whitman and Spalding, and between Gray and Spalding, and stated that Whitman "was very sanguine in his expectations that Mr. Spalding would in the future do better." The reconciliations effected at the July meeting did not seem to have moved Smith, for on September 28 he wrote again to Greene and recommended that Spalding be "recalled to the States and dismissed from the service of the Board." Smith felt the same way about Gray. Smith's letter of the 28th contains the following serious charge:

From what I have seen and know of him Spalding I greatly fear that the man will become deranged should any heavy calamity befall him. These remarks I have just read to Dr. Whitman and he concurs in what I have written, and says, moreover, that Mr. Spalding has a disease in his head, which may result in derangement, especially if excited by external circumstances.

It would be unwise to accept this secondhand report of what Whitman said as a medical diagnosis, especially when we remember the venom into which Smith was dipping his pen when he wrote about Spalding. Whitman may have made such a statement in a half-joking manner. Whitman visited Smith at Kamiah during the latter part of October, 1840, and it is possible that he and Smith then had opportunity to discuss Spalding and that Smith added to the letter dated September 28.

THE FIRST WAGONS TO THE COLUMBIA

After the return of the Whitmans to Waiilatpu following the July mission meeting, several events of interest took place. On August 8, Joseph Maki, the faithful Hawaiian in their employ, died "of inflammation of the bowels," probably appendicitis. [Letter 78.] Both Marcus and Narcissa were deeply affected as another grave was dug in the little mission cemetery. Mrs. Maki was sent back to Honolulu.

When the American Fur Company disbanded in 1840, many of the mountain men were left stranded in the Rockies. Even in the best of times they seemed to have led a precarious existence. Many were killed. Others married Indian women and were adopted into the various tribes. Farnham gives the following description of Joseph Meek, whom he saw in the summer of 1839:

Meek was evidently very poor; he had scarcely clothing enough to cover his body; and while talking with us the frosty winds which sucked up the valley made him shiver like an aspen leaf. He reverted to his destitute condition, and complained of the injustice of his former employers; the little remumeration he had received for the toils and dangers he had endured on their account, etc.—a complaint I heard from every trapper whom I met on my journey.[13]

In 1840 another party of independent missionaries started for Oregon, of whom mention will be made later. They left their two wagons at Fort Hall and continued the journey on horseback. The wagons became the property of a mountain man, Dr. Robert Newell (1807-1869), who accepted them in payment for services rendered the party as guide. A third wagon had been abandoned at Fort Hall that year by Joel P. Walker, who with his wife and five children constituted the

---

[13] Farnham, *Travels*, p. 292.

first emigrant family bound for Oregon. This wagon passed into the possession of Caleb Wilkins. Newell sold one of his wagons to Ermatinger, who was then in charge of Fort Hall, and Ermatinger employed William Craig, another mountain man, to be the driver for that wagon. These men, realizing that their trapping days in the mountains were over, had resolved to go to the Willamette.

Newell induced Joe Meek to join the party. Meek's Nez Perce wife had deserted him, leaving him with a half-breed daughter then two or three years old. Meek had read Porter's *Scottish Chiefs* and admired the character of Helen Mar, so he had named his daughter after her.[14]

The party left Fort Hall on August 5 and reached Waiilatpu the first part of September. They were the first to take wagons west of Fort Boise over the Blue Mountains into the Columbia River Valley. Because of trouble with the heavy sage they were obliged to discard the wagon beds. Dr. Newell described their arrival at Waiilatpu as follows:

In a rather rough and reduced state we arrived at Dr. Whitman's mission station in the Walla Walla Valley, where we were met by that hospitable man and kindly made welcome and feasted accordingly. On hearing me regret that I had undertaken to bring the wagons, the Doctor said, "O you will never regret it. You have broken the ice, and when others see that wagons have passed they too will pass, and in a few years the valley will be full of people."

Newell stated that the Indians were much interested in the wagons, which were minutely examined. The Indians called them "land canoes."[15] Meek has left the record of how Dr. Whitman joked with him about his (Meek's) "missionary labors among the Nez Perces," and killed a fat hog with the remark that "fat pork was good for preachers."[16]

Meek still entertained great admiration for Mrs. Whitman and induced her to accept the care of little Helen Mar Meek. Mrs. Whitman later wrote that when she received the child she found her fretful, stubborn, and difficult to manage. The child's body was in a terrible condition. She was dirty, covered with lice, half-starved, and poorly clad. More than a year later Narcissa wrote that Helen Mar, then "subdued," was a comfort to her and her husband. [Letter 105.] To a certain degree the little half-breed girl satisfied

---

[14] Victor, *River of the West*, p. 238.

[15] *T.O.P.A.*, 1877, p. 22.

[16] Victor, *op. cit.*, p. 280.

the aching hearts of those who remembered their own little girl who was drowned.

"THE MAN WHO CAME WITH US"

The trouble within the mission which had come to a focus at the mission meeting held in July and had apparently been satisfactorily settled, still seethed underneath. Mrs. Whitman wrote to her father on October 10, 1840, and gave the most outstanding bit of criticism of Spalding to be found in any of her extant letters. She wrote:

Our trials dear father knows but little about. The missionaries' greatest trials are but little known to the churches. I have never ventured to write about them for fear it might do hurt. The man who came with us is one who never ought to have come. My dear husband has suffered more from him in consequence of his wicked jealousy, and his great pique towards me, than can be known in this world. But he suffers not alone—the whole mission suffers, which is most to be deplored. It has nearly broken up the mission.

This pretended settlement with father, before we started, was only an excuse, and from all we have seen and heard, both during the journey and since we have been here, the same bitter feeling exists. His principal aim has been at me; as he said, "Bring out her character," "Expose her character," as though I was the vilest creature on earth. It is well known I never did anything before I left home to injure him, and I have done nothing since, and my husband is cautious in speaking and thinking evil of him or treating him unkindly, as my own dear father would be, yet he does not, nore has he, received the same kindness from him since we have been missionaries together.

At the close of this letter, Narcissa added: "Part of the contents of this sheet, ought not to be circulated; it may do hurt. I do not wish it made public, for any one to make ill use of it." This is the only written statement of Narcissa's yet known which refers to the love affair with Spalding, and here the reference is indirect.

Following the July mission meeting, the Grays had moved to Waiilatpu. Mrs. Gray was pregnant, and since no buildings had been erected upon the approved site at Shimnap, there was nothing for them to do but to stay with the Whitmans after they left Lapwai. Gray still harbored a grudge against Spalding. Later Whitman wrote to Greene, saying that both Gray and Smith failed to bring out all of their grievances against Spalding at the July, 1840, meeting and for that reason the same distrust continued which had characterized their work before that meeting was held. [Letter 92.]

On October 14, 1840, Gray wrote to Greene and gave

considerable detail regarding the quarrel. The next day Whitman wrote to Greene and referred directly to his differences with Spalding. Whitman wrote:

Mr. Gray has lately informed me that letters have been sent by him & others, setting forth difficulties that have existed in this mission. It was never my intention to trouble you with them. I have thought them of such a nature that Mrs. Whitman & myself must leave the Mission; & so strong was this feeling that I should have left, previous to the convening of the Mission in Sept. 1839, had not the Providence of God arrested me in my deliberate determination to do so by taking away our dear child in so sudden a manner by drowning. Since that time many appearances have changed, & I have not seen it my duty to leave.

Thus the case stood against Spalding. Smith had written four letters against Spalding; Gray, three; Rogers and Hall, one each. Whitman in his letter of March 27, 1840, had tried to shift blame to Spalding for the extravagant demands made in 1838, and then in his letter of October 15, 1840, had made a restrained statement of the case. Whitman's last letter was received by Greene on October 2, 1841. Greene was dismayed when he read the accumulating criticisms against Spalding. On the basis of that evidence, Greene appeared before the Prudential Committee of the American Board the following spring and recommended that Spalding be dismissed; that Gray and Smith be advised to return to the States; and that Whitman and Rogers move to Tshimakain to live with Walker and Eells. Both Lapwai and Waiilatpu were to be closed. It was the arrival of this order from the Board in the fall of 1842 which inspired Whitman to leave at once for Boston.

The year 1839-40 was a critical year in the mission. It was then that the internal dissensions reached their climax. Spalding was the focal point of trouble. Letters containing some sixty thousand words, mostly in criticism of "that man Spalding," piled up on Greene's desk. Spalding was ignorant of these letters. He sent in not one word of criticism of his fellow workers until he was told what the others had done.

The last of the complaining letters which arrived in time to affect the Board's decision were written in October, 1840. It took two years before the consequences of those complaints were felt back in Oregon, and by that time the situation had vastly changed.

CHAPTER TWELVE

DISCOURAGEMENTS

1840-1841

THE FIFTH year of the Oregon mission brought many discouragements to the Whitmans. Difficulties seemed to crop up on all sides, both within and without the mission. The old quarrel with Spalding was renewed. Some members left the mission. Both of the Whitmans were sick for a time. All in all it was a hard year.

Early in the fall of 1840 Walker wrote to Whitman and mentioned the possibility of selling the whole American Board mission to the Methodists. Walker later claimed that Whitman misinterpreted what was written. However, we find Whitman writing to Greene on October 15, 1840, saying:

> Mr. Walker writes me that he has written you in favour of the Boards withdrawing this Mission on account of so many coming in among & around us. I feel to say, No; Do not withdraw it. We have not done what we could, & ought to do. It could not be withdrawing the Mission, so to speak; but abandoning the cause of the Indians. Rather let us be *reenforced* to enable us to act more efficiently.
>
> I feel it a great trial to be in the most responsible part of the field, to fill alone, as I have done, the station of a public teacher or minister, school teacher, Physician, farmer, &c.

The Board was conscious of the need for additional workers and sent out the Rev. and Mrs. J. D. Paris and Mr. and Mrs. W. H. Rice in November, 1840. However, when this party reached the Sandwich Islands on May 21, 1841, they met such discouraging reports of the condition in the Oregon mission, given largely by E. O. Hall, that they decided to go no farther. They remained in the Islands.

About the middle of August six more independent missionaries unexpectedly appeared at Waiilatpu. They were the Rev. and Mrs. Harvey Clark, Mr. and Mrs. Alvin T. Smith, and Mr. and Mrs. Philo B. Littlejohn. Narcissa had known Mrs. Littlejohn back in New York State as Adeline Sadler. [Letter 217.] Of all the missionaries Mrs. Littlejohn was the only one whom Narcissa referred to by her first name. As has been mentioned, the missionaries habitually referred to each other by the proper title and the last name. There is no reason to believe that even in hours of closest fellow-

ship either of the Whitmans ever called Mr. Spalding
"Henry." They kept the formalities of their Eastern training in Old Oregon. The fact that Mrs. Whitman referred
to Mrs. Littlejohn as Adeline indicates a former acquaintance
of a friendly nature.

These new missionaries, like the Griffins and the Mungers, believed that it was possible to establish a mission
among the Indians without the aid of a mission board and
with a limited financial reserve. They soon saw their error.
Whitman was perplexed. He did not know what was the
right thing to do. The Griffins had left Lapwai about the
time the mission meeting was held there and had gone to
Waiilatpu. Thus all five families of the independent missionaries were at Waiilatpu in addition to the Grays and the
Whitmans, making seven families in all. Fortunately the
new mission house was ready and the old house was still
usable.

Narcissa probably objected to the crowded conditions
more than did her husband. She wrote to her mother, saying:
"We have no less than seven missionary families in our two
houses. We feel that we need much patience and wisdom
to get along with so many, and much strength." [Letter 78.]

Whitman reported to Greene regarding his crops. With
the aid of some of the independent missionaries, he harvested "two hundred & fifty bushels of wheat, one hundred
& thirty of corn, peas not known & a good supply of potatoes." Whitman's letter of October 15 contains four pages
of itemized purchases from the Hudson's Bay Company
totaling £112.15.11.

During the early part of October, A. B. Smith at Kamiah
had trouble with the Indians there and sent a message to
Spalding and Whitman, imploring them to come immediately.
Spalding received his letter on the 15th and left at once.
Whitman probably received his message a couple of days
later. He left Waiilatpu on a mild day and did not take
sufficient bedding with him. Narcissa wrote to her sister
Harriet on the 20th, saying: "Think of him traveling alone
this cold weather. The first [day] after he left his warm
home, the wind blew very hard and cold—he with but two
blankets, sleeping on the ground alone; and since, it has
rained almost every day, and sometimes snowed a little. I
do not know when he will come home." [Letter 81.]

Whitman found Smith thoroughly discouraged and ready
to return to the States. Smith was entirely unfitted by dis-

position for the pioneer life demanded by the circumstances under which he was living. The house he erected at Kamiah was a rude affair. Mrs. Smith was in poor health and desperately lonely. Whitman wrote: "I think they both suffer much from this cause. I regret much that Mr. Smith should have been so anxious to go where he is, as he so easily falls into loneliness & despondency." [Letter 83.] Whitman also stated that Smith felt "he brought it on himself as a judgment for being in so much haste to be sent out (or in other words to get married.)"

It appears that Whitman had written to Smith and passed on the statement of Walker's regarding the possibility of selling out to the Methodists. As soon as Spalding reached Kamiah, Smith brought up the proposal. Spalding was astonished. "My mind is thrown into confusion," he wrote in his diary for October 15.

Whitman reached Kamiah on the 22nd with some horses to pack out Smith's belongings. However, it appears that the trouble with the Indians had been greatly magnified by the despondent Smith and that Spalding had encouraged him to remain. Whitman had suffered from exposure on his 180-mile trip and was, therefore, in a mood to sympathize with Smith. Even though he had written but a few days earlier to Greene emphatically advising against giving up the mission, now he changed his mind. Smith was determined to leave the field. Whitman felt that Gray would also leave, and that he and Spalding would be alone in the Nez Perce work. Under those conditions, Whitman felt it best to give up the whole work.

Spalding emphatically declared that he would never leave, even if the Board did sell to the Methodists. The discussion must have waxed warm. Finally it was decided that Smith would remain, at least until spring, and that Mr. and Mrs. Harvey Clark should be sent to Kamiah to give companionship and to assist in the work. It was also agreed that Mr. and Mrs. A. T. Smith should be sent to Lapwai.

Spalding hastened to send a messenger to Walker as soon as possible to discover whether or not Walker had been misquoted. The messenger returned on November 2 with word to the effect that "the Doct. must have misunderstood them as they never have thought of giving up the Mission." The following extract from Mrs. Walker's diary for October 28 reflects the attitude of the Walkers and the Eells to the proposition: "We are astonished and somewhat indignant to think they should think of such a thing." We have no evidence that the Methodists were ever aware of this suggestion.

Whitman spent the night of October 24 at Lapwai on his way back home. The next day Griffin arrived with letters from Jason Lee which had nothing to do with the proposed sale but informed them that Dr. Elijah White, the physician for the Methodist mission, had been dismissed from the mission and was returning to the States. Lee expressed the fear that White would do "all he can to injure them, but trusts all to the Lord."[1] White was a member of the first re-enforcement of the Methodist mission in Oregon. His party sailed from Boston in July, 1836. After serving as mission doctor for three years, he left because of differences of opinion with Lee and returned to the States on the *Lausanne,* which had brought out Lee and his party of some fifty missionaries that summer. The *Lausanne* reached Fort Vancouver June 1.

Whitman got back to Waiilatpu on October 28 and the next day wrote a seven-page letter to Greene, in which he told of his trip to Kamiah and recommended the sale of the mission to the Methodists—a direct reversal of his opinion expressed to Greene in a letter written just two weeks earlier. Whitman wrote:

I would that the true causes were given for relinquishing the mission, as they exist in us & not altogether in the people & things more remote. It does not become me to speak by way of complaint of any one; but I may safely say we are greatly wanting in spirituality faith prayer and expectation of success.

He was in favor of concentration of forces. Why should each minister spend so much time in farming and building? Let him take care of the secular affairs at Waiilatpu, and in turn be relieved of teaching and preaching. It was a reasonable position to take. Whitman wrote: "If you sell out the mission you will be at liberty to send me to any field where I may be needed as Physician." If there was no place open, he expressed his expectation of either returning to the States or settling in the Lower Columbia country.

Nothing ever came of the idea of selling out to the Methodists. Both Walker and Eells expressed themselves as being so strongly opposed that the idea was dropped as far as the Oregon mission of the American Board was concerned.

---

[1] Spalding diary, Oct. 25, 1840.

THE WINTER OF 1840-41

The Mungers and the Littlejohns spent the winter of 1840-41 with the Grays and the Whitmans at Waiilatpu. Mr. and Mrs. Griffin went to the Willamette Valley about the time the Clarks went to Kamiah and the A. T. Smiths to Lapwai. Mr. Munger gave Whitman and Gray considerable concern because of his increasing insanity.

Both Dr. and Mrs. Whitman were ill during the winter. Dr. Whitman suffered from exposure on his Kamiah trip and from the excessive labor he put upon his millrace after his return. For a time he was obliged to rest. Then he was summoned to Fort Walla Walla on a sick call. Mrs. Whitman rode with him. On their return trip they found that the water in one of the streams which had to be forded had risen. Dr. Whitman's horse stumbled in midstream and threw him into the water. After getting out, the doctor wrapped himself in some blankets while his clothes dried by a fire. He tried to shake off the effects of the plunge into the cold stream but finally went to his bed, where he remained three weeks. Writing to Greene on March 28, 1841, he said: "From that time to this I have not been able to do anything that requires much effort."

In September, 1840, Narcissa was "taken with inflammation of the kidneys and brought very low." [Letter 78.] Writing to her mother in October, she confessed that she felt too indisposed to attempt teaching in the school that winter. In March, 1841, she stated in a letter to Mrs. Walker: "My health is quite poor—yet I keep about most of the time." According to her husband, Narcissa resumed some of her duties in the schoolroom the latter part of March. [Letter 86.]

Narcissa also suffered from weak eyes. As early as September 30, 1839, she referred to this. On March 1, 1842, she wrote: "My eyes are much weaker than when I left home and no wonder, I have so much use for them. I am at times obliged to use the spectacles Brother J. G. so kindly furnished me."

With this burden of ill-health, Narcissa frequently suffered spells of depression. To her father she wrote: "I suffer from dejection considerably—feel the want of society, especially since the death of our dear Alice." [Letter 75.] Marcus was frequently called away on business or on medical calls. Whenever possible Narcissa would go with him, especially if there were no white people at the mission during his absence expect herself. Writing to her sister Jane on March 1, 1842, she made the following reference to her loneliness: "Jane, I wish you were here to sleep with me, I am such a timid creature about sleeping alone that sometimes I suffer considerably, especially since my health has been not very good."

During the winter of 1840-41, the work of the mission at Waiilatpu was carried on by the Grays and the independent missionaries. Mrs. Gray had charge of the schoolroom. Gray himself was very slow in acquiring the language and so could do little in direct instruction. He took care of the outside work.

The construction of the mill was completed during the winter. The waters of the little stream which emptied into the Walla Walla River near the mission house were dammed and a millpond formed, the outlines of which can still be seen. On March 28, 1841, Whitman stated that the mill would grind about a bushel and a half an hour. It was a small clumsy affair, yet it was able to make flour, for which they were duly grateful.

THE SPRING OF 1841

Walker visited Waiilatpu in the early part of March, 1841, and persuaded Gray to return with him and assist in the erection of another house at Tshimakain. Gray went reluctantly, for he was eager to begin work at his new station. He remained at Tshimakain for about a month. In spite of the vote of the mission at its last annual meeting, the sentiment was strong against the establishment of a new station. Whitman was opposed, as is indicated in the following statement he wrote to Greene: "It will not be long before it will be apparent to all how foolish this extending system has been." [Letter 86.]

Whitman was convinced that all of the cultivating should be done at Waiilatpu. He felt that the blacksmith shop, the printing shop, and mills should be located there. He then could supply the needs of the ministers, thus giving them more time for their specialized duties.

When Walker and Gray left for Tshimakain, Mr. Walker carried a letter from Mrs. Whitman addressed to his wife. It seems that early that spring Mrs. Whitman had a moving religious experience which led her to examine her own heart. "For two or three days," she wrote to Mrs. Walker, "my distress was very great." Inspired by a deep feeling of self-humiliation, she poured out her penitent feelings. No one ever condemned her as strongly as Narcissa in this letter condemned herself.

> I think I have not for a long time had so clear view of the state of my heart as I have for a few weeks past—Perhaps never in my whole life have I been led to see so distinctly the hidden iniquity & secret evils of my heart.
> Of all persons I see myself to be the most unfit for the place I occupy on heathen ground. I wonder that I was ever permitted to come. ...I see now as I *never* have before wherein I have been a grief to his children by indulging in unholy passions & exhibiting so little of the meek lowly & quiet spirit of our blessed Saviour. I have been blind to my own faults & have not known what manner of spirit I was of.
> Proud & self confident have I been. I do not wonder that brother Spalding if he saw this trait in my character felt that he could not come into the field if I did.—Neither is it strange that the other members of the Mission should feel that they could not live with us. [Letter 85.]

After a full and frank confession, Narcissa begged the forgiveness of the Walkers and the Eells. The letter undoubtedly did much to establish that good feeling which thereafter existed between the Whitmans and their coworkers at Tshimakain.

The spring planting season came, with the Indians, much to Whitman's encouragement, showing greater interest than ever in agriculture. In 1838 Whitman had written to his brother Augustus, asking for fifty plows and three hundred hoes. Augustus was authorized to draw upon some of Dr. Whitman's personal funds to the extent of two hundred dollars. The appeal for plows seems to have inspired the people of Rushville to donate twenty-five, for on May 24, 1841, Marcus wrote again to his brother, acknowledging receipt of the plows at Vancouver. He also stated that the Board had sent out ten. "The Indians are not backward in using them," he wrote, "I help them make collars & harness of a good quality & they have plenty of fine horses." [Letter 89.]

In April, 1841, A. B. Smith decided that he would rather endure the stigma of leaving the mission than continue to live where both he and his wife were so thoroughly unhappy. According to Clark, Smith gave up the study of the Nez Perce language early in the spring of 1841 and began "to prepare himself for preaching in the States." [Letter 86.] In April, Smith had some further unpleasant experiences with the Indians and he made them an occasion to leave. His wife was too sick to ride horseback, so Smith loaded a few possessions in a canoe, and with his wife made the trip down the Clearwater to Lapwai, arriving there on the 21st.

In the meantime sickness had visited Lapwai. Mrs. Spalding was ill during March, and the fore part of April. Little Henry Hart Spalding became ill on the 16th, and the next day Cornelius Rogers was stricken. Spalding sent an express to Waiilatpu, requesting Whitman's immediate assistance. The doctor reached Lapwai on Wednesday, April 21, shortly before Mr. and Mrs. Smith arrived. Smith bluntly told Whitman and Spalding that he was through. He declared that he would leave the mission in disgrace rather than remain any longer with the Indians. All idealism was gone. As far as he was concerned the Nez Perces were doomed, and he did not care.[2]

Rogers, sick and likewise discouraged, listened to what Smith had to say and confessed that he felt the same way. As early as February 27, 1841, Rogers had written to Greene about his desire to leave the mission. Rogers declared: "I will simply say that Mr. Spalding is felt by me to be the principal cause of my course."

Smith had sent his animals, loaded with most of his goods, overland. On the 22nd the Smiths in one canoe and Dr. Whitman and Rogers in another started for Fort Walla Walla. Gray, who happened to be at Lapwai at the time, took Smith's pack train and Dr. Whitman's horses and went overland. The Smiths took the first opportunity to go to Fort Vancouver. There they remained for several months under the care of the doctors at the Fort. They sailed for the Sandwich Islands, arriving there January 25, 1842, and remained in the Islands doing missionary work until 1845. They then returned to the States by way of China.[3] Smith's most important contribution to the Nez Perce mission work, during the two and a half years he was a part of the mission, was along linguistic lines. At the time he left he had mastered the difficult language better than any of the other missionaries. He did excellent work on a Nez Perce grammar and dictionary.

Rogers did not immediately leave the mission. He went to Waiilatpu, where he could be under Dr. Whitman's care. For a time he was very sick. Whitman wrote to Walker on April 19, saying that he feared "Brother Rogers may not recover." However, in time he regained his health and was

---

[2] Spalding diary, April 21, 1841.
[3] Eells, *Marcus Whitman*, p. 232.

soon in the saddle riding to Fort Walla Walla. Pambrun conceived the plan of having Rogers marry his daughter Maria, and to the surprise and dismay of the missionaries, Rogers entertained the idea. The Whitmans felt that since Maria was an uneducated half-breed, she was not worthy of him. Besides, she was a Catholic. Pambrun's heart was set on the idea, and he worked assiduously to win Roger's approval.

On May 11, Rogers and Pambrun were riding together. Pambrun was guiding his horse by a rope in the horse's mouth, Indian fashion. The animal managed to get the rope out and began to run and buck. Pambrun was thrown repeatedly against the horn of the saddle and finally upon the ground, too bruised and maimed in the abdomen to walk. He was carried into his home where, after four days of terrible suffering, he died. Dr. Whitman was called at once. He wrote to Walker from the Fort on May 12, reporting on Pambrun's condition. Pambrun pled for some medicine which would put him out of his sufferings, but this Whitman refused to give. [Letter 91.]

Pambrun died on May 15, and his body was taken to Fort Vancouver for burial.[4] Rogers was willed a hundred pounds sterling, and Maria was given more than would have been her fair share of the property. The Pambrun family with Rogers removed to Vancouver. According to Mrs. Whitman, Maria finally refused to marry Rogers. [Letter 96.] He turned back the property he had received, and in September of the year following married Miss Satira Leslie, a daughter of a member of the Methodist mission. Rogers visited the Upper Columbia country again in the capacity of an interpreter both for the Wilkes party and for Elijah White, of whom mention will be made later. On February 1, 1843, Rogers with his wife and several others were accidentally drowned when their boat was carried over the Willamette Falls. Maria Pambrun had married Dr. Forbes Barclay, of the Hudson's Bay Company, in 1842.

In his letter to Walker, Whitman reported that A. T. Smith, Harvey Clark,[5] and their wives had left with Mr.

---

4 John Work, *Journal*, p. 174.

5 Letter from W. A. Tenny, Jan. 19, 1897, to Myron Eells, Coll. W.: "It is a significant fact that the first church organized for white emigrants was at Oregon City in 1844 by Rev. Harvey Clark, & was Presbyterian, & the second church for emigrants was in 1845 at Forest Grove & was Congregational. Mr. Clark was for some time the itinerant pastor of both churches at the same time."

Ermatinger for Vancouver on May 11. Much of the personal possessions of the independent missionaries were left stored at Fort Walla Walla. On October 3, 1841, a fire swept through part of the Fort, destroying that part which contained their goods. It was a heavy loss for the missionaries. In 1845 the Littlejohn family returned to the States. The others of this group went to the Willamette Valley and entered into the life of the growing American community there.

On May 24, 1841, Whitman found time to write a letter to his former preceptor, Dr. Ira Bryant, from which the following extracts are taken:

My Dear Doct, and Mrs. Bryant:

For the first time I sit down to write you. I do not see as you will be likely to write me first. You do not know how it seems at this distance to be so much in the dark about old friends. Among my correspondents I get very imperfectly any account of my own dear Friends and Native Village. All forget to tell me who is President or Governor.

The Region seems inexhaustible in its stores of pasturage. But it will not be easy to settle the Indians in this region for it will require the resource & enterprise of the white man to develop its resources by means of saw mills in the mountains to furnish timber for fences as well as building.

The upper Columbia will not likely ever to be inhabited by a Settled People for if herding is stopped they must move around more or less for grass. We have a delightful climate in the upper Columbia. Not having as in the lower country a wet & dry Season.

In order to get established I have labored most excessively but I am now so far broken that I cannot expect to accomplish much more manual labour. My Medical duties call me much from home as I have to go one hundred & eighty miles to the remotest Stations.

In a summary way let me say we have a good convenient new house. That the old one yet stands occupied generally for two families & besides a house for company, that is people who want to stay a while or for passers is nearly finished. Then we have a good flour mill & some outhouses such as corn crib, granary, harness house, smoke & hen house, double back house Cow & Horse pen.

I have little hope of ever returning to the U States. I have just heard that Harrison is President. The United States Pacifick Squadron was at the Islands a short time since & is soon expected in the Columbia. We are all in the dark as to the intention of the U S Government about this country.

This is the earliest letter of Whitman's that we have in which we read of his political interests. Whitman was still thinking of the Upper Columbia as a grazing country. At first Spalding had the same idea, not dreaming that the hills of the Palouse country would ever be covered with wheat fields.[6] It is interesting to note that it took almost seven months for the results of the Presidential election of November, 1840, to reach Oregon. William Henry Harrison was inaugurated into office on March 4, 1841, but died a month later and was succeeded by the Vice President, John Tyler. Several months had to elapse before Whitman learned of this.

THE ANNUAL MEETING OF 1841

The 1841 annual meeting of the Oregon mission was held at Waiilatpu from Wednesday, June 9, to Monday, the 14th. The diaries of both Spalding and Walker throw considerable light on the events of those days. Walker went to Fort Colville and made the trip to Fort Walla Walla by boat. While waiting for the doctor to come to take him out to the mission, Walker wrote to his wife on May 31, giving her the news of the day. He was much concerned about the proposed marriage of Rogers with Maria Pambrun. Regarding A. B. Smith's departure, he wrote: "It is very plain that he has worked all manner of wags to get off without appealing to the Mission for advice or consent." He also reported that: "The Dr is not in very good spirits but is not discouraged."[7]

Whitman reached the Fort that night and the next day they rode out to the mission. Walker wrote in his diary for June 1: " . . . found Mrs. Whitman cleaning her house. Took tea at Mr. Gray's. After that we rode out to see the mill race." Walker was not in good health and had arrived early in order to receive medical care. During these days he had several opportunities to talk with Dr. Whitman, and, judging by Walker's diary, it seems evident that the two men did not always agree. On the 4th he wrote: "Had more conversation with the Dr. and are more convinced that his course is wrong." Walker found Gray in a mood to justify Smith's conduct.

Eells arrived on Monday, the 7th, and on the 8th, Mr.

---

[6] Since the publication of the author's biography of Henry Harmon Spalding, a new Spalding letter of about thirty-six hundred words, dated "Clearwater Aug. 17, 1842" has been discovered. The letter was addressed to "Mrs. Theo. Hinsdale Winchester Litchfield Co Conn." and was purchased by a stamp collector in a stamp shop in Boston. A copy is in the Oregon Historical Society. In this Spalding wrote about the development of the Upper Columbia country: "It can never become an agricultural country by reason of the scarcity of tillable land. . . . Though it is thought by good judges that many of the high plains might produce wheat."

[7] Coll. Wn.

and Mrs. Spalding arrived, much to the surprise of those at Waiilatpu. Walker felt that Mrs. Spalding's presence was an "omen for good." The mission meeting opened that night. Walker was Moderator; Eells was Scribe. It was soon apparent that an undercurrent of jealousy and dissatisfaction still existed. Walker wrote in his diary that evening: "I fear there is not much of the Spirit of prayer in the Mission."

On Wednesday the financial report was studied. The total bill was four hundred pounds, which was about one-third less than the bill for the preceding year.[8] That night Walker again wrote in his diary: "The day passed quite pleasantly. There was a little sharp talk about some things, but ended pretty well." The next day was also given over to a consideration of financial matters.

On Friday the tension increased when Dr. Whitman made some charges against Spalding, mentioning especially Spalding's alleged refusal to co-operate with Rogers in language study. Spalding resented the accusation. He wrote in his diary that all of the charges made "except one or two small things which occurred in the States and were long since settled" were either false or were due to misunderstood Indian reports. From this we judge that the old statement Spalding made about "Mrs. Whitman's judgment" again came up for discussion. The echoes of the old love affair were heard again.

Walker wrote that night: "Spent most of the day in conversation. It came on so sharp that I was compelled to leave. It is enough to make one sick to see what is the state of things in the mission."

The next day Spalding was shocked to learn that letters of complaint had been sent to the Board regarding him. He learned that Smith, Gray, Rogers, Hall, and even Dr. Whitman, had sent in their criticisms. Walker made the following entry in his diary:

I felt as did the rest that it was impossible for the Mission to ever come together in such a manner as to work more harmoniously together; and nothing can, as it seems, bring peace but the removing of some of its members. What is to be the end of these things, I know not. . . . Notwithstanding a meeting was appointed this afternoon, and there was none on account of a conversation between Dr & his wife and Mr. Spalding & his wife.

Spalding was stunned and humbled by the turn of events.

---

[8] *See* financial summary, Appendix 2.

He wrote that night in his diary: "The Lord in great mercy look upon these men and forgive their sins to sustain his unworthy servant to kindness under these accumulating trials." The next day he sought out another interview with the Whitmans. According to his diary, Spalding confessed to Narcissa that he had said many things which had better been left unsaid and begged her forgiveness. Spalding wrote: "But was astonished at self-righteousness manifested by our bro and sister." Whitman's account of this interview is to be found in a letter he wrote to Greene on July 13, 1841, from which the following is taken:

We had a most plain talk with Mr. Spalding which resulted in his acknowledging himself to have been in the wrong in the leading causes of complaint & that he had been very jealous. I understood this to apply of the Mission as well as of ourselves. I will not be too sanguine of the future but this much I can say he has pledged himself that he will not be so jealous & that he will cooperate with the Mission & most especially with Mrs. Whitman & myself.

That day Mr. Eells officiated at the communion service. The Littlejohns were present and had their little boy, Leverett, who was later drowned in the millrace at Lapwai, baptized.[9] The Grays brought forward their little daughter, who was born at Waiilatpu the previous fall. She was given the name Caroline, and later became Mrs. Caroline Kamm, of Portland, Oregon. And the Whitmans came forward with Helen Mar Meek, the half-breed daughter of Joe Meek, then about three years old.

The next day the business sessions were resumed, and adjournment was reached in time for those who lived elsewhere to leave early in the afternoon. On Saturday the mission had taken up Gray's case again. All seem to have felt that it was most inadvisable for Gray to begin a new station. Gray was asked to remain at Waiilatpu and cooperate with Dr. Whitman. While Gray appears to have been reconciled to the necessity of giving up his pet idea of a separate establishment, yet he was unhappy to occupy what he considered to be a subordinate place in the mission. The next year when he found an opportunity to work elsewhere, he did not hesitate to resign.

THE SUMMER OF 1841

Much to the joy of the Whitmans, Archibald McKinlay, a good Scotch Presbyterian, succeeded Pambrun at Fort

---

9 Drury, *Spalding*, p. 198.

Walla Walla. For some time the Whitmans had been worried about the Catholics. Pambrun had in various ways extended favors to the priests. Pambrun was especially friendly with Young Chief, also called Tawatowe or Tauitau, and
had built a house for him on the Umatilla about twenty-five
miles from Waiilatpu, in the fall of 1840. This act of kindness was used by the Catholic priests to gain a foothold
among the Umatilla Indians.[10]

In a letter to her father, written October 1, 1841, Narcissa made reference to this incident in saying:

> Now we have Catholics on both sides of us, and, we may say, right
> in our midst, for Mr. Pambrun, while he was alive, failed not to secure
> one of the principal Indians of this tribe to that religion, and had his
> family baptized. He acts upon his band, and holds from us many who
> would be glad to come and hear us. And then, the Indians are acted
> upon constantly through the servants of the Company, who are all,
> scarcely without exception, Catholics.

Pambrun was accustomed to pay responsible Indians for
keeping the peace. [Letter 97.] When McKinlay was placed
in charge of Fort Walla Walla in the summer of 1841, a
different policy was adopted. Whitman was unable finan-
cially to keep the good will of the Indians through constantly
giving things to them and was, therefore, greatly relieved
when McKinlay refused to continue Pambrun's practices.
Once Narcissa wrote:

> From the commencement of this station until the present time, it
> has constantly been a point with one or more of them to be urging for
> property to be given them to keep them in subjection to order.
> It is difficult for them to feel but that we are rich and getting rich
> by the houses we dwell in and the clothes we wear and hang out to
> dry after washing from week to week, and the grain we consume in
> our families. [Letter 97.]

Even the long line of the family wash drying in the sun
awakened suspicion and jealousy in the hearts of the natives.
Any kind of woven cloth was expensive to them, and, lo! the
white people had it in abundance!

The coming of the Catholics gave great concern to both
Marcus and Narcissa, as well as to the other members of the
Oregon mission. Narcissa wrote as early as September 30,
1839: "A Catholic priest has recently been at Walla Walla
and held meetings with the Indians and used their influence

---

[10] J. S. Griffin to Myron Eells, Feb. 4, 1884, Coll. W.: "I then told
Whitman his cause was doomed to failure, as the Indians would from
that time onward hold the H. B. Co & *not* himself, as their benefactors.
That was the hinge upon which the death & the break up of the station
finally turned."

to draw all the people away from us." The Protestant missionaries had followed the idea of baptizing none except those who showed evident signs of a changed heart. This accounts for the small number of Indians who joined the mission church. The Catholics, on the other hand, were freer in administering this rite. Whitman wrote to his brother Augustus on May 24, 1841, and said: "There is likely to be a strong Catholic division here for one thing. It has been fostered more or less by our late neighbor Mr. Pambrun."

For various reasons, therefore, the Whitmans welcomed Mr. McKinlay to Fort Walla Walla.

The United States Government sent out an exploring expedition under Lieutenant Charles Wilkes in 1838 which reached the mouth of the Columbia in April, 1841. During the summer of that year members of this expedition penetrated into the interior and visited the various mission stations, including Waiilatpu. The Whitman letters for the summer and fall of 1841 contain several references to members of this expedition.

Joseph Drayton, who spent some time at Waiilatpu, has left for us a good description of the mission property and premises as he saw them. The following is an extract from his report:

All the premises look very comfortable. They have a fine kitchen-garden, in which grow all the vegetables raised in the United States, and several kinds of fine melons. The wheat, some of which stood seven feet high, was in full head, and nearly ripe; Indian corn was in tassel, and some of it measured nine feet in height. They will reap this year about three hundred bushels of wheat, with a quantity of corn and potatoes. The soil, in the vicinity of the small streams, is a rich black loam, and very deep.

These missionaries live quite comfortably, and seem contented; they are, however, not free from apprehension of Indian depredations. Dr. Whitman, being an unusually large and athletic man, is held in much respect by the Indians, and they have made use of his services as a physician, which does not seem to carry with it so much danger here, as among the tribes in the lower country, or farther north.

Drayton reported that the price of a good horse was then about twenty dollars. He claimed that Whitman had 124 Indians on his school roll, but because of the wandering habits of the tribe, the average daily attendance was but 25. He noted that a number of the Indians had small farms from which they were securing sufficient food.[11]

During the latter part of July, Dr. and Mrs. Whitman

---

[11] Wilkes, *Expedition*, Vol. 4, p. 399.

rode to Tshimakain, arriving there on July 21. On July 27, Mrs. Eells gave birth to her first-born, a son whom they named Edwin. The Whitmans remained for several weeks before starting back. Walker mentions in his diary an excursion that the doctor and he made to Spokane Falls, now in the city of Spokane, Washington. Walker wrote for Saturday, August 14: "The Dr. has been as full of Geology as if he had eaten some half dozen quarto volumns on this subject." The Whitmans started back on the 16th, and Walker confessed in the privacy of his diary: "I must say I did not regret to see them depart."

On August 9, while still at Tshimakain, Whitman wrote to his brother Samuel and discussed several items of interest. He wrote: "I am no more of an Abolitionist that I was for years before I left home. . . . I do not feel as much attachment to Illinois as I did & I think it is the last State I would live in on account of its heavy debt & taxes. . . . Tell mother we are eating cheese of Mrs. Whitman's make; that milk & butter are most abundant with us & so will cheese be if we choose to make it. Calves rennet is a scarce article for we value a calf the same as an old cow or ox for it costs nothing to raise them."

Shortly after their return to Waiilatpu, six-year-old Mary Ann Bridger, the half-breed daughter of Jim Bridger, arrived and was received into the Whitman household.[12] It is possible that she was brought by the Mungers, who had endeavored that summer to return to the States. Munger had become hopelessly insane by the spring of 1841. Arrangements were made to have the Munger family go to the rendezvous with a Hudson's Bay party in the hope that some escort would be available to take them to the States from that point. However, the American Fur Company had dissolved in 1840, and no other group had been organized of a like nature. Hence, no caravan crossed the Plains in 1841, and the Mungers were obliged to return. They went to the Willamette Valley, where Mr. Munger secured a position with the Methodist mission at Salem. In December he committed suicide. The whole affair was a trying experience for the Whitmans.

---

[12] Narcissa wrote on Oct. 6, 1841: "My two little girls are a comfort to me, in his absence, especially; they are both of them natives of the Rocky Mountains, and poor little outcasts when I took them. One of them is called Mary Ann and is the daughter of James Bridger, the man out of whose back the doctor cut an arrow point when he was up to the mountains the first time."

CHAPTER THIRTEEN

SPALDING IS DISMISSED
1841-1842

IN THE FALL of 1841 the first party of emigrants bound for the Willamette Valley passed the Whitman station. Narcissa wrote that they were "twenty-four in number—two families with small children from Missouri." [Letter 96.] They had left their wagons behind, so all were on horseback. Narcissa made special mention of one family with six children. "It was very pleasing to me," she wrote, "to see such a mother with so many children around her, having come so far—such a dreadful journey." [Letter 97.]

Marcus and Narcissa had often talked of the strategic location of the mission. With the passing of the years, the importance of the Oregon Trail began to be emphasized, with the ever-increasing migrations which passed their door. As early as May, 1840, Narcissa wrote:

A tide of immigration appears to be moving this way rapidly. What a few years will bring forth we know not. A great change has taken place even since we first entered the country, and we have no reason to believe it will stop here. Instead of two lonely American females we now number fourteen, and soon may twenty or forty more, if reports are true.

We are emphatically situated on the highway between the states and the Columbia river, and are a resting place for the weary travelers, consequently a greater burden rests upon us than upon any of our associates—to be always ready.

Whitman hired two of the men of the emigration to work for him. [Letter 101.] Each year thereafter he was able to secure some from each emigration to work at the mission station. Gray was busy building a house, which was later known as the mansion house. Because of the shortage of lumber, the walls were made of adobe bricks, and were a story and a half high, thus providing a low-roofed attic. By November 11, Gray had his new house roofed, and the walls were then being "hewed and plastered." [Letter 100.] Whitman has left no record as to what became of the first old adobe house. None of the reconstructed drawings of the Waiilatpu site indicate the presence of this building. It certainly was not used as a dwelling during the days before the massacre, when Waiilatpu was crowded with emigrants. It may have been used as a storehouse or workshop.

TROUBLE WITH THE INDIANS

On November 11, 1841, Whitman wrote a long letter to Greene in which he related some of the difficulties they had been having with the Indians. Mrs. Whitman copied this entire letter when writing to her father under date of November 18.

Whitman reported that during the summer some of the Indians had been most insolent to him when he sought to remove their horses from his cornfield. One of the trouble-makers by the name of Tilkanaik claimed that the land belonged to the Indians and wanted to know what Whitman had given for the land. Whitman refused to give anything, knowing that such a practice once begun would degenerate into an endless system of blackmail. He reminded the malcontents of the eagerness of the Indians to have missionaries settle in their midst and of the promises made them.

Tilkanaik was in an argumentative mood, and became belligerent. He struck Whitman twice severely upon the breast and commanded him to stop talking. "I told him," wrote Whitman, "that I had been in the habit of talking from my childhood and intended to keep on talking. This Indian Tilkanaik has for the year past been practicing the ceremonies of the Papists."

Other incidents followed, the most serious of which was one which involved W. H. Gray and Joe Gray, a half-breed Iroquois who had been in the service of the Hudson's Bay Company but was then living with the Indians near Waiilatpu. Whitman claimed that Joe Gray was a Catholic and had fomented trouble among the Indians by telling them that the missionaries ought to pay the Indians for the use of the land. Whitman wrote to Mr. McKinlay on September 30, 1841, and said: "I fear Joe Gray may have been the cause of much of the present excitement. An Indian told me he had been telling Tiloukaikt how the Indians did in his country and raised disturbances and by that means got property."

It seems that the trouble came to a climax on Saturday, September 25, when W. H. Gray forcibly ejected an Indian from the kitchen upon complaint of the Hawaiian woman cook. The Indian then went to the horse pen and tried to take one of Gray's horses. Gray put him out of the pen, but in the afternoon the Indian returned and succeeded in getting the horse. Whitman saw the deed and asked him "if he made himself a thief how he expected to cleanse himself." [Letter 95.]

A group of Indians gathered before the mansion house. where Gray was working. Tiloukaikt ordered Gray to leave the mission premises. Whitman induced Gray to keep still for he was afraid of Gray's impetuosity in a critical situation. Let Whitman tell the story.

> He said again that Mr. G. was laboring in vain for he must leave. I told him it was natural for us to labor, and we would not desist although we might labor in vain. I told him, also, that if Indians came into Mr. G's house or my house and refused to do as we desired, it was right for us to put them out.
>
> He then took hold of my ear and pulled it and struck me on the breast, ordering me to hear—as much as to say, we must let them do as they pleased about our houses. When he let go I turned the other to him and he pulled that, and in this way I let him pull first one and then the other until he gave over and took my hat and threw it into the mud. I called on the Indians who were at work for Mr. G. to give it to me and I put it on my head—when he took it off again and threw it in the mud and water, of which it dipped plentifully. Once more the Indians gave it back to me and I put it on, all mud as it was, and said to him, "Perhaps you are playing." At this he left us. [Letter 100.]

When McKinlay learned of the incident, he sent his interpreter to find out what actually had taken place. McKinlay was quick to espouse Whitman's rights. Through his interpreter he told the Indians that he considered those who so conducted themselves as dogs, a most uncomplimentary term to be used, and he warned them that the Company stood ready to avenge any wrong.

The Indians were much wrought up over being called dogs, and a group of them called on Whitman on Saturday, October 2. The Whitmans were accustomed to restrict the Indians to the Indian room of the mission house, but on this occasion they pushed themselves into the dining room. Whitman tried to lock out some of the unruly individuals and as a result one of them took an ax and broke a door. The chiefs did nothing to restore order. One Indian grabbed Whitman by the collar, tore his clothes, and struck him with his fist. Another advanced with a club, and when Whitman dodged the blow, ridiculed him for fearing death. A gun was presented at the doctor, and he was asked if he were afraid to die.

Whitman remained calm throughout the trying experience. He showed them the consequences which would come if they killed him. The Indians wanted the Whitmans to leave the doors open for the Indians to come and go through the house as they pleased, but this Dr. Whitman refused to do. They demanded some property, which Whitman refused to give. Whitman bluntly told them that Joe Gray was at the bottom of the trouble, and this they admitted. Finally the Indians withdrew, leaving the Whitmans and the Grays to wonder what the next day would bring forth.

Whitman tried to conduct worship the next day, but only a few came. Many about the grounds were insolent and committed acts of vandalism, such as the breaking of windows in the house. When some of them left for the Fort, Whitman sent a messenger to warn McKinlay to be prepared for them. McKinlay called a number of the prominent Indians together, including Tiloukaikt, and told them that if any harm befell the Whitmans, Dr. McLoughlin would send up a sufficient number to avenge their deaths and that the white men would take the Indians' horses in compensation.

McKinlay wrote to Whitman on October 4 and told him of the conference. "This is the first time," he wrote, "I have heard of Indians in any part of the country treating missionaries so, and that I never heard in any country of missionaries being obliged to pay for the lands they occupied." McKinlay felt that the Indians would do better. He warned Whitman against the custom of "paying them for their bad conduct."

On the Tuesday following, Whitman called the Indians together for a conference and frankly told them "unless they were ready to protect us and enforce good order, we would leave them; that we did not come to fight them but to teach them." Tiloukaikt, who still smarted under the rebuke given him by McKinlay, and especially because he had been called a dog, felt it expedient to preserve order.[1]

Narcissa, in a letter to her sister Jane, dated February 2, 1842, speaks of another incident which did not become quite so serious, yet was very threatening. When Dr. Whitman had rebuked the Indians about some matter, a dozen or so with rope, bows and arrows, and war clubs gathered to

---

[1] Allen, *Ten Years in Oregon*, p. 176, gives Elijah White's version of this incident. White gives the following: "It is generally thought, and possibly with truth, that, on this occasion, Dr. W. would have been killed, had not a party of white men arrived just at this moment." Whitman makes no mention of such a party.

frighten him. Narcissa was much alarmed, but again Dr. Whitman succeeded in calming them. These incidents foreshadowed coming events.

THE OLD QUARREL AGAIN

In August, Spalding had received two letters from Greene which not only cheered him up but made him feel justified in some of his positions. Spalding made a special trip to Tshimakain to show the letters to Walker and Eells. During October, Spalding and Eells visited Waiilatpu to get supplies. Spalding, fortified by the feeling that Greene approved of his ideas, became self-confident. Whitman, writing to Greene on October 22, said: "When I last wrote you I told you I thought we were prepared to cooperate together—but more recent facts have shown that hope to be vain, for Mr. & Mrs. Spalding have proved it otherwise." Spalding wanted to make a reconciliation, but Whitman refused since Mrs. Spalding was not present. "We did not go any further," he wrote to Greene, "than to agree, to act as being under covenant relations."

From Spalding's diary we learn that Dr. Whitman and a Mr. Cook, who was then in Whitman's employ, reached Lapwai on the evening of November 26, to help Spalding build his mill. On the Sunday following, November 28, Whitman addressed the natives assembled there for worship. Spalding had conducted special evangelistic meetings during October with good results. He brought forward several Indians who were ready to join the church, but Dr. Whitman was reluctant to receive them. On December 3, Spalding wrote in his diary:

Doct. W. is not willing that these persons who have been examined & who give satisfactory evidence that they are new creatures in Christ should be received into the church till our difficulties are settled. He read over a long list of charges against me many of which were true and for which I told him I was willing and anxious to make any concessions or do anything he wished if he would let me know his wish as most of them had been often rehersed & I as often intended to acknowledge my faults, but thought he did not directly say what he wanted still he gave us plainly to understand that nothing short of excission from the Mission would satisfy him & Mr. Gray. Many of the charges were facts perverted and many of them direct falsehoods got up by somebody.

The old quarrel, like a restless volcano, was about to erupt again. Spalding's mention of Gray indicates that Gray was helping to keep the issue alive. However, it seems strange that Whitman should have permitted this quarrel to keep deserving Indians from joining the church.

While at Lapwai, Dr. Whitman had the blacksmith shop dismantled. The equipment was to be taken to Waiilatpu. Whitman promised to send back a small set of tools for Spalding's use. Chief Joseph returned with Whitman and Cook on December 7 to bring back four plows which Whitman had promised to give Spalding.

After their return to Waiilatpu, Whitman and Gray built a blacksmith shop between their two dwellings. The next February, Whitman requested Spalding to send some bolting cloth for the mill and some apple trees. Spalding sent fifty young trees on the 23rd.[2] During the winter of 1841-42, Spalding had a troubled conscience over his relationships with others in the mission, so when he sent the apple trees to Whitman he also sent letters to the various members of the mission in which he again confessed his sins and begged their forgiveness. These letters were addressed to "Doct. Whitman and wife, Mr. Gray and wife, Mr. Walker and wife, Mr. Eells and wife and Mr. Rogers." Spalding mentioned this in his diary and added: "I trust by the grace of God I humbly repent of my sins against these brethren and sisters."[3]

On March 5, Spalding received an answer from the Whitmans and the Grays. He wrote in his diary for that day: "Instead of complying the requirement of Jesus in Luke 17:4 [And if he sin against thee seven times in the day, and seven times turn again to thee, saying, I repent; thou shalt forgive him.] they partly grant our request but wish us to meet them in answer to whatever charges they may wish to bring against us." Whitman was willing to turn the other cheek to the Indians, and even let them pull both ears and repeatedly throw his hat into the mud, but his patience with Spalding seems to have become exhausted.

THE SPRING OF 1842

The winter of 1841-42 passed quietly at Waiilatpu with no further difficulties with the Indians. The Walkers were

---

[2] On October 13, 1936, while visiting the site of Spalding's first home at Lapwai with Dr. A. H. Limouze, of New York City, and Dr. and Mrs. J. M. Cornelison, of Pendleton, Oregon, the author found a shoot growing out of an old apple-tree stump on which were some apples. These were identified as the Genitan, a fall apple common in New York State one hundred years ago.

[3] Spalding diary, Feb. 23, 1842.

expecting their third child in March, and Whitman was asked to be present. The doctor reached Tshimakain on March 5 and remained there until the 21st. Mrs. Walker gave birth on the 17th to a boy who was named Marcus Whitman Walker. This was the third boy to be named after Whitman during his lifetime. A few years later he was honored a fourth time in the same manner.[4] Whitman spent his spare time at Tshimakain in checking a translation of the first ten chapters of Matthew which Spalding had sent to him to be corrected. Spalding was able to print between four and five hundred copies of the Gospel according to Matthew on the mission press in 1845. Although Whitman could do little along literary lines, yet his assistance was sought in making the translation as accurate as possible.

On March 2, the day after Dr. Whitman left Waiilatpu, two Indian women called on Mrs. Whitman, bringing with them a "miserable looking child, a boy between three and four years old," and requested her to care for him. The child was a half-breed, with a Spanish father who was once in the employ of the Hudson's Bay Company, and a native mother. It appears that his parents had deserted him and that his Indian grandmother had cared for him for a time. The poor little lad was in a worse condition than was Helen Mar Meek when she was left at Waiilatpu. He was nearly naked, half-starved, and his body was covered with dirt and lice. Some Indian boys had shaved a strip "as wide as your finger . . . from ear to ear, and also from his forehead to his neck, crossing at right angles," in order to make him look ridiculous. One of his feet had been badly burned where he had been pushed into a fire.

At first Narcissa felt that she could not add to her duties, for she then had two half-breed girls with her. The forlorn boy was taken by his grandmother that night, but the next day she brought him back again. Narcissa found that she could not shut her heart against such need. "I washed him, oiled and bound up his wounds, and dressed him and cleaned his head of lice," she wrote. [Letter 105.] She found that he was much younger than she had first thought, being not much more than two years old. The hardships through which he had already passed made him appear older. As she cared for him, she wondered what she would call him. In memory she went back to her schooldays at Prattsburg and

---

[4] The fourth boy was Marcus Whitman Saunders, born May 8, 1846.

she thought of a schoolmate, David Malin, who had married her friend, Mary Porter. She called the lad David Malin.[5]

While Dr. Whitman was still absent, or on the morning of March 12, Mrs. W. H. Gray gave birth to a baby girl. Mrs. Whitman was far from well. The day before, she had been seized with severe pains in her stomach, yet when the call came for help she dressed and went over to the mansion house. She spent the whole day there assisting in the care of the mother and child. That evening she went back to her own rooms. On the 14th she wrote in her letter to her sister:

> I have this day entered upon my thirty-fifth year, and had my dear Alice C. been alive she would have been five years old, for this was her birthday as well as mine. Precious trust!... Spent the day with Sister G., although not able to do much. Have been taking medicine and feel some better this eve.... [Letter 105.]

Whitman returned on the 26th, much to Narcissa's joy. Mr. Eells came with him to get some supplies. After his return, Whitman busied himself with the spring planting. The Indians were cultivating more than ever. Writing to Mrs. Parker on July 25 of that year, Narcissa said: "The success of the Kayuses in farming is pleasing beyond description. There is scarcely an individual of them but what has his little farm some where & every year is extending it farther & farther." She admitted that the Nez Perces were more industrious than the Cayuses. Spalding was having remarkable success in his endeavors to settle the Indians.

The annual meeting of 1842 was scheduled to meet at Waiilatpu on Monday, May 16. Whitman and Gray sent a joint letter to Greene on May 12. The letter was written by Whitman. From it the following extracts are taken:

> In relation to the internal affairs of the mission there is no change, at least all things remain as they were last fall & no better understanding with Mr. Spalding. The proposed meeting for a settlement in the winter he refused to attend.
> The natives at this station have never appeared better & more quiet than at present. They have gone on with the cultivation with their usual energy & are gradually enlarging their little farms....

In this letter we also read the significant statement:

---

[5] David Malin, b. Jan. 21, 1805, attended Franklin Academy. His name is found with Spalding's on the Academy roll, April 23-Sept. 23, 1829. A.B., Hamilton College, 1833. Attended both Auburn and Princeton Theological Seminaries. Was pastor of 15th St. Presbyterian Church, Philadelphia, 1870-1878, where Spalding visited him. (*See* Drury, *Spalding*, p. 391.) Died, Dec. 25, 1885. Mrs. Pringle in Clark, *Pioneer Days*, Vol. 2, p. 521, claims that David's last name was Cortez.

"There will probably be a large party of emigrants coming to this country in the spring of 1843. Some young men are now returning with the expectation of bringing out a party next spring." In the light of the extravagant claims made for Whitman in regard to the 1843 emigration, it is interesting to note that he was aware of the possibility of the coming of a large party a year before they arrived.

THE ANNUAL MEETING OF 1842

The Walkers and their three children, the youngest but a few months old, and the Eells with their little boy, made the long trip down to Waiilatpu. Spalding, embittered over the turn of events, notified the brethren that he would not be present. The mission opened on schedule time. Walker and Eells were re-elected to their respective offices of Moderator and Scribe. Spalding's letter of explanation regarding his absence was read. Those present felt that the time had come for a final settlement. Whitman had expressed his feelings to Greene in his letter of May 12, when he wrote: "We hope soon to be able to say *all* are *united* either in a final separation, or in everlasting *union & cooperation.*" The members of the mission felt that Spalding's reasons were insufficient and sent a messenger requesting his immediate attendance. They then adjourned to await his coming. Spalding appeared on Thursday, May 26, and the mission resumed its meetings the next day.

Greene's letters of November, 1840, and March, 1841, were read, and Walker, Eells, and Spalding were appointed to reply. It appears that the women were invited to listen in on the frank discussions which were held. Mrs. Walker wrote in her diary for Monday, May 30: "We all attend the services and hear much to make our ears tingle." It was finally decided that each would write out what he considered to be the chief difficulties, and then each would give specifications as to how the difficulties could be solved. On Tuesday, May 31, Walker wrote in his diary:[6] "Had a hard session to day and there was so much bad feeling manifested that I said that I thought it was an abomination for us to meet and pray."

A review of the account of those eight days as given to

---

[6] The original of Walker's diary is in the Huntington Library, San Marino, California, with the exception of the entries for 1842, which part is in the Oregon Historical Society. His diary covers the dates Mar. 7, 1838-Oct. 4, 1838; Jan. 5, 1841-Oct. 13, 1848.

us by Walker in his diary shows that he placed most of the blame for the unhappy condition of the mission on Whitman. On June 1, Walker and Eells took a long ride in the rain "and felt that all hope was gone." On the 2nd, the mission faced the consequences which would follow if a reconciliation were not reached. Walker then wrote: "I felt much and said considerable, and hope that it was not in vain. I think there was a better state of feeling than there has been since the session began." The next day was another hard day. Walker wrote in his diary: "My feelings have been anything but calm. I have been much moved by some threats the Doctor made, that if he was not allowed to pursue his own course he would leave the Mission. The Doctor asked to be allowed to go on in his own way without being checked."

Walker could scarcely sleep that night for worry. What would the mission do without a doctor? Mrs. Walker's diary contains the following entry for June 3:

> Soon after the opening of the session Dr. W. began to call Mr. Spaulding to account. Mr. Rogers thought Dr. W. wrong. Much talk followed and the Dr. was allowed to proceed. The appearance is such as to excite much concern on the part of some if not all and lead us to fear there will be no sound settlement effected.
> If any restraint is laid on the Dr. or if he suspects he is not to have his own way entirely, he immediately threatens to leave the mission.[7]

The next day Whitman and Spalding had a private conference, after which they asked all to assemble, whereupon Spalding began his confession, which Mrs. Walker described was "as humble as could be wished." She also added: "The minds of all were relieved." Unfortunately the last entry in Spalding's diary closes with March 1, 1842, so we do not know how he felt those days. It seems, however, that Whitman and Spalding had gone to the root of their grievances and settled them for all time, for this is the last time we hear of the unpleasant dispute.

Worship services were held on Sunday with Mr. Walker as the preacher. The mission continued its business sessions for two days more. Spalding started back to his station on Wednesday the 8th. Before he left he signed a letter prepared by Walker, Eells, and himself which was sent to Greene. In this they stated that an eight-day mission meeting had been held, and after a full investigation, all difficulties had been settled.

---

[7] It is not clear just what Rogers was doing at this meeting. He may have been in the vicinity and was called in as a witness.

The members of the mission discussed the possibility of the Board's taking some serious action on the basis of the complaints sent in, so, to forestall any order disastrous to the welfare of the mission, decided that before any such action would be binding the Prudential Committee should be informed of the new developments. Hence the following paragraph in the letter to Greene of June 8:

It was the unanimous opinion at the close of the investigation that, should the Prudential Committee have taken any action on any communication yet unanswered, that the Mission ought to wait until this communication can be answered.

As later events proved, this vote was of the utmost importance to Spalding. The following motion, introduced by Gray, was also accepted at this mission meeting:

Resolve. That in view of the state of this Mission, especially the station at Lapwai, we deem it advisable that Rev. H. H. Spalding remove to Waiilatpu to take charge of the natives at this place for the present, and that Dr. Whitman remove to Lapwai to take charge of that station till circumstances shall warrant a return.[8]

That was a strange action to take and evidence is lacking to fully explain it. In July both Walker and Spalding were at Waiilatpu to get some supplies. For various reasons, Whitman, Walker, and Spalding all felt that the exchange of stations should not be made. Spalding reported some new developments at Lapwai which made a transfer unwise at that time. Eells, writing to Greene on October 3, 1842, declared that Gray "strongly urged it be made even if the life of Dr. W. should be endangered, also expressed a regret that he was connected with a mission which had not courage to carry out such a vote." Gray was adamant and refused to reconsider. Walker was asked to talk the matter over with Eells and send back a reply.

Under date of August 10, 1842, Walker and Eells sent back their reply, in which they recommended that the exchange be not made.[9] Gray, who was ready to leave the mission, grasped this incident as an occasion to resign. Either Whitman and Spalding would exchange stations or he would go. Whitman felt it best to make the long trip to Tshimakain to talk to Walker and Eells about it. He arrived at their place on August 24. Gray sent a message strongly urging Walker and Eells to reconsider. Whitman let it be known that if the exchange were not made Gray

---

[8] Quoted from Marshall, *Acquisition of Oregon*, Vol. 2, p. 112.
[9] *Frontier*, Nov., 1930, p. 76.

A picture of the resolution, slightly reduced, adopted by the Oregon mission on the eve of Whitman's departure for the East. Whitman carried the original with him. The resolution was written by Whitman.

By courtesy of the American Board.

would probably go to the Willamette. Walker and Eells refused to change their minds.

Whitman returned to his station on the 29th. Gray half expected what the verdict would be and had made preparations to visit the Lower Columbia country. He left on the 31st to see what arrangements he could make there for himself and his family. Whitman informed Walker and Eells of the developments and said that if Gray could find no opening in the Willamette he would return to the States the next spring.

DR. ELIJAH WHITE

During the absence of Gray, Dr. Elijah White arrived at Waiilatpu with the emigration of 1842, consisting of 114 people. After White's dismissal from the Methodist mission, he returned to the States, where he succeeded in securing an appointment as Indian Agent for the United States Government for Oregon Territory. This was the first time that the United States Government had appointed any person in any official capacity for the Pacific Northwest. As was subsequently proved, White lacked the fundamental qualifications to make a successful agent. He was somewhat pompous and delighted in showing his authority. On the other hand, it must be stated that the Government gave him very little active assistance. The Methodist missionaries of Oregon were rather dismayed to see one of their former number returned in a governmental capacity.

Judging by White's letters to the Commissioner of Indian Affairs, we learn that White was intensely interested in the Linn bill, which was then being considered by Congress.[10] White was a politician, and saw what he thought was a fine chance to get a political appointment. He accepted the office of Indian Agent with the hope that it would lead to something much better.

The second session of the Twenty-seventh Congress sat from December 6, 1841, to August 31, 1842. The Oregon question was then becoming one of the main issues of the day. President Tyler, in his message to Congress, approved the recommendation of John C. Spencer, then Secretary of War, for the establishment of a "chain of military posts from Council Bluffs to some point on the Pacific Ocean within our limits."[11] This, he pointed out, would benefit those engaged

---

[10] Old Indian Files, Washington, D. C.
[11] Marshall, *op. cit.*, Vol. 1, p. 212.

in the fur trade, and be the means of establishing safe intercourse "between the American settlements at the mouth of the Columbia River and those on this side of the Rocky Mountains."

On December 16, 1841, Senator Lewis F. Linn, of Missouri, introduced his bill, which was designed to hasten the occupation and settlement of Oregon. It promised a section of land to every settler. On April 13 and 15, 1842, Senator Linn spoke at length in favor of the bill and said: "There could be no dispute about the right of the United States to all the region south of the Columbia River, a right which Great Britain had fully conceded. The only question was to the right of the United States to the territory north of the Columbia River."[12]

The arrival on April 4, 1842, of Lord Ashburton from England to negotiate a treaty with the United States caused Congress to postpone definite action on the Oregon question until after the treaty had been signed. The Webster-Ashburton Treaty was concluded on August 9, 1842. Even though Lord Ashburton had instructions from his government to deal with the Oregon boundary question, the treaty had nothing to say about it. Rather, it dealt with the boundary question affecting Maine and Canada. Webster felt that the time was not ripe to settle the Oregon issue and deliberately kept it out of their discussions.

These were some of the issues in which Elijah White was tremendously interested. He had been in Oregon and he felt that the day was rapidly approaching when the United States would extend its full jurisdiction over that country. His letters reveal his eagerness to get a political appointment as soon as the Linn bill passed. White wrote to the Commissioner of Indian Affairs from Independence, Missouri, on May 11, 1842, and referred to the great interest manifested on the frontier in the Linn bill.

On May 15, White left Independence with the 1842 emigration to Oregon, which then numbered 105. There were many who were unable to make their arrangements in time to go that year but declared they would be in the 1843 party. The great movement which sent thousands over the Oregon Trail was fully launched.

White wrote to the Commissioner of Indian Affairs from Fort Laramie on July 2 and from Fort Hall on August 15. In the latter letter he stated:

_____
12 *Ibid.*, p. 426.

Our party instead of diminishing has now increased to one hundred and twelve. . . .

To get this large company through I had been under the necessity of expending in order to their comfort and safety, some eleven hundred Dollars of my own funds, I hope and trust I will be excused from drawing on the Treasury for the Pilotage for $250.00 which at this date we could not raise among us to save our heads—all other pilotage has been at my expense—shall this be at Government's or mine? . . .

My reception at this one of the "Hudson's Bay posts" has been kind and handsome showing their usual hospitality notwithstanding they were previously made acquainted with the strength of our party and my appointment.

The members of the 1842 emigration started out with nineteen wagons, none of which were taken west of Fort Hall. From White's letter of August 15, it appears that he had secured Government funds to subsidize the 1842 emigration. This is a most interesting fact if true. According to Bancroft, Jason Lee received a subsidy from the "secret-service fund" of the Government to assist in the cost of taking the great missionary re-enforcement of 1839 to Oregon.[13] It is possible that White received financial assistance from the same source.

On October 15, White wrote to the Commissioner of Indian Affairs from the Willamette Valley stating that 114 persons had reached their destination. Six of those who started died on the way. Several joined the party en route, thus accounting for the fact that more reached the Willamette Valley than started from Independence.

On August 23, White left the main party of the emigrants and pushed on ahead. We do not have the exact date of his arrival at Waiilatpu, but he did leave this brief account of his interview with Whitman: "The visit was very agreeable to both, as he had much to tell Dr. White of Oregon affairs, and the Dr. him of his two years' residence in the States."[14] There can be no doubt about White's telling Whitman of the proposed treaty with Great Britain, in which it was expected that the Oregon boundary question would be settled. White was full of information regarding the Linn bill and the excitement along the frontier, all of which he probably passed on to Whitman.

Like any other normal Oregon resident of that day, Marcus Whitman was tremendously interested in the political developments as they affected Oregon. He had reason to

[13] Bancroft, *Oregon*, Vol. 1, p. 177.
[14] Allen, *Ten Years in Oregon*, p. 166.

be more interested than the average person because his home was on the Oregon Trail and it was destined to be a resting place for the weary. Neither White nor Whitman knew that the Webster-Ashburton Treaty had been signed and that Congress had adjourned without taking action on the Linn bill. When White left the frontier, the prospects were bright that something would be done, and he gave that optimistic report to Whitman.

The main party of the emigrants reached Waiilatpu on the afternoon of September 14. Among the emigrants was Medorem Crawford, who wrote in his journal that he was never more pleased to see a house or white people in his life. He reported that Dr. and Mrs. Whitman treated them with the utmost kindness and sold provisions on "very reasonable terms." After spending the night at Waiilatpu, the emigrants continued their journey. On September 20, when Crawford was forty-five miles below Fort Walla Walla, he wrote in his journal: "Mr. Spalding & Lady over took us at noon. . . . Mr. Gray called at camp on his return from Vancouver." We do not know just why Mr. and Mrs. Spalding were there at that time. As a result of some information given by Gray, the Spaldings turned back and accompanied him to Waiilatpu.

Another member of this emigration who also kept a diary was L. W. Hastings, and in it we read:

. . . the next place of note, at which we arrived, was a presbyterian mission, in charge of which, is a Dr. Whitman, who is a very kind and hospitable gentleman. He received us with the utmost kindness and attention, and insisted upon our remaining a few days with him, in order to obtain some relaxation of both body and mind.[15]

Hastings spent a Sunday there and attended a service where the doctor "delivered a discourse to the Indians, in their own language." Hastings also wrote: "The doctor is not only a very kind and hospitable gentleman, but he is no doubt, a very good man, and a devoted Christian. He appears to be rendering great service in christianizing and civilizing the natives."

THE FATEFUL ORDER

White carried out to the Oregon mission the fateful order of the Board, dated February 25, 1842. Greene wrote a general letter to the mission, in which he gave orders to abandon Waiilatpu and Lapwai and asked for the return of

---

15 Hastings, *A New Description of Oregon and California*, p. 21.

the Spaldings, preferably by the overland route. Greene also wrote a personal letter to Whitman in which he said: "In everything that relates to Mr. Spalding, you will need to act with much discretion and kindness." Greene suggested that should the Spaldings prefer to remain in Oregon, they were to receive from five to six hundred dollars in property as the equivalent of their travel expenses home.

Whitman's heart sank as he read the letter. Greene did not understand! The Board did not know the facts. Give up Waiilatpu and Lapwai and go to Tshimakain! That was the poorest station in the whole field. Agricultural conditions there were most unfavorable. The Indians were unresponsive. Besides, the emigrants were beginning to come. Waiilatpu was strategically located. Above all other stations it should be kept. The Board could not afford to abandon it.

Moreover, the conditions within the mission had vastly changed. Smith and Rogers were out, and Gray was then making plans to leave. A reconciliation had been effected with Spalding. The Board's order was out of date. It did not apply. Then, too, how foolish of the Board to order Spalding to take his family overland! That was impossible, because there were no longer any caravans going eastward. The American Fur Company no longer existed. The tide was westward. How could they send a man with his wife and small children unescorted across the Plains?

It is quite possible that Whitman communicated the facts of the order to White, who in turn told Gray, although in 1885, Gray declared that: "The order to abandon the Mission I confess is new to me."[16] Gray certainly knew something of importance to communicate to the Spaldings to make them turn back when they were with Medorem Crawford. It seems incredible that Gray could have been present those days at Waiilatpu when the special meeting of the mission was held to discuss the order, and not know of the particulars. In later years Gray was active in claiming that the sole cause of Whitman's ride East in 1842 was to save Oregon. The order to dismiss Spalding and to abandon Waiilatpu did not fit in with that theory, so it seems that Gray forgot all about it.

Whitman appears to have known that Spalding was absent from Lapwai. Whitman, therefore, sent Greene's letter for Spalding to Walker and Eells along with his own

16 Quoted by Marshall, *op. cit.*, Vol. 2, p. 138.

request to have them come at once. The messenger reached
Tshimakain on Tuesday, September 20. Mrs. Walker wrote
that day in her diary:

> The express we are looking for arrived, bringing letters from
> D.W. Dr. Whitman and Mr. Greene, stating that the Board have
> concluded to recall Mr. Spalding, Smith and Gray and to discontinue
> the southern branch of this Mission. But as we have already written
> that the difficulties are settled and that we should wait a reply to the
> last. Mr. G. had already determined to leave and do not know as
> anyone has any objections.

Walker made a similar notation in his journal for that
day, but added: "The Doctor sent Mr. Spalding's letter to
us, and we felt it was wrong in him not to forward it."
Walker and Eells left at nine o'clock the next morning and
reached Waiilatpu on Monday, September 26, having camped
on the Touchet River over Sunday. They found both Spalding and Gray already there. As a result of Gray's fortuitous
meeting with Spalding, the latter had learned of the mission
meeting. Otherwise he might not have been present. Gray
and Spalding had reached Waiilatpu on Thursday, September 22.

The special meeting of the mission was opened Monday
evening, September 26. Greene's letters of February 28,
1842, were read and along with it a copy of the letter sent
to him on June 8. The men felt that the last paragraph of
that letter, in which they requested the Board to postpone
final decision until the Board was made acquainted with the
new developments in the mission, automatically took care
of the order dismissing Spalding and calling for the closing
of the mission work at Lapwai and Waiilatpu. The men,
therefore, turned their attention to Gray's case.

Gray submitted a written statement regarding his plan
to accept a position offered by the Methodist mission in the
Willamette Valley. This statement closed with the following
resolutions:

> That we approve Mr. Gray's engaging in the school as above in-
> timated.
> That we sanction his request to withdraw from his connection with
> the A.B.C.F.M. in view of the object above specified.[17]

Whitman seconded the motion. Spalding and Eells voted
in the negative. Walker as Moderator cast his vote with the
opposition, and the motion was lost. How strange! One

---

[17] Marshall, *op. cit.*, Vol. 2, pp. 126 ff., gives the minutes of meeting.
Original records in Coll. A.

would have thought that Spalding especially would have
been only too glad to see Gray go.

On Tuesday, September 27, Walker wrote in his journal:
"We did not do much today. The Doctor preferred some
charges against myself and Mr. Eells which we did not admit
and held him to the talk I had with him last Summer." So
far nothing had been said about Whitman's going East. On
the 28th, Walker wrote: "Rose this morning with the determination to leave, and found Mr. Spalding had the same
view, and was making preparations to leave as he felt that
nothing could be done. At breakfast the Doctor let out what
was his plan in view of the state of things. We persuaded
them to get together and talk matters over."

According to Spalding, Whitman was called to Fort Walla
Walla to see a patient while the mission was in session.[18]
Since Walker reported that nothing much had been accomplished on Tuesday, September 27, it seems reasonable to
believe that Whitman was absent that day. Archibald Mc-
Kinlay later made reference to a visit of Dr. Whitman's
shortly before he went East but did not indicate the exact
date.[19] The long ride to the Fort and return would have
given Whitman plenty of time to think about the disastrous
order. He became convinced that a personal intercession
on behalf of the mission was necessary. This we know:
Whitman proposed going to Boston on Wednesday morning
to the surprise of the other members of the mission.

If Whitman went to the Fort on Tuesday, it is possible
that he discussed the situation existing within the mission
with his friend McKinlay. We find the following statement
in McKinlay's letter of January 19, 1885, to Myron Eells:
"Whitman did say to me before his departure east that his
objects in going were to frustrate unfavorable reports sent
the Board by discontented members of the Mission—he mentioned Mr. C. Rogers, W. H. Gray, and I think Revd Mr.
Smith as the parties who had sent the communications."

According to Walker, Whitman and Spalding first talked
about the idea, and then Whitman submitted the proposal
to Walker and Eells. It appears that Spalding's consent
was secured. In Walker's diary we read: "Then the question
was submitted to us of the Doctor's going home, which we

---

[18] *Senate Doc. No. 37*, p. 20; also undated clipping from collection
of Mrs. Ross of Portland gives letter of Perrin Whitman in which it
is stated: "On the 29th of September, 1842, Dr. Whitman was called
to Wallula."

[19] McKinlay to Myron Eells, Jan. 19, 1885, Coll. W.

felt that it was one of too much importance to be decided in a moment, but finally came to the conclusion that if he could put things in such a state that it would be safe we could consent to his going, and with that left them and made a start home."

Walker and Eells, with their customary reluctance to make any move without deliberate thought, were hesitant. They wanted time to think and pray about it. Dr. Whitman, on the other hand, felt the need for immediate action. If he could leave that fall it meant that he could return with the 1843 emigration. If he waited to go East in the spring, it meant that he would not be able to return until the fall of 1844. By leaving in the fall of 1842, he could return a year earlier. However, if he were to go that autumn, it meant that he would have to hurry, in order to cross the mountains before winter came. As soon as Whitman began to consider seriously the matter of going, it is easy to understand why he wanted to hurry.

Walker and Eells brought up the question of the care of the Waiilatpu property, and made their vote dependent upon some satisfactory arrangements being made to care for it. Whitman then hastily wrote out the following resolution, which was signed by Walker, Eells, and Spalding:

Resolved, That if arrangements can be made to continue the operation of this station that Dr. Marcus Whitman be at liberty & advised to visit the United States as soon as practicable to confer with the Committee of the A.B.C.F.M. in regard to the interests of this mission.
Waiilatpu September 28th 1842

It appears that by this time Gray had succeeded in winning the consent of the other members of the mission for his dismissal, so, before Walker and Eells left, they also signed the following resolution, together with Whitman and Spalding:

Resolved, That we approve of the withdrawal and removal of Mr. W. H. Gray and wife from this Mission, in order to become the Secular Agent of and General Superintendent of the Oregon Institute, to be located in the Willamette Valley, as set forth in a prospectus for the same.
Waiilatpu, September 28, 1842

Before Walker and Eells left, it was agreed that they would each write a letter to Greene which Whitman would carry should he go East. According to Walker's diary, these letters left Tshimakain on October 11 in plenty of time to reach Waiilatpu by the date agreed.[20] The final arrange-

---

[20] Eells, *Marcus Whitman*. Cushing Eells in 1883 claimed that they agreed to have the letters at Waiilatpu by October 5. However, Cush-

ments seem to have been made in haste, for both Walker
and Eells were anxious to be on their way. After their return home they wrote their letters. Eells wrote about the
Gray case, while Walker touched on the reasons why Whitman wanted to go East. The following are extracts from
Walker's letter:

If necessity demanded that one branch of the Mission should be
abandoned, the north part could have been given up with far less
disastrous consequences both as respects white settlers and the
natives. . . .

. . . as we were about starting for our place, a proposition was made
by Dr. Whitman for him to return to the States this Winter, and
confer with the Prudential Committee, and conduct a reinforcement
out next summer, if it was thought best to continue the Mission. . . .

We do not approve of the hasty manner in which this question was
decided. Nothing it seemed to us but stern necessity induced us to
decide in the manner we did. It seemed death to put the proposition in
force, and worse than death to remain as we were.

Furthermore we need a good reinforcement especially of laymen.
. . . We want those who are willing to be such all their days, and not
feel as soon as they get to the field that they can be more useful in some
other department of labor.

The last sentence quoted was evidently aimed at Gray.
These letters did not reach Waiilatpu until after Whitman
left. Greene did not receive them until May 3, 1843, when
Whitman was already on his way back to Oregon.[21]

WHITMAN LEAVES FOR BOSTON

Within twenty-four hours after the members of the mission had departed to their respective stations, Marcus Whitman had decided to start on Monday, October 3, nearly two
weeks earlier than he had first planned. We can be sure that
had he proposed leaving on the 3rd before Walker and Eells
left, they would have objected. On Thursday, September 29,
Narcissa said in a letter she wrote to Jane and Edward:

I sit down to write you, but in great haste. My beloved husband
has about concluded to start next Monday to go to the United States,
the dear land of our birth; but I remain behind. . . . He hopes to reach
the borders in less than three months, if the Lord prospers his way.
It is a dreadful journey, especially at this season of the year; and as

---

ing Eells dated his letter to Greene October 3, and judging from
Walker's diary, he worked on it several days. The probable date
agreed upon was October 15. Walker to Greene, Feb. 28, 1843: "We
sent our letters at the time agreed upon."

[21] *See* Appendix 3 for a more detailed discussion of the causes
of Whitman's ride.

much as I want to see you all, I cannot think of ever crossing the mountains again—my present health will not admit of it....

If you are still in Quincy you may not see him until his return, as his business requires great haste. He wishes to reach Boston as early as possible so as to make arrangements to return next summer, if prospered. The interest of the missionary cause in this country calls him home.

Jane and Edward were then associated with one of Narcissa's former Prattsburg teachers, the Rev. William Beardsley, in the Mission Institute at Quincy, Illinois. Jane may have been a teacher in the Institute, while Edward seems to have been studying for the ministry. Narcissa begged her sister to return with Marcus the next spring. In a postscript to this letter we can read: "I have forgotten to speak of husband's company in travel. He is Mr. A. L. Lovejoy, a lawyer who came up from the States this summer, and now is willing and anxious to return for the good he may do in returning."

Asa Lawrence Lovejoy[22] (1808-1882) had been a member of the 1842 emigration. Writing on February 14, 1876, Lovejoy related how he happened to return with Whitman as follows:

My party camped some two miles below Dr. Whitman's place. The day after our arrival Dr. Whitman called at our camp and asked me to accompany him to his house, as he wished me to draw up a memorial to Congress to prohibit the sale of ardent spirits in this country... after numerous conversations with the Doctor touching the future prosperity of Oregon, he asked me one day in a very anxious manner, if I thought it would be possible for him to cross the mountains at that time of the year. I told him I thought he could. He next asked, "Will you accompany me?" After a little reflection, I told him I would.[23]

It is very unlikely that Whitman would have proposed the Eastern trip without the assurance of a companion. Lovejoy was at the Fort at the time of the mission meeting. If the theory be true that Whitman went to the Fort on Tuesday, September 27, it is possible that he won Lovejoy's consent then. Lovejoy might have ridden to Waiilatpu the next day to find out what Whitman intended to do. Learning of his intention to go, Lovejoy might have insisted upon an earlier departure than that suggested by Walker and Eells. This is but a theory, yet it gives a plausible explanation as to why

---

[22] Asa is often confused with his son Amos, who was born in 1856. Asa was a nephew of the Hon. Abbott Lawrence, once minister to England.

[23] Nixon, *How Marcus Whitman Saved Oregon*, p. 306

Whitman should have set forward the date of his departure by almost two weeks.

Narcissa took advantage of the occasion to send letters to loved ones. She added a postscript to the letter she had written to the Rev. and Mrs. Asa S. Allen, of Cuba, New York, on August 23. She wrote to her parents on the 30th, saying: "You will be surprised if this letter reaches you to learn that the bearer is my dear husband, and that you will, after a few days, have the pleasure of seeing him. May you have a joyful meeting." She briefly reviewed the circumstances leading up to his decision to go, and added: "He goes with the advice and entire confidence of his brethren in the mission, and who value him not only as an associate, but as their physician, and feel, as much as I do, that they know not how to spare him; but the interest of the cause demands the sacrifice on our part." The letter to the Allens, the one to Jane and Edward, and the one to her parents are the only letters of hers that we now have which Dr. Whitman carried.

Gray wrote to Greene on October 3, giving his account of his withdrawal from the mission. Whitman carried that letter and the resolution which Walker, Eells, and Spalding had signed on the 28th, authorizing his departure. So far as we know these were the only letters for Greene or the American Board that he carried.

Early on Monday morning, October 3, 1842, Whitman kissed his wife goodbye, and mounted his horse. The Grays were still at Waiilatpu. Gray was instructed to find somebody in the Willamette Valley who would come up and take care of the station during Whitman's absence. Whitman wanted Rogers and his wife. Feeling confident that suitable arrangements would be made, Whitman rode with Lovejoy down the trail that led to the Blue Mountains. They had at least one baggage animal with them, and perhaps more. The dog called Trapper, once the playmate of Alice Clarissa, went along.[24] An Indian by the name of Aps accompanied them for a short distance, returning the next day with a letter from Marcus. It is possible that a few other Indians went with them for a part of the journey through the Blue Mountains.

With a heavy but brave heart, Narcissa watched the party go down the trail until it was lost to view. Her

---

[24] Story given by Mrs. Edmund Bowden, of Seattle, a personal friend of the Rev. Cushing Eells.

anxious thoughts formed themselves into a prayer for God's protection for her husband. As she thought of the long and lonely months before her, she felt timid and afraid. She prayed not only for her husband. She prayed that God would give her strength to carry on.

CHAPTER FOURTEEN

"SHEEP WITHOUT A SHEPHERD"

1842-1843

DURING the year that Dr. Whitman was away, several important events occurred which affected the work of the American Board's mission in Oregon. Narcissa bemoaned the fact that the first official contact of the Cayuses with the United States Government through Indian Agent White had to come when her husband was absent. She wrote saying that the Indians were like "sheep without a shepherd" and knew not whom they could trust.

Mrs. Whitman's letters during this period give us the best review of her experiences. On Tuesday, October 4, Aps, one of the Indians who had started out with Whitman and Lovejoy, returned with a letter from the doctor for his wife. Narcissa sat down at once and wrote an answer, although we do not know if her husband ever saw it. She told of the departure of the Grays that morning.[1] The next day she added another section to the letter and mentioned the difficulty the Grays experienced in getting to Fort Walla Walla. "The cart broke," she stated. This is the first mention of the presence of a wheeled vehicle at the Waiilatpu station. It may be that Whitman got one of the wagons which was brought over the Blue Mountains by the Meek party in 1840.

We are interested in the following items: "I am sorry we forgot your pencil, comb and journal. Aps brought back Mr. Lovejoy's—said you left it in camp."[2] On the 5th she wrote: "In arranging the cupboard to-day, I found that you had not taken the compass as you designed to."[3] Dr. Whitman left in such haste that a number of little things were overlooked. After his departure Narcissa remembered her need for spectacles. "I intended to have spoken to you

---

[1] Gray, Eells, Ross, *The Whitman Controversy*, p. 36, states that Gray claimed he left Waiilatpu on October 15 and that Dr. Whitman's departure caused him to delay going to the Willamette Valley. Gray was mistaken in his recollection of the date.

[2] Lovejoy MS., Bancroft Coll., p. 18: "I had notes all along but I lost them."

[3] Whitman College museum claims to have Dr. Whitman's compass, perhaps the one he left behind on this trip.

about purchasing one or two pair of spectacles," she wrote. "Perhaps you will think of it."

After the departure of the Grays on the 4th, Mrs. Whitman was the only white person at the mission station. On the night of October 6, she was awakened at midnight by someone trying to enter her room. Hearing the latch raised, she jumped from her bed, slammed the door shut, and fastened the latch again. The intruder succeeded in raising it and was able to push the door partly open, Mrs. Whitman's strength not being equal to his. All the time she was calling for John, who appears to have been a faithful Indian whom she trusted. Finally the ruffian became alarmed and ran through the dining room out of doors. Narcissa hastened to lock the outside door. She lit a candle and returned to her bed trembling and cold. But she could not rest. She rose again and called John and had him sleep in the kitchen. She described this experience to her husband in the entry in her journal letter for October 7. [Letter 118.]

The next day Mungo, who happened to arrive from Tshimakain, carried the news of the intrusion to McKinlay. The Grays were still at the Fort and shared in McKinlay's anxiety for her safety. Mungo was sent back with a message strongly urging her to leave at once for the Fort. Mrs. Whitman consulted with some of the chiefs regarding the advisability of leaving. Among those with whom she discussed the situation was Feathercap. [Letter 118.] According to one writer, Feathercap, also called Tamsucky, was the one who attempted the assault.[4] We marvel at the amazing courage of Narcissa, who on previous occasions had written of her timidity about staying at the mission station without her husband, even when other white people were on the grounds. But now she was all alone! And she discussed the attempted assault with the culprit himself!

On Tuesday, October 11, Mr. McKinlay took a wagon and drove out to Waiilatpu to get Mrs. Whitman. She was not feeling well and did not want to attempt the journey, but McKinlay would not take a refusal. He arranged a bed in the wagon, on which Mrs. Whitman reclined while they made the trip to the Fort. She took with her the three half-

---

[4] Cannon, *Waiilatpu*, p. 67: "Later investigation developed evidence that the Indian who attempted the assault upon Mrs. Whitman was a second chief of Tilaukait's village, named Tamsuky." Also, p. 103, Cannon states that Mrs. Whitman identified Feathercap with Tamsucky. Gray, *Oregon*, p. 189, claims that Feathercap and Tiloukaikt were the same.

breed children. The Indians regretted her departure, but Narcissa in a letter to her husband confessed that the "anxiety was wearing upon me too much."

Another letter from Marcus reached Narcissa on Friday, October 14. Although she was relieved of the worry of being alone at the mission station, still she suffered at the Fort from the want of the conveniences of her home, primitive as it was as judged by modern standards. Her room at the Fort was cold, and some of the bedding was damp. After she had been there about a week, Mr. McKinlay put up a stove for her, which made her much more comfortable. Her poor health increased her discomfort.

In her imagination she followed her husband's course across the country. She pictured him reaching Fort Boise, where he would see Mr. Payette, the Hudson's Bay trader in charge. Then would come the long trip across the desert to Fort Hall. Stage by stage she retraced the journey they had made in 1836, and then in her daydreams she painted the picture of his arrival at his home. "How will you feel, dear husband," she asked, "when you seat yourself in Sister Julia's house, or with our mothers, and not see the windows filled with Indians, and the doors also; will you not feel lost?"

On the 22nd of October she began another letter from Fort Walla Walla to her husband which she expected to send with the express across Canada. In this letter she made the following reference to the motive which took him from her side: "Stay as long as it is necessary to accomplish all your heart's desire respecting the interest of this country, so dear to us both—our home." This letter also contains the following intimate passage:

Read this letter, my husband, and then give it to my mother— perhaps she would like once more to peep into one of the sacred chambers of her daughter's heart—it may comfort her, seeing she can not see her face again in the flesh.

This letter was sent to the American Board in Boston, where it still remains. It arrived after Whitman had left, and we have no reason to believe that Marcus or any of her relatives ever saw it.

Spalding went to Waiilatpu during the latter part of October to look after a number of things but was suddenly called back to Lapwai by the serious illness of his wife.[5] Gray was delayed in leaving the Fort, and after he reached

---

[5] Drury, *Spalding*, p. 291. Spalding and an Indian companion rode the 120 miles from Waiilatpu to Lapwai in nineteen hours.

the Willamette Valley he found difficulty in engaging someone to go to Waiilatpu. Rogers was otherwise employed.
Mr. Littlejohn, thoroughly discouraged, was planning to
return to the States the next spring with his family. Finally
Gray was able to hire William Geiger.

Mrs. Whitman was not very comfortable at the Fort, and
was happy, therefore, when she received an invitation
from the mission families at the Methodist station at The
Dalles, or Waskopum, to spend the winter with them. She
secured passage in one of the Hudson's Bay express boats
which left Fort Walla Walla on October 27 and arrived at
Waskopum on the 29th, where she was hospitably received
by the Rev. and Mrs. H. K. W. Perkins, Mr. and Mrs. Daniel
Lee, and Mr. and Mrs. Henry B. Brewer. [Letter 122.] The
Dalles station was the first branch to be established by the
Methodists. The buildings were located on the south bank
of the Columbia, about a mile from the river.

Shortly after her departure from the Fort, the gristmill
at Waiilatpu was burned. McKinlay wrote to Mrs. Whitman, telling of the occurrence and expressing his belief that
the mill was deliberately destroyed. Commenting on this
disaster in a letter to her parents, Mrs. Whitman said:
"Probably there was more than two hundred bushels of
wheat and corn burnt and some flour. The mill bolt and
threshing mill, even to a part of the wheel, was burnt. My
poor husband will feel this sadly." [Letter 121.]

On November 24, Mr. and Mrs. Littlejohn and Mr. Geiger
reached Waskopum en route to Waiilatpu. While Littlejohn
was unwilling to accept responsibility for the mission station, it appears that he was ready to spend some time there
before starting for the States. The Littlejohns and Geiger
were with the White party. Mrs. Littlejohn and her infant
son remained at Waskopum while the others continued their
journey.

DR. WHITE'S CONFERENCE

When the news of the attempted assault on Mrs. Whitman and the destruction of the mill reached Dr. White, he
felt it his duty to go at once and investigate. Securing the
services of Tom McKay, Cornelius Rogers, Baptiste Dorion,
and six armed men to form a proper escort, White set out
for the Upper Columbia country on November 15. The
weather was bitterly cold, and they were delayed by strong
head winds. Spalding in a letter written to A. T. Smith on

December 15, 1842, said that the week beginning November 14 was the coldest he had ever experienced in the country.[6] For three days the mercury was from six to fifteen below zero. Of course it was not that cold in the Willamette Valley, and yet the journey up the Columbia was a trying experience for members of the party. McKay called it a "voyage of misery."[7]

Dr. White found Mrs. Whitman in poor health and very much depressed. Horses were secured at The Dalles, and the party completed their journey on horseback, reaching Fort Walla Walla on the 30th. The next day they went out to Waiilatpu, where White was shocked "at beholding the sad work of savage destruction upon this hitherto neat and commodious little establishment." White tried to have a conference then with the Indians but only a few were to be seen. He left word that he wished to meet with them upon his return from Lapwai.

White and his party reached Lapwai on December 3, where Spalding gave them a royal welcome. The Spaldings reported but one unpleasant experience with their Indians which had taken place nearly a year previous. The Nez Perces were therefore in a better frame of mind than were the Cayuses and willingly met in conference with Dr. White. As a result Dr. White succeeded in having the Nez Perces accept eleven laws, which were subsequently printed by Spalding on the mission press at Lapwai. This was the first lawbook to be printed in Old Oregon, and it marked the beginning of the effort of the United States Government to extend its jurisdiction over the natives of Oregon Territory.[8] The Littlejohns remained at Lapwai until the fall of 1843.

The White party started back to Waiilatpu on December 20, where they met some, but not all, of the Cayuse chiefs. White wrote: "Learning what the Nez Perces had done, gave them great concern and anxiety."[9] One of the chiefs confessed to White that the mill had been burnt deliberately. In White's account of these days we find the following item: "They had not proceeded far before Feathercap, so far as we know, for the first time in life, commenced weeping, and wished to see me; said his heart was sick, and he could not live long as he now felt."[10]

---

6 Original in Spokane Public Library.

7 Allen, *Ten Years in Oregon*, p. 179.

8 Drury, *Spalding*, p. 296.

9 Allen, *op. cit.*, p. 179.

10 *Ibid.*, p. 191.

However, the Cayuse Indians were suspicious of the laws and would then not accept them. White agreed to return in the spring and resume the deliberations, when he hoped more of the chiefs would be present. Being favored with good traveling conditions on their return trip, White and his party reached Waskopum on December 25.

THE WINTER OF 1842-43

Mrs. Whitman remained at Waskopum during the winter of 1842-43. Although she greatly missed the presence of her husband, she thoroughly enjoyed her lengthy visit with the Methodist families at The Dalles. Writing to Mrs. Walker on December 16, 1842, she declared: "I am treated with the utmost kindness & attention & could not be so happyly & comfortably situated for the winter as here both for my health & spirits perhaps in the country."

During the winter she suffered much from ill-health, which would bring times of depression. On March 6, she wrote: "My eyes are almost gone—my poor health affects them materially and writing is very injurious to me. I can neither read, write or sew without spectacles, the most of the time, and sometimes with them I suffer considerable pain." [Letter 121.] Mrs. Whitman had with her Helen Mar Meek and Mary Ann Bridger. David Malin was left at the Fort in the care of Mrs. McKinlay.

On February 1, 1843, Cornelius Rogers,[11] his wife, and several others were drowned when their boat was swept over Willamette Falls. The Rev. George Abernathy, a member of the Methodist mission, who later served as the first Governor of Oregon (1845-1849), sent word of the accident to Mrs. Whitman on February 4. She forwarded the letter to her husband with a short note from herself on March 4. It is doubtful that Dr. Whitman ever saw these letters, which now rest in the archives of the American Board. Greene received the letters on August 9, 1843.

On March 14, her thirty-fifth birthday, Narcissa wrote to Augustus Whitman and his wife, Julia. "Need I ask you how do you enjoy the society of your dear brother," she asked, thinking that her husband had long since reached Rushville. In fact Dr. Whitman did not reach his home until about a month later. Narcissa tells how much she

---

[11] An account of the tragedy is found in the Cleveland *Weekly Plain Dealer*, Aug. 23, 1843, being reprinted from the Cincinnati *Sun*. Rogers was a native of Cincinnati.

missed Marcus in these words: "His society was my life, and while I had him I never knew that I was lonely. Now I am restless and uneasy, numbering the past, anxiously looking forward, struggling between hope and fear." [Letter 124.] Yet she was able to write in the same letter: "Notwithstanding all our adversities I have no occasion to feel the least regret that husband has gone and left me here; the causes demanded it increasingly."

DR. WHITE RETURNS TO WAIILATPU

On March 29, 1843, Narcissa wrote a long letter to her husband, in which she reviewed the excitement which existed among the Cayuses. The letter was sent to the American Board with the request that should Dr. Whitman be gone the letter should be forwarded to Augustus Whitman. Since the letter is still in the files of the American Board it is to be doubted that it was ever forwarded.

The fact that the Nez Perces had adopted the laws and had appointed a head chief while the Cayuses had not, was the focal point of trouble. Narcissa wrote:

The principal cause of the excitement is; the Kayuses do not wish to be *forced* to adopt the laws recommended by the Agent. They say the laws in themselves are good, they do not object to them—but do not wish to be compelled to adopt them (enforce them). This arises from what was said at the meeting to this effect; We advise you to adopt these laws, but if you do not *we will put you in a way to do it*.

They took exceptions to such language as this. Call it threatening them—and are jealous and complain of Ellis—the High Chief and the Nez Perces for so soon and so readily entering into the new measures of the Americans. This together with time for talk and the summing up of various remarks carelessly made by unwise Americans and taken to be facts has caused a very great commotion.

Rumors were rife among the Cayuses to the effect that American troops were expected. Geiger wrote to Mrs. Whitman and said that some of the Indians believed that Dr. Whitman had gone to the States to get men to fight them. "Poor creatures," wrote Narcissa, "they know not what they do nor whither they are hastening." The excitement was so great that Geiger felt that between fifteen hundred and two thousand Indians would assemble at the expected meeting with White.

H. K. W. Perkins wrote to White telling him of the excitement which existed. He said that the Indians were wrought up over the great numbers of white people who were entering their country each year and felt that these

white people would seize the land. Perkins claimed that a
Nez Perce chief had been sent to visit the Indians in the
buffalo country east of Fort Hall "for the purpose of excit-
ing them to cut off the party that it is expected Dr. Whitman will bring back with him to settle the Nez Perce country."[12] Here we see the beginning of the suspicion on the
part of the Indians that Dr. Whitman was more the white
man's friend than theirs.

While Baptiste Dorion was at Waiilatpu with the White
party in the fall of 1842, he spread several reports which
caused the Cayuses to take alarm. Of him Narcissa wrote:
"They have heard many unwise remarks which have been
made by designing persons, especially a half-breed that
came up with the agent last fall. Such as troops are coming
into the river this spring and are coming up with Dr. White
to fight them." [Letter 126.]

The situation became so threatening that the Methodist
missionaries at The Dalles joined in requesting White to
hasten and settle the trouble. Narcissa longed for her husband to be present for the critical hour and wrote:

I have some fears as to the consequences. But perhaps you will
say they are womanish fears, I grant it. Yet I cannot help feeling
that you should be present at the transaction of so important business
to the people among whom we are called to spend our lives. I am
requested by the Agent to be there.

Mrs. Whitman accurately summed up the characteristics of
the Cayuses when she wrote: "There are redeeming qualities in the character of the Kaiuses notwithstanding they
are insolent, proud, domineering, arrogant and ferocious."
[Letter 125.]

Mrs. Whitman left The Dalles on Monday, April 3, with
her two girls, for Fort Walla Walla. They reached their
destination on Saturday noon. They remained at the Fort
until the 24th, when they left for Waiilatpu, taking David
Malin with them. Mrs. Whitman found everything peaceful
at the mission station. Geiger had done very well with the
farm. The Indians were busy with their spring farm work.
The one marring feature of the whole situation was the
blackened ruins of the mill.

The Indians had inquired of Dr. McLoughlin as to his
attitude in regard to the proposed war against them and
learned that the Hudson's Bay Company would have no
part in such a war, nor did he believe that the Americans

---

[12] Hines, *History of the Oregon Mission*, pp. 143-4.

had any like intentions. This quieted the Indians. Narcissa inquired about the rumor that her husband had gone East to get soldiers to fight them, and wrote to Marcus: "The report of your going home and returning with men to fight has no weight in the minds of the people generally."

On May 9, Dr. White appeared rather unexpectedly at Waiilatpu. Mrs. Whitman had heard that he was not coming. Dr. McLoughlin had strongly advised against it, for he felt it most unwise to force the Cayuses to accept the laws. Narcissa wrote that Dr. White was "quite ignorant of the Indian character and especially of the character of the Kaiuses." [Letter 126.] She too felt that relations with them would be much better if he stayed away. White had Mr. Perkins and the Rev. Gustavus Hines with him to serve as interpreters.

Mr. Hines has given us an account of his experiences on that trip. He states that he found about sixty Cayuses cultivating small farms in the vicinity of the mission station. Among the Indians present were Peupeumoxmox, also called Yellow Serpent, and his son, who had been educated in the Methodist mission school in the Willamette and had received the name of Elijah Hedding, after the Methodist bishop of that name.

After remaining a few days at Waiilatpu, White and his companions set out for Lapwai. On May 18, while White was still away, Mrs. Whitman wrote to her husband, giving the details of what was taking place. Whitman received this letter on July 20 of that summer, when he was one hundred miles west of Laramies Fork on his way back. After reading it, Whitman sent it on to Greene, and it, too, now rests in the archives of the American Board.

Narcissa told of the efforts Dr. White was making to quiet the fears of the Indians. Tiloukaikt remarked to White that he felt it was most unfortunate that Dr. Whitman was not present at the discussions. "They have had no one to talk with," wrote Narcissa, "in whom they feel so much confidence as in their long tried friend Doct. Whitman. I have every reason to believe that all hearts are filled with anxiety to see you back again and none perhaps more so than the one that pulled your ears." It was this letter that said that the Indians "seem to be and feel 'like sheep without a shepherd.'"

In the hope and expectation that there would be a large emigration in the fall of 1843, Spalding and Geiger made

plans to send a pack train with flour to Fort Boise and to
Fort Hall. Spalding wrote to Geiger about this on May 10,[13]
and Mrs. Whitman in her letter of May 18 to her husband
wrote: "The Snake party have started and are camped a
little below here. . . . The mission sent four horse loads of
flour to Fort Boise and Fort Hall for you and your company."
Since the average load for a pack horse was 250 pounds, this
means that a thousand pounds of flour were sent to meet
the emigrant train of 1843. Narcissa sent her letter of
May 18 with this train.

On Friday, May 19, Dr. White returned to Waiilatpu,
accompanied by four or five hundred Nez Perces. The Cayuses and Walla Wallas were present "in mass," as Dr. White
described it. After a five- or six-day conference, the Cayuses
and Walla Wallas agreed to accept the laws. Five Crows,
sometimes called Hezekiah, was made head chief of the
Cayuses. Dr. White then ordered two fat oxen slain and
the meat given to the Indians, together with wheat, salt,
and other food items. White went contrary to all Indian traditions by inviting the women to the feast, much to their
joy.[14]

Hines has given some intimate glimpses into the events
of that conference. Once Yellow Serpent asked whether the
laws were from God or not. Dr. White replied that laws in
all civilized countries had God's approval. This satisfied the
Indian chief, who said: "He was very glad to learn that it
was so, because many of his people and been angry with him
when he had whipped them for crime, and had told him that
God would send him to hell for it, and he was glad to know
that it was pleasing to God."[15]

Having accomplished his objectives, Dr. White started
back to the Fort on Saturday, May 27, Mrs. Whitman and
the children going along. Although Mrs. Whitman was in
better health that spring than she had been during the winter, Dr. White as a physician could see that she was not
well and advised her to go to Fort Vancouver and place
herself under the care of Dr. Barclay of that place. This
she decided to do. Taking Helen Mar Meek with her, she
left Fort Walla Walla on June 1 for Vancouver. Mary Ann
Bridger and David Malin were left with Mrs. Littlejohn and

---

13 Original, Coll. O.
14 Allen, *op. cit.*, p. 215.
15 Hines, *op. cit.*, p. 178.

Mrs. Eells. [Letter 141.] The Hudson's Bay brigade reached Fort Vancouver Sunday evening, June 4. Of that trip Narcissa wrote:

I had a very fatiguing journey down; came near drowning in the portage once. One of the boats upset, but no lives lost. The boat I was in just escaped capsizing. We arrived here just before sunset, Sabbath; displeased with myself and every one around me because of the profanation of the holy day of the Lord. [Letter 137.]

After an examination of her condition, Dr. Barclay advised her to remain under his care for at least a month. We can rest assured that Dr. McLoughlin also urged her to stay. It was the first time that Mrs. Whitman had been to the Fort since her arrival in the fall of 1836. Writing to Mrs. Walker on June 27, Narcissa referred to "the tumor in my side."[16] She remained at the Fort until about the middle of July, when she left to visit some of the Methodist missionaries in the Willamette Valley. [Letter 139.]

THE SUMMER OF 1843

Narcissa loved to be with people, and the summer of 1843, when she met so many under congenial circumstances, was one of the happiest experiences of her life in Old Oregon. After spending about two months at Fort Vancouver, she went to be a guest in the home of Mr. and Mrs. George Abernathy at Willamette Falls. She also spent some days with the Rev. and Mrs. Alvin F. Waller. She was delighted to learn that when Mr. Waller rode a circuit out of Friendship, Allegany County, New York, he had known her father. The historic dispute of Dr. McLoughlin with the Methodist mission over land to which Waller also laid claim, was in its early stages at this time. Narcissa became very friendly with the Wallers and undoubtedly gave them her sympathy. This may account for the lack of cordiality which thereafter existed between the Whitmans and Dr. McLoughlin. While there is no evidence that anything happened to mar their friendship, yet we do not find Mrs. Whitman making the kindly references to Dr. McLoughlin which she did when they first met. The fact that Dr. McLoughlin had joined the Roman Catholic Church on November 18, 1842, also affected their relationships.

About the time Mrs. Whitman arrived at Willamette Falls,

---

[16] Narcissa to her father, April 12, 1844, speaks of Dr. Barclay and states: "He discovered that I had an enlargement of the right ovary and gave me iodine to remove it."

the Methodists were having a camp meeting at Tualatin Plains, about thirty-five miles distant, with Jason Lee, Gustavus Hines, and H. K. W. Perkins in charge. On Sunday, July 16, sixty people were present, including the majority of the residents of the valley, and in all probability Mrs. Whitman was there. Jason Lee preached, and to such effect that sixteen out of the nineteen nonprofessors of religion were converted. Among them was the old mountain man, Joseph Meek. The conversion was real, and Meek exclaimed: "Tell everybody you see that Joseph Meek, that old Rocky Mountain sinner, has turned to the Lord."[17]

In a letter written to her father on April 12, 1844, Narcissa made no mention of the July camp meeting but did refer to another meeting held in August, which she described as a "precious season" for her soul. She wrote: "It continued four days and resulted in the conversion of almost all the impenitent on the ground." She declared that those weeks spent with her Christian friends in the Willamette Valley were "among the happiest in my life."

Narcissa left the Abernathys on Monday, August 7, to go to Fort George (Astoria) to say goodbye to the Rev. and Mrs. Daniel Lee and some other missionaries who were about to sail for the States. While at the Fort, Narcissa was entertained in the home of James Birnie, resident trader in charge of that Hudson's Bay post. On Sunday, August 13, both Jason Lee and Daniel Lee preached, the last of many services jointly conducted by uncle and nephew in Old Oregon.[18] Narcissa spent a few days on board the ship *Diamond* with Mrs. Lee before it sailed. It was her first view of the Pacific Ocean. The boat lifted anchor on Tuesday, August 15, and Narcissa returned with the Rev. Jason Lee and the Rev. David Leslie to Willamette Falls. During the weeks immediately following she visited in the home of Mr. and Mrs. W. H. Gray. [Letter 149.] During the middle of September, she returned to Willamette Falls, and while she was there the cheering news came that her husband was on his way to Oregon with a large party of emigrants, who had with them 140 wagons.

Narcissa made immediate preparations to return to Waiilatpu. She was able to leave during the last week of September in company with Jason Lee, who was bound for The Dalles. The trip up the river was most disagreeable,

---

[17] *O.H.Q.*, Vol. 23, p. 326.
[18] Brosnan, *Jason Lee*, p. 205.

for it rained while they were making the portage at the Cascades, and Mrs. Whitman caught a severe cold. They reached Waskopum on Saturday evening, October 7. Her husband was not there.

After his return from the East, Whitman had been called to Lapwai to minister to the Spaldings who were critically ill with scarlet fever. When he reached Waiilatpu, he received an urgent appeal from Tshimakain to go there to attend Mrs. Eells, who was expecting another child. Even though Whitman was eager to meet his wife again, he mounted his horse and made the long trip of 140 miles to the north. Mrs. Eells gave birth to a son, whom they named Myron, on October 7. Eager to see Narcissa, Marcus started back the day the child was born. When Narcissa arrived with Jason Lee at The Dalles, Marcus was riding the trail that led back to Waiilatpu. Upon arriving at the mission station, he was further delayed by some of the emigrants who needed supplies.

As soon as possible Whitman hastened on to The Dalles, arriving there on or about the 26th of October. In a letter to her father, written the next spring, Narcissa said: "It was a joyful and happy meeting and caused our hearts to overflow with love and gratitude to the Author of all our mercies, for permitting us to see each other's faces again in the flesh." [Letter 149.] Narcissa also noted the meeting of Marcus Whitman and Jason Lee, two of the pioneer missionaries of Old Oregon. She wrote: "It was pleasing to see the pioneers of the two Missions meet and hold counsel together."

While in New York City, Whitman had seen Edward R. Ames, secretary of the Methodist Board, who told him that Lee had been dismissed. Whitman seems to have been the first to carry this distressing news to Lee,[19] who naturally resented that means of conveying such information. Soon afterwards he started back to the States, so this was the last time that Whitman and Lee met.

By the first of November, the Whitmans were at Walla Walla on their way back to Waiilatpu. Days and weeks passed before each had the opportunity to learn of the events which had come within the experience of the other during the year's separation. It is easy to imagine Narcissa eagerly inquiring: "Now tell me, dear husband, all that has happened to you."

---

[19] Brosnan, *op. cit.*, p. 206.

CHAPTER FIFTEEN

WHITMAN RIDES
1842-1843

WHITMAN and Lovejoy left Waiilatpu on Monday, October 3, 1842, for the States. In later years Lovejoy wrote three accounts describing the trip, two of which have been published. The first was a letter dated November 6, 1869, directed to W. H. Gray, which appeared in Gray's *Oregon*.[1] The second, also a letter, was dated February 14, 1876, and was sent to Dr. G. H. Atkinson, who was sent by the American Home Missionary Society to Oregon in 1848.[2] The third account was written by Lovejoy in 1878 for the historian H. H. Bancroft.[3] The earliest of these three descriptions was written twenty-seven years after the events described took place. We must, therefore, make due allowance for the fallibility of human memory in our acceptance of these accounts.

Lovejoy stated that Whitman would not travel on Sunday, except for one instance during the latter part of the journey. In both of his letters, Lovejoy declared that they reached Fort Hall in eleven days. Supposing that Lovejoy meant eleven days of travel, this means that they reached Fort Hall by Saturday, October 15. However, an earlier record of the trip is to be found in a letter Spalding wrote to A. T. Smith on January 7, 1843, in which we read: "Doct Whitman and Lovejoy arrived at Fort Hall, 18 of Oct., left 20 with guide to Paiute, expecting to go by way of the Arkansas or Sante Fe."[4] This means that they reached the Fort on a Tuesday, having spent two Sundays en route. This would have given them fourteen days of travel to cover a distance of about 528 miles, or an average of about 37 miles a day. It had taken the Whitman-Spalding party a month to cover that same distance going westward in 1836.

---

[1] Pp. 324 ff.

[2] *Pioneer and Historical Society of Oregon*, 1876, pp. 13 ff. Reprinted in Nixon, *How Marcus Whitman Saved Oregon*, pp. 305 ff.

[3] Original, Bancroft Library, Berkeley, Calif. Photostat in Coll. O.

[4] Original, Spokane Library. It is not clear what Spalding meant by the words "to Paiute," as there was no place by that name. Perhaps the reference is through the "Paiute" Indian country.

At Fort Hall they met Richard Grant, Hudson's Bay trader in charge of that post, who advised them not to follow the usual route eastward through South Pass. In Lovejoy's account to Bancroft we read:

He said it was just perfect folly. The Indians had been up there and murdered the Snake Indians that very season. He told us not to do it.... So then Whitman changed his course and goes by way of Uintah, away out to Taos and around to Sante Fe.... We were all winter. We made terrible work of it. When we got to Fort Hall we took men from the Fort, a half-breed from St. Louis by the name of Rogers. We went right through the Salt Lake Country. There was not a house nor a thing there, and it was a perfect waste. It looked to us then as though there never would be any thing there. We went on then down to Fort Uintah. This was about as far as this fellow knew. Then we got a new pilot. I think it was an Iroquois Indian, and he went on with us.

Any reports about Indian wars would have made Lovejoy uneasy, for on the way out that fall he and another member of the 1842 emigration, L. W. Hastings, were captured and held prisoner for a time by the Sioux Indians. So Whitman was persuaded to take the long detour to the south. According to another report, Whitman secured Black Harris, also known as Moses Harris, as a guide for a part of the journey.[5]

There had long been a trail, in what is now New Mexico, connecting Taos and Sante Fe with the headwaters of the Platte River. As early as 1761, Don Juan Maria de Rivera reached the mouth of the Uncompahgre River, where Delta, Colorado, now is. In 1776, Father Escalante passed that way and continued farther north through the Uintah Basin to the Great Salt Lake. The old Spanish trail thus blazed was much used by the early traders and trappers, among whom was Antoine Robidoux,[6] who seems to have been in the Uintah Basin as early as 1831.

Several forts were built along the trail. Going north from the south, one met first the fort at the mouth of the Uncompahgre known as Fort Uncompahgre or Fort Robi-

---

[5] *O.H.Q.*, Vol. 2, p. 268. A. Hinman refers to Black Harris as "the guide who had conducted Doctor Whitman across the Rocky Mountains." Harris was one of Ashley's men and was one of the four who circumnavigated Great Salt Lake in 1825. Bancroft, *Oregon*, Vol. 1, p. 515.

[6] A brother of Joseph Robidoux, who founded the city of St. Joseph, Missouri. Whitman and Parker encamped with Joseph Robidoux in May, 1835. *See O.H.Q.*, Sept., 1927, p. 243. Antoine Robidoux was with Frémont in California. Robidoux Mountain at Riverside, California, is named for him.

doux. This seems to have been Robidoux's principal post. No remains of it are to be seen today. Robidoux had another trading point on the Uintah River near where it emerges from the Uintah Mountains and near the present site of White Rocks, Utah. These two posts were at least 150 miles apart. In between was a point of lesser importance at the junction of White River with Green River, opposite the mouth of the Uintah River, which is now called the Duchesne. An old map shows a Fort Robidoux there. All evidence points to a short occupancy. Recently an inscription in French was discovered at the mouth of Westwater Canyon, in the Book Cliffs, north of Cisco, Utah, which reads when translated:

> Antoine Robidoux passed here November 13, 1837, to establish a trading house on the rivers Green or White.[7]

This inscription seems to date the fort at the mouth of White River and at the same time indicates the probable course of the old trail which connected Fort Uncompahgre with Fort Uintah.

When Whitman and Lovejoy decided that it was best for them to go the southern way,[8] their first problem was to get to Fort Uintah. They had the choice of two routes from Fort Hall. They could go to where Alexander, Idaho, is now located, follow the Bear River to the Great Salt Lake, go around the west end of the Uintah and Wasatch Mountains, and then work eastward to Fort Uintah. The alternative route would lead them to what is now Soda Springs, Idaho, and Sage, Wyoming. At the latter point the trail followed Hams Fork to Blacks Fork, down to Green River. From there the trail led through Browns Hole to Fort Uintah.

According to the vague impressions left by Lovejoy's accounts, the men took the western route along the Great Salt Lake. Whitman, however, told Horace Greeley that his route lay by way of "Soda Springs, Brown's Hole, Colorado of the West, the Wina, and the waters of the del Norte."[9]

---

[7] Discovered by Charles Kelly, of Salt Lake City. The Westwater Canyon is not the Westwater found on Utah maps, but a local name.

[8] Eells, *Marcus Whitman*, p. 158, states: "When they reached Fort Hall Captain Grant, desirous to prevent the Doctor from going, told him a falsehood that a war had broken out between the Pawnees and Cheyennes, and that it was not safe for him to proceed." There is no evidence to justify this accusation. Whitman stated they went south to avoid "hostile Indians." *See* New York *Spectator*, article by Civis, April 5, 1843.

[9] New York *Tribune*, March 29, 1843.

This account is much to be preferred to Lovejoy's. Both Whitman and Lovejoy agreed about going to Fort Uintah, and from that place on there was but one trail they could have taken to get to Sante Fe.

When Whitman, Lovejoy, and Grant discussed the various routes at Fort Hall during those days, October 18-20, 1842, they had firsthand information available as to the relative merits of the different routes. Farnham had traveled over the Browns Hole route in 1839, and so had Meek. Even though Lovejoy seems to have indicated the choice of the western route, it appears certain from Whitman's testimony that they went the eastern way.

A fairly clear description of the trail they followed is to be found in Rufus B. Sage's book, *Rocky Mountain Life*. Sage left Taos with Robidoux on October 7, 1842, for Fort Uintah. It appears that Robidoux remained at Fort Uintah while Sage pushed on to Fort Hall. It is possible that Sage met Whitman and Lovejoy on the trail or at Fort Uintah.

After studying all of the available records regarding this trail, the following is suggested as the probable route followed by Whitman and Lovejoy. The trail crossed the Green River near the mouth of Blacks Fork and followed along the southern bank for a time. Then to avoid some hills it crossed the river to the north bank, and then recrossed to the south. The trail then entered the mountains in order to avoid the river canyon and led in a southwestward direction toward the point where the present states of Wyoming, Utah, and Colorado meet. Coming to either Red Creek or Ewing Creek, the trail led southward down into a valley located on the north and east banks of the Green River which was known as Browns Hole.

As has already been pointed out, an unusually severe cold wave swept over the Pacific Northwest in November, 1842. Spalding reported that the thermometer dropped to fifteen degrees below zero at Lapwai. All traditions, together with Lovejoy's accounts, state that the two men met with deep snows and severe weather while crossing the mountains. Lovejoy wrote: "On our way from Fort Hall to Fort Uintah, we had terribly severe weather. The snows retarded our progress and blinded the trail so we lost much time."[10] While they may have had a difficult time in Browns Hole, yet it seems clear that they had passed that place when the November cold wave came.

---

[10] Nixon, *How Marcus Whitman Saved Oregon*, p. 307.

At Browns Hole, Whitman and Lovejoy found themselves on the north side and east end of the Uintah Mountains. Since they could not follow the Green River through
its canyon, they were obliged to cross what is now known
as Diamond Mountain. The trail leading to the top of this
mountain went up the canyon either of Sears Creek or Kettle
Creek. It emerged on the top of a high treeless plateau
which was open to the wild winds of winter.

The trail led for twenty miles across this plateau before
dropping down into the Uintah Basin. For a time it followed Ashley Creek, and then at about the mouth of Dry
Fork it led in a southwestwardly direction to Fort Uintah.[11]
Judging by the rate of speed they made going from Waiilatpu to Fort Hall, the men could have reached Fort Uintah
by about the first of November.

About that time, perhaps at Fort Uintah, Whitman met
Miles Goodyear, who had joined the Whitman-Spalding
party in 1836 when it crossed the plains and the mountains.
Goodyear had stayed with the party, rendering valuable
service until Fort Hall was reached. After an interval of
six years Whitman and Goodyear met again.

Goodyear took advantage of the occasion to send a letter
by Dr. Whitman to a brother. The letter is dated: "Frontier
of Mexico Rocky Mountains November 1, 1842," and from
it the following extracts are taken:

Suffice to say that my time nor my paper admit of me giving you
an entire narrative of my adventures for the last eight years. Time
has rolled on; from youth I have arrived at manhood. I have gotten
on with indifferent success so far through the world, but have always
found honesty the best policy.

I have for the last six years been in the Rocky Mountains, far
from the land of civilization—to use the words of the poet—"as free
as native air."

Tell my friends and associates in youth, that my home's amid the
mountain wild, the land I fancied from a child, to climb the cliff or
tread the vale, where care nor trouble ne'er prevail, to hunt the roe,
the stag, the deer, or breathe the mountain air so clear, or chase the
buffalo o'er the plain for here I am and here remain.[12]

He stated that he then had property worth about twenty-

---

11 Uintah was sometimes spelt Wintee, Winty, and Winta. Greeley
refers to it as Wina. Greeley's "Colorado of the West" was the old
name for Green River, and "the waters of del Norte" means the Rio
Grande del Norte or Rio Grande.

12 *Genealogy of the Goodyear Family*, p. 192. This letter was called
to my attention by M. L. Howe, of Ogden, Utah, and Charles Kelly, of
Salt Lake City. See their book *Miles Goodyear*, p. 43.

five hundred dollars, and requested that they direct their letters to him "to Independence P.O., care of Dr. Whitman, missionary to the west of the Rocky Mountains." Since the United States did not then have sovereignty over that part of the country, Fort Uintah would have been on the "Frontier of Mexico." Would that Goodyear had given his brother more information about Dr. Whitman.[13]

After making a few purchases and securing a new guide at the Fort,[14] Whitman and Lovejoy pressed on. The trail led down the Uintah River to the Green, which it crossed at the confluence. It is quite possible that Whitman and his companions spent a night in the abandoned fort at the mouth of White River. The trail then led up White River to a branch which brought the men out on the crest of Book Cliffs. They had to cross a divide to the headwaters of Bitter Creek, locally known as Westwater, which led southward down out of Book Cliffs to a point about twelve miles west of the present Utah-Colorado line, and about twenty miles north of the highway which today runs through Cisco, Utah, and Mack, Colorado. This part of the trail has been established by Kelly's discovery of the Antoine Robidoux inscription.

The trail then followed the Grand River, now called the Colorado, upstream to the junction of the Gunnison at what is now Grand Junction, Colorado, where it crossed the Grand and followed the Gunnison to the mouth of the Uncompahgre, where Fort Uncompahgre was located. Lovejoy is confused in his description of this part of the trip. He speaks of their experiences in crossing the Grand after referring to their arrival at Fort Uncompahgre. After leaving the Fort, the trail followed the waters of the Uncompahgre to Montrose, and then up a branch to where Ouray, Colorado, now is.

Both Whitman and Sage refer to going by the west side of the "Anahuac" Range, now called the La Plata Mountains. A pass, now used by a railroad, cut across these mountains east of what is now Mancos, Colorado, in the south-

---

[13] Andrew Goodyear, the brother of Miles, went West in 1847 to look for Miles. Both went to California during the gold rush. Miles died in 1850. Andrew became wealthy. Miles Goodyear's cabin is still standing at Ogden, Utah.

[14] Cannon, *Waiilatpu*, p. 62: "Fremont, who passed there in 1844, says that the fort was attacked shortly afterwards by Utah Indians and all its occupants massacred except Robidoux, who happened to be absent."

western part of the state. The trail then led southwestward
around the southern end of the San Juan Mountains over
the Continental Divide to the Rio Grande and thence to
Taos and Sante Fe. In all probability the men went to
Sante Fe before going to Taos.

According to Lovejoy's account, it took them more than
a month to go from Fort Uintah to Taos, which would have
put them in Taos sometime about the middle of December.
This was by far the most difficult and the most dangerous
part of their journey, and it was along this part that they
almost lost their lives. The first obstacle of threatening importance which they faced was the Colorado River, which
was crossed at the present site of Grand Junction, Colorado.
The water was frozen on either side about one third of the
way across the river. The following is Lovejoy's description
of the crossing:

This stream was some one hundred and fifty, or two hundred yards
wide, and looked upon by our guide as very dangerous to cross in its
present condition. But the Doctor, nothing daunted, was the first to
take the water. He mounted his horse, and the guide and myself
pushed them off into the boiling, foaming stream. Away they went
completely under water—horse and all; but directly came up, and
after buffeting the waves and foaming current, he made to the ice on
the opposite side, a long way down the stream—leaped from his horse
upon the ice, and soon had his noble animal by his side. The guide
and myself forced in the pack animals; followed the doctor's example,
and were soon drying our frozen clothes by a comfortable fire.[15]

About twenty years ago the Grand Junction chapter of
the Sons of the American Revolution placed a bronze tablet
upon a granite boulder near the place of the crossing to
commemorate the daring feat.

Lovejoy states that a new guide, a Spaniard, was secured
at Fort Uncompahgre, and the men pushed on toward the
most difficult and hazardous part of their journey. Their
trail led them up into high mountains, where they encountered a severe snowstorm. The guide became so confused
that finally he confessed that the deep snows had so changed
the face of the country that he could no longer find the trail.
Lovejoy wrote:

This was a terrible blow to the Doctor. He was determined not to
give up without another effort. And we at once agreed that the Doctor
should take the guide and make his way back to the fort, and procure
a new guide, and that I should remain in the camp with the animals
until his return, which was on the seventh day with a new guide.[16]

---

[15] Gray, *Oregon*, p. 325.
[16] *Ibid.*

With a new guide they started again at a snail's pace. Soon they ran out of provisions. One by one the pack mules were slain and eaten, and even the dog was not spared. Just as they faced the unpleasant prospect of dying for want of food, they had the good fortune to meet a party of hunters from Taos. "I never shall forget that time," wrote Lovejoy. "I know the old Dr ate so much it liked to have killed him. We were nearly starved to death."[17]

Whitman and Lovejoy reached Taos about the middle of December, 1842, perhaps passing through Sante Fe en route. There they secured a new outfit and continued their journey as soon as possible. Their next objective was Bents Fort, which had been established by the Bent brothers, of St. Louis, on the left bank of the Arkansas River, about midway between what is now La Junta and Las Animas, Colorado. A new guide, a Spaniard, was secured at Taos. [Letter 136.]

When they were out from Taos fifteen days or more, Whitman and Lovejoy met George Bent, who was on his way to Taos. Bent informed them that a party of mountain men were about ready to leave the Fort for St. Louis. After discussing the matter, Whitman decided to push on ahead of Lovejoy and the guide in the hope of reaching the Fort in time to go with the party. He took the best horses and with his blankets and a limited supply of provisions, started out ahead.

On January 3, Lovejoy and the guide with the pack animals arrived at the Fort only to find to their dismay that Whitman had not arrived. The party of mountain men were then camped at Big Cottonwood, about forty miles east of the Fort. Urgent word was sent to them to tarry until Dr. Whitman could be located. Lovejoy then set out to find Dr. Whitman. He was found on or about January 6, quite convinced that he had gotten lost because he had traveled on a Sunday. Although very despondent and fatigued, Dr. Whitman hurried to join the party of mountain men.

Lovejoy and Whitman parted company at Bents Fort. Lovejoy remained at the Fort that spring and joined the 1843 emigration to Oregon the following summer. He met Dr. Whitman again near Fort Laramie in July.

Not a single reference can be found to the four-hundred-mile trip that Dr. Whitman took from Bents Fort to Westport, Missouri. The trail he followed probably

---

[17] Lovejoy MS., Bancroft Collection.

lay along the banks of the Arkansas to Great Bend, then across the country to the Smoky Hill River, then down it to where the Kansas River joins the Missouri, and then to Westport.[18]

The dates of Whitman's arrival at various points along his way can not be fixed with certainty because of lack of sufficient evidence. Whitman told Greene that he reached Westport on February 15. [Letter 127.] In the archives of Whitman College we find the following letter of introduction which harmonizes with the date Whitman gave Greene:

Westport, Feby. 22nd, 43

C. W. Boyers
Independence
Dr. Sir
      Allow me to introduce to you the bearer, Doctor Whitman, Supr. Intd. of American Boards Missions Oregon and of the Presbyterian order. Your attention to him will be duly acknowledged by your friend & Obt. Svt.

A. G. Boone[19]

Boyers, to whom this letter was addressed, was an old freighter well qualified to advise Whitman on the subject of supplies. According to Perrin Whitman, the doctor left his animals at Independence, Missouri, until his return in the spring.[20] Not having enough money to settle with his guide, Whitman promised to pay after his return from Boston. [Letter 136.]

A new date in Dr. Whitman's progress across the country can be fixed through a postmark on a letter which Dr. Whitman mailed for his wife at St. Louis. Among the letters he carried across the mountains was one from Narcissa to her sister and brother, Jane and Edward, then living at Quincy, Illinois. Narcissa had hoped that her husband would reach the States in time for him to pay a personal visit to Quincy before going East. However, the long detour and the severe weather had so delayed him that he found this impracticable, so the letter was forwarded from St. Louis.

---

[18] Spalding, *Senate Document No. 37*, p. 21, gives an incident which occurred "on the head-waters of the Arkansas," evidently before Whitman reached Bents Fort. One day when Whitman desired some wood on the opposite side of a stream, he stretched himself out over the thin ice, and carefully slid over. That night a wolf carried off the axe for the leather string about the helve.

[19] Boyers was a charter member and elder in the Presbyterian church of Independence, Mo., also postmaster of the town.

[20] Whitman to Eells, Feb. 10, 1882, Coll. W.

On the back of the letter addressed by Mrs. Whitman to Edward Prentiss, we find this note in Dr. Whitman's handwriting: "Narcissa Whitman, Rocky Mountains, March 9/43," and also the postmark of St. Louis of the same date. From this evidence we conclude that Dr. Whitman was in that city on that date.[21]

POLITICAL DEVELOPMENTS

While in St. Louis, Whitman was a guest in the home of Dr. Edward Hale, a dentist. It may be that Dr. Whitman had known Hale as a young man in the East, although no record has been found of Hale's medical training. On July 19, 1871, when Hale was seventy years old, he wrote from North Cornwall, Connecticut, to H. H. Spalding, saying:

I had the pleasure of entertaining Dr. Whitman at St. Louis on his last visit eastward to confer with the President & heads of department in relation to the settlement of the N.W. boundary question with Gr. Britain by bartering away for a song the whole N.W. Pacific Territory. Also on his return to Oregon my house was [his] home while in St. Louis.[22]

Hale's testimony regarding the purpose of Whitman's ride is of especial interest because Hale was one of the very first to speak of Whitman's interest in political matters. Even though Hale wrote some twenty-eight years later, still he gave his testimony before any Whitman controversy was started to warp people's memories and influence their judgment.[23]

From another witness we also learn of Whitman's interest in the political affairs of the day as they affected Oregon. Boarding at the Hale home was a young schoolteacher by the name of William Barrows, who was tremendously interested in the strangely dressed visitor from the Far West. Barrows in later years was asked to write the Oregon volume in the American Commonwealth Series, edited by Horace E. Scudder. In this volume we find an interesting record of Whitman's visit to St. Louis.

As soon as the news of Whitman's arrival became known,

---

[21] Spalding once claimed that Whitman reached Washington by March 3, 1843. Of course that was a mistake.

[22] Original in Coll. W. Also published in Myron Eells, *A Reply to Professor Bourne*, pp. 64-65.

[23] It is rather significant that W. I. Marshall, who has been the severest critic of the Whitman-Saved-Oregon story, should have refrained from commenting on Hale's letter.

many trappers, traders, and adventurers hurried to talk with him. Those who had friends or relatives in the 1842 emigration were eager for the latest news. Others who were thinking about going to Oregon asked innumerable questions about the route and the opportunities in Oregon. Questions were also asked about the Hudson's Bay Company, treaties with the Indians, and so forth. Dr. Whitman was an enthusiastic "booster" for Oregon. We have ample evidence to show that he encouraged people to go. He advised prospective emigrants regarding what they should take along. A few months later, when Whitman was back again on the western frontier after his trip to Washington and Boston, he wrote back to his brother-in-law Jonas Galusha Prentiss, and said: "A great many cattle are going, but no sheep, from a mistake of what I said in passing. Next year will tell for sheep." [Letter 135.]

Whitman was eager to learn the latest developments regarding the Linn bill and the Webster-Ashburton Treaty, of which White had spoken. He learned that the Linn bill had not passed the second session of the Twenty-seventh Congress because of the negotiations then under way in regard to the treaty. President Tyler in his message to Congress of December 5, 1842, had pointed out the fact that since there was no prospect of an agreement on the question of the Oregon boundary, all reference to it had been omitted in the treaty. Tyler pointed out the necessity of settling one point at a time. The treaty did settle the Maine boundary dispute.

With the treaty out of the way, the Linn bill was reintroduced in the third session of the Twenty-seventh Congress. The bill called for the erection of a line of forts from the Western frontier to the mouth of the Columbia for the protection of the emigrants. It granted 640 acres of land to every white male over eighteen years of age. It also provided for the extension of the civil and criminal jurisdiction of the courts of the Territory of Iowa over the citizens of Oregon.[24]

Two of the strongest champions of Oregon were Senators Linn and Benton, of Missouri. Benton accused Webster of being willing to accept the Columbia River as the boundary line for the United States and Canada in Oregon. Rufus Choate, speaking for his friend Webster, replied to this by claiming that Webster was never willing to accept "any

---

[24] Winters, *Congress and the Oregon Question*, p. 289.

line south of the 49th parallel of latitude, as a negotiable boundary line."[25] This is the line which was finally accepted.

An examination of the *Congressional Globe* shows that the Oregon question received considerable attention in Congress during the winter of 1842-43. The Linn bill came to a vote in the Senate on February 3, 1843, and was passed by a vote of twenty-four to twenty-two. The opposition claimed that the proposals of the bill violated the Treaty of Joint Occupation which our government had made with Great Britain. After passing the Senate, the bill was sent to the House, where it was lost in the jam of business which is characteristic of the closing days of Congress. The third session of the Twenty-seventh Congress adjourned on March 4, 1843, without action by the House.

This was the situation as it was told to Whitman when he reached St. Louis on March 9, although the citizens of the city did not then know what had happened to the Linn bill during the closing days of Congress. It was generally believed that the Linn bill would eventually pass, even though it might fail in that Congress. This optimistic feeling, together with the favorable reports that had been sent back to the States from those who had gone to Oregon, were some of the primary reasons why so many were willing to go past the rich prairie lands of the Midwest to settle in distant Oregon. Lindsay Applegate, one of the emigrants of 1843, stated that he had received such favorable reports of Oregon from Robert Shortess, who went out in 1839, that he inserted a notice in the Booneville *Herald* about March 1, 1843, to the effect that an emigration party for Oregon would be organized that spring.[26] Another factor which prompted men to emigrate was the economic condition on the frontier. The farmers found themselves far removed from an adequate market. The rapid increase of settlers in the Midwest only made matters worse. At this opportune time, when men were looking hopefully towards Oregon, Whitman arrived, ready to tell the very story they were eager to hear.

A debatable issue regarding Whitman's trip East has been the degree of influence exercised by him in raising the 1843 emigration. Of course there would have been such an emigration had Whitman never gone East. On the other hand, it seems quite clear that Whitman was instrumental

---

[25] *Congressional Globe*, 27th Congress, 3d Session, p. 172.
[26] Eells, *Marcus Whitman* (Pamphlet), p. 27.

in getting many to go to Oregon who otherwise might not have gone. Two different people refer to a pamphlet which Whitman wrote on the advantages of Oregon.[27] Unfortunately no copy of the pamphlet has been found. An examination has been made of the two daily St. Louis newspapers then being published without finding a reference to Whitman's arrival.[28]

Before Myron Eells wrote his pamphlet on Marcus Whitman, which was issued in 1883, he wrote to some of the survivors of the 1843 emigration to find out the extent of Whitman's influence in getting people to go to Oregon. His conclusions were that while Dr. Whitman did not influence all the emigrants to go, he was instrumental in getting some. Four out of fourteen witnesses claimed that they went because of Dr. Whitman's representations.

Among those who were induced by Whitman to go to Oregon were the Hobson, Eyers, and Thomas Smith families, and a young lawyer by the name of John Ricord. Eyers owned a shop in St. Louis at the time Whitman passed through the city, which was a meeting place for many who were thinking of going to Oregon. It was there that John Hobson met Dr. Whitman.[29] It is easy to accept the statement of Barrows regarding the interest in Oregon which Whitman's visit aroused.

Whitman was anxious to be on his way. The time was short, for he felt that he should be back in St. Louis by the first of May.[30] Even though he knew that he would reach Washington after the adjournment of Congress, Whitman decided to adhere to his original plan of visiting that city. If Congress had been in session, anything that Whitman might have done to influence Oregon legislation would be a matter of pure speculation.

---

[27] *Ibid.*, p. 30. Mrs. C. B. Cary wrote: "It was a pamphlet Dr. Whitman wrote that induced me to come to Oregon." Spalding, *Senate Document No. 37*, p. 26. John Zachrey declared: "The occasion of my father starting that season for this country, as also several of our neighbors, was a publication by Dr. Whitman, or from his representations, concerning Oregon.... In the pamphlet...."

[28] Marshall, *op. cit.*, Vol. 2, pp. 280-81.

[29] *Oregonian*, Jan. 24, 1886, and Eells, *Marcus Whitman* (Pamphlet), p. 31.

[30] Marshall, *History vs. The Whitman Saved Oregon Story*, p. 82, claims that traffic on the Great Lakes did not begin until May 6. So Whitman must have returned to the East by stage.

THE TRIP TO WASHINGTON

We do not know just when Whitman reached Washington. He was in New York on March 28. Since he was in St. Louis on the 9th, it is reasonable to believe that he reached the capital city by the 23rd. This would have given him two weeks to make the trip from St. Louis to Washington, which would have been ample time. En route he stopped at Cincinnati, where he was a guest in the home of Dr. George L. Weed. George Ludington Weed, who was a boy at the time, wrote his memories of that event for the November, 1897, issue of the *Ladies' Home Journal*. Weed wrote:

Most unexpected was his appearance at my father's in Cincinnati, where he was a welcome visitor when on his journeys across the continent, and where he had brought his bride seven years before. We thought him on the banks of the Columbia. It fell to me to receive him at the door. My memory of that morning is still fresh with boyish wonderment. I stared at what seemed an apparition.

He was dressed in his mountain garb, His fur garments, buckskin breeches, fur leggins, boot moccasins and buffalo overcoat with head hood, had been poor protection from the cold and storms of the fearful ride. His face and hands and feet had been frozen. I still hear his earnest question for my father, who was at a morning prayer-meeting in the church of Dr. Lyman Beecher, whither he immediately went. His presence there created a sensation. He tarried in Cincinnati but a few hours, long enough to be provided with some of the comforts and appearances of civilization.

This description of Whitman's dress harmonizes with other accounts. Barrows likewise mentions the frozen hands, feet, and parts of the face. He states that Whitman had a four months' growth of beard, and that he wore "coarse fur garments and vesting, and buckskin breeches." He had a buffalo overcoat with a head hood, and heavy fur leggins with boot moccasins. Barrows declared: "If memory is not at fault with me, his entire dress, when on the street, did not show one square inch of woven fabric."[31] Whitman called on Horace Greeley in New York on March 28, and Greeley, after giving a similar description of Whitman's dress, wrote that he was "the roughest man that we have seen this many a day."[32] Whitman later told Cushing Eells that he sometimes wore "a blue English duffle coat" beneath the buffalo coat and that the duffle coat was several inches longer. Whitman laughingly remarked that it was

---

[31] Barrows, *Oregon*, p. 176.
[32] New York *Tribune*, Mar. 29, 1843.

"rather fantastic for a missionary, a buffalo coat with a blue border."[33]

Whitman's visit to Washington has been a focal point for discussion in the Whitman controversy. Some have doubted that he ever went to Washington. The adherents of the Whitman-Saved-Oregon story have stressed the point that Whitman visited Washington before going to Boston, and have drawn the conclusion that his political interests were more important than the missionary cause. Marshall, the fiery opponent of this theory, wrote: "It is altogether probable that he went to Washington from Boston."[34] Whitman was still in Boston on April 8, and he left Rushville for the West again on April 20. In this interval of twelve days there would not have been sufficient time for him to go to Washington and then to Rushville and have any time to visit relatives and friends. Therefore, it seems conclusive from a study of the known chronology of the period, that Whitman went to Washington first. However, it should be pointed out that this fact does not prove that a political motive was the all-important factor that caused him to go East. Whitman knew that his time was limited and that if he went to Washington he would have to do so while en route to Boston.

That he actually visited Washington seems to be proved without a doubt from the following evidence:

1. A letter from the Hon. Alexander Ramsey to Myron Eells, dated August 15, 1883, in which he claims that he met Dr. Whitman in Washington at a boardinghouse on Capitol Hill "in the winter of 1842-43."[35]

2. The Hon. James M. Porter, Secretary of War, received a letter on June 22, 1844, from Dr. Whitman which contains this sentence: "In compliance with the request you did me the honor to make last Winter, while in Washington...." [Letter 143.]

3. At least two different persons received letters from Dr. Whitman which were written by him in Washington. Unfortunately in both cases the originals have been lost, so the exact date of Whitman's presence there can not be ascertained through them. William C. McKay, then a medical student at Willoughby, Ohio, claimed in a letter written January 30, 1885, and published in the 1889 *Transactions of the Oregon Pioneer Association* that Whitman wrote to him from Washington.

A letter written to General O. F. Marshal, Wheeler, New York,

---

33 Mowry, *Marcus Whitman*, p. 166.

34 Marshall, *op. cit.*, Vol. 2, p. 68.

35 Original, Coll. W. Published in Eells, *Marcus Whitman* (Pamphlet), p. 16.

remained in the family for a number of years and was seen by a living grandson.[36]

4. Perrin Whitman visited Washington in 1868 at which time he met a man who claimed that he met Dr. Whitman "on that famous trip to Washington."[37]

In addition to the above evidence we have the testimony concerning the interviews that Whitman had with President Tyler and members of the cabinet. According to a claim made by William Geiger, Whitman was a friend of John C. Spencer (1788-?), who was Secretary of the Treasury in Tyler's cabinet when Whitman was in Washington.[38] Spencer settled in Canandaigua, the county seat of Ontario County, New York, in 1809, where he practiced law. He took an active part in the anti-Masonic agitation of 1827 and following years. After holding a number of political offices, he was made Secretary of War on October 12, 1841. This position he held until March 3, 1843, when he became Secretary of the Treasury. James Madison Porter (1793-1862) succeeded him as Secretary of War.[39]

Since Rushville is but ten miles from Canandaigua, it is altogether probable that Whitman, as a medical student riding with Dr. Bryant, had frequent opportunities to meet Spencer. The very first entry in the diary of Jonathan Pratt, made January 1, 1824, states that Jonathan had been to Canandaigua to hear an oration by Mr. J. C. Spencer. This connection of Whitman with Spencer may have been a reason which influenced Whitman to go to Washington. White undoubtedly told Whitman of Spencer's position in the cabinet, and since all Indian affairs were then placed under the jurisdiction of the Secretary of War, Spencer would have been the person most concerned with the welfare of the Oregon Indians. Moreover, since the Oregon Trail went through Indian country, the Secretary of War would be the official most interested in the welfare of the emigrants. Whitman was no ordinary visitor to Washington. He had a friend in the President's cabinet through whom he could quickly and effectively present his case.

---

[36] The grandson, O. F. Marshal, of Wheeler, wrote to Dr. Pratt, March 3, 1898, and referred to this letter. (Original, Coll. Wn.) The author met the grandson in the summer of 1935 and again in 1936. The grandson claims the letter was sent to some church board in New York or Philadelphia. The original has not been located.

[37] Portland *Oregonian*, obituary notice of Perrin Whitman, Jan. 29, 1899.

[38] Clark to Eells, April 29, 1901, Coll. W.

[39] Eells, *Marcus Whitman*, p. 160, confuses Spencer with Porter.

According to Geiger, Spencer introduced Whitman to Mr. Porter, then Secretary of War, and to Daniel Webster, Secretary of State, and also to President Tyler. There can be no doubt but that Whitman saw Porter, as is proved by Whitman's letter to Porter. [Letter 143.] Spalding claimed that Whitman secured an interview with Tyler through Senator Linn. Spalding also claimed that Tyler was about to trade off Oregon for a codfishery but that Whitman persuaded the President to wait until he demonstrated the feasibility of taking emigrants with their wagons through to Oregon.[40]

Gray, who evidently built on Spalding's account, wrote in his *Oregon:*

> Mr. Tyler, after listening to the Doctor's statements with far more candor and interest than Mr. Webster was disposed to do, informed him that, notwithstanding they had received entirely different statements from gentlemen of the Hudson's Bay Company and the British minister, then in Washington, yet he would trust to his personal representation and estimate of the value of the country to the American people. He said: "Dr. Whitman, in accordance with your representations and agreeable to your request, this question shall be deferred. An escort shall be furnished for the protection of the emigration you propose to conduct to that distant country."[41]

Barrows, Nixon, Eells, and all others who have accepted the Whitman-Saved-Oregon story have gone back to Spalding and Gray for their final authority. Whitman never made any such extensive claims for himself in any of his known letters still extant. Just where Spalding got the idea that Tyler was about to negotiate a treaty with Great Britain in which the United States would relinquish its claim to Oregon for some codfisheries is not known. This theory has no documentary foundation whatever.

From the testimony of several who received their information direct from Dr. Whitman, it seems clear that Whitman did have an interview with the President. Lovejoy wrote:

> He often expressed himself to me about the remainder of the journey, and the manner in which he was received at Washington, and by the Board of Foreign Missions at Boston. He had several in-

---

[40] San Francisco *Pacific,* Nov. 9, 1865. *See* also Marshall, *op. cit.,* Vol. 2, pp. 64 ff.

[41] P. 316. Whitman visited Gray at Oregon City in the fall of 1843 at which time he told of his Washington trip. Eells, *Marcus Whitman* (Pamphlet), p. 9.

terviews with President Tyler, Secretary Webster, and a good many members of Congress—Congress being in session at that time.[42]

Geiger claimed that Whitman saw the President.[43] Perrin Whitman likewise referred to the interview.[44] It is inconceivable to believe that such different characters as Spalding, Gray, Lovejoy, and Perrin Whitman should have deliberately concocted the story of Whitman's interview with President Tyler. Spalding and Perrin Whitman became rather antagonistic to each other in later years, yet neither of them ever wavered in his conviction that Marcus Whitman saw President Tyler.

Mowry in his *Marcus Whitman* adds a new note to the discussion by quoting from correspondence received from Lyon Gardiner Tyler, LL.D., then President of William and Mary College, who was a son of President Tyler by his second marriage. Among other things, L. G. Tyler claimed that his older half-brother, John Tyler, who served as private secretary for his father, said that "he remembered Whitman very well, that he was in Washington, 1842-43, full of his project to carry emigrants to Oregon, that he waited on the President and received from him the heartiest concurrence in his plans, etc."[45] Since this recollection was given about forty years afterward, it is possible that John Tyler confused Whitman with Dr. White, who was in Washington the previous year.[46] W. I. Marshall, the author of *Acquisition of Oregon*, had some correspondence with L. G. Tyler and succeeded in getting a retraction from him on several points.[47] However, L. G. Tyler did not retract his statement regarding his brother's impression of an interview that Dr. Marcus Whitman had with the President.

In a letter to Myron Eells, dated January 10, 1902, L. G. Tyler declared:

---

[42] Nixon, *op. cit.*, pp. 310-311. Lovejoy was mistaken in stating that Congress was in session at the time.

[43] Eells, *op. cit.*, p. 4.

[44] *Ibid.*, p. 13. Another to make this claim was David Lennox. *See* his *Overland to Oregon*, p. 60. "It was my lot as a boy of sixteen, both to see Dr. Whitman on his return trip to Oregon, and to hear him tell how he had crossed the mountains in 1842, to see President Tyler and Daniel Webster."

[45] Mowry, *op. cit.*, p. 172.

[46] New York *Tribune*, May 25, 1848, quoting from the Pittsburgh *Chronicle*, stated: "Dr. White and . . . others were killed." The reference is to the Whitman Massacre and shows how Whitman and White were confused. Bourne, *Essay*, p. 97.

[47] Marshall, *op. cit.*, Vol. 2, p. 313.

As to the influence of Whitman upon the government, I do not
believe his interviews had any determining effect. The attitude of
the government would have been the same, had Whitman never showed
up. It had certainly no effect upon the President when early messages
show that he was keenly alive to the importance of Oregon.[48]

Just what Whitman said and how much influence he had
upon Tyler in later events as they dealt with Oregon will
never be known. Undoubtedly, many at Washington, including the President, were much interested in talking with
Dr. Whitman, who had so much firsthand information to
give. Perhaps the feasibility of taking wagons through to
Oregon came up, and if so, Dr. Whitman certainly would
have affirmed his belief that it could be done, for it had
been done. If we may judge Whitman's interests by the
contents of the proposed bill which he later submitted, then
Whitman talked about the necessity of the Government's
establishing a chain of forts from the frontier to the Willamette Valley for the protection of the emigrants. This
suggestion had already been incorporated in the Linn bill.
He probably talked about the possibility of establishing
what later became known as the Pony Express. In his
letter to Porter which accompanied the bill he wrote: "I
need only add that contracts for this purpose will be readily
taken at reasonable rates for transporting the mail across
from Missouri to the mouth of the Columbia in forty days,
with fresh horses at each of the contemplated posts." The
first time the Pony Express was established to carry mail
from St. Louis to San Francisco was in April, 1860. It
appears that Whitman's suggestion, made seventeen years
earlier, is the first time the possibility of such a plan was
brought to official notice.

Whitman also talked about the advisability of having
the emigrants take sheep with them to Oregon. Writing
later to Jonas Galusha, Whitman said that he meant to
impress the Secretary of War that sheep were more important to Oregon than soldiers. [Letter 135.] It appears that
Porter requested Whitman to draw up a bill and submit
it to him. The original of this is now on file in the War
Department marked: "rec. June 22, 1844."[49] It bears no
date and the supposition is that Whitman drew it up and

---

[48] Coll. W. Also, Marshall, op. cit., Vol. 2, p. 315, for a similar
quotation made by Tyler to Marshall.

[49] Mowry, Marcus Whitman, pp. 274 ff., gives a copy of the bill.
The bill was discovered in the files of the War Department by Dr.
J. S. Parker, son of Samuel Parker, in 1891.

mailed it after he returned to Oregon. When the copy of his bill reached Washington, the Atchison bill was before Congress with similar proposals, so nothing was done with Whitman's bill but to file it away.

The Oregon question became a burning political issue in the Presidential campaign of 1844. Polk was elected on the slogan of "Fifty-four forty or fight."[50] While the Oregon question was much discussed during the first session of the Twenty-eighth Congress, no definite action was taken. The second session, which met 1844-45, again took up the Oregon question without coming to a definite conclusion. The Twenty-ninth Congress, 1845-46, also wrestled with the problem. On August 6, 1846, Congress was notified that the boundary line had been settled at the 49th parallel. The Mexican War was then engaging the attention of Congress, so nothing was done about encouraging emigrants to go to Oregon by promising free land. About two years later, under circumstances which will be subsequently outlined, Oregon became a territory.

Leslie M. Scott has admirably summed up the purpose of Whitman's visit to Washington in the following words:

In view of the very great interest in Oregon, his evident purpose was to lay before the proper authorities his conclusions, derived from his experience, as to the practicability of a wagon route to the Columbia; and also to urge the desirability of the government establishing a mail route from the Missouri to the Columbia, with government posts or stations along the way, not only for protecting and aiding the immigrants, but also for the purpose of extending a measure of civil government over the vast region between these two rivers.[51]

Although Marcus Whitman rode East on mission business, his deep interest in the political destinies of Oregon caused him to turn aside to visit Washington while en route to Boston. There was a political purpose in Whitman's visit to Washington, for how else is it possible to explain his presence in that city? However, it does not appear that his visit there was effective in shaping any government policy involving Oregon. No treaty affecting the Pacific Northwest was then under consideration. The Oregon emigration movement had already started without Whitman's influence, and there were many in the East who were just as con-

---

[50] Bancroft, *Oregon*, Volume 1, pp. 369 ff., gives a good review of the history of the various Oregon bills presented before the different sessions of Congress.

[51] *O.H.Q.*, 13, p. 172, from Scott's article, "John Fiske's Change of Attitude on the Whitman Legend."

cerned about Oregon's future as Whitman was himself. Whitman's visit to Washington was that of an enthusiastic friend of Oregon eager to pass on information which he considered of value to those occupying positions of high authority. The final bond which made Oregon a part of the Union was the presence of thousands of emigrants in that territory. Whitman was destined to play an important part in the emigrant movement, and in this respect he did more than any other single individual to save Oregon.

WHITMAN'S VISIT TO NEW YORK AND BOSTON

Whitman probably left Washington in order to arrive in New York on Saturday, March 25, 1843. We know of his reluctance to travel on Sunday and we also know that he took passage on the *Narragansett* on Monday, March 27, for Boston.

In New York, Whitman again took time to turn aside because of his political interests. He sought out Horace Greeley, editor of the New York *Tribune*, on Monday, March 27. When he knocked at the entrance of Greeley's home or office, a woman came to the door. She was surprised to see a man standing before her clad in such strange garb. Whitman did not make a good first impression, and when he inquired whether or not Mr. Greeley was in, he was curtly told that Mr. Greeley was not at home. Disappointed, Whitman turned to go away.

In the meantime Greeley inquired regarding the visitor and was probably told that the stranger, dressed worse than a tramp, had been turned away. Greeley hurried to the window and caught a glimpse of his visitor. Greeley himself was none too particular in matters of dress and saw something in Whitman which attracted his attention. He immediately asked that his visitor be called back, and after due apologies were made, Whitman was invited into the house, where the two men had a long talk.[52]

The next day Greeley wrote an editorial of about five hundred words, which appeared in the New York *Tribune* on March 29. After mentioning the arrival of Dr. Whitman, Greeley wrote: "A slight glance at him when he entered our office would convince any one that he had seen all the hardships of a life in the wilderness." Greeley continued:

---

[52] The details of this visit were given by Alan Hinman, who evidently received them direct from Dr. Whitman, in a letter to Myron Eells, dated June 8, 1883. Eells, *Marcus Whitman* (Pamphlet), p. 14.

A noble pioneer we judge him to be, a man fitting to be chief in rearing a moral empire among the wild men of the wilderness. We did not learn what success the worthy man had in leading the Indians to embrace the Christian faith, but he very modestly remarked that many of them had begun to cultivate the earth and to raise cattle.

After repeating some of the news Whitman brought concerning the American settlements in Oregon and outlining his trip, Greeley concluded his editorial with the following paragraph:

We give the hardy and self-denying man a hearty welcome to his native land. We are sorry to say that his first reception on arriving in our city was but slightly calculated to give him a favorable impression of the morals of his kinsmen. He fell into the hands of one of our vampire cabmen who in connection with the keeper of a tavern house in West street, three or four doors from the corner near the Battery fleeced him out of two of the last few dollars which the poor man had.[53]

While in New York, Whitman called at the offices of the Foreign Board of the Methodist Church, where he met Edward R. Ames, secretary in charge of the Oregon mission of that denomination. Ames spoke of the dissension which existed in the Methodist mission and informed Whitman that Jason Lee had been recalled. Perhaps a letter from that Board was on its way to Oregon with the news, but it so happened that Whitman was the first to break it to Lee.[54]

Further information regarding Dr. Whitman's movements and incidentally also his experiences with the cabman, is to be found in an article signed "Civis" which appeared in the New York *Spectator* on April 5, 1843. "Civis" was a passenger on the *Narragansett*, which left New York "at the usual time" on Monday. The boat met with rough weather in the Sound, and the captain was obliged to put in at New Haven at midnight. Tuesday, March 28, was spent in port. The next morning they lifted anchor and continued on their way to Boston, arriving there on the 29th. "Civis" remarked on Whitman's dress. "Rarely have I seen such a spectacle as he presented," he wrote. "His dress should be preserved as a curiosity." Yet Whitman made an impression upon the newspaper correspondent as the following quotation proves:

He is about thirty-six or seven years of age, I should judge, and has stamped on his brow a great deal of what David Crockett would call "God Almighty's common sense."

[53] Reprinted in *O.H.Q.*, 1903, pp. 168-69.
[54] Brosnan, *Jason Lee*, p. 213.

"Civis" also referred to Whitman's experience in New York with the cabman for he wrote: "A rascally hackman took him in at New York, and carried him from place to place at his whim and finally put him down near the Battery, and it being midnight he succeeded in the vile extortion."[55]

The fact that "Civis" thought Dr. Whitman was but thirty-six or thirty-seven years old when he was then in his fortieth year speaks well for Whitman's youthful appearance.

In the files of the American Board in Boston is the resolution signed by Walker, Eells, and Spalding on September 28, 1842, which authorized Whitman to go East. On the back is a notation to the effect that it was received in Boston on March 30, 1843. Since Whitman carried this paper with him, we can accept the date as the time when he first called at the American Board offices.

No one has given us an account of the first meeting of Whitman and Greene. It is easy to imagine the surprise which Greene must have experienced when he first saw his buckskin-clad visitor. He must have been even more surprised when the stranger introduced himself as Dr. Marcus Whitman, of Waiilatpu. Among the first questions asked by Greene was this: "Why did you leave your station?" Whitman told of the arrival of the order dated February 25, 1842, which dismissed Spalding and closed the mission stations of Lapwai and Waiilatpu. From references found in some of Whitman's later letters, we assume that Greene gave him a cool reception.[56]

In a letter written on June 5, 1883, to Myron Eells, William Geiger gives this picture of Whitman's reception by Mr. Hill, the treasurer of the Board: "Mr. Hill received him quite roughly. Mr. Hill said 'what are you here for, leaving your posts.' & at last said in not a very pleasant way as he offered him some money. 'Go get some decent clothes.' "[57]

On Friday, March 31, Whitman was back in the offices of the American Board, where the reception was a bit more

---

[55] Reprinted in the *O.H.Q.*, 1903, pp. 169-70. The Boston *Recorder* for April 6 reprinted Greeley's editorial with a few words of comment, including the following statement: "The station where Dr. Whitman formerly labored, Waulatpu, was some time since abandoned, for various reasons."

[56] Lovejoy MS. to Bancroft: "They censured him for going on."

[57] Coll. W.

cordial. He was soon made acquainted with the new developments in the Oregon mission case. Greene had written to Whitman on April 28, 1842, about two months after the fateful order had been sent forth dismissing Spalding and closing Waiilatpu. In all probability Greene handed a copy of the letter to Whitman to read. If so he then read the following:

When the case of your mission came up in February it seemed to be a perfectly clear case that the Committee should decide upon it as mentioned in my letters to yourself and the mission written about the first of March.... But had your letter of the 13th of July and Mr. Spaldings of the same date, 1841, been before the Com. they would almost necessarily decided differently.

In this letter Greene authorized Whitman "to go on as you were going before those instructions were received." The letters of Whitman and Spalding, which were so influential in changing Greene's attitude, were written shortly after the Waiilatpu mission meeting of June, 1841, at which time a reconciliation had been effected with Spalding. Spalding had learned for the first time of the letters of complaint which had been sent in about him, and was duly humbled.

Greene informed Whitman that he would resubmit the matter relating to the Oregon Mission to the Prudential Committee. This was done in March, 1843, shortly before Whitman arrived in Boston. In the meantime Greene had received the letter of June 8, 1842, which was signed by Walker, Eells, and Spalding. This letter was submitted to the Prudential Committee. The members of the Committee were not as lenient as Greene and refused to repeal their former order dismissing Spalding and closing the stations of Lapwai and Waiilatpu. Greene, therefore, on March 21, 1843, wrote again to Whitman, saying in part:

Our latest dates now are a joint letter of Messrs. Walker, Eells & Spalding of June 8, 1842. The statements there made do not seem to be of sufficient importance to lead this Committee to change what they had before done & communicated to you in March of last year.[58]

---

[58] In Drury, *Spalding*, p. 289, the author gave a different interpretation to the action of the Committee of March 21, 1843. Greene refers to the letter sent to Whitman "in March of last year." The order of the Committee was dated February 25, 1842, while Greene's letter temporarily suspending the order was dated April 28, 1842. However, in a letter of Greene to Spalding, dated April 28, 1842, he refers to the order of February as having been written "about the first of March." Thus the author feels it necessary to reverse his former interpretation. The Committee in March, 1843, confirmed its action of February, 1842.

This was the situation which Whitman faced when he reached Boston. The disastrous order of February, 1842, was still in effect and if Whitman had not gone to Boston to intercede in behalf of the mission, the changes ordered would have been made just at the time when Waiilatpu was most needed to minister to the emigrants bound for the Willamette Valley.

On Tuesday, April 4, the Prudential Committee of the American Board met in the Board rooms. Mr. Greene laid before the Committee a memorandum of information received from Dr. Whitman. This, in Mr. Greene's handwriting, may still be seen in the files of the American Board.[59] This memorandum contained the latest word regarding the status of the mission personnel and set forth Whitman's desire for re-enforcements and for pious settlers who would go out not as appointed missionaries but as interested citizens to settle in the vicinity of the mission stations and render such assistance in material things as was possible.

Whitman had talked with Greene about the advisability of taking steps to get indemnity from the United States Government for property taken by the Sioux Indians from W. H. Gray in the summer of 1837. Greene submitted this question to the Committee. In Greene's memorandum we read: "Rev. H. H. Spalding requests that he may be allowed to remain in the mission, in which request the other brethren unite."

Whitman was called before the Committee to answer questions and give an oral report.[60] Whitman made a good impression, and the minutes of the Prudential Committee show that favorable action was secured on every point desired, as the following extracts will prove:

Resolved, That Doct. Marcus Whitman and the Rev. H. H. Spalding be authorized to continue to occupy the stations at Waiilatpu and Clear Water, as they did previous to the adoption of the resolutions referred to above. [i.e. to the resolutions of the 15th and 23rd of Feb. 1843.]

Resolved. That a missionary be sent to strengthen the Oregon mission, if a suitable person can be found.

Permission was given to Gray to leave the mission, and also to Whitman to take out to Oregon "a small company of intelligent and pious laymen" if this could be done without

---

[59] Greene stated in this that Whitman reached Boston on March 30.

[60] Those present were Samuel T. Armstrong, Charles Stoddard, Nehemiah Adams, Silas Aiken, Henry Hill, Rufus Anderson, David Greene, and Selah B. Treat. Treat later succeeded Greene.

expense to the Board. Whitman did his best to arouse
Greene's interest in this plan of inducing "pious laymen"
to go to Oregon, but Greene remained rather indifferent to
the idea.

Although the minutes of the Prudential Committee make
no reference to the Gray affair, we find that Whitman wrote
to the Commissioner of Indian Affairs from Boston on Saturday, April 8. [Letter 129.] Gray had rendered an account
of the incident to Major Pilcher on August 7, 1837. On
September 16, 1837, Gray had addressed a claim for $2,096.-
45 to General William Clark at St. Louis to pay for horses
and supplies stolen by the Sioux. The Indian Commissioner
at Washington had other papers relating to the case, among
them being a report from Major Pilcher dated March 4,
1839, in which Pilcher declared that after a full investigation he was convinced that "the difficulty arose from Mr.
Gray's own imprudence, and that most of the claim is altogether unfounded." Pilcher recommended that nothing be
done.[61]

The Indian Commissioner, T. H. Crawford, was evidently guided by Pilcher's recommendations even after he
received Whitman's letter, for nothing was done by the
Government to reimburse the Board, Gray, or the Nez
Perces for property lost on that occasion. Whitman's request for indemnity was courteously worded. "We do not
wish to press the subject," he wrote, "but leave it with your
department to do what you deem proper."

Judging from a paper written by Whitman and received
by Greene on April 7, 1843, Whitman was requested by the
Prudential Committee to write a paper on the Indians west
of the Rockies. In this paper he went into some detail regarding their medical practices, superstitions, and so forth.
From the dates on this paper and on the letter to the Indian
Commissioner, we assume that Whitman remained in Boston until Saturday, April 8.

In the *Thirty-Fourth Annual Report of the American
Board,* which appeared in September, 1843, we find the
following comment on the purpose of Whitman's ride:

Early in the autumn of last year, and immediately after receiving
instructions of the Prudential Committee to discontinue the southern
branch of the Oregon mission, a meeting of the missionaries from all
the stations was held to consider the course to be adopted. In their
estimation, the circumstances of the mission and its prospects were

<hr>

[61] Originals in Old Indian Files, Washington, D. C. Photostat
copies in Coll. Wn.

so far changed, that they should be justified in going forward with the mission as it then was, until the case could be again referred to the Committee; and it was thought expedient that Doct. Whitman should proceed immediately to Boston with the hope that he might return to his labors again early in the ensuing spring.

Nothing is said about Whitman's visit to Washington or about any possible political motives which may have inspired him to leave his work at that time. As far as the Board was concerned, Whitman rode on mission business, and he was successful in obtaining the desired changes in the Board's order.[62]

One other item from this annual report is worthy of mention. Whitman had given Greene a vision of the future development of Oregon and had stressed the strategic location of the Waiilatpu station. Greene then wrote: "In view of the subject, the importance of sustaining the mission becomes much more obvious & great. It is seen to have new, wider and more permanent bearings. . . . They anticipate the wave of white population which is rolling westward."

---

[62] *See* Appendix 4 for a discussion of the literature bearing upon the Whitman controversy.

CHAPTER SIXTEEN

"WESTWARD HO"

1843

DURING the spring of 1843 there was an awakened interest in Oregon throughout the States, as is evidenced by the frequency with which editorials and articles on that subject appeared in the press. Oregon was called "the pioneer's land of promise,"[1] and "a country of the largest liberty, the only known land of equality on the face of the earth."[2] The accounts of Oregon found in the published books of such travelers as Farnham or in letters sent back from the Oregon Country were eagerly read. For instance, the Cleveland *Daily Herald* of March 1, 1843, quoted from a letter written by Dr. Elijah White on August 17, 1842, while en route to Oregon. Dr. White gave good advice to those intending to migrate to Oregon.

A typical editorial is the following which appeared in the Painesville, Ohio, *Telegraph* for May 24, 1843:

WESTWARD HO

The tide of emigration flowing westward this season must be overwhelming. Besides the hundreds and thousands that daily throng the steamboats on the Lakes there is a constant stream of "movers" on land. From ten to fifteen teams have passed through this town every day for the last three weeks, winding their way to Wisconsin and Iowa, and some, we understand are bound for the "far west" which in these latter days means a country somewhere between the Rocky Mountains and sundown. Those we noticed had the appearance generally of intelligence, respectability and wealth and gave indication of that enterprising and energetic character which alone takes upon itself the hardships and privations incident to the settlement of a new country.[3]

Several papers referred to "the Oregon fever." The *Iowa Gazette* declared: "The Oregon fever is raging in al-

---

[1] Boston *Daily Evening Transcript*, April 4, 1843. Since Whitman was in Boston at the time this appeared, it is possible that he had interviewed the editor.

[2] Cleveland *Plain Dealer*, March 8, 1843.

[3] I am indebted to Dr. F. C. Waite, of Cleveland, for this item. *See* also the *Ohio Statesman*, Mar. 14, 1843; Chillicothe *Intelligencer*, Mar. 17, 1843; *National Intelligencer*, Wash., D. C., June 7, 1843; and *O.H.Q.*, 1903, p. 175.

most every part of the Union. Companies are forming . . .
will make a pretty formidable army. This, if nothing else,
will compel Congress to act upon the matter."[4]

Such newspaper references are indicative of the wide-
spread interest in Oregon which existed through the country. Along the frontier, especially in Iowa and Missouri,
the interest was keen. "The Oregon fever had broken out,"
and it was "Westward Ho" for the most daring and the
most courageous.

WHITMAN RETURNS TO RUSHVILLE

Whitman remained in Boston for about ten days. He
was restless to be on his way, for it had been his intention
to get back to Westport soon after the first of May. It
would have taken him, under normal traveling conditions
then existing, about a month to travel from Boston to Westport. Every day he spent in Boston meant one day less that
he could spend with his relatives and friends on his westward journey. Since the Prudential Committee of the Board
met on April 8 and acted upon his requests, we are at a
loss to understand why he tarried in Boston until the 8th
of the month.

While in Boston, Whitman had a silhouette made by a
Mr. R. K. Cummings. He considered the result so unsatisfactory that he did not even get a copy for his mother.[5] All
efforts to locate this silhouette have failed. Daguerreotypes
were then being taken but the cheapest as then advertised
in the papers cost $3.50. Whitman undoubtedly felt that
this was more than he could afford. Somewhere along the
line of travel, perhaps in New York or Philadelphia, a Rev.
William Chester presented Whitman a copy of D'Aubigné's
History of the Great Reformation, which is one of the few
relics to survive the destruction which took place at the time
of the massacre.[6]

The claim has been made that Whitman called on the
Rev. Samuel Parker while he was East.[7] In view of the
fact that Whitman was pressed for time and probably went
to Rushville from Boston by a route divergent from Ithaca,
it is hardly possible that such a visit was made. After

---

[4] Quoted by the *Ohio Statesman*, April 26, 1843.
[5] Mary Alice Wisewell to Myron Eells, Mar. 10, 1882, Coll. W.
[6] Coll. W.
[7] *W.C.Q.*, Vol. 1, No. 3, p. 23.

Whitman was on his way back to Oregon, Parker wrote to Greene for information about Whitman. His letter was dated in June, 1843, and in it we read: "I had wished to have known something more definite about Doct Whitman; his object of returning and prospects etc. I have heard from his brother in Rushville that he is on his way back to the station."[8] This letter implies that Parker had not seen Whitman.

There was a railroad in the spring of 1843 which connected Boston with Buffalo. The trains averaged from fifteen to twenty miles an hour. The fare from Boston to Albany, a distance of about two hundred miles, was advertised to be four dollars. A train leaving Boston at eight o'clock in the morning would not arrive in Albany until late that same evening. The trains did not run on Sunday.

We do not know just when Whitman left Boston. Judging from the letter he wrote to the United States Indian Bureau, he was in the city on Saturday, April 8. It is possible that he did not leave until Monday, April 10, and that he then went by train as far west as Canandaigua where he could have taken a stage for Rushville. By this method he could have reached Rushville by Wednesday or Thursday of that week. If he traveled by stage, his progress would of necessity have been slower. We do not know with certainty the date of Whitman's arrival in Rushville. It must have been sometime between April 12 and April 17.[9]

Only a few meager and scattered references are to be found regarding that visit which must have created considerable interest and excitement for the whole village. Martha Wisewell, the daughter of Whitman's sister, Alice, wrote that the first indication her mother had of the presence of the doctor in the States was through reading the account of his visit with Horace Greeley.[10] Perrin Whitman claims that the doctor's mother gently rebuked her son for going to Boston first, and that Marcus replied: "Business before pleasure, mother, but I am here now to visit you."[11] Ac-

---

[8] Original or copy owned by L. Alex. Mack, New York. *See* also, Marshall, *op. cit.*, Vol. 2, p. 310, for comment on this supposed visit.

[9] Information about trains furnished by Dr. F. C. Waite. The Cleveland *Herald*, April 15, 1843, advertises the fare from Boston to Albany as being $4.00. Perrin Whitman implies that Whitman had but three days to visit his relatives. *W.H.Q.*, Vol. 2, No. 3, p. 138, and Eells, *Marcus Whitman* (Pamphlet), p. 13.

[10] *Sunday School Times*, Jan. 10, 1903.

[11] Portland *Oregonian*, Jan. 29, 1899.

cording to a statement made by Frank Wisewell, a nephew, so great was the pressure of time that Dr. Whitman "spent only a single night under his mother's roof, and one night at his sister's home in Naples."[12] It is possible that Whitman spent a night or so with other relatives in Rushville.

Whitman spoke one evening in the Congregational church at Rushville. Among those present was a seventeen-year-old boy, James Clark Strong, the son of the Rev. Henry P. Strong, who had served as pastor of the Rushville church for about three years before his death on August 28, 1835.[13] In later years James Clark Strong became a General in the United States Army. In his published autobiography, General Strong gives an interesting account of Whitman's plea for Oregon and stated: "He described the Indians, the country and the climate so vividly that when he said he wanted to get as many as he could to go back with him to settle in the country, I asked him to take me, but he said he wanted only married men."[14]

Whitman no doubt expressed his appreciation for the twenty-five plows which had been sent by the people of Rushville in 1840. A collection which amounted to twelve dollars was received and turned over to Dr. Whitman. [Letter 131.]

Another lad who was fascinated with the story of Oregon and who was attracted by Whitman's personality, was Perrin, the eldest son of Samuel Whitman, a younger brother of Marcus. When the doctor was on his way West in 1835, he visited in his brother's home at Danville, Illinois. Perrin was then five years old. Samuel Whitman returned with his family to Rushville in September, 1841. Mrs. Whitman died on September 29 of the following year, leaving her husband with four children, Perrin, the eldest, being but twelve years old.

In later years Perrin told how his uncle's story of the midwinter ride filled him with wonder. "His personality captivated me," Perrin wrote. "He seemed to have drawn me by some power, for he at once began to plead with my father to gain his consent for me to accompany him on his return trip to Oregon." The difficult condition under which Samuel was laboring with four motherless children was an

---

[12] Naples (N. Y.) *Record*, Sept. 19, 1913.
[13] Strong, *Biographical Sketch*, p. 4.
[14] *Ibid.*, p. 20.

important factor in favor of Dr. Whitman's plan. No doubt
Marcus remembered how he had been sent to live with
relatives when he was a boy. Perrin wrote:

My father reluctantly consented, after three days' pleading, that
the doctor should adopt me and take me with him if I was willing
to go. My boyish instincts were aroused, and with the promise of a
gun, a saddle and a donkey, my consent was not delayed. Papers of
adoption were made and filed.[15]

Since there was no provision in the law for legal adoption in New York State before 1873, it is probable that
Marcus and Samuel drew up a contract similar to that used
when a boy was hired out as an apprentice. A family tradition states that Samuel gave Marcus five hundred dollars
to be invested for Perrin. Later this money was invested
in horses and cattle. So it was arranged for Perrin to go
to Oregon with his Uncle Marcus. Twenty-five years later,
or in July, 1868, Perrin Whitman returned to New York
State and visited his father and brothers.[16]

One of Whitman's nieces, Martha Wisewell, the daughter of his sister, Alice, wrote the recollections of her uncle's
visit to her home at Naples. Martha wrote:

I remember standing opposite him in the room when he had a lasso
in his hand. This he threw over my head and drew me up to him, to
show the manner of catching animals in the West. And I have not
forgotten how this frightened me....[17]

While in the Wisewell home, Dr. Whitman had the opportunity of becoming acquainted with a nephew who was
born on May 23, 1838, and who was named Marcus Whitman Wisewell.

Whitman spoke in the Presbyterian church at Naples
one evening, and those present indicated their interest in
his work by pledging one hundred dollars to the cause.[18]
Most interesting to relate—there was still living in the fall

---

[15] *W.H.Q.*, Vol. 2, pp. 138 ff. Also *Spokesman-Review*, Dec. 26, 1895.

[16] Some of Perrin Whitman's property was taken by the Government troops at the time of the Whitman Massacre. A claim was put
in which was finally settled for $750, the check for which was received
by his family the day after he died—Jan. 27, 1899. The money was
used to buy the tombstone to be seen today over his grave in the Lewiston, Idaho, cemetery. Samuel Whitman's Toll Book, recently discovered,
has this item, p. 159: "July, 1868, Perrin B. Whitman came home—
to see me twenty five yrs. gone." Information by courtesy of R. E.
Moody, Rushville, N. Y.

[17] *S. S. Times*, June 10, 1903. According to a statement in the
Centennial Celebration, p. 36, Dr. Whitman left his heavy buffalo coat
in Rushville.

[18] Information by kindness of Miss Caroline Housel, of Naples.

of 1936, a woman who remembered Dr. Whitman's visit. Her name is Mrs. Eliza Ann Housel, and she was between eight and nine years old when Whitman visited Naples.

According to two reports, Dr. Whitman spent a night in Prattsburg, where lived some of the relatives of Mrs. Whitman.[19] Undoubtedly Whitman also visited old friends at Wheeler. Whitman felt the necessity of returning at once to the frontier, so after a short visit of not more than five days at the most, left for the West. Perrin claims that they started for Oregon on April 20.[20]

Marcus found it most difficult to say goodbye to his mother, who worried about his safety and wanted him to stay longer. Among the recently discovered letters of Dr. Whitman is one written to his mother on May 27 from Westport, Missouri. This letter reveals his concern over the fact that his mother was not a professing Christian. Deep in his heart he knew her to be a wonderfully good woman, firm and true as ever a woman could be. But she was a woman of independent thought, and something had happened to cause her to lose sympathy with the organized church. While we have evidence that she sometimes attended church, we find no record that she ever joined. This failure to make a public confession of faith troubled her son Marcus, and he closed his letter of May 27 with a fervent appeal, to which reference was made in the first chapter of this book, for her to make a public confession of faith.

After leaving Rushville for the last time, Whitman and his nephew went to West Almond in the adjoining county of Allegany to visit Jonas Galusha Prentiss, who owned a store there. In a letter written to Myron Eells on November 18, 1883, Jonas referred to Dr. Whitman's eagerness to get him and others to go to Oregon.[21] Marcus wrote back to his brother-in-law on May 28, and made reference to a Government "secret service fund" which might be at the disposal of Oregon emigrants.[22] It is possible that Dr. White,

---

[19] F. Fay to S. W. Pratt, Feb. 26, 1902. Coll. Wn. F. Fay wrote: "I now distinctly remember hearing Mark Whitman tell my father that the authorities at Washington promised him nothing should be settled about the boundary until the matter had been thoroughly investigated." *See* also, J. H. Hotchkin, Prattsburg *News*, April 10, 1890.

[20] Eells, *Marcus Whitman* (Pamphlet), p. 13.

[21] Original, Coll. W.

[22] Jason Lee had secured assistance from this fund for his *Lausanne* expedition to the extent of fifty dollars a passenger. Bancroft, *Oregon*, Vol. I, p. 177.

who knew of such a fund, had talked to Whitman about it. White received some aid from this source in 1842.

Jonas Galusha took Dr. Whitman and Perrin to Cuba, about thirty-five miles west of West Almond, where Whitman visited his wife's parents. He there delivered the letters Narcissa had written to her parents and to the Rev. and Mrs. Asa S. Allen.[23] Narcissa's sisters Clarissa and Harriet were also living at Cuba. Clarissa was then married to Norman Kinney and was the mother of a four-year-old son. Harriet was married to John Jackson.[24] Whitman did his best to get the Kinneys and the Jacksons to go to Oregon.

Dr. Whitman's visit was all too short for Narcissa's satisfaction. Writing to her sister more than a year later, Narcissa declared: "My husband's visit was very short, too much so to gain all the information I was in hopes he would bring me." [Letter 155.] When Dr. Whitman started for Oregon, he carried with him a number of letters and small gifts for his wife from her relatives and friends in the East. In a letter written to Mrs. Lydia Porter on May 18, 1844, Narcissa referred to the joy which such remembrances had brought to her. She mentioned receiving a book entitled *The Pastor's Wife,* which her friend David Malin had sent.

BACK TO WESTPORT

While we have very little evidence to indicate the route Whitman and his nephew took on the return trip, it seems probable that they went by stage through northern Ohio to Cleveland, and then to Cincinnati, where passage could have been secured on a river steamer for St. Louis. Perrin Whitman once stated that they went by way of Olean, New York, and "by the Allegheny and Ohio and Mississippi Rivers."[25]

In a letter written by B. F. Whitman, a grandson of Whitman's uncle, Freedom Whitman, we read:

---

[23] Allen was pastor of the Cuba church 1837-46. We have no evidence to show that Narcissa ever met either Mr. Allen or his wife. Her letter was one of general interest.

[24] Binney, *Genealogy of Prentiss Family,* p. 75. The Jacksons later settled at Oberlin, Ohio. Clarissa's son was killed in Oregon in 1855. Clarissa is reported to have moved to San Francisco where Elizabeth Sager Helm saw her. See her letter in Yates County, N. Y., *Chronicle,* Mar. 18, 1914.

[25] Marshall, *op. cit.,* Vol. 2, p. 301. Marshall quoted indirectly from Perrin. There was no boat traffic on the Allegheny River.

I have heard from my mother of a visit of Marcus Whitman to my father in this city in 1843, when Dr. Whitman was on his way west to organize the first wagon train to cross the Rocky Mountains, at which time he spent a day and a night here, at our home, almost persuading my father to join the new enterprise.[26]

If Whitman and his nephew took only the day stages, they could have reached Cleveland in four days after leaving Cuba. Allowing a day or so for a visit with relatives at Chester, Ohio, Whitman and his nephew could have reached Cleveland by the 27th or 28th of April. Since they reached St. Louis about May 6, this means that they left Cincinnati on or about May 3.[27]

Upon arriving in St. Louis, Whitman was again a guest in the home of his dentist friend, Dr. Edward Hale,[28] and while there Dr. Whitman had a tooth filled with gold. Perrin stood by, seriously watching the first dentistry he had ever seen. Years later he was able to identify his uncle's skull by that gold-filled tooth.[29]

Finding that he had some extra time, Whitman went to Quincy, Illinois, where he enjoyed a visit with Jane Prentiss. Edward Prentiss happened to be absent at the time. It is interesting to note that one of the founders of the Mission Institute at Quincy, in which Jane served as a teacher, was the Rev. Moses Hunter, once pastor of the Presbyterian church at Angelica. The principal was the Rev. William Beardsley, once principal of Franklin Academy at Prattsburg.[30]

Dr. Whitman was sorry to have missed Edward. On On May 27 he wrote to his brother-in-law from the Shawnee mission school and gave the following advice:

I suppose you think yourself a man now, and perhaps are not anxious for advice. I will venture, however, to let you know how anxious I am for you to complete your education. Entering the ministry a year or two sooner will not avail for any good purpose. We ought to aim at the greatest usefulness.

---

[26] Cleveland *Plain Dealer*, May 7, 1895. By courtesy of the Rev. W. F. Whitman, of Nashotah, Wisconsin, who sent the item to Dr. F. C. Waite, of Cleveland, who sent it to the author.

[27] Talbot, a member of Frémont's expedition of 1843, left Cincinnati on May 4 and reached St. Louis on the 7th. *See* his journal, p. 3.

[28] Hale was one of the first three early dentists in St. Louis who remained any length of time. He stopped practice in 1864.

[29] *W.C.Q.*, Vol. 2, No. 3, p. 36. Also Delaney, *Whitman Massacre*, p. 45.

[30] *General Congregational Association of Illinois*, pp. 115 ff., has information relating to the Mission Institute of Quincy.

While in St. Louis, Whitman bought a copy of De Smet's *Indian Sketches*, which seemed to have made a deep impression upon him, for he recommended the book to Greene, to Jonas Galusha, and to his brother Augustus. To Jonas he wrote: "You will see what way the Society of Jesus do their missionary work and what we have to content with in Oregon." [Letter 135.] De Smet was a pioneer Roman Catholic missionary to Oregon, who then happened to be in Europe seeking for more workers and money for his mission.

Whitman wrote to Greene on May 12 while in St. Louis and reported that he had found it impracticable to attempt to take any families with him that year, except those who were expecting to go. This is an acknowledgment that he had not succeeded in finding any "pious settlers" who would emigrate to Oregon with the intention of settling near the mission stations. The only one whom Whitman succeeded in persuading to do this was Perrin, a thirteen-year-old boy. Yet Whitman had not dropped the idea and in this letter to Greene stated: "It is requisite that more good pious men & Ministers go to Oregon without delay as Citizens or our hope there is greatly clouded if not destroyed."

Greene replied to this letter on July 21, 1843, and asked Whitman if it were not possible for him to find some good men "in that great company" who might be relied upon for employment at the mission station. Thus Greene gave his approval to a practice which Whitman followed thereafter. Greene wrote: "When we shall be able to send you out any helpers I do not know."

It is quite possible that Whitman saw Colonel John Frémont and members of his expedition in St. Louis, for Talbot states that Frémont was in the city on May 7. The expedition did not embark for Westport until Saturday, May 13, and in all probability Dr. Whitman and his nephew were on the same boat. Frémont reached Westport on May 18. This is about the time that Whitman arrived.

W. H. Gray claimed that "Fremont was sent here at the request of Dr M Whitman . . . to protect the emigration of 1843 to explore the country & report its value."[31] No contemporary document has been discovered to support such a claim.[32] It is possible that Whitman requested troops to

---

[31] Myron Eells to J. M. Vale, July 20, 1885, Coll. W.

[32] An unsuccessful search has been made in the files of the War Department for the original order which sent Frémont on his second expedition.

protect the emigrants, but others had made the same request. On March 25, 1843, J. M. Shively, of St. Louis, sent a letter to Washington in which he asked for a company of troops to escort his party to Oregon.[33] However, Frémont's expedition did not accompany the 1843 emigration, but followed it. The presence of these troops may have exercised a subduing effect upon the Indians.

THE EMIGRANTS GATHER

Because of the unusual lateness of the season, the emigrants did not start until the last of May, and Whitman found that he was on hand nearly three weeks too early. He regretted that he had hurried on after being with his relatives and friends so short a time. "I might about as well have been three weeks later," he wrote his mother, "but as I could not know before hand, it was better to be safe." [Letter 134.] Incidentally, this letter proves that Whitman felt no special responsibility in getting up or organizing the emigration of 1843.

As soon as there was sufficient grass to give pasturage to livestock, the emigrants for Oregon began to assemble at a rendezvous about twelve miles west of Independence, Missouri, and just over the state line. Peter Burnett, who was a prominent member of the emigration, arrived there on May 17. He states in his journal that a meeting was held by the emigrants on the 18th and a committee appointed to see Dr. Whitman. Another committee was appointed to inspect wagons and a third to draw up rules and regulations to govern the group on the journey.[34]

A question much discussed was regarding the possibility of taking wagons through to the Columbia River Valley. There were many who said it could not be done. The *New Era* of St. Louis of May 25, 1843, carried two columns of fine print containing a letter of P. L. Edwards, dated September 15, 1842, in which Edwards stated his belief that wagons could not be taken into the Columbia River Valley and that the emigrants should make their plans accordingly.[35] J. W. Nesmith, also a prominent member of the emigration, wrote: "Dr. Whitman was persistent in his

33 *O.H.Q.*, June, 1903, p. 172.

34 Burnett, *Recollections of a Pioneer*, p. 101. Also *T.O.P.A.*, 1875, pp. 42 ff., for Nesmith's account.

35 Eells, *Reply to Bourne*, p. 110. Edwards was a member of the Methodist mission who had gone to Oregon with Lee in 1834.

asserting that wagons could proceed as far as the Grand Dalles of the Columbia river, from which point he asserted they could be taken down by rafts or batteaux to the Willamette valley."[36]

On May 20 another meeting was held among the emigrants at Fitzhugh's mill to complete the organization. Dr. Whitman was present and met many of the men, although some of the members of that emigration did not hear about Dr. Whitman until they were along the Platte. This fact is not surprising, because most of the men were strangers to one another, having come from widely separated places in the States. Since there were about one thousand people altogether, it naturally took some time for them to know each other.[37] Another difficulty in this respect was the fact that the company divided into two parts until after they reached Fort Hall, and then, feeling free of any danger from hostile Indians, they divided into smaller units.

Captain John Gantt, a former army officer and a mountain man, was engaged to serve as pilot as far as Fort Hall, and it was agreed that all should be ready to start by Monday, May 22. On that day most, if not all, of the emigrants moved fifteen miles west to Elm Grove, where they camped. Burnett gives an interesting description of that encampment. The grove was then reduced to but two elm trees and a few dogwoods. Burnett wrote:

> The place where we encamped was very beautiful; and no scene appeared to our enthusiastic vision more exquisite than the sight of so many wagons, tents, fires, cattle, and people, as were here collected. At night the sound of joyous music was heard in the tents. Our long journey thus begun in sunshine and song, in anecdote and laughter; but these all vanished before we reached its termination.[38]

The emigration continued on its way, reaching the Kansas River on the 31st. Whitman tarried behind the emigration. When he wrote to Edward Prentiss on May 27, he dated his letter from the Shawnee mission school. We have extant four of his letters written from that place, the last of which was dated May 30. The mission station was

---

[36] *T.O.P.A.*, 1875, pp. 42 ff.

[37] Authorities differ as to the number of people in this emigration. Nesmith claimed that a roll made May 20, 1843, of the men capable of bearing arms, including all over 16, numbered 295. *T.O.P.A.*, 1875, p. 48. Nineveh Ford (MS., Coll. Wn.) claims the emigration numbered 900. McClane listed 999. *See* Bancroft, *Oregon*, Vol. 1, p. 395.

[38] Burnett, *op. cit.*, p. 101.

established by the Methodists in 1830, and was then located about nine miles west of Westport.

Writing to his mother on the 27th, Marcus said that his health was good and that he had lost ten pounds since being in Rushville. The next day in his letter to Jonas Galusha he reported that though the main body of the emigrants had started about a week previous, stragglers were even then passing by. He said that Frémont was camped about two miles away. Whitman was disappointed in that no sheep were taken, but was much encouraged to see how many people were on the road. "It is now decided," he wrote, "that Oregon will be occupied by American citizens. Those who go only open the way for more another year." [Letter 135.]

On the 30th, Whitman wrote another letter to Greene, in which he stated his intention to start the next day. Referring to the money he had drawn, he said that he used it to complete buying his outfit and to pay what he owed to a Spaniard "who came in with me from Taos." Whitman repossessed the animals which he had left at Westport the preceding February.

Whitman and his nephew left the Shawnee mission on Thursday, June 1, and spent that night with the Frémont party. Talbot wrote the following in his journal about their visitor:

Dr. Whitman, the Baptist Missionary established at Wallawallah on the Columbia, was our guest tonight. He is behind the main body of emigrants, but can of course easily overtake them. He expresses much anxiety for their safe journey, and is determined to do all in his power to assist them, a promise of much value, as well from his practical good sense as his general knowledge of the route.[39]

Whitman took little baggage besides his blankets and personal effects. Daniel Waldo, who went to Oregon that year, wrote:

I fed him the first part of the road. He had nothing to start with but a boiled ham. . . . I reckon he expected that ham to last him and his boy all the way across. After we crossed the Snake River we had to feed him again. I did not like it much. But he was a very energetic man and I liked his perseverance. He had not much judgment but a great deal of perseverance. He expected the emigrants to feed him and they did.[40]

---

[39] Talbot, *op. cit.*, p. 9. Of course Talbot was mistaken about Whitman's being a Baptist missionary.

[40] Original MS., in Bancroft Coll., U. of C., Berkeley. Partly reprinted in Bancroft, *Oregon*, Vol. 1, p. 405.

Perhaps Whitman expected to live on wild game as he had done when he crossed in 1835 and 1836. However, the buffalo were scarce along the way in 1843, so that the emigrants were obliged to live on the provisions they took or kill some of their cattle. A member of the emigration wrote a letter on June 3, 1843, published in the July 8 issue of the *Iowa Gazette,* in which we read the following:

There are over 3,000 and perhaps 5,000 head of cattle, mules and horses attached to the company. Captain Applegate has over 200 head, and others over 100 head.

The presence of so many cattle became a bone of contention because those without cattle did not want to help guard or drive them, and they wanted to move faster than the cattle could go. Therefore the emigrants divided into two main groups after crossing the Big Blue River in what is now the state of Kansas. The group with the cattle was called the "Cow Column." Dr. Whitman seems to have remained with this group most of the way across the prairies. He then pushed on ahead, and by the time they left Fort Hall, he was in the lead.

The emigration consisted of a fine type of people. The *Liberty Banner* of Clay County, Missouri, described the men as being of "fine intelligence and vigorous and intrepid character, admirably calculated to lay the firm foundations of a future empire.[41] The emigrants learned before their journey was over that oxen were better than horses to pull the heavily loaded covered wagons, of which there were about 125.[42]

"TRAVEL, TRAVEL, TRAVEL"

Instead of going up along the Missouri to the mouth of the Platte, as the mission party of 1836 had done, the emigrants of 1843 cut across what is now the northeastern part of Kansas and southwestern Nebraska and did not strike the south branch of the South Fork of the Platte until about the first of July. Wagon boxes were covered with skins and made into boats. It was about this time that Dr. Whitman overtook the main body of the emigrants. He rendered valiant service in aiding them to cross the river.

Dr. Whitman insisted on constant travel. When the spirit of song had left even the young, and they were willing

[41] Reprinted in the *National Intelligencer,* June 6, 1843, and the *Globe* (Wash., D. C.) June 8, 1843.

[42] Perrin Whitman's estimate, *W.C.Q.,* Vol. 2, No. 2, p. 33. *See* also Bancroft, *Oregon,* Vol. 1, p. 395.

to remain in camp and rest, it was Dr. Whitman who urged them to keep moving. Perrin Whitman said: "He never allowed them to stay two nights in one place. Kept them moving every day, if it was only for a little way, so as to change grass for the stock.[43] Jesse Applegate in the following statement stressed the same fact:

From the time he joined us on the Platte until he left us at Fort Hall, his great experience and indomitable energy were of priceless value to the migrating column. His constant advice, which we knew was based upon a knowledge of the road before us was "travel, *travel*, TRAVEL". . . nothing else will take you to the end of your journey; nothing is wise that does not help you along. Nothing is good for you that causes a moment's delay.[44]

Col. J. W. Nesmith described Whitman in these words: "He was of a powerful physical organization, and possessed a great and good heart, full of charity and courage, and utterly destitute of cant, hypocrisy, shams and effeminancy, and always terribly in earnest." Nesmith likewise pays tribute to Whitman's services:

While with us he was clad entirely in buckskin, and rode one of those patient long-eared animals said to be "without pride of ancestry or hope of posterity." The Doctor spent much of his time in hunting out the best route for the wagons, and would plunge into streams in search of practical fords, regardless of the depth or temperature of the water, and sometimes after the fatigue of a hard day's march, would spend much of the night in going from one part to another to minister to the sick.[45]

Jesse Applegate also refers to Whitman's services as a doctor. He tells of how one day a wagon swung out of the wagon train and stopped. Dr. Whitman had been riding beside the wagon for some time. A tent was pitched and a fire kindled. The other wagons passed by, people in them wondering what was wrong and wondering why one family should pause on the line of march to make camp. The emigrant train continued, leaving the lone covered wagon far in the rear, but here is Applegate's description:

There are anxious watchers for the absent wagon, for there are many matrons who may be afflicted like its inmate before the journey is over; and they fear the strange and startling practice of this Oregon doctor. But as the sun goes down, the absent wagon rolls into camp, the bright, speaking face and cheery look of the doctor, who

---

[43] *W.C.Q., op. cit.,* p. 35.

[44] Applegate, "A Day with the Cow Column in 1843," *T.O.P.A.,* 1876.

[45] *T.O.P.A.,* 1880, p. 22.

rides in advance, declare without words that all is well, and both mother and child are comfortable.[46]

Applegate stated that the successful delivery of the child to the emigrant mother firmly established Dr. Whitman's reputation and gave confidence to the whole group. He called Dr. Whitman a "noble and devoted man" and added this tribute: " ... and it is no disparagement to others to say, that to no other individual are the emigrants of 1843 so much indebted for the successful conclusion of their journey as to Dr. Marcus Whitman." He also gave this incident of the trail, which occurred at the end of the day when the first baby of the 1843 emigration was born. The doctor was at the tent of the pilot with whom he lived. Many of the men of the column were gathered around "listening to his wise and energetic counsel." To one side sits the pilot, "quietly smoked his pipe, for he knows the brave doctor is 'strengthening his hands.' "

The question of food supplies became acute before the journey was over. At first the people threw away scraps of food, as bacon rinds, and were generous in inviting others to eat with them. But they soon learned that everything, even the rinds of the bacon, had to be conserved. Captain Gantt killed an old buffalo bull on June 15. The wantonness on the part of hunters who had slaughtered the shaggy beasts of the prairies for the thrill of killing was already beginning to tell in the reduced herds.

Toward the end of June plenty of fresh buffalo meat was secured, and once the emigrants saw a herd estimated to contain three thousand head plunge over a twenty-foot embankment into the Platte. Scores of them fell and were trampled by the others or were drowned in the river.[47] S. M. Gilmore, who went out to Oregon that year, wrote back from Fort Vancouver on November 11, 1843, and gave the following advice to those who expected to go over the Oregon Trail:

You should bring 200 pounds of flour, 100 pounds of bacon, for every member of the family that can eat, besides other provisions. Make no calculation on getting buffalo or other wild meat, for you are only wasting time and killing horses and mules to get it. Have your wagon beds made in such a manner that they can be used for boats; you will find them of great service in crossing streams—have your

---

[46] Applegate, op. cit., p. 63.

[47] Lennox, Overland to Oregon, p. 33. Lennox was also a member of this emigration.

wagons well covered, so they will not leak, or your provisions and clothes will spoil.[48]

The light column, traveling before the cow column, reached Fort Laramie on July 14. Burnett claims that he found the following food prices at the Fort: "Coffee, $1.50 a pint; brown sugar, the same; flour, unbolted, 25 cents a pound; powder, $1.50 a pound; lead, 75 cents a pound; percussion caps, $1.50 a box; calico, very inferior, $1.00 a yard."[49]

The Laramie River was high with the waters of melting snows. It could not be forded, so the wagon boxes had to be used as boats. Waldo claimed: "No one was willing to risk himself in swimming the river and carrying the line but Dr. Whitman, which he did successfully."[50] We marvel at the amazing endurance of the man, and praise his willingness to serve.

On July 20, while at "Bigbute Creek, 100 miles west of Laramie's Fork," Marcus received the letter which Narcissa had written on May 18. Therein he learned for the first time of the burning of the mill and of Dr. White's endeavor to establish laws among the Cayuses. As he read Narcissa's remark that the Cayuses were "like sheep without a shepherd," he was all the more eager to get back. He also learned that Spalding and Geiger had sent the pack train with provisions to meet the emigration. Whitman added a note to his wife's letter and sent it to Greene with some messenger who was returning to St. Louis. Fearing that Greene might be concerned about the loss of the mill, Whitman wrote optimistically: "I am in no way solicitous for the loss of the Mill or on account of the excitement & hope no change will be made in the Mission & that you will be able to reinforce us next year."

Whitman pushed on ahead of the light column and learned of a new way from the Continental Divide to Fort Hall, which he recommended to those behind him. The party with whom Peter Burnett traveled crossed the divide on the 5th, 6th, and 7th of August. Burnett wrote: "On the 12th of August we were informed that Doctor Whitman had written a letter, stating that the Catholic missionaries had discovered, by the aid of their Flathead Indian pilot,

[48] *O.H.Q.*, 1903, p. 282.

[49] Burnett, *op. cit.*, p. 112. His recollections dealing with the trail were reprinted in the *O.H.Q.*, March, 1904.

[50] Quoted by Eells, *Marcus Whitman*, p. 215.

a pass through the mountains by way of Fort Bridger, which was shorter than the old route."[51] Burnett's party arrived at Fort Bridger on Blacks Fork of the Green River on August 14, and reached Fort Hall on the 27th. This route was not only shorter than that which the Whitman-Spalding party followed in 1836, but was evidently much better for the wagons.

At Fort Hall, Whitman met Captain Grant, in charge of that post, and received further information about Mrs. Whitman. Grant had escorted Mrs. Whitman from Waskopum to Fort Walla Walla with the Hudson's Bay express early in April of that year. Lennox reports that Whitman received a letter from his wife on August 28 which contained the plea: "Do hurry home."[52]

WAGONS WEST

A critical situation arose at Fort Hall when Captain Grant advised the emigrants to leave their wagons and cattle there and complete the journey on horseback as the members of the 1842 emigration had done. He showed them the abandoned vehicles and told them that he felt it was impossible to take wagons the remainder of the way. Grant had always traveled the trail by horseback and seems to have been sincere in the advice given. Adherents of the Whitman-Saved-Oregon story maintain that Grant saw the significance of a wagon road to Oregon and was doing his best to prevent the accomplishment of that objective.

Burnett wrote: "I consulted Mr. Grant as to his opinion of the practicability of taking our wagons through. He replied that, while he would not say it was impossible for us Americans to make the trip in our wagons, he could not himself see how it could be done." When Perrin Whitman heard Captain Grant give such advice, he reported the situation to his uncle, who gathered some of the emigrants together and reassured them that wagons could be taken through.[53] J. B. McClane, also a member of the 1843 emigration, told Bancroft that Whitman was persistent in this claim.[54]

It is hard to imagine the disaster which would have

---

[51] *O.H.Q.*, March, 1904, p. 76.
[52] *W.C.Q.*, Vol. 2, No. 2, p. 31.
[53] *W.C.Q.*, Vol. 2, No. 2, p. 35.
[54] McClane, MS., Bancroft Coll.

overtaken the party if Grant's advice had prevailed. There were many women and children in the 1843 party. Nesmith claimed that they did not have enough horses to carry all of them. He wrote: "Had we followed Grant's advice, and abandoned the cattle and wagons at Fort Hall, much suffering must have ensued . . . besides, wagons and cattle were indispensable to men expecting to live by farming in a country destitute of such articles."[55] After considerable debate, the emigrants decided to follow Whitman's advice. This decision had far-reaching effects, for the Oregon emigration movement would have received a serious blow if word had been carried back to the States that the members of the 1843 emigration had found it necessary to abandon their wagons and cattle at Fort Hall.

It is assumed that Whitman found some of the supplies sent by Spalding and Geiger at Fort Hall. These he could have sold without difficulty to the emigrants. At Fort Hall the emigrants hired Dr. Whitman to be their pilot for the remainder of the distance. Lennox claimed that a purse of four hundred dollars was raised and given to Dr. Whitman for this service.[56] There was no attempt at organization within the emigration after reaching Fort Hall. Individual groups pushed on as fast as they could. Whitman with a few others, including John Ricord, Nimrod Ford, A. L. Lovejoy, and Perrin, formed a small party to blaze the way. Writing to Greene on November 1, Whitman said:

My journey across the mountains was very much prolonged by the necessity for me to pilot the emigrants. I tried in vain to come ahead at different points, but found it would be at the risk of disaster to the emigrants of having to leave their wagons without the possibility of obtaining sufficient number of horses to take any considerable part of their families and necessary food and clothing.

In the vicinity of the present city of American Falls, Idaho, the trail branched. The main trail followed the Snake River, while a branch led to California. Here sixteen men, including Captain Gantt, left for California. The Snake River was crossed at Salmon Falls, where one of the emigrants, Miles Eyres, whom Whitman met in St. Louis and encouraged to go to Oregon, was drowned. Eyres had all of his money in a belt around his waist, and since his body was not recovered, his family was left almost destitute. They spent the winter of 1843-44 with the Whitmans at

---

[55] Eells, *Reply to Bourne*, p. 112.
[56] *W.C.Q.*, Vol. 2, No. 2, p. 30. Also Lennox, *op. cit.*, p. 17.

Waiilatpu, being among the first of many unfortunate victims of the Oregon Trail to seek the hospitality of the mission station.

By September 20, some of the emigrants reached Fort Boise, where they were kindly received by Francis Payette, Hudson's Bay trader in charge. While the emigrants had some difficulty in getting their wagons across the desert, yet the hardest part of the journey lay before them in the Blue Mountains. Since it was getting late in the season, Dr. Whitman urged the group not to tarry. With a few friends in a light wagon, Whitman continued his way ahead of the main body of the emigrants.

While in the Grande Ronde Valley, Whitman received a letter carried by an Indian messenger from the Rev. Elkanah Walker, written from Lapwai. Both Mr. and Mrs. Spalding were critically ill with scarlet fever. Believing that he was about to die, Spalding sent word to Geiger and to Walker and Eells asking them to come to attend his funeral. Geiger reached Lapwai on September 14 and Walker arrived on the 15th. Feeling certain that Whitman was nearly back, Walker sent a message to him urging him to come at once to Lapwai.

Whitman turned the care of the emigrants over to faithful Stickus, and left at once for Lapwai. He arrived there on September 25. He found the Spaldings on their way to recovery, but their children were ill with the same disease. He stayed at Lapwai but one night and left on Tuesday, September 26, for his own station. [Letter 142.] He felt the necessity of getting back to Waiilatpu and making some preparations for the emigrants. Writing to Greene on November 1, Whitman said in regard to Spalding: "He has expressed a much better state of feeling towards the members of the mission and the Board since his sickness, the reception of your letter and my return, than ever before." Contemporaneous documents do not indicate any further friction between Whitman and Spalding during the remaining years of the mission.

Whitman reached his station perhaps on Thursday, September 28. Since Geiger had been called to Lapwai, only an Indian remained in charge of Waiilatpu. Whitman discovered that some of the advance parties of the emigrants had arrived and had broken into the mission house and then left it open to the Indians. Whitman was provoked over this, for there was an abundance of garden vegetables and other food outside.

In the meantime the main body of the emigrants led by Stickus, who could speak little or no English, was crossing the Blue Mountains. Nesmith wrote that Stickus was "a faithful old fellow . . . he succeeded by pantomime in taking us over the roughest wagon route I ever saw." Nesmith also has the following incident to relate:

> I once dined with Sticus, in his camp, upon what I supposed to be elk meat. I had arrived at that conclusion because, looking at the cooked meat and then at the old Indian interrogatively, he held up his hands in a manner that indicated elk horns; but, after dinner, seeing the ears, tail, and hoofs of a mule near camp, I became satisfied that what he meant to convey by his pantomime was "ears" not "horns."[57]

While Whitman was buried in work trying to get ready for the emigrants, an urgent message arrived from Tshimakain. Mrs. Eells was expecting to give birth to a child, and Dr. Whitman was needed. So after but a day or so at Waiilatpu, Whitman mounted his horse again and started for the Tshimakain station 140 miles to the north.

When Mr. Walker returned to his home from Lapwai, he told his wife and Mr. and Mrs. Eells of Whitman's return. Mrs. Walker noted in her journal: "Dr. Whitman . . . has brought no reinforcement but expects one next year." Evidently the members of the mission were disappointed that his trip East seemed to be so fruitless. By hard riding Whitman was able to reach Tshimakain late either Sunday night, October 1, or on the following night. The babe was not born until late on the evening of the 6th. He was called Myron (1843-1907), and in later years became the outstanding champion of the Whitman-Saved-Oregon story.

During those five or six days of waiting at Tshimakain, Whitman was restless. He was constantly thinking of the emigrants streaming by Waiilatpu needing food, medical attention, and advice. He wanted to start back. Moreover he had the natural desire to see his wife as soon as possible. It was extremely irritating for him to wait. Mrs. Walker wrote in her journal on the 6th: "Dr. W. very uneasy, regrets he came so soon." Mrs. Walker tried to make him as comfortable as possible. Her own children then had the scarlet fever. She filled a straw tick with new straw from

---

[57] *T.O.P.A.*, 1875, p. 48.

the freshly threshed oats, corded a bedstead, and placed it in what she called "the study" for her guest.

At noon after the babe was born, or on Saturday, October 7, Whitman started back to Waiilatpu. Even though he was in a hurry, he rested on Sunday and did not get to his station until about eight o'clock Tuesday evening, October 10. He found that the main body of the emigrants had already passed. Geiger had been there to minister to their needs. "All came in their turns," wrote Whitman to Greene, "and were supplied with provisions." [Letter 142.]

Later Whitman was criticized for the high prices he charged for provisions. Burnett wrote in his defense:

This foolish, false, and ungrateful charge was based upon the fact that he asked us a dollar a bushel for wheat, and forty cents for potatoes. As our people had been accustomed to sell their wheat at from fifty to sixty cents a bushel, and their potatoes at from twenty to twenty-five cents, in the Western States, they thought the prices demanded by the doctor amounted to something like extortion, not reflecting that he had to pay at least twice as much for his own supplies of merchandise, and could not afford to sell his produce as low as they did theirs at home.[58]

Burnett stated that some felt so deeply about the high prices Whitman charged that they refused to buy and as a result ran out of food before they got to the Willamette Valley and were obliged to borrow from others.

About a year and a half later, when Dr. Whitman was in Oregon City, he met Dr. White on the street. Hearing that White had repeated the criticisms, Whitman asked for an explanation. The following account of the controversy has been left for us:

I was present in Oregon City, some time in the month of June, 1845, when Dr. Whitman and Dr. White had what you might call a public controversy. Dr. White from a sectarian jealousy, had written a letter to some of the eastern papers, charging Whitman with misusing immigrants. Dr. Whitman came down and happened to meet Dr. White in Oregon City, when they had a dispute. Dr. White proposed to establish what he had said, so a meeting for a public investigation was called at the Red House. Dr. White called Mr. Geiger, who still lives in Oregon City, as his first witness.

---

[58] Burnett, *Recollections*, p. 127. In White's report of Nov. 15, 1843, (now in Old Indian Files, Wash., D. C.) we read: "The Presbyterian Mission however for the first time have fallen very heavily under censure from the immigrating party this fall, from the fact principally as I understand of their exacting most exorbitant prices for supplies of provisions. I have only ex-parte statements, which known if but half true they deserve the just retrobation of mankind...." Miss Allen omitted this when editing her book, *Ten Years in Oregon*.

When asked to state how Dr. Whitman had treated the immigrants, Mr. Geiger told a very different story than White had counted on. Instead of telling how Dr. Whitman had misused them, he told of his many kindnesses to them, and what a friend he had always been to them. When White saw that the tables were turned against him by his own witnesses, he jumped up and said: "Mr. Geiger, you can take your seat, sir; I will acknowledge that you can outlie me." He failed to prove a single allegation that he had made, so the investigation proved to be a great triumph for Dr. Whitman.[59]

Others criticized Whitman because of his terms in the trading of their worn-out cattle for his fresh fat animals. Daniel Waldo said:

Whitman lied to me like hell at Waiilatpu. He wanted my cattle and told me the grass was all burnt between his place and the Dalles. I told him I would try it anyhow. The first night I left the Dalles I found the finest grass I ever saw, and it was good every night. He did not try to buy mine, but he did try to buy others.[60]

Lennox wrote in a less critical spirit and said: "My father found it necessary to get new oxen, ours were so worn out, so we traded our five oxen for two fresh ones with Mr. Geiger, working our cows to make out a full team."[61] McClane also refers to Whitman's trading fat steers, some weighing fifteen hundred pounds, for two head of the emigrants' cattle, but McClane did not criticize what he evidently thought was a fair transaction.

According to several witnesses, Dr. Whitman frequently extended credit, and there were many cases where he was never paid or was unjustly criticized. In this respect his experience was similar to that of Dr. John McLoughlin, who likewise extended credit to some of the emigrants who failed to appreciate such courtesies.[62] Whitman sold so much of his produce that he was obliged to call upon Spalding to furnish him supplies for the winter. [Letter 142.] He sold beef, pork, potatoes, wheat, and corn. He settled with Geiger at the rate of thirty dollars a month and secured the services of Mr. Littlejohn in his place.

Most of the emigrants went overland to The Dalles, where they secured boats or made rafts to carry themselves, their wagons, and their equipment the rest of the way down the river. The cattle and horses were driven through the

[59] B. F. Nichols in *W.C.Q.*, Vol. 2, No. 1, pp. 33-34.

[60] Waldo MS., Bancroft Coll.

[61] Lennox, *op. cit.*, p. 54.

[62] *See* McClane MS., Bancroft Coll.; *W.C.Q.*, Vol. 2, No. 1, p. 33, and Vol. 2, No. 2, p. 37; Bancroft, *Oregon*, Vol. 1, p. 406.

heavy forests which cloak the sides of Mt. Hood down into the Willamette Valley. Thus the first great emigration to Oregon came to an end. The feasibility of taking wagons through to the Columbia River Valley had been demonstrated. The Oregon Trail was opened!

AN APPRAISAL

It is most interesting to scan through Whitman's letters written after his return and look for those passages which reflect his conclusions regarding the results of his trip East. Writing to Greene on November 1 from Fort Walla Walla, he said:

If I never do more than to have been one of the first to take white women across the mountains and prevent the disaster and reaction which would have occurred by the breaking up of the present emigration, and establishing the first wagon road across to the border of the Columbia River I am satisfied.... I am determined to exert myself for my country and to procure such regulations and laws as will best secure both the Indians and white men in their transit and settlement intercourse.

And again on April 8, 1844, in a letter to Greene, he returned to this subject:

Perhaps in some way, as we have so eminently aided the Government by being among the first to cross the mountains and the first to bring white women over, and last but not least, as I brought the late emigration on to the shores of the Columbia with their wagons contrary to all former assertions of the impossibility of the route, we may be allowed the rights of private citizens, by taking lands in the country.

On May 16, 1844, Whitman wrote to his wife's parents:

As I hold the settlement of this country by Americans rather than by an English colony most important, I am happy to have been the means of landing so large an emigration on to the shores of the Columbia, with their wagons, families and stock, all in safety.

In a letter to Greene, dated July 22, 1844, he stated that "No one but myself was present to give them the assurance of getting through," referring to the members of the 1843 emigration. Two more quotations are pertinent. On April 1, 1847, he outlined his reasons for going East.

... and may not fail to demonstrate what I did in making my way to the States in the winter of '42 and '43, after the 3d of October. It was to open a practical route and safe passage, and to secure the favorable report of the journey from emigrants, which in connection with other objects, caused me to leave my family and brave the toils and dangers of the journey....

In connection with this let me say the other great object for which I went was to save the Mission from being broken up just then, which it must have been, as you will see by a reference to the doings of the Committee which confirmed the recall of Mr. Spalding only two weeks before my arrival in Boston.

And again in the last letter Whitman wrote Greene, dated October 18, 1847, we find:

Two things, and it is true those which were the most important, were accomplished by my return to the States. By means of the establishment of the wagon road, which is due to that effort alone, the emigration was secured and saved from disaster in the fall of '43. Upon that event the present acquired rights of the United States by her citizens hung. And not less certain is it that upon the result of emigration to this country the present existence of this Mission and of Protestantism in general hung also.

Here in these statements by Whitman himself we find the germ of the Whitman-Saved-Oregon story. All of his claims were true. Looking backward, he felt considerable pride in the remembrances of his services to the 1843 emigration. The emigrants of 1844 and succeeding years knew that those of 1843 got through, but those of 1843 had no precedent to guide them except the three wagons which crossed in 1840 and Whitman's assurance that it could be done.

Spalding commented on the results of Whitman's trip in a letter to Levi Chamberlain, dated October 10, 1843. He then had nothing to say about any proposed treaty with Great Britain, but told of the delays that the doctor had experienced and that "consequently [he] did not have time to collect a colony of pious settlers for this country but simply obtained the consent of the Board to forward such a settlement."[63] One of the earliest published comments on the purpose of the ride appeared in Lee and Frost's *Ten Years in Oregon*, where we can read: "Dr. Whitman visited the United States, to obtain further assistance, in order to strengthen the efforts that had already been made."[64]

Another early statement is to be found in a French work entitled *Voyages en California et Dans L'Oregon*, by M. de Saint-Amant, which was published in Paris in 1854. A pertinent sentence, translated, reads: "Having come before his fellow citizens had taken possession of the country, he had made himself a very active agent of the American interests, and had contributed not a little to urging annexa-

---

[63] *O.H.Q.*, Dec., 1932.
[64] P. 213. This work appeared in 1844.

tion...."[65] Since this was written in 1851 or 1852, the advocates of the Whitman-Saved-Oregon story have quoted it to prove that Whitman's political interests were early known. However, it should be pointed out that the author of this work makes no mention of Whitman's trip East in 1842-43, and that his statement applies to the whole of Whitman's residence in Oregon.

One of the best tributes ever paid to the memory of Marcus Whitman was that given by Peter H. Burnett, who became the first Governor of the State of California. He wrote:

In my judgment he made greater sacrifices, endured more hardships, and encountered more perils for Oregon, than any other one man; and his services were more practically efficient than those of any other, except perhaps those of Senator Linn, of Missouri. I say *perhaps*, because I am in doubt as to which of these two men did more in effect for Oregon.[66]

---

[65] Pp. 226-228.

[66] Portland *Oregonian*, Nov. 26, 1897; reprinted in *W.C.Q.*, Vol. 2, No. 1, p. 32.

CHAPTER SEVENTEEN

A CHANGING OREGON
1843-1846

A NEW DAY in Oregon's history began with the arrival of the 1843 emigration. The wagon road from Fort Hall to Fort Walla Walla was the magic key which unlocked Oregon's doors to the restless thousands on America's frontiers who were eagerly looking for new lands to settle. Whitman remembered with glowing pride the part he had played in the opening of that road.

In the light of later events we now realize that Whitman's greatest service to his generation was not to the Indians of Oregon, to whom he went as a Christian missionary, but rather to his own countrymen who followed him over the Oregon Trail. Whitman's letters after his return indicate his changing interests. Gradually he came to the conviction that the Indians could never keep control of the land. He felt that in the providence of God, Oregon was meant for the white man.

History is never static. Mankind is always passing from one era to another. Sometimes the process of transition is accelerated, as it was in Oregon during those years from 1843 to 1847. Whitman returned to a changing Oregon. He and his co-workers were so intimately bound up with those changing political and social conditions that they became the victims of forces they had helped to start but could not stop or control.

1843-1844

After supplying the needs of the last of the emigrants, Whitman left for The Dalles, arriving there sometime during the latter part of October, for he and his wife were back at Fort Walla Walla on November 1. Dr. Whitman found Narcissa in poor health. Reporting her condition to Greene on November 1, Whitman stated that while his wife was somewhat relieved of her trouble, still she had not fully recovered.

The trip from The Dalles to Fort Walla Walla by boat meant inevitable exposure to rain and cold. Narcissa suffered. They paused for a time at the Fort before undertaking the last stage of their journey. Dr. Whitman secured the use of a wagon, perhaps one that the mission owned, and the trip to Waiilatpu was made in one day. Because of Narcissa's weakened condition, they proceeded slowly and did not reach Waiilatpu until late in the evening. [Letter 145.] Even so, her health was not equal to the trip, and for six weeks thereafter she was confined to her room, spending most of the time in bed.

During Dr. Whitman's absence from Waiilatpu, Frémont and his men arrived. Frémont was hoping to obtain flour at the mission but was unable to do so because all had been sold to the emigrants. He was obliged to be satisfied with some of the "excellent potatoes."[1] He left some of the extra cannon balls which he had carried with him for his one lone howitzer, and this fact was remembered by the Indians at the time of the massacre.[2] He also left a big mule which the Whitman's later called Uncle Sam, and which was mentioned by Narcissa in the last letter she wrote to her sister Jane. [Letter 220.]

Narcissa was overjoyed to be with Marcus again, and yet she went back to Waiilatpu with a heavy heart. Her ill-health contributed to the spirit of dejection. She referred to her return in the following words: "I turned my face with my husband toward this dark spot, and dark, indeed, it seemed to be to me when compared with the scenes, social and religious which I had so recently been enjoying with so much zest." [Letter 149.] And again: "I felt such a dread to return to this place of moral darkness, after enjoying so much of civilized life and Christian privileges." [Letter 145.]

However, Marcus and Narcissa did not return to a lonely station. They found the two dwelling houses at Waiilatpu so crowded with emigrants that even the kitchen of the main building was used for a bedroom at night. The Whitmans had their family of the three half-breed children, Mary Ann Bridger, Helen Mar Meek, and David Malin. Perrin Whitman increased their responsibilities to four. Then while passing through Walla Walla, they were induced to accept the care of two motherless girls, Emma and Ann

---

[1] Frémont, *Narrative of the Exploring Expedition*, p. 249.
[2] Statement by Catherine Sager Pringle. *See* Eells MS., Coll. W., bearing date, "Oct. 1885."

Hobson, age six and thirteen years, who had come out with their father in the 1843 emigration.

Before leaving Waiilatpu for Waskopum, Whitman had made arrangements for the Littlejohns to live at Waiilatpu and assist in the mission work. Mrs. Littlejohn gave birth to a child shortly before the Whitmans returned. Because of the crowded conditions, she had been using the Whitmans' bedroom; thus when Narcissa arrived, tired and sick, she and her husband had to turn the dining room into a bedroom.

Five emigrant families and two single men were crowded into the other available space. Jesse Looney and his family of six occupied the Indian room together with a young man by the name of Smith. John W. East and his family, including four small children, had the schoolroom, east of the kitchen. An uninvited mountain man, a Frenchman, whom Narcissa called Alex, slept in the kitchen.

In the mansion house were three families, including the widow Eyres and her three children. There was another family with four children and an old couple. It does not appear that the first house built in 1836-37 was then suitable for habitation. Twenty-six were living in the main mission house and twelve in the mansion house, making a total of thirty-eight. With the exception of the Looney family, all others in the main dwelling, nineteen in all, ate at the Whitman table. Narcissa, writing on January 31, 1844, said that the fare was scanty: " . . . potatoes and corn meal, with a little milk occasionally, and cakes from the burnt wheat." [Letters 146 and 150.] At times Narcissa felt a little resentful to think that the best of the provisions had been sold to the emigrants.

Whenever possible, Whitman gave employment to the able-bodied men to compensate for food and lodging. Yet he was frequently obliged to care for some whom misfortune had left in his dooryard who were unable to pay either in money or service for his hospitality. The widow of Miles Eyres with her children belonged to this group. Whitman probably felt a special responsibility to this family because of his influence in getting Mr. Eyres to migrate.

Within five weeks after their return, the Whitmans were able to move into their own bedroom, suitable quarters having been prepared for the Littlejohns in a new room built "over the cellar." Narcissa's health became worse. During the latter part of December she was brought low "with a severe attack of inflammation of the bowels." [Letter 149.] Dr. Barclay at Fort Vancouver had treated her for an enlarged ovary, and after she came under her husband's care, he felt that she had "an aneurism of the main aorta below the heart." [Letter 149.] These former troubles with new complications brought Narcissa to death's door, and for a time even her husband despaired of her life. For three weeks her health remained in a precarious condition. About the first of February, 1844, she rallied, and by May she was able to write that she was better than she had been for a long time. [Letter 155.]

Dr. Whitman himself was handicapped through the winter of 1843-44 because of a lame foot. Writing to his mother on May 20, 1844, he said: "I had a lame foot on the road which left me with a tumor on my instep which has given me solicitude & may give me still much more inconvenience." With his wife sick, the burden of conducting the household, as well as directing all other activities, rested back on his shoulders.

Mr. Littlejohn likewise suffered from ill-health and could do little. Mrs. Littlejohn taught a school of fifteen white scholars. Dr. Whitman conducted the Sunday services for both the natives and the white people. Mrs. Whitman was never able to do much missionary work after her husband's return. For one thing her health would not permit it, and then, too, her household had so increased that she found it necessary to give her strength to those committed to her care.

While Whitman was able to do but little actual mission work with the natives at Waiilatpu, Spalding was having good success with the Nez Perces at Lapwai. During Whitman's absence, Spalding had welcomed ten new members into the mission church, including Five Crows, renamed Hezekiah. Five Crows became principal chief of the Cayuses, having received that appointment from Dr. White. This brought the native membership of the First Church of Oregon up to twelve. The fact that Spalding won the influential chiefs to his cause accounted in part for the success of his mission at Lapwai. The conversion of Five Crows, chief of the Cayuses, was a good omen for the work at Whitman's station.

Whitman spent June 20-23, 1844, at Lapwai, where he examined with Spalding a number of candidates for church membership. With these additions the native membership rose to twenty-two. No other natives were received into the church during the history of the American Board mission. With the exception of Five Crows, who was half Nez Perce and half Cayuse, it appears that all of the natives were from the Nez Perce tribe.

When Whitman was East he had opportunity to see the new medical books then available. Evidently he kept a list of the books which attracted his attention, for we find him sending back to Greene on April 8, 1844, for some sixteen works. At the same time he requested a copy of "Miss Leslie Complete Cookery."

In his letter of April 8, 1844, to Greene, Whitman mentions Tom Hill, a Delaware Indian, who was causing trouble. Hill settled among the Nez Perces about 1839 and by 1846 had secured a dominant position in the tribe. He was a bitter critic of the white men and of the Protestant missionaries in particular. He told the Indians that the emigrants would take their lands, as the white man had done in the East. According to Whitman, Tom Hill was friendly to the Catholic priests, and fostered a spirit of rivalry and bitterness among the Indians. He told the Indians that the Protestant missionaries should "expend more liberally on them and that it is peculiarly our duty to do so." He accused them of getting rich from the produce they sold to the emigrants. In many subtle and annoying ways, Tom Hill made mission work difficult.[3] Spalding called him a "blasphemous and debassed infidel."[4] Spalding felt the effects of his nefarious influence more than did Whitman, for Tom Hill lived among the Nez Perces, yet the Cayuses were especially receptive to the ideas he was promulgating.

Following his return, Whitman's letters carried frequent references to the Catholic priests. On April 8, 1844, he wrote:

The Indians say they have been told by the Papists not to be afraid that we should leave them.... One of them told me that Mr. Blanchet told him if they would send me away he would send a mission among

---

[3] Clark, *Pioneer Days*, Vol. 1, p. 525, refers to a visit that Tom Hill made to Waiilatpu in the fall of 1846. Fee, *Chief Joseph*, pp. 256-259, mentions Tom Hill as being an interpreter for Chief Joseph at the time of his surrender. Frank P. Corbett, a Nez Perce, now of the U. S. Indian Service, claims that this Tom Hill died in 1924. Evidently the interpreter was the son of the first Tom Hill, and with the same name. There is a reference to a "half-breed Delaware Indian, considered a very dangerous man" in Hickman's *Brigham's Destroying Angel*, p. 101, for about the year 1854.

[4] Spalding to Greene, Jan. 24, 1846.

them. I tell them all plainly that I do not refuse to go away if they prefer the Papists to us, and urge them to decide if they wished me to do so, but that I should not go except at the full expression of the people, desiring me so to do. None of them as yet have been found to express such a desire.

Whitman found the laws that White had tried to institute among the Cayuses to be but empty forms because of the lack of a law-enforcing agency. He reported that William Craig, a mountain man living near Spalding at Lapwai, was busy "trying to incite the people against the laws as recommended by Doctor White." Thus the undercurrents were beginning to move in an ominous way.

Beginning with Whitman's letter of November 1, 1843, we find that his every letter back to the Board carried some reference to the political question. Whitman was tremendously concerned about the importance of getting the right kind of people to emigrate. He never gave up hope regarding his plan of having "pious laymen" settle in the vicinity of the mission stations. Even though the tendency at first was to settle the Willamette Valley, Whitman saw that the tide of white people would someday cover the Upper Columbia country, and as early as November 1, 1843, expressed that belief. Whitman wanted to make sure that the mission had a clear title to the land it occupied, and mentioned this in his letter to Greene of July 20, 1843.

Greene replied to Whitman on April 12, 1844, saying that he would write to Washington about the land claims. Greene wrote: "I see not why you will not have as good right to preemption as any later immigrants." Whitman brought up this subject again in his letter of April 8, 1844, and suggested that Greene take some steps to get Congress to approve the idea of granting land to each mission station in order to forestall any attempt on the part of settlers to claim mission property. In fact this scheme was tried in 1845 by Craig, who laid claim to the Lapwai site.[5]

Practically all of Whitman's letter of May 18, 1844, is given over to a discussion of the land question and its relationship to the Indians and the emigrants. Whitman called the emigration movement "one of the onward movements of the world and it is quite in vain for us to wish it to stand still." Even though the Indians had made great progress in cultivation and in raising cattle, still he saw

---

[5] Drury, *Spalding*, p. 324.

that they would be wholly unable to stand before an aggressive white population. He wrote:

> For where has it been known that an ignorant, indolent man has stood against Money, inteligence & enterprise? . . . For the command is multiply & replenish the earth neither of which the Indians obey. Their indolence, violence & blood shed prevent the first & indolence & improvidence the second. How then can they stand in the way of others who will do both?

Whitman repeated this same argument in his letter to his brother of May 21, 1844. He wrote: "For I believe it is a part of the onward movements of the world and therefore more to be moulded than to be turned aside. After this you will see why I came home in hopes to get good men to speck the country with settlements, & aid as the Providence of God indicated by supporting religion (Protestant Christianity) & education, both for the Colonists & the Indians."

Whitman expressed himself as follows in a letter to his wife's parents, dated May 16, 1844: "I have no doubt our greatest work is to be to aid the white settlement of this country to found its religious institutions." The day came when the Indians realized that Marcus Whitman held such convictions, and they lost faith in him.

1844-45

Profiting by his experience in the fall of 1843, when the emigrants drained him of all provisions excepting potatoes, Whitman made every possible effort to be ready for those who came in 1844. Writing to Greene on October 25, 1844, he stated that he had from fifteen to seventeen beeves which he expected to sell at six cents a pound. With the aid of Mr. East, he fashioned and placed a pair of granite millstones which measured forty inches across, and even though no building was erected over them, they were used to turn the wheat into flour.[6] This Whitman expected to sell at five dollars a hundred for the unbolted flour and six dollars for the bolted.

Narcissa looked forward to the coming of the emigrants with a heavy heart. The previous year she had seen the hundreds go by The Dalles, hungry, tired, and travel-worn. Some were almost destitute. Writing to her friend, Mrs. Brewer, on August 5, 1844, she said:

---

[6] The Portland *Oregonian*, Sept. 27, 1936, carried a picture of a millstone in the garden of Mrs. S. W. Eustice, of Yamhill, which is supposed to have been one of the stones Whitman used.

We are all of us, I suppose, on the eve of another such scene as last fall—the passing of the emigrants—and as it falls the heavier upon my friends at the Dalls, I hope they have laid in a good stock of strength, patience and every needed grace for the siege.

The Indians had likewise profited by the previous year's experience. In their desire to get American cattle, they rode forth to meet the emigrants, some of them going as far east as Fort Hall, where they traded their fresh horses for the travel-worn cattle. The emigrants were usually in a hurry to get over the Blue Mountains, while the Indians could take their time, thus giving opportunity for the cattle to recuperate.

On Tuesday, October 1, the vanguard of the 1844 emigration reached Waiilatpu. This group consisted of some young men, and, to the surprise of Dr. Whitman, he found Newton Gilbert, of Rushville, among them. Years before, Gilbert had been one of his students in the day school and also in the Sunday school. [Letter 178.] Gilbert went on down to the Willamette but later returned to the mission to assist Whitman.

The emigration of 1844 was so late that hundreds were caught by the snows in the Blue Mountains. Writing on October 25, 1844, Narcissa declared:

It is now the last of October and they have just begun to arrive with their wagons. The Blue Mountains are covered with snow, and many families, if not half of the party, are back in or beyond the mountains, and what is still worse, destitute of provisions and some of them of clothing. Many are sick, several with children born on the way. One family arrived here night before last, and the next morn a child was born; another is expected in the same condition.

Here we are, one family alone, a way mark, as it were, or center post, about which multitudes will or must gather this winter. And these we must feed and warm to the extent of our powers. Blessed be God that He has given us so abundantly of the fruit of the earth that we may impart to those who are thus famishing.

The emigration of 1844 totaled about fifteen hundred, some of whom reached the mission station in an exhausted condition. Every possible preparation was made for them. Most of those who had spent the previous winter at Waiilatpu had gone to the Willamette Valley. The Littlejohns had left in September. Emma Hobson went to live with the Walkers at Tshimakain in April, 1844, and remained until March, 1845.[7] The empty rooms at Waiilatpu were soon filled when the emigrants arrived.

---

[7] Mrs. Walker's diary.

By the 25th of October, long before the major part of the migration had passed, Narcissa wrote that all of the house room was then taken by needy families. There was still to come the Sager family of seven orphans, regarding whom word had been sent in advance to the Whitmans. [Letter 163.] Since the orphans had not a relative in the country, interested parties in the emigration looked to the mission to take care of the children. Writing on October 25, Narcissa confessed she did not know what they could do. A closing paragraph reflects the burdens of those days:

I cannot write any more, I am so thronged and employed that I feel sometimes like being crazy, and my poor husband, if he had a hundred strings tied to him pulling in every direction could not be any worse off. [Letter 163.]

Among the first to arrive who elected to stay were a blacksmith, a hatter, and two Methodist preachers. [Letter 164.] Whitman remembered his need for a schoolteacher and hired a young man from Chenango County, New York, by the name of Alanson Hinman, who proved to be most helpful and reliable. Altogether, twelve families, besides the Sager orphans, from the emigration of that year found it necessary to spend the winter at Waiilatpu. Every spare room was crowded. Fortunately the winter was mild, thus permitting some to live either in their wagons or in tents.

Special mention must be made of the Sager children, who were made orphans on the trail. Originally from Virginia, Henry Sager was infected with the emigrating fever and made several moves, always westward. First he took his family to Ohio, then to Indiana, then to Missouri, and in April, 1844, he started for Oregon. He then had six children, two boys, John, aged 14, and Francisco, 10; and four girls—Catherine, 9; Elizabeth M., 7; Matilda Jane, 5; and Hannah Louise, 3. Mrs. Sager was about to give birth to another and did not want to go to Oregon. With prophetic insight she declared she would never live to get through. In the latter part of May after they had started, she gave birth to a baby girl, who was later called Henrietta. Mrs. Sager was in miserable health thereafter.

A series of misfortunes dogged the trail of the Sagers. At Fort Laramie, Catherine caught her dress just as she was about to jump out of a moving wagon. She was thrown under a wheel which ran over her, breaking a leg.[8] A German

---

[8] Lockley, *Oregon Trail Blazers*, pp. 325 ff., gives statement by Elizabeth that her father set the leg. Catherine herself made a similar

doctor set the leg, which healed without leaving any out-
ward trace of the injury.[9] However, Catherine was confined
to the wagon for the most of the remainder of the journey.
Mr. Sager was taken sick before they crossed the Continental Divide, and died on August 27 as his family was
camped on the bank of the Green River. Before he passed
away, he is reported to have said: "Well, if I should die,
I would want my family to stop at the station of Dr. Whitman." He committed his sick wife and children to the care
of William Shaw, captain of that section of the wagon train.
The kind-hearted German doctor, referred to by the Sager
girls as Dr. Dagen, although that does not seem to have
been his true name, took the place of the deceased father
on the driver's seat and drove the oxen the rest of the way.

About four weeks later, in the vicinity of what is now
Twin Falls, Idaho, the mother, realizing that her end was
near, bade her children a sad farewell and committed them
to the care of Dr. Dagen, with the charge that he should
turn them over to Dr. Whitman. Some of the women of
the wagon train, moved by compassion in the tragic situation, came to Dr. Dagen's help in caring for the children.
The four-wheeled wagon was reduced to a two-wheeled cart,
and thus they continued on their way. Sometime during
the latter part of the month,[10] Dr. Dagen brought to a halt
near the door of the Whitman home the oxcart bearing the
seven Sager children. Captain Shaw, who had preceded
them, was in the house at the time. Noticing their arrival,
he turned to Mrs. Whitman and said: "Your children have
come; will you go out and see them?"

Catherine Sager has given us a word-picture of their
appearance:

Foremost stood the little cart, with the tired oxen that had been
unyoked lying near it. Sitting in the front end of the cart was John,
weeping bitterly; on the opposite side stood Francis, his arms on the
wheel and his head resting on his arms, sobbing aloud; on the near side

---

statement in a letter dated Dec. 21, 1854, which was printed in *O.H.Q.*,
Vol. 37, p. 355. Yet in Clark, *Pioneer Days*, Vol. 2, p. 505, quoting
from Catherine's journal, we learn that the German doctor set the leg,
which is more probably the true story.

[9] *See* Appendix No. 5 for a list of the articles written by the Sager
girls, from which the information is drawn for this account.

[10] In several of the Sager accounts we read their claim that they
reached Waiilatpu on October 17. This is evidently an error because
Mrs. Whitman states it was October 25. In two of Mrs. Whitman's
letters (187 and 191) she speaks of their arrival as being "in Oct.
1844."

the little girls were huddled together, bareheaded and barefooted, looking at the boys and then at the house, dreading we knew not what. By the oxen stood the good German doctor, with his whip in his hand, regarding the scene with suppressed emotion.[11]

When Mrs. Whitman appeared, her heart was touched. The little girls, embarrassed and afraid, ran to the other side of the wagon. Narcissa at once tried to make them feel welcome. Noticing Catherine's lameness, she began to assist her into the house. Captain Shaw asked if she had any children of her own. Narcissa paused, and then pointing to Alice Clarissa's grave, she said: "All the child I ever had sleeps yonder."

If there had been any reluctance on Narcissa's part to assume new and heavy responsibilities, her heart melted as she faced the desperate need of the forlorn children. One of the women of the emigration had cared for the little babe, which was placed in Mrs. Whitman's arms. The following is Narcissa's description of the babe:

> She arrived here in the hands of an old filthy woman, sick, emaciated and but just alive. She was born some where on the Platte river in the first part of the journey, on the last day of May. Her mother died on the 25th of September. She was five months old when she was brought here—had suffered for the want of proper nourishment until she was nearly starved. The old woman did the best she could, but she was in distressed circumstances herself, and a wicked, disobedient family around her to see to.
>
> Husband thought we could get along with all but the baby—he did not see how we could take that; but I felt that if I must take any, I wanted her as a charm to bind the rest to me. So we took her, a poor, distressed little object, not larger than a babe three weeks old. [Letter 192.]

Surely the child would have died within a few days had it not been for the tender care which Mrs. Whitman bestowed upon her. While Dr. Whitman at first did not care to assume responsibility for the little babe, his wife felt that the five girls were enough for them to take and suggested that the boys could be given to others. However, Dr. Whitman felt that the boys should stay with the girls and said: "All or none." So it was agreed to keep them all.

Catherine Sager wrote her memories of Mrs. Whitman's appearance as follows: "She was a large, well-formed woman, fair complexioned, with beautiful auburn hair, nose rather large, and large gray eyes. She had on a dark calico dress and gingham sunbonnet. We thought as we

---

[11] Clark, *op. cit.*, Vol. 2, p. 508.

shyly looked at her that she was the prettiest woman we had ever seen."[12] Elizabeth remembered her hair as being "a copper gold," and said: "She had a matronly figure—I think she weighed between 150 and 160 pounds."[13]

The Whitmans found Mr. Hinman to be not only a good schoolteacher, but also one who could relieve Mrs. Whitman of many of the duties of the household connected with the oversight of the children. A year later Mrs. Whitman wrote: "I feel that I never can be too thankful for the mercies of the Lord in placing such a good young man in our family to do this work for us when my health was so inadequate." [Letter 176.]

When Dr. Whitman wrote to Greene on October 25, 1844, and reported on the work of the mission, he mentioned the school. "This is a place," he wrote, "most advantageous for the commencement of what may soon be an Academy & College." Today Whitman College stands within seven miles of his mission station, a living memorial to his faith and devotion. In this letter he requested that a threshing mill for his wheat, and a corn thresher be sent to him. These articles arrived in the summer of 1847.

On April 8, Whitman wrote again to Greene and gave a summary of his financial dealings with the emigrants. He had received enough money to pay cash for some supplies needed from the Hudson's Bay Company, and had $507.07 in notes which he had taken from those who were unable to pay at the time they needed provisions. He had also received ten or twelve oxen by way of exchange. During the winter of 1844-45, he had used some of the men who had wintered with him to build a sawmill about twenty miles away in the Blue Mountains. Whitman had the necessary irons at hand and needed the sawed lumber. He was then dreaming about a settlement which he expected would grow up in that vicinity. Moreover, he needed new roofs on his buildings. They were still using the old dirt roofs, which were very unsatisfactory.

In replying to Whitman's letter of October 25, 1844, Greene wrote on April 6, 1846: "Still we are not quite sure that you ought to devote so much time and thought to feeding the emigrants, and thus make your station a great *restaurant* for the weary pilgrim on their way to their promised land." Greene felt that Whitman was giving too much time and

---

12 *Ibid.*
13 Lockley, *op. cit.*, p. 329.

attention to secular activities. "There is a danger also," wrote Greene, "that your mission, like that of the Methodists, will get the name and character of a trading or money making establishment and thus bring discredit." As will be seen, Whitman resented the suggestion that he could have done otherwise as far as meeting the needs of the emigrants was concerned.

Tuesday, April 8, 1845, was a letter-writing day for both Marcus and Narcissa; four of their letters written then have come down to us. In one Whitman referred to the fact that he then had eighty sheep, a large part of which were ewes.[14] "All these," he wrote, "came from one ewe brought from the Sandwich Islands in '38 and two more brought in '39." [Letter 170.] In another letter he reported on his wife's health: "I cannot think Mrs. Whitman's health will ever be good again." On October 25 of the preceding fall Narcissa told her family that she weighed "one hundred and sixty-seven pounds; much higher than ever before in my life." [Letter 163.]

In Whitman's letter of April 8, 1845, he told of the old Indian superstition of sorcery which was then giving him considerable concern. It so happened that a young man had died of apoplexy, and it was claimed that Dr. Whitman had caused his death. Dr. Whitman wrote that if such a conviction were widely accepted it would make " ... my stay among them useless and dangerous—and might induce me to leave at once." He referred again to the Indian custom of killing a te-wat who failed to cure a patient. Another matter giving him concern was the report that the Jesuit missionaries were planning to establish a station in that vicinity. A third cause for worry was the death of Elijah Hedding, the son of a prominent Walla Walla chief, Peupeumoxmox, also known as Yellow Serpent.

When Dr. Elijah White arrived in Oregon as a Methodist missionary in May, 1837, he reported seeing a number of Indian boys in the mission school there who had been named after well-known characters in the Methodist Church, and among these boys was the son of the Walla Walla chief, who was given the name of a famous Methodist bishop, Elijah Hedding.[15] In 1844 a party of Indians from the vi-

---

[14] Whitman letter 174 states that members of the 1844 emigration had brought some sheep with them. This is the first evidence that sheep were driven across country to Oregon.

[15] Allen, Ten Years, p. 74.

cinity of Waiilatpu, including Elijah Hedding, went to Sutter's Fort in California in the hope of trading furs and horses for cattle. While they were there, a dispute arose about the ownership of a mule, which resulted in the killing of Elijah by a white man. The other Indians hastily returned, leaving their cattle behind. Their report of what took place greatly excited the other members of their tribe. Whitman immediately informed White of the situation.

The Indians were not disposed to drop the matter. They demanded retribution, which, indeed, was their right under the very laws which Dr. White had instituted among them. The first of Dr. White's laws read: "Whoever wilfully takes life shall be hung," and the tenth stated: "If an Indian raise a gun or other weapon against a white man, it shall be reported to the chiefs, and they shall punish him. If a white person do the same to an Indian, it shall be reported to Dr. White, and he shall redress it." Ellis, chief of the Nez Perces, was appointed to visit Dr. White in the spring of 1845 to talk the matter over. White sought to pacify the Indians by making some generous promises, one of which related to the establishment of a boarding school among the Indians of the Upper Columbia country. The unfulfilled promises remained, after White left Oregon, for the repeated embarrassment of both Spalding and Whitman.

Sometime during the spring of 1845, Whitman visited the Lower Columbia country. Nesmith once wrote:

I know that Dr. Whitman had cause to dread the vengeance of the Indians long before it overtook him. I heard him, in the spring of 1845, express his apprehension on that subject to Dr. McLaughlin, at Oregon City, and the latter agreed with him upon the danger of his situation, and advised him to come to the Willamette valley....[16]

These superstitions about Dr. Whitman's supposed power as a sorcerer and the early stages of the Elijah Hedding affair were the beginnings of the gathering of the storm clouds which were to unleash their fury upon the Whitmans and their companions about two and a half years later.

The 1845 mission meeting was held at Waiilatpu from May 9-14, inclusive. All were present except Mrs. Spalding. A meeting of the church was held on Sunday, May 11, and Alan Hinman was received into its membership.[17] Dr.

---

[16] *T.O.P.A.*, 1880, p. 23. For a reference by Dr. McLoughlin to his word of warning to Whitman *see ibid.*, p. 53.

[17] Mrs. Walker's diary, May 11, 1845: "Mr. Hinman was received

Whitman was appointed a committee to investigate Charles Compo,[18] who was then living in the Willamette Valley. James Conner, who had been received into the mission church on November 17, 1839, and who had been suspended on February 4, 1843, "for the sin of Sabbath breaking, neglect of religious duties & fighting," was formally excommunicated. Spalding added this note in the church records: "It has since proven that he has been guilty of polygamy, sending a challenge to fight a duel, and vending liquor."[19]

Reporting on the events of the meeting in his letter of May 20 to Greene, Whitman declared that the utmost harmony prevailed. This good feeling among all members of the mission had been apparent, he stated, ever since his return in 1843. The missionaries were fully aware of the dangers that surrounded them. On May 31, Mrs. Walker summed up her impressions of the mission meeting in her diary and gave the following comment about Dr. Whitman: "Dr. Whitman entertains fears that his people intend taking his life. We think they will not do it but it is very trying to have them conduct as they do."

The mission requested Whitman to go to the Willamette to look after some supplies. Consequently he left soon after the meeting was over and was away from Waiilatpu for at least six weeks. Whitman wrote to his brother-in-law, Frank Wisewell, from Fort Vancouver on June 29 and urged him to migrate to Oregon. In this letter we read: "Narcissa has written me since I left home and says she will not allow me to leave home again without she goes with me. She is not in strong health and her spirits flag when I am from home and so much care comes upon her."

While in the valley Whitman had his controversy with Dr. White, to which reference has already been made, in regard to the prices charged by Whitman for supplies. White started back to the States on July 12, leaving a tangled political situation behind him, fraught with much

---

into our church and baptized. Dr. W. had the four orphan sisters and Harry B. baptised, and a Mr. Thomas, a blacksmith had a child baptized."

[18] Later Spalding wrote in the church record book: "Dr. Whitman visited Compo in summer of 47. He appears well, has withstood the efforts of the Catholics to draw him back again, refused to give up his bible to the priest who wished to burn it. Since died in Cal., Jan., 1865."

[19] Bancroft, *Oregon*, Vol. 1, p. 281.

trouble. Such incidents as the Elijah Hedding affair had not been settled. On his way eastward,[20] White and his party met with the 1845 emigration. According to one witness, White advised some of the emigrants to go to Waiilatpu for supplies.[21] However, it appears that he advised others to take a short cut and go direct to The Dalles, thus avoiding both Waiilatpu and Fort Walla Walla. Whitman wrote to Greene on October 26, 1845, and stated that most of the emigrants had missed his station. He was ready to sell flour for five dollars a hundred, while at The Dalles the emigrants had to pay eight dollars for the same amount. It may be that Whitman's controversy with White was one reason why White urged the emigrants to go direct to The Dalles.

When the Whitmans took the Sager children into their home, it was understood that Captain Shaw was to return and get them the next spring. However, after a few days, Dr. Whitman mounted his horse and caught up with the wagon train and sent word to Shaw that they wished to keep the children. When in Oregon City, Whitman appeared before Probate Judge J. W. Nesmith on June 3, 1845, and requested that he be appointed the legal guardian of the Sager children. Appraisers appointed by the court reported that the total value of Henry Sager's estate was $262.50. Dr. Whitman posted bonds for twice that sum and became the legally appointed guardian of the children.[22]

When Whitman was in the Willamette Valley in the fall of 1847, he called on Captain Shaw, who was then living at Howell Prairie near Salem. He informed Shaw that he and Mrs. Whitman were planning to adopt the Sager girls and have their names changed to Whitman. Captain Shaw advised to the contrary, feeling that the girls as well as the boys should retain their family name.[23] Evidently Captain Shaw's advice prevailed, for there is no record of any action being taken by Dr. Whitman to adopt any of the Sager children. He remained their legally appointed guardian.

---

[20] Allen, *op. cit.*, p. 265. White tried to find a new route to the Willamette Valley over the Cascade Mountains, but failed. On this exploring trip he named a prominent peak after John C. Spencer, Secretary of the Treasury.

[21] Lockley, *op. cit.*, p. 352.

[22] *O.H.Q.*, Vol. 11, pp. 312 ff.

[23] Lockley, *op. cit.*, p. 331.

1845-1846

The 1845 emigration was the first to feel the full effects of the successful termination of the emigration of 1843, for it took about a year for letters to get back to the States to inform others that wagons could be taken over the Blue Mountains. The emigration of 1844 was 50 per cent larger than that of 1843, but in 1845 the numbers were 300 per cent greater. Thus the tide rolled westward, and with the increasing American population there came the ever-growing conviction that Oregon was being bound to the Union by indissoluble ties. The optimistic emigrant still hoped that Congress would pass the bill giving a section of land to each settler.

The emigration of 1845 was much earlier than that of the previous year, having enjoyed more favorable weather conditions. Consequently the emigrants did not arrive in such a destitute condition. Whitman, writing to Walker on September 29, 1845, said: "Few of the Immigrants call on us. Four hundred and fifty wagons passed Fort Hall but from seventy to one hundred went to California."

A rare pamphlet, entitled *Autobiography and Reminiscences by* Sarah J. Cummins, a member of the 1845 emigration, tells how Dr. Whitman piloted a large section of this emigration over the Blue Mountains in the fore part of September. Learning from some friendly Indians of the intention of some of the Cayuses to attack the emigration, Whitman with a few Nez Perces made a forced ride by night. He met the emigrants while they were on the Powder River. While they were in the Grande Ronde Valley, a large war party of the Cayuses and Walla Wallas appeared, who were somewhat surprised to find that the emigrants had been warned.

One of the Cayuse chiefs sullenly defied "all settlers and all authority of government." The following account is taken from Mrs. Cummins' story:

Ere the twilight faded, and as it was apparent that great numbers of the Indians were gathering within range, Dr. Whitman began to talk to the chief of the Walla Walla's. The chief made no reply but shook his head defiantly. The chief of the Cayuses now spoke vehemently in the style of true Indian eloquence. The Doctor spoke again and again, and the chief replied, still defying us to go on. Then Doctor Whitman rose to almost super-human heighth and, in a stern voice, told them in emphatic terms that the Great Father of the "Bostons" would send men to defend these travelers, and that ship

loads of soliders and guns would arrive to kill all the Indians who
molested his people on their way to the distant valley.[24]

Fearful of an attack during the night, Dr. Whitman succeeded in keeping the Cayuse chief in the emigrants' camp
as a hostage. Mrs. Cummins called it "a night of terror
to all." The next day the emigrants continued on their way
under the watchful care of Dr. Whitman. In this incident
we find one of the first indications of the growing hostility
of the Indians to the emigrants. The fact that Dr. Whitman
had taken the side of the white men undermined the faith
of the Indians in their missionary.

The April, 1907, issue of the *Washington Historical
Quarterly* contains the diary of John Ewing Howell, another
member of the 1845 emigration. On September 17, 1845,
Howell made this entry:

Trav. and camped on the Umatallow river.... Dr. Whitman and
lady visited our camp this morning and travelled with us and camped
with us. He had a wagon-load of flour along not bolted $8 pr. 100 lbs.

About two hundred families tried a new cut-off to the
Willamette Valley under the guidance of Stephen H. L.
Meek, a brother of Joseph L. Meek. They followed the
Malheur River to its headwaters, hoping to find a pass into
the Willamette Valley. They suffered indescribable hard-
ships and at least twenty of the emigrants died. Meek was
obliged to flee for his life. It may be that White's enthusi-
asm for such a cut-off was responsible for the venture, but
Meek got all the blame. The party finally reached The
Dalles, where they were back on the main route again.

Most of the 1845 emigrants, following White's advice,
followed the Umatilla River past the present site of Pendleton, Oregon, to the Columbia River. Thereafter, both Waiilatpu and Fort Walla Walla were on a detour. Only those
in immediate need of supplies turned aside to visit the
Whitman station. This was a very logical development of
the trail, yet Whitman was disappointed. He had made
extensive preparations to supply the emigrants and then
found himself with but few customers. Writing to Greene
on October 26, he declared that most of the emigrants had
already passed. He wrote: "The money I took from them
was less than one hundred and fifty dollars and about fifteen
dollars trust. Three cows and two small steers."

Whitman also referred to White's plan to establish a

_____
[24] Cummins, *op. cit.*, p. 40.

manual labor school among the Nez Perces and requested Greene "to keep a look out for Doct White's course in the states." He claimed that White had involved the Oregon mission of the American Board by his rash promises. On April 13, 1846, Whitman returned to the subject of Dr. White and blamed him for telling the emigrants that "they could get a full supply of flour at the Dalls." Not only did the emigrants have to pay more, but many found the supply exhausted. It is evident that Whitman was not happy over this incident with White.

Several families and individuals found it necessary to spend the winter at Waiilatpu. Among them was Josiah Osborn, a millwright, whose services Whitman was glad to get,[25] and Tom Summers, a blacksmith. Both men had their families with them, as did Isaac Cornelius, who also wintered at Waiilatpu. Whitman engaged two young men, Jacob Rynearson and Andrew Rodgers, to teach. Rynearson tried to teach English to the Indians, but after a month's effort the experiment was abandoned. Writing to Greene on April 13, 1846, Whitman said: "We also sent a teacher to spend the winter at Kamiah where he had a school of about twenty five among which were two Delawares & Ellis. . . . " This seems to have been the last effort by the Oregon mission to do work in Kamiah. It may be that Rynearson was the one who was sent to Kamiah. Andrew Rodgers was employed to teach the school for white children at Waiilatpu.

In the Whitman College museum is the account book of Josiah Osborn which he kept when in Dr. Whitman's employ. The records begin on August 21 and continue through to March 7, 1846. It appears that Dr. Whitman paid him at the rate of $1.50 a day, for the most part in produce. The following items taken from Osborn's accounts indicate the prices that Whitman was charging:

25 lbs flour at 5 cts per pound	$1.25
1 bus. beats	.40
1 potatoes	.40
69 lbs. beaf	3.79½
8 squashes	1.00
20 lbs pork	1.40

---

[25] An account of the Osborn (sometimes spelt Osborne) family was given by Nancy Osborn Jacobs in a paper read May 12, 1912, and printed in the Waitsburg *Times*, Feb. 2, 1934; in an interview given to Fred Lockley and printed in *Oregon Trail Blazers*, pp. 351 ff.; and in a letter of Mr. Osborn's dated April 7, 1848, which is in Coll. W.

1 lb shugar .... .20
51 lbs meal 2.04
6 ft tobacco .... .60

The tobacco, which came in twisted strands and was sold by the foot, was used in trading with the Indians. There is every reason to believe that these were the usual prices charged, and they furnish the refutation, if any be needed, to the accusation that Whitman was exorbitant in his demands.

Among those who visited Waiilatpu in the fall of 1845 was Joel Palmer, who later wrote a book on his experiences in the Oregon Country. According to Palmer, Dr. and Mrs. Whitman visited his encampment on September 17 with provisions. He wrote: "The doctor & lady remained with us during the day; he took occasion to inform us of the many incidents that marked his ten years' sojourn in this wilderness region, of a highly interesting character." Palmer reported that Whitman had killed thirty-two horses for food during his Oregon residence.[26]

Writing on April 13, 1846, to Greene, Whitman commented on the difficulty of getting much work out of the emigrants. To begin with, they were strangers, and it was difficult to check up on their abilities. Again, the winter weather often prevented out-of-doors work. With the coming of spring, when their services were most needed, they usually left for the Willamette to begin farming for themselves. However, during the winter of 1845-46 Whitman managed to get his sawmill operating in the mountains, although he still did not have enough boards to put a decent roof on his house. He also needed a building over the flour mill. He reported that he then had over one hundred ewes in addition to the sheep furnished the Indians.

Reporting on the health of members of the mission, he wrote: "Mrs. Whitman's health is quite poor just now." He reported that the expenses of the mission to be paid by the Board would be £303.7.4. He begged again for a mission reinforcement, but such pleas were without result.[27]

From time to time the Whitmans heard rumblings of discontent among the Indians. Writing in the fall of 1845, Mrs. Whitman declared: "It may be that we shall be obliged

---

[26] Palmer, *Journal of Travels*, p. 57.

[27] The Rev. G. H. Atkinson was sent out to Oregon as a home missionary to labor among the white people in the fall of 1847. He went by sea, arriving in the early part of 1848.

to leave here in the spring. The state of things looks now very much as though we should be required to." [Letter 183.] And in April, 1846, Whitman wrote to Greene about their difficulties with the Catholics. He claimed that he had told the natives that he would give them until spring to decide whether or not the mission was to be abandoned. Whitman wanted to settle the question. He wrote: "I was not long left in doubt as to duty, for they came forward at once and said they had no sympathy with the adherants of the Papist who had treated me in the manner to cause me thus to appeal to them." [Letter 191.]

The Walkers at Tshimakain expected an addition to their family in February or March, 1846, and wrote to Dr. Whitman, urging him to be present. Dr. Whitman replied on February 23, saying that it was impossible for him to make the trip because of an injury received early in the preceding December when a horse fell with him, hurting his knee joint." Mrs. Walker gave birth to her fifth child, a son, on March 7. He was called Jeremiah.

None of Mrs. Whitman's letters written in the fall of 1845, except one to Mrs. Brewer, has been preserved. Writing to her father on April 10, 1846, she began her letter with these words: "I have received no letters from father, mother or any of the sisters or brothers in Alleghany county since husband returned."[28] Why did they not write? In a letter to Harriet, written April 13, 1846, Narcissa wrote at some length regarding her care of the children. She told how she and the girls would go every day in the summer to bathe in the river.[29] With the passing of the months, she found herself becoming more and more bound up with the Sager children. She could not have been a better mother to them had they been her own. In her letter of April 10 to her father she referred to the responsibilities of rearing eleven children "in a heathen land." She wrote: "To be in a country among a people of no law, even if they are from a civilized land, is the nearest like a hell on earth of anything I can imagine."

Narcissa wrote repeatedly to members of her family,

---

[28] On Nov. 3, 1846, Narcissa wrote to her mother: "Mothers dated Mar. 26, 1846, was sent from Boston to Westport and reaches me in about five months after it was mailed. This brings me very near home. Indeed it is the first I have received since those sent by Husband."

[29] Delaney, *Whitman Massacre*, p. 9, gives Matilda's version of the summer swims.

especially to Jane and Edward, begging them to go to
Oregon. Each fall she would hope that some one of her
loved ones would be among the emigrants, and each time
she felt the disappointment a little more keenly.

Writing to her brother Edward on April 2, 1846, Narcissa acknowledged receipt of a box of things he had sent
but confessed that she was disappointed in not finding a
"louse trap." "I had hopes," she wrote, "of finding one
little article more that is needed more than most any other
because it cannot be obtained here; name pi-la-ain, as the
Indians call it (louse trap)." She referred to a fine-toothed
comb. The lodges of the Indians were always infested with
various kinds of vermin which made life miserable for all
whites living in too close proximity.

When Mrs. Whitman received the Sager children into
her home, she found them rather undisciplined. Narcissa
had decided opinions regarding the value of discipline in
the home and began at once to train the children according
to her New England ideas. Matilda Jane Sager later gave
this description of her life at Waiilatpu:

> There was no danger of any of us becoming spoiled. She would
> point to one of us, then point to the dishes or the broom, and we would
> instantly get busy with our assigned tasks. She didn't scold much, but
> we dreaded that accusing finger pointed at us.[30]

Matilda Sager wrote: "We never had anything but corn
meal mush and milk for our suppers and they were very
particular in our being regular in our habits of eating and
sleeping."[31] Occasionally the family would go on a picnic.
Matilda's reminiscences published in 1920 contain many
references to their happy life in the Whitman home. She
wrote: "Mrs. Whitman taught us the love of flowers. We
each had a flower garden, which we had to weed and care
for. She taught us a great deal about things of that kind
and instilled in us a love of the beautiful."[32]

The children went barefooted in the summer and wore
moccasins in the winter. Mrs. Whitman made dresses for
the girls out of the "hickory shirting" purchased from the
Hudson's Bay Company. For three happy, fleeting years
the Sager children lived at Waiilatpu. Dr. and Mrs. Whitman were father and mother to them, and were so called.

---

[30] Lockley, *op. cit.*, p. 345.
[31] Delaney, *op. cit.*, p. 8.
[32] *Ibid.*, p. 12.

The tenth year of the Whitmans' residence in Oregon came to a close under favorable circumstances. Mrs. Whitman was enjoying better health. The Indians were quiet. Dr. Whitman was making new improvements about the station to add to their comfort and effectiveness. All was well—but it was like the calm which sometimes precedes the storm.

CHAPTER EIGHTEEN

THE LAST YEAR

1846-1847

ALL WAS WELL at Waiilatpu in the fall of 1846. On September 8 Whitman wrote: "I think we have at no time been as much in the affections of the people as now. A much kinder disposition is manifested toward us, now more than at any former period. . . . " The Indians continued to observe morning and evening worship in their lodges, and Whitman wrote that "a blessing is strictly regarded as being a duty to be asked upon taking food." [Letter 209.] On November 3 Narcissa wrote to her mother and stated that: "Husband has just written to our Board. He says he never has felt more contented."

Even the Catholic influence did not seem so menacing to the Whitmans in the fall of 1846 as it had previously. The priests had sought for an invitation from the Cayuse Indians to settle among them, but such an invitation had not been given. [Letter 208.] On February 8, 1847, Narcissa wrote to Mrs. A. T. Smith, of Tualatin Plains, and mentioned the fact that she and her husband had sometimes talked about retiring to the Willamette, "not that we wish to leave the Indians," she explained, "so long as they will let us stay among them—but if the necessity should come that we must leave them then we shall find it pleasant to seek some quiet spot among the society of our friends where we may enjoy something of the fortaste of our eternal rest." In that same letter she also stated: "As it regards the Indians at this station we feel that our influence for good was never greater, among them, than now."

It should be remembered that these conditions prevailed after Dr. McLoughlin, Nesmith, and others had advised Whitman to move away from Waiilatpu. The fact that Whitman had weathered several crises gave him a feeling of false security. He relied too much on the good will of the Indians.

THE EMIGRATION OF 1846

The emigration of 1846 was not so large as that of the preceding year. Bancroft estimated that about twenty-five hundred persons went to the Pacific Coast that year, of whom fifteen or seventeen hundred went to Oregon.[1] The others went to California. Some of those who went to Oregon followed what was called the southern route to the Willamette and, therefore, did not pass near the Whitman station. Their trail left the main Oregon Trail before reaching Fort Boise.

Whitman wrote to Greene on September 8, saying that he had then received no calls from the emigrants for supplies. This was a disappointment, for he hoped to become self-supporting through his sale of provisions to the emigrants. On that day Horace Hart, a brother of Mrs. Henry Spalding, arrived. He left at once for Lapwai to make his home with the Spaldings.

Among the emigrants that year was Anson Sterling Cone, who in later years told how he and his brother Aaron had visited Waiilatpu about the middle of October, and, being in need of a pack horse, proposed to Whitman that they be allowed to work out the price of the horse. "Boys," replied Whitman, "you had better take 'Bob' there and all the provisions you need and go at once. At the end of the season there will be those coming who will have to stay here anyhow and I had better have the work for them." So the Cone brothers took "Bob," a trusty white Cayuse pony, and the next summer paid Dr. Whitman twenty-five dollars for the horse and the provisions received.[2] Anson Cone remembered the doctor as being "sociable and a good joker." Later Anson served on the jury which convicted the Whitman murderers.

From previous experience Whitman knew that he could expect some needy families from the tail end of the emigration to call on him for help. Such was the case in 1846. By November 3, six families and eight young men had found it necessary to stay at Waiilatpu. Of this number four were very sick, and Whitman wrote that two or three of these would certainly have died if they had not paused for medical aid and rest. Three babies were born to this group of emigrants while they were at Waiilatpu. [Letter 212.] Whitman sent three of the families to live in the log cabin which had been erected at the sawmill in the Blue Mountains. Writing on April 1, Whitman reported that his saw-

---

1 Bancroft, *Oregon*, Vol. I, p. 552.
2 Walla Walla *Union*, Aug. 12, 1936.

mill had been in operation during the winter, thus providing sufficient lumber for many needed improvements.

Greene had written to Whitman on April 6, 1846, and suggested that he was spending too much time and thought on the emigrants. Greene advised against turning the station into a restaurant or a trading point. Whitman replied on April 1, 1847, by saying: "If we are not legally, religiously nor morally bound to relieve the passing Immigrants we are necessiarly; for the sick and hungry cannot be sent away however penyless." He added that he possibly could have found farmers when he was East in 1843, but that meant he would have had to protract his stay, which in turn "would have endangered the Emigrants to come without a safe pilot and myself with the possibility of another years stay in the States."

THE WINTER OF 1846-47

The services of William Geiger were secured to teach the school of about twenty white children at Waiilatpu during the winter of 1846-47. Narcissa told her mother that Geiger was "an excellant young man and superior teacher." She also wrote: "We set the table for more than twenty every day three times—and it is a pleasing sight." [Letter 207.]

Under the influence of the Whitmans, Andrew Rodgers had decided to enter the ministry and was studying at the mission station to that end. Rodgers was a good singer and in him Narcissa found a companion that cheered many a lonely hour for her. She felt that he would have made a good husband for her sister Jane and was instrumental in getting the two to write to each other. Writing to Jane on April 15, 1847, she said:

I can assure you it is no small comfort to have some one to sing with who knows how to sing, for it is true, Jane, I love to sing just as well as ever. From what I have heard of Edward, it would be pleasant to hear him again; as for you, *kala tilapsa kunku* (I am longing for you continually to sing with), and it may be, put us all together, with the violin which Mr. Rogers plays, we should make music such as would cause the Indians to stare.

The winter of 1846-47 was unusually severe for that country. Both the missionaries and the natives lost heavily of their cattle and horses, which were left, as was the custom, in the open without shelter. Whitman in his letter of April 1, 1847, to Greene stated: "At our station we have had a heavy loss in sheep, calves and some cattle (old cows) colts and horses." It is reported that the Nez Perces lost one half of their total stock of horses, and, what was worse, the wild game in the mountains likewise suffered, which meant that the Indians were later unable to find their usual food. It seemed that Nature herself was conspiring to arouse feelings of restlessness and even of blind resentfulness in the hearts of the Indians.

THE SPRING AND SUMMER OF 1847

In the spring of 1847 Whitman found it necessary to make another trip to the Willamette Valley to see about supplies for the mission. His letter of April 1, 1847, was written from Fort Vancouver. Whitman must have heard much political discussion about Oregon's future on this trip, for his letter contains a lengthy explanation of his reasons for going East in 1842. He felt quite satisfied with the turn of events and must have found some pleasure in pointing out the important results of the journey for which he was censured by Greene.

On June 19, 1846, the United States Senate confirmed a treaty with Great Britain which fixed the Oregon boundary at the forty-ninth degree parallel, which is the present boundary line between the states of Washington and Idaho and Canada. The news of the ratification of the treaty was made known to Oregon citizens through an extra edition of Oregon's first newspaper, the *Oregon Spectator*, on November 4, 1846.

In his letter of April 1, Whitman wrote: "American interests acquired in the country, which the success of the immigration of '43 alone has and could have secured, have become the foundation and cause of the late treaty with England and the United States in regard to Oregon." Whitman was quite right in claiming that the one thing which made the treaty possible was the large influx of American citizens into Oregon. If the 1843 emigration had failed, later emigrations would have been much smaller, and the claim of the United States to Oregon would thereby have been weakened. Even though the boundary question was settled, Congress failed to take any steps to erect a territorial government. We must remember that the United States became involved in a war with Mexico in 1846 and that Congress was then too busy with other matters to be giving much time to Oregon. So the provisional government formed by interested citizens in the Willamette Valley carried on for more than a year after the boundary question was settled.

Soon after Whitman's return to his station, he was obliged to leave for Tshimakain to attend the annual meeting of 1847. Narcissa had not made a journey on horseback so far for six or seven years, but she felt strong enough to attempt the trip. Mr. Eells had been at Waiilatpu for some supplies, so he, Mr. Rodgers, and Mrs. Whitman left sometime after May 18. They made the journey by easy stages and arrived at Tshimakain on Thursday, May 28. Dr. Whitman, who was able to travel much faster than his wife, remained behind several days to assist the emigrants who had spent the winter at Waiilatpu and who were then preparing to leave for the Willamette Valley. The doctor reached Tshimakain on June 2.

This meeting of the mission considered the important matter suggested by Mr. Greene in his letter of February 25, 1846, regarding the closing of the station at Tshimakain. Greene thought that perhaps one of the families could move to Waiilatpu and another to Kamiah. "All seemed to feel," wrote Narcissa, "that we had come to an important crisis and that God alone could and must direct us." [Letter 217.] Shortly after the arrival of Greene's letter, there came the offer from the Methodists to sell their station at The Dalles. When Whitman was in Oregon City in the spring of 1847, he called on the Rev. George Gary, superintendent of the Methodist mission, and discussed with him the transfer of the property. Whitman told Gary that if the Methodists had not been at The Dalles in 1838, some of the re-enforcement sent out that year by the American Board would certainly have settled there. Whitman's letter of May 19 to Greene deals in part with the advisability of buying the property. Whitman wrote:

Yesterday letters came to hand... offering us the station without charge for the buildings and improvements and informing us that the station was to be given up by them in the course of the summer, or early in the fall. This will open a new field for our Mission and one we can by no means fail to occupy. For if we allow the Papists to take this station we might as well give up this also.

This proposal caused considerable discussion at the mission meeting held at Tshimakain. Walker and Eells were loath to accept Greene's suggestion that they abandon Tshimakain. The associations of nine years had bound them there, and they did not want to leave. It was finally decided that the Walkers should move to The Dalles, and that the Eells family should move to Waiilatpu. [Letter 217.]

On Sunday, June 6, all met in worship, and Mr. Spalding administered the sacrament. Everyone was present, four men and four women. It was the last time the full mission was assembled. On the Monday following, the Whitmans started back to their station. Mr. Walker left on the 9th, for he was asked to inspect The Dalles station with Whitman. They reached Waiilatpu on Saturday, June 12.

Whitman and Walker visited the station at The Dalles, and Walker seemed satisfied, so Whitman informed the Methodists that they would take over the station in September. However, when Walker got back to his home and talked the matter over with his wife, he sent back a negative reply. It appears that his wife was pregnant and did not want to move to a new location under these conditions. Moreover, they did not like the idea of learning a different language. The refusal of the Walkers to move meant that both families would remain at Tshimakain for at least another winter.

Whitman wrote to Greene on August 3, 1847, and reported the change of plans. He did not then know what could be done. He had promised the Methodists that the American Board mission would take the station, and yet he knew not whom to send. Both he and Narcissa were convinced of the strategic importance of the station and felt that if it was not occupied, it would fall into the hands of the Catholics. [Letter 217.]

In this letter of August 3, Whitman mentioned several other items of interest. He told of how permission had been granted to Hinman to take the mission press to the Willamette Valley, where Hinman planned to publish a paper devoted to temperance and religion. Thus this historic press escaped the looting which took place at the time of the massacre. The press is now safely preserved in the rooms of the Oregon Historical Society at Portland, Oregon. Whitman told of the retirement of Dr. McLoughlin, who was then living at Oregon City, and said that he was a zealous advocate for Papacy. McLoughlin was succeeded at Fort Vancouver by James Douglas.

According to a note made by Narcissa on August 23, Dr. Whitman then planned to hire Mr. and Mrs. Hinman to take charge of the secular affairs at The Dalles. [Letter 217.] Whitman found it necessary to go to Oregon City and The Dalles in August to complete the arrangements incident to the exchange of property. On September 7, 1847, the Methodists turned Waskopum over to Dr. Whitman, and on September 13, Whitman reported the situation to Greene. The whole cost to the American Board was $721.13. Only a small payment was then made, the balance of $651.38 to be paid the following year. The fact that the full sum was not paid left the title still in the hands of the Methodists, with the result that they later received a substantial indemnity from the Government. The mission site was occupied for military purposes after the massacre, and in 1860 Congress authorized a payment of $20,000.00 to the Methodist Church.[3]

Whitman succeeded in getting the Hinmans to go to The Dalles station. Having no one else to turn to for help in religious work, Whitman left his seventeen-year-old nephew, Perrin, to stay with the Hinmans and do what he could with the natives. Whitman wrote of Perrin's command of the Indian language: "Neither Mr. Spalding nor myself can at all compare with him in speaking or reading the Nez Perce language." Whitman was optimistic over the outlook at The Dalles. He prophesied that it would be their best station and spoke of the strategic location that it promised for a college. Again he pleaded for more workers. "We must have help from home," he wrote.

Another event of interest which took place during the summer of 1847 was the visit of Paul Kane, a Canadian artist, to Fort Walla Walla and Waiilatpu. Kane was painting pictures of the Indians of the Northwest. He visited the Whitman mission on July 18, and in his published work he speaks of the cordial reception extended to him by Dr. and Mrs. Whitman. Kane noted that Dr. Whitman then had from forty to fifty acres under cultivation and had more of the comforts of life than "one would expect in such an isolated spot." In view of later events we find Kane's description of the method by which he got the pictures of Tomahas very interesting. He wrote:

Dr. Whitman took me to the lodge of an Indian called To-ma-kus, that I might take his likeness. We found him in his lodge sitting perfectly naked. His appearance was the most savage I ever beheld, and his looks, as I afterwards heard, by no means belied his character.

[3] Photostats of documents in Coll. W.

He was not aware of what I was doing until I had finished the sketch. He then asked to look at it, and inquired what I intended doing with it, and whether I was not going to give it to the Americans, against whom he bore a strong antipathy superstitiously fancying that their possessing it would put him in their power. I in vain told him that I should not give it to them; but, not being satisfied with this assurance, he attempted to throw it in the fire, when I seized him and appeared greatly enraged, but before he had time to recover his surprise I left the lodge and mounted my horse, not without occasionally looking back to see if he might not send an arrow after me.[4]

During Kane's four-day sojourn at Waiilatpu he also secured a picture of Tiloukaikt. These two pictures along with others made by Kane are to be found today in the Royal Ontario Museum at Toronto, Canada.

The day after Kane's return to the Fort, one of the sons of Peupeumoxmox, also a brother of the murdered Elijah Hedding, appeared at the Fort. He was the advance agent of a war party of some two hundred Cayuse and Walla Walla Indians who had left for Sutter's Fort in California about February 1, 1846, to avenge the death of Elijah Hedding. The war party had been gone for eighteen months, and the rumor was that all had been killed. Walker referred to this rumor in his letter to his wife of June 15, 1847. The arrival of the messenger was the occasion for the greatest excitement among the Indians, who immediately gathered about him to hear the news. Kane happened to be present and heard his tale of the failure of the expedition. The following is Kane's account of the dramatic event:

No sooner had he dismounted from his horse than the whole camp, men, women, and children, surrounded him, eagerly inquiring after their absent friends, as they had hitherto received no intelligence, beyond a report, that the tribe had been cut off by hostile tribes. His downcast looks and silence confirmed the fears that some dire calamity must have happened, and they set up a tremendous howl, whilst he stood silent and dejected with the tears streaming down his face. At length, after much coaxing and entreaty on their part, he commenced the recital of their misfortunes.

After describing the progress of the journey to the time of the disease (the measles) making its appearance, during which he was listened to in breathless silence, he began to name its victims one after another. On the first name being mentioned, a terrific howl ensued, the women loosening their hair and gesticulating in a most violent manner. When this had subsided, he, after much persuasion, named a second and a third, until he had named upwards of thirty. The

---

[4] Kane, *Wanderings of an Artist*, p. 194.

same signs of intense grief followed the mention of each name, presenting a scene which accustomed as I was to Indian life, I must confess affected me deeply....[5]

All of the latent fears concerning the Americans were aroused. Even the ravages of the disease were blamed on them. The Indians had built up in their bodies no resistance to such a disease as measles, so when it visited their tribes it struck with devastating power. It was a white man's disease! Messengers were immediately dispatched by the Indians to neighboring tribes to inform them of the tragic circumstances.

At that time, William McBean, a Roman Catholic, was in charge of Fort Walla Walla. Archibald McKinlay had retired in February, 1846. Kane consulted with McBean, and both agreed that Dr. Whitman and his family were in the gravest danger, and should be warned. Kane left the Fort at six o'clock in the evening and rode the twenty-five miles in three hours. He told Whitman the full story and advised him to move his family to the Fort at once. Somewhat to Kane's surprise, Whitman took the news very calmly and remarked that he had lived among them so long that he did not fear they would injure him. After a visit of an hour or less, Kane remounted his horse and returned to the Fort.

It so happened that Whitman correctly evaluated the attitude of the Indians toward him at that time. McLoughlin and others had warned him of the danger of remaining at Waiilatpu, and yet somehow every crisis had blown over. Whitman had a streak of obstinacy in him. He knew of the danger that he constantly faced, but at the same time he felt that he had done too much for the Indians for them to molest him. He counted too much on a shallow gratitude. Moreover, Whitman was remembering that another emigration was then on its way to Oregon. He felt that he was needed at Waiilatpu. A high sense of duty, plus a strong faith in the providence of God, kept him at his station.

THE COMING OF THE CATHOLICS

While Whitman was still at The Dalles, the first of the emigrants of 1847 began passing. He heard reports of the thousands who were on their way, and he became anxious over the food question. The Dalles station had nothing to

---

[5] *Ibid.*, pp. 196-7.

sell, and his own farm at Waiilatpu had not produced as
much as usual that year. As soon as possible Whitman
hurried back. He reached Fort Walla Walla on September
23, where he found a number of Roman Catholic missionaries under the newly appointed Bishop of Walla Walla,
A. M. A. Blanchet, ready to open a mission station in that
vicinity. Whitman was visibly disturbed. One of the Catholics, the Rev. J. B. A. Brouillet, wrote as follows regarding
Whitman's attitude:

His countenance bore sufficient testimony of the agitation of his
heart. He soon showed by his words that he was deeply wounded by
the arrival of the Bishop. 'I know very well,' said he, 'for what purpose
you have come.' 'All is known,' replied the Bishop, 'I come to labor
for the conversion of the Indians, and even of Americans, if they are
willing to listen to me.' The Doctor then continued in the same tone
to speak of many things. He attributed the coming of the Bishop to
the Young Chief's influence—made a furious charge against the Catholics, accusing them of having persecuted Protestants.... He refused
to sell provisions to the Bishop, and protested he would not assist the
missionaries unless he saw them in starvation.[6]

The Catholics had been cordially received by William
McBean, who assisted them in making contacts with the
Indians favorable to the Roman Catholic faith. Young
Chief, who had received a house on the Umatilla River
from Pambrun, was the one most eager for the Catholic
missionaries. However, even Tiloukaikt and Five Crows
were interested enough to meet with the Bishop and his
party. According to Brouillet, Young Chief "suggested the
idea of establishing the mission near Dr. Whitman's at
the camp of Tilokaikt, saying that there was more land
there than near his house, and that it was more central;
that, by his wife, he had a right to the land of Tilokaikt, and
that he was disposed to give it to the mission, if Tilokaikt
was willing."

A meeting was held at the Fort on October 26, with
Tiloukaikt, Tamsucky, and other Indians present. After a
long conference Tiloukaikt assured the Bishop that he would
not object to the establishment of a Catholic mission near
Waiilatpu. The Bishop said that he did not want Whitman's
property but felt there was room for both missions. If he
had known the Indian character, he would have realized that
two missions of rival beliefs would certainly cause trouble

---

6 Cannon, *Waiilatpu*, pp. 93-94, quoting from Brouillet's *Authentic
Account*.

when established as close together as he then proposed.[7]

Brouillet visited the proposed site near Waiilatpu on November 8 and learned that Tiloukaikt had changed his mind. Brouillet wrote: "[He] refused to show it to me, saying that it was too small. He told me that he had no other place to give me but that of Dr. Whitman's whom he intended to send away." Brouillet then declared that the Bishop was not willing to take the place of Dr. Whitman.[8]

Brouillet returned to the Fort on the 10th of November and reported the new turn of events. The Catholic missionaries then decided to accept Young Chief's offer and live in his house on the Umatilla about twenty-five miles from Waiilatpu. The Bishop, his secretary Rousseau, and Brouillet left Fort Walla Walla for their new station on November 27. The Bishop had in the meantime sent four priests and two lay brothers to the Yakimas. Although Father De Smet was a Jesuit, none of these later Catholic missionaries belonged to that order. Whitman, Spalding, and Gray referred to all of them as Jesuits.[9]

It was an unfortunate circumstance that prompted the Roman Catholics to establish a mission station in the immediate vicinity of Waiilatpu at that particular time. The twenty-five miles which separated Waiilatpu from Young Chief's house was not a great enough distance to insure peace. One of the greatest authorities on the history of Oregon, H. H. Bancroft, wrote:

I have in previous chapters stated my belief that the interference of the Catholics augmented Whitman's troubles with the Cayuses; but it is evident to my mind that had there not been a Catholic in the country the catastrophe would have come in the identical shape that it did come, from Indian jealousy alone.[10]

Bishop Blanchet was quite aware of the concern he was giving Dr. Whitman, for he wrote as follows:

The arrival of the bishop of Walla Walla with his clergy to the fort was a thunderbolt to the Presbyterian ministers, especially to Dr. Whitman. He was wounded to the heart by it. He could not refrain from expressing his dissatisfaction saying he would do all in his power to thwart the bishop.[11]

---

[7] Gray, *Oregon*, p. 462.

[8] Eells, *Marcus Whitman*, p. 278; Gray, *op. cit.*, p. 463, quoting from Brouillet, *op. cit.*, p. 44.

[9] Bancroft, *op. cit.*, Vol. 1, p. 654. Four of them belonged to the "order of the Oblates of Mary Immaculate, with two lay brothers, two secular priests, Brouillet and Rosseau; and Guillaume Leclaire, a deacon."

[10] *Ibid.*, p. 698.

[11] *Ibid.*, p. 654.

Commenting on this statement, Bancroft wrote: " ... but whether in Catholic or Protestant, religious zeal knows no mercy ... Protestant and Catholic alike believed the other the emissary of Satan, whom to afflict was doing God service."[12]

THE EMIGRATION OF 1847

The emigration of 1847 numbered between four and five thousand. Very few went to California that year. As early as August 23, Mrs. Whitman was able to write: "For the last two weeks immigrants have been passing, probably 80 or 100 wagons have already passed." [Letter 217.] Each year many suffered along the trail, some dying, and the emigration of 1847 was no exception. The very size of the party going westward was an embarrassment, for the first on the trail exhausted the grass and those who brought up the rear found that their animals suffered for want of pasture.

The members of the emigration of 1847 suffered greatly from the depredations of the Indians, especially along the Columbia. Several cases were reported of the Indians' stripping the white people of all of their clothes and leaving them naked. There were repeated instances of the Indians' stealing livestock. Because of the difficulties experienced by the emigrants of 1846, who went by the southern route to the Willamette, most of the emigrants of 1847 went by Umatilla and The Dalles, thus making it necessary for them to pass the camps of the thieving Indians.

Whitman was indefatiguable in his endeavors to smooth the way for the emigrant and to prevent clashes with the natives. The following account is indicative of his attitude:

Harriet Tibbetts Kennedy (my husband's grandmother) was four years old when she crossed the plains, leaving Iowa April first, 1847. Some time in October the wagon train camped near the Whitman mission. To little Harriet Tibbetts, Marcus Whitman seemed a "tolerable tall man" as he came riding into their camp to warn them to hurry on, that he was "afraid of his own Indians." He was the first white man that they had seen on the trip outside of their own party. Great-grandmother Tibbetts put the children to bed so that she and her husband could talk to Marcus Whitman. Later she told Harriet that he had said his Indians were causing him trouble and he was afraid of the consequences.[13]

Another account by a member of the 1847 emigration tells how Dr. Whitman secured the return of some stolen goods.

---

12 *Ibid.*

13 Henriette Baker Kennedy's letter of Mar. 12, 1936, to the author.

Upon our robbery being reported to Dr. Whitman he called the Indians together; they gathered in a half-circle in front of the doctor, wrapped in their blankets, many with their faces painted with war paint and the doctor began to arraign them about the theft. I looked on, standing beside father (John Fenn) and holding his hand.

As the doctor proceeded and the guilty consciences of the Indians were awakened from time to time a knife, fork or frying pan would be dropped by an Indian from beneath his blanket and when Dr. Whitman had finished most of the stolen property was lying about on the ground at the feet of the Indians. One of the Indians threw down a skillet with considerable force and as I thought threw it at the doctor, but father said, "No, they are mad."[14]

While bringing back two wagons loaded with supplies from The Dalles in September, Whitman found a better route than that formerly used. The new road was inland from the river and had the advantages of avoiding some hills, of being shorter, of providing more grass for the livestock, and of missing a number of Indian camps frequently found along the river.

After returning to Waiilatpu, Whitman left almost immediately to guide a party of emigrants over his new road to The Dalles. Among them was P. W. Crawford, who has left a manuscript, entitled "Narrative of the Overland Journey," in which he refers to Dr. Whitman's "mission of benevolence." Here is one testimony among many regarding Whitman's willingness to be of service. Crawford refers to him as being a stout, robust-looking man with a strong and intelligent mind.[15]

On October 7, when Whitman was on his way back to his station after conducting this party to The Dalles, he camped a little beyond the house owned by Young Chief, near a party of emigrants, among whom was Judge L. W. Saunders and his family from Oskaloosa, Iowa. With Dr. Whitman were two men, a Mr. Bear and a Mr. Glenday, both of whom were on their way back to the States. Mr. Saunders invited the men with Dr. Whitman to his camp for both supper and breakfast. Dr. Whitman was seeking a teacher for his school for white children and offered such strong inducements to Judge Saunders that he agreed to turn back and spend the winter at Waiilatpu. This decision of Saunders involved Mr. Isaac Gilliland, a tailor, who was driving one of the Saunders wagons. Whitman and his two companions hur-

---

[14] Account of Elizabeth Ann Coonc in Walla Walla *Union*, Aug. 12, 1936.

[15] Bancroft, *op. cit.*, Vol. 1, p. 647.

ried on to Waiilatpu, while the Saunders party followed more leisurely.

In a published account of her experiences by Mrs. Saunders we read that their party reached Waiilatpu on October 12, where they found Mr. Bear and Mr. Glenday "waiting for Dr. Whitman and the Rev. Spaulding to write a paper to the government at Washington, D. C., asking to have soldiers stationed between Fort Laramie and Oregon for the protection of the next emigration to Oregon." Since Mr. Saunders had legal training, he was asked to draw up the papers.[16]

The continued and serious depredations of the Indians on the emigrants aroused Whitman. He was ready to join his appeal with many others to Congress in an effort to get the much needed protection. A six-page memorial was written, dated October 16, 1847, and addressed to "The Honorable Secretary of War, to the Committees on Indian Affairs and Oregon, in the Senate and House of Representatives of the United States." The memorial suggested that the United States Government establish a line of posts along the Oregon Trail for the protection of the emigrants. The memorial incorporated many of the ideas to be found in Whitman's proposed bill written after his return to Oregon in 1843 and in other bills relating to Oregon. The various posts were to have food supplies and were to be used as stations for the carrying of mails by horseback. It was stated that with frequent change of horses, the mails could be carried at the rate of "one hundred to one hundred and fifty miles in twenty-four hours."

Regarding the attacks of the Indians, we read:

The Indians along the line take courage from the forbearance of the immigrants. The timid Indians on the Columbia, have this year in open day, attacked several parties of waggons, numbering from two to seven, & robbed them, being armed with guns, bows & arrows, knives & axes. Mr. Glenday from St. Charles, Mo., the bearer of this communication to the States, with Mr. Bear, his companion, rescued seven waggons from being plundered & the people from gross insults, rescuing one woman, when the Indians were in the act of taking all the clothes from her person. The men were mostly stripped of their shirts & pantaloons at the time. [Letter 221.]

---

[16] Saunders, *The Whitman Massacre*, p. 7. Mrs. Saunders states that Bear and Glenday left Waiilatpu for the States on Oct. 15. Whitman's last letter to Greene, carried by Mr. Glenday, is dated October 18. A mistake was made either by Mrs. Saunders or Dr. Whitman.

Whitman sent a copy of his memorial to Greene with the request: "Please send copies of the above to such members of Congress & other influential men as you think will favor the object proposed."

It appears that copies of this memorial were sent to many different people. The following quotation is taken from a letter written by I. I. Rodgers, a sister of Andrew Rodgers, to Myron Eells:

I have in my possession an article of this description signed by Marcus Whitman and written by my brother. This was written and sent about two months or less, before the murder of all at Dr. Whitman's station. This was sent to an uncle of mine who had been in public life to some extent at different periods of life, was a warm personal friend of Col. H. T. Benton, and in a letter this was sent to my uncle for him to correct and send it in some way that it would reach the attention of the Government and bring about some such results as suggested by the paper sent.[17]

On the very day that Whitman was writing out his memorial, Dr. John McLoughlin wrote to the Secretary of War from Oregon City and gave similar recommendations for the protection of the Oregon emigrants. He wrote: "I am convinced that the manner in which the Immigrants travel from Fort Hall to this place will lead to trouble unless the Measures I suggested to Dr. White when he left here to go home are adopted." McLoughlin advised the Government to establish a post at Fort Hall, and in this connection he recommended Robert Newell "as a person well qualified for the office of Agent."[18]

LAST LETTERS

The last of Narcissa's letters that we have was written October 12 to her sister Jane. Again she made an earnest appeal for her sister to come to Oregon. Narcissa wrote: "You know not how much you are all needed here this present moment; yes, I may say, we are suffering and shall suffer for the want of your assistance and presence here this winter." In 1846, Mr. and Mrs. J. Quin Thornton, of Quincy, Illinois, had migrated to Oregon. Narcissa was deeply disappointed that Jane had not taken advantage of the opportunity to come with them. It seems that Jane wrote to Narcissa, saying that she could not go on short notice since she wanted first to see her parents. To this excuse Narcissa replied in the closing paragraph of that last letter:

---

[17] Not dated but postmarked Nov. 20, 1891, Coll. W.
[18] Original in files of Old Indian Bureau, Wash., D. C.

Jane, there will be no use in your going home to see ma and pa before you come here—it will only make the matters worse with your heart. I want to see her as much as you. If you will all come here it will not be long before they will be climbing over the Rocky Mountains to see us. The love of parents for their children is very great. I see already in their movements, indications that they will ere long come this way, for father is becoming quite a traveller. Believe me, dear Jane, and come without fail, when you have so good an opportunity.

Farewell, N. W.

Elizabeth Sager later told how eagerly Narcissa had expected Jane to arrive in the fall of 1847. In anticipation of that great event, Mrs. Whitman gave her house a thorough cleaning. Elizabeth then asked: "This isn't spring, Mother —why are we cleaning the house now?" Narcissa replied: "Didn't you know that we are looking for your Aunt Jane to come out soon?"[19] But Jane didn't come.

Whitman's last letter to Greene was dated October 18. So far as we know, it was the last letter he ever wrote. From this letter the following extracts are taken:

I have now been at home two Sabbaths only since my return from completing the wagon road from the Utilla to the Dalls. . . .

A Bishop is set over this part of the work whose seat as the name indicates will be at Walla Walla. . . . I cannot blame myself that the plan I laid down when I was in Boston was not carried out. If we could have had good families say two or three together to have placed in select spots among the Indians the present crisis which I feared would not have come.

Whitman again reverted to the subject of the good accomplished by his return to the States and emphasized the importance to Oregon of the 1843 emigration. "Upon that event," he wrote, "the present acquired rights of the U. States hung." He again urged Greene to do something about sending out colonies of good men to settle in the vicinity of the mission stations. He wrote:

My plan is for you to confer with the Pastors and individuals in some way and lay the matter open before them. Let there be a selection of men for the work or volunteers. Let them be of the best of Pastors and church members for it is a work that needs good men. . . . Can a mind be found so narrow as not to part with a church member simply because they are good men and useful where they are. I fear this is the feeling.

Again he dwelt upon the charms and advantages of Oregon to the settler. He praised the climate and boasted of the endless ranges for the grazing of sheep and cattle. He saw that the day was quickly coming when the interior

---

19 Lockley, *op. cit.*, p. 332.

would be as much sought after as the Willamette Valley. His last words to Greene were: "I hope the want of a man for the Dalls Station will not escape your notice."

Greene was patient with Whitman's continued insistence that something be done to send out pious settlers, but he did little. Writing to Whitman on April 14, 1845, he said he did not know what could be done to induce "moral and intelligent men to go as settlers to the Oregon country," and then added: "I doubt very much if we ought to attempt anything of the kind." He felt that the matter as to who should fill the Oregon Country was one which could be left "to the providence of God."

Whitman was not satisfied with that reply. He felt that the churches had a duty to fulfill; hence his repeated requests that something be done. Whitman's last letter to Greene was another effort to inspire the churches to action. Greene received the letter with the memorial several months after Whitman had been killed, and on March 17, 1848, he replied. Greene wrote:

> The memorial relating to the establishment of military posts on the route to Oregon, I send immediately to Mr. Baldwin of the U. S. Senate, with a letter of my own, asking him to give attention to it. . . .
>
> As to the sending or obtaining men to emigrate to the Oregon country, respecting which you write with much earnestness and apparently with the impression that I must feel impelled by a sense of duty & regard to every great interest to make immediate and strenuous efforts, whatever other interests may suffer from my turning away from them, I must say that I cannot regard it as my duty to make any efforts at all in any form. . . .
>
> Do not feel that all Oregon is on your hands, & that the planning, providing & laboring for all its interests are developed on you. . . .

But the man who was thus being rebuked for an excess of patriotic zeal was already dead.

CROWDED WAIILATPU

Waiilatpu was crowded with emigrants after the long wagon trains of 1847 had passed. The Saunders family with their five children was assigned two large rooms in the mansion house which Gray had built. Mrs. Saunders reports that Mr. and Mrs. Nathan Kimball, of Laporte, Indiana, with their four children occupied a room in the same building on one side of them, and that Mr. and Mrs. Peter Hall, of Illinois, with five children occupied a room on the other side. A widow, Mrs. Rebecca Hays, and her young son, of Platte County, Missouri, lived with the Halls.

Upstairs in the same building were quartered Mr. Walter
Marsh, his daughter, and an infant grandson, from Sanga-
mon County, Illinois. Also Isaac Gilliland, of Long Island,
New York; Joe Stanfield, a French Canadian, probably
once in the employ of the Hudson's Bay Company; and
Jacob Hoffmann, of Elmira, New York. Thus there were at
least twenty-eight staying in the mansion house, all of whom
except Standfield were emigrants.

Two families, Mr. and Mrs. Joseph Smith and their five
children, of Du Page County, Illinois, and Mr. and Mrs. Elam
Young, of Osage County, Missouri, were living at the sawmill
in the Blue Mountains. Other members of the emigration
who had elected to stay were Crocket Bewley and his sister
Lorinda, of Missouri, and Amos Sales, all three of whom
were sick at the time of their arrival or soon afterwards.
Lorinda Bewley was given a bed in the upstairs room of the
main mission dwelling, while her brother and Sales occupied
a sleeping room off the kitchen. Later Sales moved to the
blacksmith shop. This brought the total number of emigrants
to forty-three.

On Monday, October 18, Josiah Osborn and his wife with
their four children arrived. The Osborn family had wintered
with the Whitmans during the winter of 1845-46, and Whitman had a high opinion of Osborn as a millwright and mechanic. When Whitman was in the Willamette Valley in
August, 1847, he called on Osborn at Salem and persuaded
him to return to Waiilatpu that fall to build two mills which
Whitman needed. Whitman agreed to pay him three hundred dollars a year, and Osborn went for a two-year period.
This shows that Whitman then had no intention of moving
away from Waiilatpu.

On April 7, 1848, Osborn wrote a letter to relatives in
the East which throws some light upon the events leading
up to the tragedy of November 29. After passing through
great dangers and many sorrows, Osborn regretfully wrote:
"Dr. Whitman came down and wanted me to undertake to
build two mills for the Mission—not being satisfied when
doing well, I consented to go."[20] He left with his family the
latter part of September and reached Fort Walla Walla
about October 15. Dr. Whitman sent Crocket Bewley with
a wagon to bring the Osborn family to the mission. They

[20] Original, Coll. W.

received the Indian room in the main mission building for their quarters.

Mrs. Saunders reported that her husband opened his school "on Monday, the nineteenth of October."[21] About that time the half-breed Joe Lewis appeared "sick, and in need of clothing." According to Spalding, Lewis was born in Canada and educated in Maine. He proved to be another Tom Hill. He spoke the English language and was, according to Spalding, a "devoted Catholic."[22] Some of the emigrants first saw him at Fort Hall.

After Lewis had been at the station but a few days, Dr. Whitman learned through the Sager boys that he was stirring up trouble among the Indians. Whitman made an effort to send him on his way. Learning of the need of a driver for an emigrant wagon, Whitman gave Lewis clothing and induced him to drive the team. Within three days he was back again, and remained as an unwelcome guest. He refused to leave.[23] All accounts of him picture him as a treacherous, unprincipled scoundrel.

There happened to be another half-breed living in an Indian lodge on the mission grounds, who was of the same stamp as Joe Lewis. His name was Nicholas Finley, once in the employ of the Hudson's Bay Company. His lodge became the headquarters for the conspirators. It seems that Whitman had hired both Stanfield and Finley to work for the mission that winter.

On November 7, W. D. Canfield, of Oskaloosa, Iowa, arrived with his wife and five children.[24] Every available room was taken and for a time they had to camp out. Finally quarters, such as they were, were found in the blacksmith shop which stood about midway between the two main buildings. With their arrival the total number of emigrants was raised to fifty.

On Monday, November 22, Spalding arrived at Waiilatpu with his daughter Eliza, who was to be placed in the school. Earlier in the fall, the two half-breed sons of Donald Manson, an employee of the Hudson's Bay Company, were sent to attend the Whitman school. Thus the list of those at the

---

[21] Saunders, *The Whitman Massacre*, p. 19. She made a mistake as to the day. Monday was the 18th.

[22] Warren, *Memoirs*, p. 119.

[23] Gray, *Oregon*, pp. 468 and 500.

[24] Bancroft, *Oregon*, Vol. 1, p. 662, states that Canfield had laid out the town of Oskaloosa, Iowa.

station on the fateful Monday, November 29, 1847, was completed. They included the following, the ages of the children being given in parentheses:[25]

Main mission house   Total 23

Dr. and Mrs. Marcus Whitman

The seven Sager children—John (17), Francisco (15), Catherine (13), Elizabeth (10), Matilda (8), Louise (6), and Henrietta (4)

Five half-breed children—Mary Ann Bridger (11), Helen Mar Meek (10), David Malin (8), and the two Manson boys (17) and (16)

Eliza Spalding (10)

Andrew Rodgers, Crocket Bewley, Lorinda Bewley

Mr. and Mrs. Josiah Osborn—Nancy A. (9), John L. (9), Alexander (2)

Mansion house   29

Mr. and Mrs. L. W. Saunders—Helen M. (14), Phoebe (10), Alfred (6), Nancy (4), and Mary A. (2)

Mrs. Rebecca Hays—Henry Clay (4)

Mr. and Mrs. Peter D. Hall—Gertrude (10), Mary C. (8), Ann E. (6), Rebecca (3), Rachel (1)

Mr. and Mrs. Nathan L. Kimball—Susan M. (16), Nathan (12), Byron E. (8), Sarah S. (?), and Mina A. (1)

Mr. Walter Marsh—Mary E. (11), and grandson, Alba Lyman (2)

Isaac Gilliland, Jacob Hoffmann, Joseph Stanfield

Blacksmith shop   8

Mr. and Mrs. W. D. Canfield—Ellen (16), Oscar (9), Clarissa (7), Sylvia (5), and Albert (3)

Amos Sales

Sawmill cabin   12

Mr. and Mrs. Elam Young—James (24), Daniel (21), and John Q. (19)

Mr. and Mrs. Joseph Smith—Mary (15), Edwin (13), Charles (11), Nelson (6), and Mortimer (4)

Others   2

Nicholas Finley and Joe Lewis

Grand total—74

Not counting the adult half-breeds and the French Canadian, the Whitmans found themselves responsible for the welfare of sixty-nine men, women, and children, besides themselves. Fifty of these were emigrants. The other nine-

---

[25] One of the Osborn children died of the measles after the arrival of the family at Waiilatpu. One name usually omitted from this list is that of Alba Lyman, the grandson of Walter Marsh. *Oregon Statesman*, Nov. 6, 1936, gives his story.

teen included the members of their family, the schoolchildren entrusted to their care, and the Osborn family. All of the actors in that final tragic scene were on the stage.[26]

---

[26] For lists of the people at Waiilatpu *see:* Spalding, *Senate Document No. 37,* p. 27 (gives seventy-two names omitting Alba Lyman and Finley) ; Cannon, *Waiilatpu,* pp. 106-7 (gives seventy-two names omitting Alba Lyman and Nathan Kimball, Jr.) ; Bancroft, *Oregon,* Vol. 1, pp. 647-8 (lists only sixty-eight, omitting Alba Lyman, Gilliland, Joe Lewis, Nicholas Finley, Joseph Stanfield, and one of the Sager children). For other lists *see* Eells, *Marcus Whitman,* pp. 287-8, and *T.O.P.A.,* 1896.

CHAPTER NINETEEN

THE MASSACRE

1840

BOTH the covered wagon and the tepee were to be seen at Waiilatpu. The one carried an aggressive people who were seeking new lands to settle, while the other sheltered an indolent people who looked with suspicion upon the ever-increasing encroachments of the whites. Waiilatpu became the focal point of trouble because of its geographical location. There two civilizations overlapped, with the inevitable clash of ideas.

The massacre, which was started on November 29, 1847, came as the inevitable result of a combination of causes. The presence of the Catholics may have, unwittingly on their part, fanned the flames, but the tragedy would surely have occurred if the Catholics had never been present. Whitman's deep interest in the political affairs of Oregon was certainly an important cause for the tragedy. Gradually the conviction grew in his heart that the Indian race was doomed. It never could hold the country before the aggressive whites. In time the Indians came to suspect his position. Latent fears regarding the white man's intentions prepared their minds for the vile slanders whispered by rascally half-breeds. They came to believe that Marcus Whitman was their enemy.

One of the strongest ties which bound the Whitmans to their mission station in the face of repeated dangers and even of the warnings of friends was the emigrant. Each year, beginning with 1843, the Whitman mission had been a place of refuge. The naked were clothed, the hungry fed, the sick were cared for, the orphans were sheltered, and the gospel of Christ's redeeming love was preached to all who would pause to listen. The Whitmans looked into the years ahead and realized that the westward movement had but begun. Thousands upon thousands more were still to come, and perhaps for them the Whitmans stayed.

The emigration of 1847 brought in a virulent form of measles and a dysentery which spread with devastating rapidity through all of Old Oregon, leaving in its wake an appalling list of dead. The appearance of these diseases was like the proverbial straw which broke the camel's back. According to one report the disease made its appearance among the Cayuses during the first part of October, when an Indian child died at Fort Walla Walla.[1] By the first of November many were sick, and some of the emigrants at Waiilatpu were likewise prostrated.

The fact that the white people usually recovered, while the Indians did not, increased the resentment of the Indians against those who introduced the disease. Moreover, its being a white man's disease, as they thought, they expected Dr. Whitman to be able to cure all cases. Dr. Whitman's work was complicated by the insistence of many of the Indians on taking the old sweat-bath cure. Mrs. Saunders reported that this method of treatment almost always resulted in death.[2]

On November 8, Mrs. Osborn was taken seriously ill with the disease and on the 14th gave birth to a girl, who died shortly afterwards and was buried the next day. On the 16th little six-year-old Salvijane Osborn became ill, and she died on the 24th. All of the other Osborn children were likewise ill for a time, but they recovered. Years afterward Nancy Osborn wrote of the death of her sister as follows:

An Indian came into the room where the form of my sister lay. Mrs. Whitman asked leave to show him the dead child. She wanted the Indians to know the measles were killing the white people as well as the Indians and thus hoped to allay the growing distrust of the red men. The Indian looked long at my sister, then cruelly he laughed, to see the pale face dead.[3]

Mrs. Saunders in her account of the tragedy mentions the death of the Osborn child. She tells of how Mrs. Whitman tried to comfort the grief-stricken mother by saying: "Perhaps God thought it for the best that your little child should be called away; it may calm the Indians to see a white child taken as well as so many natives, for otherwise we may all be compelled to leave within two weeks." Mrs. Saunders reports that the child was buried on the 24th and that Tiloukaikt was among those who attended the funeral.

---

[1] Nancy Osborn Jacobs, Waitsburg *Times*, Feb. 2, 1934.

[2] Saunders, *The Whitman Massacre*, p. 9. According to this custom, a sick Indian would get into a small hut in which water would be thrown upon hot stones, thus causing steam. After spending some time in the steam, he would run out and plunge into a cold stream.

[3] Jacobs, *op. cit.*

We regret that we have no writings of either of the
Whitmans during the month or six weeks prior to the final
tragedy. The story of what took place must be gleaned
from the testimony of others. Two or more witnesses of
the same event will not always tell the same story, so we find
differences in the various accounts which have come down
to us of the closing days of the mission at Waiilatpu. Sometimes these differences can be reconciled, and sometimes
they cannot. Moreover, some of the accounts were written
many years later by those who were but children at the
time the events described took place. Due allowance must
be made for the fallibility of human memory.

Of this we can be assured, both Dr. and Mrs. Whitman
were aware of the growing danger but saw no way out except to stay where they were and do the best they could
to minister to the sick and keep the Indians peaceful. Even
if they considered moving—how were they to move so
many without arousing the Indians and precipitating trouble, and, besides, where were they to go? To the Fort?
As later events proved, McBean would have given them a
reluctant welcome. He was not prepared to defend so many
from a hostile tribe. While McBean may not have been
the scoundrel he was painted to be, yet even Bancroft declares that: "McBean was 'below the salt' when compared
with other gentlemen in the company."[4] Whitman no doubt
realized his attitude and felt that it was useless to look in
that direction for aid in a crisis. The fact that Mrs. Saunders quoted Mrs. Whitman as saying that they might have
to move within two weeks is proof that Marcus and Narcissa had discussed that possibility. Whitman has been
criticized for remaining at Waiilatpu under the circumstances, but perhaps that was the lesser of two evils and
gave greater promise of security than attempting to flee.

With anxious hearts and prayerful souls, the Whitmans
gave themselves to their ministry. Nancy Osborn in her
adult life recalled an incident of those days which has been
handed down by word of mouth to this generation. One
day Dr. Whitman entered the house very tired. His wife
in an endeavor to cheer him up, said: "Come Marcus, let
us sing." She gave him a book, but the Doctor sank down
on a chair and said: "I can't sing. I am so tired I could
not hold up the book." Then little nine-year-old Nancy
went to him and said: "Lean on me. I will help you to

---

4 Bancroft, *op. cit.*, Vol. 1, p. 661.

stand up." The heart of the Doctor was touched by the
child's solicitude, and he gathered her in his arms and put
her on his lap.[5]

According to Mrs. Saunders, five of the children in the
Whitman home, some of whom were the Sager children,
became ill. She also states that Dr. Whitman spoke of the
danger involved in the Indians' method of treatment. Bancroft gives one little incident which may have seemed very
important to the Indians. On August 23, some Cayuses
and Walla Walla Indians at The Dalles had killed an emigrant by the name of Sheppard. Later, after Whitman's
return to his station, he happened to meet one of the Cayuse
Indians who was perhaps involved in the murder. Whitman
to rebuke him refused to shake hands with him. It so happened that the young man choked that night on a piece
of dried buffalo meat and died. Many of the Indians believed that Whitman had worked some evil magic upon
him and blamed the doctor for his death. Mrs. Whitman
gave a feast for the dead in an effort to regain the confidence of the natives. Among those who remained hostile
was a "villain of an Indian called Tamsucky who fomented
discontent, and threatened Whitman that he would be
killed."

It was Joe Lewis who brought matters to a crisis. In
Osborn's letter of April 7, 1848, we can read the following:

> In the last company there was a half-breed came to the Doctor's
> and hired to work through the winter. One day he was at work for
> Indian named Tamsicky, harrowing in wheat and told him that the
> Doctor and Mrs. Whitman were scattering poison into the air, and
> would kill them all off—that he was not working for him, but for the
> Doctor—that he (the Dr) knew they would all die and he would get
> their wheat and all they had. He then proposed that if they would
> agree to it, he would help them kill the Doctor and his wife, and all
> the Americans in their country. As they had a disposition to murder,
> and wanted satisfaction for the loss of women and children, it was
> no difficult matter to incite them against the Americans.

Such reports soon reached Dr. Whitman's ears through
friendly Indians, and naturally troubled him. There seemed
to be no way to get rid of Joe Lewis. Another lie that
Lewis circulated was that he had heard Dr. and Mrs. Whitman plot together to poison the Indians. According to the
deposition of Daniel Young, the story is as follows:

> Stanfield said ... that Joe Lewis had heard from an adjoining room
> one night the Doctor and Mrs. Whitman talking of poisoning them, and

---

[5] Told by Mrs. Stephen B. L. Penrose to the author.

that the Doctor had said it was best to destroy them by degrees, but that Mrs. Whitman said it was best to do it at once, and they would be rid of them, and have all their land and horses as their own; and that he (Joe Lewis) had told the Indians this before the massacre.[6]

Another version of this story is to be found in the testimony of William Craig, of Lapwai:

Joe Lewis said that Dr Whitman and Mr Spalding had been writing for two years to their friends in the east, where Joe Lewis lived, to send them poison to kill off the Cayuses and the Nez Perces; and they had sent them some that was not good, and they wrote for more that would kill them off quick and that the medicine had come this summer.

Joe Lewis said he was lying on the settee in Dr. Whitman's room, and he heard a conversation between Dr Whitman, Mrs Whitman and Mr Spalding, in which Mr Spalding asked the doctor why he did not kill the Indians off faster. 'O,' said the doctor, 'they are dying fast enough; the young ones will die off this winter, and the old ones next spring. . . . " The Indian messenger said that Joe Lewis made this statement in a council of the Cayuses. . . .[7]

According to this same Indian messenger, whom William Craig quoted, the Cayuses had lost 197 of their number. Craig further stated: "He said that there were 6 buried on Monday morning, and among the rest his own wife; he said he knew they were poisoned." Catherine Sager wrote: "I have known five to be buried in one day."[8] And Spalding, who reached Waiilatpu on November 22, later wrote:

It was most distressing to go into a lodge of some 10 fires, and count 20 or 25, some in the midst of measles, others in the last stages of dysentery, in the midst of every kind of filth of itself sufficient to cause sickness, with no suitable means to alleviate their inconceivable sufferings, with perhaps one well person to look after the wants of 2 sick ones.[9]

If the estimate given by the Indian messenger of 197 deaths among the Cayuses be correct, then that tribe lost about one half of its total number during the epidemic. Is it any wonder that the natives were alarmed?

Further light is thrown upon the situation by an article by Dr. Wm. Frazer Tolmie which appeared in the 1884 issue of the *Transactions of the Oregon Pioneer Association.* Dr. Tolmie quoted at length from a letter he had received

[6] Gray, *Oregon*, p. 475.

[7] Bancroft, *op. cit.*, Vol. 1, pp. 652-3, quoting from Brouillet's *Authentic Account*, pp. 35-6.

[8] *O.H.Q.*, Dec., 1936, p. 356.

[9] Bancroft, *op. cit.*, Vol. 1, p. 652, quoting from *Oregon American*, July 19, 1848.

from McKinlay, who gave his memories of those days. Mc-
Kinlay wrote of the time that Gray had injected a drug
into some watermelons to punish the Indians for stealing:

> The drugging of the melons, to the best of my recollection, occurred
> in 1841. Gray spoke of the act as a clever method he had taken to
> prevent the Indians from stealing melons. After this Whitman was
> suspected of being a dangerous *medicine man*.

> The melon affair occurred in 1841. The seriousness of the act was
> little thought of at the time, but it became known to the Indians, and
> they frequently referred it not only to me but to Whitman also.

McKinlay also informed Dr. Tolmie that he considered
the Cayuse and the Walla Walla Indians to be the most
superstitious of any of the coast tribes, and added: "They
shot seven of their own medicine men by the fort during
my five years' stay there, and probably over three times
that number altogether."
Surely both Dr. and Mrs. Whitman were mindful of the
old Indian superstition that if the *te-wat* could not cure
the patient and the patient died, then the relatives of the
deceased could kill the *te-wat*. In one of Narcissa's first
letters home, she had made reference to the custom. [Let-
ter 41.] Inflamed by the lies of Joe Lewis, aroused by the
intense grief at the loss of so many of their loved ones,
the Cayuse chiefs in the vicinity of Waiilatpu sat about
the council fires and debated what should be done. Under
such circumstances it was easy for old superstitions to
assert themselves again. They who proposed killing the
white *te-wat* found ready listeners. Some advised caution,
and a few seem to have definitely opposed the plan. Finally
a few of the most influential agreed on the dreadful decision
—both Dr. and Mrs. Whitman were to be killed!

THE LAST WEEK

Spalding and his daughter reached Waiilatpu on Monday, November 22, just a week before the final tragedy
took place. He brought with him a pack of seventeen animals loaded with grain to supplement Whitman's diminishing store. This pack train was sent back to Lapwai under
the care of a Mr. Jackson, then in Spalding's employ, on
the morning of the ill-fated day. Writing to the parents
of Mrs. Whitman on April 6, 1848, Spalding described the
conditions at Waiilatpu as he found them. He wrote:

All the doctor's family had been sick, but were recovering; three of the children were yet dangerously sick; besides Mr. Osborn, with his sick family, were in the same house. Mrs. Osborn and three children were dangerous; one of the children died during the week. A young man, Mr. Bewley, was also very sick. The doctor's hands were more than full among the Indians; three and sometimes five died in a day. Dear sister Whitman seemed ready to sink under the immense weight of labor and care. But like an angel of mercy, she continued to administer with her ever-ready hand to the wants of all. Late and early, night and day, she was by the bed of the sick, the dying, and the afflicted.[10]

On Thursday, November 25, Spalding and Rodgers rode to Fort Walla Walla, where they spent the night in the lodge of Peupeumoxmox, who was friendly to the Protestants. While there, a Nez Perce entered the lodge and asked: "Is Dr. Whitman killed?" as though he were expecting an affirmative answer. The incident troubled Spalding. During the night a niece of the chief died and was buried the next day, Spalding officiating at the funeral. On Friday, the 26th, Spalding had an interview with the Catholic missionaries. Of this Spalding wrote:

They asked for and I cheerfully agreed to furnish them all needed supplies from my station. With the Bishop, the Vicar and the priests I had an animated discussion on changing the biscuit into "God." I showed them plainly they must be deceivers or cannibals. . . . I also called their attention to their Catholic "ladders," beautifully printed and scattered among the Indians, representing the Catholic as the only church leading to Heaven, and all Protestans (Whitman and Spalding's name on that line), starting from Luther leading down to hell, filled with horned devils and big fires all graphically painted in colors. I told them they would probably cause our death and that of our helpless families.[11]

In all fairness it should be pointed out that Spalding had devised a "ladder" to counteract the effect of the Catholic "ladder" which was just as graphic as those of his religious opponents. The September, 1936, issue of the *Oregon Historical Quarterly* carried a reproduction of this Protestant "ladder," together with Spalding's description.

On Saturday, November 27, Spalding and Rodgers returned to Waiilatpu. On the same day the Bishop and his two companions left for Young Chief's house on the Umatilla. Upon Spalding's arrival at the mission station, he found Dr. Whitman ready to go to Umatilla to see some patients in the lodge of Five Crows, which was near the

---

[10] *T.O.P.A.*, 1893, pp. 93-94.
[11] *Oregon American and Evangelical Unionist*, Aug., 1848.

Catholic mission house. Whitman urged Spalding to accompany him. Mrs. Whitman was reluctant to see them go and with tears in her eyes bade her husband goodbye about dusk. It was the last time that Spalding saw Narcissa, the one he had loved in his youth.

It was a stormy night. The rain blew in their faces as they urged their horses over the trail they, had followed eleven years before when they first entered the country. As they rode along they talked about the past—their high hopes, their thrilling interests, and then of the menacing demands of the Indians, who wanted pay for land and wood and water. Whitman told Spalding that he felt their lives were in danger, and perhaps Spalding told of the incident which occurred in the lodge of Peupeumoxmox, when an Indian asked if Dr. Whitman were dead. Whitman said that probably he would be killed, and then added: "But my death will probably do as much good to Oregon as my life can."[12] During the night, Spalding's horse slipped and fell. Spalding was badly bruised.

They reached the camp of Stickus on the Umatilla River, near the present city of Pendleton, Oregon, just before dawn on Sunday morning, the 28th. Dr. Whitman busied himself at once with his professional duties, while Spalding welcomed the opportunity to rest and recover from his injuries. The two men ate breakfast with the faithful chief who had guided the 1843 emigration over the Blue Mountains. Everything in the vicinity of the lodge of Stickus was quiet and orderly. The chief and his people were not a part of the conspirators. Spalding conducted religious services.

Whitman visited the camps of Young Chief (Tauitau or Tawatowe) and Five Crows (Hezekiah) on the south side of the Umatilla, and, after ministering to the sick, he called on the Catholic missionaries, where he had tea.[13] It is quite possible that Whitman discussed with the priests the possibility of selling the Waiilatpu station to them. Whitman had repeatedly declared to the Cayuses that he would leave whenever the majority of them wished it, but as often he was requested to stay. Brouillet wrote: "Dr.

---

[12] Warren, *op. cit.*, p. 118.

[13] Bancroft, *op. cit.*, Vol. 1, p. 657. Spalding claims that Whitman took tea. *Senate Document No. 37*, p. 26. Spalding himself dined with the Catholic missionaries the next day. Bagley, *Early Catholic Missions in Old Oregon*, p. 192.

Whitman held himself ready to sell the Waiilatpu station to the Catholic mission whenever a majority of the Cayuses might wish it."[14]

Dr. Whitman returned to the camp of Stickus about sundown. He felt it absolutely necessary to return to Waiilatpu even though he had spent the previous night in the saddle. Spalding undoubtedly would have returned with him but for his injuries. Whitman's horse was worn out, so he borrowed a mule from Stickus for the return journey.[15] According to one report, Stickus told Whitman just before he left that: "Joe Lewis was making trouble; that he was telling his (Stickus') people that the Doctor and Mr. Spalding were poisoning the Indians." Stickus advised Whitman to go away "until my people have better hearts."[16]

Whitman was troubled. The warning from Stickus was all the more reason why he should hasten back. He took Spalding by the hand and bade him farewell, then mounted his borrowed animal and rode away into the coming night. It was their last meeting. Their long road which started at Howard, New York, and which they had traveled together for nearly twelve years, had come to an end.

THE MASSACRE

Catherine Sager has given us the following description of Dr. Whitman's return:

Doctor Whitman arrived at home about 10 o'clock that night, having ridden twenty-five miles after sundown. He sent my two brothers, who were sitting up with the sick, to bed, saying that he would watch the remainder of the night. After they had retired he examined the patients one after the other. (I also was lying sick at the time.) Coming to Helen, he spoke and told his wife, who was lying on the bed, that Helen was dying. He sat and watched her for some time, when she rallied and seemed better. I had noticed that he seemed to be troubled when he first came home, but concluded that it was anxiety in reference to the sick children.

Taking a chair, he sat down by the stove and requested his wife to arise, as he wished to talk with her. She complied, and he related to her what Stickas had told him that day; also that he had learned that the Indians were holding councils every night. After conversing for some time his wife retired to another room, and the doctor kept his lonely watch.[17]

---

[14] Bancroft, *ibid.*

[15] Spalding, *Senate Document No. 37,* p. 26.

[16] Eells, *Marcus Whitman,* p. 282.

[17] Clark, *Pioneer Days,* Vol. 2, pp. 529-30. Spalding, *op. cit.,* p. 27, claims that Dr. Whitman sent for Nicholas Finley and asked him: "Finley, I understand the Indians are to kill me and Mr. Spalding; do you know anything about it?" Finley professed ignorance.

Matilda Sager remembered that the morning of the 29th was dark and dreary. Catherine said it was a cold, foggy morning. When Matilda entered the kitchen that morning she found Dr. Whitman broiling a steak for breakfast. Matilda put her arms about his neck and greeted him with a kiss and the words: "Good morning, father."[18] Soon the family gathered for breakfast, but Mrs. Whitman was not present. One of the girls prepared something for her to eat and carried it into her room. According to Catherine: "She was sitting with her face buried in her hankerchief, sobbing bitterly. Taking the food, she motioned the child to leave. The food was there, untouched, next morning."[19]

Early in the morning an Indian appeared and reported the death of a child. While awaiting the arrival of the corpse, which was to be buried on the mission grounds, Whitman discussed the threatening situation with Rodgers. Whitman officiated at the funeral and noticed that while many Indians were about the premises, only a few were present at the burial. This disturbed him, and he commented on the fact to his wife when he returned to the house. A beef had been brought in that morning to be butchered, and Dr. and Mrs. Whitman felt that perhaps that event had attracted the natives.

Mrs. Saunders, in her reminiscences of the tragedy, stated that Dr. Whitman was called upon to bury three of the children of Chief Tiloukaikt on that Monday morning. If this triple tragedy had struck into the family life of the principal chief, surely others would have mentioned it also. It is possible, however, that the child buried that morning was from Tiloukaikt's lodge and that on previous occasions Whitman had officiated at the funeral services of his children. If the chief lost three children by the disease, regardless of when they died, we can the more easily understand the blind rage of the grief-stricken Indian who was convinced that Dr. Whitman was poisoning his children.

After the funeral, Dr. Whitman called at the room of Mrs. Saunders and showed that he was much disturbed. He spoke again about the "unwisdom of the Indian method of treating the measles." While there, an Indian with a green cap entered, apparently on an inspection trip. Mrs. Saunders offered him a chair. He remained seated for a few moments and then arose and, crossing the room, looked

---

[18] Delaney, *Whitman Massacre*, p. 14.
[19] Clark, *op. cit.*, p. 530.

into the next room. He then returned to his chair. When the Doctor left, he left.

Surely there were enough suspicious signs to alarm Dr. Whitman, but if he sensed the gravity of the situation he gave no warning to the emigrants to put them on their guard. For this failure he has been severely criticized. It should be remembered, however, that Dr. Whitman did not believe in the use of force for protection. Repeatedly he had demonstrated his faith in nonresistance. Besides, if he had resorted to force or had encouraged others to do so, it probably would have meant the death of many of the women and children, if not all, for the Americans were far outnumbered and had no one to come to their rescue if besieged. He may have felt that in case the Indians killed any, he would be the only victim.

Noon came, and all partook of their midday meal. Afterwards Francis Sager shot the beef. Kimball, Hoffmann, and Canfield began dressing it. They were working between the two houses, in front of the blacksmith shop. Marsh was busy grinding at the mill. Saunders, the schoolteacher, had reopened his school that morning after an enforced vacation occasioned by the illness of so many of his pupils. He called his scholars together for their afternoon session. Gilliland was at work on a suit of clothes for Dr. Whitman in the mansion house. Osborn was in his room with his family in the mission building. Hall was laying a floor on a room which was being built at the east end of the "L" of the main mission building. Bewley and Sales were both confined to their beds with illness. Rodgers went to the river to get some water just before the trouble broke out.

After lunch, when the men had resumed their tasks and the children returned to their studies, Mrs. Osborn ventured to get up out of her bed and walk about. This was the first time she had walked for three weeks. She went from the Indian room in which her family was staying, into the living room, where both of the Whitmans were with some of the sick children. About that time Mrs. Whitman began bathing Elizabeth Sager. Dr. Whitman was seated on a settee near the stove, reading, when Mrs. Osborn entered. There came a knock on the door leading from the dining room into the kitchen. Mrs. Whitman answered and then said: "Doctor, you are wanted." An Indian in the kitchen desired medicine. When Dr. Whitman opened the door, the Indian endeavored to force his way into the

THE ASSASSINATION OF MARCUS WHITMAN.
From Victor, *River of the West.*

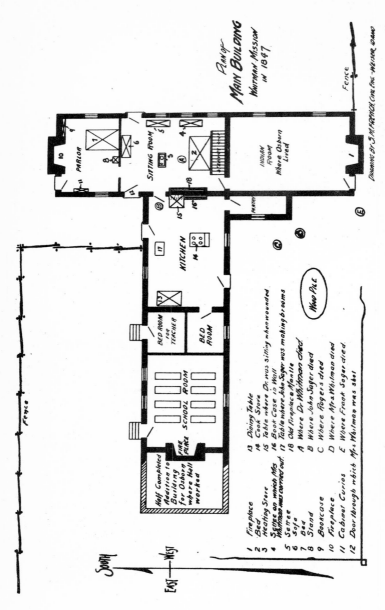

PLAN OF THE MISSION HOUSE DRAWN UNDER THE DIRECTION OF MRS. ELIZABETH SAGER HELM.

This drawing was not made to scale as was the plan drawn by Asahel Munger which Mrs. Whitman sent to her parents with her letter of May 2, 1840. Elizabeth Sager Helm omits the room marked B on Munger's drawing. In general, however, the two drawings agree very closely. From Cannon, *Waiilatpu*.

TOMAHAS.

TILOUKAIKT.

THE MURDERERS OF DR. MARCUS WHITMAN.
From Kane, *Wanderings of an Artist.*

THE ASSASSINATION OF DR. WHITMAN.
From Nixon, *Whitman's Ride Through Savage Lands.*

room, but the Doctor succeeded in keeping him out. Whitman then went to the medicine closet under the stairway, got what he wanted, and went into the kitchen, asking his wife to lock the door behind him.[20] It was then about two o'clock in the afternoon.

Elizabeth declared that she remembered loud words between the Indians and Dr. Whitman. Mrs. Whitman and Mrs. Osborn were talking in low tones, when suddenly they heard a volley of shots in the kitchen. Mrs. Whitman exclaimed in great agitation: "The Indians will murder us all!" Little Elizabeth climbed out of the tub and started to run out of the room. Mrs. Whitman hastily collected herself, called Elizabeth back, and began to assist her to dress. Mrs. Osborn hurried back to her room. Mrs. Whitman called to them to lock the outside door. Osborn drove a nail with a flatiron over the latch. In the meantime Mary Ann Bridger burst excitedly into the west door of the dining room and cried: "They have killed father."

Available records do not give us a clear picture of what took place in the kitchen. It seems that John Sager, who was just recovering from the measles, was sitting there, winding some twine which was to be made into brooms. Mary Ann Bridger was also in the room and was the only one who saw the Indians begin the attack on Dr. Whitman. It seems that Tiloukaikt and Tomahas had come on the pretext of wanting medicine. Several writers have confused Tomahas with Tamsucky, but the earliest accounts state that the villain who crept up behind the doctor while he was talking with Tiloukaikt was Tomahas.[21] When the doctor's attention was fully engaged, Tomahas struck him on the head with a pipe tomahawk.[22]

According to the testimony of Mrs. Eliza Hall, given at the trial of the murderers, part of the struggle took place

---

[20] *See* Appendix 5 for a list of the eyewitness accounts of the massacre and captivity from which writings the details have been taken for this account. Every statement here made can be verified in one or more of these accounts.

[21] Catherine Sager, Elizabeth Sager, and Spalding all refer to Tomahas, who was later captured, tried on the charge of killing the doctor, and executed. Cannon, Gray, and a later statement of Elizabeth Sager state that the villain was Tamsucky. Cannon followed Gray. Elizabeth Sager gave her statement in her old age to Fred Lockley.

[22] Both Whitman College and the Oregon Historical Society claim to have the original tomahawk. The claims of the latter seem to be the most trustworthy.

out of doors. She claimed that she saw Tiloukaikt strike Dr. Whitman three times with a hatchet. Several have testified that Whitman's face was mutilated. Very evidently he was struck after he had fallen.

Gertrude Hall Denny, who was ten years old at the time, later wrote:

Mother told me that on the way she saw Chief Tiloukite trying to hit Dr. Whitman on the head, but the latter kept dodging from side to side and missing the blows, although he had already been shot and was bleeding.[23]

It appears, therefore, that Dr. Whitman made a desperate effort to escape and that he managed to get outside before he fell, mortally wounded.

When John Sager saw what was happening, he reached for a pistol, but watchful Indians quickly shot him. He, too, fell mortally wounded. It was then that little Mary Ann Bridger climbed out of a window and ran around the end of the building to the west entrance to warn Mrs. Whitman. The sound of the shots in the kitchen seemed to have been the signal for a general attack to begin on all of the white men on the mission grounds. The Indians standing around watching the butchering dropped their blankets and with guns and tomahawks began their murderous attack.

All was confusion. When the attack commenced, Mrs. Hayes and Mrs. Hall ran from the mansion house to the mission house. There they found Mrs. Whitman bending over the stricken form of her husband. Together the women half carried and half dragged his body into the dining room, where they placed it on a settee. Mrs. Whitman tried to stop the bleeding. She asked him if he knew her, and he murmured a "Yes." She wanted to know if she could do anything to stop the bleeding. He said: "No." "Can you speak to me?" she cried. Again: "No." Mrs. Whitman took a towel and some ashes from the stove and tried to staunch the blood.

About this time Rodgers, who had been out by the river, burst into the door, being chased by some Indians. He had been struck on the head with a club or a tomahawk, and had been shot in the arm. Mr. Rodgers, seeing Dr. Whitman prostrated and bleeding, asked if he were dead. Dr. Whitman rallied to answer for them. "No," he said. Nar-

---

[23] *Ore. Nat. Son.*, Vol. 1, p. 63. The skull of Dr. Whitman showed that he received two blows. One cut out a piece of skull in the back about the size of a dollar. The other cracked the skull on top.

cissa, realizing that the end was at hand, cried out: "I am a widow! I am a widow!" She also said: "That Joe! That Joe! He has done it all."

About this time Nathan Kimball, one of the men engaged in preparing the beef, entered, wounded in the arm. He came into the room where Mrs. Whitman and the others were, holding his bleeding arm and said: "The Indians are killing us—I don't know what the damned Indians want to kill me for—I never did anything to them. Get me some water." Mrs. Whitman hurried for water. Since Nathan Kimball was a very religious man and never used profane language, and since Mrs. Whitman never countenanced swearing in her hearing, ten-year-old Elizabeth giggled when she heard Kimball speak of "the damned Indians." She expected Mrs. Whitman to reprove him, but nothing was said.

Elizabeth heard shots outside and looked out of the window in time to see the Indians shooting at Mr. Saunders. She cried out excitedly: "Mother, they are killing Mr. Saunders." Mrs. Whitman went to the door, the upper part of which was of glass, to look out. While standing there, she saw Joe Lewis and cried out to him: "Is it you, Joe, who are doing this?" At this a young Indian by the name of Frank Escaloom, who was standing on the steps leading into the schoolroom, fired at Mrs. Whitman, the bullet entering "under her left arm." She screamed and fell to the floor, but soon staggered to her feet again. She began praying aloud: "Lord, save these little ones," and she is also reported to have said: "This will kill my poor mother."

The Indians were then beating down the doors in an effort to gain admission to the living room. Mrs. Whitman suggested that they go upstairs. There were then with the Whitmans in the room or in the chamber above, Rodgers and Kimball, both of whom were wounded, Mrs. Hayes, Mrs. Hall, Lorinda Bewley, Mary Ann Bridger, Helen Mar Meek, and four of the Sager girls. Matilda Sager was in the schoolroom. Louise Sager and Helen Meek were very ill and had been carried up by Mr. Rodgers. No effort was made to move Dr. Whitman, who was then unconscious.

They had barely got upstairs before the Indians broke into the room below. Soon they had forced open the door leading to the stairway and were about to rush upstairs when they suddenly became very docile as they saw the

end of a gun pointed in their direction. After getting upstairs, Mrs. Whitman rested across the end of Miss Bewley's
bed. She called to Rodgers to take an old gun barrel which
happened to be in the room. "Hold the end of the muzzle
over the top of the stairs," she cried, "so the Indians will
think you have a gun." It was this broken weapon which
so quickly quieted the murderers.

Tamsucky then appeared and asked them all to come
down. He promised that all would be spared and told them
they could go to Finley's lodge. He said that the house was
about to be burned and as he was their friend, he wanted
to protect them. The walls of the house were made of
adobe, and therefore would not burn, but the Indians could
have built a fire within the dwelling and burned the rafters
and floors of the upstairs room, so the threat to burn was
very real. After considerable parley, Tamsucky went upstairs. He was fearful of being shot, and it took considerable pleading to cause him to venture. Upstairs he
expressed such sympathy that he completely won Mrs. Whitman's confidence. She placed full trust in his promises and
said: "God has raised us up a friend." It was finally arranged that the adults should go first, and the children
should remain for a time. Kimball decided to hide, and
so escaped for the time being. Elizabeth Sager followed
Mrs. Whitman downstairs.

Lorinda Bewley and Rodgers helped Mrs. Whitman go
downstairs. She was then so weak from loss of blood that
she found it necessary to lie down on a settee. Elizabeth
Sager noticed that Mrs. Whitman "averted her face from
the Dr. who was still breathing." The body of John Sager
was then lying in the doorway connecting the living room
with the kitchen. Mrs. Hall, Mrs. Hayes, and Miss Bewley
went out and crossed the grounds to the mansion house.
Since Mrs. Whitman was so weak, it was decided to carry
her on the settee. Rodgers took one end, and Joe Lewis
entered to take the other.

The Indians crowded about the north door. A space
was cleared, and just after they got the settee outside, Rodgers having the front end, the Indians began firing. Rodgers
dropped his end and cried out: "O my God!" and fell mortally wounded. Lewis dropped his end and stepped back
into the crowd and likewise began firing. One bullet hit
Mrs. Whitman in the cheek, another in the body. She may
have received many more. One of the Indians pushed the

settee over, throwing her body into the mud. Another raised her head by the hair and struck her face with his leather quirt.

Rodgers was shot at least three times, but even so life lingered on into the night. The members of the Osborn family from their hiding place, but a few feet away, heard the dying groans of Rodgers. Among his last words were: "Come, Lord Jesus, come quickly," and "Sweet Jesus." Mrs. Whitman died before Rodgers. In all probability she passed away before her husband. Elizabeth Sager remembered hearing Dr. Whitman's moans and heavy breathing in the early part of the night. These gradually became lower, and then ceased.

Mrs. Whitman was the only woman to lose her life in the tragedy. She was then in her thirty-ninth year. Gifted, devoted, and talented, she literally gave her life, as did her husband, for the unregenerate savages of Oregon.[24] Dr. Whitman was in his forty-sixth year. He was a man of tireless energy, of high ideals, and of consecrated purpose.

THE FATE OF OTHERS

The story of the massacre is incomplete without a brief review of what happened to the other white people who were at Waiilatpu at the time. Mrs. Saunders reports that the Indian with the green cap returned to her rooms shortly before the trouble began. He left the door open, and when the signal to fire was given, another Indian entered, dropped his blanket, and fired at Mr. Gilliland, who was sitting on top of a table, sewing. Gilliland, fatally wounded, managed to get into the bedroom, where he flung himself on the bed. He died about two o'clock that night. Mrs. Saunders declared that the one who shot Gilliland was the one who was the first to shoot at Mrs. Whitman.

The Indians who were gathered about the beef attacked Kimball, Canfield, and Hoffmann. Let Mrs. Saunders tell the story:

I saw Mr. Hoffman fighting with his ax, and an Indian killing someone with his tomahawk, at the rail fence which enclosed a few

---

[24] Spalding wrote in *Senate Document No. 37*, p. 30: "Thus fell at her post the devoted Mrs. Whitman, daughter of Judge Prentiss of Prattsburg, New York, alone, under the open heavens, no mother's hand or husband's voice to soothe her last moments—the cold earth her dying pillow, her own blood her winding sheet. The companion of my youth, we were members of the same school, of the same church, of the same hazardous journey, of the same mission."

acres between the Mission and the Manor House where we lived. I saw the Indian who shot Mr. Gilliland, upon a haystack. He afterwards shot thru a glass door and wounded Mrs. Whitman. I saw Mr. Hall who was laying a floor on the second-story of a house, put his hands on the window sill and slide down and run towards the willows. Several Indians gave chase to him but soon returned. At the same time Mr. Marsh had been shot at the grist mill. . . .

I saw old Chief Beardy coming in great haste on horseback. Knowing him to be a member of Dr. Whitman's church, I call to him repeatedly. He turned his head and looked at me. . . . We could also hear old Chief Beardy, who often had come to visit Dr. Whitman, talking very loudly to the Indians trying to persuade them to stop their slaughter.[25]

Mrs. Saunders was mistaken about Beardy being a member of the church. The only member of the Cayuse tribe who was a member of the First Church of Oregon was Five Crows, and he was not a party to the massacre.

Hoffmann appears to have been the only one who offered resistance. With his ax he inflicted a painful wound on Tamsucky in the foot. Spalding quotes Canfield as saying: "Saw Hoffman fall several times, but would arise amid the flying tomahawks, till he was backed up in the corner of the doctor's house, when two Indians came up on horses with long-handled tomahawks, over-reached, cut him down, and he rose no more."[26] The man whom Mrs. Saunders saw being killed at the fence was her own husband, who had left the schoolroom and was endeavoring to get to his wife. In the description given of the massacre by his daughter Helen, we read: "I looked through the window and saw two Indians holding him and another trying to shoot him. I tried to get to him but the older scholars pulled me back and shut the door. . . . I found him afterward lying dead about half way to the Mansion House."

Kimball succeeded in finding temporary refuge in the mission house and for a time remained in hiding upstairs. He was severely wounded, and Elizabeth Sager remembered his groaning through the night. Some of the sick children cried for water during the long night. Shortly before daybreak, Kimball decided to make the desperate effort of going to the river for water. He asked Catherine Sager to tear up a sheet and make some bandages. Catherine replied: "Mother wouldn't want the sheets torn up." "Child," replied the wounded man, "your mother will never need sheets. She is dead."

---

[25] Saunders, *op. cit.*

[26] Spalding, *Senate Document No. 37*, p. 28.

He sought to disguise himself by wrapping a blanket about his body, Indian-fashion. The unfortunate man was discovered by some Indians and shot. His body was left lying by a fence. Later the Indians permitted some of the girls to get water.

Canfield, the third man about the beef, succeeded in secreting himself in the blacksmith shop until darkness came. He then left on foot for Lapwai, 120 miles distant, to warn Mrs. Spalding and those there. He succeeded in reaching his destination on December 4. He had never been over the trail before.[27] This was a remarkable trip, and the man deserves great praise.

Hall, who was at work on the new addition to the mission house, succeeded in escaping. He ran to the river and hid in the willows that lined the banks. During the night he made his way to Fort Walla Walla, where he arrived early Tuesday morning and gave McBean and those at the Fort the first news of the tragedy. Some controversy has centered about McBean's treatment of Hall. Suffice it to say, Hall left for the Willamette Valley, and it is reported that he was drowned while crossing the Columbia River at the Upper Falls.[28]

McBean claimed that he had but five men with him at the Fort, thus making it impossible for him to send a rescue party. He did send his interpreter at once to the mission grounds to inform Tiloukaikt "that his young men had already gone too far by killing Dr. Whitman, his lady, and the rest ... and that I wanted him to spare the poor women and children."[29] It is possible that this intercession on McBean's part was effective in giving protection to the women and children.

McBean's interpreter met Nicholas Finley en route to the Fort with the two Manson boys and David Malin. The interpreter continued to Waiilatpu, made his investigation, and upon his return reported to McBean that Dr. and Mrs. Whitman had been killed with nine others and that three had been wounded. McBean immediately wrote to his superior officers at Fort Vancouver, informing them of the tragedy. This is the first written account of the massacre.[30] For fear

---

[27] Drury, *Spalding*, p. 341.

[28] Cannon, *op. cit.*, p. 120.

[29] Marshall, *op. cit.*, Vol. 2, pp. 233 ff., gives a letter of McBean, dated Mar. 12, 1866, in which he gives his side of the story.

[30] *Ibid.*, p. 235.

of arousing the Indians on the Lower Columbia. McBean gave strict orders to his messenger to tell no one about the affair. It seems that McBean should have permitted the messenger to warn the Hinmans and Perrin Whitman at The Dalles.

About the time of the shooting of Mrs. Whitman and Mr. Rodgers, Joe Lewis discovered Francis Sager hiding with some of the school children in the rafters over the schoolroom. The two Manson boys and David Malin, being sons of Hudson's Bay men, were sent to the lodge of Finley. They were safe. Francis had a feeling that he would be killed, and after he had seen the dead body of his brother, he said: "I will soon follow my brother." Conflicting stories are told about his death. Matilda Sager speaks of two Indians' arguing over what should be done. One pled for his life, but the other insisted on killing him. Nathan Kimball, Jr., later wrote: "I saw him [Joe Lewis] take a boy about fifteen years old, named Sager, by the nose and shoot him in the head with a pistol, while I was a prisoner there." In all probability Lewis was provoked by the Sager boys' telling Dr. Whitman what he had been saying, and thus had a special grudge against them.

Shortly after the arrival of the Osborn family at Waiilatpu, Dr. Whitman, with plenty of lumber on hand, ordered the laying of a new floor in the Indian room. Sleepers had been placed about three feet above the ground, on which the new floor boards were laid. Some of these were loose, so that when the trouble broke out, Mr. Osborn raised some of the boards, thus affording a hiding place for himself and his family. They succeeded in secreting themselves just before the room was filled with Indians. Little two-year-old Alexander heard the Indians rummaging through their belongings and said aloud: "Mother, the Indians are taking all of our things." In fear and haste the mother clapped her hand over the child's mouth. From their hiding place, they heard the shooting of Mrs. Whitman, Mr. Rodgers, and then a little later that of Francis Sager. They could hear their dying groans.

With the coming of night and when everything was quiet, the Osborns decided to go to the Fort. Leaving everything behind, and with Mr. Osborn carrying the two boys, they started out. Poor Mrs. Osborn, who had but that day risen from her sickbed, was totally unequal to the task. She managed to struggle along for two miles and then found

THREE WHITMAN RELICS.

Narcissa's writing desk, thought to have been brought across the Plains; a medicine jar which Dr. Whitman once used; and a piece of broken plate. These relics are on exhibit in the Oregon Historical Society, by whose courtesy this picture has been made.

WHITMAN RELICS IN THE WHITMAN COLLEGE MUSEUM.

Bible that Whitman gave to the Rev. Elkanah Walker; tomahawk claimed to have been the one used to kill Dr. Whitman; compass, with lid, carried across the continent in 1836 and given by Dr. Whitman to the Rev. Cushing Eells; coffee box used in the Whitman home; and broken earthenware container used for medicines.

By courtesy of Whitman College.

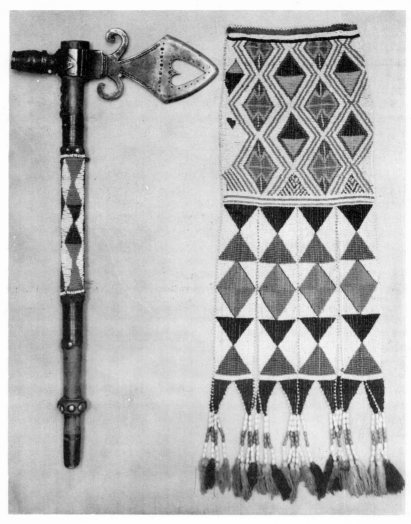

Tomahawk owned by the Oregon Historical Society which it claims is the one used by Tomahas to kill Dr. Whitman. The beadwork is supposed to have once been the property of Tomahas.

Picture by courtesy of the Oregon Historical Society.

herself completely exhausted. She was left with Nancy and
the youngest boy, while her husband with John on his back
started for the Fort more than twenty miles distant. He
reached the Fort at nine o'clock the next morning. Osborn
had bitter words to say about the treatment accorded him
by McBean. After receiving some supplies from an American, J. M. Stanley, who had arrived the previous day from
Tshimakain, Osborn started back with a friendly Indian to
get his wife and children. After some difficulty they were
located. Mrs. Osborn was so weak that she had to be tied to
her horse. They got back to the Fort at ten o'clock that
night.

Thus we find that at the close of the first day the following had been killed—Dr. and Mrs. Whitman, John and
Francis Sager, Hoffmann, Gilliland, Saunders, Marsh, and
Rodgers. Kimball was killed the second day, bringing the
total of deaths to ten. Canfield, Hall, and the Osborn family
escaped. Left without the ministering care of the Whitmans,
Louise Sager died on December 5, and Helen Mar Meek died
on the 8th. It is possible that they would have died even if
the Whitmans had remained alive to care for them, for the
girls were very ill at the time of the massacre.

Following the events of Monday, the Indians withdrew
to their camp on what is now known as Stone Creek, about
three miles distant. Each day they would go back to the
mission station, where they held the survivors captives.
These were given plenty of food, and the women were made
to cook for the Indians. Those were days of feasting when
no restraint whatever was placed upon the stores of food
which Dr. Whitman had so laboriously and carefully gathered.[31] On Tuesday, Stanfield dug a shallow grave, about
three feet deep on the edge of the Indian cemetery and to
the north of the mission house.

The Indians did not scalp any of the victims, although
they did brutally mutilate some of the bodies. During that
first night the bodies lay where they had fallen. Some of
the Indians threw blankets over the corpses. Elizabeth Sager
remembered seeing the body of Dr. Whitman lying in the
dining room, his face gashed and his eyes wide open.

---

[31] Cannon, *op. cit.*, pp. 130-153. Cannon tells the story of a kind-
hearted Cayuse by the name of Beardy, who got sick from eating too
much peach pie. For a time he was afraid he had been poisoned by the
whites. When he finally understood his trouble, "his mirth was un-
bounded, and he never tired of telling the story in after years."

On Tuesday, November 30, Father Brouillet left the
Umatilla to visit Tiloukaikt's camp. He arrived there about
seven or eight o'clock in the evening and learned then the
dreadful news. The priest was aghast at what had happened.
Wednesday morning he baptized three sick children and
then hastened to the scene of the tragedy.[32] In Brouillet's
account we read:

> I found five or six women and over thirty children in a condition
> deplorable beyond description. Some had lost their husbands, and the
> others their fathers, whom they had seen massacred before their eyes,
> and were expecting very moment to share the same fate.
>
> After the first few words that could be exchanged under the cir-
> cumstances, I inquired after the victims, and was told that they were
> yet unburied. Joseph Stanfield ... had been spared by the Indians,
> was engaged in washing the corpses, but being alone he was unable
> to bury them. I resolved to go and assist him, so as to render to those
> unfortunate victims the last service in my power to offer them.
> What a sight did I then behold! Ten bodies lying here and there,
> covered with blood and bearing the marks of the most atrocious cruelty
> —some pierced with balls, others more or less gashed by the hatchet.
> Dr. Whitman had received three gashes on the face. Three others had
> their skulls crushed so that their brains were oozing out.[33]

The bodies were buried in the grave prepared the previous day by Stanfield. A few days after burial it was discovered that the wolves had dug into the grave and had
eaten all of the flesh from one of Mrs. Whitman's legs. Stanfield reburied the bodies and piled more dirt on the grave.
However, when the soldiers came the next spring they found
that wolves had dug up all of the bodies and had scattered
the bones.

On Tuesday morning James Young from the sawmill was
sent to the mission station with a load of lumber. Some Indians killed the unsuspecting young man about two miles
from the mission station. Later Stanfield buried the body
where it lay. On Wednesday, Spalding started for Waiilatpu
and would have met the same fate had he not been warned by
Brouillet, who chanced to meet him shortly before he reached
Waiilatpu. Though pursued, Spalding managed to escape

---

[32] Bagley, *Early Catholic Missions in Old Oregon*, p. 192. T. C.
Elliott, of Walla Walla, has examined Brouillet's original record of
baptisms without finding mention of these. However, since Brouillet
in his *Authentic Account* claimed that he baptized the children, we
must accept his statement. Mrs. Saunders likewise refers to it. Spalding, who may not have understood the importance the Catholics place
upon this sacrament, could never understand why the priests should
have baptized the children of the murderers at that time.

[33] *Ibid.*, pp. 192-3.

and succeeded in making his way to Lapwai, where he arrived on December 6, two days after Canfield, having made most of the journey on foot.

Since James Young had not returned, the families at the sawmill became concerned. On the Sunday following, December 5, Daniel Young, his brother, went down on horseback to investigate. Upon his arrival at the mission station, he learned to his horror what had happened. The Indians then needed someone to operate the gristmill and sent back to the sawmill for the two families. They were promised immunity if the men would grind the wheat.

After the arrival of these families, the Indians massacred in a most brutal way Crocket Bewley and Amos Sales. According to the deposition of Daniel Young, Bewley had said that he believed that "Joe Lewis was one of the leaders and the Catholic priests were the cause of it." Stanfield warned him that he should not let the Indians hear him say that.[34] It may be that as a result of such outspoken criticism, both Bewley and Sales lost their lives, thus bringing the total of deaths to thirteen. Hall's death, perhaps by drowning, accounted for the final total of fourteen.

The following table outlines the fate of the seventy-four people who were at the mission station when the tragedy occurred:

	Men	Women	Children	Total
Killed (including Hall)	11	1	2	14
Died			2	2
Escaped	2	1	3	6
Released (Mansons-Malin)			3	3
Adult half-breeds	2			2
Captives (including Stanfield)	5	8	34	47
	20	10	44	74

The only families to come through the tragedy without the loss of at least one were the Osborns and Smiths.

---

[34] Gray, *Oregon*, p. 476. Spalding wrote *Senate Document No. 37*: "On the eighth day after the first butchery, three Indians ... tore off the table-legs and commenced beating Sailes and Bewley, and were full half an hour in killing them."

EPILOGUE

McBEAN'S messenger with the first news of the Whitman massacre arrived at Fort Vancouver on the evening of December 6.[1] The messenger had stopped at The Dalles, where Hinman joined him. Perrin Whitman and Mrs. Hinman were left at the mission station in ignorance of what had taken place at Waiilatpu. When Hinman later learned of the tragedy he was bitter in his criticism of McBean for having given such strict orders to the messenger. If Hinman had not hastened back to The Dalles, a tragedy might have occurred there also.[2]

Sir James Douglas, the successor of Dr. McLoughlin at Fort Vancouver, lost no time in sending Peter Skene Ogden with a party of sixteen men and a supply of goods to seek release of the captives. They reached Fort Walla Walla on December 19. Ogden succeeded in ransoming the captives, and they arrived at Fort Walla Walla on December 29. On the whole, they were well treated by the Indians, although Miss Bewley and some of the older girls were taken by the Indians for their wives. Miss Bewley especially had a horrifying experience with Five Crows, who wished her for his wife. She fled to the priests for protection, but they felt that they could do nothing except advise her to go with the chief.

The Nez Perces escorted the Spaldings and those of their household to the Fort on January 1. Mrs. Spalding suffered much from exposure, particularly as she was not in strong health at the time. She died at Brownsville, Oregon, on January 7, 1851.

Ogden, with the men, women, and children, left Fort Walla Walla on January 2 for the Willamette Valley. David Malin was left behind because he was the son of a former employee of the Hudson's Bay Company. One of the Sager girls remembered him standing on the river bank as the

---

[1] McBean's account, written in haste and with secondhand information, contained many inaccuracies, as, for instance, the accusation that Rodgers, in order to save his life, had confessed that he had heard Dr. Whitman and Mrs. Spalding plotting to poison the Indians. Strange to say, even Bancroft, *Oregon*, Vol. 1, p. 663, accepted this story. Miss Bewley denied it. Gray, *Oregon*, p. 488.

[2] For discussion of this incident *see* Bancroft, *op. cit.*, Vol. 1, p. 667. For Hinman's account *see* *O.H.Q.*, Vol. 2, pp. 268-83.

FAMILY RECORD.

DEATHS.

DEATHS.

PAGE FROM THE WHITMAN FAMILY BIBLE.
The fifth entry in the left-hand column records the death of Marcus Whitman.
By courtesy of Mrs. Minnie A. Dayton.

boats pulled away from the Fort, crying as though his heart would break. Peter Ogden delivered his charges over to Governor Abernathy at Oregon City on January 10. The Sager children, reduced now to four in number and made orphans a second time, were taken into different homes. The Spaldings took Matilda. Mary Ann Bridger passed away in March of that spring. Thus, out of the happy group of eleven children once a part of the Whitman household, two were killed, three died, and the others were scattered throughout the Willamette Valley.

The faithful Spokanes protected the missionaries in their midst, but it was not until the next spring that Walker and Eells and their families were able to go to the Willamette. Thus all three stations of the American Board's mission in Oregon were closed. The Walkers and the Eells settled at Oregon City for a time. In 1850 the Walkers moved to Forest Grove, where they lived thereafter and where their youngest son, Samuel T. Walker, still resides. The Eells family lived in Hillsboro and Forest Grove, Oregon, and then in 1860 Mr. Eells went to Walla Walla. Eells was active in organizing Congregational churches throughout the Inland Empire.

The two families at Tshimakain learned of the Whitman Massacre through a letter written by J. M. Stanley, an American painter, who had been visiting them and who was en route to Waiilatpu when he heard what had taken place. On December 2, 1847, Stanley notified Walker and Eells.[3] This is the second known account of the massacre and was carried to Tshimakain by Solomon. In Mrs. Walker's diary for December 9, we read:

We are hoping to have Dr. Whitman with us for supper to-night. But about sunset old Solomon arrived bringing the sad intelligence that Dr. and Mrs. Whitman, Mr. Rogers, John and Francis Sager and others have been murdered by the Indians. Mr. Stanly was apprised of it at the Soda mines and went to Walla Walla instead of Waiilatpu or he too might have been killed.

Dr. Whitman was expected at Tshimakain in December to attend Mrs. Walker, who gave birth to a son on December 31. He was called John.

While in Oregon, Stanley painted a number of pictures, including one entitled *Massacre of Dr. Whitman's family*

---

[3] Original owned by F. W. Skiff, of Portland, Oregon. Published, Mowry, *Marcus Whitman*, p. 292, and Skiff, *Adventures in Americana*, p. 197.

at the Wailetpu Mission in Oregon, 29th of November 1847,
also one entitled *Abduction of Miss Bewley from Dr. Whit-*
man's Mission. In 1852 a catalog of 151 of Stanley's paintings was made. Most of these pictures were destroyed at
the time the Smithsonian Institution in Washington, D. C.,
burned, on January 24, 1865. Five of Stanley's paintings
happened to be elsewhere at the time and thus escaped.
They now hang in the National Museum at Washington.[4]

CAPTURE OF THE MURDERERS

In the meantime Governor George Abernathy, head of
the provisional government of Oregon, received word regarding the massacre on December 8 from Sir James Douglas. The legislature was then meeting, and with surprising
alacrity a company of fifty riflemen was enrolled and
equipped to be sent to the upper country to punish the
murderers. All of lower Oregon was stirred to the depths
by the news of the atrocity. It was soon realized that fifty
riflemen would not be enough, so the Governor issued a
call for five hundred. News of the determination of the
Americans to avenge the massacre was carefully kept from
the Indians until the captives were released.

After considerable difficulty in raising money to finance
the undertaking, the punitive expedition under the command of Colonel Cornelius Gilliam mobilized at Oregon
City on December 25 and left as soon as possible for the
upper country. By the last of January about 130 men were
at The Dalles.[5] This grew to 537 by the 12th of February.
On the 24th of that month the expedition started for the
Umatilla. During that day they had an encounter with
some Indians which resulted in the death of a chief called
Gray Eagle and the wounding of Five Crows. Stickus remained neutral during the hostilities and endeavored to
bring about peace.[6]

The soldiers proceeded to the Walla Walla River, which
was reached on the 28th, and the next day camp was made
near the Whitman mission. There the men found the deserted and destroyed buildings. The Indians had looted all
that could be easily taken. The bodies of the victims had
been dug up by the wolves and the bones scattered about

4 *Smithsonian Report*, 1924, pp. 507-512; *O.H.Q.*, Vol. 33, pp. 250 ff.

5 Clark, *Pioneer Days*, Vol. 2, p. 556.

6 Clark, *Pioneer Days*, Vol. 2, devotes Chapter LIV to "Istachus,
the Christianized Indian."

the grounds. Perrin Whitman was present and has left
the following account of what he saw:

We found everything swept from the site of the Mission, the building burned and everything in ruins. The bodies had been buried, but
the coyotes had dug into the graves considerable. I found what I satisfied myself was Doctor's skull. There were two hatchet marks in
the back of the head.[7]

Perrin was able to identify the skull by the gold-filled
tooth. When the bodies were disinterred in 1897, Dr. Whitman's skull was found cut in two by a fine-tooth saw. The
dividing line started above the nose and continued straight
across the head. Dr. Stephen B. L. Penrose, president
emeritus of Whitman College, wrote:

Perrin B. Whitman told me positively that it had not been sawn
when he helped to rebury it in 1848. The matter is a mystery for
which I have no explanation, but the fact is undisputed.[8]

When Perrin was asked in 1897 whether or not the Indians would have so mutilated the skull, he said: "No, The
Indians are the most superstitious people in the world about
touching the dead. The Indians would not have molested
the body in that way for any cause."[9]

The soldiers found a considerable portion of Mrs. Whitman's golden hair, from which locks were cut by several
members of the expedition. The remains were gathered together again and reinterred, a wagon box being used as
a coffin. In 1860 the Rev. Cushing Eells visited the site and
made a rude fence to encircle the grave. In 1863 Myron
Eells erected a board fence to replace the earlier one
erected by his father. In 1885 the students of Whitman College built a picket fence which remained until the grave
was opened in October, 1897.[10]

The Cayuses fled before the soldiers after one or two
insignificant skirmishes. The Nez Perces manifested friend-
liness and were not molested. It was impossible to follow
the Cayuses across the mountains. After spending the
spring and part of the summer of 1848 in the vicinity of

---

[7] *W.C.Q.*, Vol. 2, No. 3, p. 36.

[8] Letter to the author dated Aug. 26, 1936. During the winter of
1897-98, photographs were taken of the skulls of both Dr. and Mrs.
Whitman. The picture of Dr. Whitman's skull clearly shows the division. Had more than one picture been taken of the skulls from different angles, an attempt could have been made to reconstruct facial
features.

[9] *W.C.Q.*, Vol. 2, No. 3, p. 36.

[10] Eells, *Marcus Whitman*, p. 295.

Waiilatpu, a guard of fifty men was left, and the rest returned to their homes in the Willamette Valley.

Several years passed before any of the perpetrators of the crime were taken. Joe Lewis, the most notorious of all, was never apprehended. According to one report, Lewis was mortally wounded in 1862 when he attempted to rob the express which was being carried from Auburn to Boise. He was buried in an unmarked grave on the bank of the Payette River.[11] Horace Hart, in a letter dated May 12, 1848, to his brother-in-law, H. H. Spalding, reported that Five Crows was not expected to recover from the wound he received in the first encounter with the soldiers.[12] It is reported that Tamsucky was killed at the time of his arrest.[13]

After two years of wandering, always fearful of the soldiers and never daring to return to the Walla Walla, the Cayuses finally decided to deliver up five men to the whites for the welfare of the tribe. No record remains of the suffering endured during these years by members of the tribe, both innocent and guilty, as they wandered in the mountains. Already they had become dependent upon their farms and were ill prepared to be driven from their native haunts.

The five who voluntarily gave themselves up were Tiloukaikt, Tomahas, Klokamas, Isaiachalakis, and Kiamasumpkin. When Tiloukaikt was once asked why he had given himself up, he is reported to have replied: "Did not your missionaries teach us that Christ died to save his people? So die we to save our people."

The trial began on May 22, 1850, at Oregon City. The Indians were represented by counsel, but such efforts as he was able to put forth were futile. Witnesses included Mrs. Eliza Hall, Elizabeth Sager, Mrs. Lorinda Bewley Chapman, and Josiah Osborn, whose testimony involved all of the defendants except Kiamasumpkin, who, although admitting that he was present at the time of the massacre, persistently denied any part in taking the life of any white person. As part of the defense, the counsel for the accused tried to prove that Dr. Whitman had received warning, and called Dr. John McLoughlin, Stickus, and Henry Spalding as witnesses to prove this point.

---

[11] Arnold, *Indian Wars of Idaho*, p. 101.

[12] Coll. W. Hart also reported that Lewis had then fled to the Mormons.

[13] Nixon, *Marcus Whitman*, p. 230.

SARAH MINTHORN or IPNATS OLATALKT.
Born about 1830, died, 1907. Thought to have been the last of the pupils
of the Whitman mission school to pass away.
Picture by courtesy of Mrs. J. M. Cornelison, of Pendleton.

HYMN OF OUR SIRES

Anniversary Hymn

"MARCUS WHITMAN"

ROBERT FREEMAN, 1927

WILLIAM PIERSON MERRILL, 1927

1. Brav-ing the wilds all un - ex-plored, Dream-ers of dreams and pi - o - neers, Wield-ing the sick-le, goad, and sword, They marched with the sun to the last fron-tiers— God of the val-iant, grant that we, Their sons, do fol-low val - iant - ly!
2. Fair knights of jus-tice and of good, They gave to e - vil bat - tle gage; Bear-ing their souls in rec - ti - tude, They left a good - ly her - it - age— God of the righteous, grant that we, Their sons, do fol-low right-eous - ly!
3. Guards of the sa - cred al - tar flame, Bring-ers of learn-ing and of faith, They lu-mined life in the Bless - ed Name And hope they flared in the day of death— God of the faith-ful, grant that we, Their sons, do fol-low faith-ful - ly!
4. Theirs was the Pres-ence ev - er sure, Theirs was the all a - bound-ing grace, Theirs was the pas - sion ev - er pure To hon - or the Lord in all their ways— God of the Christlike, grant that we Do fol - low, fol-low worth - i - ly! A - men.

All five, including Kiamasumpkin, who appears to have been innocent, were sentenced to be hanged on Monday, June 3. Tiloukaikt pled earnestly to be shot, as he considered hanging an ignominious fate.[14] The condemned preferred the spiritual ministrations of a Roman Catholic priest, Father Veyret, to the offered services of H. H. Spalding. The sentence was carried out as ordered, Joseph Meek, then U. S. Marshal, serving as executioner.

THE INVENTORY

Spalding made out an itemized statement of the property belonging to the Whitmans or to the American Board, which was lost, destroyed, or stolen at the time of the tragedy. This statement was sworn to on September 1, 1849, by both Spalding and Perrin Whitman. This inventory gives a clear picture of the material welfare of the Whitmans at the time of the massacre.

Spalding listed a farm of thirty acres fenced and cultivated; a log cabin at the sawmill; 40,000 feet of sawed lumber, enough for 2 houses, one third of which had been transported to Waiilatpu; an orchard of 75 apple trees[15] with an irrigation ditch, also a nursery of apple and peach trees; a flour mill, without a millhouse; a blacksmith shop; granaries; the mission house and mansion house, with detailed information regarding the number and size of windows and doors, and so forth; furniture to include 4 settees, 2 rocking chairs, listed at $5.00 each, and 12 more at $1.50 each; 84 chairs, 3 feather-beds, bedding for 20 people, tables, bookcases, beds, stands, 1 cookstove, 1 box stove; 1 threshing machine, 1 corn sheller, 300 pounds of nails; 2 large prairie plows, 23 cast plows, 1 harrow, 1 wagon, 12 ox yokes, 2 grain cradles, 6 sickles, 300 bushels of wheat, 60 of corn, 250 of potatoes, and 20 of onions.

The livestock included 290 head of cattle, 46 head of horses, and 92 head of sheep with a total valuation of $3,980.00. These were listed as follows:

100 milch cows at $16.00 each	1600
80 young cattle at $5.00 each	400
11 yoke of oxen at $50	550

---

[14] *Oregon Spectator*, May 30 and June 27, 1850.

[15] In Mrs. Walker's diary for October 2, 1846, we find mention made of Dr. Whitman's apples. She wrote: "Mr. E. returned. He brought three apples. They grew on Dr. W's trees and are very nice. The first any of our children except Cyrus have seen since they were old enough to remember."

```
80 calves at $4 each ................................................................320
8 beef cattle at 20 ................................................................160
8 broke horses at 20 .............................................................160
2   "      "    at 30 ..............................................................  60
6 Unbroke at $12 .................................................................. 72
30 mares & coalts at $12 .....................................................360
80 Sheep at $3 .......................................................................240
12 Bucks South down Imported ........................................ 60
```

Spalding listed Dr. Whitman's wearing apparel at $378.00 and his wife's at $300.00. The library was valued at $180.00. He also listed trunks, saddlebags, riding saddles (including one lady's), 200 pounds of wool, a grindstone, cheese press, tools, medicines, and so forth. The total value was $21,583.26, as compared with an inventory of $10,-448.44 for his station at Lapwai.[16] An effort was made to collect these sums from the United States Government, but no evidence has been discovered to show that any part of the claims was ever paid.

OREGON TERRITORY CREATED

As soon as the inhabitants of the Lower Columbia country heard of the massacre, many felt the necessity of appealing to Washington for aid. Joseph L. Meek was delegated to carry the news to the States and make an appeal for help. Meek accompanied the Volunteers to Waiilatpu, where he parted company with them on March 4, 1848, and with a few companions started eastward. His companions remained with him for only a part of the journey.

Mrs. Frances Fuller Victor in her *River of the West,* which was based upon Meek's personal recollections, gives the following description of his arrival at Waiilatpu:

Arrived at Waiilatpu, the friends and acquaintances of Dr. Whitman were shocked to find that the remains of the victims were still unburied, although a little earth had been thrown over them. Meek, to whom, ever since his meeting with her in the train of the fur-trader, Mrs. Whitman had seemed all that was noble and captivating, had the melancholy satisfaction of bestowing, with others, the sad rite of burial upon such portions of her once fair person that murder and the wolves had not destroyed. Some tresses of golden hair were severed from the brow so terribly disfigured, to be given to her friends in the Wallamet as a last and only memorial.

Not only had Meek to discover and inter the remains of Dr. and Mrs. Whitman, but also of his little girl, who was being educated at the mission.[17]

---

[16] Originals in Old Indian Files, Washington, D. C. Copies in American Board.

[17] P. 433.

Meek reached St. Louis May 17, with the first news of the massacre and of the Indian war in Oregon. After many interesting experiences, he reached Washington and was welcomed to the White House by President Polk. Meek was a distant relative of the President and enjoyed the hospitality of the White House during his visit in Washington. He was a picturesque figure and created a sensation wherever he went.

On the day following his arrival, the President sent a message to Congress in which he recommended the immediate organization of a territorial government. The Oregon bill, so long before Congress in some form or another, had been held up by Southern Congressmen who insisted on making Oregon a slave state. Senator Benton again spoke in Oregon's behalf on May 31. It so happened that another representative of Oregon was in Washington, J. Quin Thornton, Chief Justice of the Provisional Government, who had been sent by sea to the States before the massacre occurred. Meek and Thornton, though differing in many ways, had one thing in common, and that was their devotion to Oregon.

In spite of the Presidential recommendation for immediate action and the fervent efforts of such men as Benton, there was great delay. The House of Representatives finally approved the bill on August 2. The Senate delayed action until August 13, the day before adjournment, when it, too, took favorable action. When the bill was signed by the President, Old Oregon became Oregon Territory. The law giving a section of land to each settler was passed at a subsequent session of Congress.

Whitman had said to Spalding on the Saturday night before his death: "But my death will probably do as much good to Oregon as my life can." Whitman in his martyrdom rendered the last service to his beloved Oregon in that he brought the Oregon question to a focus in Congress and insured passage of the Oregon bill. The Whitman Massacre moved a dilatory Congress to action, and thus extended the full sovereignty of the United States over that important territory.

WHY DID IT HAPPEN?

The news of the massacre as carried by Meek appeared in the papers and through these columns the loved ones in the East first read of the dreadful tragedy. The Rev. David Greene wrote to the Commissioner of Indian Affairs on

May 27, 1848, requesting a confirmation or contradiction of the report.[18]

The Rev. Joel Wakeman served as pastor of the Presbyterian church at West Almond from 1844 to 1865. It so happened that Judge and Mrs. Stephen Prentiss were living with their son Jonas Galusha in that village when the news arrived. Wakeman picked up his paper one day and was startled to read the news of the tragedy in far-off Oregon. Taking the paper with him, he hastened to the store which Jonas conducted to break the sad news to him and to his parents. Wakeman found Jonas and his father in the store and was about to tell them when Mrs. Prentiss entered with her copy of the paper in her hand and said: "Marcus and Narcissa have been murdered by the Indians."[19]

Dr. Whitman's niece, Mary Alice Wisewell, has given the following description of the grief of Whitman's loved ones:

His Mother received the news of his massacre, with the stony grief without tears, and sat alone for days without speaking, and his sister, Mrs. Wisewell, was made sick by the news, and could not eat for weeks, and went out into the orchard and cried, until she could cry no more.[20]

In the Whitman family Bible we find this entry, possibly written by the grief-stricken mother:

Marcus Whitman
was killed by the Indians of Oregon
together with his wife and several others
November 29th   1847

Naturally, loved ones in the East, far removed from the scene of trouble, wondered why the Indians should do such a horrible deed. Why? Why? Why? Among the aching hearts which yearned for more information was that of Jane Prentiss. Some time prior to the summer of 1849, the Rev. H. K. W. Perkins, in whose home Narcissa had lived for a time at Waskopum when her husband was on his Eastern trip, returned to his home at Hallowell, Maine. On August 29, 1849, Jane wrote to Mr. Perkins, asking for

---

[18] Original in files of Old Indian Bureau.

[19] Prattsburg *News*, Jan. 27, 1898.

[20] Statement by Mary Alice Wisewell Caulkins to Dr. S. W. Pratt, Coll. Wn.

any letters[21] that her sister had written to him or his wife, and for any light which he might throw on the tragedy.

Perkins replied on October 19 and gave such a detailed and enlightening description of the fundamental causes leading up to the massacre that the letter is given in its entirety in an appendix.[22] Perkins was very frank, yet kind, as he stated his conviction that neither Dr. nor Mrs. Whitman were fitted by disposition to be missionaries to the Indians. This is no reflection upon their devotion. They tried to make the adjustment, but never did. He claimed that the Indians grew to fear Dr. Whitman. They felt that he was the white man's friend rather than theirs. Mrs. Whitman was "considered haughty." He wrote: "Mrs. Whitman was not adapted to savage but *civilized* life." His discerning letter heightens our admiration for these two, who, in spite of fundamental disqualifications, remained at their post because of their high sense of duty.

However, their ministry for the Indians was not altogether in vain. Only a small part of the Cayuses actually took part in the massacre. Many, including faithful Stickus, deeply mourned the unfortunate occurrence. Catherine Sager states that Stickus "never tired of talking of Dr. W. & tears would roll down his cheeks when speaking of his tragic death."[23] Others of the Cayuse tribe maintained their daily devotions and continued to observe Sunday with puritan strictness for years after the massacre.

Although the Indians did not realize it at the time, the day was inevitably approaching for them when they would have to make an adjustment with Western civilization. While that adjustment was hard, it would have been infinitely harder for them had the Whitmans never lived at Waiilatpu. As it was, the majority of the tribes of the Walla Wallas, the Umatillas, and the Cayuses settled on the reservation provided for them by the Government at Pendleton, Oregon, without disturbance. The massacre and the events subsequent thereto broke the spirit of the Cayuses, once so proud and haughty. Decimated in numbers by disease and shorn of their prestige and influence, as well as of

---

[21] The letters from Mrs. Whitman to Mrs. Perkins, now in Coll. O., were evidently sent by Mr. Perkins to Miss Prentiss. Later they passed into the hands of a descendant of the Prentiss family and were given to the Oregon Historical Society.

[22] *See* Appendix 6.

[23] Statement of Catherine Sager copied by Myron Eells, Dec. 1, 1884, Coll. W.

their lands, they became docile and peaceful. Fifty years after the massacre about seven hundred full-blooded Indians were reported living on the reservation at Pendleton. Of these, 350 claimed to be Cayuses, 175 were Umatillas, and a like number were Walla Wallas. In addition, there were about 300 half- and quarter-breeds.[24] With the passing of the years tribal lines have faded. Gradually the English language is supplanting the old tongues. Old customs and costumes are giving away before the white man's ways. Today, according to the 1936 census, there are 1,151 Indians living on the Pendleton Reservation, including those of part Indian blood. Of this number, 374 are Cayuses; 663, Walla Wallas; 126, Umatillas; and 18 others.

H. H. Spalding returned to Lapwai as an appointed missionary of the Presbyterian Church in the fall of 1871, on the eve of a great spiritual awakening which seemed to affect the whole Nez Perce tribe. Hundreds upon hundreds of the Nez Perces were baptized and the foundations laid for the seven Protestant churches, six Presbyterian, and one Methodist, which are still in existence among that people. During the summer of 1873, Spalding visited the Spokane Indians and baptized 253 adults and 81 infants. Two Presbyterian churches among the Spokanes carry on the work which Walker and Eells started. In his old age Spalding and his associates baptized over 1,000 Indians.

The Cayuses and the other Indians in the vicinity of Waiilatpu did not share in this spiritual awakening that visited the Nez Perces and Spokanes. We do find, however, that Spalding had several contacts with the Indians near Pendleton. In the official record book of the First Church of Oregon he noted that on September 27, 1872, nine Indians were baptized at Wild Horse, which is the name of a creek which flows into the Umatilla River.[25] Rev. H. K. Hines was present and took part in the ceremony.

In the spring of 1874, Spalding fell sick at Kamiah. He passed away at Lapwai on August 3, 1874, and was buried on the old mission site. Today the State of Idaho has converted part of the original site into a state park. An entry in the record book of the church for May 11, 1874, gives another account of a contact with the Indians among whom

---

[24] For details of this *see* Drury, *Spalding*, pp. 402 ff.

[25] The original record is lost, but a certified copy appeared in the 1903 minutes of the Synod of Washington (Presbyterian). These were reprinted in the 1936 minutes of the Synod.

Dr. and Mrs. Whitman labored. The Rev. H. T. Cowley, a colleague of Spalding's, wrote:

Today the deeply interesting event occurred of the baptism by Bro. Spalding apparently on his death bed, of the Umatilla Chief Umhawalish, who came all the way from his country, 210 miles for Protestant baptism. He was one of the early pupils of the Martyr Whitman and the name of Marcus Whitman was given to him in his new relation as a member of the household of faith.

Spalding was then so weak that Cowley had to support him in his bed when the sacrament was administered. The chief's wife was baptized and received the name of Narcissa Whitman. On another occasion some of the Nez Perces took the Whitman family name, and one of the first of the Nez Perce ordained ministers was the Rev. Silas Whitman.

On June 17, 1882, a Presbyterian Church was organized on the Pendleton Reservation for the Indians by the Rev. George L. Deffenbaugh, a Presbyterian missionary, and the Rev. Robert Williams, the first ordained Nez Perce minister. Twenty-six members were enrolled, among them being Sarah Tsalapihai (or Ipnatsolatalkt), who was a girl about seventeen years old at the time of the massacre and who had attended the Whitman school for the natives. She lived until 1907. The church now enrolls sixty-five members and has for its pastor a Presbyterian missionary, the Rev. J. M. Cornelison, D.D.

Even though members of the Cayuse tribe today remember with chagrin and sorrow the part some of their ancestors played in the final tragedy, yet at the same time they remember with pride the fact that the Whitmans once lived among them. The martyrdom of the missionaries but deepened the love and respect in which they were held by many within the tribe. The story is told of how an old Indian visited the home of a white settler in the vicinity of Walla Walla many years after the massacre. The Indian had known the Whitmans. The white man asked many questions about them, and finally asked this: "What was the color of Mrs. Whitman's hair?" For a long time the Indian sat looking into the burning fire in the fireplace without saying a word, and then replied: "It was like the gold of the sunset."

The Roman Catholics endeavored to establish a mission in the vicinity of Waiilatpu several years after the massacre. Father Brouillet founded what he called the Santa Rosa Mission about three miles from Waiilatpu. Later the site was claimed by Burwell W. Bussell, a settler. In an endeavor to get title to the land, the Catholics carried the case to the courts. It was finally settled sometime during the seventies in favor of Bussell. On August 21, 1876, Bussell made "Preemption Cash Entry, Walla Walla series, No. 505, covering the land embraced in the said donation claim, for which a patent was issued to him April 10, 1882." It appears that during the absence of Father Brouillet, Bussell filed on the land and succeeded in getting title. This incident shows that the Catholics made the effort to open mission work among the Cayuses after the massacre.[26]

MONUMENTS, MEMORIALS, RELICS

The fame of the Whitmans has grown with the passing of the years. The greatest of all monuments erected to perpetuate the Whitman memory is Whitman College at Walla Walla, which was begun by the Rev. Cushing Eells as Whitman Seminary in 1859. The college has been sponsored by the Congregational Church. The first building was erected in 1866. After going through many vicissitudes, the college is now well established and is reflecting credit to the honored name which it bears. Among the buildings on the campus is a hall for girls named Narcissa Prentiss Hall.

In 1897 the college sponsored a fitting commemoration of the fiftieth anniversary of the massacre. Among the first to conceive the idea of erecting a monument at Waiilatpu to the Whitmans was W. H. Gray, who during the seventies collected about eight hundred dollars for that purpose. Mr. Gray did not live to see his ideal realized. Others took up the project, and finally a monument thirty feet high with the name WHITMAN inscribed on its base was erected at a cost of about $2,250. The College planned to dedicate this monument at the time of the fiftieth anniversary of the massacre, November 29, 1897.[27]

The bodies of the victims were disinterred on October 22, 1897, to be reburied in a more fitting tomb. Unfortunately the stones did not arrive in time for the ceremonies. The monument was erected on top of the hill near the site of the mission home and can be seen today for many miles

---

[26] Information received from Dept. of Interior in a letter to the author dated Dec. 30, 1936. The contest papers have been lost.

[27] An account of this commemorative occasion is to be found in Vol. 1, No. 4 and Vol. 2, No. 1, of the *Whitman College Quarterly*.

THE WHITMAN GRAVE IN 1858

THE GRAVE TO-DAY

THE GRAVE OF MARCUS WHITMAN (early views).
From Eells, *Marcus Whitman.*

THE GRAVE OF MARCUS WHITMAN TODAY.

The victims of the Whitman massacre lie buried under the marble slab. The monument to the left marks the grave of Mr. and Mrs. W. H. Gray, and the Whitman monument is on the brow of the hill to the right, in the distance.

in all directions. The remains of the victims were reburied in a different location at the foot of the hill on January 29, 1898, where a heavy marble slab was placed over the large metal casket. The names of the fourteen victims were inscribed on the slab.[28]

Among those present at the fiftieth anniversary of the massacre were eight survivors of the tragedy, including Catherine Sager Pringle, Matilda Sager Delaney, Elizabeth Sager Helm, Nancy Osborn Jacobs, Susan Kimball Wirt, Sophia Kimball Munson, Nina Kimball Megler, and Byron S. Kimball. The last of the survivors to pass away was Mrs. Gertrude Jane Hall Denny, who died in Portland, August 5, 1933.[29] Among those who took part in the commemorative ceremonies was the Rev. Samuel Greene, of Seattle, a son of the Rev. David Greene, of the American Board.[30] Another present was the Rev. L. H. Hallock, D.D., believed to be a descendant of Moses Hallock.

When Mr. and Mrs. W. H. Gray died, their bodies were buried at Astoria, Oregon. Years later it was felt that their remains should be removed to Waiilatpu, and this was done in the fall of 1916. Suitable commemorative exercises were held on November 1, 1916. The Grays were buried near the grave containing the victims of the massacre, and a monument was erected to them.

An effort is now being made to restore Waiilatpu. Cushing Eells secured title to the mission site through purchase from the American Board. He sold the land to Charles Moore. The title was clouded, so the Kiwanis Club of Walla Walla instituted steps to clear it. On June 21, 1926, the Congress of the United States passed an act turning over 646.89 acres of land to the American Board, which in turn deeded it to the present owners, thus clearing the title. Eight acres were kept out as a public park. This lot included the hill with the monument and the graves. In the summer of 1936, Congress passed a law providing for the restoration and maintenance of the Whitman mission, contingent upon the site's being purchased and donated to the government. The Chamber of Commerce of Walla Walla succeeded during

---

[28] Eells, *Marcus Whitman*, p. 296. Mowry, *Marcus Whitman*, p. 232.

[29] Mrs. Denny was the wife of Judge Denny who served in various important diplomatic posts in China and Korea. While U. S. Consul General at Shanghai, he became interested in the ring-necked Chinese pheasant and was the one who introduced the birds into Oregon.

[30] Greene retired from the Board in 1848. He died on April 7, 1866. *Missionary Herald*, Aug., 1866, contains his picture and obituary.

the summer of 1936 in raising the amount needed to buy about thirty-seven acres of the land. This site is to become a part of the National Park Service, and soon duplicates of the mission buildings will be erected there.

In 1855 the Hudson's Bay Company gave up Fort Walla Walla. In 1857 United States troops established a fort at the present site of Walla Walla, about five miles distant from the mission premises. Nothing remains at the old site of Fort Walla Walla except the outlines of the foundation walls.

Whitman's name and memory are perpetuated by the Whitman National Forest in the Blue Mountains; also by Whitman County in the state of Washington, which has a population, according to the last census, of 28,014, and an area of 2,108 square miles. This county is almost as large as the state of Delaware.

A statue of Dr. Whitman, by Alexander S. Calder, was placed on the façade of the Witherspoon Building in Philadelphia, which is the headquarters of the Board of Christian Education of the Presbyterian Church, U. S. A. The building was dedicated October 24, 1896. The statue is about twelve feet high and represents Whitman clad in frontier dress, standing beside a wheel. It is said that the statue was modeled after Perrin Whitman, who resembled his uncle in many ways.

The highway connecting Prattsburg with Naples in New York State is called the Narcissa Prentiss Highway, and that connecting Penn Yan with Rushville is called the Marcus Whitman Highway. A number of plaques and monuments have been erected to the Whitmans at Prattsburg, Wheeler, Rushville, and Ithaca, New York.

A monument along the old Oregon Trail at Hagerman, Idaho, contains the following inscription:

COMMEMORATING THE MEMORY OF
MARCUS WHITMAN
PIONEER MISSIONARY WHO IN 1836
BROUGHT THE FIRST WAGON OVER THE TRAPPERS PATH
THAT AFTERWARD BECAME THE OREGON TRAIL

ERECTED BY SONS AND DAUGHTERS
OF IDAHO PIONEERS 1934

The authentic Whitman relics are but few. In the rooms of the Oregon Historical Society at Portland are to be found a broken fragment of a plate found at Waiilatpu, Mrs. Whitman's writing desk, and a medicine jar once owned by Dr.

Whitman and given by him to the Osborns. The Presbyterian Historical Society, with rooms in the Witherspoon
Building, Philadelphia, owns the saddlebags that Dr. Whitman used when a physician at Wheeler, New York. The
collection at Whitman College contains the following items:
Dr. Whitman's compass, a Bible given by Mrs. Whitman
to Lorinda Bewley, coffee box used by the Whitmans, butcher
knife carried across the plains, various articles dug up on
the site of the blacksmith shop, and various other incidental
articles. The Whitman College collection is especially rich
in original letters, diaries, and much valuable source material.

During 1936, celebrations in honor of the centennial of
the arrival in Old Oregon of the members of the Whitman-
Spalding party were held in many places throughout the
country. The Presbyterian Church, U. S. A., was especially
active in promoting centennial observances. Special exercises were held at Rushville and Prattsburg, New York,
on June 4, 1936, following the meeting of the Presbyterian
General Assembly at Syracuse.

Such communities as Lewiston, Idaho, and Walla Walla,
Washington, staged elaborate celebrations which continued
over several days. The Lewiston celebration was held May
8-10 inclusive and centered about the Spaldings. The Whitmans were well remembered when Walla Walla observed
the centennial on August 13-16. The United States Post
Office Department issued a special Oregon stamp during
the summer of 1936 in honor of the Whitman-Spalding centennial, although their names did not appear on the stamp.
The first-day covers mailed from Walla Walla on July 14,
1936, totaled 106,150, while 252,350 stamps were also sold
in addition to those used on the covers.[31]

The monuments we erect, the commemorative exercises
we hold, and the relics we carefully preserve give testimony
to the depth of our affection for the Whitmans. More enduring than monuments of stone are the memories cherished
by all who delight in stories of courage, of adventure, and
of high idealism. The greatest guarantee that we have of
the imperishable fame of the Whitmans is the simple fact
that so much of the good and the true and the beautiful was
woven into their characters. They died as Christian martyrs
in the service of their Lord, and they died as patriots in

---

[31] *Spokesman-Review*, Spokane, July 23, 1936.

the service of their country. Though their spirits have been called from this world, their influence remains to strengthen and inspire. In this sense Marcus and Narcissa Whitman still live and serve whenever their story is known.

The tragic and barbarous scenes connected with their death arouse sympathy whenever and wherever told. One cannot help asking—was such a sacrifice wholly in vain? The answer to this question must be left to a wisdom superior to that of man. We see but dimly and partially. This much is certain—Marcus and Narcissa Whitman are enshrined in the hearts of the people of the Pacific Northwest as are no other two who lived in Oregon's yesterdays. Their fame is as enduring as human appreciation of the self-sacrificing lives they lived. They belong to the saints!

> *"Or lose thyself in the continuous woods*
> *Where rolls the Oregon, and hears no sound,*
> *Save his own dashings—yet the dead are there...."*

Appendices

APPENDIX 1

INDEX TO THE LETTERS OF DR. AND MRS. MARCUS WHITMAN

THE LETTERS of Dr. and Mrs. Marcus Whitman are referred to in the text by numbers in brackets. By finding the corresponding number in the following list, one can learn the date of the letter, to whom it was written, from what place, the location of the original, if known, and the book or magazine which contains the letter, if printed.

The following key designates the various collections which contain source material:

Coll. A.—American Board, Boston, Mass.
Coll. M.—Methodist Collection, care of the Rev. John Canse, Portland, Ore.
Coll. O.—Oregon Historical Society, Portland, Ore.
Coll. P.—Presbyterian Historical Society, Philadelphia, Penna.
Coll. W.—Whitman College, Walla Walla, Wash.
Coll. Wn.—Washington State College, Pullman, Wash.
Coll. U.—Miss Elona Underwood, Salt Lake City, Utah.

A few Whitman letters are in private possession, and where known the names of the owners are given. The letters of Mrs. Whitman are designated by putting the dates in italics. This list does not include twelve letters which Dr. Whitman sent to Henry Hill, Treasurer of the American Board, dealing almost entirely with financial matters, and being usually nothing more than a notification of moneys drawn. Neither does it include a letter of Mrs. Whitman's (April 15, 1845) to Mr. Hill regarding subscriptions to the *Mother's Magazine*. These letters to Hill are on file with the American Board.

Edward Eberstadt, a bookdealer in New York, claims that he secured a lot of about eighty Whitman letters for one of his clients. It is believed that this lot includes the originals of some of the letters listed below, copies of which are in the Oregon Historical Society. This lot of eighty letters was not accessible for the preparation of this work.

The following is the key used to designate the persons to whom the letters were addressed:

1—Members of the American Board.
2—Members of Dr. Whitman's family.
3—Members of Mrs. Whitman's family.
4—The Rev. or Mrs. Samuel Parker.
5—The Rev. or Mrs. Elkanah Walker.
6—The Rev. or Mrs. H. K. W. Perkins.
7—Mr. or Mrs. H. B. Brewer.

See bibliography for fuller information regarding books or magazines.

No.	Place of Writing	To Whom	Date	Present Location	Magazine or Book
			1827		
1	Rushville	Pratt	Sept. 11	Wn.	
			1828		
2	Rushville	Pratt	Feb. 5	P.	
			1834		
3	Wheeler	1	June 3	A.	Hulbert, *Oregon Crusade*, p. 258
4	Wheeler	1	June 27	A.	Hulbert, *Oregon Crusade*, p. 262
5	Wheeler	1	Dec. 2	A.	Hulbert, *Oregon Crusade*, p. 269
			1835		
6	Wheeler	1	Feb. 2	A.	Hulbert, *Oregon Crusade*, p. 281
7	Amity	1	*Feb. 23*	A.	Hulbert, *Oregon Crusade*, p. 139
8	Liberty	Narcissa	April 30		Mowry, *Marcus Whitman*, p. 56
9	Liberty	1	May 13	A.	Hulbert, *op. cit.*, p. 144
10		1	*No date*		Mowry, *op. cit.*, p. 65
11		Mrs. Hull	May 14-Oct. 26	A. & U.	*O.H.Q.*, Sept., 1927
12	Bellevue	1	June 21		Mowry, *op. cit.*, p. 58
13	St. Louis	1	Nov. 7	A.	Hulbert, *op. cit.*, p. 167
14	Rushville	1	Dec. 17	A.	Hulbert, *op. cit.*, p. 171
15	Cohocton	1	Dec. 28	A.	Hulbert, *op. cit.*, p. 173
			1836		
16	Rushville	1	Jan. 6	A.	*Marcus Whitman, Crusader*, p. 179
17	Rushville	1	Jan. 29	A.	*Marcus Whitman, Crusader*, p. 185
18	Rushville	1	Feb. 15	A.	*Marcus Whitman, Crusader*, p. 186
19	Rushville	1	Mar. 3	A.	*Marcus Whitman, Crusader*, p. 193
20	Steamboat *Siam*	3	*Mar. 15*	O.	*T.O.P.A.*, 1891, p. 79
21	Steamboat *Chariton*	3	*Mar. 31*	O.	*T.O.P.A.*, 1891, p. 83
22	Leavenworth	1	May 5	A.	*Marcus Whitman, Crusader*, p. 200
23	Platte	(Harriet) 3	*June 3*	O.	*T.O.P..A*, 1893, p. 104

No.	Place of Writing	To Whom	Date	Present Location	Magazine or Book
			1836—(Continued)		
24	Platte	(Parents) 3	June 4	O.	T.O.P.A., 1893, p. 109
25	Platte	(Parents) 2	June 6	U.	
26	Platte	(Augustus) 2	June 27	U.	T.O.P.A., 1891, p. 40
27	Rendezvous	(Bro. & Sis.) 3	July 15 Mack Coll., N. Y. City	A.	
28	Rendezvous	1	July 16		
29		(Diary) 2 & 3	July 18-Oct. 22	W. & U.	Marcus Whitman, Crusader, p. 204
30	Walla Walla	1	Sept. 5		O.H.Q., Vol. 27
31	Vancouver	4	Sept. 18		Marcus Whitman, Crusader, p. 212
32	Walla Walla	4	Oct. 8		W.C.Q., June, 1899
33	Vancouver	(Mother) 2	Oct. 13	(Copy, Coll. Wn.)	W.C.Q., June, 1899
34	Vancouver	(Oren & Nancy) 2	Oct. 24	(Copy, Coll. Wn.)	
35	Vancouver	4	Oct. 24	Parker MS., Ithaca (Cornell U. Lib.)	
36	Vancouver	4	Oct. 25	Parker MS., Ithaca (Cornell U. Lib.)	
			1837		
37	Vancouver	The Rev. & Mrs. Hull	Oct. 25	W.	Marcus Whitman, Crusader, p. 242
38	Vancouver	3	Nov. 1	W.	O.H.Q., Vol. 27, p. 189
39	Walla Walla	(Mother) 3	Dec. 5	O.	T.O.P.A., 1891, p. 86
			1838		
40	Waiilatpu	(Parents) 3	Mar. 30	O.	T.O.P.A., 1891, p. 90
41	Waiilatpu	(Parents) 3	May 2	O.	T.O.P.A., 1891, p. 93
42	Waiilatpu	1	May 5	A.	Marcus Whitman, Crusader, p. 278 and O.H.Q., Vol. 37, p. 121
43	Waiilatpu	1	Mar. 12	A.	Marcus Whitman, Crusader, p. 291
44	Waiilatpu	(Parents) 3	Mar. 14	O.	T.O.P.A., 1891, p. 97
45	Columbia River	1	Mar. 17	A.	Marcus Whitman, Crusader, p. 301*
46	Waiilatpu	(Parents) 3	April 11	A.	T.O.P.A., 1891, p. 101
47	Waiilatpu	1	April 21	A.	Marcus Whitman, Crusader, p. 302*
48	Waiilatpu	1	May 8	A.	Marcus Whitman, Crusader, p. 311
49	Waiilatpu	1	May 15	A.	Marcus Whitman, Crusader, p. 317*

* Joint letter with Spalding.

No.	Place of Writing	To Whom	Date	Present Location	Magazine or Book
			1838—(Continued)		
50	Waiilatpu	6	July 4	O.	T.O.P.A., 1893, p. 110
51	Waiilatpu	(Jane) 3	Sept. 18	(Copy, O.)	T.O.P.A., 1891, p. 106
52	Waiilatpu	(Mary Ann) 3	Sept. 25	O.	T.O.P.A., 1891, p. 109
53	Waiilatpu	(Father) 3	Sept. 28	(Copy, O.)	T.O.P.A., 1891, p. 113
54	Waiilatpu	(Judson) 3	Sept. 29	W.	Marcus Whitman, Crusader, p. 319
55	Waiilatpu	4	Oct. 3	(Copy, O.)	T.O.P.A., 1891, p. 116
56	Vancouver	1	Oct. 5	A.	Marcus Whitman, Crusader, p. 316
57	Waiilatpu		Oct. 30	A.	Marcus Whitman, Crusader, p. 325
58	Waiilatpu	Chamberlain	Oct. 30	Honolulu	
59	Waiilatpu	6	Nov. 5	O.	T.O.P.A., 1893, p. 112
			1839		
60	Waiilatpu	6	Feb. 18	O.	T.O.P.A., 1893, p. 114
61	Waiilatpu	6	Mar. 23	O.	T.O.P.A., 1893, p. 116
62	Waiilatpu	1	May 10	A.	
63	Waiilatpu	(Jane) 3	May 17	O.	T.O.P.A., 1893, p. 118
64	Waiilatpu	6	June 25		T.O.P.A., 1893, p. 123
65	Waiilatpu	6	June 26	O.	T.O.P.A., 1893, p. 126
66	Waiilatpu	5	July 29	(Copy, O.)	
67	Waiilatpu	(Father) 3	Sept. 30	(Copy, O.)	T.O.P.A., 1891, p. 120
68	Waiilatpu	(Mother) 3	Oct. 9		T.O.P.A., 1891, p. 124
69	Waiilatpu	Chamberlain	Oct. 17	Honolulu	
70	Waiilatpu	1	Oct. 22	A.	
71	Waiilatpu		Nov. 25	A*	
72	Waiilatpu	Gray 5	Dec. 3		Frontier, Nov., 1930, p. 74
			1840		
73	Waiilatpu	6	Jan. 1	O.	T.O.P.A., 1893, p. 127
74	Waiilatpu	1	Mar. 27	A.	T.O.P.A., 1891, p. 130
75	Waiilatpu	(Father) 3	April 30		

* Joint letter with Spalding.

No.	Place of Writing	To Whom	Date	Present Location	Magazine or Book
			1840— (Continued)		
76	Waiilatpu	(Mother) 3	May 2	A.	T.O.P.A., 1891, p. 133
77	Waiilatpu	1	July 6	A.	(Unsigned. Whitman's writing.)
78	Waiilatpu	(Mother) 3	Oct. 9	O.	T.O.P.A., 1893, p. 133
79	Waiilatpu	(Father) 3	Oct. 10		T.O.P.A., 1893, p. 128
80	Waiilatpu	1	Oct. 15	A.	
81	Waiilatpu	(Harriet) 3	Oct. 20	O.	T.O.P.A., 1893, p. 137
82	Waiilatpu	(Father) 3	Oct. 21	O.	
83	Waiilatpu	1	Oct. 29	A.	
			1841		
84	Waiilatpu	6	Mar. 2	O.	T.O.P.A., 1893, p. 139
85	Waiilatpu	5	Mar. 8	W.	
86	Waiilatpu	1	Mar. 28	A.	
87	Waiilatpu	5	April 19	W.	
88	Walla Walla	5	May 12	(Copy, O.)	
89	Waiilatpu	(Augustus) 2	May 24	(Copy, W.)	
90	Waiilatpu	Dr. Bryant	May 24	Miss Barrett, Evanston, Ill.	
91	Waiilatpu	(Edward) 3	May 30	A.	T.O.P.A., 1893, p. 140
92	Waiilatpu	1	July 13	A.	
93	Waiilatpu	(Samuel) 3	Aug. 9	Miss Barrett	
94	Waiilatpu	5	Sept. 20	W.	Walla Walla Union, Aug. 12, 1936
95	Waiilatpu	McKinley	Sept. 30	G. H. Plummer, Seattle	
96	Waiilatpu	(Jane) 3	Oct. 1	O.	T.O.P.A., 1891, p. 138
97	Waiilatpu	(Parents) 3	Oct. 6	O.	T.O.P.A., 1891, p. 145
98	Waiilatpu	7	Oct. 12	M.	
99	Waiilatpu	1	Oct. 22	A.	
100	Waiilatpu	1	Nov. 11	A.	T.O.P.A., 1891, p. 154
101	Waiilatpu	(Father) 3	Nov. 18	O.	T.O.P.A., 1891, p. 154

No.	Place of Writing	To Whom	Date	Present Location	Magazine or Book
			1842		
102	Waiilatpu	5	Jan. 24	......	Frontier, Nov., 1930, p. 75
103	Waiilatpu	7	Feb. 1	...M.	
104	Waiilatpu	(Jane) 3	Feb. 2	......	T.O.P.A., 1891, p. 140
105	Waiilatpu	(Jane & Ed) 3	Mar. 1	......	T.O.P.A., 1893, p. 143
106	Waiilatpu	7	Mar. 25	...M.	
107	Waiilatpu	1	Mar. 30	...M.	
108	Waiilatpu	7	May 12	...A.	(Joint letter with Gray.)
109	Waiilatpu	(Jane) 3	May 17	......	T.O.P.A., 1893, p. 143
110	Waiilatpu	5	June 12	Copy, U. of W., Seattle	
111	Waiilatpu	Marie Pambrun	July 7	......	Ore. Nat. Son., I, p. 27
112	Waiilatpu	7	July 9	...M.	
113	Waiilatpu	7	July 22	...O.	T.O.P.A., 1893, p. 154
114	Waiilatpu	4	July 25	...O.	
115	Waiilatpu	Allens	Aug. 23	...O.	T.O.P.A., 1893, p. 162
116	Waiilatpu	(Jane & Ed) 3	Sept. 29	...O.	T.O.P.A., 1893, p. 165
117	Waiilatpu	(Parents) 3	Sept. 30	...O.	T.O.P.A., 1893, p. 167
118	Waiilatpu	Marcus	Oct. 4	...O.	T.O.P.A., 1891, p. 162
119	Walla Walla	Marcus	Oct. 22	......	T.O.P.A., 1891, p. 167
120	Waskopum	Marcus 5	Dec. 16	...Wn.	
			1843		
121	Waskopum	(Parents) 3	Feb. 7	......	T.O.P.A., 1891, p. 170
122	Waskopum	Marcus	Mar. 4	...A.	
123	Waskopum	(Harriet) 3	Mar. 11	...O.	T.O.P.A., 1893, p. 154
124	Waskopum	(Augustus) 2	Mar. 14	Miss Barrett	
125	Waskopum	Marcus	Mar. 29	...A.	
126	Waskopum	(Jonas) 3	Mar. 31	......	T.O.P.A., 1893, p. 158
127	Boston	1	April 4	...A.	
128	Boston	1	April 7	...A.	
129	Boston	U. S. Ind. Bur.	April 8	U. S. Ind. Office	Mowry, op. cit., p. 256
130	Walla Walla	(Jonas) 3	April 14	...O.	T.O.P.A., 1893, p. 160

No.	Place of Writing	To Whom	Date	Present Location	Magazine or Book
			1843—(Continued)		
131	St. Louis	1	May 12	A.	
132	Waiilatpu	Marcus	May 18	A.	
133	Shawnee Mission	(Ed) 3	May 27	O.	T.O.P.A., 1891, p. 177
134	Shawnee Mission	(Mother) 2	May 27	U.	
135	Shawnee Mission	(Galusha) 3	May 28		T.O.P.A., 1891, p. 178
136	Shawnee Mission	1	May 30	A.	Mowry, op. cit., p. 262
137	Vancouver	6	June 8	O.	T.O.P.A., 1893, p. 169
138	Vancouver	5	June 27	W.	
139	Vancouver	(Jane) 3	July 11	O.	T.O.P.A., 1893, p. 53
140	Black Hills	3	July 20	A.	
141	Ft. George	(Parents) 3	Aug. 11		T.O.P.A., 1893, p. 156
142	Ft. Walla Walla	1	Nov. 1	A.	Mowry, op. cit., p. 264
143		Hon. J. M. Porter	Dec. (?)		Mowry, op. cit., p. 274
			1844		
144	Waiilatpu	7	Jan. 29	M.	
145	Waiilatpu	7	Jan. 30	O.	T.O.P.A., 1893, p. 170
146	Waiilatpu	6	Jan. 31	O.	T.O.P.A., 1893, p. 173
147	Waiilatpu	7	Mar. 5	M.	
148	Waiilatpu	1	April 8	A.	Mowry, op. cit., p. 268
149	Waiilatpu	(Father) 3	April 12	O.	T.O.P.A., 1893, p. 56
150	Waiilatpu	7	April 24	O.	T.O.P.A., 1893, p. 175
151	Waiilatpu	7	April 25	M.	
152	Waiilatpu	(Parents) 3	May 16	A.	T.O.P.A., 1893, p. 64
153	Waiilatpu	1	May 18	A.	
154	Waiilatpu	Mrs. Porter	May 18		T.O.P.A., 1893, p. 176
155	Waiilatpu	(Clarissa) 3	May 20		T.O.P.A., 1893, p. 179
156	Waiilatpu	(Mother) 2	May 20	U.	
157	Waiilatpu	(Augustus) 2	May 21	Miss Barrett	
158	Waiilatpu	Mrs. Leslie	May 28	(Copy, W.)	
159	Waiilatpu	Mr. & Mrs. Waller	May 31		
160	Waiilatpu	1	July 22	A.	
161	Waiilatpu	7	July 29	M.	

No.	Place of Writing	To Whom	Date	Present Location	Magazine or Book
			1844—(Continued)		
162	Waiilatpu	7	Aug. 5	O.	T.O.P.A., 1893, p. 181
163	Waiilatpu	(Parents) 3	Aug. 9	O.	T.O.P.A., 1893, p. 66
164	Waiilatpu	1	Oct. 25	A.	
165	Waiilatpu	7	Nov. 27	M.	
			1845		
166	Waiilatpu	7	Feb. 20	O.	T.O.P.A., 1893, p. 182
167	Waiilatpu	Mrs. Leslie	Feb. 20	(Copy, W.)	
168	Waiilatpu	1	April 8	A.	
169	Waiilatpu	(Henry) 2	April 8		R. L. Robinson, Dundee, New York
170	Waiilatpu	(Father) 3	April 8		T.O.P.A., 1893, p. 68
171	Waiilatpu	(Parents) 3	April 8		T.O.P.A., 1893, p. 70
172	Waiilatpu	7	May 19		T.O.P.A., 1893, p. 184
173	Waiilatpu	1	May 20	A.	
174	Vancouver	(Mrs. Wisewell) 2	June 29	W.	
175	Ft. Vancouver		June 30	A.	W.C.Q., Dec., 1898
176	Waiilatpu	7	Aug. 9		
177	Waiilatpu	7	Sept. 20	M.	T.O.P.A., 1893, p. 184
178	Waiilatpu	5	Sept. 29	W.	
179	Waiilatpu	1	Oct. 26	A.	
180	Waiilatpu	1	Nov. 1	A.	
181	Waiilatpu	5	Nov. 20		Frontier, Nov., 1930, p.86
182	Waiilatpu	7	Nov. 27	M.	
183	Waiilatpu	7	Nov. 28		T.O.P.A., 1893, p. 187
			1846		
184	Waiilatpu	7	Feb. 6	M.	
185	Waiilatpu	5	Feb. 23	(Copy, O.)	
186	Waiilatpu	(Ed) 3	April 2	O.	T.O.P.A., 1893, p. 188
187	Waiilatpu	(Jane) 3	April 2	O.	T.O.P.A., 1893, p. 191
188	Waiilatpu	7	April 7	M.	

No.	Place of Writing	To Whom	Date	Present Location	Magazine or Book
			1846—(Continued)		
189	Waiilatpu	(Mother) 3	April 9	O.	T.O.P.A., 1893, p. 71
190	Waiilatpu	(Father) 3	April 10	O.	T.O.P.A., 1893, p. 75
191	Waiilatpu	1	April 13	A.	(Written by Perrin Whitman.)
192	Waiilatpu	(Harriet) 3	April 13	O.	T.O.P.A., 1893, p. 79
193	Waiilatpu	Mothers Mag.	April 16		Mothers Magazine, Vol. 14, No. 9
194	Waiilatpu	1	May 15	A.	
195	Waiilatpu	(Ed & Jane) 3	May 15	O.	T.O.P.A., 1893, p. 194
196	Waiilatpu	7	July 17	O.	T.O.P.A., 1893, p. 196
197	Waiilatpu	7	July 20	M.	
198	Waiilatpu	Mrs. Osborn	Aug. 29	Huntington Lib.	
199	Waiilatpu	Waller	Sept. 7	O.	
200	Waiilatpu	1	Sept. 8	A.	
201	Waiilatpu	5	Sept. 9		Frontier, Nov., 1930, p. 86
202	Waiilatpu	(Bro. & Sis.) 3	Sept. 11		T.O.P.A., 1893, p. 86
203	Waiilatpu	Mrs. Gilbert	Oct. 15	U.	
204	Waiilatpu	7	Oct. 19	(Copy, O.)	
205	Waiilatpu	Mrs. Spalding	Nov. 2	W.	T.O.P.A., 1893, p. 88
206	Waiilatpu	(Clarissa) 3	Nov. 3		
207	Waiilatpu	(Mother) 3	Nov. 3	(Copy, O.)	
208	Waiilatpu	1	Nov. 3	A.	
209	Waiilatpu	(Judson) 3	Nov. 5	W.	T.O.P.A., 1893, p. 198
210	Waiilatpu	7	Dec. 7		
			1847		
211	Waiilatpu	Mrs. Smith	Feb. 8	W.	
212	Ft. Vancouver	1	April 1	A.	
213	Waiilatpu	(Jane) 3	April 15	O.	T.O.P.A., 1893, p. 205
214	Waiilatpu	Mrs. Gilbert	May 3	U.	
215	Waiilatpu	1	May 19	A.	
216	Waiilatpu	Spalding	May 20	W.	
217	Waiilatpu	(Mother) 3	July 4	O.	T.O.P.A., 1893, p. 208
218	Waiilatpu	1	Aug. 3	A.	

No.	Place of Writing	To Whom	Date	Present Location	Magazine or Book
			1847—(Continued)		
219	Waskopum	1	Sept. 13	A.	
220	Waiilatpu	(Jane) 3	Oct. 12	O.	T.O.P.A., 1893, p. 216
221	Waiilatpu	U. S. Sec. War	Oct. 16		Nixon, *Marcus Whitman*, p. 332
222	Waiilatpu	1	Oct. 18	A.	Mowry, *op. cit.*, p. 284

Total: Dr. Whitman's letters—115; Mrs. Whitman's letters—107.

APPENDICES

The Whitman College collection contains some notes made by the Rev. Myron Eells, among which are extracts from some Whitman letters, the originals of which could not be located. They are as follows:

1. Whitman letter of Aug. 22, 1838: "By the fostering care of a kind providence we were permitted to receive Bro Gray & lady last evening. We felt like Paul when he met the brethren from Rome We thank God & took courage."

2. June 30, 1839: "I had concluded to take the consequences of leaving the mission." Had been reading Henry on Meekness.

3. "Letter of July 29, 1839 Mrs. W. gives an interesting acct. of the death of 2 Ind Children."

4. "May 1841 Dr. W despairs of agreeing with Mr. Sp. thinks it hard to get rid of him & has made up his mind to ask dismission fr Board."

5. "July 15, '44, Dr. W. says—Spent 4 days in examining candidates for ch. membership 10 admitted others putt off on probation."

6. "Fr. Mrs. Whitman to her mother, 1847 fr original by M. Eells 1883 . . . like him for their help is greatly needed. I wrote to him to come but do not know as he got my letter. Husband is wearing out fast."

7. Eells, *Marcus Whitman*, p. 262, gives quotation for a letter of Mrs. Whitman's dated April 11, 1843.

APPENDIX 2

A FINANCIAL SUMMARY

THE FOLLOWING is a summary of the expenses of the Oregon mission of the American Board, especially as they concern Dr. Marcus Whitman and the Waiilatpu station. The statistics were gleaned from references in letters sent by members of the mission to the Board, and from the records of the Board found in Treasury Department records, Volume No. D 29-192, 1822-1846. Since money was cleared through the Hudson's Bay Company, the figures are in English money.

Date of draft or report	Cost for whole mission	Whitman's share
April 28, 1836	$800.00[1]	
Nov. 20, 1836	£381. 8. 1	£188. 7. 2
March 18, 1837	102.13. 1	26.12.10
March 20, 1838	133.15.11	46. 9. 0
March 27, 1838	58. 3.10	58. 3.10
May 10, 1839	595. 1. 0	118.19.10
March 30, 1840	634. 6. 7	104. 4. 1
March 18, 1841	400. 0. 0	?
1842	?	?
April 20, 1843	342.11. 6[2]	
May 30, 1843		$100.00[3]
April 9, 1844	296. 4.11	?
March 29, 1845	345.15. 2	?
April 4, 1846	353. 6. 9	?

---

[1] The total cost of getting the members of the Whitman-Spalding party to Oregon in 1836 was $3,273.76.

[2] Reported by Spalding.

[3] The Board's accounts show that this sum was drawn at Westport, Missouri, but Whitman in his letter of May 27, 1843, to Greene, stated that he drew $100.00 at Cincinnati. These two may be separate items, and they may be the same.

APPENDIX 3

THE CAUSE OF WHITMAN'S RIDE

CONSIDERABLE has been written during the heat of the Whitman controversy on the cause of Whitman's ride. Henry Harmon Spalding in a lecture printed in the Sacramento *Union*, October 19, 1865, and reprinted in his *Senate Document No. 37, 41st Congress, 3d session*, seems to have been the first to claim a political motive for the ride. He stated that while Dr. Whitman was at Fort Walla Walla during the time the mission meeting was held at Waiilatpu during the latter part of September, 1842, he attended a dinner party at the Fort at which there were a number of Hudson's Bay men and some Catholic priests. Spalding wrote:

> While this great company were at dinner, an express arrived from Fort Colville, announcing the (to them) glad news that the colony from Red River had passed the Rocky Mountains and were near Colville. An exclamation of joy burst from the whole table, at first unaccountable to Doctor Whitman, till a young priest, perhaps not so discreet as the older, and not thinking that there was an American at the table, sprang to his feet, and swinging his hand, exclaimed: "Hurrah for Columbia! (Oregon) America is too late; we have got the country." In an instant, as by instinct, Dr. Whitman saw through the whole plan, clear to Washington, Fort Hall, and all.[1]

According to Spalding, Whitman immediately excused himself from the table, sprang on his horse, and rode to Waiilatpu. Upon his arrival there, his horse white with foam, he dramatically declared: "I am going to cross the Rocky Mountains and reach Washington this winter, God carrying me through, and bring out an emigration over the mountains next season, or this country is lost."

Spalding's account was written in the heat of controversy and bears more evidence of an eloquent imagination than it does of historical accuracy. To begin with, the Red River emigration came in 1841 and not in 1842, as Spalding's diary itself bears testimony. Archibald McKinlay indignantly denied that any such dinner party was ever held or any such taunt ever given. When the Rev. Myron Eells published his pamphlet in 1883, setting forth his view of

---

[1] P. 20.

Whitman's services, he used this extract from Spalding's lectures. A year or so later, he was moved to write to Mc-Kinlay about the dinner party, and on January 19, 1885, McKinlay replied:

> You address me as a stranger—I remember you many years ago when you were quite young. Had you wished for correct information regarding the *celebrated* taunt at Walla Walla I think it would have been better to have addressed me before publishing the Pamphlet....
>
> However I may add that I do not believe that Whitman ever originated that dastardly story.... I considered myself on intimate and confidential terms with all the missionaries particularly so with Whitman. Why then such a malicious and utterly foundless fabrication should have been promulgated by any one of these gentlemen at my expense is more than I can possibly conceive....[2]

In this letter McKinlay repeated his conviction that Whitman's primary purpose for going East was on mission business. In a letter written by Ranald McDonald, son of Archibald McDonald, dated February 25, 1891, we find the following statement:

> ...I had seen the Doctors correspondence with Mr. McKinlay for they were intimate friends & I had Mr. McKinlay's words of their last interview at Wallawalla H.B.C. Post. Their was nothing said of going to Washington & saving Oregon   his sole object was on business with the Board....[3]

Yet on May 28, 1866, the Rev. Cushing Eells wrote: "According to the understanding of the members of the Mission, the single object of Dr. Whitman in attempting to cross the continent in the winter of 1842-43 ... was to make a desperate effort to save this country to the United States."[4] Gray, Spalding, and Eells were all active in stressing this point. Walker was silent on the subject. It seems incredible that these three missionaries should have deliberately banded themselves together to spread a falsehood. They came to believe, honestly and sincerely, that Whitman's primary purpose for going East was to save Oregon.

It should be remembered that there was a basis in fact for their theory. Whitman was eager for "pious settlers." All of the Protestant missionaries were much concerned about the coming of the Catholic missionaries. Whitman had a plan of getting small groups of Protestant laymen to settle in the vicinity of the mission stations. Whitman's services to the 1843 emigration were of the greatest value,

---

2 Coll. W.

3 Original in Provincial Library and Archives, Victoria, B. C.

4 *Missionary Herald*, Dec., 1866, pp. 370-72.

and this emigration was of strategic importance to all later emigrations because it succeeded in taking wagons through to the Columbia.

However, it should be pointed out that some of these developments were subsequent to the special mission meeting held in the later part of September, 1842. We must distinguish between the cause and the effect of Whitman's ride. This Gray, Spalding, and Eells did not always do. They confused the two and claimed that Whitman rode to save Oregon.

It should also be remembered that these missionaries were loath to talk about the unfortunate quarrels which had disturbed the peace and effectiveness of the mission for more than three years. In none of his public lectures did Spalding ever make mention of the fact that he had been dismissed. Gray, likewise, was silent on his part in the affair. Eells was a mild-mannered Christian gentleman who abhorred controversy. Any endeavor to explain Whitman's trip East on the basis of mission business would have necessitated the revelation of dissension within the mission. Therefore we can see how easy it was for all three to slur over the mission cause for Whitman's ride and major upon Whitman's desire to bring out Protestant settlers to save Oregon from becoming Catholic.

Except for the references to the desire for "pious settlers" in Walker's letter to Greene of October 3, 1842, there is nothing in the contemporaneous documents which would indicate that any of the missionaries attached any political significance to Whitman's departure. Mrs. Walker undoubtedly reflected her husband's opinion as to the cause for the journey when she wrote in her diary on October 1, after her husband's return: "The mission have concluded to send Dr. Whitman to the States to represent the Mission and obtain a reinforcement or settlers or do something."

Whereas the evidence seems to prove conclusively that the primary reason why Whitman went East when he did was to intercede with the Board regarding its disastrous order of February 28, 1842, yet it is possible that Whitman had a political motive in mind which he did not communicate at the time to his brethren, and which would not, therefore, appear in contemporaneous documents.

White's reports concerning the Linn bill and the proposed Ashburton Treaty undoubtedly excited Whitman's mind as he visualized the effect that such political moves might have on Oregon. From a letter written by White to the Commissioner of Indian Affairs on April 1, 1843, we learn that Whitman had decided to visit Washington before he left Waiilatpu. Dr. White wrote: "Their country is well watered gently undulating extremely healthy and admirably adapted to grazing as Doctor Marcus Whitman may have informed you who resides in their midst."[5]

Since Whitman intended visiting Washington, it must have been for a political motive. Mission business would not have called him there. Granting that there was this motive in Whitman's mind not then made known to his co-workers, we then can ask ourselves this question: "Would Whitman have made the perilous ride when he did if the fateful order of the Board had never been issued?" The documentary evidence indicates that he would *not* have done so. The primary cause for his departure on October 3, 1842, was mission business, but as a patriotic American citizen, Whitman planned before he left Waiilatpu to visit Washington to lay before authorities there some information he possessed and to speak in behalf of a cause dear to his heart.

---

[6] Allen, *Ten Years in Oregon*, p. 174.

APPENDIX 4

THE WHITMAN CONTROVERSY

M OST of the literature dealing with Marcus Whitman centers about the causes and the effects of his famous trip East in 1842-43. For the benefit of students who might wish to study the issues involved in the controversy, a brief outline of the more important publications, with a concise critique, is here given. The term "Whitman legend" is here used to include all or part of the following claims:

1. That the primary cause of Whitman's ride was political. That he rode to prevent the signing of a treaty which would have traded Oregon for a codfishery.

2. That Whitman reached Washington by March 3, 1843, and that he was successful in his pleading with President Tyler and Secretary Webster, who promised him that action would be deferred until he proved that wagons could be taken through to Oregon.

3. That Whitman was mainly instrumental in raising the big emigration of 1843.

It should be remembered that the author of this work accepts the view that the first and primary cause of Whitman's ride was mission business. We have no evidence which would lead us to believe that Whitman would have gone East when he did if the Board's order of February, 1842, had not been sent. The writer believes that a political motive took Whitman to Washington, but that his visit there had little or no significance on any legislation or treaty affecting Oregon, as far as we are able to learn from contemporary documents. Whitman rendered valiant service to the 1843 emigration, serving as pilot from Fort Hall to the Grande Ronde Valley. Whitman was one link in a chain which bound Oregon to the United States. He was an important link, but not the whole chain. This conception of the cause and effect of his ride naturally colors the following review of the works bearing on the Whitman controversy.

The first known published version of the Whitman-Saved-Oregon story was written by S. A. Clark and appeared in the Sacramento *Union*, November 16, 1864.[1] This

---

[1] Marshall, *Acquisition of Oregon*, and Bourne, *Essays in Historical Criticism*, give a detailed review of the literature bearing on the controversy, reprinting some of the articles.

account was short and rather vague, but it gives the supposed conversation between Whitman and Webster. This account was reprinted in the Dansville *Advertiser*, Dansville, New York, May 4, 1865. Beginning with the May 23, 1865, issue of the San Francisco *Pacific,* a series of lectures by H. H. Spalding appeared. The tenth and eleventh of the series, which were published on October 19 and November 9 of that year, gave fuller development to the theory that Whitman rode to save Oregon.[2]

The Astoria *Marine Gazette* for July and August, 1866, carried a similar account of Whitman's ride by W. H. Gray. These three accounts laid the basis of the Whitman legend. Myron Eells wrote: "Rev. H. H. Spalding was about the first person to make known the fact of Dr. Whitman's going east on a political errand."[3] The story came to the ears of the Rev. G. H. Atkinson, who first reached Oregon as a home missionary in June, 1848. Atkinson visited Boston in 1865 and told the secretaries of the American Board "that while they had been accustomed to look upon their Oregon mission as a failure, it was a grand success."[4] They were somewhat sceptical of his story. Atkinson advised them to write to the Rev. Cushing Eells, which was done. Eells replied on May 28, 1866, and his letter was published in the December issue of that year of the *Missionary Herald,* the official publication of the American Board.

In the meantime, before the publication of the account of Eells, Secretary S. B. Treat of the American Board prepared an address on "Early Indian Missions" which included this story. Treat was a member of the committee before whom Whitman appeared on April 4, 1843, to intercede in behalf of the Oregon mission. Treat's address was given at the Pittsfield, Massachusetts, meeting of the Board, September 27, 1866, and subsequently appeared in the October 5, 1866, issue of the *Congregationalist.* Treat built on Eells' version of the ride, which differed from the Spalding version in a few particulars. The New York *Evening Post* copied Treat's lecture from the *Congregationalist,* and it was in turn copied by the *Oregon Herald,* November 17, 1866.

---

[2] Drury, *Spalding,* chapters 16 and 17, gives the background of Spalding's attitude. He wrote in the heat of controversy and made exaggerations which he believed, but which could not be proved.

[3] Eells, *Father Eells,* p. 106.

[4] *Ibid.*

About the same time more of Spalding's lectures were appearing. The Walla Walla *Statesman* printed nine lectures, beginning with the issue of February 9, 1866. Another series was printed in the *States Rights Democrat,* of Albany, Oregon, in the fall of 1866. These lectures and articles developed the idea that Whitman rode to save Oregon.

Eells wrote: "According to the understanding of the members of the mission, the single object of Dr. Whitman, in attempting to cross the continent in the winter of 1842-43, amid mighty peril and suffering, was to make a desperate effort to save this country to the United States."[5] Dr. G. H. Atkinson became a devout believer in the theory and gave a thrilling address on the subject before the annual meeting of the American Board in 1868, which was printed in the *Congregationalist,* October 15, 1868, and in the *Missionary Herald,* March, 1869.

The story found a readier reception in the East than it did in Oregon. To answer some doubters, W. H. Gray wrote to A. L. Lovejoy, who was Whitman's companion on the famous ride for part of the journey. Lovejoy replied on November 6, 1869, and while Lovejoy failed to confirm the essential parts of the Spalding story, still his letter is most valuable for the light it throws upon the famous ride.[6] On February 14, 1876, Lovejoy wrote to Atkinson on the same subject and copied parts of his letter to Gray.[7] In 1870, Gray issued his *Oregon,* which set forth the Whitman legend for the first time in book form.

By this time the secretaries of the American Board held the theory without hesitancy. In the files of the American Board is a large volume, written by hand, which contains the biographies or the official records of its missionaries for the period 1810-1870. The record for Marcus Whitman includes the following statement:

Dr. Whitman established himself at Waiilatpu, among the Kayuses, about 25 miles from Walla Walla. Having frequent occasion to visit the post of the Hudson Bay Co. at that place, he perceived that it was designed to hold that immense and valuable territory as a British possession. To forstall that design, in part, and in compliance with a resolve of the mission in Oct. 1842, he crossed the Rocky Mountains in midwinter, on horseback, arrived in Missouri, in Feb. 1843, visited Washington, called upon Mr. Webster, then Secretary of State,

---

[5] *Missionary Herald,* 1866, p. 371.

[6] Gray, *Oregon,* pp. 324 ff.

[7] Nixon, *How Marcus Whitman Saved Oregon,* pp. 305 ff.

and President Tyler, and by his earnest representations prevailed on them not to cede Oregon to the British government (which they were about to do.) [8]

In the fall of 1870, the Rev. H. H. Spalding visited the East. He went to Washington and succeeded in having the United States Senate issue a document which he had prepared. This document is entitled "Letter from the Secretary of the Interior," and bears the official designation, "Senate, 41st Congress, 3d Session, Ex. Doc. No. 37." It sets forth Spalding's side of his quarrel with the Catholics and included several accounts by various people of the Whitman-Saved-Oregon story.[9]

The decade 1870-80 passed without many new contributions to the subject. The fifth annual report of the Pioneer and Historical Society of Oregon (Astoria, 1876), contains an address by Dr. G. H. Atkinson about Whitman's ride, while the report for the following year contains Gray's lecture on the same subject.

Bitter controversy broke out in the decade 1880-90. In 1882, the Rev. Myron Eells, son of the Rev. Cushing Eells, issued his *Indian Missions,* in which the legend of Whitman's saving Oregon again appeared. In 1883, the Oregon volume of the American Commonwealth series, by William Barrows, appeared. Barrows had met Whitman in St. Louis in March, 1843, and was a firm believer in the theory which then had found no opponents. Barrows had written a series of articles which appeared in *The Observer* in December, 1882, and January and February, 1883. These articles became the basis for his volume on Oregon. Barrows drew largely from Gray's *Oregon* and Spalding's *Senate Document No. 37.*

By this time the Whitman legend was so widely accepted that it was included without hesitation in school histories, as, for example, in E. E. Scudder's *History of the United States.* Barrows wrote the article on Oregon for the 1884 edition of the *Encyclopedia Britannica* and of course included the legend. Bourne declared: "Never were confiding scholars and a more confiding public so taken in.... The propagation of the legend of Marcus Whitman after the publication of Barrows' *Oregon* is simply amazing."[10]

---

[8] Called to attention of the author by the kindness of Miss Dorothy Cole, of the American Board staff.

[9] This was reprinted in 1903.

[10] Bourne, *Essays,* pp. 41-42.

But the tide had reached its full crest. Two prominent students of Northwest history, namely, the Hon. Elwood Evans and Mrs. F. F. Victor, both of whom once accepted the Whitman legend, had come to doubt it. Evans announced his views in Seattle as early as 1878. Mrs. Victor had published her *River of the West* in 1870, in which she accepted in good faith the legend. Soon afterwards she changed her opinions. Both Evans and Mrs. Victor worked with H. H. Bancroft in the preparation of his two-volume *History of Oregon,* which appeared in 1884, and which still remains a standard work on Oregon. According to Mrs. Victor's claim, most of Bancroft's *Oregon* came from her pen.[11] Mrs. Victor appears to have been the first to issue a contradiction to the Whitman-Saved-Oregon story.

Sensing the growing sentiment against the legend, Myron Eells in 1883 issued his pamphlet entitled *Marcus Whitman, M.D., Proofs of His work in Saving Oregon to the United States, and in Promoting the Immigration of 1843.* In his opening sentence he refers to the subject as being "widely discussed." Eells gathered some valuable firsthand testimony to support the old view.

Then came a controversy which was carried on through the columns of the Portland *Oregonian.* Mrs. Victor wrote on November 6 and 7, 1884, questioning Whitman's political influence. E. C. Ross replied on December 9. Elwood Evans in the December 26 issue took his stand with Mrs. Victor. On January 11, 1885, Myron Eells replied to Mrs. Victor and Elwood Evans, and so the arguments appeared in the January, February, and March, 1885, issues of the *Oregonian.*[12]

The controversy spread to other papers. A letter from Evans appeared in the January 16, 1885, issue of the Tacoma *Weekly Ledger.* This was one of the causes for the two articles by Dr. Thomas Laurie which appeared in the February and September, 1885, issues of the *Missionary Herald.* Various articles of Perrin Whitman, Matthew P. Deady, and others appeared in the *Oregonian* during the years 1886-88.

The decade beginning with 1890 produced two biographies of Dr. Whitman, both of which were written by ad-

---

[11] Powers, *History of Oregon Literature,* pp. 546 ff.

[12] The articles by Gray, Eells, and Ross were issued in pamphlet form in 1885 at Portland under the title *The Whitman Controversy.* A copy of this rare Whitman item is in the Congressional Library.

herents of the Whitman legend. The first appeared in 1895
and was written by the Rev. J. G. Craighead, who titled
his book *The Story of Marcus Whitman.* It is not a scholarly
work. In June of the same year, O. W. Nixon's *How Marcus
Whitman Saved Oregon* appeared and received a large reading public. Nixon also accepted all of the old claims of the
Whitman legend, and became the standard authority of
thousands who were interested in this subject. In a letter
dated March 8, 1898, Nixon wrote: "In fact it was with
great difficulty I snatched the Mo of April, 1895 to write
the Book, & was too busy when it was issued to even read
a line of proof, or many errors of the earlier editions would
have been corrected."[13] Thus a book that was written in
a month became a chief authority!

The appearance of the Nixon book caused another series
of articles to appear in the *Oregonian* in which Myron Eells
again figured. The wide celebration of the semicentennial
of the Whitman massacre in the fall of 1897 was another
occasion for a wide dissemination of the Whitman legend.
A number of articles on various aspects of the Whitman
story appeared in the *Whitman College Quarterly* beginning
with January, 1897.[14]

In 1899, Marcus Whitman's name was voted on for the
New York University Hall of Fame. Of this Bourne wrote:

Fifty-two years later (i.e. after the massacre), in the most careful
appraisal of human achievement in America that has ever been made,
the voting for the Hall of Fame at New York University, Marcus
Whitman received nineteen out of a possible ninety-eight votes to be
ranked as one of the fifty greatest Americans. In the class of missionaries and explorers he stood fourth, being surpassed by Adoniram
Judson with thirty-five, Daniel Boone with thirty-four, and Elisha
Kent Kant with twenty-one votes, and followed by Fremont and George
Rogers Clark with seventeen....

History will be sought in vain for a more extraordinary growth
of fame after death.[15]

The decade beginning 1900 gave new contributions to
the Whitman controversy. Two men, Edward Gaylord
Bourne, Professor of History at Yale University, and W.
I. Marshall, Principal of a school in Chicago, independently

---

[13] Original in Coll. Wn. Letter addressed to the Rev. S. W. Pratt.
W.C.Q., Vol. 1, No. 1, p. 21: "Dr. Nixon wrote his famous book, 'How
Marcus Whitman Saved Oregon,' intending it as a campaign document
to help the College in its work."

[14] The Jan., 1897, issue was Vol. 1, No. 1. It was reprinted in Vol.
12, No. 4, 1909, under the title *The Story of Marcus Whitman.*

[15] Bourne, *Essays*, p. 4.

reached the same conclusion about the same time, to the effect that the Whitman-Saved-Oregon story was without historical foundation. Bourne and Marshall met at the meeting of the American Historical Society held in Detroit, December 27-29, 1900, where Bourne read his paper: *The Legend of Marcus Whitman*. Bourne had not studied the subject as long as Marshall but anticipated him in the publication of his conclusions. Bourne's paper appeared in the January, 1901, issue of the *American Historical Review*. It was later revised and appeared in a fuller version in *Essays in Historical Criticism,* in 1901.

Marshall had assembled a wealth of material, but, because of lack of funds, was unable to publish it. His large two-volume work entitled *Acquisition of Oregon* appeared in Seattle, after his death, in 1911. Bourne and Marshall together completely demolished the Whitman legend. Bourne is more restrained than Marshall, who is at times vitriolic and denies too much.

Myron Eells issued a pamphlet in 1902, entitled *A Reply to Professor Bourne's The Whitman Legend*. Eells accepted some of Bourne's conclusions, admitting that in some cases too much had been claimed for Whitman, but he challenged Bourne on several points. Eells produced new evidence to show that Whitman visited Washington. In 1904 Marshall issued a pamphlet entitled *History vs. The Whitman Saved Oregon Story* which contained three essays, the first of which was a criticism of W. A. Mowry's *Marcus Whitman,* which appeared in 1901. Mowry's book was a great improvement over Nixon's, although he accepted the larger part of the Whitman legend. Mowry had not read Bourne's article before he wrote his book.

Marshall's second essay was a criticism of Myron Eells, whom he accused of suppressing valuable source material bearing upon the Whitman story, including the diary of H. H. Spalding. The third essay was a discussion with commendation of Bourne's article.

Marshall died October 30, 1906. The Rev. Myron Eells died early in January, 1907. In each case their final work was published by friends after their death. As has been noted, Marshall's *Acquisition of Oregon* appeared in 1911. Eells' *Marcus Whitman* appeared in 1909 at Seattle. It is by far the best biography of Marcus Whitman which has heretofore appeared. Eells sought to be fair-minded and was willing to admit that the old Spalding story contained many errors of fact, but to the last he advocated the political cause for the ride and stressed the political consequences.

Twenty-five years have passed since Marshall's work was published. During this time many articles and a few pamphlets on Marcus Whitman have appeared. Authors of school books, convinced of the unreliability of the old legend, eliminated the Whitman story from their textbooks. The true was thrown out with the false. What a misfortune! Stripped of all its embellishments, the Whitman story remains worthy to be included in the schoolbooks of America.

On the other hand, clergymen and writers for the religious press, seemingly unmindful of the works of Bourne and Marshall, continued from time to time to repeat the old legend in mission-study books, Sunday school lessons, editorials, sermons, and so forth. Craighead, Nixon, Barrows, and Eells were for them the final and standard authorities.

The coming of the Whitman centennial in 1936 awakened new interest in the subject. The passing of the years has removed the animosities and prejudices which a discussion of this subject once aroused. We of this generation can read more impartially the records of the past. We see how both sides went to extremes. Too much was claimed for Whitman and too much was denied. New evidence has been discovered which has cleared up some disputed points. While the consensus today is that Whitman rode on mission business, we also believe that he visited Washington on political business. While contemporary documents prove that the chief cause for his departure for the East was the receipt of the Board's order of February, 1842, yet Whitman may have then had definite plans regarding his proposed visit to Washington which were never recorded. Until further discoveries throw new light on what occurred in Washington, this part of the story must remain open to speculation, and hence to continued differences of opinion.

In recent years a new school of writers on this subject has appeared, which includes Archer Butler Hulbert, now deceased, and his wife Dorothy Printup Hulbert, who is carrying on the work he started. The first volume of a three-volume edition entitled *Marcus Whitman, Crusader*, rich in source material, appeared in 1936. This set, when completed, will make available the bulk of the Whitman correspondence.

In the East is Herbert D. Winters, Professor of History,

Keuka College, Keuka Park, New York, who has made an intensive study of the political phases of the question and has written such articles as "Tyler, Webster and the Oregon Question," issued in the October, 1930, number of the *Journal of the New York State Historical Association,* and "Congress and the Oregon Question," which appeared in Vol. IX of the Rochester Historical Society's publication. These have been reprinted in pamphlet form.

Melvin Clay Jacobs, Professor of History of Whitman College, Walla Walla, Washington, has in manuscript a fine study entitled *The Winning of Oregon Territory Considered as a Frontier Movement,* in which he shows that the missionary influences in the Oregon emigration movement were greatly overrated.

The writer's recent book on the life of Henry Harmon Spalding (Caxton, Caldwell, Idaho, 1936) furnishes new light from original sources on the causes for Whitman's ride. Thus we of this generation are revaluating the story of Marcus Whitman. Perhaps, in the new light of his accomplishments, Marcus Whitman may yet be deemed worthy of being included in the New York University Hall of Fame.

APPENDIX 5

EYEWITNESS ACCOUNTS OF THE MASSACRE AND
OF THE CAPTIVITY

THE FOLLOWING list of accounts of the massacre and of the captivity by eyewitnesses may not be complete. It does not include the testimony of the witnesses given at the trial of the murderers, a brief review of which appeared in the May 30, 1850, issue of the *Oregon Spectator*. Incidentally the accounts given by the Sager children throw considerable light upon their own later history.

By adults:

1. Josiah Osborn, (a.) letter of April 7, 1848, to "Dear Brother and sister," original, Coll. W.; (b.) *Senate Ex. Doc. No. 37*, pp. 31-33, reprinted in Warren, *Memoirs*, pp. 126-128.

2. Daniel Young, deposition, January 20, 1849. Gray, *Oregon*, pp. 474-479.

3. Elam Young, deposition, January 20, 1849. *Ibid.*, pp. 482-485.

4. Lorinda Bewley, (a.) deposition, December 12, 1848, *ibid.*, pp. 486-489; (b.) *Senate Ex. Doc. No. 37*, pp. 34-37; (c.) Walker, J. E., *Esther Among the Cayuses*, Coll. O.

5. Mrs. Mary Saunders, *The Whitman Massacre*. (A copy is in the Library of Congress.)

6. Mr. and Mrs. W. D. Canfield gave an account to Dr. F. F. Ellinwood, who wrote two articles which appeared in the May and June, 1886, issues of *The Foreign Missionary*. These articles were reprinted in pamphlet form under the title: *Marcus Whitman and the Settlement of Oregon*.

By those who were children at the time. Ages indicated in parentheses:

7. Eliza Spalding Warren (10), *Memoirs of the West*, pp. 22-32.

8. Catherine Sager Pringle (13), (a.) Clark, *Pioneer Days*, Vol. 2, pp. 528-544; (b.) *O.H.Q.*, Dec., 1936, pp. 354-360, gives letter written Dec. 21, 1854.

9. Elizabeth M. Sager Helm (10), (a.) *W.C.Q.*, April, 1897, pp. 17-28, gives article by Mrs. E. M. Wilson, being an interview with Mrs. Helm; (b.) Lockley, *Oregon Trail Blazers*, pp. 325-350, also an interview; (c.) *T.O.P.A.*, 1896, pp. 120 ff., *The Last Day at Waiilatpu;* (d.) letter dated January 17, 1885, to her uncle Frederick Sager, Paradise City, Iowa, printed in several newspapers, including *Oregonian*, Oct. 30, 1932, and *Standard Examiner*, Ogden, Utah, summer of 1934; (e.) letter of Mar. 3, 1913, to Dr. James Wightman, *Yates County Chronicle*, Mar. 18, 1914.

10. Matilda J. Sager Delaney (8), (a.) *The Whitman Massacre;* (b.) Lockley, *op. cit.*, pp. 344-351; (c.) interview for *Oregonian*, reprinted in Walla Walla *Union*, Aug. 12, 1936.

11. Helen M. Saunders Church (14), *W.C.Q.*, Dec., 1898, pp. 21-26.

12. Nathan Kimball (12), *T.O.P.A.*, 1903, pp. 189-195.

13. Nancy Osborn Jacobs (9), (a.) paper read before a pioneer re-
union at Walla Walla, May 29, 1912, printed in Waitsburg *Times*,
Feb. 2, 1935; (b.) Lockley, *op. cit.*, pp. 351-363; (c.) interview
for *East Oregonian*, Pendleton, May 19, 1919.

14. Sarah Sophia Kimball Munson (6), short statement given in
Cannon, *Waiilatpu*, pp. 157-8.

15. Mary E. Marsh Cason (11), *Oregon Statesman*, Nov. 6-Nov. 10,
1936, articles by R. J. Hendricks.

16. Gertrude Hall Denny (10), *Oregon Native Son*, June, 1899.

17. Oscar F. Canfield, (9), Lewiston *Tribune*, Jan. 1, 1908; also unidentified clipping in author's possession for July 21, 1894.

APPENDIX 6

IN THE ARCHIVES of Whitman College is to be found a hitherto unpublished letter of the Rev. H. K. W. Perkins, dated "Hallowell, Me. Oct. 19, 1849." This letter bears the notation: "Copied by M. Eells Oct. 17, 1883. . . . Copied by M. Eells 1883 from Original." The copy was made on very thin paper and is most difficult to read. The original was addressed to "Miss Jane Prentiss, West Almond Allegany County New York." It may be that the news of the massacre was the occasion for the return of Jane to New York State. The letter in part is as follows:

Dear Sister

Yours of Aug 29 was recd in due time but owing to a press of business & absence in Boston of late I have not had time to attend to your request concerning your dear sisters letters until today.

You write that Mrs. Whitman was a dear Sister of yours. She was a dear sister of ours also. The acquaintance we formed with her was very intimate. For several months during her husband's last visit to the U. States she was a member of our family. The circumstances that induced her to spend so long a season with us, I presume you must be familiar with as she kept up a constant correspondence I believe with her friends in the United States. If so you will recollect that even then, her situation among the natives at Waiilatpu was far from being *safe*. The truth is Miss Prentiss your lamented sister was far from happy in the situation she had chosen to occupy.

She no doubt felt a strong desire for the salvation of the Indian race & perhaps it might have been said of her: "She hath done what she could," but if I may be allowed the liberty of expressing my own opinion, I should say, unhesitatingly that both herself & husband were out of their proper sphere. They were not adapted to their work. They could not possibly interest & gain the affections of the natives. I know for a long time before the tragedy that closed their final career that many of the natives around them looked upon them suspiciously. Though they *feared* the Doctor they did not *love* him. They did not love your sister. They could appreciate neither the one nor the other.

The Doctor I presume you knew familiarly. And *knowing him* as *I knew him* you would not need to be told that an Oregon Indian & he could never get along well together. It was "the last place," to use a familiar phrase, that he ought to have occupied. And first, I need hardly tell you he cared for no man under heaven,—perfectly fearless & independent. Secondly he could never stop to *parley*. It was always *yes* or *no*. In the 3d place he had no sense of *etiquette* or personal dignity—manners, I mean. 4. And in the fourth place *he was always at work*.

Now I need not tell you that he & an Indian would never agree.

How could they? What would such a man have in common with an Indian? How could they sympathize with each other? In connection with some other man, perhaps, Sister Whitman, would have done better. Perhaps she would have been more familiar—sympathizing—open hearted. That she felt a deep interest in the welfare of the natives, no one who was at all acquainted with her could doubt. But the affection was manifested under false views of Indian character. Her carriage towards them was always considered *haughty*. It was the common remark among them that Mrs. Whitman was "very proud."

Now I do not really suppose that this was the case or that she ever suspected that she conveyed such an impression. But so the natives always spoke of it. Sister Whitman partook a good deal of her husband's independent spirit. She doubtless supposed also that it was necessary to maintain considerable *reserve*.

What contributed still more I presume to increase the distance between her & the natives was her *ill health & increasing nervousness*. Her constitution was a good deal impaired, toward the close of her labors & she could not in reality bear much. Her hopes of success also, were very much weakened and melancholy musings occupied her more than at her first setting out in missionary life.

I wish I could tell you just how it was. And yet I cannot do it, without seeming somewhat severely to reflect upon the Doctor. Again I am afraid that you will never get at the real truth in the case if I do not tell you. The published accounts of that melancholy catastrophe which cut short so many lives, are all one sided. They fail almost entirely to account for the proceedings of the natives. I will briefly state a few things which ought to be kept in view with the whole affair.

And first Dr. Whitman in pursuing his missionary labors never so identified himself with the natives as to make their interests *paramount*. He looked upon them as an inferior race & doomed at no distant day to give place to a settlement of enterprising Americans. With an eye to this he laid his plans & acted. His American feelings even while engaged in his missionary toils, were unfortunately suffered to predominate. Indeed it might almost be doubted whether he felt half the interest in the natives that he did in the *prospective* white population. He wanted to see the country settled. The beautiful valley of the Walla Walla he wanted to see teeming with a busy, bustling white population. Where were scattered a few Indian huts, he wanted to see thrifty farm houses. Where stalked abroad a few broken-down Indian horses, cropping the rich grasses of the surrounding plain, he wanted to see grazing the cow, the ox, & the sheep of a happy Yankee community. With his eye bent on this he was willing meantime to do what he could incidentally, for the poor, weak, feeble doomed Oregonians.

And now, Miss Prentiss, what would be the natural result? Why what every sensible man must have seen. *Jealousy on the part of the natives*. And in meeting death in the way that he did, it might be said with more truth that he died a martyr to the progress of American civilization than to the cause of Missions.

Had Dr. Whitman given himself up wholly to the interests of the natives, with all his natural unfitness for the place he occupied, he no doubt would have been *safe*, safe as anywhere in Christendom.

(2) It has been said that the natives are dying very rapidly & that

Dr. Whitman was suspected as the cause of their rapid decrease. No doubt this suspicion might operate to some extent but then why seek their vengeance on the poor unsuspecting white settlers? The fact was the natives identified the Doctor with the whites. While they were rapidly coming in year by year & occupying their rich lands, they looked upon the Doctor as at the head of the concern. They saw him entering no protest,—making no remonstrance, but rather aiding & abetting,—planning & directing, & all the family of course including Mrs. W. concurring apparently in their displaceance. What would they do? They would do what they did do,—"strike for their altars & their fires." They wanted their *lands*, their *homes*, the *graves of their fathers*, their *rich hunting grounds & horse ranges*. They did not look upon the man or men who would connive at the usurpation of all these as their real friends. They looked upon the Doctor & wife as not missionaries to them but to the Americans. With these brief statements of facts I need not add another word explanatory. You see everything at a glance. The result could have hardly been otherwise than it was.

In your letter you remark that I doubtless have recollections of her (Mrs. W.) which if expressed would greatly interest her acquaintances & friends. Yes, Miss Prentiss, I have recollections of her,—interesting recollections which I shall always cherish. But they are not recollections of her as a *missionary* but as a *woman*. Mrs. Whitman was not adapted to savage but *civilized* life. She would have done honor to her sex in a polished & exalted sphere, but never in the low drudgery of Indian toil. The natives esteemed her as proud, haughty, as *far above them*. No doubt she really seemed so. It was her *misfortune*, not her *fault*. She was adapted to a different destiny. She wanted something exalted—communion with *mind*. She longed for society, *refined society*. She was intellectually & by association fitted to do good only in such a sphere. She should have been differently situated. I think her stay with us including her visit to the Willamette the pleasantest portion of her Oregon life. She saw considerable company & really seemed to *enjoy it*. She had leisure also for reading & writing, which she also seemed always to enjoy. She loved company, society, excitement & ought always to have enjoyed it. The self-denial that took her away from it was suicidal. Perhaps, however, more good was accomplished by it than could have been accomplished by pursuing a different course. Certain it is that we needed such minds to keep us in love with civilized life, to remind us occasionally of *home*. As for myself I could as easily have become an Indian as not. I completely sympathized with them in all their plans & feelings. I could gladly have made the wigwam my home for life if duty had called. But it was not so with Mrs. W. She had nothing apparently with them in common. She kept in her own original sphere to the last. She was not a *missionary* but a *woman*, an American highly gifted, polished American lady. And such she died.

I desire with you her death may be sanctified to the cause of God. I think it more likely to be when the truth in the case is really known. I sympathize with you. I sympathized with her. I would that with her it might have been otherwise. But so it was. May we ever be found in our lot & place that when the Master calls for us we may be found waiting. Yours truly, H. K. W. Perkins.[1]

---

[1] The words in italics were underlined in the copy.

BIBLIOGRAPHY

THE FOLLOWING books and periodicals have been consulted in the preparation of this work. A few items, mentioned in the text, footnotes, or appendices, have not been listed. The October, 1908, issue of the *Washington Historical Quarterly* contains an article by Charles W. Smith entitled "A Contribution Toward a Bibliography of Marcus Whitman," which is very good. Since the Whitman controversy was by that time a matter of history, the bibliography he prepared covering fifty-five pages is quite complete.

Allen, Miss A. J.—*Ten Years in Oregon* (being the record of Dr. Elijah White), Ithaca, N. Y., 1848.

Allen, Edward—*History of Bridgewater*, Bridgewater, 1897.

Alter, J. Cecil—*James Bridger*, Salt Lake City, 1925.

Bagley, C. B.—*Early Catholic Missions in Oregon* (containing Brouillet's pamphlet of 1848), Seattle, 1932.

Bancroft, H. H.—*History of Oregon*, 2 vols., San Francisco, 1886.

Barrows, William—*Oregon*, Boston, 1884.

Benton, Nathaniel S.—*History of Herkimer County*, Albany, 1856.

Binney, C. F. J.—*History and Genealogy of the Prentice or Prentiss Family*, 2nd ed., Boston, 1883.

Bourne, E. G.—*Essays in Historical Criticism*, New York, 1901.

Bowden, Angie Burt—*Early Schools of Washington Territory*, Seattle, 1935.

Bradley, W. A.—*Wm. Cullen Bryant*, New York, 1905.

Brosnan, C. J.—*Jason Lee*, New York, 1932.

Brouillet, J. B. A.—*Authentic Account (See* Bagley).

Burnett, Peter—*Recollections of an old Pioneer*, New York, 1880.

Canniff, William—*The Medical Profession in Upper Canada*, Toronto, 1894.

Cannon, Miles—*Waiilatpu*, Boise, 1915.

Carver, Jonathan—*Travels through the Interior Parts of North America in the years 1766, 1767 and 1768*, London, 2nd ed., 1779.

Centennial Celebration of the Rushville Church, Rushville, 1902.

Clark, S. A.—*Pioneer Days of Oregon History*, 2 vols., Portland, 1905.

Clayton, W. W.—*History of Steuben County*, New York, 1879.

Cummins, Sarah J.—*Autobiography and Reminiscences*, La Grande, Oregon, 1908.

Defenbach, Byron—*Red Heroines of the Northwest*, Caldwell, 1929.

Delaney, Matilda Sager—*The Whitman Massacre*, Spokane, 1920.

De Smet, Pierre Jean—*Letters and Sketches*, Philadelphia, 1843.

Douthit, Mary Osborn—*Souvenir of Western Women*, Portland, 1905.

Drury, Clifford Merrill—*Henry Harmon Spalding*, Caldwell, 1936.

Dyer, Charles N.—*History of the Town of Plainfield*, Northampton, 1891.

Eells, Myron—*Indian Missions*, Philadelphia, 1882; *Marcus Whitman, Proofs of his Work in Saving Oregon* (Pamphlet), Portland, 1883; *Father Eells*, Boston, 1894; *Reply to Professor Bourne's "The Whitman Legend,"* Walla Walla, 1902; *Marcus Whitman*, Seattle, 1909.

Ellinwood, F. F.—*Marcus Whitman and the Settlement of Oregon* (Pamphlet), 1886.

Evans, Elwood—*History of the Pacific Northwest*, Portland, Vol. I, p. 16, 1889.

Fairbanks, Mrs. A. W.—*Emma Willard and her Pupils*, New York, 1898.

Farnham, Charles H.—*History of the Descendants of John Whitman*, New Haven, 1889.

Farnham, T. J.—*Travels Across the Great Western Prairies*, Cleveland, 1906.

Frémont, J. C.—*Narrative of the Exploring Expedition to the Rocky Mountains in the year 1842*, Syracuse, 1848.

Ghent, W. J.—*The Road to Oregon*, Longmans, New York, 1929.

Gray, W. H.—*History of Oregon*, Portland, 1870.

Hafen, L. R., and Ghent, W. J.—*Broken Hand*, Denver, 1931.

Hastings, L. W.—*A New Description of Oregon & California*, Cincinnati, 1857.

Hines, Gustavus—*Oregon*, Buffalo, 1851.

History of the Connecticut Valley in Massachusetts, Philadelphia, 1879.

History of the Synod of Washington, 1909.

Hotchkin, James H.—*History of the Purchase and Settlement of Western New York*, New York, 1848.

Hulbert, A. B., and Hulbert, Dorothy P.—*The Oregon Crusade*, and *Marcus Whitman, Crusader*, Vols. 5 and 6 of *Overland to Pacific*, Denver, 1935 and 1936.

Irving, Washington—*Astoria*, Philadelphia, 1836.

Johnson, Robert C.—*John McLoughlin*, Portland, 1935.

Kane, Paul—*Wanderings of an Artist*, Toronto, 1925.

Kirkman, Grace Goodyear—*Genealogy of the Goodyear Family*, San Francisco, 1899. (A copy is in the Sutro branch of the California State Library.)

Laurie, Thomas—*The Whitman Controversy* (Pamphlet), Astoria, 1886.

Lee, D., and Frost, J. H.—*Ten Years in Oregon*, New York, 1844.

Lennox, Edward Henry—*Overland to Oregon*, Oakland, 1904.

Lockley, Fred—*Oregon Trail Blazers*, New York, 1929.

Marshall, W. I.—*The Acquisition of Oregon*, 2 vols., Seattle, 1911; *History vs. The Whitman Saved Oregon Story*, Chicago, 1904.

McBeth, Kate C.—*The Nez Perces since Lewis and Clark*, New York, 1908.

Miller, James A.—*Presbyterianism in Steuben and Allegany*, Angelica, New York, 1897.

Mowry, W. A.—*Marcus Whitman*, New York, 1901.

Nixon, O. W.—*How Marcus Whitman Saved Oregon*, Chicago, 1895; *Whitman's Ride through Savage Lands*, Winona Pub. Co., 1895.

One Hundred Years of the Presbyterian Church in Ithaca, Ithaca, 1904.

Palmer, Joel—*Journal of Travels*, Cleveland, 1906.

Parker, Henry W.—*How Oregon Was Saved to the United States* (Pamphlet in Library of Congress), Funk & Wagnalls, 1901.

Parker, Samuel—*Journal of an Exploring Tour from Beyond the Rocky Mountains*, Ithaca, 1838.

Parker, S. J.—*The History of Oregon and the Pacific Coast* (In manuscript. Presented to Cornell Library, Ithaca, 1892).

Penrose, Stephen B. L.—*Whitman, an Unfinished Story*, Walla Walla, 1935.

Porter, Jacob—*Historical Sketch of Plainfield*, Greenfield, 1834.

Powers, Alfred—*History of Oregon Literature*, Portland, Ore., 1935.

Pratt, S. W.—*History of the Presbyterian Church of Prattsburg*, 1876.

Ross, E. C., Eells, M., and Gray, W. H.—*The Whitman Controversy* (Pamphlet), Portland, 1885.

Rix, Guy S.—*History & Genealogy of the Eastman Family*, Concord, 1901.

Saunders, Mrs. Mary—*The Whitman Massacre, A true story by a Survivor*, Oakland, 1916. (Pamphlet. A copy is in the Congressional Library.)

Schafer, Joseph—*History of the Pacific Northwest*, New York, 1905.

Schenck, J. S., and Rann, W. S.—*History of Warren County*, Syracuse, 1887.

Scott, L. M.—*History of the Oregon Country*, 6 vols., Cambridge, 1924.

Seymour, Flora Warren—*Story of the Red Man*, New York, 1934.

Skiff, Frederick W.—*Adventures in Americana*, Portland, 1935.

Sylvester, Nathaniel B.—*History of Rennsalaer Co.*, New York, 1880.

Spalding, Henry Harmon—*See U. S. Senate Document No. 37, 41st Congress, 3rd Session.*

Strong, James Clark—*Biographical Sketch*, Los Gatos, Calif., 1910.

Strong, Wm.—*The Story of the American Board*, Boston, 1910.

Talbots, Theodore—*Journal*, Portland, 1931.

Thompson, Samuel—*New Guide to Health or Botanic Family Physician*, Boston, 1835.

Tucker, Sarah—*Rainbow in the North*, London, 1851.

U. S. House, 30th Congress, 1st session, Misc. Report, No. 98, Serial No. 523. (Memorial of Oregon Legislature, Jan. 25, 1848.)

U. S. Senate Executive Document No. 37, 41st Congress, 3rd session, Serial No. 1440 (Being Spalding's document).

Victor, Frances Fuller—*River of the West*, Hartford, 1870.

Waite, F. C.—*John Delamater*, Bulletin of the Cleveland Academy of Medicine, May, 1930.

Warren, Eliza Spalding—*Memoirs of the West*, Portland, 1916.

Wilkes, Charles—*Narrative of the U. S. Exploring Expedition*, Philadelphia, 1845.

Winters, Herbert D.—*Congress and the Oregon Question* (Pamphlet, being a reprint from Vol. IX, Rochester Historical Society, 1931).

PERIODICALS CONSULTED

The abbreviations used in the footnotes are indicated in the parentheses.

Bath, N. Y., *Plaindealer*
Boston *Recorder*
Boston *Daily Evening Transcript*
Burlington, Iowa, *Gazette*
Christian Advocate and Journal
Cleveland *Weekly Plain Dealer*
Cleveland *Daily Herald*
Congregationalist
Congressional Globe
Corning, New York, *Leader*
Foreign Missionary
Frontier Magazine
General Congregational Association of Illinois
Golden Rule
Journal of the Department of History, Presbyterian Church U. S. A.
Magazine of American History
Minutes of the Presbyterian (U. S. A.) General Assembly
Minutes of the Synod of Washington, 1903
Missionary Herald
Mississippi Valley Historical Review
Mother's Magazine, Vol. 14
Naples, New York, *Recorder*
New York *Spectator*
New York *Tribune*
Oregon American and Evangelical Unionist
Oregon Historical Quarterly (O.H.Q.)
Oregon Native Son
Oregon Spectator
Ogden, Utah, *Standard Examiner*
Pacific Northwest Historical Quarterly
Penn Yan, New York, *Chronicle & Express*
Pioneer and Historical Society of Oregon
Portland *Oregonian*
Prattsburg *Advertiser*
Prattsburg *News*
Rochester *Democrat-Chronicle*
San Francisco *Pacific*
Spokesman-Review
St. Louis *Argus*
Sunday School Times
Sunset Magazine, 1909
Transactions of the Oregon Pioneer Association (T.O.P.A.)
Waitsburg *Times*

Walla Walla *Union*
Washington, D. C., *Daily National Intelligencer*
Washington *Globe*
Washington Historical Quarterly (W.H.Q.)
Whitman College Quarterly (W.C.Q.)
Yates County Chronicle

Also, church records, vital statistics, school catalogs, county records, and family Bibles. Original and unpublished source material was examined in the archives of the American Board (Coll. A.) ; the Oregon Historical Society (Coll. O.) ; Hammond Library, Chicago Theological Seminary; Bancroft Library, Berkeley; Washington State College, Pullman (Coll. Wn.) ; Whitman College (Coll. W.) ; Old Indian Files, Washington, D. C.; and in individual collections.

INDEX

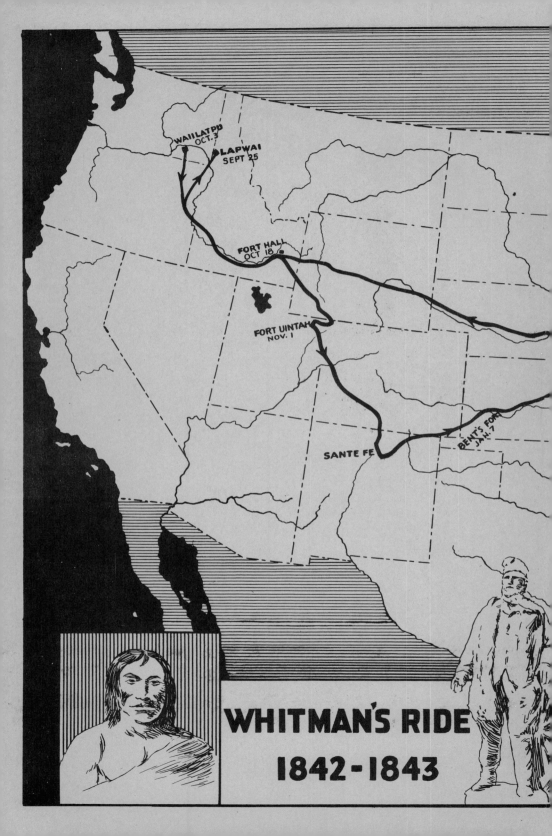